Rogers Cadenhead

Sams **Teach Yourself**

Java

(Covers Java 7 and Android)

in **21 Days**

 SAMS | 800 East 96th Street, Indianapolis, Indiana 46240

Sams Teach Yourself Java in 21 Days
(Covering Java 7 and Android)

Copyright © 2013 by Pearson Education, Inc.

ISBN-13: 978-0-672-33574-7
ISBN-10: 0-672-33574-3

Library of Congress Cataloging-in-Publication Data:
Cadenhead, Rogers.
 Sams teach yourself Java in 21 days : covering Java 7 and Android / Rogers Cadenhead.—6th ed.
  p. cm.
 ISBN 978-0-672-33574-7 (pbk.)
 1. Java (Computer program language) 2. Android (Electronic resource) I. Title.
 QA76.73.J38C315 2013
 005.13'3--dc23

                        2012022262

Printed in the United States of America

First Printing August 2012

Trademarks

Warning and Disclaimer

Bulk Sales

Sams Publishing offers excellent discounts on this book when ordered in quantity for bulk purchases or special sales. For more information, please contact

U.S. Corporate and Government Sales
1-800-382-3419
corpsales@pearsontechgroup.com

For sales outside of the U.S., please contact

International Sales
international@pearsoned.com

Editor-in-Chief
Mark Taub

Acquisitions Editor
Mark Taber

Development Editor
Songlin Qiu

Managing Editor
Kristy Hart

Project Editor
Anne Goebel

Copy Editor
Gayle Johnson

Indexer
Tim Wright

Proofreader
Chrissy White, Language Logistics, LLC

Technical Editor
Boris Minkin

Editorial Assistant
Vanessa Evans

Cover Designer
Anne Jones

Compositor
Nonie Ratcliff

Contents at a Glance

Table of Contents

About the Author

Rogers Cadenhead is a programmer and author. He has written more than 20 books on programming and web publishing, including *Sams Teach Yourself Java in 24 Hours*. He also publishes the Drudge Retort and other websites that receive more than 20 million visits a year. He maintains this book's official website at www.java21days.com and a personal weblog at http://workbench.cadenhead.org.

Dedication

To my mom, Gail Cadenhead. I'm disappointed you abandoned the beehive hairdo you had in the '60s, but that's the last time you ever disappointed me in the 45 years of my life. Thank you for the room and board, for the love and support, and for introducing me to Ryan's Hope *and* One Life to Live *when I was 8.*

Acknowledgments

A book of this scope (and heft!) requires the hard work and dedication of numerous people. Most of them are at Sams Publishing in Indianapolis, and to them I owe considerable thanks—in particular, to Boris Minkin, Gayle Johnson, Songlin Qiu, Anne Goebel, and Mark Taber. Most of all, thanks to my wife, Mary, and my sons, Max, Eli, and Sam.

I'd also like to thank readers who have sent helpful comments about corrections, typos, and suggested improvements regarding this book and its prior editions. The list includes the following people: Dave Barton, Patrick Benson, Ian Burton, Lawrence Chang, Jim DeVries, Ryan Esposto, Kim Farr, Sam Fitzpatrick, Bruce Franz, Owen Gailar, Rich Getz, Bob Griesemer, Jenny Guriel, Brenda Henry-Sewell, Ben Hensley, Jon Hereng, Drew Huber, John R. Jackson, Bleu Jaegel, Natalie Kehr, Mark Lehner, Stephen Loscialpo, Brad Kaenel, Chris McGuire, Paul Niedenzu, E.J. O'Brien, Chip Pursell, Pranay Rajgarhia, Peter Riedlberger, Darrell Roberts, Luke Shulenburger, Mike Tomsic, John Walker, Joseph Walsh, Mark Weiss, P.C. Whidden, Chen Yan, Kyu Hwang Yeon, and J-F. Zurcher.

We Want to Hear from You!

As the reader of this book, *you* are our most important critic and commentator. We value your opinion and want to know what we're doing right, what we could do better, what areas you'd like to see us publish in, and any other words of wisdom you're willing to pass our way.

We welcome your comments. You can email or write to let us know what you did or didn't like about this book—as well as what we can do to make our books better.

Please note that we cannot help you with technical problems related to the topic of this book.

When you write, please be sure to include this book's title and author as well as your name and email address. We will carefully review your comments and share them with the author and editors who worked on the book.

Email: errata@informit.com

Mail: Addison-Wesley/Prentice Hall Publishing
          ATTN: Reader Feedback
          1330 Avenue of the Americas
          35th Floor
          New York, New York, 10019

Reader Services

Visit our website and register this book at informit.com/register for convenient access to any updates, downloads, or errata that might be available for this book.

Introduction

Some revolutions catch the world by surprise. Twitter, the Linux operating system, and *Cupcake Wars* all rose to prominence unexpectedly.

The remarkable success of the Java programming language, on the other hand, caught nobody by surprise. Java has been a source of great expectations since its introduction 17 years ago. When Java was introduced in web browsers, a torrent of publicity welcomed the arrival of the new language.

Sun Microsystems cofounder Bill Joy proclaimed, "This represents the end result of nearly 15 years of trying to come up with a better programming language and environment for building simpler and more reliable software."

Sun, which created Java in 1991 and first released it to the public four years later, was acquired by Oracle in 2010. Oracle, which has been committed to Java development since its earliest years, has continued to support the language and produce new versions.

In the ensuing years, Java lived up to a considerable amount of its hype. The language has become as strong a part of software development as the beverage of the same name. One kind of Java keeps programmers up nights. The other kind enables programmers to rest easier after they have developed their software.

Java was originally offered as a technology for enhancing websites with programs that run in browsers. Today, it's more likely to be found on servers, driving dynamic web applications backed by relational databases on some of the web's largest sites. It's also found on Android cell phones running popular apps such as Angry Birds and Words with Friends.

Each new release of Java strengthens its capabilities as a general-purpose programming language for a wide range of environments. Today, Java is being put to use in desktop applications, Internet servers, personal digital assistants, mobile devices, and many other environments. It's even making a comeback in the browser with sophisticated applications created in Java that are deployed using the Google Web Toolkit.

Now in its eighth major release—Java 7—the Java language has matured into a full-featured competitor to other general-purpose development languages, such as C++, Python, Ruby, and Visual Basic.

You might be familiar with Java programming tools such as Eclipse, Borland JBuilder, and NetBeans. These programs make it possible to develop functional Java programs, and you also can use Oracle's Java Development Kit. The kit, which is available for free on the Web at http://oracle.com/technetwork/java, is a set of command-line tools for writing, compiling, and testing Java programs. NetBeans, another free tool offered by Oracle, is an integrated development environment for the creation of Java programs. It can be downloaded from http://netbeans.org.

This book introduces you to all aspects of Java software development using the most current version of the language and the best available techniques in the Java Standard Edition, the most widely used version of the language and Java Class Library. Programs are prepared and tested using NetBeans, so you can quickly demonstrate the skills you master each day.

Reading this book will help you understand why Java has become the most widely employed programming language on the planet.

How This Book Is Organized

Sams Teach Yourself Java in 21 Days teaches you about the Java language and how to use it to create applications for any computing environment and Android apps that run on cell phones and other mobile devices. By the time you have finished the book, you'll have well-rounded knowledge of Java and the Java class libraries. Using your new skills, you will be able to develop your own programs for tasks such as web services, database connectivity, XML processing, and mobile programming.

You learn by doing in this book, creating several programs each day that demonstrate the topics being introduced. The source code for all these programs is available on the book's official website at www.java21days.com, along with other supplemental material such as answers to reader questions.

This book covers the Java language and its class libraries in 21 days, organized into three weeks. Each week covers a broad area of developing Java programs.

In the first week, you learn about the Java language itself:

- Day 1 covers the basics—what Java is, why you should learn the language, and how to create software using a powerful style of development called object-oriented programming. You create your first Java application.
- On Day 2, you dive into the fundamental Java building blocks—data types, variables, and expressions.

- Day 3 goes into detail about how to deal with objects in Java—how to create them, use their variables, call their methods, and compare them.
- On Day 4, you give Java programs some brainpower using conditionals and work with arrays and loops.
- Day 5 fully explores creating classes—the basic building blocks of any Java program.
- On Day 6, you discover more about interfaces and packages, which are useful for grouping classes and organizing a class hierarchy.
- Day 7 covers three powerful features of Java—exceptions, the ability to deal with errors and threads, and the ability to run different parts of a program simultaneously.

Week 2 is dedicated to the most useful classes offered by Oracle for use in your own Java programs:

- Day 8 introduces data structures that you can use as an alternative to strings and arrays—array lists, stacks, hash maps, and bit sets. It also describes a special for loop that makes them easier to use.
- Day 9 begins a five-day exploration of visual programming. You learn how to create a graphical user interface using Swing classes for interfaces, graphics, and user input. Your programs adopt the Nimbus look and feel introduced in Java 7.
- Day 10 covers more than a dozen interface components you can use in a Java program, including buttons, text fields, sliders, scrolling text areas, and icons.
- Day 11 explains how to make a user interface look marvelous using *layout managers*, a set of classes that determine how components on an interface are arranged.
- Day 12 concludes the coverage of Swing with event-handling classes, which enable a program to respond to mouse clicks and other user interactions.
- On Day 13, you learn about drawing shapes and characters on user interface components.
- Day 14 demonstrates how to use Java Web Start, a technique that makes installing a Java program as easy as clicking a web page link. It also describes `SwingWorker`, a class that improves application performance by using threads.

Week 3 moves into advanced topics:

- Day 15 covers input and output using *streams*, a set of classes that enable file access, network access, and other sophisticated data handling.

- Day 16 introduces object *serialization*, a way to make objects exist even when no program is running. You learn how to save them to a storage medium such as a hard disk, read them into a program, and then use them again as objects.

- On Day 17, you extend your knowledge of streams to write programs that communicate with the Internet, including socket programming, buffers, channels, and URL handling.

- Day 18 shows you how to connect to relational databases using Java Database Connectivity (JDBC) version 4.1. You learn how to exploit the capabilities of Derby, the open source database that's included with Java.

- Day 19 covers how to read and write RSS documents using the XML Object Model (XOM), an open source Java class library. RSS feeds, one of the most popular XML dialects in use today, enable millions of people to follow site updates and other new web content.

- Day 20 explores how to write web services clients with the language and the Apache XML-RPC class library.

- Day 21 covers the fastest-growing area of Java programming: developing apps for Android phones and mobile devices. Using Eclipse as a development environment and a free Android development kit, you create apps that can be deployed and tested on a phone.

Who Should Read This Book

This book teaches the Java language to three groups:

- Novices who are relatively new to programming
- People who have been introduced to earlier versions of Java
- Experienced developers in other languages, such as Visual C++, Visual Basic, or Python

When you're finished with this book, you'll be able to tackle any aspect of the Java language. You'll also be comfortable enough to tackle your own ambitious programming projects, both on and off the Web.

If you're somewhat new to programming or have never written a program, you might wonder whether this is the right book for you. Because all the concepts in this book are illustrated with working programs, you'll be able to work your way through the subject regardless of your experience level. If you understand what variables and loops are, you'll be able to benefit from this book. You might want to read this book if any of the following are true:

- You had some beginning programming lessons in school, you grasp what programming is, and you've heard that Java is easy to learn, powerful, and cool.
- You've programmed in another language for a few years, you keep hearing accolades for Java, and you want to see whether it lives up to its hype.
- You've heard that Java is great for web application and Android programming.

If you've never been introduced to object-oriented programming, which is the style of programming that Java embodies, don't be discouraged. This book assumes that you have no background in object-oriented design. You'll get a chance to learn this development methodology as you're learning Java.

If you're a complete beginner to programming, this book might move a little fast for you. Java is a good language to start with, though, and if you take it slowly and work through all the examples, you can still pick up Java and start creating your own programs.

Conventions Used in This Book

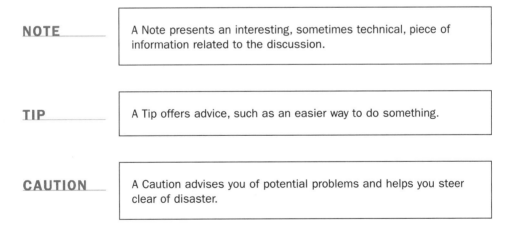

NOTE — A Note presents an interesting, sometimes technical, piece of information related to the discussion.

TIP — A Tip offers advice, such as an easier way to do something.

CAUTION — A Caution advises you of potential problems and helps you steer clear of disaster.

Text that you type and text that appears onscreen is presented in a `monospace` font:

`It looks like this.`

This font represents how text looks onscreen. Placeholders for variables and expressions appear in `monospace italic`.

The end of each lesson offers several special features: answers to commonly asked questions about that day's subject matter, a quiz to test your knowledge of the material, two exercises that you can try on your own, and a practice question in case you're preparing for Java certification. Answers to the questions can be found at the end of the book. Solutions to the exercises and the answer to the certification question can be found on the book's official website at www.java21days.com.

WEEK 1:
The Java Language

DAY 1
Getting Started with Java

The thing that Java tries to do and is actually remarkably successful at is spanning a lot of different domains, so you can do app server work, you can do cell phone work, you can do scientific programming, you can write software, do interplanetary navigation, all kinds of stuff...

—Java language creator James Gosling

When the Java programming language was unleashed on the public in 1995, it was an inventive toy for the Web that had the potential to be more.

The word "potential" is a compliment that comes with an expiration date. Sooner or later, potential must be realized, or new words and phrases are used in its place, such as "slacker," "letdown," "waste," and "major disappointment to your mother and me."

As you develop your skills throughout this book's 21 one-day tutorials, you'll be in a good position to judge whether the language has lived up to more than a decade of hype.

You'll also become a Java programmer with a lot of potential.

The Java Language

Now in its eighth major release, Java has lived up to the expectations that accompanied its arrival. More than four million programmers have learned the language and are using it in places such as NASA, IBM, Kaiser Permanente, and Google. It's a standard part of the academic curriculum at many computer science departments around the world. First used to create simple programs on web pages, Java can be found today in the following places (and many more):

- Web servers
- Relational databases
- Orbiting telescopes
- E-book readers
- Cell phones

Although Java remains useful for web developers, its ambitions today extend far beyond the Web. Java has matured into one of the most popular general-purpose programming languages.

History of the Language

The story of the Java language is well known by this point. James Gosling and a team of developers were working on an interactive TV project at Sun Microsystems in the mid-1990s when Gosling became frustrated with the language being used. C++ was an object-oriented programming language developed a decade earlier as an extension of the C language.

To address some of the things that frustrated him about C++, Gosling holed up in his office and created a new language that was suitable for his project.

Although that interactive TV effort flopped, Gosling's language had unforeseen applicability to a new medium that was becoming popular at the same time: the Web.

Java was released to the public for the first time in fall 1995. Although most of the language's features were primitive compared with C++ (and Java today), special Java programs called applets could be run as part of web pages on the most popular web browser, Netscape Navigator.

This functionality—the first interactive programming available on the Web—drew so much attention to the new language that several hundred thousand programmers learned Java in its first six months.

Even after the novelty of Java web programming wore off, the overall benefits of the language became clear, and the programmers stuck around. There are more professional Java programmers today than C++ programmers.

Sun Microsystems controlled the development of the Java language from its inception until 2010, when the company was acquired by the database and enterprise software giant Oracle in a $7.4 billion deal. Oracle, a longtime user of the language on its own products, has a strong commitment to supporting Java and increasing its capabilities with new releases.

Introduction to Java

Java is an object-oriented, platform-neutral, secure language designed to be easier to learn than C++ and harder to misuse than C and C++.

Object-oriented programming (OOP) is a software development methodology in which a program is conceptualized as a group of objects that work together. Objects are created from templates called *classes*, and they contain data and the statements required to use that data. Java is primarily object-oriented, as you see later today when you create your first class and use it to create objects.

Platform neutrality is a program's ability to run without modification in different computing environments. Java programs are transformed into a format called *bytecode* that can be run by any computer or device equipped with a Java virtual machine. You can create a Java program on a Windows Vista machine that runs on a Linux web server, an Apple Mac using OS X, and a Samsung Android phone. As long as a platform has a Java virtual machine, it can run the bytecode.

Although the relative ease of learning one language over another is always a point of contention among programmers, Java was designed to be easier than C++ primarily in the following ways:

- Java automatically takes care of memory allocation and deallocation, freeing programmers from this error-prone and complex task.
- Java doesn't include pointers, a powerful feature for experienced programmers that can be easily misused and introduce major security vulnerabilities.
- Java includes only single inheritance in object-oriented programming.

The lack of pointers and the presence of automatic memory management are two key elements of Java security.

1

Selecting a Development Tool

Now that you've been introduced to Java as a spectator, it's time to put some of these concepts into play and create your first Java program.

If you work your way through the 21 days of this book, you'll become well versed in Java's capabilities, including graphics, file input and output, XML processing, and Android app development. You will write programs that run on web pages and others that run on your computer, web servers, or other computing environments.

Before you get started, you must have software on your computer that can be used to edit, prepare, and run Java programs that use the most up-to-date version of the language: Java 7.

Several popular integrated development environments (IDEs) for Java support version 7, including IntelliJ IDEA and the open source software Eclipse.

If you are learning to use these tools at the same time as you learn Java, it can be a daunting task. Most IDEs are aimed primarily at experienced programmers who want to be more productive, not new people who are taking their first forays into a new language.

The simplest tool for Java development is the Java Development Kit, which is free and can be downloaded from www.oracle.com/technetwork/java/javase/downloads.

Whenever Oracle releases a new version of Java, it also makes a free development kit available over the Web to support that version. The current release is Java SE Development Kit 7.

For the sake of a few trees, in this book the language is usually referred to as simply Java and the kit as the JDK.

The drawback of developing Java programs with the JDK is that it is a set of command-line tools. Therefore, it has no graphical user interface for editing programs, turning them into Java classes, and testing them. (A command line is simply a prompt for typing text commands. The Windows command line is accessible on the Start menu under Accessories, Command Prompt or Accessories, System Tools, Command Prompt.)

Oracle offers a free IDE for Java programmers called NetBeans from the website www.netbeans.org. Because NetBeans is easier to use for most people than the JDK, it's employed throughout this book.

If you don't have a Java development tool on your computer yet and you want to try NetBeans, you can find out how to get started with the software in Appendix A, "Using the NetBeans Integrated Development Environment." The appendix covers how to download and install the kit and use it to create a sample Java program to make sure it works.

As soon as you have a Java development tool on your computer that supports Java 7, you're ready to dive into the language.

TIP _____ For more information on the other IDEs for Java, visit the IDEA site at www.jetbrains.com/idea and the Eclipse site at www.eclipse.org. Eclipse also is used for Android programming in Day 21, "Writing Android Apps for Java."

Object-Oriented Programming

The biggest challenge for a new Java programmer is learning object-oriented programming while learning the Java language.

Although this might sound daunting if you are unfamiliar with this style of programming, think of it as a two-for-one discount for your brain. You will learn object-oriented programming by learning Java. There's no other way to make use of the language.

Object-oriented programming is an approach to building computer programs that mimics how objects are assembled in the physical world.

By using this style of development, you can create programs that are more reusable, reliable, and understandable.

To get to that point, you first must explore how Java embodies the principles of object-oriented programming.

If you already are familiar with object-oriented programming, much of today's material will be a review for you. Even if you skim over the introductory material, you should create the sample program to get some experience in developing, compiling, and running Java programs.

There are many different ways to conceptualize a computer program. One way is to think of a program as a series of instructions carried out in sequence, which commonly is called *procedural programming*. Some programmers start by learning a procedural language such as a version of BASIC.

Procedural languages mirror how a computer carries out instructions, so the programs you write are tailored to the computer's manner of doing things. One of the first things a procedural programmer must learn is how to break a problem into a series of simple steps followed in order.

Object-oriented programming looks at a computer program from a different angle, focusing on the task the program was created to perform, not on how a computer handles tasks.

In object-oriented programming, a computer program is conceptualized as a set of objects that work together to accomplish a task. Each object is a separate part of the program, interacting with the other parts in highly controlled ways.

For a real-life example of object-oriented design, consider a stereo system. Most systems are built by hooking together a bunch of different objects, which are more commonly called components, such as the following:

- Speaker components play midrange and high-frequency sounds.
- A subwoofer component plays low bass frequency sounds.
- A tuner component receives radio broadcast signals.
- A CD player component reads audio data from CDs.
- A turntable component reads audio data from vinyl records.

These components are designed to interact with each other using standard input and output connectors. Even if you bought the speakers, subwoofer, tuner, CD player, and turntable from different companies, you could combine them to form a stereo system—as long as each component has standard connectors.

Object-oriented programming works under the same principle: You put together a program by creating new objects and connecting them to each other and to existing objects provided by Oracle or another developer. These objects are each a component in the larger program and are combined in a standard way. Each object plays a specific role in the larger program.

An *object* is a self-contained element of a computer program that represents a related group of features and that is designed to accomplish specific tasks.

Objects and Classes

Object-oriented programming is modeled on the observation that in the physical world, objects are made up of many kinds of smaller objects.

The ability to combine objects is only one aspect of object-oriented programming. Another important feature is the use of classes.

A *class* is a template used to create an object. Every object created from the same class has similar features.

Classes embody all features of a particular set of objects. When you write a program in an object-oriented language, you don't define individual objects. Instead, you define classes used to create those objects.

If you were writing a networking program in Java, you could create a Modem class that describes the features of all computer modems. Most modems have the following common features:

- They connect to a computer's serial port.
- They send and receive information.
- They dial phone numbers.

The Modem class serves as an abstract model for the concept of a modem. To actually have something concrete you can manipulate in a program, you need an object. You must use the Modem class to create a Modem object. The process of creating an object from a class is called *instantiation*, which is why objects also are called *instances*.

A Modem class can be used to create different Modem objects in a program, each with different features such as the following:

- Some are internal modems, and others are external modems.
- Some use the COM1 port, and others use the COM2 port.
- Some have error control, and others don't.

Even with these differences, two Modem objects still have enough in common to be recognizable as related objects. Figure 1.1 shows a Modem class and several objects created from that template.

Here's another example: Using Java, you could create a class to represent all command buttons—the clickable rectangles that appear on windows, dialog boxes, and other parts of a program's graphical user interface.

When the CommandButton class is developed, it could define these features:

- The text displayed on the button
- The size of the button
- Aspects of its appearance, such as whether it has a 3D shadow

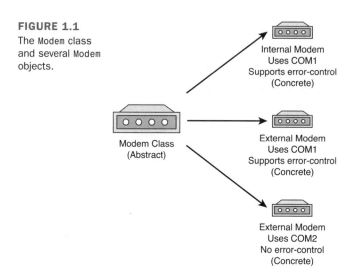

Internal Modem
Uses COM1
Supports error-control
(Concrete)

Modem Class
(Abstract)

External Modem
Uses COM1
Supports error-control
(Concrete)

External Modem
Uses COM2
No error-control
(Concrete)

The CommandButton class also could define how a button behaves, deciding the following things:

- Whether the button requires a single click or a double-click
- Whether it should ignore mouse clicks
- What it does when clicked

After you define the CommandButton class, you can create instances of that button—in other words, CommandButton objects. The objects all take on the basic features of a button as defined by the class. But each one could have a different appearance and slightly different behavior, depending on what you need that object to do.

By creating a CommandButton class, you don't have to keep rewriting the code for each button you want to use in your programs. In addition, you can reuse the CommandButton class to create different kinds of buttons as you need them, both in this program and in others.

When you write a Java program, you design and construct a set of classes. When your program runs, objects are created from those classes and used as needed. Your task as a Java programmer is to create the right set of classes to accomplish what your program needs to accomplish.

Fortunately, you don't have to start from scratch. The Java language includes the Java Class Library, more than 3,900 classes that implement most of the functionality you will need. These classes are installed along with a development tool such as the JDK.

When you're talking about programming in the Java language, you're actually talking about using this class library and some standard keywords and operators defined in Java.

The class library handles numerous tasks, such as mathematical functions, text, graphics, user interaction, and networking. Working with these classes is no different from working with the Java classes you create.

For complicated Java programs, you might create a whole set of new classes that form their own class library for use in other programs.

Reuse is one of the fundamental benefits of object-oriented programming.

1

NOTE

> In the Java Class Library, one of Java's standard classes, JButton in the javax.swing package, encompasses all the functionality of this hypothetical CommandButton example, along with a lot more. You get a chance to create objects from this class during Day 9, "Working with Swing."

Attributes and Behavior

A Java class consists of two distinct types of information: attributes and behavior.

Both of these are present in VolcanoRobot, a project you will implement today as a class. This project, a simple simulation of a volcanic exploration vehicle, is inspired by the Dante II robot used by NASA's Telerobotics Research program to do research inside volcanic craters.

Before you create the program, you need to learn some things about how object-oriented programs are designed in Java. The concepts may be difficult to understand as you're introduced to them, but you get plenty of practice with them throughout the book.

Attributes of a Class of Objects

Attributes are the data that differentiates one object from another. They can be used to determine the appearance, state, and other qualities of objects that belong to that class.

A volcanic exploration vehicle could have the following attributes:

- **Status**—Exploring, moving, returning home
- **Speed**—Measured in miles per hour
- **Temperature**—Measured in degrees Fahrenheit

In a class, attributes are defined by *variables*—places to store information in a computer program. *Instance variables* are attributes that have values that differ from one object to another.

An instance variable defines an attribute of one particular object. The object's class defines what kind of attribute it is, and each instance stores its own value for that attribute. Instance variables also are called *object variables*.

Each class attribute has a single corresponding variable. You change that attribute of the object by changing the value of the variable.

For example, the `VolcanoRobot` class defines a `speed` instance variable. This must be an instance variable because each robot travels at a different speed. The value of a robot's `speed` instance variable could be changed to make the robot move more quickly or slowly.

Instance variables can be given a value when an object is created and then stay constant throughout the life of the object. They also can be given different values as the object is used in a running program.

For other variables, it makes more sense to have one value that is shared by all objects of that class. These attributes are called *class variables*.

A class variable defines an attribute of an entire class. The variable applies to the class itself and to all its instances, so only one value is stored, no matter how many objects of that class have been created.

An example of a class variable for the `VolcanoRobot` class would be a variable that holds the current time. If an instance variable were created to hold the time, each object could have a different value for this variable. That could cause problems if the robots are supposed to perform tasks in conjunction with each other.

Using a class variable prevents this problem because all objects of that class share the same value automatically. Each `VolcanoRobot` object would have access to that variable.

Behavior of a Class of Objects

Behavior refers to the things that a class of objects can do to themselves and other objects. Behavior can be used to change an object's attributes, receive information from other objects, and send messages to other objects, asking them to perform tasks.

A volcano robot could have the following behavior:

- Check the current temperature
- Begin a survey

- Accelerate or decelerate its speed
- Report its current location

Behavior for a class of objects is implemented using methods.

Methods are groups of related statements in a class that perform a specific task. They are used to accomplish specific tasks on their own objects and on other objects and are comparable to functions and subroutines in other programming languages. A well-designed method performs only one task.

Objects communicate with each other using methods. A class or object can call methods in another class or object for many reasons, including the following:

- To report a change to another object
- To tell the other object to change something about itself
- To ask another object to do something

For example, two volcano robots could use methods to report their locations to each other and avoid collisions, and one robot could tell another to stop so that it can pass by safely.

Just as there are instance and class variables, there are also instance and class methods. Instance methods, which are usually just called methods, are used when you are working with an object of the class. If a method changes an individual object, it must be an instance method. Class methods apply to a class itself.

Creating a Class

To see classes, objects, attributes, and behavior in action, you will develop a VolcanoRobot class, create objects from that class, and work with them in a running program.

NOTE

The main purpose of this project is to explore object-oriented programming. You learn more about Java programming syntax during Day 2, "The ABCs of Programming."

NetBeans organizes Java classes into projects. It will be useful to have a project to hold the classes you create in this book. If you have not done so already, create a project:

1. Choose the menu command File, New Project. The New Project dialog box appears.

2. In the Categories pane, choose Java.

3. In the Projects pane, choose Java Application and click Next. The New Java Application dialog box opens.

4. In the Project Name text field, enter the name of the project (I used Java21). The Project Folder field is updated as you type the name. Make a note of this folder—it's where your Java programs can be found on your computer.

5. Click Finish.

The project is created. You can use it throughout the book.

If you created a project earlier, it already should be open in NetBeans. A new class you create will be added to this project.

To begin creating your first class, run NetBeans and start a new program:

1. Choose the menu command File, New File. The New File dialog box opens.

2. In the Categories pane, choose Java.

3. In the File Types pane, choose Empty Java File and click Next. The Empty Java File dialog box opens.

4. In the Class Name text field, enter VolcanoRobot. The file you're creating is shown in the Created File field, which can't be edited. This file has the name VolcanoRobot.java.

5. Click Finish.

The NetBeans source code editor opens with a blank file. Enter the code shown in Listing 1.1. When you're done, save the file using the menu command File, Save. The file VolcanoRobot.java will be saved.

NOTE — Don't type the numbers at the beginning of each line in the listing. They're not part of the program. They are included so that individual lines can be described for instructive purposes in this book.

LISTING 1.1   The Full Text of VolcanoRobot.java.

```
 1: class VolcanoRobot {
 2:     String status;
 3:     int speed;
 4:     float temperature;
 5:
 6:     void checkTemperature() {
 7:         if (temperature > 660) {
 8:             status = "returning home";
 9:             speed = 5;
10:         }
11:     }
12:
13:     void showAttributes() {
14:         System.out.println("Status: " + status);
15:         System.out.println("Speed: " + speed);
16:         System.out.println("Temperature: " + temperature);
17:     }
18: }
```

When you save this file, if it has no errors, NetBeans automatically creates a VolcanoRobot class. This process is called *compiling* the class, and it uses a tool called a compiler. The compiler turns the lines of source code into bytecode that the Java virtual machine can run.

The class statement in line 1 of Listing 1.1 defines and names the VolcanoRobot class. Everything contained between the opening brace ({) on line 1 and the closing brace (}) on line 18 is part of this class.

The VolcanoRobot class contains three instance variables and two instance methods.

The instance variables are defined in lines 2–4:

```
String status;
int speed;
float temperature;
```

The variables are named status, speed, and temperature. Each is used to store a different type of information:

- status holds a String object—a group of letters, numbers, punctuation, and other characters.
- speed holds an int, a numeric integer value.
- temperature holds a float, a floating-point number.

String objects are created from the String class, which is part of the Java Class Library.

TIP

As you might have noticed from the use of String in this program, a class can use objects as instance variables.

The first instance method in the VolcanoRobot class is defined in lines 6–11:

```
void checkTemperature() {
    if (temperature > 660) {
        status = "returning home";
        speed = 5;
    }
}
```

Methods are defined in a manner similar to a class. They begin with a statement that names the method, identifies the type of information the method produces, and defines other things.

The checkTemperature() method is contained within the opening brace on line 6 of Listing 1.1 and the closing brace on line 11. This method can be called on a VolcanoRobot object to find out its temperature.

This method checks to see whether the object's temperature instance variable has a value greater than 660. If it does, two other instance variables are changed:

- The status variable is changed to the text "returning home," indicating that the temperature is too hot and the robot is heading back to its base.

- The speed is changed to 5. (Presumably, this is as fast as the robot can travel.)

The second instance method, showAttributes(), is defined in lines 13–17:

```
void showAttributes() {
    System.out.println("Status: " + status);
    System.out.println("Speed: " + speed);
    System.out.println("Temperature: " + temperature);
}
```

This method calls the method System.out.println() to display the values of three instance variables, along with some text explaining what each value represents.

If you haven't saved this file yet, choose File, Save. This command is disabled if the file hasn't been changed since the last time you saved it.

Running the Program

Even if you typed the VolcanoRobot program in Listing 1.1 correctly and compiled it into a class, you can't do anything with it. The class you have created defines what a VolcanoRobot object is like, but it doesn't actually create one of these objects.

There are two ways to put the VolcanoRobot class to use:

- Create a separate Java program that creates an object belonging to that class.
- Add a special class method called main() to the VolcanoRobot class so that it can be run as an application and create an object of that class in that method.

The first option is chosen for this exercise.

Listing 1.2 contains the source code for VolcanoApplication, a Java class that creates a VolcanoRobot object, sets its instance variables, and calls methods. Following the same steps as in the preceding listing, create a new Java file in NetBeans and name it VolcanoApplication.

Enter the code shown in Listing 1.2 into the NetBeans source code editor.

LISTING 1.2   The Full Text of VolcanoApplication.java

```
 1: class VolcanoApplication {
 2:     public static void main(String[] arguments) {
 3:         VolcanoRobot dante = new VolcanoRobot();
 4:         dante.status = "exploring";
 5:         dante.speed = 2;
 6:         dante.temperature = 510;
 7:
 8:         dante.showAttributes();
 9:         System.out.println("Increasing speed to 3.");
10:         dante.speed = 3;
11:         dante.showAttributes();
12:         System.out.println("Changing temperature to 670.");
13:         dante.temperature = 670;
14:         dante.showAttributes();
15:         System.out.println("Checking the temperature.");
16:         dante.checkTemperature();
17:         dante.showAttributes();
18:     }
19: }
```

When you choose File, Save to save the file, NetBeans compiles it into the VolcanoApplication class, which contains bytecode for the Java virtual machine to run.

After you have compiled the application, run the program by choosing the menu command Run, Run File. The output displayed by the VolcanoApplication class appears in an Output pane in NetBeans, as shown in Figure 1.2.

FIGURE 1.2

The output of the Volcano Application class.

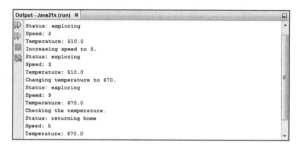

```
Output - Java21x (run)
Status: exploring
Speed: 2
Temperature: 510.0
Increasing speed to 3.
Status: exploring
Speed: 3
Temperature: 510.0
Changing temperature to 670.
Status: exploring
Speed: 3
Temperature: 670.0
Checking the temperature.
Status: returning home
Speed: 5
Temperature: 670.0
```

Using Listing 1.2 as a guide, you can see the following things taking place in the main() class method of this application:

- **Line 2**—The main() method is created and named. All main() methods take this format, as you learn during Day 5, "Creating Classes and Methods." For now, the most important thing to note is the static keyword, which indicates that the method is a class method shared by all VolcanoRobot objects.

- **Line 3**—A new VolcanoRobot object is created using the class as a template. The object is given the name dante.

- **Lines 4–6**—Three instance variables of the dante object are given values: status is set to the text "exploring," speed is set to 2, and temperature is set to 510.

- **Line 8**—On this line and several that follow, the showAttributes() method of the dante object is called. This method displays the current values of the instance variables status, speed, and temperature.

- **Line 9**—On this line and others that follow, a call to the System.out.println() method displays the text in parentheses.

- **Line 10**—The speed instance variable is set to the value 3.

- **Line 13**—The temperature instance variable is set to the value 670.

- **Line 16**—The checkTemperature() method of the dante object is called. This method checks to see whether the temperature instance variable is greater than 660. If it is, status and speed are assigned new values.

NOTE

> If for some reason you can't use NetBeans to write Java programs and must instead use the Java Development Kit, you can find out how to install it in Appendix D, "Using the Java Development Kit," and how to compile and run Java programs with it in Appendix E, "Programming with the Java Development Kit."

Organizing Classes and Class Behavior

Object-oriented programming in Java also requires three more concepts: inheritance, interfaces, and packages. All three are mechanisms for organizing classes and class behavior.

Inheritance

Inheritance, one of the most crucial concepts in object-oriented programming, has a direct impact on how you design and write your own Java classes.

Inheritance is a mechanism that enables one class to inherit all the behavior and attributes of another class.

Through inheritance, a class automatically picks up all the functionality of an existing class. The new class must only define how it is different from that existing class.

With inheritance, all classes—including those you create and the ones in the Java Class Library—are arranged in a strict hierarchy.

A class that inherits from another class is called a *subclass*. The class that gives the inheritance is called a *superclass*.

A class can have only one superclass, but it can have an unlimited number of subclasses. Subclasses inherit all the attributes and behavior of their superclass.

In practical terms, this means that if the superclass has behavior and attributes that your class needs, you don't have to redefine the behavior or copy that code to have the same behavior and attributes. Your class automatically receives these things from its superclass, the superclass gets them from its superclass, and so on, all the way up the hierarchy. Your class becomes a combination of its own features and all the features of the classes above it in the hierarchy.

The situation is comparable to how you inherited traits from your parents, such as your height, hair color, and love of peanut-butter-and-banana sandwiches. They inherited some of these things from their parents, who inherited from theirs, and backward through time to the Garden of Eden, Big Bang, giant spaghetti monster, or *[insert personal belief here]*.

Figure 1.3 shows how a hierarchy of classes is arranged.

FIGURE 1.3
A class hierarchy.

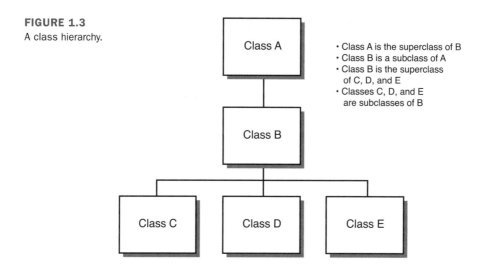

• Class A is the superclass of B
• Class B is a subclass of A
• Class B is the superclass of C, D, and E
• Classes C, D, and E are subclasses of B

At the top of the Java class hierarchy is the class Object.

All classes inherit from this superclass. Object is the most general class in the hierarchy. It defines behavior inherited by all the classes in the Java Class Library.

Each class further down the hierarchy becomes more tailored to a specific purpose. A class hierarchy defines abstract concepts at the top of the hierarchy. Those concepts become more concrete further down the line of subclasses.

Often when you create a new class in Java, you want all the functionality of an existing class except for some additions or modifications of your own creation. For example, you might want a new version of CommandButton that makes a sound when clicked.

To receive all the CommandButton functionality without doing any work to re-create it, you can define your new class as a subclass of CommandButton.

Because of inheritance, your class automatically inherits behavior and attributes defined in CommandButton as well as the behavior and attributes defined in the superclasses of

CommandButton. All you have to worry about are the things that make your new class different from CommandButton itself. Subclassing is the mechanism for defining new classes as the differences between those classes and their superclass.

Subclassing is the creation of a new class that inherits from an existing class. The only task in the subclass is to indicate the differences in behavior and attributes between the subclass and its superclass.

If your class defines entirely new behavior and isn't a subclass of another class, you can inherit directly from the Object class.

If you create a class that doesn't indicate a superclass, Java assumes that the new class inherits directly from Object. The VolcanoRobot class you created earlier today did not specify a superclass, so it's a subclass of Object.

Creating a Class Hierarchy

If you're creating a large set of classes, it makes sense for your classes to inherit from the existing class hierarchy and to make up a hierarchy themselves. This gives your classes several advantages:

- Functionality common to multiple classes can be put into a superclass, which enables it to be used repeatedly in all classes below it in the hierarchy.
- Changes to a superclass automatically are reflected in all its subclasses, their subclasses, and so on. There is no need to change or recompile any of the lower classes; they receive the new information through inheritance.

For example, imagine that you have created a Java class to implement all the features of a volcanic exploratory robot. (This shouldn't take much imagination.)

The VolcanoRobot class is completed and works successfully. Your boss at NASA asks you to create a Java class called MarsRobot.

These two kinds of robots have similar features. Both are research robots that work in hostile environments and conduct research. Both keep track of their current temperature and speed.

Your first impulse might be to open the VolcanoRobot.java source file, copy it into a new source file called MarsRobot.java, and then make the necessary changes for the new robot to do its job.

A better plan is to figure out the common functionality of MarsRobot and VolcanoRobot and organize it into a more general class hierarchy. This might be a lot of work just for the classes VolcanoRobot and MarsRobot, but what if you also want to add MoonRobot,

1

UndeseaRobot, and DesertRobot? Factoring common behavior into one or more reusable superclasses significantly reduces the overall amount of work you must do.

To design a class hierarchy that might serve this purpose, start at the top with the class Object, the pinnacle of all Java classes.

The most general class to which these robots belong might be called Robot. A robot, generally, could be defined as a self-controlled exploration device. In the Robot class, you define only the behavior that qualifies something to be a device, to be self-controlled, and to be designed for exploration.

There could be two classes below Robot: WalkingRobot and DrivingRobot. The obvious thing that differentiates these classes is that one travels by foot and the other by wheel. The behavior of walking robots might include bending over to pick up something, ducking, running, and the like. Driving robots would behave differently. Figure 1.4 shows what you have so far.

FIGURE 1.4
The basic Robot
hierarchy.

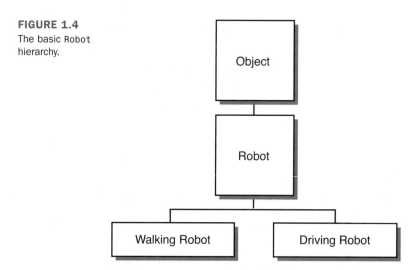

Now the hierarchy can become even more specific.

With WalkingRobot, you might have several classes: ScienceRobot, GuardRobot, SearchRobot, and so on. As an alternative, you could factor out still more functionality and have intermediate classes for TwoLegged and FourLegged robots, with different behaviors for each (see Figure 1.5).

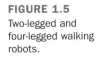

FIGURE 1.5
Two-legged and
four-legged walking
robots.

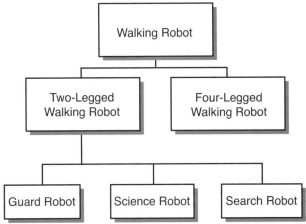

1

Finally, the hierarchy is done, and you have a place for VolcanoRobot. It can be a sub-class of ScienceRobot, which is a subclass of WalkingRobot, which is a subclass of Robot, which is a subclass of Object.

Where do attributes such as status, temperature, and speed come in? At the place they fit into the class hierarchy most naturally. Because all robots need to keep track of the temperature of their environment, it makes sense to define temperature as an instance variable in Robot. All subclasses would have that instance variable as well. Remember that you need to define a behavior or attribute only once in the hierarchy and it is inherited automatically by each subclass.

NOTE   Designing an effective class hierarchy involves a lot of planning and revision. As you attempt to put attributes and behavior into a hierarchy, you're likely to find reasons to move some classes to different spots in the hierarchy. The goal is to reduce the number of repetitive features (and redundant code) needed.

Inheritance in Action

Inheritance in Java works much more simply than it does in the real world. No wills or courts are required when inheriting from a parent.

When you create a new object, Java keeps track of each variable defined for that object and each variable defined for each superclass of the object. In this way, all the classes combine to form a template for the current object, and each object fills in the information appropriate to its situation.

Methods operate similarly. A new object has access to all method names of its class and superclass. This is determined dynamically when a method is used in a running program. If you call a method of a particular object, the Java virtual machine first checks the object's class for that method. If the method isn't found, the virtual machine looks for it in the superclass of that class, and so on, until the method definition is found. This is illustrated in Figure 1.6.

FIGURE 1.6
How methods are located in a class hierarchy.

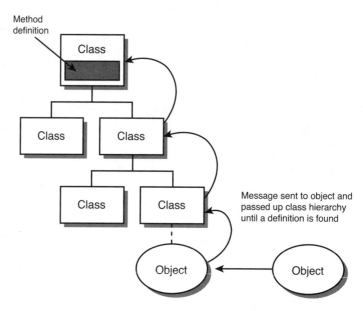

Things get complicated when a subclass defines a method that matches a method defined in a superclass in name and other aspects. In this case, the method definition found first (starting at the bottom of the hierarchy and working upward) is the one that is used.

Because of this, you can create a method in a subclass that prevents a method in a superclass from being used. To do this, you give the method the same name, return type, and arguments as the method in the superclass. This procedure, shown in Figure 1.7, is called *overriding*.

FIGURE 1.7
Overriding
methods.

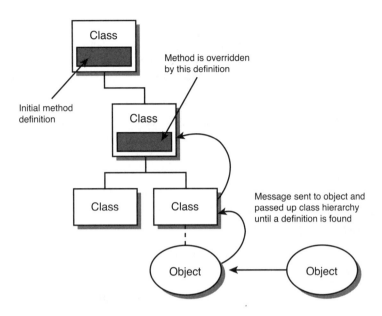

NOTE

Java's form of inheritance is called single inheritance because each Java class can have only one superclass, although any given superclass can have multiple subclasses.

In other object-oriented programming languages such as C++, classes can have more than one superclass, and they inherit combined variables and methods from all those superclasses. This is called multiple inheritance. Java makes inheritance simpler by allowing only single inheritance.

Interfaces

Single inheritance makes the relationship between classes and the functionality they implement easier to understand and design. However, it also can be restrictive, especially when you have similar behavior that needs to be duplicated across different branches of a class hierarchy. Java solves the problem of shared behavior by using interfaces.

An *interface* is a collection of methods that indicate a class has some behavior in addition to what it inherits from its superclasses. The methods included in an interface do not define this behavior; that task is left for the classes that implement the interface.

For example, the Comparable interface contains a method that compares two objects of the same class to see which one should appear first in a sorted list. Any class that implements this interface shows other objects that it knows how to determine the sorting order for objects of that class. This behavior would be unavailable to the class without the interface.

You learn about interfaces during Day 6, "Packages, Interfaces, and Other Class Features."

Packages

Packages in Java are a way to group related classes and interfaces. They enable groups of classes to be referenced more easily in other classes. They also eliminate potential naming conflicts among classes.

Classes in Java can be referred to by a short name such as Object or a full name such as java.lang.Object.

By default, your Java classes can refer to the classes in the java.lang package using only short names. The java.lang package provides basic language features such as string handling and mathematical operations. To use classes from any other package, you must refer to them explicitly using their full package name or use an import command to import the package in your source code file.

Because the Color class is contained in the java.awt package, you normally refer to it in your programs with the notation java.awt.Color.

If the entire java.awt package has been imported using import, the class can be referred to as Color.

Summary

If today was your first exposure to object-oriented programming, it probably seemed theoretical and a bit overwhelming.

Because your brain has been stuffed with object-oriented programming concepts and terminology for the first time, you might be worried that no room is left for the Java lessons of the remaining 20 days.

Don't panic. Stay calm and carry on.

At this point, you should have a basic understanding of classes, objects, attributes, and behavior. You also should be familiar with instance variables and methods. You use these right away tomorrow.

The other aspects of object-oriented programming, such as inheritance and packages, are covered in more detail in upcoming days.

You work with object-oriented programming in every remaining day of the book. There's no other way to create programs in Java.

By the time you finish the first week, you'll have working experience with objects, classes, inheritance, and all other aspects of the methodology.

Q&A

Q **Methods are functions defined inside classes. If they look like functions and act like functions, why aren't they called functions?**

A Some object-oriented programming languages do call them functions. (C++ calls them member functions.) Other object-oriented languages differentiate between functions inside and outside the body of a class or object because in those languages the use of the separate terms is important to understanding how each function works. Because the difference is relevant in other languages and because the term *method* now is in common use in object-oriented terminology, Java uses the term as well.

Q **What's the distinction between instance variables and methods and their counterparts, class variables and methods?**

A Almost everything you do in a Java program involves instances (also called objects) rather than classes. However, some behavior and attributes make more sense if stored in the class itself rather than in the object.

For example, the Math class in the java.lang package includes a class variable called PI that holds the approximate value of pi. This value does not change, so there's no reason why different objects of that class would need their own individual copy of the PI variable. On the other hand, every String object contains a method called length() that reveals the number of characters in that String. This value can be different for each object of that class, so it must be an instance method.

Class variables occupy memory until a Java program is finished running, so they should be used with care. If a class variable references an object, that object will remain in memory as well. This is a common problem causing a program to take up too much memory and run slowly.

Q When a Java class imports an entire package, does it increase the compiled size of that class?

A No. The use of the term "import" is a bit misleading. The import keyword does not add the bytecode of one class or one package to the class you are creating. Instead, it simply makes it easier to refer to classes within another class.

The sole purpose of importing is to shorten the class names when they're used in Java statements. It would be cumbersome to always have to refer to full class names such as javax.swing.JButton and java.awt.Graphics in your code instead of calling them JButton and Graphics.

Quiz

Review today's material by taking this three-question quiz. Answers are at the end of the book.

Questions

1. What is another word for a class?
    A. Object
    B. Template
    C. Instance

2. When you create a subclass, what must you define about that class?
    A. Nothing. Everything is defined already.
    B. Things that are different from its superclass
    C. Everything about the class

3. What does an instance method of a class represent?
    A. The attributes of that class
    B. The behavior of that class
    C. The behavior of an object created from that class

Certification Practice

The following question is the kind of thing you could expect to be asked on a Java programming certification test. Answer it without looking at today's material.

Which of the following statements is true?

A. All objects created from the same class must be identical.

B. All objects created from the same class can be different from each other.

C. An object inherits attributes and behavior from the class used to create it.

D. A class inherits attributes and behavior from its subclass.

1

The answer is available on the book's website at www.java21days.com. Visit the Day 1 page and click the Certification Practice link.

Exercises

To extend your knowledge of the subjects covered today, try the following exercises:

1. In the `main()` method of the `VolcanoRobot` class, create a second `VolcanoRobot` robot named `virgil`, set up its instance variables, and display them.

2. Create an inheritance hierarchy for the pieces of a chess set. Decide where the instance variables `color`, `startingPosition`, `forwardMovement`, and `sideMovement` should be defined in the hierarchy.

Where applicable, exercise solutions are offered on the book's website at www.java21days.com.

DAY 2
The ABCs of Programming

A Java program is made up of classes and objects, which, in turn, are made up of methods and variables. Methods are made up of statements and expressions, which are made up of operators.

At this point, you might be worried that Java is like a set of Russian nesting *matryoshka* dolls. Each doll except the smallest one has a smaller doll inside it, as intricate and detailed as its larger companion.

Today's lesson clears away the big dolls to reveal the smallest elements of Java programming. You will set aside classes, objects, and methods for a day and examine the basic things you can do in a single line of Java code.

The following subjects are covered:

- Java statements and expressions
- Variables and primitive data types
- Constants
- Comments
- Literals
- Arithmetic
- Comparisons
- Logical operators

Statements and Expressions

All the tasks you want to accomplish in a Java program can be broken into a series of statements. In a programming language, a *statement* is a simple command that causes something to happen.

Statements represent a single action taken in a Java program. Here are three simple Java statements:

```
int weight = 225;
System.out.println("Free the bound periodicals!");
song.duration = 230;
```

Some statements can convey a value, such as when two numbers are added or two variables are compared to find out if they are equal.

A statement that produces a value is called an *expression*. The value can be stored for later use in the program, used immediately in another statement, or disregarded. The value produced by a statement is called its *return value*.

Some expressions produce a numeric return value, as when two numbers are added or multiplied. Others produce a Boolean value—either `true` or `false`—or even can produce a Java object. They are discussed later today.

Although many Java programs contain one statement per line, this is a formatting decision that does not determine where one statement ends and another one begins. Each statement in Java is terminated with a semicolon character (`;`). A programmer can put more than one statement on a line and it will compile successfully, as in the following example:

```
dante.speed = 2; dante.temperature = 510;
```

To make your program more readable to other programmers, you should follow the convention of putting only one statement on each line.

Statements in Java are grouped using an opening brace (`{`) and a closing brace (`}`). A group of statements organized between these characters is called a block (or block statement). You learn more about them during Day 4, "Lists, Logic, and Loops."

Variables and Data Types

In the VolcanoRobot application created during Day 1, "Getting Started with Java," you used variables to keep track of information. A variable is a place where information can be stored while a program is running. The value can be changed at any point in the program—hence the name.

To create a variable, you must give it a name and identify the type of information it will store. You also can give a variable an initial value at the same time you create it.

Java has three kinds of variables: instance variables, class variables, and local variables.

Instance variables, as you learned yesterday, define an object's attributes.

Class variables define the attributes of an entire class of objects and apply to all instances of it.

Local variables are used inside method definitions or even smaller blocks of statements within a method. You can use them only while the method or block is being executed by the Java virtual machine. They cease to exist afterwards.

Although all three kinds of variables are created in much the same way, class and instance variables are used in a different manner than local variables. You will learn about local variables today and explore instance and class variables during Day 3, "Working with Objects."

Creating Variables

Before you can use a variable in a Java program, you must create the variable by declaring its name and the type of information it will store. The type of information is listed first, followed by the name of the variable. The following all are examples of variable declarations:

```
int loanLength;

String message;

boolean gameOver;
```

In these examples, the int type represents integers, String is an object that holds text, and boolean is used for Boolean true/false values.

Local variables can be declared at any place inside a method, like any other Java statement, but they must be declared before they can be used.

In the following example, three variables are declared at the top of a program's main() method:

```
public static void main(String[] arguments) {
    int total;
    String reportTitle;
    boolean active;
}
```

If you are creating several variables of the same type, you can declare all of them in the same statement by separating the variable names with commas. The following statement creates three `String` variables named `street`, `city`, and `state`:

```
String street, city, state;
```

Variables can be assigned a value when they are created by using an equals sign (=) followed by the value. The following statements create new variables and give them initial values:

```
String zipCode = "02134";
int box = 350;
boolean pbs = true;
String name = "Zoom", city = "Boston", state = "MA";
```

As the last statement demonstrates, you can assign values to multiple variables of the same type by using commas to separate them.

You must give values to local variables before you use them in a program, or the program won't compile successfully. For this reason, it is good practice to give initial values to all local variables.

Instance and class variable definitions are given an initial value depending on the type of information they hold, as in the following:

- Numeric variables: `0`
- Characters: `'\0'`
- Booleans: `false`
- Objects: `null`

Naming Variables

Variable names in Java must start with a letter, an underscore character (_), or a dollar sign ($).

Variable names cannot start with a number. After the first character, variable names can include any combination of letters or numbers.

<table>
<tr>
<td>NOTE</td>
<td>In addition, the Java language uses the Unicode character set, which includes thousands of character sets to represent international alphabets. Accented characters and other symbols can be used in variable names as long as they have a Unicode character number.</td>
</tr>
</table>

When naming a variable and using it in a program, it's important to remember that Java is case-sensitive—the capitalization of letters must be consistent. Because of this, a program can have a variable named X and another named x (and a Rose is not a rose is not a ROSE).

In programs in this book and elsewhere, Java variables are given meaningful names that include several joined words. To make it easier to spot the words, the following rules of thumb are used:

- The first letter of the variable name is lowercase.
- Each successive word in the variable name begins with a capital letter.
- All other letters are lowercase.

The following variable declarations follow these naming rules:

```
Button loadFile;

int localAreaCode;

boolean quitGame;
```

Variable Types

In addition to a name, a variable declaration must include the data type of information being stored. The type can be any of the following:

- One of the primitive data types, such as int or boolean
- The name of a class or interface
- An array

You learn how to declare and use array variables on Day 4. Today's lesson focuses on the other variable types.

Data Types

Java has eight basic data types that store integers, floating-point numbers, characters, and Boolean values. These often are called *primitive types* because they are built-in parts of the language rather than objects, which makes them easier to create and use. These data types have the same size and characteristics no matter what operating system and platform you're on, unlike some data types in other programming languages.

You can use four data types to store integers. Which one you use depends on the integer's size, as shown in Table 2.1.

TABLE 2.1   Integer Types

Type	Size	Values That Can Be Stored
byte	8 bits	−128 to 127
short	16 bits	−32,768 to 32,767
int	32 bits	−2,147,483,648 to 2,147,483,647
long	64 bits	−9,223,372,036,854,775,808 to 9,223,372,036,854,775,807

All these types are *signed*, which means that they can hold either positive or negative numbers. The type used for a variable depends on the range of values it might need to hold. None of these integer variables can reliably store a value that is too large or too small for its designated variable type, so take care when designating the type.

Another type of number that can be stored is a floating-point number, which has the type float or double. *Floating-point* numbers are numbers with a decimal point. The float type should be sufficient for most uses because it can handle any number from 1.4E-45 to 3.4E+38. If not, the double type can be used for more precise numbers ranging from 4.9E-324 to 1.7E+308.

The char type is used for individual characters, such as letters, numbers, punctuation, and other symbols.

The last of the eight primitive data types is boolean. As you have learned, this data type holds either true or false.

All these variable types appear in lowercase, and you must use them as such in programs. Some classes have the same names as some of these data types, but with different capitalization, such as Boolean and Char. These are created and referenced differently in a Java program, so you can't use them interchangeably in most circumstances. Tomorrow you will see how to use these special classes.

NOTE There's actually a ninth primitive data type in Java, void, which represents nothing. It's used in methods to indicate that they do not return a value.

Class Types

In addition to the primitive data types, a variable can have a class as its type, as in the following examples:

```
String lastName = "Hopper";
Color hair;
VolcanoRobot vr;
```

When a variable has a class as its type, the variable refers to an object of that class or one of its subclasses.

The last statement in the preceding list creates a variable named vr that is reserved for a VolcanoRobot object. You learn more tomorrow about how to associate objects with variables.

Assigning Values to Variables

After a variable has been declared, a value can be assigned to it with the assignment operator, which is an equals sign (=). The following are examples of assignment statements:

```
idCode = 8675309;
accountOverdrawn = false;
```

Constants

Variables are useful when you need to store information that can be changed as a program runs.

If the value never should change during a program's runtime, you can use a type of variable called a constant. A *constant* is a variable with a value that never changes. This might seem like an oxymoron, given the meaning of the word "variable."

Constants are useful in defining shared values for the use of all methods of an object. In Java, you can create constants for all kinds of variables: instance, class, and local.

2

To declare a constant, use the `final` keyword before the variable declaration and include an initial value for that variable, as in the following:

```
final float PI = 3.141592;

final boolean DEBUG = false;

final int PENALTY = 25;
```

Constants can be handy for naming various states of an object and then testing for those states. Suppose you have a program that takes directional input from the numeric keypad on the keyboard—press 8 to go up, 4 to go left, and so on. You can define those values as constant integers:

```
final int LEFT = 4;
final int RIGHT = 6;
final int UP = 8;
final int DOWN = 2;
```

Constants often make a program easier to understand. To illustrate this point, consider which of the following two statements is more informative as to its function:

```
guide.direction = 4;

guide.direction = LEFT;
```

 NOTE

In the preceding statements, the names of the constants such as DEBUG and LEFT are capitalized. This is a convention adopted by many Java programmers to make it clear that the variable is a constant. Java does not require that constants be capitalized in this manner.

Today's first project is a Java application that creates several variables, assigns them initial values, and displays two of them as output. Run NetBeans and create a new Java program by selecting the menu command File, New File. Choose the category Java and the file type Empty Java File, and then name the class `Variables`. Enter the code shown in Listing 2.1 into the source code editor.

LISTING 2.1   The Full Text of `Variables.java`

```
1: public class Variables {
2:
3:     public static void main(String[] arguments) {
4:         final char UP = 'U';
```

LISTING 2.1   Continued

```
 5:            byte initialLevel = 12;
 6:            short location = 13250;
 7:            int score = 3500100;
 8:            boolean newGame = true;
 9:
10:            System.out.println("Level: " + initialLevel);
11:            System.out.println("Up: " + UP);
12:        }
13: }
```

2

Save the file by choosing File, Save. NetBeans automatically compiles the application if it contains no errors. Run the program by choosing Run, Run File. This program produces two lines of output:

Output ▼

```
Level: 12
Up: U
```

This class uses four local variables and one constant, making use of `System.out.println()` in lines 10 and 11 to produce output.

`System.out.println()` is a method called to display strings and other information to the standard output device, which usually is the screen.

This method takes a single argument within its parentheses: a string. To present more than one variable or literal as the argument to `println()`, the + operator combines the elements into a single string.

Java also has a `System.out.print()` method, which displays a string without terminating it with a newline character. You can call `print()` instead of `println()` to display several strings on the same line.

Comments

One of the most effective ways to improve a program's readability is to use comments. These are text included in a program that explains what's going on in the code. The Java compiler ignores comments when preparing a version of a Java source file that can be run as a class, so there's no penalty for using them.

You can use three different kinds of comments in Java programs.

A single-line comment is preceded by two slash characters (//). Everything from the slashes to the end of the line is considered a comment and is disregarded by the compiler, as in the following statement:

```
int creditHours = 3; // set up credit hours for course
```

Everything from the slashes onward is ignored. As far as the compiler is concerned, the preceding line is the same as this:

```
int creditHours = 3;
```

A multiline comment begins with /* and ends with */. Everything between these two delimiters is considered a comment, as in the following:

```
/* This program occasionally deletes all files on
your hard drive and renders it unusable
forever when you click the Save button. */
```

A Javadoc comment begins with /** and ends with */. Everything between these delimiters is considered to be official documentation on how the class and its methods work.

Javadoc comments are designed to be read by utilities such as javadoc, a tool that's part of the JDK. This program uses official comments to create a set of web page records that document the functionality of a Java class, show its place in relation to its superclass and subclasses, and describe each of its methods.

TIP

All the official documentation on each class in the Java Class Library is generated from Javadoc comments. You can view current Java documentation at http://docs.oracle.com/javase/7/docs/api.

Literals

In addition to variables, you can work with values as literals in a Java statement. A *literal* is any number, text, or other information that directly represents a value.

The following assignment statement uses a literal:

```
int year = 2012;
```

The literal 2012 represents the integer value 2012. Numbers, characters, and strings are all examples of literals. Java has some special types of literals that represent different kinds of numbers, characters, strings, and Boolean values.

Number Literals

Java has several integer literals. The number 4, for example, is an integer literal of the int variable type. It also can be assigned to byte and short variables because the number is small enough to fit into those integer types. An integer literal larger than an int can hold automatically is considered to be of the type long. You also can indicate that a literal should be a long integer by adding the letter L (upper- or lowercase) to the number. Here's an example:

```
pennyTotal = pennyTotal + 4L;
```

This statement adds the value 4, formatted as a long, to the current value of the pennyTotal variable.

To represent a negative number as a literal, prepend a minus sign (–), as in –45.

2

NOTE

Java also supports numeric literals that use binary, octal, and hexadecimal numbering.

Binary numbers are a base-2 numbering system in which only the values 0 and 1 are used. Values made up of 1s and 0s are the simplest form for a computer and are a fundamental part of computing. Counting up from 0, binary values are 0, 1, 10, 11, 100, 111, and so on. Each digit in the number is called a bit. The combination of eight numbers is a byte.

Octal numbers are a base-8 numbering system, which means that they can represent only the values 0 through 7 as a single digit. The eighth number in octal is 10 (or 010 as a Java literal).

Hexadecimal is a base-16 numbering system that can represent 16 numbers as a single digit. The letters A through F represent the last six digits, so the first 16 numbers are 0, 1, 2, 3, 4, 5, 6, 7, 8, 9, A, B, C, D, E, F.

The octal and hexadecimal systems are better suited for certain tasks in programming than the normal decimal system. If you have ever edited a web page to set its background color, you could have used hexadecimal numbers for green (001100), blue (000011), or butterscotch (FFCC99).

If you need to use a literal integer with octal numbering, prepend a 0 to the number. For example, the octal number 777 would be the literal 0777. Hexadecimal integers are used as literals by prepending the number with 0x, as in 0x12 or 0xFF.

The use of literals to specify binary values was introduced in Java 7. You prepend the number with 0b. For example, 0b101 is the binary value 101, and 0b11111111 is binary 11111111.

Floating-point literals use a period character (.) for the decimal point, as you would expect. The following statement uses a literal to set up a `double` variable:

```
double myGPA = 2.25;
```

All floating-point literals are considered to be of the `double` variable type instead of `float`. To specify a literal of `float`, add the letter F (upper- or lowercase) to the literal, as in the following example:

```
float piValue = 3.1415927F;
```

You can use exponents in floating-point literals by using the letter e or E followed by the exponent, which can be a negative number. The following statements use exponential notation:

```
double x = 12e22;
double y = 19E-95;
```

Java 7 adds the ability to include an underscore character (_) in a large integer literal to make it more readable to humans. The underscore serves the same purpose as a comma in a large number, making its value more apparent. Consider these two examples, one of which uses underscores:

```
int jackpot = 3500000;
int jackpot = 3_500_000;
```

Both examples equal 3,500,000, which is easier to see in the second statement. The Java compiler ignores the underscores.

CAUTION If you use a feature of Java 7 in NetBeans and it displays an error message, make sure the project has been set up to use the current version of the language. Choose File, Project Properties to open the Project Properties dialog, choose the category `Libraries`, and make sure the Java Platform drop-down is set to JDK `1.7`.

Boolean Literals

The Boolean literals `true` and `false` are the only two values you can use when assigning a value to a `boolean` variable type or using a Boolean in a statement.

The following statement sets a boolean variable:

```
boolean chosen = true;
```

2

CAUTION If you have programmed in other languages, you might expect that a value of 1 is equivalent to true and 0 is equivalent to false. This isn't the case in Java; you must use the values true and false to represent Boolean values.

Note that the literal true does not have quotation marks around it. If it did, the Java compiler would assume that it is a string of characters.

Character Literals

Character literals are expressed by a single character surrounded by single quotation marks, such as 'a', '#', and '3'. You might be familiar with the ASCII character set, which includes 128 characters, including letters, numerals, punctuation, and other characters useful in computing. Java supports thousands of additional characters through the 16-bit Unicode standard.

Some character literals represent characters that are not readily printable or accessible from a keyboard. Table 2.2 lists the codes that can represent these special characters as well as characters from the Unicode character set.

TABLE 2.2   Character Escape Codes

Escape	Meaning
\n	New line
\t	Tab
\b	Backspace
\r	Carriage return
\f	Formfeed
\\	Backslash
\'	Single quotation mark
\"	Double quotation mark
\d	Octal
\xd	Hexadecimal
\ud	Unicode character

In Table 2.2, the letter _d_ in the octal, hex, and Unicode escape codes represents a number or a hexadecimal digit (a through f or A through F).

String Literals

The final literal you can use in a Java program represents strings of characters. A string in Java is an object rather than a primitive data type. Strings are not stored in arrays as they are in languages such as C.

Because string objects are real objects in Java, methods are available to combine strings, modify strings, and determine whether two strings have the same value.

String literals consist of a series of characters inside double quotation marks, as in the following statements:

```
String quitMsg = "Are you sure you want to quit?";
String password = "drowssap";
```

Strings can include the character escape codes listed in Table 2.2, as shown here:

```
String example = "Socrates asked, \"Hemlock is poison?\"";
System.out.println("Sincerely,\nMillard Fillmore\n");
String title = "Sams Teach Yourself Ruby on Rails in the John\u2122";
```

In the last example, the Unicode code sequence \u2122 produces a ™ symbol on systems that have been configured to support Unicode.

CAUTION	Although Java supports the transmission of Unicode characters, the user's system also must support it for the characters to be displayed. Unicode support provides a way to encode its characters for systems that support the standard. Java supports the display of any Unicode character that can be represented by a host font.
	For more information about Unicode, visit the Unicode Consortium website at www.unicode.org.

Although string literals are used in a manner similar to other literals in a program, they are handled differently behind the scenes.

With a string literal, Java stores that value as a String object. You don't have to explicitly create a new object, as you must when working with other objects, so they are as easy to work with as primitive data types. Strings are unusual in this respect—none of the basic types are stored as an object when used. You learn more about strings and the `String` class later today.

Expressions and Operators

An *expression* is a statement that can convey a value. Some of the most common expressions are mathematical, such as in the following examples:

```
int x = 3;
int y = x;
int z = x * y;
```

2

All three of these statements can be considered expressions; they convey values that can be assigned to variables. The first assigns the literal 3 to the variable x. The second assigns the value of the variable x to the variable y. In the third expression, the multiplication operator (*) is used to multiply the x and y integers, and the result is stored in the z integer.

Expressions can be any combination of variables, literals, and operators. They also can be method calls because methods send back a value to the object or class that called the method.

The value conveyed by an expression is called a *return value*. This value can be assigned to a variable and used in many other ways in your Java programs.

Most of the expressions in Java use operators such as *. *Operators* are special symbols used for mathematical functions, assignment statements, and logical comparisons.

Arithmetic

Five operators are used to accomplish basic arithmetic in Java, as shown in Table 2.3.

TABLE 2.3 Arithmetic Operators

Operator	Meaning	Example
+	Addition	3 + 4
-	Subtraction	5 - 7
*	Multiplication	5 * 5
/	Division	14 / 7
%	Modulus	20 % 7

Each operator takes two operands, one on each side of the operator. The subtraction operator also can be used to negate a single operand, which is equivalent to multiplying that operand by −1.

One thing to be mindful of when performing division is the type of numbers being used. If you store a division operation in an integer, the result is truncated to the next-lower whole number because the int data type can't handle floating-point numbers.

For example, the expression 31 / 9 results in 3 if stored as an integer.

Modulus division, which uses the % operator, produces the remainder of a division operation. The expression 31 % 9 results in 4 because 31 divided by 9, with the whole number result of 3, leaves a remainder of 4.

Note that many arithmetic operations involving integers produce an int regardless of the original type of the operands. If you're working with other numbers, such as floating-point numbers or long integers, you should make sure that the operands have the same type you're trying to end up with.

The next project is a Java class that demonstrates simple arithmetic in the language. Create a new empty Java file in NetBeans called Weather, and enter the code shown in Listing 2.2 into the source code editor. Save the file when you're done.

LISTING 2.2   The Full Text of Weather.java

```
 1: public class Weather {
 2:     public static void main(String[] arguments) {
 3:         float fah = 86;
 4:         System.out.println(fah + " degrees Fahrenheit is ...");
 5:         // To convert Fahrenheit into Celsius
 6:         // begin by subtracting 32
 7:         fah = fah - 32;
 8:         // Divide the answer by 9
 9:         fah = fah / 9;
10:         // Multiply that answer by 5
11:         fah = fah * 5;
12:         System.out.println(fah + " degrees Celsius\n");
13:
14:         float cel = 33;
15:         System.out.println(cel + " degrees Celsius is ...");
16:         // To convert Celsius into Fahrenheit
17:         // begin by multiplying by 9
18:         cel = cel * 9;
19:         // Divide the answer by 5
20:         cel = cel / 5;
21:         // Add 32 to the answer
```

LISTING 2.2 Continued

```
22:          cel = cel + 32;
23:          System.out.println(cel + " degrees Fahrenheit");
24:      }
25: }
```

Run the program by selecting Run, Run File. It produces the following output in the NetBeans Output pane:

Output ▼

```
86.0 degrees Fahrenheit is ...
30.0 degrees Celsius

33.0 degrees Celsius is ...
91.4 degrees Fahrenheit
```

In lines 3–12 of this Java application, a temperature in Fahrenheit is converted to Celsius using the arithmetic operators:

- **Line 3**—The floating-point variable fah is created with a value of 86.
- **Line 4**—The current value of fah is displayed.
- **Line 5**—The first of several comments explains what the program is doing. The Java compiler ignores these comments.
- **Line 7**—fah is set to its current value minus 32.
- **Line 9**—fah is set to its current value divided by 9.
- **Line 11**—fah is set to its current value multiplied by 5.
- **Line 12**—Now that fah has been converted to a Celsius value, fah is displayed again.

A similar thing happens in lines 14–23 but in the reverse direction. A temperature in Celsius is converted to Fahrenheit.

More About Assignment

Assigning a value to a variable is an expression because it produces a value. Because of this feature, you can combine assignment statements in the following way:

```
x = y = z = 7;
```

In this statement, all three variables x, y, and z end up with the value 7.

The right side of an assignment expression always is calculated before the assignment takes place. This makes it possible to use an expression statement as in the following code:

```
int x = 5;
x = x + 2;
```

In the expression x = x + 2, the first thing that happens is that x + 2 is calculated. The result of this calculation, 7, is then assigned to x.

Using an expression to change a variable's value is a common task in programming. Several operators are used strictly in these cases.

Table 2.4 shows these assignment operators and the expressions they are functionally equivalent to.

TABLE 2.4   Assignment Operators

Expression	Meaning
x += y	x = x + y
x -= y	x = x - y
x *= y	x = x * y
x /= y	x = x / y

CAUTION

These shorthand assignment operators are functionally equivalent to the longer assignment statements for which they substitute. If either side of your assignment statement is part of a complex expression, however, there are cases where the operators are not equivalent. For example, if x equals 20 and y equals 5, the following two statements do not produce the same value:

```
x = x / y + 5;
x /= y + 5;
```

When in doubt, simplify an expression by using multiple assignment statements, and don't use the shorthand operators.

Incrementing and Decrementing

Another common task required in programming is to add 1 to or subtract 1 from an integer variable. These expressions have special operators, which are called increment and decrement operators. *Incrementing* a variable means adding 1 to its value, and *decrementing* a variable means subtracting 1 from its value.

The increment operator is ++, and the decrement operator is --. These operators are placed immediately after or immediately before a variable name, as in the following code example:

```
int x = 7;
x = x++;
```

In this example, the statement x = x++ increments the x variable from 7 to 8.

These increment and decrement operators can be placed before or after a variable name. This affects the value of expressions that involve these operators.

Increment and decrement operators are called *prefix* operators if listed before a variable name and *postfix* operators if listed after a name.

In a simple expression such as count--;, using a prefix or postfix operator produces the same result, making the operators interchangeable. When increment and decrement operations are part of a larger expression, however, the choice between prefix and postfix operators is important.

Consider the following code:

```
int x, y, z;
x = 42;
y = x++;
z = ++x;
```

The three expressions in this code yield different results because of the difference between prefix and postfix operations.

When you use postfix operators on a variable in an expression, the variable's value is evaluated in the expression before it is incremented or decremented. So in y = x++, y receives the value of x before it is incremented by 1.

When using prefix operators on a variable in an expression, the variable is incremented or decremented before its value is evaluated in that expression. Therefore, in z = ++x, x is incremented by 1 before the value is assigned to z.

The end result of the preceding codes example is that y equals 42, z equals 44, and x equals 44.

If you're still having some trouble figuring this out, here's the example again with comments describing each step:

```
int x, y, z; // x, y, and z are all declared
x = 42;      // x is given the value of 42
y = x++;     // y is given x's value (42) before it is incremented
```

2

```
                // and x is then incremented to 43
z = ++x;        // x is incremented to 44, and z is given x's value
```

CAUTION

Using increment and decrement operators in complex expressions can produce results you might not have expected.

The concept of "assigning x to y before x is incremented" isn't precisely right because Java evaluates everything on the right side of an expression before assigning its value to the left side.

Java stores some values before handling an expression to make postfix work the way it has been described in this section.

If you're not getting the results you expect from a complex expression that includes prefix and postfix operators, try breaking the expression into multiple statements to simplify it.

Comparisons

Java has several operators for making comparisons among variables, variables and literals, or other types of information in a program.

These operators are used in expressions that return Boolean values of true or false, depending on whether the comparison being made is true or not. Table 2.5 shows the comparison operators.

TABLE 2.5 Comparison Operators

Operator	Meaning	Example
==	Equal to	x == 3
!=	Not equal to	x != 3
<	Less than	x < 3
>	Greater than	x > 3
<=	Less than or equal to	x <= 3
>=	Greater than or equal to	x >= 3

The following example shows a comparison operator in use:

```
boolean isHip;
int age = 45;
isHip = age < 25;
```

The expression age < 25 produces a result of either `true` or `false`, depending on the value of the integer age. Because age is 45 in this example (which is not less than 25), isHip is given the Boolean value `false`.

Logical Operators

Expressions that result in Boolean values, such as comparison operations, can be combined to form more complex expressions. This is handled through logical operators, which are used for the logical combinations AND, OR, XOR, and logical NOT.

For AND combinations, the & or && logical operator is used. When two Boolean expressions are linked by these operators, the combined expression returns a `true` value only if both Boolean expressions are true.

Consider this example:

```
boolean extraLife = (score > 75000) & (playerLives < 10);
```

This expression combines two comparison expressions: score > 75000 and playerLives < 10. If both expressions are true, the Boolean value `true` is assigned to the variable extraLife. In any other circumstance, the value `false` is assigned to the variable.

The difference between & and && lies in how much work Java does on the combined expression. If & is used, the expressions on both sides of the & are evaluated no matter what. If && is used and the left side of the && is false, the expression on the right side of the && never is evaluated.

For OR combinations, the | or || logical operator is used. These combined expressions return a `true` value if either Boolean expression is true.

Consider this example:

```
boolean extralife = (score > 75000) || (playerLevel == 0);
```

This expression combines two comparison expressions: score > 75000 and playerLevel == 0. If either of these expressions is true, the Boolean value `true` is assigned to the variable extraLife. Only if both of these expressions are false is the value `false` assigned to extraLife.

Note the use of || instead of |. Because of this usage, if score > 75000 is true, extraLife is set to `true`, and the second expression is never evaluated.

The XOR combination has one logical operator, ^. This results in a `true` value only if the Boolean expressions it combines have opposite values. If both are true or both are false, the ^ operator produces a `false` value.

2

The NOT combination uses the ! logical operator followed by a single expression. It reverses the value of a Boolean expression in the same way that a minus sign reverses the positive or negative sign on a number. For example, if age < 30 returns a true value, !(age < 30) returns a false value.

The logical operators may seem illogical when you first encounter them. You get plenty of opportunities to work with them during the rest of this week, especially on Day 5, "Creating Classes and Methods."

Operator Precedence

When more than one operator is used in an expression, Java has an established precedence hierarchy to determine the order in which operators are evaluated. In many cases, this precedence determines the expression's overall value.

For example, consider the following expression:

```
y = 6 + 4 / 2;
```

The y variable will equal the value 5 or the value 8, depending on which arithmetic operation is handled first. If the 6 + 4 expression comes first, y has the value of 5. Otherwise, y equals 8.

In general, the order of evaluation from first to last is as follows:

1. Increment and decrement operations
2. Arithmetic operations
3. Comparisons
4. Logical operations
5. Assignment expressions

If two operations have the same precedence, the one on the left in the expression is handled before the one on the right. Table 2.6 shows the specific precedence of the various operators in Java. Operators higher up in the table are evaluated first.

TABLE 2.6 Operator Precedence

Operator	Notes
. [] ()	Parentheses (()) are used to group expressions. A period (.) is used for access to methods and variables within objects and classes. Square brackets ([]) are used for arrays.
++ -- ! ~ instanceof	The instanceof operator returns true or false based on whether the object is an instance of the named class or any of that class's subclasses.

TABLE 2.6 Continued

Operator	Notes
new (*type*)*expression*	The new operator is used to create new instances of classes. The parentheses in this case are for casting a value to another type.
* / %	Multiplication, division, modulus
+ -	Addition, subtraction
<< >> >>>	Bitwise left and right shift
< > <= >=	Relational comparison tests
== !=	Equality
&	AND
^	XOR
|	OR
&&	Logical AND
||	Logical OR
? :	Ternary operator
= += -= *= /= %= ^=	Various assignments
&= |= <<= >>= >>>=	More assignments

Several of the operators listed in Table 2.6 are covered later this week.

Returning to the expression y = 6 + 4 / 2, Table 2.6 shows that division is evaluated before addition, so the value of y is 8.

To change the order in which expressions are evaluated, place parentheses around the expressions that should be evaluated first. You can nest one set of parentheses inside another to make sure that expressions are evaluated in the desired order; the innermost parenthetic expression is evaluated first.

The following expression results in a value of 5:

y = (6 + 4) / 2

The value of 5 is the result because 6 + 4 is calculated first, and then the result, 10, is divided by 2.

Parentheses also can improve an expression's readability. If an expression's precedence isn't immediately clear to you, adding parentheses to impose the desired precedence can make the statement easier to understand.

String Arithmetic

As stated earlier, the + operator has a double life outside the world of mathematics. It can concatenate two or more strings.

Concatenate means to link two things. For reasons unknown, it is the verb of choice in computer programming when describing the act of combining two strings, winning out over paste, glue, affix, combine, link, and conjoin.

In several examples, you have seen statements that look something like this:

```
String brand = "Jif";
System.out.println("Choosy mothers choose " + brand);
```

These two lines result in the display of the following text:

```
Choosy mothers choose Jif
```

The + operator combines strings, other objects, and variables to form a single string. In the preceding example, the literal "Choosy mothers choose" is concatenated to the value of the String object brand.

Working with the concatenation operator is made easier in Java by the fact that the operator can handle any variable type and object value as if it were a string. If any part of a concatenation operation is a String or a string literal, all elements of the operation are treated as if they were strings:

```
System.out.println(4 + " score and " + 7 + " years ago");
```

This produces the output text "4 score and 7 years ago", as if the integer literals 4 and 7 were strings.

There also is a += shorthand operator to append something to the end of a string. For example, consider the following expression:

```
myName += " Jr.";
```

This expression is equivalent to the following:

```
myName = myName + " Jr.";
```

In this example, += changes the value of myName, which might be something like "Efrem Zimbalist," by adding "Jr." at the end to form the string "Efrem Zimbalist Jr."

To summarize today's material, Table 2.7 lists the operators you have learned about. Be a doll and look them over carefully.

TABLE 2.7   Operator Summary

Operator	Meaning
+	Addition
-	Subtraction
*	Multiplication
/	Division
%	Modulus
<	Less than
>	Greater than
<=	Less than or equal to
>=	Greater than or equal to
==	Equal to
!=	Not equal to
&&	Logical AND
||	Logical OR
!	Logical NOT
&	AND
|	OR
^	XOR
=	Assignment
++	Increment
--	Decrement
+=	Add and assign
-=	Subtract and assign
*=	Multiply and assign
/=	Divide and assign
%=	Modulus and assign

Summary

Anyone who pops open a set of *matryoshka* dolls has to be a bit disappointed upon reaching the smallest doll in the group.

Today you reached Java's smallest nesting doll. Using statements and expressions enables you to begin building effective methods, which makes effective objects and classes possible.

Today you learned about creating variables and assigning values to them. You also used literals to represent numeric, character, and string values and worked with operators. Tomorrow, you put these skills to use developing classes.

Q&A

Q **What happens if I assign an integer value to a variable that is too large for that variable to hold?**

A Logically, you might think that the variable is converted to the next-larger type, but this isn't what happens. Instead, an *overflow* occurs—a situation in which the number wraps around from one size extreme to the other. An example of overflow would be a byte variable that goes from 127 (an acceptable value) to 128 (unacceptable). It would wrap around to the lowest acceptable value, which is –128, and start counting upward from there. Overflow isn't something you can readily detect in a program, so be sure to give your variables plenty of living space in their chosen data type.

Small data types like byte were more necessary when computers had much less memory than they do today and every byte counted. Today, with plentiful memory and hard disk space measured in gigabytes, it is better to use larger data types like int to ensure that you have enough space to store all possible values in a particular variable.

Q **Why does Java have all these shorthand operators for arithmetic and assignment? It's really hard to read that way.**

A Java's syntax is based on C++, which is based on C (more Russian nesting doll behavior). C is an expert language that values programming power over readability, and the shorthand operators are one of the legacies of that design priority. Using them in a program isn't required because effective substitutes are available, so you can avoid them in your own programming if you prefer.

Quiz

Review today's material by taking this three-question quiz. Answers are at the end of the book.

Questions

1. Which of the following is a valid value for a boolean variable?

  A. "false"

  B. false

  C. 10

2. Which of these is not a convention for naming variables in Java?

    A. After the first word in the variable name, each successive word begins with a capital letter.

    B. The first letter of the variable name is lowercase.

    C. All letters are capitalized.

3. Which of these data types holds numbers from –32,768 to 32,767?

    A. `char`

    B. `byte`

    C. `short`

2

Certification Practice

The following question is the kind of thing you could expect to be asked on a Java programming certification test. Answer it without looking at today's material.

Which of the following data types can hold the number 3,000,000,000 (3 billion)?

A. `short, int, long, float`

B. `int, long, float`

C. `long, float`

D. `byte`

The answer is available on the book's website at www.java21days.com. Visit the Day 2 page and click the Certification Practice link.

Exercises

To extend your knowledge of the subjects covered today, try the following exercises:

1. Create a program that calculates how much a $14,000 investment would be worth if it increased in value by 40% during the first year, lost $1,500 in value the second year, and increased 12% in the third year.

2. Write a program that displays two numbers and uses the `/` and `%` operators to display the result and remainder after they are divided. Use the `\t` character escape code to separate the result and remainder in your output.

Where applicable, exercise solutions are offered on the book's website at www.java21days.com.

DAY 3
Working with Objects

Java is primarily an object-oriented programming language. When you do work in Java, you use objects to get the job done. You create objects, modify them, change their variables, call their methods, and combine them with other objects. You develop classes, create objects out of those classes, and use them with other classes and objects.

Today, you work extensively with objects as the following topics are covered:

- Creating objects
- Testing and modifying their class and instance variables
- Calling an object's methods
- Converting objects from one class to another

Creating New Objects

When you write a Java program, you define a set of classes. As you learned during Day 1, "Getting Started with Java," classes are templates used to create objects. These objects, which also are called instances, are self-contained elements of a program with related features and data. For the most part, you use the class merely to create instances and then work with those instances. In this section, you learn how to create a new object from any given class.

When using strings on Day 2, "The ABCs of Programming," you learned that using a string literal (a series of characters enclosed in double quotation marks) creates a new instance of the class String with the value of that string.

The String class is unusual in that respect. Although it's a class, it can be assigned a value with a literal as if it were a primitive data type. This shortcut is unavailable for other classes. To create instances for them, the new operator is used.

NOTE

What about the literals for numbers and characters? Don't they create objects too? Actually, they don't. The primitive data types for numbers and characters create numbers and characters, but for efficiency they actually aren't objects. On Day 5, "Creating Classes and Methods," you learn how to use objects to represent primitive values.

Using new

To create a new object, you use the new operator with the name of the class that should be used as a template. The name of the class is followed by parentheses, as in these three examples:

```
String name = new String("Hal Jordan");

URL address = new URL("http://www.java21days.com");

VolcanoRobot robbie = new VolcanoRobot();
```

The parentheses are important and can't be omitted. The parentheses can be empty, however, in which case the most simple, basic object is created. The parentheses also can contain arguments that determine the values of instance variables or other initial qualities of that object.

The following examples show objects being created with arguments:

```
Random seed = new Random(606843071);
Point pt = new Point(0, 0);
```

The number and type of arguments to include inside the parentheses are defined by the class itself using a special method called a *constructor*. (You learn more about constructors later today.) If you try to create a new instance of a class with the wrong number or wrong type of arguments, or if you give it no arguments and it needs them, an error occurs when the program is compiled.

Here's an example of creating different types of objects with different numbers and types of arguments. The StringTokenizer class in the java.util package divides a string into a series of shorter strings called *tokens*.

You divide a string into tokens by applying a character or characters as a delimiter. For example, the text "02/20/67" could be divided into three tokens—"02", "20", and "67"—using the slash character (/) as a delimiter.

3

Today's first project is a Java application that uses string tokens to analyze stock price data. In NetBeans, create a new empty Java file for the class TokenTester, and enter the code shown in Listing 3.1 as its source code. This program creates StringTokenizer objects by using new in two different ways and then displays each token the objects contain.

LISTING 3.1   The Full Text of TokenTester.java

```
 1: import java.util.StringTokenizer;
 2:
 3: class TokenTester {
 4:
 5:     public static void main(String[] arguments) {
 6:         StringTokenizer st1, st2;
 7:
 8:         String quote1 = "GOOG 604.43 -0.42";
 9:         st1 = new StringTokenizer(quote1);
10:         System.out.println("Token 1: " + st1.nextToken());
11:         System.out.println("Token 2: " + st1.nextToken());
12:         System.out.println("Token 3: " + st1.nextToken());
13:
14:         String quote2 = "RHT@60.39@0.78";
15:         st2 = new StringTokenizer(quote2, "@");
16:         System.out.println("\nToken 1: " + st2.nextToken());
```

LISTING 3.1 Continued

```
17:          System.out.println("Token 2: " + st2.nextToken());
18:          System.out.println("Token 3: " + st2.nextToken());
19:     }
20: }
```

Save this file by choosing File, Save or clicking Save All on the NetBeans toolbar. Run the application by choosing Run, Run File to see the output:

Output ▼

```
Token 1: GOOG
Token 2: 604.43
Token 3: -0.42

Token 1: RHT
Token 2: 60.39
Token 3: 0.78
```

Two different StringTokenizer objects are created using different arguments to the constructor.

The first object is created using new StringTokenizer() with one argument, a String object named quote1 (line 9). This creates a StringTokenizer object that uses the default delimiters, which are blank spaces, tabs, newlines, carriage returns, or formfeed characters.

If any of these characters is contained in the string, it is used to divide the string. Because the quote1 string contains spaces, these are used as delimiters dividing each token. Lines 10–12 display the values of all three tokens: "GOOG", "604.43", and "-0.42".

The second StringTokenizer object in this example has two arguments when it is constructed in line 14—a String object named quote2 and an at-sign character (@). This second argument indicates that the @ character should be used as the delimiter between tokens. The StringTokenizer object created in line 15 contains three tokens: "RHT", "60.39", and "0.78".

How Objects Are Constructed

Several things happen when you use the new operator. The new instance of the given class is created, memory is allocated for it, and a special method defined in the given class is called. This special method is called a constructor.

A *constructor* is a special way to create a new instance of a class. A constructor initializes the new object and its variables, creates any other objects that the object needs, and performs any additional operations the object requires to initialize itself.

A class can have several different constructors, each with a different number or type of arguments. When you use new, you can specify different arguments in the argument list, and the correct constructor for those arguments is called.

Multiple constructor definitions enable the TokenTester class to accomplish different things with different uses of the new operator. When you create your own classes, you can define as many constructors as you need to implement the behavior of the class.

No two constructors in a class can have the same number and type of arguments because this is the only way constructors are differentiated from each other.

If a class defines no constructors, a constructor with no arguments is called by default when an object of the class is created. The only thing this constructor does is call the same constructor in its superclass.

3

A Note on Memory Management

If you are familiar with other object-oriented programming languages, you might wonder whether the new statement has an opposite that destroys an object when it is no longer needed.

Memory management in Java is dynamic and automatic. When you create a new object, Java automatically allocates the proper amount of memory for that object. You don't have to allocate any memory for objects explicitly. Java does it for you.

Because Java memory management is automatic, you don't need to deallocate the memory an object uses when you're finished using the object. Under most circumstances, when you are finished with an object you have created, Java can determine that the object no longer has any live references to it. (In other words, the object isn't assigned to any variables still in use or stored in any arrays.)

As a program runs, the Java virtual machine periodically looks for unused objects and reclaims the memory that those objects are using. This process is called *garbage collection* and occurs without any programming on your part. You don't have to explicitly free the memory taken up by an object; you just have to make sure that you're not still holding onto an object you want to get rid of.

Using Class and Instance Variables

At this point, you can create your own object with class and instance variables defined in it, but how do you work with those variables? They're used in largely the same manner as the local variables you learned about yesterday. You can use them in expressions, assign values to them in statements, and so on. You just refer to them slightly differently.

Getting Values

To get to the value of an instance variable, you use *dot notation*, a form of addressing in which an instance or class variable name has two parts:

- A reference to an object or class on the left side of a dot operator (.)
- A variable on the right side

Dot notation is how you refer to an object's instance variables and methods.

For example, if you have an object named `customer` with a variable called `orderTotal`, here's how that variable could be referred to in a statement:

```
float total = customer.orderTotal;
```

This statement assigns the value of the `customer` object's `orderTotal` instance variable to a local floating-point variable named `total`.

Accessing variables in dot notation is an expression (meaning that it returns a value). Both sides of the dot also are expressions. This means that you can chain instance variable access.

Extending the preceding example, suppose the `customer` object is an instance variable of the `store` class. Dot notation can be used twice, as in this statement:

```
float total = store.customer.orderTotal;
```

Dot expressions are evaluated from left to right, so you start with `store`'s instance variable `customer`, which itself has an instance variable `orderTotal`. The value of this variable is assigned to the `total` local variable.

Setting Values

Assigning a value to an instance variable with dot notation employs the = operator just like local variables:

```
customer.layaway = true;
```

This example sets the value of a `boolean` instance variable named `layaway` to `true`.

The PointSetter application shown in Listing 3.2 tests and modifies the instance variables in a `Point` object. `Point`, a class in the `java.awt` package, represents points in a coordinate system with (x, y) values.

Create a new empty Java file in NetBeans with the class name `PointSetter`, and then type the source code shown in Listing 3.2 and save the file.

LISTING 3.2   The Full Text of `PointSetter.java`

```
 1: import java.awt.Point;
 2:
 3: class PointSetter {
 4:
 5:     public static void main(String[] arguments) {
 6:         Point location = new Point(4, 13);
 7:
 8:         System.out.println("Starting location:");
 9:         System.out.println("X equals " + location.x);
10:         System.out.println("Y equals " + location.y);
11:
12:         System.out.println("\nMoving to (7, 6)");
13:         location.x = 7;
14:         location.y = 6;
15:
16:         System.out.println("\nEnding location:");
17:         System.out.println("X equals " + location.x);
18:         System.out.println("Y equals " + location.y);
19:     }
20: }
```

When you run this application, the output is the following:

Output ▼

```
Starting location:
X equals 4
Y equals 13

Moving to (7, 6)

Ending location:
X equals 7
Y equals 6
```

In this application, you first create an instance of `Point` where x equals 4 and y equals 13 (line 6). These individual values are retrieved using dot notation.

3

The value of x is changed to 7 and y to 6. Finally, the values are displayed again to show how they have changed.

Class Variables

Class variables, as you have learned, are variables defined and stored in the class itself. Their values apply to the class and all its instances.

With instance variables, each new instance of the class gets a new copy of the instance variables that the class defines. Each instance then can change the values of those instance variables without affecting any other instances. With class variables, only one copy of that variable exists when the class is loaded. Changing the value of that variable changes it for all instances of that class.

You define class variables by including the static keyword before the variable itself. For example, consider the following partial class definition:

```
class FamilyMember {
    static String surname = "Mendoza";
    String name;
    int age;
}
```

Each instance of the class FamilyMember has its own values for name and age, but the class variable surname has only one value for all family members: Mendoza. If the value of surname is changed, all instances of FamilyMember are affected.

NOTE

Calling these static variables refers to one of the meanings of the word "static": fixed in one place. If a class has a static variable, every object of that class has the same value for that variable.

To access class variables, you use the same dot notation as with instance variables. To retrieve or change the value of the class variable, you can use either the instance or the name of the class on the left side of the dot operator. Both lines of output in this example display the same value:

```
FamilyMember dad = new FamilyMember();
System.out.println("Family's surname is: " + dad.surname);
System.out.println("Family's surname is: " + FamilyMember.surname);
```

Because you can use an object to change the value of a class variable, it's easy to become confused about class variables and where their values are coming from. Remember that the value of a class variable affects all objects of that particular class.

For this reason, it's a good idea to use the name of the class when you refer to a class variable. It makes your code easier to read and makes strange results easier to debug.

Calling Methods

Calling a method in an object also makes use of dot notation. The object whose method is being called is on the left side of the dot, and the name of the method and its arguments are on the right side:

```
customer.addToCart(itemNumber, price, quantity);
```

All method calls must have parentheses after them, even when the method takes no arguments, as in this example:

```
customer.cancelOrder();
```

In Listing 3.3, the StringChecker application shows an example of calling some methods defined in the String class. Strings include methods for string tests and modification. Create this program in NetBeans as an empty Java file with the class name StringChecker.

LISTING 3.3   The Full Text of StringChecker.java

```
 1: class StringChecker {
 2:
 3:     public static void main(String[] arguments) {
 4:         String str = " Would you like an apple pie with that?";
 5:         System.out.println("The string is: " + str);
 6:         System.out.println("Length of this string: "
 7:             + str.length());
 8:         System.out.println("The character at position 6: "
 9:             + str.charAt(6));
10:         System.out.println("The substring from 26 to 32: "
11:             + str.substring(26, 32));
12:         System.out.println("The index of the first 'a': "
13:             + str.indexOf('a'));
14:         System.out.println("The index of the beginning of the "
15:             + "substring \"IBM\": " + str.indexOf("IBM"));
16:         System.out.println("The string in uppercase: "
17:             + str.toUpperCase());
18:     }
19: }
```

Save and run the file to display this output:

Output ▼

```
The string is: Would you like an apple pie with that?
Length of this string: 38
The character at position 6: y
The substring from 26 to 32: e with
The index of the first 'a': 15
The index of the beginning of the substring "apple": 18
The string in uppercase: WOULD YOU LIKE AN APPLE PIE WITH THAT?
```

In line 4, you create a new instance of String by using a string literal. The remainder of the program simply calls different string methods to do different operations on that string:

- Line 5 prints the value of the string you created in line 4: "Would you like an apple pie with that?"

- Line 7 calls the length() method in the new String object. This string has 38 characters.

- Line 9 calls the charAt() method, which returns the character at the given position in the string. Note that string positions start at position 0 rather than 1, so the character at position 6 is y.

- Line 11 calls the substring() method, which takes two integers indicating a range and returns the substring with those starting and ending points. The substring() method also can be called with only one argument, which returns the substring from that position to the end of the string.

- Line 13 calls the indexOf() method, which returns the position of the first instance of the given character (here, 'a'). Character literals are surrounded by single quotation marks; if double quotation marks had surrounded the 'a' in line 13, the literal would be considered a String.

- Line 15 shows a different use of the indexOf() method, which takes a string argument and returns the index of the beginning of that string.

- Line 17 uses the toUpperCase() method to return a copy of the string in all uppercase.

NOTE

If you compare the output of the StringChecker application to the characters in the string, you might be wondering how y could be at position 6 when it is the seventh character in the string. All of the methods look like they're off by one (except for length()).

The reason is that the methods are zero-based, which means they begin counting with 0 instead of 1. So 'W' is at position 0, 'o' at position 1, 'u' at position 2 and so on. This is something you encounter often in Java.

Formatting Strings

Numbers such as money often need to be displayed in a precise manner. There's only two places after the decimal (for the cents), a dollar sign ($), and commas.

This kind of formatting when displaying strings can be accomplished with the `System.out.format()` method.

The method takes two arguments: the output format template and the string to display. Here's an example that adds a dollar sign and commas to the display of an integer:

```
int accountBalance = 5005;
System.out.format("Balance: $%,d%n", accountBalance);
```

This code produces the output `Balance: $5,005`.

The formatting string begins with a percent sign (%) followed by one or more flags. The `%,d` code displays a decimal with commas dividing each group of three digits. The `%n` code displays a newline character.

The next example displays the value of pi to 11 decimal places:

```
double pi = Math.PI;
System.out.format("%.11f%n", pi);
```

The output is `3.14159265359`.

TIP   Oracle's Java site includes a beginner's tutorial for `printf`-style output that describes some of the most useful formatting codes:

http://docs.oracle.com/javase/tutorial/java/data/numberformat.html

Nesting Method Calls

A method can return a reference to an object, a primitive data type, or no value at all. In the StringChecker application, all the methods called on the `String` object `str` return values that are displayed. The charAt() method returns a character at a specified position in the string.

The value returned by a method also can be stored in a variable:

```
String label = "From";
String upper = label.toUpperCase();
```

In this example, the String object upper contains the value returned by calling label.toUpperCase(), which is the text FROM, the uppercase version of From.

If the method returns an object, you can call the methods of that object in the same statement. This makes it possible for you to nest methods as you would variables.

Earlier today, you saw an example of a method called with no arguments:

```
customer.cancelOrder();
```

If the cancelOrder() method returns an object, you can call methods of that object in the same statement:

```
customer.cancelOrder().fileComplaint();
```

This statement calls the fileComplaint () method, which is defined in the object returned by the cancelOrder() method of the customer object.

You can combine nested method calls and instance variable references as well. In the next example, the putOnLayaway() method is defined in the object stored by the orderTotal instance variable, which itself is part of the customer object:

```
customer.orderTotal.putOnLayaway(itemNumber, price, quantity);
```

This manner of nesting variables and methods is demonstrated in a method you've used frequently in the first several days of this book: System.out.println().

That method displays strings and other data to the computer's standard output device.

The System class, part of the java.lang package, describes behavior specific to the computer system on which Java is running. System.out is a class variable that contains an instance of the class PrintStream representing the system's standard output, which normally is the screen but can be a printer or file. PrintStream objects have a println() method that sends a string to that output stream. The PrintStream class is in the java.io package.

Class Methods

Class methods, like class variables, apply to the class as a whole and not to its instances. Class methods commonly are used for general utility methods that might not operate directly on an object of that class but do fit with that class conceptually.

For example, the `String` class contains a class method called `valueOf()`, which can take one of many different types of arguments (integers, Booleans, objects, and so on). The `valueOf()` method then returns a new instance of `String` containing the argument's string value. This method doesn't operate directly on an existing instance of `String`, but getting a string from another object or data type is behavior that makes sense to define in the `String` class.

Class methods also can be useful for gathering general methods in one place. For example, the `Math` class, defined in the `java.lang` package, contains a large set of mathematical operations as class methods. No objects can be created from the `Math` class, but you still can use its methods with numeric or Boolean arguments.

For example, the class method `Math.max()` takes two arguments and returns the larger of the two. You don't need to create a new instance of `Math`; it can be called anywhere you need it, as in the following:

```
int firstPrice = 225;
int secondPrice = 217;
int higherPrice = Math.max(firstPrice, secondPrice);
```

Dot notation is used to call a class method. As with class variables, you can use either an instance of the class or the class itself on the left side of the dot. For the same reasons noted earlier in the discussion of class variables, using the name of the class makes your code easier to read.

The last two lines in this example both produce strings equal to "550":

```
String s, s2;
s = "item";
s2 = s.valueOf(550);
s2 = String.valueOf(550);
```

References to Objects

As you work with objects, it's important to understand references. A *reference* is an address that indicates where an object's variables and methods are stored.

You aren't actually using objects when you assign an object to a variable or pass an object to a method as an argument. You aren't even using copies of the objects. Instead, you're using references to those objects.

To better illustrate the difference, the RefTester application shown in Listing 3.4 shows how references work. Create an empty Java file for the class `RefTester` in NetBeans, and enter the code shown in Listing 3.4 as the application's source code.

LISTING 3.4   The Full Text of RefTester.java

```
1: import java.awt.Point;
2:
3: class RefTester {
4:     public static void main(String[] arguments) {
5:         Point pt1, pt2;
6:         pt1 = new Point(100, 100);
7:         pt2 = pt1;
8:
9:         pt1.x = 200;
10:        pt1.y = 200;
11:        System.out.println("Point1: " + pt1.x + ", " + pt1.y);
12:        System.out.println("Point2: " + pt2.x + ", " + pt2.y);
13:    }
14: }
```

Save and run the application. Here is the output:

Output ▼

```
Point1: 200, 200
Point2: 200, 200
```

The following takes place in the first part of this program:

- **Line 5**—Two Point variables are created.
- **Line 6**—A new Point object is assigned to pt1.
- **Line 7**—The value of pt1 is assigned to pt2.

Lines 9–12 are the tricky part. The x and y variables of pt1 both are set to 200, and then all variables of pt1 and pt2 are displayed onscreen.

You might expect pt1 and pt2 to have different values. However, the output shows this not to be the case. As you can see, the x and y variables of pt2 also are changed, even though nothing in the program explicitly changes them. This happens because line 7 creates a reference from pt2 to pt1, instead of creating pt2 as a new object copied from pt1.

The variable pt2 is a reference to the same object as pt1, as shown in Figure 3.1. Either variable can be used to refer to the object or to change its variables.

FIGURE 3.1
References to objects.

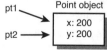

If you wanted pt1 and pt2 to refer to separate objects, you could use separate new
Point() statements on lines 6 and 7 to create separate objects, as shown here:

```
pt1 = new Point(100, 100);
pt2 = new Point(100, 100);
```

References in Java become particularly important when arguments are passed to
methods. You learn more about this later today.

NOTE

> Java has no explicit pointers or pointer arithmetic, unlike C and
> C++. By using references and Java arrays, you can duplicate most
> pointer capabilities without many of their drawbacks.

Casting Objects and Primitive Types

3

One thing you discover quickly about Java is how finicky it is about the information it
will handle. Like Morris, the perpetually hard-to-please cat in the old 9Lives cat food
commercials, Java methods and constructors require things to take a specific form and
won't accept alternatives.

When you send arguments to methods or use variables in expressions, you must use variables of the correct data types. If a method requires an int, the Java compiler responds
with an error if you try to send a float value to the method. Likewise, if you set up one
variable with the value of another, they must be of the same type.

NOTE

> There is one area where Java's compiler is decidedly flexible: the
> String object. String handling in println() methods, assignment
> statements, and method arguments is simplified by the + concate-
> nation operator. If any variable in a group of concatenated vari-
> ables is a string, Java treats the whole thing as a String. This
> makes the following possible:
>
> ```
> float gpa = 2.25F;
> System.out.println("Honest, mom, my GPA is a " + (gpa + 1.5));
> ```
>
> Using the concatenation operator, a single string can hold the text
> representation of multiple objects and primitive data in Java.

Sometimes you'll have a value in your Java class that isn't the right type for what you need. It might be the wrong class or the wrong data type, such as a `float` when you need an `int`.

In these situations, you can use a process called *casting* to convert a value from one type to another.

Although the concept of casting is reasonably simple, the usage is complicated by the fact that Java has both primitive types (such as `int`, `float`, and `boolean`) and object types (`String`, `Point`, `ZipFile`, and the like). This section discusses three forms of casts and conversions:

- Casting between primitive types, such as `int` to `float` or `float` to `double`
- Casting from an object of a class to an object of another class, such as from `Object` to `String`
- Casting primitive types to objects and then extracting primitive values from those objects

When discussing casting, it can be easier to think in terms of sources and destinations. The source is the variable being cast into another type. The destination is the result.

Casting Primitive Types

Casting between primitive types enables you to convert the value of one type to another primitive type. This most commonly occurs with the numeric types. But one primitive type can never be used in a cast. Boolean values must be either `true` or `false` and cannot be used in a casting operation.

In many casts between primitive types, the destination can hold larger values than the source, so the value is converted easily. An example would be casting a `byte` into an `int`. Because a `byte` holds values from –128 to 127 and an `int` holds from around –2,100,000 to 2,100,000, there's more than enough room to cast a `byte` into an `int`.

Often you can automatically use a `byte` or `char` as an `int`; you can use an `int` as a `long`, an `int` as a `float`, or anything as a `double`. In most cases, because the larger type provides more precision than the smaller, no loss of information occurs as a result. The exception is casting integers to floating-point values. Casting an `int` or a `long` to a `float`, or a `long` to a `double`, can cause some loss of precision.

A character can be used as an `int` because each character has a corresponding numeric code that represents its position in the character set. If the variable `i` has the value 65, the cast `(char)` `i` produces the character value `'A'`. The numeric code associated with a capital A is 65 in the ASCII character set, which Java adopted as part of its character support.

You must use an explicit cast to convert a value in a large type to a smaller type. Explicit casts take the following form:

`(typename) value`

Here `typename` is the name of the primitive data type to which you're converting, such as `short`, `int`, or `float`. `value` is an expression that results in the value of the source type. For example, in the following statement, the value of x is divided by the value of y, and the result is cast into an `int` in the following expression:

`int result = (int)(x / y);`

Note that because the precedence of casting is higher than that of arithmetic, you have to use parentheses here. Otherwise, first the value of x would be cast into an `int`, and then it would be divided by y, which could easily produce a different result.

Casting Objects

Objects of classes also can be cast into objects of other classes when the source and destination classes are related by inheritance and one class is a subclass of the other.

Some objects might not need to be cast explicitly. In particular, because a subclass contains all the same information as its superclass, you can use an object of a subclass anywhere a superclass is expected.

For example, consider a method that takes two arguments, one of type `Object` and another of type `Component` in the `java.awt` package.

You can pass an instance of any class for the `Object` argument because all Java classes are subclasses of `Object`.

For the `Component` argument, you can pass in its subclasses, such as `Button`, `Container`, and `Label` (all in `java.awt`).

This is true anywhere in a program, not just inside method calls. If you had a variable defined as class `Component`, you could assign objects of that class or any of its subclasses to that variable without casting.

This also is true in the reverse, so you can use a superclass when a subclass is expected. There is a catch, however: Because subclasses contain more behavior than their super- classes, a loss of precision occurs in the casting. Those superclass objects might not have all the behavior needed to act in place of a subclass object.

Consider this example: If you have an operation that calls methods in objects of the class Integer, using an object of its superclass Number won't include many methods specified in Integer. Errors occur if you try to call methods that the destination object doesn't have.

To use superclass objects where subclass objects are expected, you must cast them explicitly. You won't lose any information in the cast, but you gain all the methods and variables that the subclass defines. To cast an object to another class, you use the same operation as for primitive types, which takes this form:

```
(classname) object
```

In this template, *classname* is the name of the destination class, and *object* is a refer- ence to the source object. Note that casting creates a reference to the old object of the type *classname*; the old object continues to exist as it did before.

The following example casts an instance of the class VicePresident to an instance of the class Employee. VicePresident is a subclass of Employee with more information:

```
Employee emp = new Employee();
VicePresident veep = new VicePresident();
emp = veep; // no cast needed for upward use
veep = (VicePresident) emp; // must cast explicitly
```

As you'll see when you begin working with graphical user interfaces during Week 2, "The Java Class Library," casting one object is necessary whenever you use Java2D graphics operations. You must cast a Graphics object to a Graphics2D object before you can draw onscreen. The following example uses a Graphics object called screen to cre- ate a new Graphics2D object called screen2D:

```
Graphics2D screen2D = (Graphics2D) screen;
```

Graphics2D is a subclass of Graphics, and both belong to the java.awt package. You explore this subject fully during Day 13, "Creating Java2D Graphics."

In addition to casting objects to classes, you can cast objects to interfaces, but only if an object's class or one of its superclasses actually implements the interface. Casting an object to an interface means that you can call one of that interface's methods even if that object's class does not actually implement that interface.

Converting Primitive Types to Objects and Vice Versa

One thing you can't do under any circumstance is cast from an object to a primitive data type, or vice versa.

Primitive types and objects are very different things in Java, and you can't automatically cast between the two.

As an alternative, the `java.lang` package includes classes that correspond to each primitive data type: `Float`, `Boolean`, `Byte`, and so on. Most of these classes have the same names as the data types, except that the class names begin with a capital letter (`Short` instead of `short`, `Double` instead of `double`, and the like). Also, two classes have names that differ from the corresponding data type: `Character` is used for `char` variables, and `Integer` is used for `int` variables.

Using the classes that correspond to each primitive type, you can create an object that holds the same value. The following statement creates an instance of the `Integer` class with the integer value 7801:

3

```
Integer dataCount = new Integer(7801);
```

After you have created an object in this manner, you can use it as you would any object (although you cannot change its value). When you want to use that value again as a primitive value, there are methods for that as well. For example, if you wanted to get an `int` value from a `dataCount` object, the following statement shows how that would work:

```
int newCount = dataCount.intValue(); // returns 7801
```

A common translation you need in programs is converting a `String` to a numeric type, such as an integer. When you need an `int` as the result, this can be done by using the `parseInt()` class method of the `Integer` class. The `String` to convert is the only argument sent to the method, as in the following example:

```
String pennsylvania = "65000";
int penn = Integer.parseInt(pennsylvania);
```

The following classes can be used to work with objects instead of primitive data types: `Boolean`, `Byte`, `Character`, `Double`, `Float`, `Integer`, `Long`, `Short`, and `Void`. These classes are commonly called object wrappers because they provide an object representation that contains a primitive value.

CAUTION

> If you try to use the preceding example in a program, your program won't compile. The parseInt() method is designed to fail with a NumberFormatException error if the argument to the method is not a valid numeric value. To deal with errors of this kind, you must use special error-handling statements, which are introduced during Day 7, "Exceptions and Threads."

Working with primitive types and objects that represent the same values is made easier through autoboxing and unboxing, an automatic conversion process.

Autoboxing automatically converts a primitive type to an object, and *unboxing* converts in the other direction.

If you write a statement that uses an object where a primitive type is expected, or vice versa, the value is converted so that the statement executes successfully.

This feature was unavailable in the first several versions of the language.

Here's an example of autoboxing and unboxing:

```
Float f1 = new Float(12.5F);
Float f2 = new Float(27.2F);
System.out.println("Lower number: " + Math.min(f1, f2));
```

The Math.min() method takes two float values as arguments, but the preceding example sends the method two Float objects as arguments instead.

The compiler does not report an error over this discrepancy. Instead, the Float objects automatically are unboxed into float values before being sent to the min() method.

CAUTION

> Unboxing an object works only if the object has a value. If no constructor has been called to set up the object, compilation fails with an error.

Comparing Object Values and Classes

In addition to casting, you often will perform three other common tasks that involve objects:

- Comparing objects
- Finding out the class of any given object
- Testing to see whether an object is an instance of a given class

Comparing Objects

Yesterday, you learned about operators for comparing values—equal to, not equal, less than, and so on. Most of these operators work only on primitive types, not on objects. If you try to use other values as operands, the Java compiler produces errors.

The exceptions to this rule are the == operator for equality and the != operator for inequality. When applied to objects, these operators don't do what you might first expect. Instead of checking whether one object has the same value as the other, they determine whether both sides of the operator refer to the same object.

To compare objects of a class and have meaningful results, you must implement special methods in your class and call those methods.

A good example of this is the String class. It is possible to have two different String objects that represent the same text. If you were to employ the == operator to compare these objects, however, they would be considered unequal. Although their contents match, they are not the same object.

To see whether two String objects have matching values, a method of the class called equals() is used. The method tests each character in the string and returns true if the two strings have the same value. The EqualsTester application shown in Listing 3.5 illustrates this. Create the application with NetBeans and save the file, either by choosing File, Save or by clicking the Save All toolbar button.

LISTING 3.5   The Full Text of EqualsTester.java

```
 1: class EqualsTester {
 2:     public static void main(String[] arguments) {
 3:         String str1, str2;
 4:         str1 = "Free the bound periodicals.";
 5:         str2 = str1;
 6:
 7:         System.out.println("String1: " + str1);
 8:         System.out.println("String2: " + str2);
 9:         System.out.println("Same object? " + (str1 == str2));
10:
11:         str2 = new String(str1);
12:
```

LISTING 3.5   Continued

```
13:          System.out.println("String1: " + str1);
14:          System.out.println("String2: " + str2);
15:          System.out.println("Same object? " + (str1 == str2));
16:          System.out.println("Same value? " + str1.equals(str2));
17:      }
18: }
```

Here's the output:

Output ▼

```
String1: Free the bound periodicals.
String2: Free the bound periodicals.
Same object? true
String1: Free the bound periodicals.
String2: Free the bound periodicals.
Same object? false
Same value? true
```

The first part of this program declares two variables (str1 and str2), assigns the literal "Free the bound periodicals." to str1, and then assigns that value to str2 (lines 3–5). As you learned earlier, str1 and str2 now point to the same object, and the equality test at line 9 proves that.

In the second part of this program, you create a new String object with the same value as str1 and assign str2 to that new String object.

Now you have two different string objects in str1 and str2, both with the same value. Testing them to see whether they're the same object by using the == operator (line 15) returns the expected answer: false. They are not the same object in memory. Testing them using the equals() method in line 16 also returns the expected answer of true, which shows they have the same value.

NOTE   Why can't you just use another literal when you change str2, instead of using new? String literals are optimized in Java. If you create a string using a literal and then use another literal with the same characters, Java knows enough to give you back the first String object. Both strings are the same object; you have to go out of your way to create two separate objects.

Determining the Class of an Object

Want to find out what an object's class is? Here's how you do so for an object assigned to the variable key:

```
String name = key.getClass().getName();
```

The getClass() method is defined in the Object class, so it can be called in all objects. It returns a Class object that represents the object's class. That object's getName() method returns a string holding the name of the class.

Another useful test is the instanceof operator, which has two operands: a reference to an object on the left, and a class name on the right. The expression produces a Boolean value: true if the object is an instance of the named class or any of that class's sub-classes, or false otherwise, as in these examples:

```
boolean check1 = "Texas" instanceof String; // true

Point pt = new Point(10, 10);
boolean check2 = pt instanceof String; // false
```

The instanceof operator also can be used for interfaces. If an object implements an interface, the instanceof operator returns true when this is tested.

Unlike other operators in Java, instanceof is not defined as some form of punctuation. Instead, the instanceof keyword is the operator.

3

Summary

Now that you have spent three days exploring how object-oriented programming is implemented in Java, you're in a better position to decide how useful it can be in your programming.

If you are a "glass half empty" kind of person, object-oriented programming is a level of abstraction that gets in the way of using a programming language. You learn more about why OOP is thoroughly ingrained in Java in the coming days.

If you are a "glass half full" kind of person, object-oriented programming is beneficial because of its benefits: improved reliability, reusability, and maintenance.

Today, you learned how to deal with objects: creating them, reading their values and changing them, and calling their methods. You also learned how to cast objects from one class to another, cast to and from primitive data types and classes, and take advantage of automatic conversions through autoboxing and unboxing.

Q&A

Q **I'm confused about the differences between objects and the primitive data types, such as `int` and `boolean`.**

A The primitive types (`byte`, `short`, `int`, `long`, `float`, `double`, `boolean`, and `char`) are not objects, although in many ways they can be handled like objects. They can be assigned to variables and passed in and out of methods.

Objects are instances of classes and as such usually are much more complex data types than simple numbers and characters. They often contain numbers and characters as instance or class variables.

Q **The `length()` and `charAt()` methods in the StringChecker application (Listing 3.3) don't appear to make sense. If `length()` says that a string is 38 characters long, shouldn't the characters be numbered from 1 to 38 when `charAt()` is used to display characters in the string?**

A The two methods look at strings differently. The `length()` method counts the characters in the string, with the first character counting as 1, the second as 2, and so on. The `charAt()` method considers the first character in the string to be located at position number 0. This is the same numbering system used with array elements in Java. Consider the string `"Charlie Brown"`. It has 13 characters ranging from position 0 (the letter C) to position 12 (the letter n).

Q **If Java lacks pointers, how can I do something like linked lists, where there's a pointer from one node to another so that they can be traversed?**

A It's incorrect to say that Java has no pointers; it just has no *explicit* pointers. Object references are effectively pointers. To create something like a linked list, you could create a class called `Node`, which would have an instance variable also of type `Node`. To link node objects, assign a node object to the instance variable of the object immediately before it in the list. Because object references are pointers, linked lists set up this way behave as you would expect them to. (You work with the Java class library's version of linked lists on Day 8, "Data Structures.")

Quiz

Review today's material by taking this three-question quiz. Answers are at the end of the book.

Questions

1. Which operator do you use to call an object's constructor and create a new object?

    A. +

    B. new

    C. instanceof

2. What kind of methods apply to all objects of a class rather than an individual object?

    A. Universal methods

    B. Instance methods

    C. Class methods

3. If you have a program with objects named obj1 and obj2, what happens when you use the statement obj2 = obj1?

    A. The instance variables in obj2 are given the same values as obj1.

    B. obj2 and obj1 are considered to be the same object.

    C. Neither A nor B.

3

Certification Practice

The following question is the kind of thing you could expect to be asked on a Java programming certification test. Answer it without looking at today's material or using the Java compiler to test the code.

Given:

```java
public class AyeAye {
    int i = 40;
    int j;

    public AyeAye() {
        setValue(i++);
    }

    void setValue(int inputValue) {
        int i = 20;
        j = i + 1;
        System.out.println("j = " + j);
    }
}
```

What is the value of the j variable at the time it is displayed inside the `setValue()` method?

- **A.** 42
- **B.** 40
- **C.** 21
- **D.** 20

The answer is available on the book's website at www.java21days.com. Visit the Day 3 page and click the Certification Practice link.

Exercises

To extend your knowledge of the subjects covered today, try the following exercises:

1. Create a program that turns a birthday in MM/DD/YYYY format (such as 04/29/2013) into three individual strings.

2. Create a class with instance variables for `height`, `weight`, and `depth`, making each an integer. Create a Java application that uses your new class, sets each of these values in an object, and displays the values.

Where applicable, exercise solutions are offered on the book's website at www.java21days.com.

DAY 4
Lists, Logic, and Loops

Today, you learn about three of the most boring features in the Java language:

- How to organize groups of the same class or data type into lists called arrays

- How to make a program decide whether to do something based on logic

- How to make part of a Java program repeat itself by using loops

If these features don't sound boring to you, that's good. Most of the significant work that you will accomplish with your Java software will use all three.

These topics are boring for computers. They enable software to do one of the things at which it excels: performing repetitive tasks repeatedly.

Arrays

At this point, you have dealt with only a few variables in each Java program. In some cases, it's manageable to use individual variables to store information, but what if you had 20 items of related information to track? You could create 20 different variables and set up their initial values, but that approach becomes progressively more cumbersome as you deal with larger amounts of information. What if there were 100 items or even 1,000?

Arrays are a way to store a list of items that have the same primitive data type, the same class, or a common parent class. Each item on the list goes into its own numbered slot so that you can easily access the information.

Arrays can contain any type of information that is stored in a variable, but after the array is created, you can use it for that information type only. For example, you can have an array of integers, an array of String objects, or an array of arrays, but you can't have an array that contains both String objects and integers.

Java implements arrays differently than other languages—as objects treated like other objects.

To create an array in Java, you must do the following:

1. Declare a variable to hold the array.
2. Create a new array object and assign it to the array variable.
3. Store information in that array.

Declaring Array Variables

The first step in array creation is to declare a variable that will hold the array. Array variables indicate the object or data type that the array will hold and the array's name. To differentiate from regular variable declarations, a pair of empty brackets ([ ]) is added to the object or data type, or to the variable name.

The following statements are examples of array variable declarations:

```
String[] requests;
```

```
Point[] targets;
```

```
float[] donations;
```

You also can declare an array by putting the brackets after the variable name instead of the information type, as in the following statements:

```
String requests[];
```

```
Point targets[];
```

```
float donations[];
```

NOTE

> The choice of which style to use is a matter of personal prefer-
> ence. The sample programs in this book place the brackets after
> the information type rather than the variable name, which is the
> more popular convention among Java programmers.

Creating Array Objects

After you declare the array variable, the next step is to create an array object and assign it to that variable. To do this

- Use the new operator.
- Initialize the contents of the array directly.

Because arrays are objects in Java, you can use the new operator to create a new instance of an array, as in the following statement:

```
String[] players = new String[10];
```

This statement creates a new array of strings with 10 slots that can contain String objects. When you create an array object by using new, you must indicate how many slots the array will hold. This statement does not put actual String objects in the slots; you must do that later.

4

Array objects can contain primitive types, such as integers or Booleans, just as they can contain objects:

```
int[] temps = new int[99];
```

When you create an array object using new, all its slots automatically are given an initial value (0 for numeric arrays, false for Booleans, '\0' for character arrays, and null for objects).

NOTE

> The Java keyword null refers to a null object (and can be used
> for any object reference). It is not equivalent to 0 or the '\0'
> character as the NULL constant is in C.

Because each object in an array of objects has a null reference when created, you must assign an object to each array element before using it.

The following example creates an array of three Integer objects and then assigns each element an object:

```
Integer[] series = new Integer[3];
series[0] = new Integer(10);
series[1] = new Integer(3);
series[2] = new Integer(5);
```

You can create and initialize an array at the same time by enclosing the array's elements inside braces, separated by commas:

```
Point[] markup = { new Point(1,5), new Point(3,3), new Point(2,3) };
```

Each of the elements inside the braces must be the same type as the variable that holds the array. When you create an array with initial values in this manner, the array is the same size as the number of elements you include within the braces. The preceding example creates an array of Point objects named markup that contains three elements.

Because String objects can be created and initialized without the new operator, you can do the same when creating an array of strings:

```
String[] titles = { "Mr.", "Mrs.", "Ms.", "Miss", "Dr." };
```

The preceding statement creates a five-element array of String objects named titles.

All arrays have an instance variable named length that holds a count of the number of elements in the array. Extending the preceding example, the variable titles.length contains the value 5.

The first element of an array has a subscript of 0 rather than 1, so an array with five elements has array slots accessed using subscripts 0 through 4.

Accessing Array Elements

After you have an array with initial values, you can retrieve, change, and test the values in each slot of that array. The value in a slot is accessed using the array name followed by a subscript enclosed in square brackets. This name and subscript can be put into expressions, as in the following:

```
testScore[40] = 920;
```

This statement sets the 41st element of the testScore array to a value of 920. The testScore part of this expression is a variable holding an array object, although it also can be an expression that results in an array. The subscript expression specifies the slot to access within the array.

All array subscripts are checked to make sure that they are inside the array's boundaries as specified when the array was created. In Java, it is impossible to access or assign a value to an array slot outside the array's boundaries. This avoids the problems that result from overrunning the bounds of an array in other languages. Note the following two statements:

```
float[] rating = new float[20];
rating[20] = 3.22F;
```

The compiler reports an error with these lines of code. The error occurs because the rating array does not have a slot numbered 20; it has 20 slots that begin at 0 and end at 19. The Java compiler would make note of this by stopping with an ArrayIndexOutOfBoundsException error.

The Java interpreter also notes an error if the array subscript is calculated when the program is running and the subscript is outside the array's boundaries. You learn more about errors, which are called exceptions, on Day 7, "Exceptions and Threads."

One way to avoid accidentally overrunning the end of an array in your programs is to use the length instance variable. The following statement displays the number of elements in the rating object:

```
System.out.println("Elements: " + rating.length);
```

Changing Array Elements

As you saw in the previous examples, you can assign a value to a specific slot in an array by putting an assignment statement after the array name and subscript, as in the following:

```
temperature[4] = 85;

day[0] = "Sunday";

manager[2] = manager[0];
```

It's important to remember that an array of objects in Java is an array of references to those objects. When you assign a value to a slot in that kind of array, you are creating a reference to that object. When you move around values inside arrays, you are reassigning the reference rather than copying a value from one slot to another. Arrays of a primitive data type, such as int and float, do copy the values from one slot to another, as do elements of a String array, even though they are objects.

Arrays are reasonably simple to create and modify, and they provide an enormous amount of functionality for Java. The HalfDollars application, shown in Listing 4.1, creates, initializes, and displays elements of three arrays. Create a new empty Java file in NetBeans called HalfDollars, and enter the listing's source code.

LISTING 4.1   The Full Text of HalfDollars.java

```
1: class HalfDollars {
2:     public static void main(String[] arguments) {
3:         int[] denver = { 1_900_000, 1_700_000, 1_700_000 };
4:         int[] philadelphia = new int[denver.length];
5:         int[] total = new int[denver.length];
6:         int average;
7:
8:         philadelphia[0] = 1_900_000;
9:         philadelphia[1] = 1_800_000;
10:        philadelphia[2] = 1_750_000;
11:
12:        total[0] = denver[0] + philadelphia[0];
13:        total[1] = denver[1] + philadelphia[1];
14:        total[2] = denver[2] + philadelphia[2];
15:        average = (total[0] + total[1] + total[2]) / 3;
16:
17:        System.out.print("2009 production: ");
18:        System.out.format("%,d%n", total[0]);
19:        System.out.print("2010 production: ");
20:        System.out.format("%,d%n", total[1]);
21:        System.out.print("2011 production: ");
22:        System.out.format("%,d%n", total[2]);
23:        System.out.print("Average production: ");
24:        System.out.format("%,d%n", average);
25:    }
26: }
```

The HalfDollars application uses three integer arrays to store production totals for U.S. half-dollar coins produced at the Denver and Philadelphia mints. When you run the program, the following output appears:

Output ▼

```
2009 production: 3,800,000
2010 production: 3,500,000
2011 production: 3,450,000
Average production: 3,583,333
```

The class created here, HalfDollars, has three instance variables that hold arrays of integers.

The first, which is named denver, is declared and initialized on line 3 to contain three integers: 1_900_000 in element 0, 1_700_000 in element 1, and 1_700_000 in element 2. These figures are the total half-dollar production at the Denver mint for three years. The integers use an underscore character (_) after every three digits to make the numbers more human-readable, a new feature of Java 7. The compiler ignores the underscores.

The second and third instance variables, `philadelphia` and `total`, are declared in lines 4 and 5. The `philadelphia` array contains the production totals for the Philadelphia mint, and `total` is used to store the overall production totals.

No initial values are assigned to the slots of the `philadelphia` and `total` arrays in lines 4 and 5. For this reason, each element is given the default value for integers: 0.

The `denver.length` variable is used to give both of these arrays the same number of slots as the `denver` array. Every array contains a `length` variable that you can use to keep track of the number of elements it contains.

The rest of the `main()` method of this application does the following:

- Line 6 creates an integer variable called `average`.
- Lines 8–10 assign new values to the three elements of the `philadelphia` array.
- Lines 12–14 assign new values to the elements of the `total` array. In line 12, `total` element 0 is given the sum of `denver` element 0 and `philadelphia` element 0. Similar expressions are used in lines 13 and 14.
- Line 15 sets the value of the `average` variable to the average of the three `total` elements. Because `average` and the three `total` elements are integers, the average is expressed as an integer rather than a floating-point number.
- Lines 17–24 display the values stored in the `total` array and the `average` variable, using the `System.out.format()` method to display the numeric values in a more readable form using commas.

This application handles arrays inefficiently. The statements are almost identical, except for the subscripts that indicate the array element to which you are referring. If the HalfDollars application were being used to track 100 years of production totals instead of 3 years, this approach would require a lot of redundant statements.

When dealing with arrays, you can use loops to cycle through an array's elements instead of dealing with each element individually. This makes the code a lot shorter and easier to read. When you learn about loops later today, you'll see a rewrite of the current example (Listing 4.3).

Multidimensional Arrays

Arrays can be multidimensional, containing more than one subscript to store information in multiple dimensions.

A common use of a multidimensional array is to represent the data in an (x,y) grid of array elements.

Java supports this by enabling an array to hold arrays as each of its elements. Those arrays can also contain arrays, and so on, for as many dimensions as needed.

For example, consider a program that needs to accomplish the following tasks:

- Record an integer value each day for a year.
- Organize those values by week.

One way to organize this data is to create a 52-element array in which each element contains a 7-element array:

```
int[][] dayValue = new int[52][7];
```

This array of arrays contains a total of 364 integers, one for each day in 52 weeks. You could set the value for the first day of the 10th week with the following statement:

```
dayValue[9][0] = 14200;
```

Remember that array indexes start at 0 instead of 1, so the 10th week is at element 9 and the first day at element 0.

You can use the `length` instance variable with these arrays as you would any other. The following statement contains a three-dimensional array of integers and displays the number of elements in each dimension:

```
int[][][] century = new int[100][52][7];
System.out.println("Elements in the first dimension: " + century.length);
System.out.println("Elements in the second dimension: " + century[0].length);
System.out.println("Elements in the third dimension: " + century[0][0].length);
```

Block Statements

Statements in Java are grouped into blocks. The beginning and ending boundaries of a block are noted with brace characters—an opening brace ({) for the beginning and a closing brace (}) for the ending.

You have used blocks to hold the variables and methods in a class definition and define statements that belong in a method.

Blocks also are called block statements because an entire block can be used anywhere a single statement could be used. Each statement inside the block then is executed from top to bottom.

You can put blocks inside other blocks, just as you do when you put a method inside a class definition.

An important thing to note about using a block is that it creates a scope for the local variables created inside the block. Scope is the part of a program where a variable exists and can be used. If you try to use a variable outside its scope, an error occurs.

In Java, the scope of a variable is the block in which it was created. When you can declare and use local variables inside a block, those variables cease to exist after the block is finished executing. For example, the following method contains a block:

```
void testBlock() {
    int x = 10;
    { // start of block
        int y = 40;
        y = y + x;
    } // end of block
}
```

Two variables are defined in this method: x and y. The scope of the y variable is the block it's in, which is marked by the start of block and end of block comments. The variable can be used only within that block. An error would result if you tried to use the y variable in another part of the method.

The x variable was created inside the method but outside the inner block, so it can be used anywhere in the method. You can modify the value of x anywhere within the method.

Block statements are used in class and method definitions and the logic and looping structures you learn about next. The way the preceding example uses the inner block is not common.

4

If Conditionals

A key aspect of any programming language is how it enables a program to make decisions. This is handled through a special type of statement called a *conditional*, a statement executed only if a specific condition is met.

The most basic conditional in Java is if. The if conditional uses a Boolean expression to decide whether a statement should be executed. If the expression produces a true value, the statement is executed.

Here's a simple example that displays the message Not enough arguments only if the value of an instance variable is less than 3:

```
if (arguments.length < 3)
    System.out.println("Not enough arguments");
```

If you want something else to happen when an if expression produces a false value, you can use the else keyword. The following example uses both if and else:

```
String server;
int duration;
if (arguments.length < 1) {
```

```
    server = "localhost";
} else {
    server = arguments[0];
}
```

The `if` conditional executes different statements based on the result of a single Boolean test.

NOTE _____ A difference between `if` conditionals in Java and those in other languages is that Java conditionals produce only Boolean values (`true` or `false`). In C and C++, the test can return an integer.

Using `if`, you can include only a single statement as the code to execute if the test expression is true and another statement if the expression is false.

However, as you learned earlier today, a block can appear anywhere in Java that a single statement can appear. If you want to do more than one thing as a result of an `if` statement, you can enclose those statements inside a block. Note the following snippet of code, which was used on Day 1, "Getting Started with Java":

```
int temperature = 530;
if (temperature > 660) {
    status = "returning home";
    speed = 5;
}
```

The `if` statement in this example contains the test expression `temperature > 660`. If the `temperature` variable contains a value higher than 660, the block statement is executed, and two things occur:

- The `status` variable is given the value "returning home."
- The `speed` variable is set to 5.

If the `temperature` variable is equal to or less than 660, the entire block is skipped, so nothing happens.

All `if` and `else` statements use Boolean tests to determine whether statements are executed. You can use a `boolean` variable itself for this test, as in the following:

```
boolean outOfGas = true;
if (outOfGas)
    status = "inactive";
```

The preceding example uses a boolean variable called outOfGas. It functions exactly like the following:

```
if (outOfGas == true)
    status = "inactive";
```

Switch Conditionals

A common programming practice is to test a variable against a value, and if it doesn't match, test it again against a different value, and so on.

This approach can become unwieldy if you're using only if statements, depending on how many different values you have to test. For example, you might end up with a set of if statements something like the following:

```
if (operation == '+')
    add(object1, object2);
else if (operation == '-')
    subtract(object1, object2);
else if (operation == '*')
    multiply(object1, object2);
else if (operation == '/')
    divide(object1, object2);
```

This use of if statements is called a *nested if statement* because each else statement contains another if until all possible tests have been made.

A better way to handle this situation in Java is by grouping actions with the switch statement. The following example demonstrates switch usage:

```
char grade = 'D';
switch (grade) {
    case 'A':
        System.out.println("Great job!");
        break;
    case 'B':
        System.out.println("Good job!");
        break;
    case 'C':
        System.out.println("You can do better!");
        break;
    default:
        System.out.println("Consider cheating!");
}
```

A switch statement is built on a test variable. In the preceding example, the variable is the value of the grade variable, which holds a char value.

4

The test variable can be the primitive types byte, char, short, or int or, as of Java 7, the class String. The following code uses the value of a String object named command to decide which method to call:

```
String command = "close";
switch (command) {
    case "open":
        openFile();
        break;
    case "close":
        closeFile();
        break;
    default:
        System.out.println("Invalid command");
    }
}
```

The test variable is compared in turn with each case value. If a match is found, the statement or statements after the test are executed.

If no match is found, the default statement or statements are executed. Providing a default statement is optional. If it is omitted and there is no match for any of the case statements, the switch statement might complete without executing anything.

The test cases in a switch statement are limited to primitive types that can be cast to an int, such as char or strings. You cannot use larger primitive types such as long or float or test for any relationship other than equality.

The following is a revision of the nested if example shown previously. It has been rewritten as a switch statement:

```
switch (operation) {
    case '+':
        add(object1, object2);
        break;
    case '-':
        subtract(object1, object2);
        break;
    case '*':
        multiply(object1, object2);
        break;
    case '/':
        divide(object1, object2);
        break;
    }
```

After each case, you can include a single result statement or as many as you need. Unlike with if statements, multiple statements don't require a block statement.

The break statement included with each case section determines when to stop executing statements in response to a matching case. Suppose a case section has no break statement. After a match is made, the statements for that match and all the statements further down the switch are executed until a break or the end of the switch is found.

In some situations, this might be exactly what you want to do. Otherwise, you should include break statements to ensure that only the right code is executed. The break statement, which you use again later in the section "Breaking Out of Loops," stops execution at the current point. Then it jumps to the statement after the closing brace that ends the switch statement.

One handy use of falling through without a break occurs when multiple values need to execute the same statements. To accomplish this task, you can use multiple case lines with no result; the switch executes the first statement it finds.

For example, in the following switch statement, the string "x is an even number" is printed if x has a value of 2, 4, 6, or 8. All other values of x cause the string "x is an odd number" to be printed.

```
int x = 5;
switch (x) {
    case 2:
    case 4:
    case 6:
    case 8:
        System.out.println("x is an even number");
        break;
    default:
        System.out.println("x is an odd number");
}
```

The DayCounter application, shown in Listing 4.2, takes two arguments, a month and a year, and displays the number of days in that month. A switch statement, if statements, and else statements are used. Create this application in NetBeans as an empty Java file.

LISTING 4.2   The Full Text of DayCounter.java

```
 1: class DayCounter {
 2:     public static void main(String[] arguments) {
 3:         int yearIn = 2012;
 4:         int monthIn = 1;
 5:         if (arguments.length > 0)
 6:             monthIn = Integer.parseInt(arguments[0]);
 7:         if (arguments.length > 1)
 8:             yearIn = Integer.parseInt(arguments[1]);
 9:         System.out.println(monthIn + "/" + yearIn + " has "
10:             + countDays(monthIn, yearIn) + " days.");
```

4

LISTING 4.2   Continued

```
11:     }
12:
13:     static int countDays(int month, int year) {
14:         int count = -1;
15:         switch (month) {
16:             case 1:
17:             case 3:
18:             case 5:
19:             case 7:
20:             case 8:
21:             case 10:
22:             case 12:
23:                 count = 31;
24:                 break;
25:             case 4:
26:             case 6:
27:             case 9:
28:             case 11:
29:                 count = 30;
30:                 break;
31:             case 2:
32:                 if (year % 4 == 0)
33:                     count = 29;
34:                 else
35:                     count = 28;
36:                 if ((year % 100 == 0) & (year % 400 != 0))
37:                     count = 28;
38:         }
39:         return count;
40:     }
41: }
```

This application uses command-line arguments to specify the month and year to check. The first argument is the month, which should be expressed as a number from 1 to 12. The second argument is the year, which should be expressed as a full four-digit year. If the application is run without setting the arguments, it uses 1 as the month and 12 as the year, displaying this output:

Output ▼

1/2012 has 31 days.

To set command-line arguments in NetBeans, choose Run, Set Project Configuration, Customize. The Project Properties dialog opens, as shown in Figure 4.1.

FIGURE 4.1
Setting command-line arguments for an application in NetBeans.

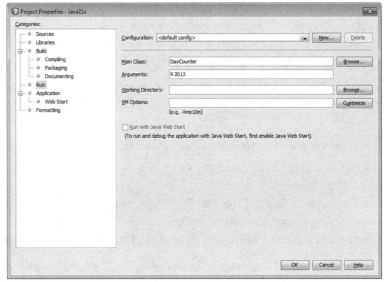

In the Main Class field, enter the name of the class that contains the `main()` method that will be run: `DayCounter`.

4

In the Arguments field, enter the command-line arguments separated by spaces, such as `9 2013`. Click OK to save this configuration.

To run the application with these arguments in NetBeans, choose Run, Run Project (instead of Run, Run File). When run with 9 and 2013 as arguments, the output is the following:

Output ▼

`9/2013 has 30 days.`

The `DayCounter` application uses a `switch` statement to count the days in a month. This statement is part of the `countDays()` method in lines 13–40 of Listing 4.2.

The `countDays()` method has two `int` arguments: `month` and `year`. The number of days is stored in the `count` variable, which is given an initial value of –1 that is replaced by the correct count later.

The `switch` statement that begins on line 15 uses `month` as its conditional value.

The number of days in a month is easy to determine for 11 months of the year. January, March, May, July, August, October, and December have 31 days. April, June, September, and November have 30 days.

The count for these 11 months is handled in lines 16–30 of Listing 4.2. Months are numbered from 1 (January) to 12 (December), as you would expect. When one of the `case` statements has the same value as `month`, every statement after that is executed until `break` or the end of the `switch` statement is reached.

February is more complex and is handled in lines 31–37. Every leap year has 29 days in February, whereas other years have 28. A leap year must meet either of the following conditions:

- The year must be evenly divisible by 4 and not evenly divisible by 100.
- The year must be evenly divisible by 400.

As you learned on Day 2, "The ABCs of Programming," the modulus operator (`%`) returns the remainder of a division operation. This is used with several `if-else` statements to determine how many days there are in February, depending on what year it is.

The `if-else` statement in lines 32–35 sets `count` to 29 when the year is evenly divisible by 4 and sets it to 28 otherwise.

The `if` statement in lines 36 and 37 uses the `&` operator to combine two conditional expressions: `year % 100 == 0` and `year % 400 != 0`. If both these conditions are true, `count` is set to 28.

The `countDays` method ends by returning the value of `count` in line 39.

When you run the DayCounter application, the `main()` method in lines 2–11 is executed.

In all Java applications, command-line arguments are stored in an array of `String` objects. This array is called `arguments` in DayCounter. The first command-line argument is stored in `argument[0]`, the second in `argument[1]`, and upward until all arguments have been stored. If the application is run with no arguments, the array is created with no elements.

Lines 3 and 4 create `yearIn` and `monthIn`, two integer variables to store the year and month that should be checked.

The `if` statement in line 5 uses `arguments.length` to make sure that the `arguments` array has at least one element. If it does, line 6 is executed.

Line 6 calls `parseInt()`, a class method of the `Integer` class, with `arguments[0]` as an argument. This method takes a `String` object as an argument, and if the string could be a valid integer, it returns that value as an `int`. This converted value is stored in `monthIn`. A similar thing happens in line 8: `parseInt()` is called with `arguments[1]`, and this is used to set `yearIn`.

The program's output is displayed in lines 9–10. As part of the output, the countDays() method is called with monthIn and yearIn, and the value returned by this method is displayed.

NOTE

At this point, you might want to know how to collect input from a user in a program rather than using command-line arguments to receive it. There isn't a method comparable to System.out. println() that receives input. Instead, you must learn a bit more about Java's input and output classes before you can receive input in a program without a graphical user interface. This topic is covered during Day 15, "Working with Input and Output."

The Ternary Operator

An alternative to using the if and else keywords in a conditional statement is to use the ternary operator, also called the conditional operator. This operator is ternary because it has three operands (the word "ternary" refers to anything with three parts).

The conditional operator is an expression, meaning that it returns a value—unlike the more general if, which can result in only a statement or block being executed. The conditional operator is most useful for short or simple conditionals and takes the following form:

```
test ? trueresult : falseresult;
```

The test is an expression that returns true or false, just like the test in the if statement. If the test is true, the conditional operator returns the value of trueresult. If the test is false, the conditional operator returns the value of falseresult. For example, the following conditional tests the values of myScore and yourScore and sets the variable ourBestScore equal to one of them:

```
int ourBestScore = myScore > yourScore ? myScore : yourScore;
```

The larger value of myScore and yourScore is copied to ourBestScore.

This use of the conditional operator is equivalent to the following if-else code:

```
int ourBestScore;
if (myScore > yourScore) {
    ourBestScore = myScore;
} else {
    ourBestScore = yourScore;
}
```

4

The conditional operator has low precedence. Usually it is evaluated only after all its subexpressions have been evaluated. The only operators lower in precedence are the assignment operators. For a refresher on operator precedence, refer to Table 2.6 in Day 2, "The ABCs of Programming."

NOTE

> The ternary operator is of primary benefit to experienced programmers creating complex expressions. Because its functionality is duplicated in simpler use of `if-else` statements, there's no need to use this operator while you're beginning to learn the language. The main reason it's introduced in this book is because you'll encounter it in the source code of other Java programmers.

For Loops

A `for` loop is used to repeat a statement until a condition is met. Although `for` loops frequently are used for simple iteration in which a statement is repeated a certain number of times, `for` loops can be used for just about any kind of loop.

The `for` loop in Java has the following structure:

```
for (initialization; test; increment) {
    statement;
}
```

The start of the `for` loop has three parts:

- The *initialization* is an expression that initializes the start of the loop. If you have a loop index, this expression might declare and initialize it, such as `int i = 0`. Variables that you declare in this part of the `for` loop are local to the loop itself. They cease to exist after the loop is finished executing. You can initialize more than one variable in this section by separating each expression with a comma. The statement `int i = 0, int j = 10` in this section would declare the variables `i` and `j`, and both would be local to the loop.

- The *test* is the test that occurs before each pass of the loop. The test must be a Boolean expression or a function that returns a `boolean` value, such as `i < 10`. If the test is `true`, the loop executes. When the test is `false`, the loop stops executing.

- The *increment* is any expression or function call. Commonly, the increment is used to change the value of the loop index to bring the state of the loop closer to returning `false` and stopping the loop. The increment takes place after each pass of the loop. Similar to the *initialization* section, you can put more than one expression in this section by separating each expression with a comma.

The *statement* part of the for loop is the statement that is executed each time the loop iterates. As with if, you can include either a single statement or a block statement. The previous example used a block because that is more common. The following example is a for loop that sets all slots of a String array to the value Mr.:

```
String[] salutation = new String[10];
int i; // the loop index variable
for (i = 0; i < salutation.length; i++)
    salutation[i] = "Mr.";
}
```

In this example, the variable i serves as a loop index; it counts the number of times the loop has been executed. Before each trip through the loop, the index value is compared with salutation.length, the number of elements in the salutation array. When the index is equal to or greater than salutation.length, the loop is exited.

The final element of the for statement is i++. This causes the loop index to increment by 1 each time the loop is executed. Without this statement, the loop would never stop.

The statement inside the loop sets an element of the salutation array equal to "Mr.". The loop index is used to determine which element is modified.

Any part of the for loop can be an empty statement; in other words, you can include a semicolon with no expression or statement, and that part of the for loop is ignored. Note that if you do use an empty statement in your for loop, you might have to initialize or increment any loop variables or loop indexes yourself elsewhere in the program.

4

You also can have an empty statement as the body of your for loop if everything you want to do is in the first line of that loop. For example, the following for loop finds the first prime number higher than 4,000. (It assumes the existence of a method called notPrime() that returns a Boolean value to indicate when i is not prime.)

```
for (i = 4001; notPrime(i); i += 2);
```

The semicolon at the end of the for statement indicates that the loop has no statements in its body.

A common mistake in for loops is to accidentally put a semicolon at the end of the line that includes the for statement:

```
int x = 1;
for (i = 0; i < 10; i++);
    x = x * i; // this line is not inside the loop!
```

In this example, the semicolon outside the parentheses in the for statement ends the loop without executing x = x * i as part of the loop. The x = x * i line is executed only once because it is outside the for loop. Be careful not to make this mistake in your Java programs.

The next project you undertake is a rewrite of the HalfDollar application that uses `for` loops to remove redundant code.

The original application works with an array that is only three elements long. The new version shown in Listing 4.3, called HalfLooper, is shorter and more flexible and returns the same output. Create an empty Java file with that class name in NetBeans.

LISTING 4.3   The Full Text of `HalfLooper.java`

```
 1: class HalfLooper {
 2:     public static void main(String[] arguments) {
 3:         int[] denver = { 1_900_000, 1_700_000, 1_700_000 };
 4:         int[] philadelphia = { 1_900_000, 1_800_000, 1_750_000 };
 5:         int[] total = new int[denver.length];
 6:         int sum = 0;
 7:
 8:         for (int i = 0; i < denver.length; i++) {
 9:             total[i] = denver[i] + philadelphia[i];
10:             System.out.format((i + 2009) + " production: %,d%n",
11:                 total[i]);
12:             sum += total[i];
13:         }
14:
15:         System.out.format("Average production: %,d%n",
16:             (sum / denver.length));
17:     }
18: }
```

The output is as follows:

Output ▼

```
2009 production: 3,800,000
2010 production: 3,500,000
2011 production: 3,450,000
Average production: 3,583,333
```

Instead of going through the elements of the three arrays one by one, this example uses a `for` loop. The following things take place in the loop, which is contained in lines 8–13:

- **Line 8**—The loop is created with an `int` variable called `i` as the index. The index increments by 1 for each pass through the loop and stops when `i` is equal to or greater than `denver.length`, the total number of elements in the `denver` array.

- **Lines 9–11**—The value of one of the `total` elements is set using the loop index and then is displayed with some text identifying the year.

■ **Line 12**—The value of a total element is added to the sum variable, which is used to calculate the average yearly production.

Using a more general-purpose loop to iterate over an array enables you to use the program with arrays of different sizes and still have it assign correct values to the elements of the total array and display those values.

> **NOTE**   Java also includes a for loop that can be used to iterate through all the elements of data structures, such as array lists, linked lists, hash maps, and other collections. This loop is covered along with those structures on Day 8, "Data Structures."

While and Do Loops

The remaining types of loops are while and do, which also enable a block of Java code to be executed repeatedly until a specific condition is met.

While Loops

The while loop repeats a statement for as long as a particular condition remains true. Here's an example:

```
while (i < 13) {
    x = x * i++; // the body of the loop
}
```

The condition that accompanies the while keyword is a Boolean expression—i < 13 in the preceding example. If the expression returns true, the while loop executes the body of the loop and then tests the condition again. This process repeats until the condition is false.

Although the preceding loop uses opening and closing braces to form a block statement, the braces are unneeded because the loop contains only one statement: x = x * i++. Using the braces does not create any problems, though, and the braces will be required if you add another statement inside the loop later.

The ArrayCopier application, shown in in Listing 4.4, uses a while loop to copy the elements of an array of integers (in array1) to an array of float variables (in array2), casting each element to a float as it goes. The one catch is that if any of the elements in the first array is 1, the loop immediately exits at that point.

4

LISTING 4.4   The Full Text of ArrayCopier.java

```
 1: class ArrayCopier {
 2:     public static void main(String[] arguments) {
 3:         int[] array1 = { 7, 4, 8, 1, 4, 1, 4 };
 4:         float[] array2 = new float[array1.length];
 5:
 6:         System.out.print("array1: [ ");
 7:         for (int i = 0; i < array1.length; i++) {
 8:             System.out.print(array1[i] + " ");
 9:         }
10:         System.out.println("]");
11:
12:         System.out.print("array2: [ ");
13:         int count = 0;
14:         while ( count < array1.length && array1[count] != 1) {
15:             array2[count] = (float) array1[count];
16:             System.out.print(array2[count++] + " ");
17:         }
18:         System.out.println("]");
19:     }
20: }
```

The output is as follows:

Output ▼

```
array1: [ 7 4 8 1 4 1 4 ]
array2: [ 7.0 4.0 8.0 ]
```

Here is what's going on in the main() method:

- Lines 3 and 4 declare the arrays. array1 is an array of integers, which are initial- ized to some suitable numbers. array2 is an array of floating-point numbers that is the same length as array1 but doesn't have any initial values.

- Lines 6–10 are for output purposes; they simply iterate through array1 using a for loop to print its values.

- Lines 12–18 are where the interesting stuff happens. This bunch of statements both assigns the values of array2 (converting the numbers to floating-point numbers along the array) and prints them. You start with a count variable, which keeps track of the array index elements. The test in the while loop keeps track of the two conditions for exiting the loop, where those two conditions are running out of ele- ments in array1 or encountering a 1 in array1. (Remember, that was part of the original description of what this program does.)

You can use the logical conditional && operator to keep track of the test; remember that && makes sure that both conditions are true before the entire expression is true. If either one is false, the expression returns false, and the loop exits.

The program's output shows that the first four elements in array1 were copied to array2, but a 1 in the middle stopped the loop from going any further. Without the 1, array2 should end up with all the same elements as array1. If the while loop's test initially is false the first time it is tested (for example, if the first element in that first array is 1), the body of the while loop will never be executed. If you need to execute the loop at least once, you can do one of two things:

- Duplicate the body of the loop outside the while loop.
- Use a do loop (which is described in the following section).

The do loop is considered the better solution.

Do-While Loops

The do loop is just like a while loop, with one major difference—the place in the loop where the condition is tested.

A while loop tests the condition before looping, so if the condition is false the first time it is tested, the body of the loop never executes.

A do loop executes the body of the loop at least once before testing the condition. So if the condition is false the first time it is tested, the body of the loop already will have executed once.

The following example uses a do loop to keep doubling the value of a long integer until it is larger than 3 trillion:

```
long i = 1;
do {
    i *= 2;
    System.out.print(i + " ");
} while (i < 3_000_000_000_000L);
```

The body of the loop is executed once before the test condition, i < 3_000_000_000_000L, is evaluated. Then, if the test evaluates as true, the loop runs again. If it is false, the loop exits. Keep in mind that the body of the loop executes at least once with do loops.

The for, while, and do loops all accomplish the same purpose in slightly different ways. When writing your own code, you may have trouble deciding which one to use. There's often no wrong answer. Whether you use a for, while, or do loop is largely a matter of programming style.

4

Breaking Out of Loops

All loops end when a tested condition is met. There might be times when something occurs during execution of a loop, and you want to exit the loop early. In that case, you can use the `break` and `continue` keywords.

You already have seen `break` as part of the `switch` statement; `break` stops execution of the `switch` statement, and the program continues. The `break` keyword, when used with a loop, does the same thing—it immediately halts execution of the current loop. If you have nested loops within loops, execution picks up with the next outer loop. Otherwise, the program simply continues executing the next statement after the loop.

For example, recall the `while` loop from Listing 4.4. It copied elements from an integer array into an array of floating-point numbers until either the end of the array or a 1 was reached. You can test for the latter case inside the body of the `while` loop and then use `break` to exit the loop:

```
int count = 0;
while (count < array1.length) {
    if (array1[count] == 1)
        break;
    array2[count] = (float) array2[count++];
}
```

The `continue` keyword starts the loop over at the next iteration. For `do` and `while` loops, this means that the execution of the block statement starts over again; with `for` loops, the increment expression is evaluated, and then the block statement is executed.

The `continue` keyword is useful when you want to make a special case out of elements within a loop. With the previous example of copying one array to another, you could test for whether the current element is equal to 1 and use `continue` to restart the loop after every 1 so that the resulting array never contains 0. Note that because you're skipping elements in the first array, you now have to keep track of two different array counters:

```
int count = 0;
int count2 = 0;
while (count++ <= array1.length) {
    if (array1[count] == 1)
        continue;

    array2[count2++] = (float)array1[count];
}
```

Labeled Loops

Both `break` and `continue` can have an optional label that tells Java where to resume execution of the program. Without a label, `break` jumps outside the nearest loop to an enclosing loop or to the next statement outside the loop. The `continue` keyword restarts the loop it is enclosed within. Using `break` and `continue` with a label enables you to use `break` to go to a point outside a nested loop or to use `continue` to go to a loop outside the current loop.

To use a labeled loop, add the label before the initial part of the loop, with a colon between the label and the loop. Then, when you use `break` or `continue`, add the name of the label after the keyword itself, as in the following:

```
out:
    for (int i = 0; i <10; i++) {
        while (x < 50) {
            if (i * x++ > 400)
                break out;
            // inner loop here
        }
        // outer loop here
    }
```

In this code snippet, the label `out` labels the outer loop. Then, inside both the `for` and `while` loops, when a particular condition is met, a `break` causes the execution to break out of both loops. Without the label `out`, the `break` statement would exit the inner loop and resume execution with the outer loop.

4

Summary

Now that you have been introduced to lists, loops, and logic, you can make a computer decide whether to repeatedly display the contents of an array.

You've learned how to declare an array variable, assign an object to it, and access and change elements of the array. With the `if` and `switch` conditional statements, you can branch to different parts of a program based on a Boolean test. You learned about the `for`, `while`, and `do` loops, and you learned that each enables a portion of a program to be repeated until a given condition is met.

It bears repeating: You'll use all three of these features frequently in your Java programs.

You'll use all three of these features frequently in your Java programs.

Q&A

Q I declared a variable inside a block statement for an `if`. When the `if` was done, the definition of that variable vanished. Where did it go?

A In technical terms, block statements form a new lexical scope. This means that if you declare a variable inside a block, it's visible and usable only inside that block.

When the block finishes executing, all the variables you declared go away.

It's a good idea to declare most of your variables in the outermost block in which they'll be needed—usually at the top of a block statement. The exception might be simple variables, such as index counters in `for` loops, where declaring them in the first line of the `for` loop is an easy shortcut.

Q Why can't I use `switch` with strings?

A This is one of the most common questions Java programmers ask after they learn about the `switch` conditional. With the release of Java 7, you can use strings with each `case` in the statement. You have to make sure that you have Java 7 installed and that your development environment has been set up to use it.

In NetBeans, to see whether the current project is set up for Java 7, choose File, Project Properties to open the properties dialog. Choose `Libraries` in the Categories pane, then set Java Platform to `JDK 7` if it isn't already. Click OK to save the change and exit the dialog.

Quiz

Review today's material by taking this three-question quiz. Answers are at the end of the book.

Questions

1. What kind of loop is used to execute the statements in the loop at least once before the conditional expression is evaluated?

     A. `do-while`

     B. `for`

     C. `while`

2. Which of the following cannot be used as the test in a `case` statement?

     A. `characters`

     B. `strings`

     C. `objects`

3. Which instance variable of an array is used to find out how big it is?

     A. `size`

     B. `length`

     C. `MAX_VALUE`

Certification Practice

The following question is the kind of thing you could expect to be asked on a Java programming certification test. Answer it without looking at today's material or using the Java compiler to test the code.

Given:

```
public class Cases {
    public static void main(String[] arguments) {
        float x = 9;
        float y = 5;
        int z = (int)(x / y);
        switch (z) {
            case 1:
                x = x + 2;
            case 2:
                x = x + 3;
            default:
                x = x + 1;
        }
        System.out.println("Value of x: " + x);
    }
}
```

4

What will be the value of x when it is displayed?

A. 9.0

B. 11.0

C. 15.0

D. The program will not compile.

The answer is available on the book's website at www.java21days.com. Visit the Day 4 page and click the Certification Practice link.

Exercises

To extend your knowledge of the subjects covered today, try the following exercises:

1. Using the countDays() method from the DayCounter application, create an application that displays every date in a given year in a single list from January 1 to December 31.

2. Create a class that takes words for the first 10 numbers ("one" to "ten") and converts them into a single `long` integer. Use a `switch` statement for the conversion and command-line arguments for the words.

Where applicable, exercise solutions are offered on the book's website at www.java21days.com.

DAY 5
Creating Classes and Methods

If you're coming to Java from another programming language, you might be struggling with the meaning of the term *class*. It seems synonymous with the term *program*, but you might be uncertain of the relationship between the two.

In Java, a program is made up of a main class and any other classes needed to support the main class. These support classes include any you might need in the Java class library, such as String, Math, and the like.

Today, the meaning of class is clarified as you create classes and methods, which define the behavior of an object or class. You learn about each of the following:

- The definition of the parts of a class

- The creation and use of instance variables

- The creation and use of methods

- The use of the main() method in Java applications

- The creation of overloaded methods

- The creation of constructors

Defining Classes

Because you have created classes during each of the previous days, you should be familiar with the basics of their creation at this point. A class is defined via the `class` keyword and the name of the class, as in the following example:

```
class Ticker {
    // body of the class
}
```

By default, classes inherit from the `Object` class. It's the superclass of all classes in the Java class hierarchy.

The `extends` keyword is used to indicate the superclass of a class, as in this example, which is defined as a subclass of `Ticker`:

```
class SportsTicker extends Ticker {
    // body of the class
}
```

Creating Instance and Class Variables

Whenever you create a class, one thing you must do is define behavior that makes the new class different from its superclass.

This behavior is defined by specifying the variables and methods of the new class. In this section, you work with three kinds of variables: instance variables, local variables, and class variables. The subsequent section covers methods.

Defining Instance Variables

On Day 2, "The ABCs of Programming," you learned how to declare and initialize local variables, which are variables inside method definitions.

Instance variables are declared and defined in almost the same manner as local variables. The main difference is their location in the class definition.

Variables are considered instance variables if they are declared outside a method definition and are not modified by the `static` keyword.

By programming custom, most instance variables are defined right after the first line of the class definition, but they could just as easily be defined at the end.

Here's a simple class definition for the class `VolcanoRobot`, which inherits from the superclass `ScienceRobot`:

```
class VolcanoRobot extends ScienceRobot {
    String status;
    int speed;
    float temperature;
    int power;
}
```

This class definition contains four variables. Because these variables are not defined inside a method, they are instance variables. The variables are as follows:

- status—A string indicating the robot's current activity (for example, "exploring" or "returning home")
- speed—An integer that indicates the robot's current rate of travel
- temperature—A floating-point number that indicates the current temperature of the robot's environment
- power—An integer indicating the robot's current battery power

Class Variables

As you learned in previous days, class variables apply to a class as a whole, rather than to a particular object of that class.

Class variables are good for sharing information between different objects of the same class or for keeping track of common information among a set of objects.

The static keyword is used in the class declaration to declare a class variable, as in the following example:

```
static int SUM;
static final int MAXOBJECTS = 10;
```

5

By convention, many Java programmers capitalize the names of class variables so that they're distinguished in code from other variables. This is not a requirement of the language.

Creating Methods

As you learned on Day 3, "Working with Objects," methods define an object's behavior—anything that happens when the object is created as well as the various tasks the object can perform during its lifetime.

This section introduces method definitions and how methods work. Tomorrow's lesson has more details about more sophisticated things you can do with methods.

Defining Methods

In Java, a method definition has four basic parts:

- The method's name
- A list of parameters
- The type of object or primitive type that the method returns
- The body of the method

The first two parts of the method definition form the method's *signature*.

 NOTE   To keep things simpler today, two optional parts of the method definition have been left out: a modifier, such as `public` or `private`, and the `throws` keyword, which indicates the exceptions a method can throw. You'll learn about these parts of method definition on Day 6, "Packages, Interfaces, and Other Class Features," and Day 7, "Exceptions and Threads."

In other languages, the name of the method (which might be called a function, subroutine, or procedure) is enough to distinguish it from other methods in the program.

In Java, you can have several methods in the same class with the same name but different signatures. This practice is called method overloading, and you'll learn more about it later today.

Here's what a basic method definition looks like:

```
returnType methodName(type1 arg1, type2 arg2, type3 arg3 ...) {
    // body of the method
}
```

The *returnType* is the primitive type or class of the value returned by the method. It can be one of the primitive types, a class name, or `void` if the method does not return a value.

The method's parameter list is a set of variable declarations separated by commas and set inside parentheses. These parameters become local variables in the body of the method, receiving their values when the method is called.

Note that if this method returns an array object, the array brackets can go after either the return type or the closing parenthesis of the parameter list. Because putting the brackets after the return type is easier to read, it is used in this book's examples. For instance, the following declares a method that returns an integer array:

```
int[] makeRange(int lower, int upper) {
    // body of this method
}
```

You can have statements, expressions, method calls on other objects, conditionals, loops, and so on inside the body of the method.

Unless a method has been declared with void as its return type, the method returns some kind of value when it is completed. This value must be explicitly returned at some exit point inside the method, using the return keyword.

Listing 5.1 contains RangeLister, a class that defines a makeRange() method. This method takes two integers—a lower boundary and an upper boundary—and creates an array that contains all the integers between those two boundaries. The boundaries themselves are included in the array of integers.

Create a new empty Java file in NetBeans for a class called RangeLister and enter the code of Listing 5.1 into it.

LISTING 5.1   The Full Text of RangeLister.java

```
 1: class RangeLister {
 2:     int[] makeRange(int lower, int upper) {
 3:         int[] range = new int[(upper-lower) + 1];
 4:
 5:         for (int i = 0; i < range.length; i++) {
 6:             range[i] = lower++;
 7:         }
 8:         return range;
 9:     }
10:
11:     public static void main(String[] arguments) {
12:         int[] range;
13:         RangeLister lister = new RangeLister();
14:
15:         range = lister.makeRange(4, 13);
16:         System.out.print("The array: [ ");
17:         for (int i = 0; i < range.length; i++) {
18:             System.out.print(range[i] + " ");
19:         }
20:         System.out.println("]");
21:     }
22:
23: }
```

5

The output is the following:

Output ▼

```
The array: [ 4 5 6 7 8 9 10 11 12 13 ]
```

The main() method in this class tests the makeRange() method by calling it with the arguments of 4 and 13. The method creates an empty integer array and uses a for loop to fill the new array with values from 4 through 13 in lines 5–7.

The this Keyword

In the body of a method definition, sometimes you might need to refer to the object that contains the method (in other words, to the object itself). You can do so to use that object's instance variables and to pass the current object as an argument to another method.

To refer to the object in these cases, use the this keyword where you normally would refer to an object's name.

The this keyword refers to the current object, and you can use it anywhere a reference to an object might appear: in dot notation, as an argument to a method, as the return value for the current method, and so on. The following are some examples of using this:

```
t = this.x;          // the x instance variable for this object

z.resetData(this);   // call the resetData method, defined in
                     // the z class, and pass it the current object


return this;         // return the current object
```

In many cases, you might not need to explicitly use the this keyword because it is assumed. For instance, you can refer to both instance variables and method calls defined in the current class simply by name because the this is implicit in those references. Therefore, you could write the first example as follows:

```
t = x;               // the x instance variable for this object
```

NOTE

The viability of omitting the this keyword for instance variables depends on whether variables of the same name are declared in the local scope. You'll read about this subject in the next section.

Because this is a reference to the current instance of a class, use it only inside the body of an instance method definition. Class methods—which are declared with the static keyword—cannot use this.

Variable Scope and Method Definitions

One thing you must know to use a variable is its scope. *Scope* is the part of a program in which a variable or another type of information exists, making it possible to use the variable in statements and expressions. When the part defining the scope has finished executing, the variable ceases to exist.

When you declare a variable in Java, that variable always has limited scope. A variable with local scope, for example, can be used only inside the block in which it was defined. Instance variables have a scope that extends to the entire class, so they can be used by any of the instance methods within that class.

When you refer to a variable, Java checks for its definition outward, starting with the innermost scope.

The innermost scope could be a block statement, such as the contents of a while loop. The second-innermost scope could be the method in which the block is contained.

If the variable hasn't been found in the method, the class itself is checked.

Because of how Java checks for the scope of a given variable, it is possible for you to create a variable in a lower scope that hides (or replaces) the original value of that variable and introduces subtle bugs into your code.

For example, consider the following Java application:

```
class ScopeTest {
    int test = 10;

    void printTest() {
        int test = 20;
        System.out.println("Test: " + test);
    }

    public static void main(String[] arguments) {
        ScopeTest st = new ScopeTest();
        st.printTest();
    }
}
```

This class has two variables with the same name, test. The first, an instance variable, is initialized with the value 10. The second is a local variable with the value 20.

The local variable test within the printTest() method hides the instance variable test. When the printTest() method is called from within the main() method, it displays that test equals 20, even though there's a test instance variable that equals 10. You can avoid this problem by using this.test to refer to the instance variable and simply using test to refer to the local variable. But a better solution might be to avoid duplicating variable names and definitions.

A more insidious example occurs when you redefine a variable in a subclass that already occurs in a superclass. This can create subtle bugs in your code. For example, you might call methods that are intended to change the value of an instance variable, but the wrong variable is changed. Another bug might occur when you cast an object from one class to another. The value of your instance variable might mysteriously change because the variable was getting that value from the superclass instead of your class.

The best way to avoid this behavior is to be aware of the variables defined in the superclass of your class. This awareness prevents you from duplicating a variable name used higher in the class hierarchy.

Passing Arguments to Methods

When you call a method with an object as a parameter, the object is passed into the method's body by reference. Any change made to the object inside the method persists outside the method.

Keep in mind that such objects include arrays and all objects contained in arrays. When you pass an array into a method and modify its contents, the original array is affected. Primitive types, on the other hand, are passed by value.

The Passer class, shown in Listing 5.2, demonstrates how this works. Create this class in NetBeans.

LISTING 5.2   The Full Text of Passer.java

```
 1: class Passer {
 2:
 3:     void toUpperCase(String[] text) {
 4:         for (int i = 0; i < text.length; i++) {
 5:             text[i] = text[i].toUpperCase();
 6:         }
 7:     }
 8:
 9:     public static void main(String[] arguments) {
10:         Passer passer = new Passer();
11:         passer.toUpperCase(arguments);
12:         for (int i = 0; i < arguments.length; i++) {
```

```
13:                 System.out.print(arguments[i] + " ");
14:             }
15:         System.out.println();
16:     }
17: }
```

This application takes one or more command-line arguments and displays them in all uppercase letters.

In NetBeans, set the arguments by choosing Run, Set Project Configuration, Customize. The Project Properties dialog appears. Enter Passer as the Main Class and Athos Aramis Porthos (or words of your choice) as the Arguments, and then click OK. Run the application by choosing Run, Run Project.

Here's an example of the application's output:

Output ▼

```
ATHOS ARAMIS PORTHOS
```

The Passer application uses command-line arguments stored in the arguments array of strings.

The application creates a Passer object and calls its toUpperCase() method with the arguments array as an argument (lines 10 and 11).

Because a reference to the array object is passed to the method, changing the value of each array element in line 5 changes the actual element (rather than a copy of it). Displaying the array with lines 12–14 demonstrates this.

5

CAUTION   If nothing happens when you run the Passer application in NetBeans, you're probably running it with the command Run, Run File instead of Run, Run Project. The Run File command does not use the arguments set up in the project configuration. The Run Project command does.

Class Methods

The relationship between class and instance variables is directly comparable to how class and instance methods work.

Class methods are available to any instance of the class itself and can be made available to other classes. In addition, unlike an instance method, a class does not require an object of the class for its methods to be called.

For example, the Java Class Library includes the System class, which defines a set of methods that are useful when displaying text, retrieving configuration information, and accomplishing other tasks. Here are two statements that use its class methods:

```
System.exit(0);

long now = System.currentTimeMillis();
```

The exit(*int*) method closes an application with a status code that indicates success (0) or failure (any other value). The currentTimeMillis() method returns a long holding the number of milliseconds since midnight on Jan. 1, 1970. This number is a representation of the current date and time.

To define class methods, use the static keyword in front of the method definition as you would in front of a class variable. For example, the class method exit() in the preceding example might have the following signature:

```
static void exit(int arg1) {
    // body of the method
}
```

Java supplies wrapper classes such as Integer and Float for each of the primitive types. By using class methods defined in those classes, you can create objects for primitive types and vice versa. The same value is represented in either form.

For example, the parseInt() class method in the Integer class can be used with a string argument, returning an int representation of that string:

```
int count = Integer.parseInt("42");
```

In the preceding statement, parseInt() returns the String value "42" as an integer with a value of 42, and this is stored in the count variable.

The lack of a static keyword in front of a method name makes it an instance method. Instance methods operate in a particular object, rather than a class of objects. On Day 1, "Getting Started with Java," you created an instance method called checkTemperature() that checked the temperature in the robot's environment.

TIP   Most methods that affect a particular object should be defined as instance methods. Methods that provide some general capability but do not directly affect an object of the class should be declared as class methods.

Class methods, unlike instance methods, are not inherited. A class method in a superclass cannot be overridden in a subclass.

Creating Java Applications

Now that you know how to create classes, objects, class and instance variables, and class and instance methods, you can put it all together in a Java program.

To refresh your memory, applications are Java classes that can be run on their own.

A Java application consists of one or more classes and can be as large or as small as you want it to be. Although all the applications you've created up to this point do nothing visually other than display characters, you also can create Java applications that use windows, graphics, and a graphical user interface.

The only thing you need to make a Java application run, however, is one class that serves as the starting point.

The class needs only one thing: a main() method. When the application is run, the Java virtual machine calls this method.

The signature for the main() method takes the following form:

```
public static void main(String[] arguments) {
    // body of method
}
```

Here's a rundown of the parts of the main() method:

- public means that this method is available to other classes and objects, which is a form of access control. The main() method must be declared public. You'll learn more about access methods during Day 6.

- static means that main() is a class method.

- void means that the main() method doesn't return a value.

- main() takes one parameter, which is an array of strings. This argument holds command-line arguments.

The body of the main() method contains any code you need to start your application, such as the initialization of variables or the creation of objects.

The main() method is a class method. An object of the class that holds main() is not created automatically when your application runs. If you want to treat that class as an object, you have to create an instance of it in the main() method (as you did in the Passer application in Listing 5.2 on line 10).

5

In a NetBeans project, one class can be designated as the main class of the project. When the project is packaged into a single Java archive (JAR) file, the main class will be run if the JAR file is executed.

To set the main class, choose Run, Set Project Configuration, Customize. In the Project Properties dialog, enter the name of this class in the Main Class field.

Helper Classes

Your Java application may consist of a single class—the one with the `main()` method— or several classes that use each other. (In reality, even a simple tutorial program uses numerous classes in the Java Class Library.) You can create as many classes as you want for your program.

As long as Java can find the class, your program uses it when it runs. Note, however, that only the starting-point class needs a `main()` method. After it is called, the methods inside the various classes and objects used in your program take over. Although you can include `main()` methods in helper classes, they are ignored when the program runs.

Java Applications and Command-Line Arguments

Because Java applications are stand-alone programs, it's useful to pass arguments to an application to customize how it operates.

You can use arguments to determine how an application will run or to enable a generic application to operate on different kinds of input. You can use program arguments for many different purposes, such as to turn on debugging input or to indicate a filename to load.

Passing Arguments to Java Applications

How you pass arguments to a Java application varies based on the computer and virtual machine on which Java is being run.

To pass arguments to a Java program with the `java` interpreter included with the JDK, the arguments would be appended to the command line when the program is run. For example:

```
java EchoArgs April 450 -10
```

Here java is the name of the interpreter, EchoArgs is the Java application, and the rest is the three arguments passed to a program: April, 450, and -10. Note that a space separates each of the arguments.

To group arguments that include spaces, surround the arguments with quotation marks. For example, consider the following command line:

```
java EchoArgs Niekro Hough Wakefield "R. A. Dickey" 49
```

Putting quotation marks around R. A. Dickey causes that text to be treated as a single argument. The EchoArgs application would receive five arguments: Niekro, Hough, Wakefield, R. A. Dickey, and 49. The quotation marks prevent the spaces within R. A. Dickey from being used to separate arguments. These spaces are not included as part of the argument when it is sent to the program and received using the main() method.

CAUTION	One thing quotation marks are not used for is to identify strings. Every argument passed to an application is stored in an array of String objects, even if it has a numeric value (such as 450, –10, and 49 in the preceding examples).

Because NetBeans runs the interpreter behind the scenes, there's no command line on which to specify arguments. Instead, they can be set in the project configuration, as you did in Listing 5.1 for the RangeLister application.

Handling Arguments in Your Java Application

When an application is run with arguments, Java stores the arguments as an array of strings and passes the array to the application's main() method. Take another look at the signature for main():

```
public static void main(String[] arguments) {
    // body of method
}
```

Here, arguments is the name of the array of strings that contains the list of arguments. You can call this array anything you want.

Inside the main() method, you then can handle the arguments your program was given by looping through the array of arguments and handling them in some manner. The Averager class, shown in Listing 5.3, is a Java application that takes numeric arguments and returns the sum and average of those arguments.

Create a new empty Java file in NetBeans for the Averager class.

5

LISTING 5.3   The Full Text of Averager.java

```
 1: class Averager {
 2:     public static void main(String[] arguments) {
 3:         int sum = 0;
 4:
 5:         if (arguments.length > 0) {
 6:             for (int i = 0; i < arguments.length; i++) {
 7:                 sum += Integer.parseInt(arguments[i]);
 8:             }
 9:             System.out.println("Sum is: " + sum);
10:             System.out.println("Average is: " +
11:                 (float)sum / arguments.length);
12:         }
13:     }
14: }
```

Before running the application in NetBeans, set arguments in the project configuration, as you did with the RangeLister application.

The Averager application makes sure that in line 5 at least one argument is passed to the program. This is handled through length, the instance variable that contains the number of elements in the arguments array.

You must always do things like this when dealing with command-line arguments. Otherwise, your programs crash with ArrayIndexOutOfBoundsException errors whenever the user supplies fewer command-line arguments than you were expecting.

If at least one argument is passed, the for loop iterates through all the strings stored in the arguments array (lines 6–8).

Because all command-line arguments are passed to a Java application as String objects, you must convert them to numeric values before using them in any mathematical expressions. The parseInt() class method of the Integer class takes a String object as input and returns an int (line 7).

If 1 4 13 were submitted as your arguments, you would see the following output:

Output ▼

```
Sum is: 18
Average is: 6.0
```

Creating Methods with the Same Name

When you work with the Java Class Library, you often encounter classes that have numerous methods with the same name.

Two things differentiate these same-named methods:

- The number of arguments they take
- The primitive type or objects of each argument

These two things are part of a method's signature. Using several methods with the same name and different signatures is called *overloading*.

Method overloading can eliminate the need for entirely different methods that do essentially the same thing. Overloading also makes it possible for methods to behave differently based on the arguments they receive.

When you call a method in an object, Java matches the method name and arguments to choose which method definition to execute.

To create an overloaded method, you create different method definitions in a class, each with the same name but different argument lists. The difference can be the number, the type of arguments, or both. Java allows method overloading as long as each argument list is unique for the same method name.

CAUTION Java does not consider the return type when differentiating among overloaded methods. If you attempt to create two methods with the same signature and different return types, the class won't compile. In addition, the variable names that you choose for each argument to the method are irrelevant. The number and the type of arguments are the two things that matter.

5

The next project you undertake creates an overloaded method. It begins with a simple class definition for a class called Box. This defines a rectangular shape with four instance variables to define the upper-left and lower-right corners of the rectangle, (x1, y1) and (x2, y2):

```
class Box {
    int x1 = 0;
    int y1 = 0;
    int x2 = 0;
    int y2 = 0;
}
```

When a new instance of the `Box` class is created, all its instance variables are initialized to 0.

A `buildBox()` instance method sets the variables to their correct values:

```
Box buildBox(int x1, int y1, int x2, int y2) {
    this.x1 = x1;
    this.y1 = y1;
    this.x2 = x2;
    this.y2 = y2;
    return this;
}
```

This method takes four integer arguments and returns a reference to the resulting `Box` object. Because the arguments have the same names as the instance variables, the keyword `this` is used inside the method when referring to the instance variables.

This method can be used to create rectangles, but what if you wanted to define a rectangle's dimensions differently? An alternative would be to use `Point` objects rather than individual coordinates because `Point` objects contain both an x and y value as instance variables.

You can overload `buildBox()` by creating a second version of the method with an argument list that takes two `Point` objects:

```
Box buildBox(Point topLeft, Point bottomRight) {
    x1 = topLeft.x;
    y1 = topLeft.y;
    x2 = bottomRight.x;
    y2 = bottomRight.y;
    return this;
}
```

For this method to work, the `java.awt.Point` class must be imported so that it can be referred to by the short name `Point`.

Another possible way to define the rectangle is to use a top corner, a height, and a width:

```
Box buildBox(Point topLeft, int w, int h) {
    x1 = topLeft.x;
    y1 = topLeft.y;
    x2 = (x1 + w);
    y2 = (y1 + h);
    return this;
}
```

To finish this example, a `printBox()` is created to display the rectangle's coordinates. A `main()` method turns `Box` into an application and tries out everything on a `Box` object. Listing 5.4 shows the completed class definition. Create this class with NetBeans.

LISTING 5.4   The Full Text of Box.java

```
 1: import java.awt.Point;
 2:
 3: class Box {
 4:         int x1 = 0;
 5:         int y1 = 0;
 6:         int x2 = 0;
 7:         int y2 = 0;
 8:
 9:         Box buildBox(int x1, int y1, int x2, int y2) {
10:                 this.x1 = x1;
11:                 this.y1 = y1;
12:                 this.x2 = x2;
13:                 this.y2 = y2;
14:                 return this;
15:         }
16:
17:         Box buildBox(Point topLeft, Point bottomRight) {
18:                 x1 = topLeft.x;
19:                 y1 = topLeft.y;
20:                 x2 = bottomRight.x;
21:                 y2 = bottomRight.y;
22:                 return this;
23:         }
24:
25:         Box buildBox(Point topLeft, int w, int h) {
26:                 x1 = topLeft.x;
27:                 y1 = topLeft.y;
28:                 x2 = (x1 + w);
29:                 y2 = (y1 + h);
30:                 return this;
31:         }
32:
33:         void printBox(){
34:                 System.out.print("Box: <" + x1 + ", " + y1);
35:                 System.out.println(", " + x2 + ", " + y2 + ">");
36:         }
37:
38:         public static void main(String[] arguments) {
39:                 Box rect = new Box();
40:
41:                 System.out.println("Calling buildBox with "
42:                         + "coordinates (25,25) and (50,50):");
43:                 rect.buildBox(25, 25, 50, 50);
44:                 rect.printBox();
45:
46:                 System.out.println("\nCalling buildBox with "
47:                         + "points (10,10) and (20,20):");
48:                 rect.buildBox(new Point(10, 10), new Point(20, 20));
49:                 rect.printBox();
```

5

LISTING 5.4   Continued

```
50:
51:            System.out.println("\nCalling buildBox with "
52:                + "point (10,10), width 50 and height 50:");
53:
54:            rect.buildBox(new Point(10, 10), 50, 50);
55:            rect.printBox();
56:    }
57: }
```

The application displays this output:

Output ▼

```
Calling buildBox with coordinates (25,25) and (50,50):
Box: <25, 25, 50, 50>

Calling buildBox with points (10,10) and (20,20):
Box: <10, 10, 20, 20>

Calling buildBox with point (10,10), width 50 and height 50:
Box: <10, 10, 60, 60>
```

You can define as many versions of a method as you need to implement the behavior needed for that class.

When you have several methods that do similar things, using one method to call another is a shortcut technique to consider. For example, the buildBox() method in lines 17–23 can be replaced with the following, much shorter method:

```
Box buildBox(Point topLeft, Point bottomRight) {
    return buildBox(topLeft.x, topLeft.y,
        bottomRight.x, bottomRight.y);
}
```

The return statement in this method calls the buildBox() method in lines 9–15 with four integer arguments, producing the same result in fewer statements.

Constructors

You also can define constructors in your class definition that are called automatically when objects of that class are created. A constructor is a method called on an object when it is created—in other words, when it is constructed.

Unlike other methods, a constructor cannot be called directly. Java does three things when new is used to create an instance of a class:

- It allocates memory for the object.
- It initializes that object's instance variables, either to initial values or to a default (0 for numbers, `null` for objects, `false` for Booleans, or `'\0'` for characters).
- It calls a constructor of the class.

If a class doesn't have any constructors defined, an object still is created when the `new` operator is used in conjunction with the class. However, you might have to set its instance variables or call other methods that the object needs to initialize itself.

When an object is created of a class that has no constructors, a constructor with no arguments is implicitly provided by Java. This constructor is called to create the object. For this reason, a constructor with no arguments can be called with `new` even when no constructors are defined.

By defining constructors in your own classes, you can set initial values of instance variables, call methods based on those variables, call methods on other objects, and set an object's initial properties.

When creating a class, you can overload constructors, as you can do with methods, to create an object that has specific properties based on the arguments you give to `new`.

If a class has a constructor that takes one or more arguments, a constructor with no arguments can be called only if one has been defined in the class.

Basic Constructors

Constructors look a lot like regular methods, with three basic differences:

- They always have the same name as the class.
- They don't have a return type.
- They cannot return a value in the method by using the `return` statement.

For example, the following class uses a constructor to initialize its instance variables based on arguments for `new`:

```
class VolcanoRobot {
    String status;
    int speed;
    int power;

    VolcanoRobot(String in1, int in2, int in3) {
        status = in1;
        speed = in2;
        power = in3;
    }
}
```

You could create an object of this class with the following statement:

```
VolcanoRobot vic = new VolcanoRobot("exploring", 5, 200);
```

The status instance variable would be set to "exploring", speed to 5, and power to 200.

Calling Another Constructor

If you have a constructor that duplicates some of the behavior of an existing constructor, you can call the first constructor from inside the body of the second. Java provides special syntax for doing this. Use the following code to call a constructor defined in the current class:

```
this(arg1, arg2, arg3);
```

The use of this with a constructor method is similar to how this can be used to access a current object's variables. In the preceding statement, the arguments with this() are the arguments for the constructor.

For example, consider a simple class that defines a circle using the (x, y) coordinate of its center and the length of its radius. The class, Circle, could have two constructors: one where the radius is defined and one where the radius is set to a default value of 1. Here's code that does this:

```
class Circle {
    int x, y, radius;

    Circle(int xPoint, int yPoint, int radiusLength) {
        this.x = xPoint;
        this.y = yPoint;
        this.radius = radiusLength;
    }

    Circle(int xPoint, int yPoint) {
        this(xPoint, yPoint, 1);
    }
}
```

The second constructor in Circle takes only the (x, y) coordinates of the circle's center. Because no radius is defined, the default value of 1 is used. The first constructor is called with the arguments xPoint, yPoint, and the integer literal 1.

Overloading Constructors

Like methods, constructors also can take varying numbers and types of parameters. This capability enables you to create an object with exactly the properties you want it to have or lets the object calculate properties from different kinds of input.

For example, the buildBox() methods that you defined in the Box class earlier today would make excellent constructors because they are used to initialize an object's instance variables to the appropriate values. So, instead of the original buildBox() method you defined (which took four parameters for the corners' coordinates), you could create a constructor.

Listing 5.5 shows a new class, Box2, that has the same functionality as the original Box class, except that it uses overloaded constructors instead of overloaded buildBox() methods. Create the Box2 class in NetBeans.

LISTING 5.5 The Full Text of Box2.java

```
 1: import java.awt.Point;
 2:
 3: class Box2 {
 4:       int x1 = 0;
 5:       int y1 = 0;
 6:       int x2 = 0;
 7:       int y2 = 0;
 8:
 9:       Box2(int x1, int y1, int x2, int y2) {
10:            this.x1 = x1;
11:            this.y1 = y1;
12:            this.x2 = x2;
13:            this.y2 = y2;
14:       }
15:
16:       Box2(Point topLeft, Point bottomRight) {
17:            this(topLeft.x, topLeft.y, bottomRight.x,
18:                 bottomRight.y);
19:       }
20:
21:       Box2(Point topLeft, int w, int h) {
22:            this(topLeft.x, topLeft.y, topLeft.x + w,
23:                 topLeft.y + h);
24:       }
25:
26:       void printBox() {
27:            System.out.print("Box: <" + x1 + ", " + y1);
28:            System.out.println(", " + x2 + ", " + y2 + ">");
29:       }
30:
31:       public static void main(String[] arguments) {
32:            Box2 rect;
33:
34:            System.out.println("Calling Box2 with coordinates "
35:                 + "(25,25) and (50,50):");
36:            rect = new Box2(25, 25, 50, 50);
```

5

LISTING 5.5   Continued

```
37:            rect.printBox();
38:
39:            System.out.println("\nCalling Box2 with points "
40:                + "(10,10) and (20,20):");
41:            rect= new Box2(new Point(10, 10), new Point(20, 20));
42:            rect.printBox();
43:
44:            System.out.println("\nCalling Box2 with 1 point "
45:                + "(10,10), width 50 and height 50:");
46:            rect = new Box2(new Point(10, 10), 50, 50);
47:            rect.printBox();
48:
49:      }
50: }
```

This application produces the same output as the Box application shown in Listing 5.4. In Listing 5.5, the second and third constructors use this in lines 17–18 and lines 22–23 to call the first constructor, giving it the task of creating the object with the specified parameters.

Overriding Methods

When you call an object's method, Java looks for that method definition in the object's class. If it doesn't find one, it passes the method call up the class hierarchy until it finds a method definition. This inheritance enables you to define and use methods repeatedly in subclasses without having to duplicate the code.

However, there might be times when you want an object to respond to the same methods but have different behavior when that method is called. In that case, you can override the method.

To override a method, define a method in a subclass with the same signature as a method in a superclass. Then, when the method is called, the subclass method is found and executed instead of the one in the superclass.

Creating Methods That Override Existing Methods

To override a method, all you have to do is create a method in your subclass that has the same signature (name and argument list) as a method defined by your class's superclass. Because Java executes the first method definition it finds that matches the signature, the new signature hides the original method definition.

Here's a simple example. Listing 5.6 contains two classes. `Printer` contains a method called `printMe()` that displays information about objects of that class. `SubPrinter` is a subclass that adds a z instance variable to the class. Create this class and name it `Printer` in NetBeans.

LISTING 5.6   The Full Text of `Printer.java`

```
 1: class Printer {
 2:     int x = 0;
 3:     int y = 1;
 4:
 5:     void printMe() {
 6:         System.out.println("x is " + x + ", y is " + y);
 7:         System.out.println("I am an instance of the class " +
 8:             this.getClass().getName());
 9:     }
10: }
11:
12: class SubPrinter extends Printer {
13:     int z = 3;
14:
15:     public static void main(String[] arguments) {
16:         SubPrinter obj = new SubPrinter();
17:         obj.printMe();
18:     }
19: }
```

When this file is compiled, there are two class files rather than one. Because the source file defines the `Printer` and `SubPrinter` classes, the compiler produces both. Run `SubPrinter` (by selecting Run, Run File in NetBeans), and you see the following output:

Output ▼

```
x is 0, y is 1
I am an instance of the class SubPrinter
```

5

CAUTION
The `Printer` class does not have a `main()` method, so it cannot be run as an application. So when you choose Run, Run File in NetBeans, it automatically runs the SubPrinter application's `main()` method because no other class has such a method. If a source code file contains more than one class with `main()`, NetBeans asks which one should be run.

A SubPrinter object was created, and the printMe() method was called in the main() method of SubPrinter. Because the SubPrinter does not define this method, Java looks for it in the superclasses of SubPrinter, starting with Printer. Printer has a printMe() method, so it is executed. Unfortunately, this method does not display the z instance variable, as you can see from the preceding output.

To correct the problem, you can override that printMe() method in SubPrinter, adding a statement to display the z instance variable:

```
void printMe() {
    System.out.println("x is " + x + ", y is " + y +
        ", z is " + z);
    System.out.println("I am an instance of the class " +
        this.getClass().getName());
}
```

Calling the Original Method

Usually, there are two reasons why you want to override a method that a superclass already has implemented:

- To replace the definition of that original method
- To augment the original method with additional behavior

Overriding a method and giving it a new definition hides the original method definition. However, sometimes behavior should be added to the original definition instead of being replaced, particularly when behavior is duplicated in both the original method and the method that overrides it. By calling the original method in the body of the overriding method, you can add only what you need.

Use the super keyword to call the original method from inside a method definition. This keyword passes the method call up the hierarchy, as shown in the following:

```
void doMethod(String a, String b) {
    // do stuff here
    super.doMethod(a, b);
    // do more stuff here
}
```

The super keyword, similar to the this keyword, is a placeholder for the class's superclass. You can use it anywhere that you use this, but super refers to the superclass rather than to the current object.

Overriding Constructors

Technically, constructors cannot be overridden. Because they always have the same name as the current class, new constructor methods are created instead of being inherited. This system is fine much of the time; when your class's constructor method is called, the constructor method with the same signature for all your superclasses also is called. Therefore, initialization can happen for all parts of a class you inherit.

However, when you are defining constructors for your own class, you might want to change how your object is initialized, not only by initializing new variables added by your class, but also by changing the contents of variables that are already there. To do this, explicitly call the constructors of the superclass and change whatever variables need to be changed.

To call a regular method in a superclass, you use super.*methodname(arguments)*. Because constructor methods don't have a method name to call, the following form is used:

```
super(arg1, arg2, ...);
```

Java has a rule for the use of super(): It must be the first statement in your constructor definition. If you don't call super() explicitly in your constructor, Java automatically calls super() with no arguments before the first statement in the constructor.

Because a call to a super() method must be the first statement, you can't do something like the following in your overriding constructor:

```
if (condition == true)
    super(1,2,3); // call one superclass constructor
else
    super(1,2); // call a different constructor
```

5

Similar to using this() in a constructor, super() calls the constructor for the immediate superclass (which might, in turn, call the constructor of its superclass, and so on). Note that a constructor with that signature has to exist in the superclass for the call to super() to work. The Java compiler checks this when a class is compiled.

You don't have to call the constructor in your superclass that has the same signature as the constructor in your class; you have to call the constructor only for the values you need initialized. In fact, you can create a class that has constructors with entirely different signatures from any of the superclass's constructors.

Listing 5.7 shows a class called NamedPoint, which extends the class Point from the java.awt package. The Point class has only one constructor, which takes an x and a y argument and returns a Point object. NamedPoint has an additional instance variable (a string for the name) and defines a constructor to initialize x, y, and the name. Create this class in NetBeans.

LISTING 5.7 The NamedPoint Class

```
1: import java.awt.Point;
2:
3: class NamedPoint extends Point {
4:     String name;
5:
6:     NamedPoint(int x, int y, String name) {
7:         super(x,y);
8:         this.name = name;
9:     }
10:
11:     public static void main(String[] arguments) {
12:         NamedPoint np = new NamedPoint(5, 5, "SmallPoint");
13:         System.out.println("x is " + np.x);
14:         System.out.println("y is " + np.y);
15:         System.out.println("Name is " + np.name);
16:     }
17: }
```

The output is as follows:

Output ▼

```
x is 5
y is 5
Name is SmallPoint
```

The constructor defined here for NamedPoint calls Point's constructor to initialize the instance variables of Point (x and y). Although you can just as easily initialize x and y yourself, you might not know what other things Point is doing to initialize itself. Therefore, it is always a good idea to pass constructors up the hierarchy to make sure that everything is set up correctly.

Summary

After finishing today's lesson, you should have a pretty good idea of the relationship among classes in Java and programs you create using the language.

Everything you create in Java involves the use of a main class that interacts with other classes as needed. It's a different programming mindset than you might be used to with other languages.

Today, you put together everything you have learned about creating Java classes. These topics were covered:

- Instance and class variables, which hold the attributes of a class and objects created from it.

- Instance and class methods, which define the behavior of a class. You learned how to define methods, including the parts of a method signature, how to return values from a method, how arguments are passed to methods, and how to use the `this` keyword to refer to the current object.

- The `main()` method of Java applications, and how to pass arguments to it from the command line.

- Overloaded methods, which reuse a method name by giving it different arguments.

- Constructors, which define the initial variables and other starting conditions of an object.

Q&A

Q My class has an instance variable called `origin`. It also has a local variable called `origin` in a method, which, because of variable scope, gets hidden by the local variable. Is there any way to access the instance variable's value?

A The easiest way to avoid this problem is to give your local variables the same names your instance variables have. Otherwise, you can use `this.origin` to refer to the instance variable and `origin` to refer to the local variable.

Q I created two methods with the following signatures:

```
int total(int arg1, int arg2, int arg3) {...}
float total(int arg1, int arg2, int arg3) {...}
```

The Java compiler complains when I try to compile the class with these method definitions, even though their signatures are different. What did I do wrong?

A Your methods have the same signature. Method overloading in Java works only if the argument lists are different in either number or type of arguments. Return type is not part of a method signature, so it's not considered when methods have been overloaded. Looking at it from the point at which a method is called, this makes sense: If two methods have exactly the same parameter list, how would Java know which one to call?

5

Q **I wrote a program to take four arguments, but when I give it too few arguments, it crashes with a runtime error. Why?**

A It's up to you to test for the number and type of arguments your program expects; Java won't do it for you. If your program requires four arguments, test that you have indeed been given four arguments by using the `length` variable of an array, which contains the count of its elements. Return an error message if you haven't.

Quiz

Review today's material by taking this three-question quiz. Answers are at the end of the book.

Questions

1. If a local variable has the same name as an instance variable, how can you refer to the instance variable in the scope of the local variable?

   A. You can't; you should rename one of the variables.

   B. Use the keyword `this` before the instance variable name.

   C. Use the keyword `super` before the name.

2. Where are instance variables declared in a class?

   A. Anywhere in the class

   B. Outside all methods in the class

   C. After the class declaration and above the first method

3. How can you send to a program an argument that includes a space or spaces?

   A. Surround the argument with double quotes.

   B. Separate the arguments with commas.

   C. Separate the arguments with periods.

Certification Practice

The following question is the kind of thing you could expect to be asked on a Java programming certification test. Answer it without looking at today's material or using the Java compiler to test the code.

Given:

```
public class BigValue {
    float result;

    public BigValue(int a, int b) {
        result = calculateResult(a, b);
    }

    float calculateResult(int a, int b) {
        return (a * 10) + (b * 2);
    }

    public static void main(String[] arguments) {
        BiggerValue bgr = new BiggerValue(2, 3, 4);
        System.out.println("The result is " + bgr.result);
    }
}

class BiggerValue extends BigValue {

    BiggerValue(int a, int b, int c) {
        super(a, b);
        result = calculateResult(a, b, c);
    }

    // answer goes here
        return (c * 3) * result;
    }
}
```

What statement should replace // answer goes here so that the result variable equals 312.0?

5

A. `float calculateResult(int c) {`

B. `float calculateResult(int a, int b) {`

C. `float calculateResult(int a, int b, int c) {`

D. `float calculateResult() {`

The answer is available on the book's website at www.java21days.com. Visit the Day 5 page and click the Certification Practice link.

Exercises

To extend your knowledge of the subjects covered today, try the following exercises:

1. Modify the VolcanoRobot project from Day 1 so that it includes constructors.

2. Create a class for four-dimensional points called FourDPoint that is a subclass of Point from the java.awt package.

Where applicable, exercise solutions are offered on the book's website at www.java21days.com.

DAY 6

Packages, Interfaces, and Other Class Features

Classes, the templates used to create objects that can store data and accomplish tasks, turn up in everything you do with the Java language.

Today, you extend your knowledge of classes by learning more about how to create them, use them, organize them, and establish rules for how other classes can use them.

The following subjects are covered:

- Controlling access to methods and variables from outside a class

- Finalizing classes, methods, and variables so that their values or definitions cannot be overridden in subclasses

- Creating abstract classes and methods for factoring common behavior into superclasses

- Grouping classes into packages

- Using interfaces to bridge gaps in a class hierarchy

Modifiers

During this week, you have learned how to define classes, methods, and variables in Java. The programming techniques you learn today involve different ways of thinking about how a class is organized. All these techniques use special modifiers in the Java language. *Modifiers* are keywords that you add to those definitions to change their meanings.

The Java language has a wide variety of modifiers, including the following:

- Modifiers for controlling access to a class, method, or variable: `public`, `protected`, and `private`
- The `static` modifier for creating class methods and variables
- The `final` modifier for finalizing the implementations of classes, methods, and variables
- The `abstract` modifier for creating abstract classes and methods
- The `synchronized` and `volatile` modifiers, which are used for threads

To use a modifier, you include its keyword in the definition of a class, method, or variable. The modifier precedes the rest of the statement, as in the following examples:

```
public class RedButton extends javax.swing.JButton {
    // ...
}

private boolean offline;

static final double WEEKS = 9.5;

protected static final int MEANING_OF_LIFE = 42;

public static void main(String[] arguments) {
    // body of method
}
```

If you're using more than one modifier in a statement, you can place them in any order, as long as all modifiers precede the element they are modifying. Be sure to avoid treating a method's return type—such as `void`—as if it were one of the modifiers. The return type must precede the method name, with no modifiers between them.

Modifiers are optional, as you might have realized after using some of them in the preceding five days. There are many good reasons to use them in your programs.

Access Control for Methods and Variables

The modifiers that you will use most often control access to methods and variables: public, private, and protected. These modifiers determine which variables and methods of a class are visible to other classes.

By using access control, you can dictate how your class is used by other classes. Some variables and methods in a class are of use only within the class itself and should be hidden from other classes. This process is called *encapsulation*: An object controls what the outside world can know about it and how the outside world can interact with it. Encapsulation is the process that prevents class variables from being read or modified by other classes. The only way to use these variables is by calling methods of the class if they are available.

The Java language provides four levels of access control: public, private, protected, and a default level specified by using none of these access control modifiers.

Default Access

Variables and methods can be declared without any modifiers, as in the following examples:

```
String version = "0.7a";

boolean processOrder() {
    // ...
    return true;
}
```

A variable or method declared without an access control modifier is available to any other class in the same package. The Java Class Library is organized into packages such as javax.swing, which is windowing classes for use primarily in graphical user interface programming, and java.util, a useful group of utility classes.

Any variable declared without a modifier can be read or changed by any other class in the same package. Any method declared the same way can be called by any other class in the same package. No other classes can access these elements in any way.

This level of access control doesn't control much access, so it's less useful when you begin thinking about how you want a class to be used by other classes.

6

NOTE

The preceding discussion raises the question of what package your own classes have been in up to this point. As you see later today, you can make your class a member of a package by using the package declaration. If you don't use this declaration, the class is put into an unnamed package with all other classes that don't belong to any other packages.

Classes should be assigned to a package so that they can be referred to clearly in other classes.

Private Access

To completely hide a method or variable and keep it from being used by other classes, use the `private` modifier. The only place these methods or variables can be accessed is within their own class.

A private instance variable can be used by methods in its own class but not by objects of any other class. Private methods can be called by other methods in their own class but cannot be called by any others. This restriction also affects inheritance: Neither private variables nor private methods are inherited by subclasses.

Private variables are useful in two circumstances:

- When other classes have no reason to use that variable
- When another class could wreak havoc by changing the variable in an inappropriate way

For example, consider a Java class called `CouponMachine` that generates discounts for an Internet shopping site. A variable in that class called `salesRatio` could control the size of discounts based on product sales. This variable has a big impact on the business's bottom line. If the variable were changed by other classes, `CouponMachine`'s performance would change significantly. To guard against this scenario, you can declare the `salesRatio` variable as private.

The following class uses private access control:

```
class Logger {
    private String format;

    public String getFormat() {
        return this.format;
    }

    public void setFormat(String format) {
```

```
        if ( (format.equals("common")) || (format.equals("combined")) ) {
            this.format = format;
        }
    }
}
```

In this code example, the `format` variable of the `Logger` class is private, so there's no way for other classes to retrieve or set its value directly.

Instead, it's available through two public methods: `getFormat()`, which returns the value of `format`, and `setFormat(String)`, which sets its value.

The latter method contains logic that allows the variable to be set to only `"common"` or `"combined"`. This demonstrates a benefit of using public methods as the only means of accessing instance variables of a class: The methods can give the class control over how the variable is accessed and limit the values it can take.

Using the `private` modifier is the main way in which an object encapsulates itself. You can't limit the ways in which a class is used without using `private` to hide variables and methods. Another class is free to change the variables inside a class and call its methods in many possible ways if you don't control access.

A big advantage of privacy is that it lets the implementation of a class change without affecting the users of that class. If you come up with a better way to accomplish something, you can rewrite the class as long as its public methods take the same arguments and return the same kinds of values.

Public Access

In some cases, you might want a method or variable in a class to be completely available to any other class that wants to use it. For example, the `Color` class in the `java.awt` package has public variables for common colors such as `black`. This variable is used when a graphical class wants to use the color black, so `black` should have no access control.

Class variables often are declared to be public. An example is a set of variables in a `Football` class that represent the number of points used in scoring. The `TOUCHDOWN` variable could equal 6, the `FIELD_GOAL` variable could equal 3, and `SAFETY` could equal 2. If these variables are public, other classes could use them in statements such as the following:

```
if (yard < 0) {
    System.out.println("Touchdown!");
    score = score + Football.TOUCHDOWN;
}
```

6

The public modifier makes a method or variable completely available to all classes. You have used it in every application you have written so far in their main() methods:

```
public static void main(String[] arguments) {
    // ...
}
```

The main() method of an application has to be public. Otherwise, it could not be called by a Java interpreter to run the class.

Because of class inheritance, all public methods and variables of a class are inherited by its subclasses.

Protected Access

The next level of access control is to limit a method and variable to use by the following two groups:

- Subclasses of a class
- Other classes in the same package

You do so by using the protected modifier, as in the following statement:

```
protected boolean outOfData = true;
```

> **NOTE**
> You might be wondering how these two groups differ. After all, aren't subclasses part of the same package as their superclass? Not always. An example is the java.sql.Date class, which represents calendar dates in a SQL database. It is a subclass of java.util.Date, a more generic date class. Protected access differs from default access in this way; protected variables are available to subclasses, even if they aren't in the same package.

This level of access control is useful if you want to make it easier for a subclass to be implemented. Your class might use a method or variable to help the class do its job. Because a subclass inherits much of the same behavior and attributes, it might have the same job to do. Protected access gives the subclass a chance to use the helper method or variable while preventing an unrelated class from trying to use it.

Consider the example of a class called AudioPlayer that plays a digital audio file. AudioPlayer has a method called openSpeaker(), which interacts with the hardware to prepare the speaker for playing. openSpeaker() isn't important to anyone outside the

AudioPlayer class, so at first glance you might want to make it private. A snippet of AudioPlayer might look something like this:

```
class AudioPlayer {

    private boolean openSpeaker(Speaker sp) {
        // implementation here
    }
}
```

This code works fine if AudioPlayer won't be subclassed. But what if later you need a class called StreamingAudioPlayer that is a subclass of AudioPlayer? That class needs access to the openSpeaker() method to override it and provide support for streaming audio devices. You still don't want the method to be generally available to random objects, so it shouldn't be public, but you want any subclasses to have access to it.

Comparing Levels of Access Control

The differences among the various protection types can be confusing, particularly in the case of protected methods and variables. Table 6.1, which summarizes exactly what is allowed where, helps clarify the differences from the least restrictive (public) to the most restrictive (private) forms of protection.

TABLE 6.1 The Different Levels of Access Control

Visibility	Public	Protected	Default	Private
From the same class	Yes	Yes	Yes	Yes
From any class in the same package	Yes	Yes	Yes	No
From any class outside the package	Yes	No	No	No
From a subclass in the same package	Yes	Yes	Yes	No
From a subclass outside the same package	Yes	Yes	No	No

6

Access Control and Inheritance

One last issue regarding access control for methods involves subclasses. When you create a subclass and override a method, you must consider the access control in place on the original method.

As a general rule, you cannot override a method in Java and make the new method more restrictively controlled than the original. You can, however, make it more public. The following rules for inherited methods are enforced:

- Methods declared public in a superclass also must be public in all subclasses.
- Methods declared protected in a superclass must be either protected or public in subclasses; they cannot be private.
- Methods declared without access control (no modifier was used) can be declared more private in subclasses.

Methods declared private are not inherited, so the rules don't apply.

Accessor Methods

In many cases, you may have an instance variable in a class that has strict rules for the values it can contain. An example would be a `zipCode` variable. A zip code in the United States must be a five-digit number. (There also is a zip+4 format that's nine digits.)

To prevent an external class from setting the `zipCode` variable incorrectly, you can declare it private:

```
private int zipCode;
```

However, what if other classes must be able to set the `zipCode` variable for the class to be useful? In that circumstance, you can give other classes access to a private variable by using an accessor method inside the same class as `zipCode`.

An accessor method provides access to a variable that otherwise would be off-limits. By using a method to provide access to a private variable, you can control how that variable is used. In the zip code example, the class could prevent anyone else from setting `zipCode` to an incorrect value.

Often, separate accessor methods to read and write a variable are available. Reading methods have a name beginning with `get`, and writing methods have a name beginning with `set`, as in `setZipCode(int)` and `getZipCode()`.

Using methods to access instance variables is a common technique in object-oriented programming. This approach makes classes more reusable by guarding against improper use.

Static Variables and Methods

A modifier that you already have used in programs is `static`, which was described in detail during Day 5, "Creating Classes and Methods." The `static` modifier is used to create class methods and variables, as in the following example:

```
public class Circle {
    public static float PI = 3.14159265F;

    public float area(float r) {
        return PI * r * r;
    }
}
```

Class variables and methods can be accessed using the class name followed by a dot and the name of the variable or method, as in `Color.black` or `Circle.PI`. You also can use the name of an object belonging to the class, but for class variables and methods, using the class name is better. This approach makes it more clear what kind of variable or method you're working with; instance variables and methods can never be referred to by a class name.

The following statements use class variables and methods:

```
float circumference = 2 * Circle.PI * getRadius();
float randomNumber = Math.random();
```

TIP

For the same reason as instance variables, class variables can benefit from being private and limiting their use to accessor methods only.

The first project you undertake today is a class called `InstanceCounter` that uses class and instance variables to keep track of how many objects of that class have been created. In NetBeans, create an empty Java file named `InstanceCounter` in the project you've been using throughout this book. Enter the code shown in Listing 6.1 in the source code file and save it when you're done.

6

LISTING 6.1   The Full Text of InstanceCounter.java

```
 1: public class InstanceCounter {
 2:     private static int numInstances = 0;
 3:
 4:     protected static int getCount() {
 5:         return numInstances;
 6:     }
 7:
 8:     private static void addInstance() {
 9:         numInstances++;
10:     }
11:
12:     InstanceCounter() {
13:         InstanceCounter.addInstance();
14:     }
15:
16:     public static void main(String[] arguments) {
17:         System.out.println("Starting with " +
18:             InstanceCounter.getCount() + " objects");
19:         for (int  i = 0; i < 500; ++i)
20:             new InstanceCounter();
21:         System.out.println("Created " +
22:             InstanceCounter.getCount() + " objects");
23:     }
24: }
```

NetBeans attempts to compile a Java class when it is saved or run. If there are no errors, you can run it to see this output:

Output ▼

```
Starting with 0 objects
Created 500 objects
```

This example demonstrates several features. In line 2, a private class variable is declared to hold the number of objects. It is a class variable (declared static) because the number of objects is relevant to the class as a whole, not to any particular object. It's private so that it can be retrieved with only an accessor method.

Note the initialization of numInstances. Just as an instance variable is initialized when its instance is created, a class variable is initialized when its class is created. This class initialization happens essentially before anything else can happen to that class or its instances so that the class in the example will work as planned.

In lines 4–6, a get method is defined so that the private instance variable's value can be retrieved. This method also is declared as a class method because it applies directly to the class variable. The `getCount()` method is declared protected, as opposed to public, because only this class and perhaps its subclasses are interested in that value; other random classes, therefore, are restricted from seeing it.

Note that there is no accessor method to set the value. The value of the variable should be incremented only when a new instance is created; it should not be set to any random value. Instead of creating an accessor method, a special private method called `addInstance()` is defined in lines 8–10 that increments the value of `numInstances` by 1.

Lines 12–14 create the constructor method for this class. Constructors are called when a new object is created, which makes this the most logical place to call `addInstance()` and to increment the variable.

The `main()` method indicates that you can run this as a Java application and test all the other methods. In the `main()` method, 500 objects of the `InstanceCounter` class are created, and then the value of the `numInstances` class variable is displayed.

Final Classes, Methods, and Variables

The `final` modifier is used with classes, methods, and variables to indicate that they will never be changed. It has different meanings for each thing that can be made final, as follows:

- A `final` class cannot be subclassed.
- A `final` method cannot be overridden by any subclasses.
- A `final` variable cannot change in value.

Variables

Final variables are often called constants (or constant variables) because they do not change in value at any time.

With variables, the `final` modifier often is used with `static` to make the constant a class variable. If the value never changes, you don't have much reason to give each object in the same class its own copy of the value. They all can use the class variable with the same functionality.

The following statements are examples of declaring constants:

```
public static final int TOUCHDOWN = 6;
static final String TITLE = "Captain";
```

6

Methods

Final methods never can be overridden by a subclass. You declare them using the `final` modifier in the class declaration, as in the following example:

```
public final void getSignature() {
    // body of method
}
```

The most common reason to declare a method final is to make the class run more efficiently. Normally, when the Java virtual machine runs a method, first it checks the current class to find the method, then it checks its superclass, and so on up the class hierarchy until the method is found. This process sacrifices some speed in the name of flexibility and ease of development.

If a method is final, the Java compiler can put the method's executable bytecode directly into any program that calls the method. After all, the method will never change because of a subclass that overrides it.

When you first develop a class, you don't have much reason to use `final`. However, if you need to make the class execute more quickly, you can change a few methods into final methods to speed up the process. Doing so removes the possibility that the method later will be overridden in a subclass, so consider this change carefully before continuing.

The Java Class Library declares many of the commonly used methods final so that they can be executed more quickly when used in programs that call them.

NOTE   Private methods are final without being declared that way because they can't be overridden in a subclass under any circumstance.

Classes

You finalize classes by using the `final` modifier in the class's declaration, as in the following:

```
public final class ChatServer {
    // body of method
}
```

A `final` class cannot be subclassed by another class. As with `final` methods, this process introduces some speed benefits to the Java language at the expense of flexibility.

If you're wondering what you lose by using `final` classes, you must not have tried to subclass anything in the Java Class Library. Many of the popular classes are final, such as `java.lang.String`, `java.lang.Math`, and `java.net.URL`. If you want to create a class that behaves like strings but with some new changes, you can't subclass `String` and define only the behavior that is different. You have to start from scratch.

All methods in a final class are automatically final themselves, so you don't have to use a modifier in their declarations.

Because classes that can provide behavior and attributes to subclasses are much more useful, you should strongly consider whether the benefit of using `final` on one of your classes is outweighed by the cost.

Abstract Classes and Methods

In a class hierarchy, the higher the class, the more abstract its definition. A class at the top of a hierarchy of other classes can define only the behavior and attributes common to all the classes. More-specific behavior and attributes fall somewhere lower down the hierarchy.

When you factor out common behavior and attributes during the process of defining a hierarchy of classes, you might at times find yourself with a class that never needs to be instantiated directly. Instead, such a class serves as a place to hold common behavior and attributes shared by their subclasses.

These classes are called abstract classes, and they are created using the `abstract` modifier. The following is an example:

```
public abstract class Palette {
    // ...
}
```

An example of an abstract class is `java.awt.Component`, the superclass of graphical user interface components. Because numerous components inherit from this class, it contains methods and variables useful to each of them. However, there's no such thing as a generic component that can be added to a user interface, so you would never need to create a `Component` object in a program.

Abstract classes can contain anything a normal class can, including constructors, because their subclasses might need to inherit them. Abstract classes also can contain abstract methods, which are method signatures with no implementation. These methods are implemented in subclasses of the abstract class. Abstract methods are declared with the `abstract` modifier. You cannot declare an abstract method in a class that isn't itself

6

abstract. If an abstract class has nothing but abstract methods, you're better off using an interface, as you see later today.

Packages

Using packages, as mentioned previously, is a way of organizing groups of classes. A package contains classes that are related in purpose, in scope, or by inheritance.

If your programs are small and use a limited number of classes, you might find that you don't need to explore packages. But as you begin creating more sophisticated projects with many classes related to each other by inheritance, you might discover the benefit of organizing them into packages.

Packages are useful for several broad reasons:

- They enable you to organize your classes into units. Just as you have folders or directories on your hard disk to organize your files and applications, packages enable you to organize your classes into groups so that you use only what you need for each program.

- They reduce problems with conflicts about names. As the number of Java classes grows, so does the likelihood that you'll use the same class name as another developer. This introduces the possibility of naming clashes and error messages if you try to integrate groups of classes into a single program. Packages provide a way to refer specifically to the desired class, even if it shares a name with a class in another package.

- They enable you to protect classes, variables, and methods in larger ways than on a class-by-class basis, as you learned today. You'll learn more about protections with packages later.

- Packages can be used to uniquely identify your work.

You've been using packages all along in this book. Every time you use the `import` command, and every time you refer to a class by its full package name (`java.util.StringTokenizer`, for example), you are using packages.

To use a class contained in a package, you can use one of three techniques:

- If the class you want to use is in the package `java.lang` (for example, `System` or `Date`), you can simply use the class name to refer to that class. The `java.lang` classes are automatically available to you in all your programs.

- If the class you want to use is in some other package, you can refer to that class by its full name, including any package names (for example, `java.awt.Font`).

- For classes that you use frequently from other packages, you can import individual classes or a whole package of classes. After a class or package has been imported, you can refer to that class by its class name.

If you don't declare that your class belongs to a package, it is put into an unnamed default package. You can refer to that class and any other unpackaged class simply by its class name from anywhere in other classes.

To refer to a class in another package, you always can use its full name: the class name preceded by its package. You do not have to import the class or package to use it in this manner, as in this example:

```
java.awt.Font text = new java.awt.Font();
```

For classes that you use only once or twice in your program, using the full name might make sense. If you use a class multiple times, you can import the class to save yourself some typing.

The import Declaration

To import classes from a package, use the import declaration as you did in earlier projects in the first week. You can import an individual class, as in this statement:

```
import java.util.Vector;
```

You also can import an entire package of classes using an asterisk (*) in place of an individual class name:

```
import java.awt.*;
```

The asterisk can be used in place of a class name only in an import statement. It does not make it possible to import multiple packages with similar names.

For example, the Java Class Library includes the java.util, java.util.jar, and java.util.prefs packages. You could not import all three packages with the following statement:

```
import java.util.*;
```

6

This merely imports the java.util package. To make all three available in a class, the following statements are required:

```
import java.util.*;
import java.util.jar.*;
import java.util.prefs.*;
```

Also, you cannot indicate partial class names (such as L* to import all the classes that begin with the letter L). Your only options when using an import declaration are to load all the classes in a package or just a single class.

The import declarations in your class definition go at the top of the file, before any class definitions but after the package declaration, as you'll see in the next section.

Using individual import declarations or importing packages is mostly a question of your own coding style. Importing a group of classes does not slow down your program or make it any larger; only the classes that you actually use in your code are loaded as they are needed. Importing specific classes makes it easier for readers of your code to figure out what classes are being used in the code.

NOTE	If you're familiar with C or C++, you might expect the import declaration to work like #include and possibly result in a large executable program because it includes source code from another file. This isn't the case in Java. The import keyword's only function is to tell the Java compiler where to look for the full name of a class when its short name is used. It doesn't actually import code from any classes.

The import statement also can be used to refer to constants in a class by name.

Normally, class constants must be prefaced with the name of the class, as in Color.black, Math.PI, and File.separator.

An import static statement makes the constants in an identified class available in shorter form. The keywords import static are followed by the name of an interface or class and an asterisk. For example:

```
import static java.lang.Math.*;
```

This statement makes it possible to refer to the constants in the Math class, E and PI, using only their names. Here's a short example of a class that takes advantage of this feature:

```
import static java.lang.Math.*;

public class ShortConstants {
    public static void main(String[] arguments) {
        System.out.println("PI: " + PI);
        System.out.println("" + (PI * 3));
    }
}
```

Class Name Conflicts

After you have imported a class or a package of classes, you usually can refer to a class simply by its name without the package identifier. However, you must be more explicit when you import two classes from different packages that have the same class name.

One situation where a naming conflict might occur is during database programming, which you'll undertake on Day 18, "Accessing Databases with JDBC 4.1 and Derby." This kind of programming can involve the java.util and java.sql packages, which both contain a class named Date.

If you're working with both packages in a class that reads or writes data in a database, you could import them with these statements:

```
import java.sql.*;
import java.util.*;
```

When both these packages are imported, a compiler error occurs when you refer to the Date class without specifying a package name, as in this statement:

```
Date now = new Date();
```

The error occurs because the Java compiler has no way of knowing which Date class is being referred to in the statement. The package must be included in the statement, like this:

```
java.util.Date = new java.util.Date();
```

Creating Your Own Packages

Creating a package for your classes in Java is not much more complicated than creating a class.

Picking a Package Name

The first step is to decide on a name. The name you choose for your package depends on how you will use those classes. Perhaps you name your package after yourself or a part of the Java system you're working on (such as graphics or messaging). If you intend to distribute your package as an open source or commercial product, use a package name that uniquely identifies its authorship.

Oracle recommends that Java developers use an Internet domain name that you control as the basis for a unique package name.

To form the name, reverse the elements so that the last part of the domain becomes the first part of the package name, followed by the second-to-last part. Following this convention, because my personal domain name is cadenhead.org, all Java packages I create

6

begin with the name `org.cadenhead`, such as `org.cadenhead.rss` and `org.cadenhead.xml`.

This convention provides a reasonable assurance that no other Java developers will offer a package with the same name, as long as they follow the same rule themselves (as most developers do).

By another convention, package names use no capital letters, which distinguishes them from class names. For example, in the full name of the class `java.lang.String`, you can easily distinguish the package name `java.lang` from the class name `String`.

Creating the Folder Structure

The second step in creating packages is to create a folder structure that matches the package name, which requires a separate folder for each part of the name. The package `org.cadenhead.rss` requires an org folder, a cadenhead folder inside org, and an rss folder inside cadenhead. The classes in the package then are stored in the rss folder.

Adding a Class to a Package

The final step of putting a class inside a package is to add a statement to the class file above any `import` declarations and the `class` declaration. The `package` declaration is followed by the full name of the package:

```
package org.cadenhead.rss;
```

The `package` declaration must be the first line of code in your source file, disregarding comments or blank lines.

Packages and Class Access Control

Earlier today, you learned about access control modifiers for methods and variables. You also can control access to classes.

Classes have the default access control if no modifier is specified, which means that the class is available to all other classes in the same package but is not visible or available outside that package. It cannot be imported or referred to by name; classes with package protection are hidden inside the package in which they are contained.

To allow a class to be visible and importable outside your package, you can give it public protection by adding the `public` modifier to its definition:

```
public class Visible {
    // ...
}
```

Classes declared as public can be accessed by other classes outside the package.

Note that when you use an `import` statement with an asterisk, you import only the public classes inside that package. Other classes remain hidden and can be used only by the other classes in that package.

Why would you want to hide a class inside a package? For the same reasons that you want to hide variables and methods inside a class: so that you can have utility classes and behavior that are useful only to your implementation, or so that you can limit your program's interface to minimize the effect of larger changes. As you design your classes, consider the whole package and decide which classes you want to declare public and which you want to be hidden.

Creating a good package consists of defining a small, clean set of public classes and methods for other classes to use and then implementing them by using any number of hidden support classes. You'll see another use for private classes later today.

Interfaces

Interfaces, like abstract classes and methods, provide templates of behavior that other classes are expected to implement. They also offer significant advantages in class and object design that complement Java's single-inheritance approach to object-oriented programming.

The Problem of Single Inheritance

As you begin turning a project into a hierarchy of classes related by inheritance, you might discover that the simplicity of the class organization is restrictive. This is especially true when you have some behavior that needs to be used by classes that do not share a common superclass.

Other object-oriented programming (OOP) languages include the concept of multiple inheritance, which solves this problem by letting a class inherit from more than one superclass, acquiring behavior and attributes from all its superclasses at once.

6

This concept makes a programming language more challenging to learn and use. Questions of method invocation and how the class hierarchy is organized become far more complicated with multiple inheritance. They also become more open to confusion and ambiguity.

Because one of the goals of Java was that it be simple, multiple inheritance was rejected in favor of single inheritance.

A Java interface is a collection of abstract behavior that can be adopted by any class without being inherited from a superclass.

An interface contains nothing but abstract method definitions and constants. It has no instance variables or method implementations.

Interfaces are implemented and used throughout the Java Class Library when behavior is expected to be implemented by a number of disparate classes. Later today, you'll use one of the interfaces in the Java class hierarchy, `java.lang.Comparable`.

Interfaces and Classes

Classes and interfaces, despite their different definitions, have a great deal in common. Both are declared in source files and compiled into `.class` files. In most cases, an interface can be used anywhere you can use a class.

You can substitute an interface name for a class name in almost every example in this book. Java programmers often say "class" when they actually mean "class or interface." Interfaces complement and extend the power of classes, and the two can be treated almost the same, but an interface cannot be instantiated: new can only create an instance of a nonabstract class.

Implementing and Using Interfaces

You can do two things with interfaces: use them in your own classes and define your own. For now, start with using them in your own classes.

To use an interface, include the `implements` keyword as part of your class definition:

```
public class AnimatedSign extends Sign
    implements Runnable {
    //...
}
```

In this example, Sign is the superclass, and the Runnable interface extends the behavior that it implements.

Because interfaces provide nothing but abstract method definitions, you then have to implement those methods in your own classes using the same method signatures from the interface.

To implement an interface, you must offer all the methods in that interface—you can't pick and choose the methods you need. By implementing an interface, you're telling users of your class that you support the entire interface.

After your class implements an interface, subclasses of your class inherit those new methods and can override or overload them. If your class inherits from a superclass that implements a given interface, you don't have to include the implements keyword in your own class definition.

Implementing Multiple Interfaces

Unlike with the single-inheritance class hierarchy, you can include as many interfaces as you need in your own classes. Your class must implement the combined behavior of all the included interfaces. To include multiple interfaces in a class, just separate their names with commas:

```
public class AnimatedSign extends Sign
    implements Runnable, Observer {

    // ...
}
```

Note that complications might arise from implementing multiple interfaces. What happens if two different interfaces both define the same method? You can solve this problem in one of three ways:

- If the methods in each interface have identical signatures, you implement one method in your class, and that definition satisfies both interfaces.

- If the methods have different argument lists, it is a simple case of method overloading; you implement both method signatures, and each definition satisfies its respective interface definition.

- If the methods have the same argument lists but different return types, you cannot create a method that satisfies both. (Remember that a method signature does not include the method's return type.) In this case, trying to compile a class that implements both interfaces would produce a compiler error message. Encountering this problem suggests that your interfaces have some design flaws that you might need to reexamine.

6

Other Uses of Interfaces

Almost everywhere that you can use a class, you can use an interface instead. For example, you can declare a variable to be of an interface type:

```
Iterator loop = new Iterator();
```

When a variable is declared to be of an interface type, it is an object that implements the interface. In this case, because loop is an object of the type Iterator, the assumption is that you can call all three of the interface's methods on that object: hasNext(), next(), and remove().

The important point to realize is that although Iterator is expected to have the three methods, you could write this code long before any classes that qualify are actually implemented. You also can cast objects to an interface, just as you can cast objects to other classes.

Creating and Extending Interfaces

After you use interfaces for a while, the next step is to define your own interfaces. Interfaces look a lot like classes; they are declared in much the same way and can be arranged into a hierarchy. However, you must follow certain rules for declaring interfaces.

New Interfaces

To create a new interface, you declare it like this:

```
interface Expandable {
    // ...
}
```

This declaration is, effectively, the same as a class definition, with the word interface replacing the word class. Inside the interface definition are methods and variables.

The method definitions inside the interface are public and abstract. You can explicitly declare them as such, or they will be turned into public and abstract methods if you do not include those modifiers. You cannot declare a method inside an interface to be either private or protected.

As an example, here's an Expandable interface with one method explicitly declared public and abstract and one declared implicitly:

```
public interface Expandable {
    public abstract void expand(); // explicitly public and abstract
    void contract(); // effectively public and abstract
}
```

Both methods are public and abstract.

Note that, as with abstract methods in classes, methods inside interfaces do not have bodies. An interface consists of only a method signature; no implementation is involved.

In addition to methods, interfaces can have variables, but those variables must be declared public, static, and final (making them constant). As with methods, you can explicitly define a variable to be public, static, and final, or it is implicitly defined as such if you don't use those modifiers. Here's that same Expandable definition with two new variables:

```
public interface Expandable {
    public static final int INCREMENT = 10;
    long CAPACITY = 15000; // becomes public static and final

    public abstract void expand(); //explicitly public and abstract
    void contract(); // effectively public and abstract
}
```

Interfaces must have either public or package protection, just like classes. Note, however, that interfaces without the public modifier do not automatically convert their methods to public and abstract nor their constants to public. A nonpublic interface also has nonpublic methods and constants that can be used only by classes and other interfaces in the same package.

Interfaces, like classes, can belong to a package. Interfaces also can import other interfaces and classes from other packages, just as classes can.

Methods Inside Interfaces

Here's one trick to note about methods inside interfaces: Those methods are supposed to be abstract and apply to any kind of class, but how can you define arguments to those methods? You don't know what class will be using them! The answer lies in the fact that you use an interface name anywhere a class name can be used, as you learned earlier. By defining your method arguments to be interface types, you can create generic arguments that apply to any class that might use this interface.

Consider the interface Trackable, which defines methods with no arguments for track() and quitTracking(). You also might have a method for beginTracking(), which has one argument: the trackable object itself.

What class should that argument be? It should be any object that implements the Trackable interface rather than a particular class and its subclasses. The solution is to declare the argument as simply Trackable in the interface:

```
public interface Trackable {
    public abstract Trackable beginTracking(Trackable self);
}
```

6

Then, in an actual implementation for this method in a class, you can take the generic `Trackable` argument and cast it to the appropriate object:

```
public class Monitor implements Trackable {

public Trackable beginTracking(Trackable self) {
    Monitor mon = (Monitor) self;
    // ...
    return mon;
}
```

Extending Interfaces

As you can do with classes, you can organize interfaces into a hierarchy. When one interface inherits from another interface, that subinterface acquires all the method definitions and constants that its superinterface declared.

To extend an interface, you use the `extends` keyword just as you do in a class definition:

```
interface PreciselyTrackable extends Trackable {
    // ...
}
```

Note that unlike classes, the interface hierarchy has no equivalent of the `Object` class—there is no root superinterface from which all interfaces descend. Interfaces can either exist entirely on their own or inherit from another interface.

Note also that unlike the class hierarchy, the inheritance hierarchy can have multiple inheritance. For example, a single interface can extend as many classes as it needs to (separated by commas in the `extends` part of the definition), and the new interface contains a combination of all its parent's methods and constants.

In interfaces, the rules for managing method name conflicts are the same as for classes that use multiple interfaces; methods that differ only in return type result in a compiler error message.

Creating an Online Storefront

To explore all the topics covered up to this point, the Storefront application uses packages, access control, interfaces, and encapsulation. This application manages the items in an online storefront, handling two main tasks:

- Calculating the sale price of each item, depending on how much of it is presently in stock
- Sorting items according to sale price

The Storefront application consists of two classes, Storefront and Item. These classes will be organized as a new package called org.cadenhead.ecommerce.

In NetBeans, choose File, New File, indicate that you're creating a new empty Java file, and then click Next. Give it the class name Item and the package name org.cadenhead.ecommerce. Click Finish to start entering the code shown in Listing 6.2.

LISTING 6.2   The Full Text of Item.java

```
 1: package org.cadenhead.ecommerce;
 2:
 3: public class Item implements Comparable {
 4:     private String id;
 5:     private String name;
 6:     private double retail;
 7:     private int quantity;
 8:     private double price;
 9:
10:     Item(String idIn, String nameIn, String retailIn, String quanIn) {
11:         id = idIn;
12:         name = nameIn;
13:         retail = Double.parseDouble(retailIn);
14:         quantity = Integer.parseInt(quanIn);
15:
16:         if (quantity > 400)
17:             price = retail * .5D;
18:         else if (quantity > 200)
19:             price = retail * .6D;
20:         else
21:             price = retail * .7D;
22:         price = Math.floor( price * 100 + .5 ) / 100;
23:     }
24:
25:     public int compareTo(Object obj) {
26:         Item temp = (Item)obj;
27:         if (this.price < temp.price)
28:             return 1;
29:         else if (this.price > temp.price)
30:             return -1;
31:         return 0;
32:     }
33:
34:     public String getId() {
35:         return id;
36:     }
37:
38:     public String getName() {
39:         return name;
40:     }
```

6

LISTING 6.2   Continued

```
41:
42:     public double getRetail() {
43:          return retail;
44:     }
45:
46:     public int getQuantity() {
47:          return quantity;
48:     }
49:
50:     public double getPrice() {
51:          return price;
52:     }
53: }
```

When you save this file, look in the Projects pane of NetBeans. The Item.java source code file has been put in a different place, as shown in Figure 6.1.

FIGURE 6.1

Grouping packages in a NetBeans project.

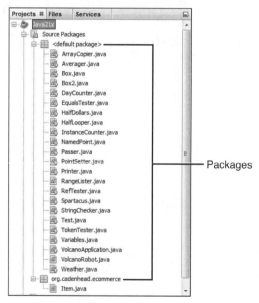

Instead of organizing the file in the <default package> category like the other programs you have created thus far, NetBeans puts it in the org.cadenhead.ecommerce category. One of the advantages of using NetBeans over the JDK is that it organizes packages properly, based on their name designated by the package declaration.

The Item class is a support class that represents a product sold by an online store. It contains private instance variables for the product ID code, name, how many are in stock (quantity), and the retail and sale prices.

Because all the instance variables of this class are private, no other class can set or retrieve their values. Simple accessor methods are created in lines 34–52 to provide a way for other programs to retrieve these values. Each method begins with get followed by the capitalized name of the variable, which is a standard convention in Java programming used throughout the Java Class Library. The getPrice() method returns a double containing the value of price. No methods are provided for setting any of these instance variables. That is handled in the constructor method for this class.

Line 1 establishes that the Item class is part of the org.cadenhead.ecommerce package.

NOTE   cadenhead.org is the personal domain of this book's coauthor, so this project follows Oracle's package-naming convention by beginning with a top-level domain (org), following it with the second-level domain name (cadenhead), and then using a name that describes the package's purpose (ecommerce).

The Item class implements the Comparable interface (line 3), which makes it easy to sort a class's objects. This interface has only one method, compareTo(*Object*), which returns an integer.

The compareTo() method compares two objects of a class: the current object and another object passed as an argument to the method. The value returned by the method defines the natural sorting order for objects of this class:

- If the current object should be sorted above the other object, return –1.
- If the current object should be sorted below the other object, return 1.
- If the two objects are equal, return 0.

6

You determine in the compareTo() method which of an object's instance variables to consider when sorting. Lines 25–32 override the compareTo() method for the Item class, sorting on the basis of the price variable. Items are sorted by price from highest to lowest.

After you have implemented the Comparable interface for an object, two class methods can be called to sort an array or a class holding those objects. You'll see this later, when the Storefront class is created.

The Item() constructor in lines 10–23 takes four String objects as arguments and uses them to set up the id, name, retail, and quantity instance variables. The last two must be converted from strings to numeric values using the Double.parseDouble() and Integer.parseInt() class methods, respectively.

The value of the price instance variable depends on how much of that item is presently in stock:

- If more than 400 are in stock, price is 50 percent of retail (lines 16 and 17).
- If between 201 and 400 are in stock, price is 60 percent of retail (lines 18 and 19).
- For everything else, price is 70 percent of retail (lines 20 and 21).

Line 22 rounds off price so that it contains two or fewer decimal places, turning a value such as $6.92999999999999 into $6.93. The Math.floor() method rounds off decimal numbers to the next-lowest integer, returning them as double values.

Next, you need a class that represents a storefront for these products. Create an empty Java file with the class name Storefront and package name org.cadenhead.ecommerce, and enter the code shown in Listing 6.3.

LISTING 6.3   The Full Text of Storefront.java

```
 1: package org.cadenhead.ecommerce;
 2:
 3: import java.util.*;
 4:
 5: public class Storefront {
 6:     private LinkedList catalog = new LinkedList();
 7:
 8:     public void addItem(String id, String name, String price,
 9:         String quant) {
10:
11:         Item it = new Item(id, name, price, quant);
12:         catalog.add(it);
13:     }
14:
15:     public Item getItem(int i) {
16:         return (Item)catalog.get(i);
17:     }
18:
19:     public int getSize() {
20:         return catalog.size();
21:     }
22:
```

```
23:        public void sort() {
24:            Collections.sort(catalog);
25:        }
26: }
```

Because it belongs to the same package as the Item class, Storefront will be listed with it in the NetBeans Projects pane.

The Storefront class is used to manage a collection of products in an online store. Each product is an Item object, and they are stored together in a LinkedList instance variable named catalog (line 6).

The addItem() method in lines 8–13 creates a new Item object based on four arguments sent to the method: the ID, name, price, and quantity of the item that is in stock. After the item is created, it is added to the catalog linked list through a call to its add(Object) method with the Item object as an argument.

The getItem() and getSize() methods provide an interface to the information stored in the private catalog variable. The getSize() method in lines 19–21 calls the catalog.size() method, which returns the number of objects contained in catalog.

Because objects in a linked list are numbered like arrays and other data structures, you can retrieve them using an index number. The getItem() method in lines 15–17 calls catalog.get(int) with an index number as an argument, returning the object stored at that location in the linked list.

The sort() method in lines 23–25 is where you benefit from the implementation of the Comparable interface in the Item class. The class method Collections.sort() sorts a linked list and other data structures based on the natural sort order of the objects they contain, calling the object's compareTo() method to determine this order.

To finish this project, the GiftShop application is a class that makes use of Item and Storefront objects. This application also belongs to the org.cadenhead.ecommerce package. Create the new Java class GiftShop with the source code shown in Listing 6.4.

6

LISTING 6.4   The Full Text of GiftShop.java

```
1: package org.cadenhead.ecommerce;
2:
3: public class GiftShop {
4:     public static void main(String[] arguments) {
5:         Storefront store = new Storefront();
6:         store.addItem("C01", "MUG", "9.99", "150");
7:         store.addItem("C02", "LG MUG", "12.99", "82");
```

LISTING 6.4   Continued

```
 8:          store.addItem("C03", "MOUSEPAD", "10.49", "800");
 9:          store.addItem("D01", "T SHIRT", "16.99", "90");
10:          store.sort();
11:
12:          for (int i = 0; i < store.getSize(); i++) {
13:              Item show = (Item)store.getItem(i);
14:              System.out.println("\nItem ID: " + show.getId() +
15:                  "\nName: " + show.getName() +
16:                  "\nRetail Price: $" + show.getRetail() +
17:                  "\nPrice: $" + show.getPrice() +
18:                  "\nQuantity: " + show.getQuantity());
19:          }
20:      }
21: }
```

The GiftShop class demonstrates each part of the public interface that the Storefront and Item classes make available. You can do the following:

- Create an online store
- Add items to it
- Sort the items by sale price
- Loop through a list of items to display information about each one

The output is as follows:

Output ▼

```
Item ID: D01
Name: T SHIRT
Retail Price: $16.99
Price: $11.89
Quantity: 90

Item ID: C02
Name: LG MUG
Retail Price: $12.99
Price: $9.09
Quantity: 82

Item ID: C01
Name: MUG
Retail Price: $9.99
Price: $6.99
Quantity: 150
```

```
Item ID: C03
Name: MOUSEPAD
Retail Price: $10.49
Price: $5.25
Quantity: 800
```

Many implementation details of these classes are hidden from GiftShop and other classes that would use the package.

For instance, the programmer who developed GiftShop doesn't need to know that Storefront uses a linked list to hold all the store's product data. If the developer of Storefront later decided to use a different data structure, as long as getSize() and getItem() returned the expected values, GiftShop would continue to work correctly.

Inner Classes

The classes you have worked with thus far are all members of a package, either because you specified a package name with the package declaration or because the default package was used. Classes that belong to a package are called top-level classes. When Java was introduced, they were the only classes that the language supported.

Adding more power to the language, you can define a class inside a class as if it were a method or variable. The class follows the same rules for how it is structured, except that it is defined within another class definition.

The following class, Zone, has an inner class called Center. Comments show where the definition of the inner class begins and ends. An object of the class is created in the constructor for Zone:

```
public class Zone {
    int x, y, width, height;
    class Center { // inner class begins
        int cx, cy;

        Center(int x, int y) {
            cx = x;
            cy = y;
        }
    } // inner class ends

    public Zone(int x1, int y1, int x2, int y2) {
        x = x1;
        y = y1;
        width = y2 - y1;
        height = x2 - x1;
        // create object of inner class
```

6

```
        Center c = new Center( (x1 + x2) / 2,
            (y1 + y2) / 2 );
    }
}
```

In this example, a `Center` object has instance variables for an (x, y) coordinate.

The SquareTool application, shown in Listing 6.5, uses an inner class called `Square` to square a floating-point number and store the result. This application does not specify a package, so it belongs to the default package in Java. When creating it in NetBeans, make sure that `org.cadenhead.ecommerce` is not in the Package field and instead is left blank. Enter the listing into the source code editor.

LISTING 6.5   The Full Text of SquareTool.java

```
 1: public class SquareTool {
 2:     public SquareTool(String input) {
 3:         try {
 4:             float in = Float.parseFloat(input);
 5:             Square sq = new Square(in);
 6:             float result = sq.value;
 7:             System.out.println("The square of " + input
 8:                 + " is " + result);
 9:         } catch (NumberFormatException nfe) {
10:             System.out.println(input
11:                 + " is not a valid number.");
12:         }
13:     }
14:
15:     class Square {
16:         float value;
17:
18:         Square(float x) {
19:             value = x * x;
20:         }
21:     }
22:
23:     public static void main(String[] arguments) {
24:         if (arguments.length < 1) {
25:             System.out.println("Usage: java SquareTool number");
26:         } else {
27:             SquareTool dr = new SquareTool(arguments[0]);
28:         }
29:     }
30: }
```

After saving the file, customize the project configuration in NetBeans to specify a number as an argument. (Choose Project, Set Project Configuration, Customize, and then enter `SquareTool` as the class name and a number as the only argument.)

If you run it with 13 as the argument, here's the output:

```
The square of 13 is 169.0
```

In this application, the `Square` class isn't functionally different from a helper class included in the same source file as a program's main class file. The only difference is that the helper is defined inside the class file. This has several advantages:

- Inner classes are invisible to all other classes, which means that you don't have to worry about name conflicts between an inner class and other classes.
- Inner classes can have access to variables and methods within the scope of a top-level class that they would not have as a separate class.

In many cases, an inner class is a short class file that exists only for a limited purpose. In the SquareTool application, because the `Square` class doesn't contain a lot of complex behavior and attributes, it is well suited for implementation as an inner class.

The name of an inner class is associated with the name of the class in which it is contained, and it is assigned automatically when the program is compiled. The Java compiler names the `Square` class `SquareTool$Square.class`.

Inner classes, although seemingly a minor enhancement, actually represent a significant modification to the language.

Rules governing the scope of an inner class closely match those governing variables. An inner class's name is not visible outside its scope, except in a fully qualified name, which helps in structuring classes within a package. The code for an inner class can use simple names from enclosing scopes, including class and member variables of enclosing classes, as well as local variables of enclosing blocks.

In addition, you can define a top-level class as a static member of another top-level class. Unlike an inner class, a top-level class cannot directly use the instance variables of any other class. The ability to nest classes in this way allows any top-level class to provide package-style organization for a logically related group of secondary top-level classes.

6

Summary

Today, you learned how to encapsulate an object by using access control modifiers for its variables and methods. You also learned how to use other modifiers such as `static`, `final`, and `abstract` to develop Java classes and class hierarchies.

To further the effort of developing and using a set of classes, you learned how to group classes into packages. These groupings better organize your programs and help you share classes with the many other Java programmers, making their code publicly available.

Finally, you learned how to implement interfaces and inner classes, two structures that are helpful when designing a class hierarchy.

Q&A

Q Won't using accessor methods everywhere slow down my Java code?

A Not always. As Java compilers improve and can create more optimizations, they will be able to make accessor methods fast automatically. But if you're concerned about speed, you can always declare accessor methods to be final, and they'll be comparable in speed to direct instance variable accesses under most circumstances.

Q Based on what I've learned, private abstract methods and final abstract methods and classes don't seem to make sense. Are they legal?

A No. They cause compiler errors, as you have guessed. To be useful, abstract methods must be overridden, and abstract classes must be subclassed, but neither of those operations would be legal if they were also private or final.

Q I've been told that I should consider using Ant to manage my Java packages and compile applications. What does Ant do?

A Apache Ant is an open source tool for compiling and packaging Java applications and class libraries that is implemented with Java and Extensible Markup Language (XML). With Ant, you create an XML file that indicates how your classes should be compiled, archived, and organized. You can specify multiple targets for each "build," the term applied to the process, and easily produce multiple builds for each stage of a project's development.

Ant, which can be downloaded from http://ant.apache.org, was created by programmers for Jakarta, the open source Java project administered by Apache. Jakarta has produced Struts, Velocity, Tomcat, and many other useful Java class libraries and technologies.

Jakarta projects are extensive, requiring the management of hundreds of Java classes, JAR archives, and other files. Ant was so useful in the creation of the Tomcat web server that it became an Apache development project in its own right. It has subsequently become the most popular build tool for Java programmers.

Quiz

Review today's material by taking this three-question quiz. Answers are at the end of the book.

Questions

1. What packages are automatically imported into your Java classes?

   A. None

   B. The classes stored in the folders of your `Classpath`

   C. The classes in the `java.lang` package

2. According to the convention for naming packages, what should be the first part of the name of a package you create?

   A. Your name followed by a period

   B. Your top-level Internet domain followed by a period

   C. The text `java` followed by a period

3. If you create a subclass and override a public method, what access modifiers can you use with that method?

   A. `public` only

   B. `public` or `protected`

   C. `public`, `protected`, or default access

Certification Practice

The following question is the kind of thing you could expect to be asked on a Java programming certification test. Answer it without looking at today's material or using the Java compiler to test the code.

Given:

```
package org.cadenhead.bureau;

public class Information {
    public int duration = 12;
    protected float rate = 3.15F;
    float average = 0.5F;
}
```

6

and:

```
package org.cadenhead.bureau;

import org.cadenhead.bureau.*;

public class MoreInformation extends Information {
    public int quantity = 8;
}
```

and:

```
package org.cadenhead.bureau.us;

import org.cadenhead.bureau.*;

public class EvenMoreInformation extends MoreInformation {
    public int quantity = 9;

    EvenMoreInformation() {
        super();
        int i1 = duration;
        float i2 = rate;
        float i3 = average;
    }
}
```

Which instance variables are visible in the EvenMoreInformation class?

   A. quantity, duration, rate, and average

   B. quantity, duration, and rate

   C. quantity, duration, and average

   D. quantity, rate, and average

The answer is available on the book's website at www.java21days.com. Visit the Day 6 page and click the Certification Practice link.

Exercises

To extend your knowledge of the subjects covered today, try the following exercises:

1. Create a modified version of the Storefront project that includes a noDiscount variable for each item. When this variable is true, sell the item at the retail price.

2. Create a ZipCode class that uses access control to ensure that its zipCode instance variable always has a five-digit value.

Where applicable, exercise solutions are offered on the book's website at www.java21days.com.

6

DAY 7
Exceptions and Threads

Your first week in the Java language ends with two of its most useful elements, threads and exceptions.

Threads are objects that implement the `Runnable` interface or extend the `Thread` class, indicating that they can run simultaneously with other parts of a Java program. Exceptions are objects that represent errors that may occur as a Java program runs.

Threads enable programs to make efficient use of resources by isolating the computing-intensive parts of a program so that they don't slow down everything else. Exceptions enable programs to recognize errors and respond to them. Exceptions even make it possible for programs to correct the conditions and continue running, when possible.

Exceptions are covered first because they're one of the things you use when working with threads.

Exceptions

Programmers in any language endeavor to write programs that are bug-free, never crash, can handle any circumstance with grace, and always recover from unusual situations.

So much for that idea.

Errors occur because programmers didn't anticipate possible problems or didn't test enough. Or programs encounter situations out of their control, such as bad data from users, corrupt files that don't have the correct data in them, network connections that don't connect, hardware devices that don't respond, sunspots, gremlins, and on and on.

In Java, the strange events that might cause a program to fail are called *exceptions*. Java defines a number of language features that deal with exceptions:

- How to handle exceptions in your code and recover gracefully from potential problems
- How to tell code that uses your classes that you're expecting a potential exception
- How to create an exception if you detect one
- How your code is limited yet made more robust by exceptions

With most programming languages, handling error conditions requires much more work than handling a program that is running properly. It can require a confusing structure of conditional statements to deal with errors that might occur.

As an example, consider the following code that could be used to load a file from disk. File input and output can be problematic because of disk errors, file-not-found errors, and the like. If the program must have the data from the file to operate properly, it must deal with all these circumstances before continuing.

Here's the structure of one possible solution:

```
int status = loadTextFile();
if (status != 1) {
    // something unusual happened; report it
    switch (status) {
        case 2:
            System.out.println("File not found");
            break;
        case 3:
            System.out.println("Disk error");
            break;
        case 4:
            System.out.println("File corrupted");
            break;
```

```
        default:
            System.out.println("Error");
    }
} else {
    // file loaded OK; continue with program
}
```

This code tries to load a file by calling the method `loadTextFile()`, which presumably has been defined elsewhere in the class. The method returns an integer that indicates whether the file loaded properly (a value of 1) or an error occurred (2, 3, 4, or higher).

The program uses a `switch` statement keyed on that error code to address the problem. The end result is a block of code in which the most common circumstance—a successful file load—can be lost amid the error-handling code. This is the result of handling only one possible error. If other errors take place later in the program, you might end up with more nested `if-else` and `switch-case` blocks.

As you can see, error management would become a major problem in larger programs. Different programmers could designate special values for handling errors, which would require that they be documented properly and used in a consistent manner.

Error-management code like this could make a Java class difficult to read and maintain.

Dealing with errors in this manner makes it impossible for the compiler to check for consistency the way it can check to make sure that you called a method with the right arguments or set a variable to the right class of object.

Although the previous example uses Java syntax, you never have to deal with errors that way with the Java language because you can use a group of classes called exceptions that work much better.

Exceptions include errors that could be fatal to your program as well as other unusual situations. By managing exceptions, you can manage errors and possibly work around them.

Errors and other conditions in Java programs can be more easily managed through a combination of language features, consistency checking at compile time, and a set of extensible exception classes.

With these features, you can add a whole new dimension to the behavior and design of your classes, your class hierarchy, and your overall system. Your classes and interface describe how your program is supposed to behave under the best circumstances. With exceptions, you can consistently describe how the program will behave when circumstances are not ideal and allow programmers who use your classes to know what to expect in those cases.

7

Exception Classes

At this point, it's likely that you've run into at least one Java exception. Perhaps you mistyped a method name or made a mistake in your code that caused a problem. Maybe you tried to run a Java application without providing the command-line arguments that were needed and saw an `ArrayIndexOutOfBoundsException` message.

Chances are, when an exception occurred, the application quit and spewed a bunch of mysterious errors to the screen. Those errors are exceptions. When your program stops without successfully finishing its work, an exception is thrown. Exceptions can be thrown by the Java virtual machine, by classes you use, or intentionally in your own programs.

Just as exceptions are thrown, they also can be caught. Catching an exception involves dealing with the exceptional circumstance so that your program doesn't crash, as you'll learn later today.

The heart of the Java exception system is the exception itself. Exceptions in Java are instances of classes that inherit from the `Throwable` class. An instance of a `Throwable` class is created when an exception is thrown.

`Throwable` has two subclasses: `Error` and `Exception`. Instances of `Error` are internal errors involving the Java virtual machine (the runtime environment). These errors are rare and usually fatal to the program; there's not much you can do about them, other than catch them or throw them yourself.

The class `Exception` is more relevant to your own programming. Subclasses of `Exception` fall into two general groups:

- Unchecked exceptions (subclasses of the class `RuntimeException`) such as `ArrayIndexOutofBoundsException`, `SecurityException`, and `NullPointerException`
- Checked exceptions such as `EOFException` and `MalformedURLException`

Unchecked exceptions, also called runtime exceptions, usually occur because of code that isn't very robust. An `ArrayIndexOutOfBounds` exception, for example, should never be thrown if you're properly checking to make sure that your code stays within the bounds of an array. `NullPointerException` exceptions happen when you try to use a variable that doesn't refer to an object yet.

CAUTION   If your program is causing unchecked exceptions, you should fix those problems by improving your code. Don't rely on exception management to handle programming mistakes that can be corrected while you're creating a Java program.

Checked exceptions indicates that something strange and out of control is happening. An EOFException, for example, happens when you're reading a file and the file ends before it was expected to. A MalformedURLException happens when a web address (also called a URL) isn't in the right format. This group includes exceptions that you create to signal unusual cases that might occur in your own programs.

Exceptions are arranged in a hierarchy just as other classes are, where the superclasses are more general kinds of problems and the subclasses are more specific. This organization becomes more important to you as you deal with exceptions in your own code.

The primary exception classes are part of the java.lang package: Throwable, Exception, and RuntimeException. Many of the other packages in the Java Class Library define other exceptions, which are used throughout the library.

The java.io package defines a general exception class called IOException. It is subclassed not only in the java.io package for input and output exceptions (EOFException and FileNotFoundException) but also in the java.net classes for networking exceptions such as MalformedURLException and in the java.util package with ZipException.

Managing Exceptions

Now that you know what an exception is, how do you deal with one in your own code? In many cases, the Java compiler enforces exception management when you try to use methods that throw exceptions; you need to deal with those exceptions in your own code, or it simply won't compile. In this section, you'll learn about consistency checking and how to use three new keywords—try, catch, and finally—to deal with exceptions that might occur.

Exception Consistency Checking

The more you work with the Java Class Library, the more likely you are to run into a compiler error (an exception!) such as this one:

Output ▼

```
Exception java.lang.InterruptedException
must be caught or it must be declared in the throws clause
of this method.
```

In Java, a method can indicate the kinds of errors it might potentially throw. For example, methods that read from files can throw IOException errors, so those methods are declared with a special modifier that indicates potential errors. When you use those methods in your own Java programs, you have to protect your code against the exceptions.

This rule is enforced by the compiler itself, in the same way that it checks to make sure that you're using methods with the correct number of arguments and that all your variable types match what you're assigning to them.

Why is this check in place? It makes programs less likely to crash with fatal errors because you know up front the kind of exceptions that can be thrown by the methods a program uses.

You no longer have to pore over documentation or an object's code to ensure that you've dealt with all the potential problems; Java does the checking for you. On the other side, if you define your methods so that they indicate the exceptions they can throw, Java can tell your objects' users to handle those errors.

Protecting Code and Catching Exceptions

Assume that you've been happily coding and an exception occurs as a class is compiled. According to the message, you have to either catch the error or declare that your method throws it.

First, we'll deal with catching potential exceptions, which requires two things:

- You protect the code that contains the method that might throw an exception inside a `try` block.
- You deal with an exception inside a `catch` block.

A `try` block tries a block of code to see if it can execute all of it without causing an exception. If it fails and an exception occurs, a `catch` block deals with it.

You've seen `try` and `catch` before. On Day 6, "Packages, Interfaces, and Other Class Features," you used the following code to create an integer from a `String` value:

```
public SquareTool(String input) {
    try {
        float in = Float.parseFloat(input);
        // ...
    } catch (NumberFormatException nfe) {
        System.out.println(input + " is not a valid number.");
    }
}
```

In this code, the `Float.parseFloat()` class method might throw an exception of the class `NumberFormatException`, which signifies that the string is not in a valid format as a number. (One situation that triggers this exception is if `input` equals `15x`, which is not a number.)

To handle the exception, the call to parseFloat() is placed inside a try block, and an associated catch block has been set up. The catch block receives any NumberFormatException objects thrown within the try block.

The part of the catch clause inside the parentheses is similar to a method definition's argument list. It contains the class of exception to be caught and a variable name. You can use the variable to refer to that exception object inside the catch block.

An exception object has a getMessage() method that displays a detailed error message describing what happened.

The following example is a revised version of the try-catch block used on Day 6:

```
try {
    float in = Float.parseFloat(input);
} catch (NumberFormatException nfe) {
    System.out.println("Oops: " + nfe.getMessage());
}
```

The examples you have seen thus far catch a specific type of exception. Because exception classes are organized into a hierarchy and you can use a subclass anywhere that a superclass is expected, you can catch groups of exceptions within the same catch statement.

As an example, when you start writing programs that handle input and output from files, Internet servers, and other places, you deal with several different types of IOException exceptions (the IO stands for input/output). These exceptions include two of its subclasses, EOFException and FileNotFoundException. By catching IOException, you also catch instances of any IOException subclass.

To catch several different exceptions that aren't related by inheritance, you can use multiple catch blocks for a single try, like this:

```
try {
    // code that might generate exceptions
} catch (IOException ioe) {
    System.out.println("Input/output error");
    System.out.println(ioe.getMessage());
} catch (ClassNotFoundException cnfe) {
    System.out.println("Class not found");
    System.out.println(cnfe.getMessage());
} catch (InterruptedException ie) {
    System.out.println("Program interrupted");
    System.out.println(ie.getMessage());
}
```

7

In a multiple `catch` block, the first `catch` block that matches is executed, and the rest is ignored.

You can run into unexpected problems by using an `Exception` superclass in a `catch` block followed by one or more of its sub-classes in their own `catch` blocks. For example, the input/output exception `IOException` is the superclass of the end-of-file excep-tion `EOFException`. If you put an `IOException` block above an `EOFException` block, the subclass never catches any exceptions.

In Java 7, you also can catch more than one class of exceptions in the same `catch` state-ment. The classes must be separated by a pipe character (|). Here's an example:

```
try {
    // code that reads a file from disk
} catch (EOFException|FileNotFoundException exc) {
    System.out.println("File error: "
        + exc.getMessage());
}
```

This code catches two exceptions, `EOFException` and `FileNotFoundException`, in the same `catch` block. The exception is assigned to the `exc` argument, and its `getMessage()` method is called.

The first class in the list that matches the thrown exception will be assigned to the argument.

The exceptions declared as alternatives in the `catch` statement cannot be superclasses or subclasses of each other unless they are in the proper order. The following would not work:

```
try {
    // code that reads a file from disk
} catch (IOException|EOFException|FileNotFoundException exc) {
    System.out.println("File error: "
        + exc.getMessage());
}
```

This code wouldn't compile because `IOException` is the superclass of the other two exceptions and it precedes them in the list. Because a superclass can catch exceptions of its subclasses, the second and third exceptions in that statement never would be caught.

Here's a fixed version that would work:

```
try {
    // code that reads a file from disk
} catch (EOFException|FileNotFoundException exc) {
    System.out.println("File error: "
        + exc.getMessage());
} catch (IOException ioe) {
    System.out.println("IO error: "
        + ioe.getMessage());
}
```

Another way to make it work would be to put the superclass last in the catch statement:

```
try {
    // code that reads a file from disk
} catch (EOFException|FileNotFoundException|IOException exc) {
    System.out.println("File error: "
        + exc.getMessage());
}
```

CAUTION   Exceptions have a `printStackTrace()` method that displays the sequence of method calls that led to the statement that generated the exception. If you use this in a program, NetBeans flags it for a warning in the source code editor. The reason is that `printStackTrace()` contains debugging information that probably should not be shared with users after a program has been finished.

A catch statement must be needed by the try block with which it is paired. The exception class in catch has to be one that could be thrown in that block (or a superclass of one that could be thrown). The compiler will fail with an error otherwise.

For example, if you used catch for FileNotFoundException in a program that did not read any files, the program would not compile.

The finally Clause

Suppose that there is some action in your code that you absolutely must do, no matter what happens, regardless of whether an exception is thrown. This is usually to free some external resource after acquiring it, to close a file after opening it, or something similar.

One example is when you are working with databases, as you do during Day 18, "Accessing Databases with JDBC 4.1 and Derby." The database connection and objects you create to access the database are closed in a finally block to free those resources because they're no longer needed.

7

Although you could put that action both inside a catch block and outside it, that would be duplicating the same code in two different places. And you should avoid this situation as much as possible in your programming.

Instead, put one copy of that code inside a special optional block of the try-catch statement that uses the keyword finally:

```
try {
    readTextFile();
} catch (IOException ioe) {
    // deal with IO errors
} finally {
    closeTextFile();
}
```

Today's first project shows how a finally statement can be used inside a method.

The HexReader application, shown in Listing 7.1, reads sequences of two-digit hexadecimal numbers and displays their decimal values. There are three sequences to read:

- 000A110D1D260219

- 78700F1318141E0C

- 6A197D45B0FFFFFF

As you learned on Day 2, "The ABCs of Programming," hexadecimal is a base-16 numbering system in which the single-digit numbers range from 00 (decimal 0) to 0F (decimal 15), and double-digit numbers range from 10 (decimal 16) to FF (decimal 255).

Create this class in NetBeans as an empty Java file and enter the source code of Listing 7.1.

LISTING 7.1   The Full Text of HexReader.java

```
 1: class HexReader {
 2:     String[] input = { "000A110D1D260219 ",
 3:         "78700F1318141E0C ",
 4:         "6A197D45B0FFFFFF " };
 5:
 6:     public static void main(String[] arguments) {
 7:         HexReader hex = new HexReader();
 8:         for (int i = 0; i < hex.input.length; i++)
 9:             hex.readLine(hex.input[i]);
10:     }
11:
12:     void readLine(String code) {
13:         try {
```

```
14:                    for (int j = 0; j + 1 < code.length(); j += 2) {
15:                        String sub = code.substring(j, j+2);
16:                        int num = Integer.parseInt(sub, 16);
17:                        if (num == 255)
18:                            return;
19:                        System.out.print(num + " ");
20:                    }
21:                } finally {
22:                    System.out.println("**");
23:                }
24:                return;
25:        }
26: }
```

The output of this program is as follows:

Output ▼

```
0 10 17 13 29 38 2 25 **
120 112 15 19 24 20 30 12 **
106 25 125 69 176 **
```

Line 15 of the program reads two characters from code, the string that was sent to the readLine() method, by calling the string's substring(*int*, *int*) method.

NOTE	In the substring() method of the String class, you select a substring in a somewhat counterintuitive way. The first argument specifies the index of the first character to include in the substring, but the second argument does not specify the last character. Instead, the second argument indicates the index of the last character plus 1. A call to substring(2, 5) for a string would return the characters from index position 2 to index position 4.

The two-character substring contains a hexadecimal number stored as a String. The Integer class method parseInt can be used with a second argument to convert this number into an integer. Use 16 as the argument for a hexadecimal (base 16) conversion, 8 for an octal (base 8) conversion, and so on.

In the HexReader application, the hexadecimal FF is used to fill out the end of a sequence and should not be displayed as a decimal value. This is accomplished by using a try-finally block in lines 13–23 of Listing 7.1.

7

The try-finally block causes an unusual thing to happen when the return statement is encountered at line 18. You would expect return to cause the readLine() method to be exited immediately.

Because it is within a try-finally block, the statement within the finally block is executed no matter how the try block is exited. The text ** is displayed at the end of a line of decimal values.

Java 7 offers a new way to ensure that resources are freed properly even when an operation inside a try block fails with an exception. The try-with-resources feature enables statements that claim resources to be declared inside parentheses in a try statement.

The following code contains two statements that read data from an Internet server using a networking socket (a type of connection):

```
Socket digit = new Socket(host, 79);
BufferedReader in = new BufferedReader(
    new InputStreamReader(digit.getInputStream()));
```

To ensure that resources are properly released, they can be declared inside the try statement, as in this example:

```
try (Socket digit = new Socket(host, 79);
    BufferedReader in = new BufferedReader(
        new InputStreamReader(digit.getInputStream()));
    ) {

    // code goes here
} catch (IOException e) {
    System.out.println("IO Error:" + e.getMessage());
}
```

No matter how the code in the try block exits, whether through success or an exception, the digit and in resources will be disposed of properly.

NetBeans issues a warning in the source code editor on any statement that ought to be in a try-with-resources statement but isn't. Take this advice whenever you can because this new feature of Java 7 is a big improvement. It eliminates the common error of forgetting to close a resource when no longer in use.

Declaring Methods That Might Throw Exceptions

In previous examples, you learned how to deal with methods that might throw exceptions by protecting code and catching any exceptions that occur. The Java compiler checks to make sure that you've dealt with a method's exceptions. But how does it know which exceptions to tell you about?

The answer is that the original method indicated the exceptions that it might possibly throw as part of its definition. You can use this mechanism in your own methods. In fact, it's good style to do so to make sure that users of your classes are alerted to the errors your methods might experience.

To indicate that a method will possibly throw an exception, you use a special clause in the method definition called throws.

The throws Clause

If some code in your method's body might throw an exception, add the throws keyword after the method's closing parenthesis, followed by the name or names of the exception that your method throws, as in this example:

```
public void getFormula(int x, int y) throws NumberFormatException {
    // body of method
}
```

If your method might throw multiple kinds of exceptions, you can declare them all in the throws clause separated by commas:

```
public void storeFormula(int x, int y)
        throws NumberFormatException, EOFException {
            // body of method
}
```

Note that, as with catch, you can use a superclass of a group of exceptions to indicate that your method might throw any subclass of that exception. For instance:

```
public void loadFormula() throws IOException {
    // ...
}
```

Keep in mind that adding a throws clause to your method definition simply means that the method might throw an exception if something goes wrong, not that it actually will. The throws clause provides extra information to your method definition about potential exceptions and allows Java to make sure that your method is being used correctly by other people.

Think of a method's overall description as a contract between the designer of that method and the caller of the method. (You can be on either side of that contract, of course.)

7

Usually the description indicates the types of a method's arguments, what it returns, and the particulars of what it normally does. By using throws, you are adding information about the abnormal things the method can do. This new part of the contract helps separate and make explicit all the places where exceptional conditions should be handled in your program, and that makes large-scale design easier.

Which Exceptions Should You Throw?

After you decide to declare that your method might throw an exception, you must decide which exceptions it might throw and actually throw them or call a method that will throw them. (You'll learn about throwing your own exceptions in the next section.)

In many instances, this is apparent from the operation of the method itself. Perhaps you're already creating and throwing your own exceptions, in which case you'll know exactly which exceptions to throw.

You don't really have to list all the possible exceptions that your method could throw. Unchecked exceptions are handled by the runtime itself and are so common that you don't have to deal with them.

In particular, exceptions of either the `Error` or `RuntimeException` class or any of their subclasses do not have to be listed in your `throws` clause.

They get special treatment because they can occur anywhere within a Java program and are usually conditions that you, as the programmer, did not directly cause.

One good example is `OutOfMemoryError`, which can happen anywhere, at any time, and for any number of reasons.

Unchecked exceptions are subclasses of the `RuntimeException` and `Error` classes and are usually thrown by the Java runtime itself. You do not have to declare that your method throws them, and you usually do not need to deal with them in any other way.

NOTE

You can, of course, choose to list these errors and runtime exceptions in your `throws` clause if you want, but your method's callers will not be forced to handle them. Only nonruntime exceptions must be handled.

All other exceptions are called *checked exceptions* and are potential candidates for a `throws` clause in your method.

Passing on Exceptions

There are times when it doesn't make sense for your method to deal with an exception. It might be better for the method that calls your method to deal with that exception. There's nothing wrong with this; it's fairly common for you to pass back an exception to the method that calls your method.

For example, consider the hypothetical example of `WebRetriever`, a class that loads a web page using its web address and stores it in a file. As you'll learn on Day 17, "Communicating Across the Internet," you can't work with web addresses without dealing with `MalformedURLException`, the exception thrown when an address is in the wrong format.

To use `WebRetriever`, another class calls its constructor method with the address as an argument. If the address specified by the other class is in the wrong format, a `MalformedURLException` is thrown. Instead of dealing with this, the constructor of the `WebRetriever` class could have the following definition:

```
public WebRetriever() throws MalformedURLException {
    // ...
}
```

This would force any class that works with `WebRetriever` objects to deal with `MalformedURLException` errors (or pass the buck with their own `throws` clause, of course).

One thing is always true: It's better to pass on exceptions to calling methods than to catch them and do nothing in response.

In addition to declaring methods that throw exceptions, there's one other instance in which your method definition may include a `throws` clause: Within that method, you want to call a method that throws an exception, but you don't want to catch or deal with that exception.

Rather than using the `try` and `catch` clauses in your method's body, you can declare your method with a `throws` clause so that it, too, might possibly throw the appropriate exception. It's then the responsibility of the method that calls your method to deal with that exception. This is the other case that tells the Java compiler that you have done something with a given exception.

Using this technique, you could create a method that deals with number format exceptions without a `try-catch` block:

```
public void readFloat(String input) throws NumberFormatException {
    float in = Float.parseFloat(input);
}
```

7

After you declare your method to throw an exception, you can use other methods that also throw those exceptions inside the body of this method without needing to protect the code or catch the exception.

NOTE

You can, of course, deal with other exceptions using `try` and `catch` in the body of your method in addition to passing on the exceptions you listed in the `throws` clause. You also can both deal with the exception in some way and then rethrow it so that your method's calling method has to deal with it anyhow. You learn how to throw methods in the next section.

throws and Inheritance

If your method definition overrides a method in a superclass that includes a `throws` clause, there are special rules for how your overridden method deals with `throws`. Unlike other parts of the method signature that must mimic those of the method it is overriding, your new method does not require the same set of exceptions listed in the `throws` clause.

Because there's a possibility that your new method might deal better with exceptions instead of just throwing them, your method can potentially throw fewer types of exceptions. It could even throw no exceptions. This means that you can have the following two class definitions and things will work just fine:

```
public class RadioPlayer {
    public void startPlaying() throws SoundException {
        // body of method
    }
}

public class StereoPlayer extends RadioPlayer {
    public void startPlaying() {
        // body of method
    }
}
```

The converse of this rule is not true: A subclass method cannot throw more checked exceptions (either exceptions of different types or more general exception classes) than its superclass method.

Creating and Throwing Your Own Exceptions

There are two sides to every exception: the side that throws the exception and the side that catches it. An exception can be tossed around a number of times to a number of methods before it's caught, but eventually it will be caught and dealt with.

Who does the actual throwing? Where do exceptions come from? Many exceptions are thrown by the Java runtime or by methods inside the Java classes themselves. You also can throw any of the standard exceptions that the Java Class Libraries define, or you can create and throw your own exceptions.

Throwing Exceptions

Declaring that your method throws an exception is useful only to your method's users and to the Java compiler, which checks to make sure that all your exceptions are being handled. The declaration itself doesn't do anything to actually throw that exception should it occur; you must do that yourself as needed in the body of the method.

You need to create a new instance of an exception class to throw an exception. After you have that instance, use the `throw` statement to throw it.

Here's an example using a hypothetical `NotInServiceException` class that is a subclass of the `Exception` class:

```
NotInServiceException nise = new NotInServiceException();
throw nise;
```

You can throw only objects that implement the `Throwable` class.

Depending on the exception class you're using, the exception also may have arguments to its constructor that you can use. The most common of these is a string argument, which enables you to describe the problem in greater detail (which can be useful for debugging purposes). Here's an example:

```
NotInServiceException nise = new
    NotInServiceException("Exception: Database Not in Service");
throw nise;
```

After an exception is thrown, the method exits immediately without executing any other code, other than the code inside a `finally` block if one exists. The method won't return a value either. If the calling method does not have a `try` or `catch` surrounding the call to your method, the program might exit based on the exception you threw.

7

Creating Your Own Exceptions

Although you can use a fair number of exceptions in the Java Class Library in your own methods, you might need to create your own exceptions to handle the different kinds of errors that your programs run into. Creating new exceptions is easy.

Your new exception should inherit from some other exception in the Java hierarchy. All user-created exceptions should be part of the Exception hierarchy rather than the Error hierarchy, which is reserved for errors involving the Java virtual machine. Look for an exception that's close to the one you're creating; for example, an exception for a bad file format would logically be an IOException. If you can't find a closely related exception for your new exception, consider inheriting from Exception, which forms the "top" of the exception hierarchy for checked exceptions (unchecked exceptions should inherit from RuntimeException).

Exception classes typically have two constructors: The first takes no arguments, and the second takes a single string as an argument.

Exception classes are like other classes. You can put them in their own source files and compile them just as you would other classes:

```
public class SunSpotException extends Exception {
    public SunSpotException() {}
    public SunSpotException(String msg) {
        super(msg);
    }
}
```

Combining throws, try, and throw

What if you want to combine all the approaches shown so far? You want to handle incoming exceptions yourself in your method, but you also want the option to pass on the exception to your method's caller. Simply using try and catch doesn't pass on the exception, and adding a throws clause doesn't give you a chance to deal with the exception.

If you want to both manage the exception and pass it on to the caller, use all three mechanisms: the throws clause, the try statement, and a throw statement to explicitly rethrow the exception.

Here's a method that uses this technique:

```
public void readMessage() throws IOException {
    MessageReader mr = new MessageReader();

    try {
```

```
    mr.loadHeader();
} catch (IOException e) {
    // do something to handle the
    // IO exception and then rethrow
    // the exception ...
    throw e;
}
}
```

This works because exception handlers can be nested. You handle the exception by doing something responsible with it but decide that it is important enough to give the method's caller a chance to handle it as well.

Exceptions can float all the way up the chain of method callers this way (usually not being handled by most of them) until finally the system itself handles any uncaught exceptions by aborting your program and printing an error message.

If it's possible for you to catch an exception and do something intelligent with it, you should.

When and When Not to Use Exceptions

Because throwing, catching, and declaring exceptions are related concepts and can be confusing, here's a quick summary of when to do what.

When to Use Exceptions

You can do one of three things if your method calls another method that has a `throws` clause:

- Deal with the exception by using `try` and `catch` statements.
- Pass the exception up the calling chain by adding your own `throws` clause to your method definition.
- Perform both of the preceding methods by catching the exception using `catch` and then explicitly rethrowing it using `throw`.

In cases where a method throws more than one exception, you can handle each of those exceptions differently. For example, you might catch some of those exceptions while allowing others to pass up the calling chain.

If your method throws its own exceptions, you should declare that it throws those methods using the `throws` statement. If your method overrides a superclass method that has a `throws` statement, you can throw the same types of checked exceptions or subclasses of those exceptions; you cannot throw any different types of checked exceptions.

7

Finally, if your method has been declared with a `throws` clause, don't forget to actually throw the exception in the body of your method using the `throw` statement.

When Not to Use Exceptions

Although they might seem appropriate at the time, there are several cases in which you should not use exceptions.

First, you should not use exceptions for circumstances you expect and could avoid easily. For example, although you can rely on an `ArrayIndexOutofBounds` exception to indicate when you've gone past the end of an array, it's easy to use the array's `length` variable to keep from going beyond the bounds.

In addition, if your users will enter data that must be an integer, testing to make sure that the data is an integer is a much better idea than throwing an exception and dealing with it somewhere else.

Exceptions take up a lot of processing time for your Java program. A simple test or series of tests will run much faster than exception handling and make your program more efficient. Exceptions should be used only for truly exceptional cases that are out of your control.

It's also easy to get carried away with exceptions and to try to make sure that all your methods have been declared to throw all the possible exceptions that they can throw. This makes your code more complex. In addition, if other people will be using your code, they'll have to deal with handling all the exceptions that your methods might throw.

You create more work for everyone involved when you get carried away with exceptions. Declaring a method to throw either few or many exceptions is a trade-off; the more exceptions your method can throw, the more complex that method is to use. Declare only the exceptions that have a reasonably fair chance of happening and that make sense for the overall design of your classes.

Bad Style Using Exceptions

When you first start using exceptions, it might be appealing to work around the compiler errors that result when you use a method that declares a `throws` statement. Although it is legal to add an empty `catch` clause or to add a `throws` statement to your own method (and there are appropriate reasons for doing so), intentionally dropping exceptions without dealing with them subverts the checks that the Java compiler does for you.

The Java exception system was designed so that if an error can occur, you're warned about it. Ignoring those warnings and working around them makes it possible for fatal errors to occur in your program—errors that you could have avoided with a few lines of code. Even worse, adding `throws` clauses to your methods to avoid exceptions means that the users of your methods (objects further up in the calling chain) will have to deal with them. You've just made your methods more difficult to use.

Compiler errors regarding exceptions are there to remind you to reflect on these issues. Take the time to deal with the exceptions that might affect your code. This extra care richly rewards you as you reuse your classes in later projects and in larger and larger programs. Of course, the Java Class Library has been written with exactly this degree of care, and that's one of the reasons it's robust enough to be used in constructing all your Java projects.

Threads

One thing to consider in Java programming is how system resources are being used. Graphics, complex mathematical computations, and other intensive tasks can take up a lot of processor time.

This is especially true of programs that have a graphical user interface, which is a style of software that you'll learn about next week.

If you write a graphical Java program that does something that consumes a lot of the computer's time, you might find that the program's graphical user interface responds slowly. Drop-down lists take a second or more to appear, button clicks are recognized slowly, and so on.

To solve this problem, you can segregate the processor-hogging functions in a Java class so that they run separately from the rest of the program.

This is possible through the use of a feature of the Java language called threads.

Threads are parts of a program set up to run on their own while the rest of the program does something else. This also is called *multitasking* because the program can handle more than one task simultaneously.

Threads are ideal for anything that takes up a lot of processing time and runs continuously.

By putting the program's workload into a thread, you free up the rest of the program to handle other things. You also make handling the program easier for the virtual machine because all the intensive work is isolated into its own thread.

Writing a Threaded Program

7

Threads are implemented in Java with the Thread class in the java.lang package.

The simplest use of threads is to make a program pause in execution and stay idle during that time. To do this, call the Thread class method sleep(*long*) with the number of milliseconds to pause as the only argument.

This method throws an exception, `InterruptedException`, whenever the paused thread has been interrupted for some reason. (One possible reason is that the user closes the program while it is sleeping.)

The following statements stop a program in its tracks for 3 seconds:

```
try {
    Thread.sleep(3000);
catch (InterruptedException ie) {
    // do nothing
}
```

The `catch` block does nothing, which is typical when you're using `sleep()`.

One way to use threads is to put all the time-consuming behavior into its own class.

A thread can be created in two ways: by subclassing the `Thread` class or implementing the `Runnable` interface in another class. Both belong to the `java.lang` package, so no `import` statement is necessary to refer to them.

Because the `Thread` class implements `Runnable`, both techniques result in objects that start and stop threads in the same manner.

To implement the `Runnable` interface, add the keyword `implements` to the class declaration followed by the name of the interface, as in the following example:

```
public class StockTicker implements Runnable {
    public void run() {
        // ...
    }
}
```

When a class implements an interface, it must include all methods of that interface. The `Runnable` interface contains only one method, `run()`.

The first step in creating a thread is to create a reference to an object of the `Thread` class:

```
Thread runner;
```

This statement creates a reference to a thread, but no `Thread` object has been assigned to it yet. Threads are created by calling the constructor `Thread(Object)` with the threaded object as an argument. You could create a threaded `StockTicker` object with the following statement:

```
StockTicker tix = new StockTicker();
Thread tickerThread = new Thread(tix);
```

Two good places to create threads are the constructor for an application and the constructor for a component (such as a panel).

A thread is begun by calling its start() method, as in the following statement:

```
tickerThread.start();
```

The following statements can be used in a thread class to start the thread:

```
Thread runner = null;
if (runner == null) {
    runner = new Thread(this);
    runner.start();
}
```

The this keyword used in the Thread() constructor refers to the object in which these statements are contained. The runner variable has a value of null before any object is assigned to it, so the if statement is used to make sure that the thread is not started more than once.

To run a thread, its start() method is called, as in this statement from the preceding example:

```
runner.start();
```

Calling a thread's start() method causes another method to be called—namely, the run() method that must be present in all threaded objects.

The run() method is the engine of a threaded class. In the introduction to threads, they were described as a means of segregating processor-intensive work so that it runs separately from the rest of a class. This kind of behavior would be contained within a thread's run() method and the methods it calls.

A Threaded Application

Threaded programming requires a lot of interaction among different objects, so it should become more clear when you see it in action.

Listing 7.2 contains a class that finds a specific prime number in a sequence, such as the 10th prime, 100th prime, or 1,000th prime. This can take some time, especially for numbers beyond 100,000, so the search for the right prime takes place in its own thread.

Enter the code shown in Listing 7.2 in NetBeans and save it as the class name PrimeFinder.

LISTING 7.2   The Full Text of PrimeFinder.java

7

```
1: public class PrimeFinder implements Runnable {
2:     public long target;
3:     public long prime;
4:     public boolean finished = false;
5:     private Thread runner;
```

LISTING 7.2   Continued

```
 6:
 7:    PrimeFinder(long inTarget) {
 8:         target = inTarget;
 9:         if (runner == null) {
10:             runner = new Thread(this);
11:             runner.start();
12:         }
13:    }
14:
15:    public void run() {
16:         long numPrimes = 0;
17:         long candidate = 2;
18:         while (numPrimes < target) {
19:             if (isPrime(candidate)) {
20:                 numPrimes++;
21:                 prime = candidate;
22:             }
23:             candidate++;
24:         }
25:         finished = true;
26:    }
27:
28:    boolean isPrime(long checkNumber) {
29:         double root = Math.sqrt(checkNumber);
30:         for (int i = 2; i <= root; i++) {
31:             if (checkNumber % i == 0)
32:                 return false;
33:         }
34:         return true;
35:    }
36: }
```

Save the PrimeFinder class when you're finished. This class doesn't have a main() method, so you can't run it as an application. Next you'll create a program that uses this class.

The PrimeFinder class implements the Runnable interface, so it can be run as a thread.

There are three public instance variables:

- target is a long that indicates when the specified prime in the sequence has been found. If you're looking for the 5,000th prime, target equals 5000.
- prime is a long that holds the last prime number found by this class.
- finished is a Boolean that indicates when the target has been reached.

There is also a private instance variable called runner that holds the Thread object that this class runs in. This object should be equal to null before the thread is started.

The PrimeFinder constructor method in lines 7–13 sets the target instance variable and starts the thread if it hasn't already been started. When the thread's start() method is called, it in turn calls the run() method of the threaded class.

The run() method is in lines 15–26. This method does most of the work of the thread, which is typical of threaded classes. You want to put the most computing-intensive tasks in their own threads so that they don't bog down the rest of the program.

This method uses two new variables: numPrimes, the number of primes that have been found, and candidate, the number that might possibly be prime. The candidate variable begins at the first possible prime number, which is 2.

The while loop in lines 18–24 continues until the right number of primes has been found.

First, it checks whether the current candidate is prime by calling the isPrime(long) method, which returns true if the number is prime and false otherwise.

If the candidate is prime, numPrimes increases by 1, and the prime instance variable is set to this prime number.

The candidate variable is then incremented by 1, and the loop continues.

After the right number of primes has been found, the while loop ends, and the finished instance variable is set to true. This indicates that the PrimeFinder object has found the right prime number and is finished searching.

The end of the run() method is reached in line 26, and the thread no longer does any work.

The isPrime() method is contained in lines 28–35. This method determines whether a number is prime by using the % operator, which returns the remainder of a division operation. If a number is evenly divisible by 2 or any higher number (leaving a remainder of 0), it is not a prime number.

Listing 7.3 is an application that uses the PrimeFinder class. Enter the code shown in Listing 7.3 in NetBeans as a new Java class named PrimeThreads.

7

LISTING 7.3 The Full Text of PrimeThreads.java

```
 1: public class PrimeThreads {
 2:     public static void main(String[] arguments) {
 3:         PrimeThreads pt = new PrimeThreads(arguments);
 4:     }
 5:
 6:     public PrimeThreads(String[] arguments) {
 7:         PrimeFinder[] finder = new PrimeFinder[arguments.length];
 8:         for (int i = 0; i < arguments.length; i++) {
 9:             try {
10:                 long count = Long.parseLong(arguments[i]);
11:                 finder[i] = new PrimeFinder(count);
12:                 System.out.println("Looking for prime " + count);
13:             } catch (NumberFormatException nfe) {
14:                 System.out.println("Error: " + nfe.getMessage());
15:             }
16:         }
17:         boolean complete = false;
18:         while (!complete) {
19:             complete = true;
20:             for (int j = 0; j < finder.length; j++) {
21:                 if (finder[j] == null) continue;
22:                 if (!finder[j].finished) {
23:                     complete = false;
24:                 } else {
25:                     displayResult(finder[j]);
26:                     finder[j] = null;
27:                 }
28:             }
29:             try {
30:                 Thread.sleep(1000);
31:             } catch (InterruptedException ie) {
32:                 // do nothing
33:             }
34:         }
35:     }
36:
37:     private void displayResult(PrimeFinder finder) {
38:         System.out.println("Prime " + finder.target
39:             + " is " + finder.prime);
40:     }
41: }
```

Save the file when you're finished, and it compiles automatically.

The PrimeThreads application can be used to find one or more prime numbers in sequence. Specify the prime numbers that you're looking for as command-line arguments and include as many as you want.

If this program is run with the command-line arguments 1 10 100 1000, it produces the following output:

Output ▼

```
Looking for prime 1
Looking for prime 10
Looking for prime 100
Looking for prime 1000
Prime 1 is 2
Prime 10 is 29
Prime 100 is 541
Prime 1000 is 7919
```

Because there's no guarantee of the order the threads will finish, here's another possible output:

Output ▼

```
Looking for prime 1
Looking for prime 10
Looking for prime 100
Looking for prime 1000
Prime 1 is 2
Prime 100 is 541
Prime 10 is 29
Prime 1000 is 7919
```

The thread looking for the 100th prime completed before the thread looking for the tenth.

The for loop in lines 8–16 of the PrimeThreads application creates one PrimeFinder object for each command-line argument specified when the program is run.

Because arguments are Strings and the PrimeFinder constructor requires long values, the Long.parseLong(*String*) class method is used to handle the conversion. All the number-parsing methods throw NumberFormatException exceptions, so they are enclosed in try-catch blocks to deal with arguments that are not numeric.

When a PrimeFinder object is created, the object starts running in its own thread (as specified in the PrimeFinder constructor).

The while loop in lines 18–34 checks to see whether any PrimeFinder thread has completed, which is indicated by its finished instance variable equaling true. When a thread has completed, the displayResult() method is called in line 25 to display the prime number that was found. The thread then is set to null, freeing the object for garbage collection (and preventing its result from being displayed more than once).

7

The call to Thread.sleep(1000) in line 30 causes the while loop to pause for 1 second during each pass through the loop. A slowdown in loops helps keep the Java interpreter from executing statements at such a furious pace that it becomes bogged down.

Stopping a Thread

Stopping a thread is a little more complicated than starting one. The Thread class includes a stop() method that can be called to stop a thread, but it creates instabilities in Java's runtime environment and can introduce hard-to-detect errors into a program. For this reason, the method has been deprecated, indicating that it should not be used in favor of another technique.

A better way to stop a thread is to place a loop in the thread's run() method that ends when a variable changes in value, as in the following example:

```
public void run() {
    while (okToRun == true) {
        // ...
    }
}
```

The okToRun variable could be an instance variable of the thread's class. If it is changed to false, the loop inside the run() method ends.

Another option you can use to stop a thread is to loop in the run() method only while the currently running thread has a variable that references it.

In previous examples, a Thread object called runner was used to hold the current thread.

A class method, Thread.currentThread(), returns a reference to the current thread (in other words, the thread in which the object is running).

The following run() method loops as long as runner and currentThread() refer to the same object:

```
public void run() {
    Thread thisThread = Thread.currentThread();
    while (runner == thisThread) {
        // ...
    }
}
```

If you use a loop like this, you can stop the thread anywhere in the class with the following statement:

```
runner = null;
```

Summary

Exceptions and threads aid your program's design and robustness.

Exceptions enable you to manage potential errors. By using try, catch, and finally, you can protect code that might result in exceptions by handling those exceptions as they occur.

Handling exceptions is only half the equation; the other half is generating and throwing exceptions. A throws clause tells a method's users that the method might throw an exception. It also can be used to pass on an exception from a method call in the body of your method.

You learned how to actually create and throw your own methods by defining new exception classes and by throwing instances of any exception classes using throw.

Threads enable you to run the most processor-intensive parts of a Java class separately from the rest of the class. This is especially useful when the class is doing something computing-intensive such as animation, complex mathematics, or looping through a large amount of data quickly.

You also can use threads to do several things at once and to start and stop threads externally.

Threads implement the Runnable interface, which contains one method: run(). When you start a thread by calling its start() method, the thread's run() method is called automatically.

Q&A

Q I'm still not sure I understand the difference between exceptions, errors, and runtime exceptions. Is there another way of looking at them?

A Errors are caused by dynamic linking or virtual machine problems. Thus, they are too low-level for most programs to care about—or to be able to handle even if they did care.

Runtime exceptions are generated by the normal execution of Java code. Although they occasionally reflect a condition you will want to handle explicitly, more often they reflect a coding mistake made by the programmer, and thus simply print an error to help flag that mistake.

Nonruntime exceptions (IOException exceptions, for example) are conditions that, because of their nature, should be explicitly handled by any robust and well-thought-out code. The Java Class Library has been written using only a few of

7

these, but those few are important to using the system safely and correctly. The compiler helps you handle these exceptions properly via its `throws` clause checks and restrictions.

Q Does Java support unit testing to make programs more reliable?

A Unit testing, a technique for ensuring the reliability of software by adding tests, is supported by the open source Java Class Library JUnit. This is the most popular unit-testing framework for Java programmers. Visit www.junit.org to download it.

With JUnit, you write a set of tests, called a suite, that create the Java objects you've developed and call their methods. The values produced by these tests are checked to see whether they're what you expected. All tests must pass for your software to pass.

Although unit testing is only as good as the tests you create, the existence of a test suite is extremely helpful when you make changes to your software. By running the tests again after the changes, you can better assure yourself that it continues to work correctly.

Some Java programmers believe so strongly in the benefits of unit testing that they write tests before any code.

Q Is there any way to get around the strict restrictions placed on methods by the *throws* clause?

A Yes. Suppose you have thought long and hard and have decided that you need to circumvent this restriction. This is almost never the case because the right solution is to go back and redesign your methods to reflect the exceptions you need to throw. Imagine, however, that for some reason a system class has you in a bind. Your first solution is to subclass `RuntimeException` to make up a new, unchecked exception of your own. Now you can throw it to your heart's content because the `throws` clause that was annoying you does not need to include this new exception. If you need many such exceptions, an elegant approach is to mix in some novel exception interfaces with your new `Runtime` classes. You're free to choose whatever subset of these new interfaces you want to catch (none of the normal `Runtime` exceptions need to be caught). Any leftover `Runtime` exceptions are allowed to go through that otherwise annoying standard method in the library.

Quiz

Review today's material by taking this three-question quiz. Answers are at the end of the book.

Questions

1. What keyword is used to jump out of a try block and into a `finally` block?

    A. catch

    B. return

    C. while

2. What class should be the superclass of any exceptions you create in Java?

    A. Throwable

    B. Error

    C. Exception

3. If a class implements the `Runnable` interface, what methods must the class contain?

    A. start(), stop(), and run()

    B. actionPerformed()

    C. run()

Certification Practice

The following question is the kind of thing you could expect to be asked on a Java programming certification test. Answer it without looking at today's material or using the Java compiler to test the code.

The AverageValue application is supposed to take up to 10 floating-point numbers as command-line arguments and display their average.

Given:

```java
public class AverageValue {
    public static void main(String[] arguments) {
        float[] temps = new float[10];
        float sum = 0;
        int count = 0;
        int i;
        for (i = 0; i < arguments.length & i < 10; i++) {
            try {
                temps[i] = Float.parseFloat(arguments[i]);
                count++;
```

7

```
        } catch (NumberFormatException nfe) {
            System.out.println("Invalid input: " + arguments[i]);
        }
        sum += temps[i];
    }
    System.out.println("Average: " + (sum / i));
  }
}
```

Which statement contains an error?

A. `for (i = 0; i < arguments.length & i < 10; i++) {`

B. `sum += temps[i];`

C. `System.out.println("Average: " + (sum / i));`

D. None of them; the program is correct.

The answer is available on the book's website at www.java21days.com. Visit the Day 7 page and click the Certification Practice link.

Exercises

To extend your knowledge of the subjects covered today, try the following exercises:

1. Modify the `PrimeFinder` class so that it throws a new exception, `NegativeNumberException`, if a negative number is sent to the constructor.

2. Modify the `PrimeThreads` application so that it can handle the new `NegativeNumberException` error.

Where applicable, exercise solutions are offered on the book's website at www.java21days.com.

WEEK 2:
The Java Class Library

DAY 8
Data Structures

During the first week, you learned about the core elements of the Java language: objects, classes, and interfaces, along with the keywords, statements, expressions, and operators they contain.

For the second week, the focus shifts from the classes you create to the ones that have been created for you. The Java Class Library is a set of standard packages from Oracle that has more than 3,900 classes you can use in your own Java programs.

Today, you start with classes that represent data.

The following data structures are covered:

- Bit sets, which hold Boolean values
- Array lists, arrays that can grow and shrink in size
- Stacks, structures stored in last-in, first-out (LIFO) order
- Hash maps, which store items using keys

Moving Beyond Arrays

The Java class library provides a set of data structures in the `java.util` package that gives you more flexibility in organizing and manipulating data.

A solid understanding of data structures and when to employ them will be useful throughout your Java programming efforts.

Many Java programs that you create rely on some means of storing and manipulating data within a class. Up to this point, you have used three structures to store and retrieve data: variables, `String` objects, and arrays.

These are just a few of the data classes available in Java. If you don't understand the full range of data structures, you'll find yourself trying to use arrays or strings when other options would be more efficient or easier to implement.

Outside of primitive data types and strings, arrays are the simplest data structure that Java supports. An array is a series of data elements of the same primitive type or class. It's treated as a single object but contains multiple elements that can be accessed independently. Arrays are useful when you need to store and access related information.

A glaring limitation of arrays is that they can't adjust in size to accommodate more or fewer elements. You can't add new elements to an array that's already full. One data structure you learn about today, array lists, does not have this limitation.

NOTE

Unlike the data structures provided by the `java.util` package, arrays are considered such a core component of Java that they are implemented in the language itself. Therefore, you can use arrays in Java without importing any packages.

Java Structures

The data structures provided by the `java.util` package perform a wide range of functions. These data structures consist of the `Iterator` interface, the `Map` interface, and classes such as the following:

- `BitSet`
- `ArrayList`
- `Stack`
- `HashMap`

Each of these data structures provides a way to store and retrieve information in a well-defined manner. The Iterator interface itself isn't a data structure, but it defines a means to retrieve successive elements from a data structure. For example, Iterator defines a method called next() that gets the next element in a data structure containing multiple elements.

8

NOTE

Iterator is an expanded and improved version of the Enumeration interface from early versions of the language. Although Enumeration is still supported, Iterator has simpler method names and support for removing items.

The BitSet class implements a group of bits, or flags, which can be set and cleared individually. This class is useful when you need to keep up with a set of Boolean values; you simply assign a bit to each value and set or clear it as appropriate. A flag is a Boolean value that represents one of a group of on/off type states in a program.

The ArrayList class is similar to a traditional Java array, except that it can grow as necessary to accommodate new elements and also shrink. Like an array, elements of an ArrayList object can be accessed via an index value. The nice thing about using an array list is that you don't have to worry about setting it to a specific size upon creation; it shrinks and grows automatically as needed.

The Stack class implements a last-in, first-out stack of elements. You can think of a stack as literally a vertical stack of objects. When you add a new element, it's stacked on top of the others. When you pull an element off the stack, it comes off the top. That element is removed from the stack, unlike a structure such as an array, where the elements always are available.

The HashMap class implements Dictionary, an abstract class that defines a data structure for mapping keys to values. This is useful when you want to access data through a particular key rather than an integer index. Because the Dictionary class is abstract, it provides only the framework for a key-mapped data structure rather than a specific implementation. A key is an identifier used to reference, or look up, a value in a data structure.

The HashMap class provides an implementation of a key-mapped data structure. HashMap organizes data based on a user-defined key structure. For example, in a zip code list stored in a hash map, you could store and sort data using each code as a key. The specific meaning of keys in a hash map depends on how the map is used and the data it contains.

The next section looks at these data structures in more detail to show how they work.

Iterator

The Iterator interface provides a standard means of progressing through a list of elements in a defined sequence, which is a common task for many data structures.

Even though you can't use the interface outside a particular data structure, understanding how the Iterator interface works helps you understand other Java data structures.

With that in mind, take a look at the methods defined by the Iterator interface:

```
public boolean hasNext();

public Object next();

public void remove();
```

These methods lack code because interfaces don't have implementations. The class that implements the interface must provide the code to define the methods.

The hasNext() method determines whether the structure contains any more elements. You can call this method to see whether you can continue iterating through a structure.

The next() method retrieves the next element in a structure. If there are no more elements, next() throws a NoSuchElementException exception. To avoid this, you can use hasNext() in conjunction with next() to make sure that there is another element to retrieve.

The following while loop uses these two methods to iterate through a data structure called users that implements the Iterator interface:

```
while (users.hasNext()) {
    Object ob = users.next();
    System.out.println(ob);
}
```

This sample code displays the contents of each list item by using the hasNext() and next() methods.

The next() method returns an object of the class Object. You can cast this to another class that the structure holds. Here's an example for a data structure that holds String objects:

```
while (users.hasNext()) {
    String ob = (String) users.next();
    System.out.println(ob);
}
```

NOTE

Because Iterator is an interface, you never use it directly as a data structure. Instead, you use the methods defined by Iterator for structures that implement the interface. This provides a consistent interface for many of Java's standard data structures, which makes them easier to learn and use.

Bit Sets

The BitSet class is useful when you need to represent a large amount of binary data—bit values that equal either 0 or 1. These also are called on-or-off values (with 1 representing on and 0 representing off) or Boolean values (with 1 representing true and 0 representing false).

With the BitSet class, you can use individual bits to store Boolean values without requiring bitwise operations to extract bit values. You simply refer to each bit using an index. Another nice feature of BitSet is that it automatically grows to represent the number of bits that a program requires. Figure 8.1 shows the logical organization of a bit set data structure.

FIGURE 8.1
The organization of a bit set.

You can use a BitSet object to hold attributes that can easily be modeled by Boolean values. Because the individual bits in a set are accessed via an index, you can define each attribute as a constant index value, as in this class:

```
class ConnectionAttributes {
    public static final int READABLE = 0;
    public static final int WRITABLE = 1;
    public static final int STREAMABLE = 2;
    public static final int FLEXIBLE = 3;
}
```

In this class, the attributes are assigned increasing values beginning with 0. You can use these values to get and set the appropriate bits in a set. First, you need to create a BitSet object:

```
BitSet connex = new BitSet();
```

This constructor creates a set with no specified size. You also can create a set with a specific size:

```
BitSet connex = new BitSet(4);
```

This creates a set containing 4 Boolean bits. Regardless of the constructor used, all bits in new sets are initially set to `false`. After you have a set, you can set and clear the bits by using `set(int)` and `clear(int)` methods with the bit constants you defined:

```
connex.set(ConnectionAttributes.WRITABLE);
connex.set(ConnectionAttributes.STREAMABLE);
connex.set(ConnectionAttributes.FLEXIBLE);

connex.clear(ConnectionAttributes.WRITABLE);
```

In this code, the `WRITABLE`, `STREAMABLE`, and `FLEXIBLE` attributes are set, and then the `WRITABLE` bit is cleared. The class name is used for each attribute because the constants are class variables in the `ConnectionAttributes` class.

You can get the value of individual bits in a set by using the `get()` method:

```
boolean isWriteable = connex.get(ConnectionAttributes.WRITABLE);
```

You can find out how many bits a set represents with the `size` method:

```
int numBits = connex.size();
```

The `BitSet` class also provides other methods for performing comparisons and bitwise operations on sets, such as `AND`, `OR`, and `XOR`. All these methods take a `BitSet` object as their only argument.

Today's first project is `HolidaySked`, a Java class that uses a set to keep track of which days in a year are holidays.

A set is employed because `HolidaySked` must be able to take any day of the year and answer the same yes/no question: Are you a holiday?

Enter the code shown in Listing 8.1 into an empty Java file in NetBeans named `HolidaySked`.

LISTING 8.1   The Full Text of `HolidaySked.java`

```
1: import java.util.*;
2:
3: public class HolidaySked {
4:     BitSet sked;
5:
6:     public HolidaySked() {
```

LISTING 8.1 Continued

```
 7:         sked = new BitSet(365);
 8:         int[] holiday = { 1, 15, 50, 148, 185, 246,
 9:             281, 316, 326, 359 };
10:         for (int i = 0; i < holiday.length; i++) {
11:             addHoliday(holiday[i]);
12:         }
13:     }
14:
15:     public void addHoliday(int dayToAdd) {
16:         sked.set(dayToAdd);
17:     }
18:
19:     public boolean isHoliday(int dayToCheck) {
20:         boolean result = sked.get(dayToCheck);
21:         return result;
22:     }
23:
24:     public static void main(String[] arguments) {
25:         HolidaySked cal = new HolidaySked();
26:         if (arguments.length > 0) {
27:             try {
28:                 int whichDay = Integer.parseInt(arguments[0]);
29:                 if (cal.isHoliday(whichDay)) {
30:                     System.out.println("Day number " + whichDay +
31:                         " is a holiday.");
32:                 } else {
33:                     System.out.println("Day number " + whichDay +
34:                         " is not a holiday.");
35:                 }
36:             } catch (NumberFormatException nfe) {
37:                 System.out.println("Error: " + nfe.getMessage());
38:             }
39:         }
40:     }
41: }
```

This application requires one command-line argument: a number from 1 to 365 that represents the day of the year, in sequence. (These numbers are defined in lines 8–9 and would be different for each year.)

Test the program with values such as 15 (Martin Luther King Day) or 103 (my birthday). The application should respond that day 15 is a holiday but that day 103, sadly, is not.

The HolidaySked class contains only one instance variable: sked, a BitSet that holds values for each day in a year.

The constructor of the class creates the sked bit set with 365 positions, with a value of 0 (lines 6–13). All bit sets are filled with 0 values when they are created.

Next, an integer array called holiday is created. This array holds the number of each work holiday in the year, beginning with 1 (New Year's Day) and ending with 359 (Christmas).

The holiday array is used to add each holiday to the sked bit set. A for loop iterates through the holiday array and calls the method addHoliday(int) with each one (lines 10–12).

The addHoliday(int) method is defined in lines 15–17. The argument represents the day that should be added. The bit set's set(int) method is called to set the bit at the specified position to 1. For example, if set(359) is called, the bit at position 359 is given the value 1.

The HolidaySked class also can determine whether a specified day is a holiday. This is handled by the isHoliday(int) method (lines 19–22). The method calls the bit set's get(int) method, which returns true if the specified position has the value 1 and false otherwise.

This class can be run as an application because of the main() method (lines 24–40). The application takes a single command-line argument: a number from 1 to 365 that represents one of the days of the year. The application displays whether that day is a holiday according to the schedule of the HolidaySked class.

Array Lists

One of the most popular data structures in Java, the ArrayList class implements an expandable and contractible array of objects, making it more flexible and useful than arrays. Because the ArrayList class is responsible for changing size as necessary, it has to decide when and how much to grow or shrink as elements are added and removed.

An array list can be created with a constructor taking no arguments:

```
ArrayList golfer = new ArrayList();
```

This constructor creates a default array list containing no elements. All lists are empty upon creation. One of the attributes that determines how a list sizes itself is its initial capacity—the number of elements for which it allocates memory to hold.

The size of an array list is the number of elements currently stored in it. A list's capacity is always greater than or equal to the size.

The following code shows how to create an array list with a specified capacity:

```
ArrayList golfer = new ArrayList(30);
```

This list allocates enough memory to support 30 elements. If the capacity fills up, the list automatically expands by half the initial size. So if a 30th element is put in `golfer`, it expands to make room for 45 elements.

8

Because allocating additional space for the list takes time and consumes memory, it's best to create a list with as many elements as you expect to use.

You can't just use square brackets (`[]`) to access the elements in an array list, as you can in an array. You must use methods defined in the `ArrayList` class.

Use the `add(Object)` method to add an element to an array list, like this:

```
golfer.add("Tseng");
golfer.add("Lewis");
golfer.add("Stanford");
```

To retrieve the last string added to the list, you can use the `lastElement()` method:

```
String s = (String) golfer.lastElement();
```

The `lastElement()` method returns an `Object` because the `ArrayList` class supports all classes of objects. You must cast it to the class that was put into the list. Here, because strings were stored in `golfer`, the returned object is cast to a string.

The `get()` method retrieves a list element using a numeric index, as shown in the following code:

```
String s1 = (String) golfer.get(0);
String s2 = (String) golfer.get(2);
```

Because array list numbering is zero-based, the first call to `get()` retrieves the `"Tseng"` string, and the second call retrieves the `"Stanford"` string.

Just as you can retrieve an element at a particular index, you also can add and remove elements at an index by using the `add(int, Object)` and `remove(int)` methods:

```
golfer.add(1, "Miyazato");
golfer.add(0, "Kerr");
golfer.remove(3);
```

The first call to `add()` inserts an element at index 1, between the `"Tseng"` and `"Lewis"` strings. The `"Lewis"` and `"Stanford"` strings are moved by an element in the list to accommodate the inserted `"Miyazato"` string. The second call to `add()` inserts an element at index 0, which is the beginning of the list. All existing elements are moved up one space in the list to accommodate the inserted "Kerr" string. At this point, the contents of the list look like this:

0. "Kerr"
1. "Tseng"
2. "Miyazato"
3. "Lewis"
4. "Stanford"

The call to remove() removes the element at index 3, which is the "Lewis" string. The resulting list consists of the following strings:

0. "Kerr"
1. "Tseng"
2. "Miyazato"
3. "Stanford"

You can use the set() method to change a specific element:

```
golfer.set(1, "Kung");
```

This method replaces the "Tseng" string with the "Kung" string, resulting in the following list:

0. "Kerr"
1. "Kung"
2. "Miyazato"
3. "Stanford"

If you want to clear out the array list, you can remove all the elements with the clear() method:

```
golfer.clear();
```

The ArrayList class also provides some methods for working with elements without using indexes. These methods search through the list for a particular element. The first of these methods is the contains(Object) method, which simply checks whether an object is in the list:

```
boolean isThere = golfer.contains("Webb");
```

Another method for searching is the indexOf(*Object*) method, which finds the index of an element matching an object:

```
int i = golfer.indexOf("Stanford");
```

The indexOf() method returns the index or –1 if the object is not in the list. The remove(*Object*) method works similarly, removing an object from the list, as in this statement:

```
golfer.remove("Kung");
```

The ArrayList class offers a few methods for determining and manipulating a list's size. First, the size method determines the number of elements in the list:

```
int size = golfer.size();
```

Recall that lists have two different attributes relating to size: size and capacity. The size is the number of elements in the list, and the capacity is the amount of memory allocated to hold all the elements. The capacity is always greater than or equal to the size. You can force the capacity to exactly match the size by using the trimToSize() method:

```
golfer.trimToSize();
```

CAUTION

The Java Class Library also includes Vector, a data structure that works a lot like array lists. When you use vectors in NetBeans 7.1, a warning is displayed that calls the class an "obsolete collection." This occurs because array lists are considered a superior version of vectors.

Looping Through Data Structures

If you're interested in working sequentially with all the elements in a list, you can use the iterator() method, which returns a list of the elements you can iterate through:

```
Iterator it = golfer.iterator();
```

As you learned earlier today, you can use an iterator to step through elements sequentially. In this example, you can work with the it list using the methods defined by the Iterator interface.

The following for loop uses an iterator and its methods to traverse an entire array list:

```
for (Iterator i = golfer.iterator(); i.hasNext(); ) {
    String name = (String) i.next();
    System.out.println(name);
}
```

Today's next project demonstrates the care and feeding of array lists. The CodeKeeper class, shown in Listing 8.2, holds a set of text codes, some provided by the class and others provided by users. Because the amount of space needed to hold the codes isn't known until the program is run, an array list is used to store the data instead of an array. Create this class in NetBeans.

LISTING 8.2   The Full Text of CodeKeeper.java

```
 1: import java.util.*;
 2:
 3: public class CodeKeeper {
 4:     ArrayList list;
 5:     String[] codes = { "alpha", "lambda", "gamma", "delta", "zeta" };
 6:
 7:     public CodeKeeper(String[] userCodes) {
 8:         list = new ArrayList();
 9:         // load built-in codes
10:         for (int i = 0; i < codes.length; i++) {
11:             addCode(codes[i]);
12:         }
13:         // load user codes
14:         for (int j = 0; j < userCodes.length; j++) {
15:             addCode(userCodes[j]);
16:         }
17:         // display all codes
18:         for (Iterator ite = list.iterator(); ite.hasNext(); ) {
19:             String output = (String) ite.next();
20:             System.out.println(output);
21:         }
22:     }
23:
24:     private void addCode(String code) {
25:         if (!list.contains(code)) {
26:             list.add(code);
27:         }
28:     }
29:
30:     public static void main(String[] arguments) {
31:         CodeKeeper keeper = new CodeKeeper(arguments);
32:     }
33: }
```

NetBeans may display a warning that this class uses "unchecked or unsafe operations." This isn't as severe as it sounds. The code works properly as written and is not unsafe.

The warning serves as a strong hint that there's a better way to work with array lists and other data structures. You learn about this technique later today.

The `CodeKeeper` class uses an `ArrayList` instance variable named `list` to hold the text codes.

First, five built-in codes are read from a string array into the list (lines 10–12).

Next, any codes provided by the user as command-line arguments are added (lines 14–16).

Codes are added by calling the `addCode()` method (lines 24–28). `addCode()` adds a new text code only if it isn't already present, using the list's `contains(Object)` method to make this determination.

You add command-line arguments in NetBeans by selecting Project, Set Project Configuration, Customize. The arguments should be a list of codes separated by spaces.

After the codes have been added to the list, its contents are displayed. Running the class with the command-line arguments `"gamma"`, `"beta"`, and `"delta"` produces the following output:

Output ▼

```
alpha
lambda
gamma
delta
zeta
beta
```

A simpler `for` loop can be employed to iterate through a data structure. The loop takes the form `for (variable : structure)`, where `structure` is a data structure that implements the `Iterator` interface. The `variable` section declares an object that holds each element of the structure as the loop progresses.

This `for` loop uses an iterator and its methods to traverse an array list named `golfer`:

```
for (Object name : golfer) {
    System.out.println(name);
}
```

The loop can be used with any data structure that works with `Iterator`.

Stacks

Stacks are a data structure used to model information accessed in a specific order. The `Stack` class in Java is implemented as a last-in, first-out stack, which means that the last item added to the stack is the first one to be removed. Figure 8.2 shows the logical organization of a stack.

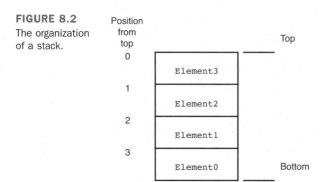

FIGURE 8.2
The organization
of a stack.

You might wonder why the numbers of the elements don't match their positions from the top of the stack. Keep in mind that elements are added to the top, so Element0, which is on the bottom, was the first element added to the stack. Likewise, Element3, which is on top, was the last element added. Also, because Element3 is at the top of the stack, it will be the first to be removed.

The Stack class defines only one constructor, which is a default constructor that creates an empty stack. You use this constructor to create a stack like this:

```
Stack s = new Stack();
```

Stacks in Java contain methods to manipulate the stack.

You can add new elements to a stack by using the push() method, which pushes an element onto the top of the stack:

```
s.push("One");
s.push("Two");
s.push("Three");
s.push("Four");
s.push("Five");
s.push("Six");
```

This code pushes six strings onto the stack, with the last string ("Six") ending up on top. You remove elements from the stack by using the pop() method, which pops them off the top:

```
String s1 = (String) s.pop();
String s2 = (String) s.pop();
```

This code pops the last two strings off the stack, leaving the first four strings and resulting in the s1 variable's containing the "Six" string and the s2 variable's containing the "Five" string.

If you want to use the top element on the stack without actually popping it off the stack, you can use the peek() method:

```
String s3 = (String) s.peek();
```

This call to peek() returns the "Four" string but leaves the string on the stack. You can search for an element on the stack by using the search() method:

```
int i = s.search("Two");
```

The search() method returns the distance from the top of the stack to the element if it is found, or –1 if not. In this case, the "Two" string is the third element from the top, so the search() method returns 2.

8

NOTE   As in all Java data structures that deal with indexes or lists, the Stack class reports element positions in a zero-based fashion: The top element in a stack has a location of 0, the fourth element down has a location of 3, and so on.

The last method defined in the Stack class is empty(), which indicates whether a stack is empty:

```
boolean isEmpty = s.empty();
```

Map

The Map interface defines a framework for implementing a key-mapped data structure, a place to store objects each referenced by a key. The key serves the same purpose as an element number in an array—it's a unique value used to access the data stored at a position in the data structure.

You can put the key-mapped approach to work by using the HashMap class or one of the other classes that implement the Map interface. You'll learn about the HashMap class in the next section.

The Map interface defines a means of storing and retrieving information based on a key. This is similar in some ways to the ArrayList class, in which elements are accessed through an index, which is a specific type of key. However, keys in the Map interface can be just about anything. You can create your own classes to use as the keys for accessing and manipulating data in a dictionary. Figure 8.3 shows how keys map to data in a dictionary.

FIGURE 8.3

The organization of a key-mapped data structure.

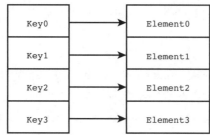

The Map interface declares a variety of methods for working with the data stored in a dictionary. Implementing classes have to implement all those methods to be truly useful. The put(*String*, *Object*) and get(*String*, *Object*) methods are used to store objects in the dictionary and retrieve them.

Assuming that look is an object that implements the Map interface, the following code shows how to use the put() method to add elements:

```
Rectangle r1 = new Rectangle(0, 0, 5, 5);
look.put("small", r1);
Rectangle r2 = new Rectangle(0, 0, 15, 15);
look.put("medium", r2);
Rectangle r3 = new Rectangle(0, 0, 25, 25);
look.put("large", r3);
```

This code adds three Rectangle objects (from the java.awt package) to the map, using strings as the keys. To get an element, use the get() method and specify the appropriate key:

```
Rectangle r = (Rectangle) look.get("medium");
```

You also can remove an element with a key by using the remove() method:

```
look.remove("large");
```

You can find out how many elements are in the structure by using the size() method, as in the ArrayList class:

```
int size = look.size();
```

You also can check whether the structure is empty by using the isEmpty() method:

```
boolean isEmpty = look.isEmpty();
```

Hash Maps

The HashMap class implements the Map interface and provides a complete implementation of a key-mapped data structure. Hash maps let you store data based on some type of key and have an efficiency defined by the map's load factor. The load factor is a floating-point number between 0.0 and 1.0 that determines how and when the hash map allocates space for more elements.

Like array lists, hash maps have a capacity, or an amount of allocated memory. Hash maps allocate memory by comparing the map's current size with the product of the capacity and the load factor. If the size of the hash map exceeds this product, the map increases its capacity by rehashing itself.

8

Load factors closer to 1.0 result in a more efficient use of memory at the expense of a longer lookup time for each element. Similarly, load factors closer to 0.0 result in more efficient lookups but tend to be more wasteful with memory. Determining the load factor for your own hash maps depends on how you use each map and whether your priority is performance or memory efficiency.

You can create hash maps in one of three ways. The first constructor creates a default hash map with an initial capacity of 16 elements and a load factor of 0.75:

```
HashMap hash = new HashMap();
```

The second constructor creates a hash map with the specified initial capacity and a load factor of 0.75:

```
HashMap hash = new HashMap(20);
```

Finally, the third constructor creates a hash map with the specified initial capacity and load factor:

```
HashMap hash = new HashMap(20, 0.5F);
```

All the abstract methods defined in Map are implemented in the HashMap class. In addition, the HashMap class implements a few others that perform functions specific to supporting maps. One of these is the clear() method, which clears a map of all its keys and elements:

```
hash.clear();
```

The containsValue(Object) method checks whether an object is stored in the hash map:

```
Rectangle box = new Rectangle(0, 0, 5, 5);
boolean isThere = hash.containsValue(box);
```

The containsKey(String) method searches a map for a key:

```
boolean isThere = hash.containsKey("Small");
```

The practical use of a hash map comes from its capability to represent data that is too time-consuming to search or reference by value. The data structure comes in handy when you're working with complex data and it's more efficient to access the data by using a key rather than comparing the data objects themselves.

Furthermore, hash maps typically compute a key for elements, which is called a hash code. For example, a string can have an integer hash code computed for it that uniquely represents the string. When a bunch of strings are stored in a hash map, the map can access the strings by using integer hash codes as opposed to using the contents of the strings themselves. This results in much more efficient searching and retrieving capabilities.

A hash code is a computed key that uniquely identifies each element in a hash map.

This technique of computing and using hash codes for object storage and reference is exploited heavily throughout the Java Class Library. The parent of all classes, `Object`, defines a `hashCode()` method overridden in most standard Java classes. Any class that defines a `hashCode()` method can be efficiently stored and accessed in a hash map. A class that wants to be hashed also must implement the `equals()` method, which defines a way of telling whether two objects are equal. The `equals()` method usually just performs a straight comparison of all the member variables defined in a class.

The next project you undertake today uses maps for a shopping application.

The ComicBooks application prices collectible comic books according to their base value and condition. The condition is described as one of the following: mint, near mint, very fine, fine, good, or poor. Each condition has a specific effect on a comic's value:

- "Mint" books are worth 3 times their base price.
- "Near mint" books are worth 2 times their base price.
- "Very fine" books are worth 1.5 times their base price.
- "Fine" books are worth their base price.
- "Good" books are worth 0.5 times their base price.
- "Poor" books are worth 0.25 times their base price.

To associate text such as "mint" or "very fine" with a numeric value, they are put into a hash map. The keys to the map are the condition descriptions, and the values are floating-point numbers such as 3.0, 1.5, and 0.25.

Enter the code shown in Listing 8.3 in NetBeans as the class `ComicBooks`.

LISTING 8.3   The Full Text of ComicBooks.java

```
 1: import java.util.*;
 2:
 3: public class ComicBooks {
 4:
 5:     public ComicBooks() {
 6:     }
 7:
 8:     public static void main(String[] arguments) {
 9:         // set up hash map
10:         HashMap quality = new HashMap();
11:         float price1 = 3.00F;
12:         quality.put("mint", price1);
13:         float price2 = 2.00F;
14:         quality.put("near mint", price2);
15:         float price3 = 1.50F;
16:         quality.put("very fine", price3);
17:         float price4 = 1.00F;
18:         quality.put("fine", price4);
19:         float price5 = 0.50F;
20:         quality.put("good", price5);
21:         float price6 = 0.25F;
22:         quality.put("poor", price6);
23:         // set up collection
24:         Comic[] comix = new Comic[3];
25:         comix[0] = new Comic("Amazing Spider-Man", "1A", "very fine",
26:             5_000.00F);
27:         comix[0].setPrice( (Float) quality.get(comix[0].condition) );
28:         comix[1] = new Comic("Incredible Hulk", "181", "near mint",
29:             240.00F);
30:         comix[1].setPrice( (Float) quality.get(comix[1].condition) );
31:         comix[2] = new Comic("Cerebus", "1A", "good", 144.00F);
32:         comix[2].setPrice( (Float) quality.get(comix[2].condition) );
33:         for (int i = 0; i < comix.length; i++) {
34:             System.out.println("Title: " + comix[i].title);
35:             System.out.println("Issue: " + comix[i].issueNumber);
36:             System.out.println("Condition: " + comix[i].condition);
37:             System.out.println("Price: $" + comix[i].price + "\n");
38:         }
39:     }
40: }
41:
42: class Comic {
43:     String title;
44:     String issueNumber;
45:     String condition;
46:     float basePrice;
47:     float price;
48:
49:     Comic(String inTitle, String inIssueNumber, String inCondition,
```

8

LISTING 8.3 Continued

```
50:            float inBasePrice) {
51:
52:            title = inTitle;
53:            issueNumber = inIssueNumber;
54:            condition = inCondition;
55:            basePrice = inBasePrice;
56:        }
57:
58:     void setPrice(float factor) {
59:            price = basePrice * factor;
60:        }
61: }
```

When you run the ComicBooks application, it produces the following output:

Output ▼

```
Title: Amazing Spider-Man
Issue: 1A
Condition: very fine
Price: $7500.0

Title: Incredible Hulk
Issue: 181
Condition: near mint
Price: $480.0

Title: Cerebus
Issue: 1A
Condition: good
Price: $72.0
```

The ComicBooks application is implemented as two classes: an application class called ComicBooks and a helper class called Comic.

In the application, the hash map is created in lines 9–22.

First, the map is created in line 10.

Next, a float called price1 is created with the value 3.00. This value is added to the map and associated with the key "mint". (Remember that hash maps, like other data structures, can hold only objects. The float value is automatically converted to a Float object through autoboxing.)

The process is repeated for each of the other comic book conditions, from "near mint" to "poor."

After the hash map is set up, an array of `Comic` objects called `comix` is created to hold each comic book currently for sale.

The `Comic` constructor is called with four arguments: the book's title, issue number, condition, and base price. The first three are strings, and the last is a `float`.

After a `Comic` has been created, its `setPrice(float)` method is called to set the book's price based on its condition. Here's an example, line 27:

```
comix[0].setPrice( (Float) quality.get(comix[0].condition) );
```

The hash map's `get(String)` method is called with the book's condition, a string that is one of the keys in the map. An `Object` is returned that represents the value associated with that key. (In line 27, because `comix[0].condition` is equal to `"very fine"`, `get()` returns the floating-point value 3.00F.)

Because `get()` returns an `Object`, it must be cast as a `Float`. The `Float` argument is unboxed as a `float` value automatically through unboxing.

This process is repeated for two more books.

Lines 33–38 display information about each comic book in the `comix` array.

The `Comic` class is defined in lines 42–61. It has five instance variables—the `String` object's `title`, `issueNumber`, and `condition`, and the floating-point value's `basePrice` and `price`.

The constructor method of the class, located in lines 49–56, sets the value of four instance variables to the arguments sent to the constructor.

The `setPrice(Float)` method in lines 58–60 sets the price of a comic book. The argument sent to the method is a `float` value. A comic's price is calculated by multiplying this `float` by the comic's base price. Consequently, if a book is worth $1,000, and its multiplier is 2.0, the book is priced at $2,000.

Hash maps are a powerful data structure for manipulating large amounts of data. The fact that these maps are so widely supported in the Java Class Library via the `Object` class should give you a clue as to their importance in Java programming.

Generics

The data structures that you learned about today are some of the most essential utility classes in the Java Class Library.

Hash maps, array lists, stacks, and the other structures in the `java.util` package are useful regardless of the kind of programs you want to develop. Almost every software program handles data in some manner.

These data structures are well suited for use in code that applies generically to a wide range of classes of objects. A method written to manipulate array lists could be written to function equally well on strings, string buffers, character arrays, or other objects that represent text. A method in an accounting program could take objects that represent integers, floating-point numbers, and other math classes, using each to calculate a balance.

This flexibility comes at a price: When a data structure works with any kind of object, the Java compiler can't display a warning when the structure is being misused.

For instance, the ComicBooks application uses a hash map named `quality` to associate condition descriptions such as "mint" and "good" with price multipliers. Here's the statement for "near mint":

```
quality.put("near mint", 1.50F);
```

By design, the `quality` map should hold only floating-point values (as `Float` objects). However, the class compiles successfully regardless of the class of the value added to a map. You might goof and unintentionally add a string to the map, as in this revised statement:

```
quality.put("near mint", "1.50");
```

The class compiles successfully, but when it is run, it fails with a `ClassCastException` error in the following statement:

```
comix[1].setPrice( (Float) quality.get(comix[1].condition) );
```

The reason for the error is that the statement tries to cast the map's "near mint" value to a `Float`, which fails because it receives the string `"1.50"` instead.

Runtime errors are much more troublesome for programmers than compiler errors. A compiler error stops you in your tracks and must be fixed before you can continue. A runtime error might creep its way into the code, unbeknownst to you, and cause problems for users of your software.

You can specify the class or classes expected in a data structure using a feature of the language called *generics*.

The expected class information is added to statements where the structure is assigned a variable or created with a constructor. The class or classes are placed within < and > characters and follow the name of the class, as in this statement:

```
ArrayList<Integer> zipCodes = new ArrayList<>();
```

This statement creates an array list that will be used to hold `Integer` objects. Because the list is declared in this manner, the following statements cause a compiler error that NetBeans will flag in the source code editor:

```
zipCodes.add("90210");
zipCodes.add("02134");
zipCodes.add("20500");
```

The compiler recognizes that String objects do not belong in this array list. The proper way to add elements to the list is to use integer values:

```
zipCodes.add(90210);
zipCodes.add(02134);
zipCodes.add(20500);
```

Data structures that use multiple classes, such as hash maps, take these class names separated by commas within the < and > characters.

The ComicBooks application can take advantage of generics by changing line 10 of Listing 8.3 to the following:

```
HashMap<String, Float> quality = new HashMap<>();
```

This sets up a map to use String objects for keys and Float objects for values. With this statement in place, a string no longer can be added as the value for a condition such as "near mint." A compiler error flags a problem of this kind.

Generics also make it easier to retrieve an object from a data structure because you don't have to use casting to convert them to the desired class. For example, the quality map no longer requires a cast to produce Float objects in statements like this one:

```
comix[1].setPrice(quality.get(comix[1].condition));
```

From a stylistic standpoint, the addition of generics in variable declarations and constructor methods is likely to appear intimidating. However, after you become accustomed to working with them (and using autoboxing, unboxing, and the new for loops), data structures are significantly easier to work with and less error-prone.

The CodeKeeper2 class, shown in Listing 8.4, is a new version of CodeKeeper that has been rewritten to use generics, type inference, and the for loop that can iterate through data structures such as array lists.

LISTING 8.4   The Full Text of CodeKeeper2.java

```
1: import java.util.*;
2:
3: public class CodeKeeper2 {
4:     ArrayList<String> list;
5:     String[] codes = { "alpha", "lambda", "gamma", "delta", "zeta" };
6:
7:     public CodeKeeper2(String[] userCodes) {
8:         list = new ArrayList<>();
```

LISTING 8.4   Continued

```
 9:          // load built-in codes
10:          for (int i = 0; i < codes.length; i++) {
11:              addCode(codes[i]);
12:          }
13:          // load user codes
14:          for (int j = 0; j < userCodes.length; j++) {
15:              addCode(userCodes[j]);
16:          }
17:          // display all codes
18:          for (String code : list) {
19:              System.out.println(code);
20:          }
21:      }
22:
23:      private void addCode(String code) {
24:          if (!list.contains(code)) {
25:              list.add(code);
26:          }
27:      }
28:
29:      public static void main(String[] arguments) {
30:          CodeKeeper2 keeper = new CodeKeeper2(arguments);
31:      }
32: }
```

The only modifications to the class are in line 4, where the new generics declaration for an array list of strings is made; line 8, where type inference figures out the proper generics declaration; and lines 18 and 19, the simpler for loop that displays all the codes.

NOTE

Prior to Java 7, a statement that used generics had to refer to the classes every time within the < and > characters, as in these examples:

```
ArrayList<Integer> zipCodes = new ArrayList<Integer>();
HashMap<String, Float> quality = new HashMap<String,
Float>();
```

One of the improvements in Java 7 is type *inference*, which enables the compiler to infer the proper class or classes whenever possible. The diamond operator (<>) appears with nothing in it:

```
ArrayList<Integer> zipCodes = new ArrayList<>();
HashMap<String, Float> quality = new HashMap<>();
```

In these statements, the <> infers the classes involved based on what they would have to be for the statement to make sense.

Summary

Today, you learned about several data structures you can use in your Java programs:

- **Bit sets**—Large sets of Boolean on-or-off values
- **Array lists**—Arrays that can change in size dynamically and be shrunken or expanded as needed
- **Stacks**—Structures in which the last item added is the first item removed
- **Hash maps**—Objects stored and retrieved using unique keys

These data structures are part of the `java.util` package, a collection of useful classes for handling data, dates, strings, and other things. The addition of generics and new `for` loops for iteration enhances their capabilities.

Learning about the ways in which you can organize data in Java has benefits in all aspects of software development. Whether you're learning the language to write servlets, desktop applications, phone apps, or something else, you need to represent data in numerous ways.

Q&A

Q **The `HolidaySked` project from today could be implemented as an array of Boolean values. Is one way preferable to the other?**

A That depends. One thing you'll find as you work with data structures is that there are often many different ways to implement something. Bit sets are somewhat preferable to a Boolean array when the size of your program matters because a bit set is smaller. An array of a primitive type such as Boolean is preferable when the speed of your program matters because arrays are somewhat faster. In the example of the `HolidaySked` class, it's so small that the difference is negligible, but as you develop your own robust, real-world applications, these kinds of decisions can make a difference.

Q **The Java compiler's warning for data structures that don't use generics is pretty ominous. It doesn't sound like a very good idea to release a class that has "unchecked or unsafe operations." Is there any reason to stick with old code or not use generics with data structures?**

A The compiler's warning about safety is a bit overstated. Java programmers have been using array lists, hash maps, and other structures for years in their classes, creating software that runs reliably and safely. The lack of generics meant that more work was necessary to ensure that runtime problems didn't occur because of wrong classes being placed in a structure.

It's more accurate to state that data structures can be made more safe through the use of generics, rather than suggesting that previous versions of Java were unsafe.

My personal rule of thumb is to use generics in new code and old code that's being reorganized or significantly rewritten and leave alone old code that works correctly.

Quiz

Review today's material by taking this three-question quiz. Answers are at the end of the book.

Questions

1. Which of the following kinds of data cannot be stored in a hash map?

    A. `String`

    B. `int`

    C. Both can be stored in a map.

2. An array list is created, and three strings, `"Tinker"`, `"Evers"`, and `"Chance"`, are added to it. The method `remove("Evers")` is called. Which of the following `ArrayList` methods retrieves the string `"Chance"`?

    A. `get(1);`

    B. `get(2);`

    C. `get("Chance");`

3. Which of these classes implements the `Map` interface?

    A. `Stack`

    B. `HashMap`

    C. `BitSet`

Certification Practice

The following question is the kind of thing you could expect to be asked on a Java programming certification test. Answer it without looking at today's material or using the Java compiler to test the code.

Given:

```
public class Recursion {
    public int dex = -1;

    public Recursion() {
        dex = getValue(17);
    }

    public int getValue(int dexValue) {
        if (dexValue > 100)
            return dexValue;
        else
            return getValue(dexValue * 2);
    }

    public static void main(String[] arguments) {
        Recursion r = new Recursion();
        System.out.println(r.dex);
    }
}
```

What will be the output of this application?

A. -1

B. 17

C. 34

D. 136

The answer is available on the book's website at www.java21days.com. Visit the Day 8 page and click the Certification Practice link.

Exercises

To extend your knowledge of the subjects covered today, try the following exercises:

1. Add two more conditions to the ComicBooks application: "pristine mint" for books that should sell at 5 times their base price and "coverless" for books that should sell at one-tenth of their base price.

2. Create an application that uses an array list as a shopping cart that holds Fruit objects. Each Fruit object should have a name, quantity, and price.

Where applicable, exercise solutions are offered on the book's website at www.java21days.com.

DAY 9
Working with Swing

Computer users today expect the software they use to feature a graphical user interface (GUI) with a variety of widgets such as text boxes, sliders, and scrollbars. The Java class library includes a set of packages called Swing that enable Java programs to offer a sophisticated GUI and collect user input with the mouse, keyboard, and other input devices.

Today, you will use Swing to create applications that feature these GUI components:

- **Frames**—Windows that can include a title bar; menu bar; and Maximize, Minimize, and Close buttons

- **Containers**—Interface elements that can hold other components

- **Buttons**—Clickable regions with text or graphics indicating their purpose

- **Labels**—Text or graphics that provide information

- **Text fields and text areas**—Windows that accept keyboard input and allow text to be edited

- **Drop-down lists**—Groups of related items that can be selected from drop-down menus or scrolling windows

- **Check boxes and radio buttons**—Small squares or circles that can be selected or deselected

- **Image icons**—Graphics that can be added to buttons, labels, and other components

- **Scrolling panes**—Panels that hold components too big for a user interface that are accessed in full with a scrollbar

Creating an Application

Swing enables you to create a Java program with an interface that adopts the style of the native operating system, such as Windows or Linux or a style that's unique to Java. Each of these styles is called a *look and feel* because it describes both the appearance of the interface and how its components function when they are used.

Java 7 introduces a distinctive new look and feel called Nimbus that's unique to Java.

Swing components are part of the `javax.swing` package, a standard part of the Java class library. To refer to a Swing class using its short name—without referring to the package, in other words—you must make it available with an `import` statement or use a catchall statement such as the following:

```
import javax.swing.*;
```

Two other packages that are used to support GUI programming are `java.awt`, the Abstract Windowing Toolkit (AWT), and `java.awt.event`, event-handling classes that handle user input.

When you use a Swing component, you work with objects of that component's class. You create the component by calling its constructor and then calling methods of the component as needed for proper setup.

All Swing components are subclasses of the abstract class `JComponent`. It includes methods to set a component's size, change the background color, define the font used for any displayed text, and set up *ToolTips* (explanatory text that appears when you hover the mouse over the component for a few seconds).

CAUTION

Swing classes inherit from many of the same superclasses as the Abstract Windowing Toolkit, so it is possible to use Swing and AWT components together in the same interface. However, the two types of components will not be rendered correctly in a container, so it's best to always use Swing components—there's one for every AWT component.

Before components can be displayed in a user interface, they must be added to a *container*, a component that can hold other components. Swing containers are subclasses of `java.awt.Container`. This class includes methods to add and remove components from a container, arrange components using an object called a layout manager, and set up borders around the edges of a container. Containers often can be placed in other containers.

Creating an Interface

The first step in creating a Swing application is to create a class that represents the main GUI. An object of this class serves as a container that holds all the other components to be displayed.

In many projects, the main interface object is a frame (the JFrame class). Frames are the window shown whenever you open an application on your computer, regardless of the language it was programmed in. Frames have a title bar; Maximize, Minimize, and Close buttons; and other features.

In a graphical environment such as Windows or Mac OS, users expect to be able to move, resize, and close the windows of programs they run. One way to create a graphical Java application is to make the interface a subclass of JFrame, as in the following class declaration:

```
public class FeedReader extends JFrame {
    // ...
}
```

The constructor of the class should handle the following tasks:

- Call a superclass constructor to give the frame a title and handle other setup procedures.
- Set the size of the frame's window, either by specifying the width and height in pixels or by letting Swing choose the right size.
- Decide what to do if a user closes the window.
- Display the frame.

The JFrame class has the simple constructors JFrame() and JFrame(*String*). One sets the frame's title bar to the specified text, and the other leaves the title bar empty. You also can set the title by calling the frame's setTitle(*String*) method.

The size of a frame can be established by calling the setSize(*int, int*) method with the width and height as arguments. A frame's size is indicated in pixels, so calling setSize(650, 550) creates a frame 650 pixels wide and 550 pixels tall, taking up most of a screen that has 800×600 resolution.

9

You also can call the method setSize(*Dimension*) to set up a frame's size. Dimension is a class in the java.awt package that represents the width and height of a user interface component. Calling the Dimension(*int, int*) constructor creates a Dimension object representing the width and height specified as arguments.

Another way to set a frame's size is to fill the frame with the components it will contain and then call the frame's pack() method. This resizes the frame based on the size of the components inside it. If the frame is bigger than it needs to be, pack() shrinks it to the minimum size required to display the components. If the frame is too small (or the size has not been set), pack() expands it to the required size.

Frames are invisible when they are created. You can make them visible by calling the frame's setVisible(*boolean*) method with the literal true as an argument.

If you want a frame to be displayed when it is created, call one of these methods in the constructor. You also can leave the frame invisible, requiring any class that uses the frame to make it visible by calling setVisible(true). As you probably have surmised, calling setVisible(false) makes a frame invisible.

When a frame is displayed, the default behavior is for it to be positioned in the upper-left corner of the computer's desktop.

You can specify a different location by calling the setBounds(*int, int, int, int*) method. The first two arguments to this method are the (x,y) position of the frame's upper-left corner on the desktop. The last two arguments set the frame's width and height.

Another way to set the bounds is with a Rectangle object from the java.awt package. Create the rectangle with the Rectangle(*int, int, int, int*) constructor. The first two arguments are the (x, y) position of the upper-left corner. The next two are the width and height. Call setBounds(*Rectangle*) to draw the frame at that spot.

The following class represents a 300×100 frame with "Edit Payroll" in the title bar:

```
public class Payroll extends javax.swing.JFrame {
    public Payroll() {
        super("Edit Payroll");
        setSize(300, 100);
        setVisible(true);
    }
}
```

Every frame has Maximize, Minimize, and Close buttons on the title bar that the user can control—the same controls present in the interface of other software running on your computer.

The normal behavior when a frame is closed is for the application to keep running. When a frame serves as a program's main GUI, this leaves a user with no way to stop the program.

To change this, you must call a frame's `setDefaultCloseOperation()` method with one of four static variables of the `JFrame` class as an argument:

- `EXIT_ON_CLOSE`—Exits the application when the frame is closed
- `DISPOSE_ON_CLOSE`—Closes the frame, removes the frame object from Java virtual machine memory, and keeps running the application
- `DO_NOTHING_ON_CLOSE`—Keeps the frame open and continues running
- `HIDE_ON_CLOSE`—Closes the frame and continues running

To prevent a user from closing a frame, add the following statement to the frame's constructor method:

```
setDefaultCloseOperation(JFrame.DO_NOTHING_ON_CLOSE);
```

If you are creating a frame to serve as an application's main user interface, the expected behavior is probably `EXIT_ON_CLOSE`, which shuts down the application along with the frame.

As mentioned earlier, you can customize the overall appearance of a user interface in Java by designating a look and feel. The `UIManager` class in the `javax.swing` package manages this aspect of Swing. To set the look and feel, call the class method `setLookAndFeel(String)` with the name of the look and feel's class as the argument. Here's how to choose Nimbus, the new look and feel introduced in Java 7:

```
UIManager.setLookAndFeel(
    "com.sun.java.swing.plaf.nimbus.NimbusLookAndFeel"
);
```

This method call should be contained within a `try-catch` block because it might generate five different exceptions. Catching the `Exception` class and ignoring it causes the default look and feel to be used in the unlikely circumstance that Nimbus can't be chosen properly.

CAUTION | Using EXIT_ON_CLOSE shuts down the entire Java virtual machine, so it only should be used in the frame for an application's main window. If anything needs to happen after the frame closes, DISPOSE_ON_CLOSE or HIDE_ON_CLOSE should be used instead.

Developing a Framework

Today's first project is an application that displays a frame containing no other interface components. In NetBeans, create a new Java file with the class name SimpleFrame and enter Listing 9.1 (shown next) as the source code. This simple application displays a frame 300×100 pixels in size and can serve as a framewok—pun unavoidable—for any applications you create that use a GUI.

LISTING 9.1 The Full Text of SimpleFrame.java

```
 1: import javax.swing.*;
 2:
 3: public class SimpleFrame extends JFrame {
 4:     public SimpleFrame() {
 5:         super("Frame Title");
 6:         setSize(300, 100);
 7:         setDefaultCloseOperation(JFrame.EXIT_ON_CLOSE);
 8:         setLookAndFeel();
 9:         setVisible(true);
10:     }
11:
12:     private static void setLookAndFeel() {
13:         try {
14:             UIManager.setLookAndFeel(
15:                 "com.sun.java.swing.plaf.nimbus.NimbusLookAndFeel"
16:             );
17:         } catch (Exception exc) {
18:             // ignore error
19:         }
20:     }
21:
22:     public static void main(String[] arguments) {
23:         setLookAndFeel();
24:         SimpleFrame sf = new SimpleFrame();
25:     }
26: }
```

When you compile and run the application, you should see the frame displayed in Figure 9.1.

FIGURE 9.1

Displaying a frame.

The SimpleFrame application isn't much to look at. The GUI contains no components, aside from the standard Minimize, Maximize, and Close (X) buttons on the title bar, as shown in Figure 9.1. You will add components later today.

In the application, a SimpleFrame object is created in the main() method in lines 22–25. If you had not displayed the frame when it was constructed, you could call sf.setVisible(true) in the main() method to display the frame.

Nimbus is set as the frame's look and feel in lines 14–16.

The work involved in creating the frame's user interface takes place in the SimpleFrame() constructor in lines 4–10. Components can be created and added to the frame within this constructor.

Creating a Component

Creating a GUI is a great way to get experience working with objects in Java, because each interface component is represented by its own class.

To use an interface component in Java, you create an object of that component's class. You already have worked with the container class JFrame.

One of the simplest components to employ is JButton, the class that represents clickable buttons.

In most programs, buttons trigger an action. You can click Install to begin installing software, click a smiley button to begin a new game of Angry Birds, click the Minimize button to prevent your boss from seeing Angry Birds running, and so on.

A Swing button can feature a text label, a graphical icon, or a combination of both.

Constructors you can use for buttons include the following:

- JButton(*String*)—A button labeled with the specified text
- JButton(*Icon*)—A button that displays the specified graphical icon
- JButton(*String*, *Icon*)—A button with the specified text and graphical icon

The following statements create three buttons with text labels:

```
JButton play = new JButton("Play");
JButton stop = new JButton("Stop");
JButton rewind = new JButton("Rewind");
```

Graphical buttons are covered later today.

Adding Components to a Container

Before you can display a user interface component such as a button in a Java program, you must add it to a container and display that container.

To add a component to a container, call the container's add(*Component*) method with the component as the argument (all user interface components in Swing inherit from java.awt.Component).

The simplest Swing container is a panel (the JPanel class). The following example creates a button and adds it to a panel:

```
JButton quit = new JButton("Quit");
JPanel panel = new JPanel();
panel.add(quit);
```

Use the same technique to add components to frames and windows.

The ButtonFrame class, shown in Listing 9.2, expands on the application framework created earlier today. A panel is created, three buttons are added to the panel, and then it is added to a frame. Enter the source code of Listing 9.2 into a new Java file called ButtonFrame in NetBeans.

LISTING 9.2   The Full Text of ButtonFrame.java

```
 1: import javax.swing.*;
 2:
 3: public class ButtonFrame extends JFrame {
 4:     JButton load = new JButton("Load");
 5:     JButton save = new JButton("Save");
 6:     JButton unsubscribe = new JButton("Unsubscribe");
 7:
 8:     public ButtonFrame() {
 9:         super("Button Frame");
10:         setSize(340, 170);
11:         setDefaultCloseOperation(JFrame.EXIT_ON_CLOSE);
12:         JPanel pane = new JPanel();
13:         pane.add(load);
14:         pane.add(save);
```

LISTING 9.2   Continued

```
15:             pane.add(unsubscribe);
16:             add(pane);
17:             setVisible(true);
18:         }
19:
20:     private static void setLookAndFeel() {
21:             try {
22:                 UIManager.setLookAndFeel(
23:                     "com.sun.java.swing.plaf.nimbus.NimbusLookAndFeel"
24:                 );
25:             } catch (Exception exc) {
26:                 System.out.println(exc.getMessage());
27:             }
28:         }
29:
30:     public static void main(String[] arguments) {
31:             setLookAndFeel();
32:             ButtonFrame bf = new ButtonFrame();
33:         }
34: }
```

When you run the application, a small frame opens that contains the three buttons, as shown in Figure 9.2.

FIGURE 9.2
The ButtonFrame
application.

The ButtonFrame class has three instance variables: the load, save, and unsubscribe JButton objects.

In lines 12–15 of Listing 9.2, a new JPanel object is created, and the three buttons are added to the panel by calls to its add(Component) method. When the panel contains all the buttons, the frame's own add(Component) method is called in line 16 with the panel as an argument, adding it to the frame.

NOTE

> If you click the buttons, nothing happens. Doing something in response to a button click is covered on Day 12, "Responding to User Input."

Working with Components

Swing offers more than two dozen different user interface components in addition to the buttons and containers you have used so far. You will work with many of these components for the rest of today and on Day 10, "Building a Swing Interface."

All Swing components share a common superclass, `javax.swing.JComponent`, from which they inherit several methods you will find useful in your own programs.

The `setEnabled(boolean)` method determines whether a component can receive user input (an argument of `true`) or is inactive and cannot receive input (`false`). Components are enabled by default. Many components change in appearance to indicate when they are not presently usable. For instance, a disabled `JButton` has light gray borders and gray text. If you want to check whether a component is enabled, you can call the `isEnabled()` method, which returns a `boolean` value.

The `setVisible(boolean)` method works for all components the way it does for containers. Use `true` to display a component and `false` to hide it. There also is a `boolean` `isVisible()` method.

The `setSize(int, int)` method resizes the component to the width and height specified as arguments, and `setSize(Dimension)` uses a `Dimension` object to accomplish the same thing. For most components, you don't need to set a size; the default is usually acceptable. To find out a component's size, call its `getSize()` method, which returns a `Dimension` object with the dimensions in `height` and `width` instance variables.

As you will see, similar Swing components also have other methods in common, such as `setText()` and `getText()` for text components and `setValue()` and `getValue()` for components that store a numeric value.

CAUTION

> When you begin working with Swing components, a common source of mistakes is to set up aspects of a component after it has been added to a container. Be sure to set up a component fully before placing it in a panel or any other container.

Image Icons

Swing supports the use of graphical `ImageIcon` objects on buttons and other components in which a label can be provided. An *icon* is a small graphic that can be placed on a button, label, or other user interface element to identify it. Examples include a garbage can or recycling bin icon for deleting files and folder icons for opening and storing files.

You can create an `ImageIcon` object by specifying the filename of a graphic as the only argument to the constructor. The following example loads an icon from the graphics file `subscribe.gif` and creates a `JButton` with the icon as its label:

```
ImageIcon subscribe = new ImageIcon("subscribe.gif");
JButton button = new JButton(subscribe);
JPanel pane = new JPanel();
pane.add(button);
add(pane);
setVisible(true);
```

Listing 9.3 is a Java application that creates four image icons with text labels, adds them to a panel, and then adds the panel to a frame. Create a new empty Java file in NetBeans for a class named `IconFrame` and enter this listing with the source code editor.

LISTING 9.3 The Full Text of `IconFrame.java`

```
 1: import javax.swing.*;
 2:
 3: public class IconFrame extends JFrame {
 4:     JButton load, save, subscribe, unsubscribe;
 5:
 6:     public IconFrame() {
 7:         super("Icon Frame");
 8:         setDefaultCloseOperation(JFrame.EXIT_ON_CLOSE);
 9:         JPanel panel = new JPanel();
10:         // create icons
11:         ImageIcon loadIcon = new ImageIcon("load.gif");
12:         ImageIcon saveIcon = new ImageIcon("save.gif");
13:         ImageIcon subscribeIcon = new ImageIcon("subscribe.gif");
14:         ImageIcon unsubscribeIcon = new ImageIcon("unsubscribe.gif");
15:         // create buttons
16:         load = new JButton("Load", loadIcon);
17:         save = new JButton("Save", saveIcon);
18:         subscribe = new JButton("Subscribe", subscribeIcon);
19:         unsubscribe = new JButton("Unsubscribe", unsubscribeIcon);
20:         // add buttons to panel
21:         panel.add(load);
22:         panel.add(save);
23:         panel.add(subscribe);
```

9

LISTING 9.3 Continued

```
24:            panel.add(unsubscribe);
25:            // add the panel to a frame
26:            add(panel);
27:            pack();
28:            setVisible(true);
29:        }
30:
31:        public static void main(String[] arguments) {
32:            IconFrame ike = new IconFrame();
33:        }
34: }
```

Figure 9.3 shows the result.

FIGURE 9.3
An interface containing buttons labeled with icons.

The icons' graphics referred to in lines 11–14 can be found on this book's official website at www.java21days.com on the Day 9 page.

In NetBeans, the graphics must be part of the project before this application runs correctly. The graphics need to be stored in the main folder of the Java21 project you've been using throughout this book to hold the classes you create. Follow these steps:

1. Save the graphics files to a temporary folder on your computer.

2. Click the Files tab to bring that pane to the front. The Files pane opens, as shown in Figure 9.4, listing the files in the project.

3. Drag and drop the four graphics files into the Java21 folder in this pane.

The IconFrame application does not set the size of the frame in pixels. Instead, the pack() method is called in line 27 to expand the frame to the minimum size required to present the four buttons next to each other.

If the frame were set to be tall rather than wide—for instance, by calling setSize (100, 400) in the constructor—the buttons would be stacked vertically.

Files tab

FIGURE 9.4

Dragging files into the NetBeans Files pane.

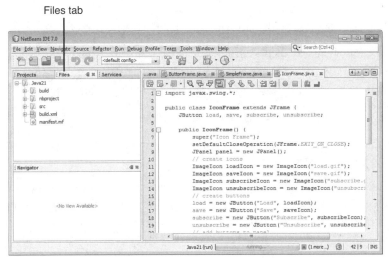

> **NOTE**
>
> Some of the project's graphics are from Oracle's Java Look and Feel Graphics Repository, a collection of icons suitable for use in your own programs. If you're looking for icons to experiment with in Swing applications, you can find some at the following address: http://java.sun.com/developer/techDocs/hi/repository.

Labels

A *label* is a user component that holds text, an icon, or both. Labels, which are created from the JLabel class, identify the purpose of other components on an interface. A user cannot edit them directly.

To create a label, you can use these simple constructors:

- JLabel(*String*)—A label with the specified text
- JLabel(*String*, *int*)—A label with the specified text and alignment
- JLabel(*String*, *Icon*, *int*)—A label with the specified text, icon, and alignment

A label's alignment determines how its text or icon is aligned in relation to the area taken up by the window. Three static class variables of the SwingConstants interface are used to specify alignment: LEFT, CENTER, and RIGHT.

You can set a label's contents with the setText(*String*) or setIcon(*Icon*) methods. You also can retrieve these things with the getText() and getIcon() methods.

The following statements create three labels with left, center, and right alignment, respectively:

```
JLabel feedsLabel = new JLabel("Feeds", SwingConstants.LEFT);
JLabel urlLabel = new JLabel("URL: ", SwingConstants.CENTER);
JLabel dateLabel = new JLabel("Date: ", SwingConstants.RIGHT);
```

Text Fields

A *text field* is a location on an interface where a user can enter and modify text using the keyboard. Text fields are represented by the JTextField class, and each can handle one line of input. The next section describes a text area component that can handle multiple lines.

Constructors for text fields include the following:

- JTextField()—An empty text field
- JTextField(*int*)—A text field with the specified width
- JTextField(*String, int*)—A text field with the specified text and width

A text field's width attribute has relevance only if the interface is organized in a manner that does not resize components. You will get more experience with this when you work with layout managers on Day 11, "Arranging Components on a User Interface."

The following statements create an empty text field that has enough space for roughly 60 characters and a text field of the same size with the starting text "Enter feed URL here":

```
JTextField rssUrl = new JTextField(60);
JTextField rssUrl2 = new JTextField(
    "Enter feed URL here", 60);
```

Text fields and text areas both inherit from the superclass JTextComponent and share many common methods.

The setEditable(*boolean*) method determines whether a text component can be edited (true) or not (false). An isEditable() method returns a corresponding boolean value.

The setText(*String*) method changes the text to the specified string, and the getText() method returns the component's current text as a string. Another method retrieves only the text that a user has highlighted in the getSelectedText() component.

Password fields are text fields that hide the characters a user types into the field. They are represented by the JPasswordField class, a subclass of JTextField. The JPasswordField constructors take the same arguments as those of the parent class.

After you have created a password field, call its setEchoChar(char) method to obscure input by replacing each input character with the specified character.

The following statements create a password field and set its echo character to #:

```
JPasswordField codePhrase = new JPasswordField(20);
codePhrase.setEchoChar('#');
```

9

Text Areas

Text areas, editable text fields that can handle more than one line of input, are implemented by the JTextArea class, which includes these constructors:

- JTextArea(int, int)—A text area with the specified number of rows and columns
- JTextArea(String, int, int) — A text area with the specified text, rows, and columns

You can use the getText(), getSelectedText(), and setText(String) methods with text areas as you would text fields. Also, an append(String) method adds the specified text at the end of the current text, and an insert(String, int) method inserts the specified text at the indicated position.

The setLineWrap(boolean) method determines whether text will wrap to the next line when it reaches the right edge of the component. Call setLineWrap(true) to cause line wrapping to occur.

The setWrapStyleWord(boolean) method determines what wraps to the next line— either the current word (true) or the current character (false).

The next project you create, the Authenticator application shown in Listing 9.4, uses several Swing components to collect user input: a text field, a password field, and a text area. Labels also are used to indicate the purpose of each text component. Create an empty Java file called Authenticator in NetBeans.

LISTING 9.4   The Full Text of Authenticator.java

```
1: import javax.swing.*;
2:
3: public class Authenticator extends javax.swing.JFrame {
```

LISTING 9.4 Continued

```
 4:    JTextField username = new JTextField(15);
 5:    JPasswordField password = new JPasswordField(15);
 6:    JTextArea comments = new JTextArea(4, 15);
 7:    JButton ok = new JButton("OK");
 8:    JButton cancel = new JButton("Cancel");
 9:
10:    public Authenticator() {
11:        super("Account Information");
12:        setSize(300, 220);
13:        setDefaultCloseOperation(JFrame.EXIT_ON_CLOSE);
14:
15:        JPanel pane = new JPanel();
16:        JLabel usernameLabel = new JLabel("Username: ");
17:        JLabel passwordLabel = new JLabel("Password: ");
18:        JLabel commentsLabel = new JLabel("Comments: ");
19:        comments.setLineWrap(true);
20:        comments.setWrapStyleWord(true);
21:        pane.add(usernameLabel);
22:        pane.add(username);
23:        pane.add(passwordLabel);
24:        pane.add(password);
25:        pane.add(commentsLabel);
26:        pane.add(comments);
27:        pane.add(ok);
28:        pane.add(cancel);
29:        add(pane);
30:        setVisible(true);
31:    }
32:
33:    private static void setLookAndFeel() {
34:        try {
35:            UIManager.setLookAndFeel(
36:                "com.sun.java.swing.plaf.nimbus.NimbusLookAndFeel"
37:            );
38:        } catch (Exception exc) {
39:            System.out.println(exc.getMessage());
40:        }
41:    }
42:
43:    public static void main(String[] arguments) {
44:        Authenticator.setLookAndFeel();
45:        Authenticator auth = new Authenticator();
46:    }
47: }
```

This application sets up components and adds them to a panel in lines 15–28. Figure 9.5 shows the application in use. The password is obscured with asterisk characters (*), which is the default when no other echo character is designated by calling the field's `setEchoChar(char)` method.

FIGURE 9.5
The Authenticator application.

The text area in this application behaves in a manner that you might not expect. When you reach the bottom of the field and continue entering text, the component grows to make more room for input (and even scrolls below the bottom edge of the frame). The next section describes how to add scrollbars to prevent the area from changing in size.

Scrolling Panes

Text areas in Swing do not include horizontal or vertical scrollbars, and there's no way to add them using this component alone.

Swing supports scrollbars through a new container that can be used to hold any component that can be scrolled: `JScrollPane`.

A scrolling pane is associated with a component in the pane's constructor. You can use these following constructors:

- `JScrollPane(Component)`—A scrolling pane that contains the specified component
- `JScrollPane(Component, int, int)`—A scrolling pane with the specified component, vertical scrollbar configuration, and horizontal scrollbar configuration

Scrollbars are configured using one of six static class variables of the `ScrollPaneConstants` interface. There are three for vertical scrollbars:

- `VERTICAL_SCROLLBAR_ALWAYS`
- `VERTICAL_SCROLLBAR_AS_NEEDED`
- `VERTICAL_SCROLLBAR_NEVER`

There also are three variables for horizontal scrollbars with similar names.

After you create a scrolling pane containing a component, you should add the pane to containers in place of that component.

The following example creates a text area with a vertical scrollbar and no horizontal scrollbar and then adds it to a container:

```
JPanel pane = new JPanel();
JTextArea comments = new JTextArea(4, 15);
JScrollPane scroll = new JScrollPane(comments,
    ScrollPaneConstants.VERTICAL_SCROLLBAR_ALWAYS,
    ScrollPaneConstants.HORIZONTAL_SCROLLBAR_NEVER);
pane.add(scroll);
add(pane);
```

NOTE   This book's website contains Authenticator2, a full application that makes use of this code. Visit www.java21days.com and open the Day 9 page to find a link to `Authenticator2.java`.

Check Boxes and Radio Buttons

The next two components, check boxes and radio buttons, hold only two possible values: selected or not selected.

Check boxes are used to make a simple choice in an interface, such as yes/no or on/off. Radio buttons are grouped so that only one button can be selected at any time.

Check boxes (the `JCheckBox` class) appear as labeled or unlabeled boxes that contain a check mark when they are selected and nothing otherwise. Radio buttons (the `JRadioButton` class) appear as circles that contain a dot when selected and nothing otherwise.

Both the `JCheckBox` and `JRadioButton` classes have several useful methods inherited from `JToggleButton`, their common superclass:

- `setSelected(boolean)`—Selects the component if the argument is `true` and deselects it otherwise
- `isSelected()`—Returns a `boolean` indicating whether the component is currently selected

The following constructors can be used for the JCheckBox class:

- JCheckBox(*String*)—A check box with the specified text label
- JCheckBox(*String, boolean*)—A check box with the specified text label that is selected if the second argument is true
- JCheckBox(*Icon*)—A check box with the specified graphical icon
- JCheckBox(*Icon, boolean*)—A check box with the specified graphical icon that is selected if the second argument is true
- JCheckBox(*String, Icon*)—A check box with the specified text label and graphical icon
- JCheckBox(*String, Icon, boolean*)—A check box with the specified text label and graphical icon that is selected if the third argument is true

The JRadioButton class has constructors with the same arguments and functionality.

Check boxes and radio buttons by themselves are *nonexclusive*, meaning that if you have five check boxes in a container, all five can be checked or unchecked at the same time. To make them exclusive, as radio buttons should be, you must organize related components into groups.

To organize several radio buttons into a group, allowing only one to be selected at a time, create a ButtonGroup class object, as demonstrated in the following statement:

```
ButtonGroup choice = new ButtonGroup();
```

The ButtonGroup object keeps track of all radio buttons in its group. Call the group's add(*Component*) method to add the specified component to the group.

The following example creates a group and two radio buttons that belong to it:

```
ButtonGroup saveFormat = new ButtonGroup();
JRadioButton s1 = new JRadioButton("JSON", false);
saveFormat.add(s1);
JRadioButton s2 = new JRadioButton("XML", true);
saveFormat.add(s2);
```

The saveFormat object groups the s1 and s2 radio buttons. The s2 object, which has the label "XML", is selected. Only one member of the group can be selected at a time. If one component is selected, the ButtonGroup object ensures that all others in the group are deselected.

Create a new empty Java file in NetBeans called FormatFrame. Enter the source code shown in Listing 9.5 to create an application with four radio buttons in a group.

9

LISTING 9.5   The Full Text of `FormatFrame.java`

```
 1: import javax.swing.*;
 2:
 3: public class FormatFrame extends JFrame {
 4:     JRadioButton[] teams = new JRadioButton[4];
 5:
 6:     public FormatFrame() {
 7:         super("Choose an Output Format");
 8:         setSize(320, 120);
 9:         setDefaultCloseOperation(JFrame.EXIT_ON_CLOSE);
10:         teams[0] = new JRadioButton("Atom");
11:         teams[1] = new JRadioButton("RSS 0.92");
12:         teams[2] = new JRadioButton("RSS 1.0");
13:         teams[3] = new JRadioButton("RSS 2.0", true);
14:         JPanel panel = new JPanel();
15:         JLabel chooseLabel = new JLabel(
16:             "Choose an output format for syndicated news items.");
17:         panel.add(chooseLabel);
18:         ButtonGroup group = new ButtonGroup();
19:         for (JRadioButton team : teams) {
20:             group.add(team);
21:             panel.add(team);
22:         }
23:         add(panel);
24:         setVisible(true);
25:     }
26:
27:     private static void setLookAndFeel() {
28:         try {
29:             UIManager.setLookAndFeel(
30:                 "com.sun.java.swing.plaf.nimbus.NimbusLookAndFeel"
31:             );
32:         } catch (Exception exc) {
33:             System.out.println(exc.getMessage());
34:         }
35:     }
36:
37:     public static void main(String[] arguments) {
38:         FormatFrame.setLookAndFeel();
39:         FormatFrame ff = new FormatFrame();
40:     }
41: }
```

Figure 9.6 shows the application running. The four `JRadioButton` objects are stored in an array in lines 10–13. In the `for` loop in lines 19–22, each element is first added to a button group and then is added to a panel. After the loop ends, the panel is added to the frame.

FIGURE 9.6
The FormatFrame application.

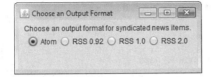

Choosing one of the radio buttons causes the existing choice to be deselected.

Combo Boxes

9

The Swing class JComboBox can be used to create combo boxes, components that present a drop-down menu from which a single value can be selected. The menu is hidden when the component is not being used, thus taking up less space in a GUI.

After a combo box is created by calling the JComboBox() constructor with no arguments, the combo box's addItem(*Object*) method adds items to the list.

Another way to create a combo box is to call JComboBox(*Object[ ]*) with an array that contains the items. If the items are text, a String array would be the argument.

In a combo box, users can select only one of the items on the drop-down menu. If the component's setEditable() method is called with true as an argument, it also supports text entry. This feature gives combo boxes their name: A component configured in this manner serves as both a drop-down menu and a text field.

The JComboBox class has several methods you can use to control a drop-down list or combo box:

- getItemAt(*int*)—Returns the text of the list item at the index position specified by the integer argument. As with arrays, the first item of a choice list is at index position 0, the second is at position 1, and so on.
- getItemCount()—Returns the number of items in the list.
- getSelectedIndex()—Returns the index position of the currently selected item in the list.
- getSelectedItem()—Returns the text of the currently selected item.
- setSelectedIndex(*int*)—Selects the item at the indicated index position.
- setSelectedIndex(*Object*)—Selects the specified object in the list.

The FormatFrame2 application, shown in Listing 9.6, rewrites the preceding radio button example. The program uses a noneditable combo box from which a user can choose one of four options.

LISTING 9.6   The Full Text of `FormatFrame2.java`

```
 1: import javax.swing.*;
 2:
 3: public class FormatFrame2 extends JFrame {
 4:     String[] formats = { "Atom", "RSS 0.92", "RSS 1.0", "RSS 2.0" };
 5:     JComboBox formatBox = new JComboBox(formats);
 6:
 7:     public FormatFrame2() {
 8:         super("Choose a Format");
 9:         setSize(220, 150);
10:         setDefaultCloseOperation(JFrame.EXIT_ON_CLOSE);
11:         JPanel pane = new JPanel();
12:         JLabel formatLabel = new JLabel("Output formats:");
13:         pane.add(formatLabel);
14:         pane.add(formatBox);
15:         add(pane);
16:         setVisible(true);
17:     }
18:
19:     private static void setLookAndFeel() {
20:         try {
21:             UIManager.setLookAndFeel(
22:                 "com.sun.java.swing.plaf.nimbus.NimbusLookAndFeel"
23:             );
24:         } catch (Exception exc) {
25:             System.out.println(exc.getMessage());
26:         }
27:     }
28:
29:     public static void main(String[] arguments) {
30:         FormatFrame2.setLookAndFeel();
31:         FormatFrame2 ff = new FormatFrame2();
32:     }
33: }
```

The combo box is created in line 5 and is filled with strings from an array in the `for` loop in lines 14–16. Figure 9.7 shows the application as the combo box is expanded so that a value can be selected.

FIGURE 9.7
The FormatFrame2
application.

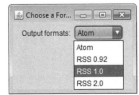

Lists

The last Swing component to be introduced today is similar to combo boxes. Lists,
which are represented by the JList class, allow you to select one or more values from
a list.

9

You can create and fill lists with the contents of an array or vector (a data structure similar to array lists). The following constructors are available:

- JList()—Creates an empty list
- JList(*Object[]*)—Creates a list that contains an array of the specified class (such
  as String)
- JList(*Vector<Class>*)—Creates a list that contains the specified
  java.util.Vector object of the specified class

An empty list can be filled by calling its setListData() method with either an array or
vector as the only argument.

Unlike combo boxes, lists display more than one of their rows when they are presented
in a user interface. The default is to display eight items. To change this, call
setVisibleRowCount(*int*) with the number of items to display.

The getSelectedValuesList() method returns a list of objects containing all the items
selected in the list. This list can be cast to an ArrayList.

The Subscriptions application, shown in Listing 9.7, displays eight items from an array
of strings.

LISTING 9.7   The Full Text of Subscriptions.java

```
1: import javax.swing.*;
2:
3: public class Subscriptions extends JFrame {
4:     String[] subs = { "0xDECAFBAD", "Cafe au Lait",
```

LISTING 9.7 Continued

```
 5:            "Hack the Planet", "Ideoplex", "Inessential", "Intertwingly",
 6:            "Markpasc", "Postneo", "RC3", "Workbench" };
 7:    JList subList = new JList(subs);
 8:
 9:    public Subscriptions() {
10:        super("Subscriptions");
11:        setSize(150, 335);
12:        setDefaultCloseOperation(JFrame.EXIT_ON_CLOSE);
13:        JPanel panel = new JPanel();
14:        JLabel subLabel = new JLabel("RSS Subscriptions:");
15:        panel.add(subLabel);
16:        subList.setVisibleRowCount(8);
17:        JScrollPane scroller = new JScrollPane(subList);
18:        panel.add(scroller);
19:        add(panel);
20:        setVisible(true);
21:    }
22:
23:    private static void setLookAndFeel() {
24:        try {
25:            UIManager.setLookAndFeel(
26:                "com.sun.java.swing.plaf.nimbus.NimbusLookAndFeel"
27:            );
28:        } catch (Exception exc) {
29:            System.out.println(exc.getMessage());
30:        }
31:    }
32:
33:    public static void main(String[] arguments) {
34:        Subscriptions.setLookAndFeel();
35:        Subscriptions app = new Subscriptions();
36:    }
37: }
```

The application is shown in Figure 9.8. The Subscriptions application has an interface with a label atop a list displaying eight items. A scroll pane is used in lines 17 and 18 to enable the list to be scrolled to see items 9 and 10.

FIGURE 9.8
The Subscriptions application.

Summary

Today you began working with Swing, the package of classes that enables your Java programs to support a GUI.

You used more than a dozen classes today, creating interface components such as buttons, labels, and text fields. You put each of these into containers: components that include panels, frames, and windows.

This kind of programming can be complicated. Swing represents the largest package of classes that a new Java programmer must deal with in learning the language.

However, as you have experienced with components such as text areas and text fields, Swing components have many superclasses in common. This makes it easier to extend your knowledge into new components and containers, along with the other aspects of Swing programming you will explore over the next three days.

Q&A

Q Is there a way to change the font of text that appears on a button and other components?

A The JComponent class includes a setFont(*Font*) method that can be used to set the font for text displayed by that component. You will work with Font objects, color, and more graphics on Day 13, "Creating Java2D Graphics."

Q **How can I find out what components are available in Swing and how to use them?**

A This is the first of two days spent introducing user interface components, so you will learn more about them tomorrow. If you have web access, you can find out what classes are in the Swing package by visiting Oracle's online documentation for Java at http://download.oracle.com/javase/7/docs/api/. Click the `javax.swing` link under Packages.

Quiz

Review today's material by taking this three-question quiz. Answers are at the end of the book.

Questions

1. Which of the following user interface components is not a container?

A. `JScrollPane`

B. `JTextArea`

C. `JPanel`

2. Which component can be placed into a scroll pane?

A. `JTextArea`

B. `JTextField`

C. Any component

3. If you use `setSize()` on an application's main frame, where will it appear on your desktop?

A. At the center of the desktop

B. At the same spot the last application appeared

C. At the upper-left corner of the desktop

Certification Practice

The following question is the kind of thing you could expect to be asked on a Java programming certification test. Answer it without looking at today's material or using the Java compiler to test the code.

Given:

```
import javax.swing.*;

public class Display extends JFrame {
    public Display() {
        super("Display");
        // answer goes here
        JLabel hello = new JLabel("Hello");
        JPanel pane = new JPanel();
        add(hello);
        pack();
        setVisible(true);
    }

    public static void main(String[] arguments) {
        Display ds = new Display();
    }
}
```

What statement needs to replace `// answer goes here` to make the application function properly?

A. `setSize(300, 200);`

B. `setDefaultCloseOperation(JFrame.EXIT_ON_CLOSE);`

C. `Display ds = new Display();`

D. No statement is needed.

The answer is available on the book's website at www.java21days.com. Visit the Day 9 page and click the Certification Practice link.

Exercises

To extend your knowledge of the subjects covered today, try the following exercises:

1. Create an application with a frame that includes several DVR controls as individual components: play, stop/eject, rewind, fast-forward, and pause. Choose a size for the window that enables all the components to be displayed on a single row.

2. Create a frame that opens a smaller frame with fields asking for a username and password.

Where applicable, exercise solutions are offered on the book's website at www.java21days.com.

DAY 10

Building a Swing Interface

Although computers can be operated in a command-line environment such as a Linux shell or the Windows command prompt, most computer users expect software to feature a graphical user interface (GUI) and to receive input with a mouse and keyboard.

GUI software can be one of the more challenging tasks for a novice programmer, but as you learned yesterday, Java has simplified the process with Swing.

Swing offers the following features:

- Common user interface components, including buttons, text fields, text areas, labels, check boxes, radio buttons, scrollbars, lists, menu items, and sliders.

- Containers—interface components that can be used to hold other components (including other containers). Containers include frames, panels, menus, menu bars, and tabbed panes.

Swing Features

Most components and containers you learned about yesterday were Swing versions of classes that were part of the Abstract Windowing Toolkit, the original Java package for GUI programming.

Swing offers many additional new components, including keyboard mnemonics, ToolTips, and standard dialog boxes.

Standard Dialog Boxes

The JOptionPane class offers several methods you can use to create standard dialog boxes: small windows that ask a question, warn a user, or provide an important message. Figure 10.1 shows an example.

FIGURE 10.1
A standard dialog box.

You have doubtless seen dialog boxes like the one shown in Figure 10.1. When your system crashes, a dialog box appears to break the bad news. When you delete files, a dialog box pops up to make sure that you really want to do so.

These windows are an effective way to communicate with a user without the overhead of creating a new class to represent the window, adding components to it, and writing event-handling methods to receive input. All these tasks are handled automatically when one of the standard dialog boxes offered by JOptionPane is used.

The four classes of the standard dialog boxes are as follows:

- ConfirmDialog—Asks a question, with buttons for Yes, No, and Cancel responses
- InputDialog—Prompts for text input
- MessageDialog—Displays a message
- OptionDialog—Comprises all three of the other dialog box types

Each of these dialog boxes has its own display method in the JOptionPane class.

Confirm Dialog Boxes

The easiest way to create a Yes/No/Cancel dialog box is by calling the showConfirmDialog(*Component*, *Object*) method. The *Component* argument specifies the container that's the parent of the dialog box, which determines where the dialog window should be displayed. If null is used instead of a container, or if the container is not a JFrame object, the dialog box will be centered onscreen.

The second argument, *Object*, can be a string, a component, or an Icon object. If it's a string, that text will be displayed in the dialog box. If it's a component or an Icon, that object will be displayed in place of a text message.

This method returns one of five possible integer values, each a class constant of JOptionPane: YES_OPTION, NO_OPTION, CANCEL_OPTION, OK_OPTION, or CLOSED_OPTION.

The following example uses a confirm dialog box with a text message and stores the response in the response variable:

```
int response = JOptionPane.showConfirmDialog(null,
    "Should I delete all of your irreplaceable personal files?");
```

This dialog box was shown in Figure 10.1.

Another method offers more options for the dialog box:
showConfirmDialog(*Component*, *Object*, *String*, *int*, *int*). The first two arguments are the same as those in other showConfirmDialog() methods. The last three arguments are the following:

- A string that will be displayed in the dialog box's title bar.
- An integer that indicates which option buttons will be shown. It should be equal to one of the class constants YES_NO_CANCEL_OPTION or YES_NO_OPTION.
- An integer that describes the kind of dialog box it is, using the class constants ERROR_MESSAGE, INFORMATION_MESSAGE, PLAIN_MESSAGE, QUESTION_MESSAGE, or WARNING_MESSAGE. (This argument is used to determine which icon to draw in the dialog box along with the message.)

For example:

```
int response = JOptionPane.showConfirmDialog(null,
    "Error reading file. Want to try again?",
    "File Input Error",
    JOptionPane.YES_NO_OPTION,
    JOptionPane.ERROR_MESSAGE);
```

Figure 10.2 shows the resulting dialog box.

FIGURE 10.2
A confirm dialog
box with Yes and
No buttons.

Input Dialog Boxes

An input dialog box asks a question and uses a text field to store the response.
Figure 10.3 shows an example.

FIGURE 10.3
An input dialog
box.

The easiest way to create an input dialog box is with a call to the
showInputDialog(*Component*, *Object*) method. The arguments are the parent component and the string, component, or icon to display in the box.

The input dialog box method call returns a string that represents the user's response. The
following statement creates the input dialog box shown in Figure 10.3:

```
String response = JOptionPane.showInputDialog(null,
    "Enter your name:");
```

You also can create an input dialog box with the showInputDialog(*Component*,
Object, *String*, *int*) method. The first two arguments are the same as the shorter
method call, and the last two are the following:

- The title to display in the dialog box title bar
- One of five class constants describing the type of dialog box: ERROR_MESSAGE,
  INFORMATION_MESSAGE, PLAIN_MESSAGE, QUESTION_MESSAGE, or WARNING_MESSAGE

The following statement uses this method to create an input dialog box:

```
String response = JOptionPane.showInputDialog(null,
    "What is your ZIP code?",
    "Enter ZIP Code",
    JOptionPane.QUESTION_MESSAGE);
```

Message Dialog Boxes

A message dialog box is a simple window that displays information, as shown in Figure 10.4.

FIGURE 10.4
A message dialog box.

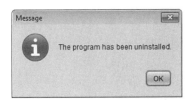

10

A message dialog box can be created with a call to the showMessageDialog(*Component*, *Object*) method. As with other dialog boxes, the arguments are the parent component and the string, component, or icon to display.

Unlike the other dialog boxes, message dialog boxes do not return a response value. The following statement creates the message dialog box shown in Figure 10.4:

```
JOptionPane.showMessageDialog(null,
    "The program has been uninstalled.");
```

You also can create a message input dialog box by calling the showMessageDialog(*Component*, *Object*, *String*, *int*) method. The use is identical to the showInputDialog() method, with the same arguments, except that showMessageDialog() does not return a value.

The following statement creates a message dialog box using this method:

```
JOptionPane.showMessageDialog(null,
    "An asteroid has destroyed the Earth.",
    "Asteroid Destruction Alert",
    JOptionPane.WARNING_MESSAGE);
```

Option Dialog Boxes

The most complex of the dialog boxes is the option dialog box, which combines the features of all the other dialog boxes. It can be created with the showOptionDialog(*Component*, *Object*, *String*, *int*, *int*, *Icon*, *Object[]*, *Object*) method.

The arguments to this method are as follows:

- The parent component of the dialog box
- The text, icon, or component to display
- A string to display in the title bar
- The type of box, using the class constant YES_NO_OPTION or YES_NO_CANCEL_OPTION, or the value 0 if other buttons will be used instead
- The icon to display, using the class constants ERROR_MESSAGE, INFORMATION_MESSAGE, PLAIN_MESSAGE, QUESTION_MESSAGE, or WARNING_MESSAGE, or the value 0 if none of these should be used
- An Icon object to display instead of one of the icons in the preceding argument
- An array of objects holding the objects that represent the choices in the dialog box if YES_NO_OPTION and YES_NO_CANCEL_OPTION are not being used
- The object representing the default selection if YES_NO_OPTION and YES_NO_CANCEL_OPTION are not being used

The final two arguments offer a wide range of possibilities for the dialog box. You can create an array of strings that holds the text of each button to display on the dialog box.

The following example creates an option dialog box that uses an array of String objects for the options in the box and the gender[2] element as the default selection:

```
String[] gender = { "Male", "Female",
    "None of Your Business" };
int response = JOptionPane.showOptionDialog(null,
    "What is your gender?",
    "Gender",
    0,
    JOptionPane.INFORMATION_MESSAGE,
    null,
    gender,
    gender[2]);
System.out.println("You chose " + gender[response]);
```

Figure 10.5 shows the resulting dialog box.

FIGURE 10.5
An option dialog
box.

Using Dialog Boxes

The next project shows a series of dialog boxes in a working program. The FeedInfo
application uses dialog boxes to get information from the user; that information is then
placed into text fields in the application's main window.

Enter the code shown in Listing 10.1 and save the result.

10

LISTING 10.1   The Full Text of FeedInfo.java

```
 1: import java.awt.GridLayout;
 2: import java.awt.event.*;
 3: import javax.swing.*;
 4:
 5: public class FeedInfo extends JFrame {
 6:     private JLabel nameLabel = new JLabel("Name: ",
 7:         SwingConstants.RIGHT);
 8:     private JTextField name;
 9:     private JLabel urlLabel = new JLabel("URL: ",
10:         SwingConstants.RIGHT);
11:     private JTextField url;
12:     private JLabel typeLabel = new JLabel("Type: ",
13:         SwingConstants.RIGHT);
14:     private JTextField type;
15:
16:     public FeedInfo() {
17:         super("Feed Information");
18:         setSize(400, 145);
19:         setDefaultCloseOperation(JFrame.EXIT_ON_CLOSE);
20:         setLookAndFeel();
21:         // Site name
22:         String response1 = JOptionPane.showInputDialog(null,
23:             "Enter the site name:");
24:         name = new JTextField(response1, 20);
25:
26:         // Site address
27:         String response2 = JOptionPane.showInputDialog(null,
```

LISTING 10.1 Continued

```
28:                    "Enter the site address:");
29:            url = new JTextField(response2, 20);
30:
31:            // Site type
32:            String[] choices = { "Personal", "Commercial", "Unknown" };
33:            int response3 = JOptionPane.showOptionDialog(null,
34:                    "What type of site is it?",
35:                    "Site Type",
36:                    0,
37:                    JOptionPane.QUESTION_MESSAGE,
38:                    null,
39:                    choices,
40:                    choices[0]);
41:            type = new JTextField(choices[response3], 20);
42:
43:            setLayout(new GridLayout(3, 2));
44:            add(nameLabel);
45:            add(name);
46:            add(urlLabel);
47:            add(url);
48:            add(typeLabel);
49:            add(type);
50:            setLookAndFeel();
51:            setVisible(true);
52:        }
53:
54:        private void setLookAndFeel() {
55:            try {
56:                UIManager.setLookAndFeel(
57:                    "com.sun.java.swing.plaf.nimbus.NimbusLookAndFeel"
58:                );
59:                SwingUtilities.updateComponentTreeUI(this);
60:            } catch (Exception e) {
61:                System.err.println("Couldn't use the system "
62:                    + "look and feel: " + e);
63:            }
64:        }
65:
66:        public static void main(String[] arguments) {
67:            FeedInfo frame = new FeedInfo();
68:        }
69: }
```

After you fill in the fields in each dialog box, you will see the application's main window, which is displayed in Figure 10.6. Three text fields have values supplied by dialog boxes.

FIGURE 10.6
The main window
of the FeedInfo
application.

Much of this application is boilerplate code that can be used with any Swing application. The following lines relate to the dialog boxes:

- In lines 22–24, an input dialog box asks the user to enter a site name. This name is used in the constructor for a JTextField object, placing it in the text field.

- In lines 27–29, a similar input dialog box asks for a site address, which is used in the constructor for another JTextField object.

- In line 32, an array of String objects called choices is created, and three elements are given values.

- In lines 33–40, an option dialog box asks for the site type. The choices array is the seventh argument, which sets up three buttons on the dialog box labeled with the strings in the array: "Personal", "Commercial", and "Unknown". The last argument, choices[0], designates the first array element as the default selection in the dialog box.

- Line 41 contains the response to the option dialog box—an integer identifying the array element that was selected. It is stored in a JTextField component called type.

The look and feel, which is established in the setLookAndFeel() method in lines 54–64, is called at the beginning and end of the frame's constructor method. Because you're opening several dialog boxes in the constructor, you must set up the look and feel before opening them.

This class designates a look and feel differently than previous examples today and on Day 9, "Working with Swing." The setLookAndFeel() method is called within the constructor in line 20. To ensure that all components in the user interface reflect the look and feel, the SwingUtilities class method
SwingUtilities.updateComponentTreeUI(*Component*) is called with this as the argument, which refers to the FeedInfo object being created.

10

Sliders

Sliders, which are implemented in Swing with the `JSlider` class, enable the user to set a number by sliding a control within the range of a minimum and maximum value. In many cases, a slider can be used for numeric input instead of a text field. This has the advantage of restricting input to a range of acceptable values.

Figure 10.7 shows a `JSlider` component.

FIGURE 10.7
A `JSlider` component.

Sliders are horizontal by default. You can explicitly set the orientation using two class constants of the `SwingConstants` interface: `HORIZONTAL` or `VERTICAL`.

You can use the following constructor methods:

- `JSlider(int)`—A slider with the specified orientation, a minimum value of 0, maximum value of 100, and starting value of 50

- `JSlider(int, int)`—A slider with the specified minimum value and maximum value

- `JSlider(int, int, int)`—A slider with the specified minimum value, maximum value, and starting value

- `JSlider(int, int, int, int)`—A slider with the specified orientation, minimum value, maximum value, and starting value

Slider components have an optional label that can be used to indicate the minimum value, maximum value, and two different sets of tick marks ranging between the values. The default values are a minimum of 0, maximum of 100, starting value of 50, and horizontal orientation.

The elements of this label are established by calling several methods of `JSlider`:

- `setMajorTickSpacing(int)`—Separates major tick marks by the specified distance. The distance is not in pixels, but in values between the minimum and maximum values represented by the slider.

- `setMinorTickSpacing(int)`—Separates minor tick marks by the specified distance. Minor ticks are displayed as half the height of major ticks.

- setPaintTicks(*boolean*)—Determines whether the tick marks should be displayed (true) or not (false).
- setPaintLabels(*boolean*)—Determines whether the slider's numeric label should be displayed (true) or not (false).

These methods should be called on the slider before it is added to a container.

Listing 10.2 contains the Slider.java source code; the application was shown in Figure 10.7.

LISTING 10.2   The Full Text of Slider.java

```
 1: import java.awt.event.*;
 2: import javax.swing.*;
 3:
 4: public class Slider extends JFrame {
 5:
 6:     public Slider() {
 7:         super("Slider");
 8:         setDefaultCloseOperation(JFrame.EXIT_ON_CLOSE);
 9:         setLookAndFeel();
10:         JSlider pickNum = new JSlider(JSlider.HORIZONTAL, 0, 30, 5);
11:         pickNum.setMajorTickSpacing(10);
12:         pickNum.setMinorTickSpacing(1);
13:         pickNum.setPaintTicks(true);
14:         pickNum.setPaintLabels(true);
15:         add(pickNum);
16:         pack();
17:         setVisible(true);
18:     }
19:
20:     private void setLookAndFeel() {
21:         try {
22:             UIManager.setLookAndFeel(
23:                 "com.sun.java.swing.plaf.nimbus.NimbusLookAndFeel"
24:             );
25:             SwingUtilities.updateComponentTreeUI(this);
26:         } catch (Exception e) {
27:             System.err.println("Couldn't use the system "
28:                 + "look and feel: " + e);
29:         }
30:     }
31:
32:     public static void main(String[] args) {
33:         Slider frame = new Slider();
34:     }
35: }
```

10

Lines 10–15 contain the code that's used to create a JSlider component, set up its tick marks to be displayed, and add the component to a container. The rest of the program is a basic framework for an application that consists of a main JFrame container with no menus.

Scroll Panes

In early versions of Java, text areas and some other components had a built-in scrollbar. The bar could be used when the text in the component took up more space than the component could display. Scrollbars could be used in either the vertical or horizontal direction to scroll through the text.

One of the most common examples of scrolling is in a web browser, where a scrollbar can be used on any page bigger than the browser's display area.

Swing changes the rules for scrollbars to the following:

- For a component to be able to scroll, it must be added to a JScrollPane container.
- This JScrollPane container is added to a container in place of the scrollable component.

Scroll panes can be created using the JScrollPane(*Object*) constructor, where *Object* represents the component that can be scrolled.

The following example creates a text area in a scroll pane called scroller and then adds it to a container called mainPane:

```
JTextArea textBox = new JTextArea(7, 30);
JScrollPane scroller = new JScrollPane(textBox);
mainPane.add(scroller);
```

As you work with a scroll pane, it often can be useful to indicate the size you want it to occupy on the interface. You do so by calling the setPreferredSize(*Dimension*) method of the scroll pane before adding it to a container. The Dimension object represents the width and height of the preferred size in pixels.

The following code builds on the previous example by setting the preferred size of scroller:

```
Dimension pref = new Dimension(350, 100);
scroller.setPreferredSize(pref);
```

You should set the dimensions before scroller is added to a container.

CAUTION
> This is one of many situations in Swing where you must do something in the proper order for it to work correctly. For most components, the order is the following: Create the component, set up the component fully, and add the component to a container.

By default, a scroll pane does not display scrollbars unless they are needed. If the component inside the pane is no larger than the pane itself, the bars won't appear. In the case of components such as text areas, where the component size might increase as the program is used, the bars automatically appear when they're needed and disappear when they're not.

To override this behavior, you can set a policy for a JScrollBar component when you create it, using one of several ScrollPaneConstants class constants:

- HORIZONTAL_SCROLLBAR_ALWAYS
- HORIZONTAL_SCROLLBAR_AS_NEEDED
- HORIZONTAL_SCROLLBAR_NEVER
- VERTICAL_SCROLLBAR_ALWAYS
- VERTICAL_SCROLLBAR_AS_NEEDED
- VERTICAL_SCROLLBAR_NEVER

10

These class constants are used with the JScrollPane(*Object*, *int*, *int*) constructor, which specifies the component in the pane, the vertical scrollbar policy, and the horizontal scrollbar policy. Here's an example:

```
JScrollPane scroller = new JScrollPane(textBox,
    VERTICAL_SCROLLBAR_ALWAYS,
    HORIZONTAL_SCROLLBAR_NEVER);
```

Toolbars

A *toolbar*, created in Swing with the JToolBar class, is a container that groups several components into a row or column. These components are most often buttons.

Toolbars are rows or columns of components that group the most commonly used program options. Toolbars often contain buttons and lists and can be used as an alternative to using pull-down menus or shortcut keys.

Toolbars are horizontal by default, but the orientation can be set explicitly with the HORIZONTAL or VERTICAL class variables of the SwingConstants interface.

Constructor methods include the following:

- `JToolBar()`—Creates a new toolbar
- `JToolBar(int)`—Creates a new toolbar with the specified orientation

After you have created a toolbar, you can add components to it with the toolbar's `add(Object)` method, where `Object` represents the component to place on the toolbar.

Many programs that use toolbars enable the user to move the bars. These are called *dockable toolbars* because you can dock them along an edge of the screen, similar to docking a boat. Swing toolbars also can be docked into a new window, separate from the original.

For best results, a dockable `JToolBar` component should be arranged in a container using the `BorderLayout` class, which is a user interface class called a layout manager. A border layout divides a container into five areas: north, south, east, west, and center. Each of the directional components takes up whatever space it needs, and the rest are allocated to the center.

The toolbar should be placed in one of the directional areas of the border layout. The only other area of the layout that can be filled is the center. (You'll learn about layout managers such as border layout during tomorrow's lesson, Day 11, "Arranging Components on a User Interface.")

Figure 10.8 shows a dockable toolbar occupying the south area of a border layout. A text area has been placed in the center.

FIGURE 10.8
A dockable toolbar and a text area.

Listing 10.3 shows the source code used to produce this application.

LISTING 10.3   The Full Text of `FeedBar.java`

```
1: import java.awt.*;
2: import java.awt.event.*;
3: import javax.swing.*;
```

```
 4:
 5: public class FeedBar extends JFrame {
 6:
 7:     public FeedBar() {
 8:         super("FeedBar");
 9:         setDefaultCloseOperation(JFrame.EXIT_ON_CLOSE);
10:         setLookAndFeel();
11:         // create icons
12:         ImageIcon loadIcon = new ImageIcon("load.gif");
13:         ImageIcon saveIcon = new ImageIcon("save.gif");
14:         ImageIcon subscribeIcon = new ImageIcon("subscribe.gif");
15:         ImageIcon unsubscribeIcon = new ImageIcon("unsubscribe.gif");
16:         // create buttons
17:         JButton load = new JButton("Load", loadIcon);
18:         JButton save = new JButton("Save", saveIcon);
19:         JButton subscribe = new JButton("Subscribe", subscribeIcon);
20:         JButton unsubscribe = new JButton("Unsubscribe", unsubscribeIcon);
21:         // add buttons to toolbar
22:         JToolBar bar = new JToolBar();
23:         bar.add(load);
24:         bar.add(save);
25:         bar.add(subscribe);
26:         bar.add(unsubscribe);
27:         // prepare user interface
28:         JTextArea edit = new JTextArea(8, 40);
29:         JScrollPane scroll = new JScrollPane(edit);
30:         BorderLayout bord = new BorderLayout();
31:         setLayout(bord);
32:         add("North", bar);
33:         add("Center", scroll);
34:         pack();
35:         setVisible(true);
36:     }
37:
38:     private void setLookAndFeel() {
39:         try {
40:             UIManager.setLookAndFeel(
41:                 "com.sun.java.swing.plaf.nimbus.NimbusLookAndFeel"
42:             );
43:             SwingUtilities.updateComponentTreeUI(this);
44:         } catch (Exception e) {
45:             System.err.println("Couldn't use the system "
46:                 + "look and feel: " + e);
47:         }
48:     }
49:
50:     public static void main(String[] arguments) {
51:         FeedBar frame = new FeedBar();
52:     }
53: }
```

10

This application uses four images to represent the graphics on the buttons—the same graphics used in the IconFrame project yesterday. If you haven't downloaded them yet, they are available on the book's official website at www.java21days.com on the Day 10 page. You also can use graphics from your own computer.

Four ImageIcon objects are created from the four graphics in lines 12–15, and then they are used to create buttons in lines 17–20. A JToolbar is created in line 22, and the buttons are added to it in lines 23–26.

The toolbar in this application starts at the top edge of the frame, but it can be moved. The component can be grabbed by its handle—the area immediately to the left of the Load button shown in Figure 10.8. If you drag it within the window, you can dock it along different edges of the application window. When you release the toolbar, the application is rearranged using the border layout manager. You also can drag the toolbar outside the application window.

If the toolbar has been dragged to its own window, when the frame is closed the toolbar also will close.

Although toolbars are most commonly used with graphical buttons, they can contain textual buttons, combo boxes, and other components.

Progress Bars

Progress bars are components used to show how much time is left before a task is complete. They are implemented in Swing through the JProgressBar class. Figure 10.9 shows a Java application that uses this component.

FIGURE 10.9
A progress bar in a frame.

Progress bars are used to track the progress of a task that can be represented numerically. They are created by specifying a minimum and a maximum value that represent the points at which the task is beginning and ending.

Consider a software program that consists of 335 different files when it is installed on a computer. This is a good example of a task that can be numerically quantified. The number of files transferred can be used to monitor the progress of the task. The minimum value is 0, and the maximum value is 335.

Constructor methods include the following:

- JProgressBar()—Creates a new progress bar
- JProgressBar(*int*, *int*)—Creates a new progress bar with the specified minimum value and maximum value
- JProgressBar(*int*, *int*, *int*)—Creates a new progress bar with the specified orientation, minimum value, and maximum value

The orientation of a progress bar can be established with the SwingConstants.VERTICAL and SwingConstants.HORIZONTAL class constants. Progress bars are horizontal by default.

You also can set the minimum and maximum values by calling the progress bar's setMinimum(*int*) and setMaximum(*int*) values with the indicated values.

To update a progress bar, you call its setValue(*int*) method with a value indicating how far along the task is at that moment. This value should be somewhere between the minimum and maximum values established for the bar. The following example tells the install progress bar in the previous example of a software installation how many files have been uploaded thus far:

```
int filesDone = getNumberOfFiles();
install.setValue(filesDone);
```

In this example, the getNumberOfFiles() method represents some code that would be used to keep track of how many files have been copied so far during the installation. When this value is passed to the progress bar by the setValue() method, the bar is immediately updated to represent the percentage of the task that has been completed.

Progress bars often include a text label in addition to the graphic of an empty box filling up. This label displays the percentage of the task that has been completed. You can set it up for a bar by calling the setStringPainted(*boolean*) method with a value of true. A false argument turns off this label.

Listing 10.4 contains ProgressMonitor, the application shown at the beginning of this section in Figure 10.9.

LISTING 10.4 The Full Text of ProgressMonitor.java

```
1: import java.awt.*;
2: import java.awt.event.*;
3: import javax.swing.*;
4:
```

LISTING 10.4   Continued

```
 5: public class ProgressMonitor extends JFrame {
 6:
 7:     JProgressBar current;
 8:     JTextArea out;
 9:     JButton find;
10:     Thread runner;
11:     int num = 0;
12:
13:     public ProgressMonitor() {
14:         super("Progress Monitor");
15:         setDefaultCloseOperation(JFrame.EXIT_ON_CLOSE);
16:         setLookAndFeel();
17:         setSize(205, 68);
18:         setLayout(new FlowLayout());
19:         current = new JProgressBar(0, 2000);
20:         current.setValue(0);
21:         current.setStringPainted(true);
22:         add(current);
23:     }
24:
25:     public void iterate() {
26:         while (num < 2000) {
27:             current.setValue(num);
28:             try {
29:                 Thread.sleep(1000);
30:             } catch (InterruptedException e) { }
31:             num += 95;
32:         }
33:     }
34:
35:     private void setLookAndFeel() {
36:         try {
37:             UIManager.setLookAndFeel(
38:                 "com.sun.java.swing.plaf.nimbus.NimbusLookAndFeel"
39:             );
40:             SwingUtilities.updateComponentTreeUI(this);
41:         } catch (Exception e) {
42:             System.err.println("Couldn't use the system "
43:                 + "look and feel: " + e);
44:         }
45:     }
46:
47:     public static void main(String[] arguments) {
48:         ProgressMonitor frame = new ProgressMonitor();
49:         frame.setVisible(true);
50:         frame.iterate();
51:     }
52: }
```

The ProgressMonitor application uses a progress bar to track the value of the num variable. The progress bar is created in line 19 with a minimum value of 0 and a maximum value of 2000.

The iterate() method in lines 25–33 loops while num is less than 2,000 and increases num by 95 each iteration. The progress bar's setValue() method is called in line 27 of the loop with num as an argument, causing the bar to use that value when charting progress.

Using a progress bar is a way to make a program more user-friendly when it will be busy for more than a few seconds. Software users like progress bars because they estimate how much more time something will take.

Progress bars also provide another essential piece of information: proof that the program is still running and has not crashed.

Menus

10

One way you can enhance a frame's usability is to give it a menu bar, a series of pull-down menus used to perform tasks. Menus often duplicate the same tasks you could accomplish by using buttons and other user interface components, giving users two ways to get work done.

Menus in Java are supported by three components that work in conjunction with each other:

- JMenuItem—An item on a menu
- JMenu—A drop-down menu that contains one or more JMenuItem components, other interface components, and separators—lines displayed between items
- JMenuBar—A container that holds one or more JMenu components and displays their names

A JMenuItem component is like a button and can be set up using the same constructor methods as a JButton component. Call it with JMenuItem(*String*) for a text item, JMenuItem(*Icon*) for an item that displays a graphics file, or JMenuItem(*String*, *Icon*) for both.

The following statements create seven menu items:

```
JMenuItem j1 = new JMenuItem("Open");
JMenuItem j2 = new JMenuItem("Save");
JMenuItem j3 = new JMenuItem("Save as Template");
JMenuItem j4 = new JMenuItem("Page Setup");
```

```
JMenuItem j5 = new JMenuItem("Print");
JMenuItem j6 = new JMenuItem("Use as Default Message Style");
JMenuItem j7 = new JMenuItem("Close");
```

A JMenu container holds all the menu items for a drop-down menu. To create it, call the JMenu(*String*) constructor with the name of the menu as an argument. This name appears on the menu bar.

After you have created a JMenu container, call its add(*JMenuItem*) to add a menu item to it. New items are placed at the end of the menu.

The item you put on a menu doesn't have to be a menu item. Call the add(*Component*) method with a user interface component as the argument. One that often appears on a menu is a check box (the JCheckBox class in Java).

To add a line separator to the end of the menu, call the addSeparator() method. Separators often are used to visually group several related items on a menu.

You also can add text to a menu that serves as a label of some kind. Call the add(*String*) method with the text as an argument.

Using the seven menu items from the preceding example, the following statements create a menu and fill it with all those items and three separators:

```
JMenu m1 = new JMenu("File");
m1.add(j1);
m1.add(j2);
m1.add(j3);
m1.addSeparator();
m1.add(j4);
m1.add(j5);
m1.addSeparator();
m1.add(j6);
m1.addSeparator();
m1.add(j7);
```

A JMenuBar container holds one or more JMenu containers and displays each of their names. The most common place to see a menu bar is directly below an application's title bar.

To create a menu bar, call the JMenuBar() constructor method with no arguments. Add menus to the end of a bar by calling its add(*JMenu*) method.

After you have created all your items, added them to menus, and added the menus to a bar, you're ready to add them to a frame. Call the frame's setJMenuBar(*JMenuBar*) method.

The following statement finishes the current example by creating a menu bar, adding a menu to it, and then placing the bar on a frame called gui:

```
JMenuBar bar = new JMenuBar();
bar.add(m7);
gui.setJMenuBar(bar);
```

Figure 10.10 shows what this menu looks like on an otherwise empty menu bar.

FIGURE 10.10
A frame with a menu bar.

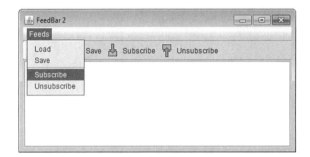

Although you can open and close a menu and select items, nothing happens in response. You'll learn how to receive user input for this component and others during Day 12, "Responding to User Input."

Listing 10.5 is an expanded version of the FeedBar project, adding a menu bar that holds one menu and four individual items.

LISTING 10.5   The Full Text of FeedBar2.java

```
 1: import java.awt.*;
 2: import javax.swing.*;
 3:
 4: public class FeedBar2 extends JFrame {
 5:
 6:     public FeedBar2() {
 7:         super("FeedBar 2");
 8:         setDefaultCloseOperation(JFrame.EXIT_ON_CLOSE);
 9:         setLookAndFeel();
10:         // create icons
11:         ImageIcon loadIcon = new ImageIcon("load.gif");
12:         ImageIcon saveIcon = new ImageIcon("save.gif");
13:         ImageIcon subscribeIcon = new ImageIcon("subscribe.gif");
14:         ImageIcon unsubscribeIcon = new ImageIcon("unsubscribe.gif");
15:         // create buttons
16:         JButton load = new JButton("Load", loadIcon);
17:         JButton save = new JButton("Save", saveIcon);
```

LISTING 10.5 Continued

```
18:          JButton subscribe = new JButton("Subscribe", subscribeIcon);
19:          JButton unsubscribe = new JButton("Unsubscribe", unsubscribeIcon);
20:          // add buttons to toolbar
21:          JToolBar bar = new JToolBar();
22:          bar.add(load);
23:          bar.add(save);
24:          bar.add(subscribe);
25:          bar.add(unsubscribe);
26:          // create menu
27:          JMenuItem j1 = new JMenuItem("Load");
28:          JMenuItem j2 = new JMenuItem("Save");
29:          JMenuItem j3 = new JMenuItem("Subscribe");
30:          JMenuItem j4 = new JMenuItem("Unsubscribe");
31:          JMenuBar menubar = new JMenuBar();
32:          JMenu menu = new JMenu("Feeds");
33:          menu.add(j1);
34:          menu.add(j2);
35:          menu.addSeparator();
36:          menu.add(j3);
37:          menu.add(j4);
38:          menubar.add(menu);
39:          // prepare user interface
40:          JTextArea edit = new JTextArea(8, 40);
41:          JScrollPane scroll = new JScrollPane(edit);
42:          BorderLayout bord = new BorderLayout();
43:          setLayout(bord);
44:          add("North", bar);
45:          add("Center", scroll);
46:          setJMenuBar(menubar);
47:          pack();
48:          setVisible(true);
49:      }
50:
51:     private void setLookAndFeel() {
52:          try {
53:              UIManager.setLookAndFeel(
54:                  "com.sun.java.swing.plaf.nimbus.NimbusLookAndFeel"
55:              );
56:              SwingUtilities.updateComponentTreeUI(this);
57:          } catch (Exception e) {
58:              System.err.println("Couldn't use the system "
59:                  + "look and feel: " + e);
60:          }
61:      }
62:
63:     public static void main(String[] arguments) {
64:          FeedBar2 frame = new FeedBar2();
65:      }
66: }
```

This application creates the menu bar in lines 27–38 and adds it to the frame in line 46. Figure 10.10 shows the application running.

Tabbed Panes

Tabbed panes, a group of stacked panels in which only one panel can be viewed at a time, are implemented in Swing by the JTabbedPane class.

To view a panel, you click the tab that contains its name. Tabs can be arranged horizontally across the top or bottom of the component or vertically along the left or right side.

Tabbed panes are created with the following three constructor methods:

- JTabbedPane()—Creates a vertical tabbed pane along the top that does not scroll
- JTabbedPane(*int*)—Creates a tabbed pane that does not scroll and has the specified placement
- JTabbedPane(*int, int*)—Creates a tabbed pane with the specified placement (first argument) and scrolling policy (second argument)

The placement of a tabbed pane is the position where its tabs are displayed in relation to the panels. Use one of four class variables as the argument to the constructor: JTabbedPane.TOP, JTabbedPane.BOTTOM, JTabbedPane.LEFT, or JTabbedPane.RIGHT.

The scrolling policy determines how tabs will be displayed when there are more tabs than the interface can hold. A tabbed pane that does not scroll displays extra tabs on their own line, which can be set up using the JTabbedPane.WRAP_TAB_LAYOUT class variable. A tabbed pane that scrolls displays scrolling arrows beside the tabs. This can be set up with JTabbedPane.SCROLL_TAB_LAYOUT.

After you create a tabbed pane, you can add components to it by calling the pane's addTab(*String, Component*) method. The String argument will be used as the tab's label. The second argument is the component that will make up one of the tabs on the pane. It's common but not required to use a JPanel object for this purpose.

The TabPanels application in Listing 10.6 displays a pane with five tabs, each holding its own panel.

LISTING 10.6   The Full Text of TabPanels.java

```
1: import java.awt.*;
2: import javax.swing.*;
3:
4: public class TabPanels extends JFrame {
5:
```

LISTING 10.6   Continued

```
 6:     public TabPanels() {
 7:         super("Tabbed Panes");
 8:         setDefaultCloseOperation(JFrame.EXIT_ON_CLOSE);
 9:         setLookAndFeel();
10:         setSize(480, 218);
11:         JPanel mainSettings = new JPanel();
12:         JPanel advancedSettings = new JPanel();
13:         JPanel privacySettings = new JPanel();
14:         JPanel emailSettings = new JPanel();
15:         JPanel securitySettings = new JPanel();
16:         JTabbedPane tabs = new JTabbedPane();
17:         tabs.addTab("Main", mainSettings);
18:         tabs.addTab("Advanced", advancedSettings);
19:         tabs.addTab("Privacy", privacySettings);
20:         tabs.addTab("E-mail", emailSettings);
21:         tabs.addTab("Security", securitySettings);
22:         add(tabs);
23:         setVisible(true);
24:     }.
25:
26:     private void setLookAndFeel() {
27:         try {
28:             UIManager.setLookAndFeel(
29:                 "com.sun.java.swing.plaf.nimbus.NimbusLookAndFeel"
30:             );
31:             SwingUtilities.updateComponentTreeUI(this);
32:         } catch (Exception e) {
33:             System.err.println("Couldn't use the system "
34:                 + "look and feel: " + e);
35:         }
36:     }
37:
38:     public static void main(String[] arguments) {
39:         TabPanels frame = new TabPanels();
40:     }
41: }
```

Five panels are created in lines 11–15. A tabbed pane is created, then the panels are added to each tab in lines 16–21. Each panel can hold its own user interface components.

Figure 10.11 shows the application running.

NOTE   The TOP, BOTTOM, LEFT, and RIGHT constants used in JTabbedPane constructors are part of the SwingConstants interface in the javax.swing package. The interface contains a set of integer constants that help position and align components.

FIGURE 10.11
A tabbed pane
with five tabs.

Summary

You now know how to paint a user interface onto a Java application window using the components of the Swing package.

Swing includes classes for many of the buttons, bars, lists, and fields you would expect to see on a program. It also includes more advanced components, such as sliders, dialog boxes, progress bars, and menu bars. You implement interface components by creating an instance of their class and adding it to a container such as a frame. You use the container's add() method or a similar method specific to the container, such as the tabbed pane's addTab() method.

Today, you developed components and added them to an interface. During the next two days, you will learn about two tasks required to make a graphical interface usable. You will see how to arrange components to form a whole interface and how to receive input from a user through these components.

Swing offers a lot more user interface components than the ones covered today and yesterday. Visit Oracle's Javadoc site at http://docs.oracle.com/javase/7/docs/api/ and click the javax.swing package link to explore these classes further.

Q&A

Q Can an application be created without Swing?

A Certainly. Swing is just an expansion on the Abstract Windowing Toolkit, so you could use only AWT classes to design your interface and receive input from a user. But there's no comparison between Swing's capabilities and those offered by the AWT. With Swing, you can use many more components, control them in more sophisticated ways, and count on better performance and more reliability.

Other user interface libraries also extend or compete with Swing. One of the most popular is the Standard Widget Toolkit (SWT), an open source GUI library created by the Eclipse project. The SWT offers components that appear and behave like the

10

interface components offered by each operating system. For more information, visit www.eclipse.org/swt.

Q In the Slider application, what does the `pack()` statement do?

A Every interface component has a preferred size, although this often is disregarded by the layout manager used to arrange the component within a container. Calling a frame or window's `pack()` method causes it to be resized to fit the preferred size of the components it contains. Because the Slider application does not set a size for the frame, calling `pack()` sets it to an adequate size before the frame is displayed.

Q When I try to create a tabbed pane, all that appears are the tabs—the panels themselves are not visible. What can I do to correct this?

A Tabbed panes won't work correctly until their contents have been fully set up with components inside them. If a tab's panes are empty, nothing appears below or beside the tabs. Make sure that the panels you are putting into the tabs display all their components.

Quiz

Review today's material by taking this three-question quiz. Answers are at the end of the book.

Questions

1. Which user interface component is common in software installation programs?
   - A. Sliders
   - B. Progress bars
   - C. Dialog boxes

2. Which Java class library includes a class for clickable buttons?
   - A. Abstract Windowing Toolkit
   - B. Swing
   - C. Both

3. Which user interface component can be picked up and moved around?
   - A. `JSlider`
   - B. `JToolBar`
   - C. Both

Certification Practice

The following question is the kind of thing you could expect to be asked on a Java programming certification test. Answer it without looking at today's material or using the Java compiler to test the code.

Given:

```java
import java.awt.*;
import javax.swing.*;

public class AskFrame extends JFrame {
    public AskFrame() {
        setDefaultCloseOperation(JFrame.EXIT_ON_CLOSE);
        JSlider value = new JSlider(0, 255, 100);
        add(value);
        setSize(450, 150);
        setVisible(true);
        super();
    }

    public static void main(String[] arguments) {
        AskFrame af = new AskFrame();
    }
}
```

What will happen when you attempt to compile and run this source code?

A. It compiles without error and runs correctly.

B. It compiles without error but does not display anything in the frame.

C. It does not compile because of the super() statement.

D. It does not compile because of the add() statement.

The answer is available on the book's website at www.java21days.com. Visit the Day 10 page and click the Certification Practice link.

10

Exercises

To extend your knowledge of the subjects covered today, try the following exercises:

1. Create an input dialog box that can be used to set the title of the frame that loaded the dialog box.

2. Create a modified version of the ProgressMonitor application that also displays the value of the num variable in a text field.

Where applicable, exercise solutions are offered on the book's website at www.java21days.com.

DAY 11
Arranging Components on a User Interface

If designing a graphical user interface (GUI) were comparable to painting, currently you could produce only one kind of art: abstract expressionism. You can put components on an interface, but you can't control where they go.

To arrange the components of a user interface in Java, you must use a set of classes called layout managers.

Today, you learn how to use layout managers to arrange components in an interface. You take advantage of the flexibility of Java's graphical user interface capabilities, which were designed to be presentable on the many different platforms that support the language.

You also learn how to put several different layout managers to work on the same interface. This approach is for the many times when one layout manager doesn't suit the exact interface you seek to design.

Basic Interface Layout

As you learned yesterday, a GUI designed with Swing is a fluid thing. Resizing a window can wreak havoc on your interface, because components move to places on a container that you might not have intended.

This fluidity is a necessary part of Java's support for different platforms, where there are subtle differences in how each platform displays things such as buttons, scrollbars, and other parts of a user interface.

With some programming languages, a component's location on a window is precisely defined by its (x,y) coordinate. Some Java development tools allow similar control over an interface through the use of their own windowing classes (and there's a way to do that in Java).

When using Swing, a programmer gains more control over the layout of an interface by using layout managers.

The platform-independent nature of Swing provides flexibility at the cost of slower performance and a user interface look-and-feel that doesn't closely match the native look-and-feel of the operating system.

Laying Out an Interface

A layout manager determines how components will be arranged when they are added to a container.

The default layout manager for panels is the `FlowLayout` class. This class lets components flow from left to right in the order in which they are added to a container. When there's no more room, a new row of components begins immediately below the first, and the left-to-right order continues.

Java includes a bunch of general-purpose layout managers: `BorderLayout`, `BoxLayout`, `CardLayout`, `FlowLayout`, `GridBagLayout`, and `GridLayout`. To create a layout manager for a container, first call its constructor to create an instance of the class, as in this example:

```
FlowLayout flo = new FlowLayout();
```

After you create a layout manager, you designate it as the layout manager for a container by using the container's `setLayout()` method. The layout manager must be set before any components are added to the container. If no layout manager is specified, the container's default layout is used. The default is `FlowLayout` for panels and `BorderLayout` for frames.

The following statements represent the starting point for a frame that uses a layout manager to control the arrangement of all the components that will be added to the frame:

```
import java.awt.*;
import javax.swing.*;

public class Starter extends JFrame {

    public Starter() {
        super("Example Frame");
        FlowLayout manager = new FlowLayout();
        setLayout(manager);
        // add components here
    }
}
```

After the layout manager is set, you can start adding components to the container it manages. For some of the layout managers, such as FlowLayout, the order in which components are added is significant. You'll see this as you work with each of the managers.

Flow Layout

The FlowLayout class in the java.awt package is the simplest layout manager. It lays out components in rows in the same way that words are laid out on a page in English—from left to right until there's no more room at the right edge, and then on to the left edge on the next row.

By default, the components in each row are centered when you use the FlowLayout() constructor with no arguments. If you want the components to be aligned along the left or right edge of the container, you can use the FlowLayout.LEFT or FlowLayout.RIGHT class variable as the constructor's only argument, as in the following statement:

```
FlowLayout righty = new FlowLayout(FlowLayout.RIGHT);
```

The FlowLayout.CENTER class variable specifies a centered alignment for components.

11

NOTE

If you need to align components for a non-English-speaking audience where left-to-right order does not make sense, you can use the FlowLayout.LEADING and FlowLayout.TRAILING variables. They set justification to the side of either the first component in a row or the last, respectively.

The Alphabet application, shown in Listing 11.1, displays six buttons arranged by the flow layout manager. Because the FlowLayout.LEFT class variable is used in the FlowLayout() constructor, the components are lined up along the left side of the application window.

LISTING 11.1   The Full Text of Alphabet.java

```
 1: import java.awt.*;
 2: import java.awt.event.*;
 3: import javax.swing.*;
 4:
 5: public class Alphabet extends JFrame {
 6:
 7:     public Alphabet() {
 8:         super("Alphabet");
 9:         setDefaultCloseOperation(JFrame.EXIT_ON_CLOSE);
10:         setLookAndFeel();
11:         setSize(360, 120);
12:         FlowLayout lm = new FlowLayout(FlowLayout.LEFT);
13:         setLayout(lm);
14:         JButton a = new JButton("Alibi");
15:         JButton b = new JButton("Burglar");
16:         JButton c = new JButton("Corpse");
17:         JButton d = new JButton("Deadbeat");
18:         JButton e = new JButton("Evidence");
19:         JButton f = new JButton("Fugitive");
20:         add(a);
21:         add(b);
22:         add(c);
23:         add(d);
24:         add(e);
25:         add(f);
26:         setVisible(true);
27:     }
28:
29:     private void setLookAndFeel() {
30:         try {
31:             UIManager.setLookAndFeel(
32:                 "com.sun.java.swing.plaf.nimbus.NimbusLookAndFeel"
33:             );
34:             SwingUtilities.updateComponentTreeUI(this);
35:         } catch (Exception exc) {
36:             System.err.println("Couldn't use the system "
37:                 + "look and feel: " + exc);
38:         }
39:     }
40:
41:     public static void main(String[] arguments) {
42:         Alphabet frame = new Alphabet();
43:     }
44: }
```

Figure 11.1 shows the application running.

The Alphabet application creates a flow layout manager in line 12 and sets it to manage the frame in line 13. The buttons added to the frame in lines 20–25 are arranged by this manager.

The manager uses the default gap of 5 pixels between each component on a row and a gap of 5 pixels between each row. You can change the horizontal and vertical gap between components with some extra arguments to the FlowLayout() constructor or by calling flow layout's setVgap(int) and setHgap(int) methods with the desired vertical or horizontal gap.

The FlowLayout(int, int, int) constructor takes the following three arguments, in order:

- The alignment, which must be one of five class variables of FlowLayout: CENTER, LEFT, RIGHT, LEADING, or TRAILING
- The horizontal gap between components, in pixels
- The vertical gap, in pixels

The following constructor creates a flow layout manager with centered components, a horizontal gap of 30 pixels, and a vertical gap of 10 pixels:

```
FlowLayout flo = new FlowLayout(FlowLayout.CENTER, 30, 10);
```

Box Layout

The next layout manager can be used to stack components from top to bottom or from left to right. Box layout, managed by the BoxLayout class in the javax.swing package, improves on flow layout by ensuring that components always line up vertically or horizontally, regardless of how their container is resized.

A box layout manager must be created with two arguments to its constructor: the container it will manage and a class variable that sets up vertical or horizontal alignment.

The alignment, specified with class variables of the BoxLayout class, can be X_AXIS for left-to-right horizontal alignment or Y_AXIS for top-to-bottom vertical alignment.

11

The following code sets up a panel to use vertical box layout:

```
JPanel optionPane = new JPanel();
BoxLayout box = new BoxLayout(optionPane,
    BoxLayout.Y_AXIS);
optionPane.setLayout(box);
```

Components added to the container will line up on the specified axis and will be displayed at their preferred sizes. In horizontal alignment, the box layout manager attempts to give each component the same height. In vertical alignment, the manager attempts to give each one the same width.

The Stacker application, shown in Listing 11.2, contains a panel of buttons arranged with box layout.

LISTING 11.2   The Full Text of `Stacker.java`

```
 1: import java.awt.*;
 2: import javax.swing.*;
 3:
 4: public class Stacker extends JFrame {
 5:     public Stacker() {
 6:         super("Stacker");
 7:         setSize(430, 150);
 8:         setDefaultCloseOperation(JFrame.EXIT_ON_CLOSE);
 9:         setLookAndFeel();
10:         // create top panel
11:         JPanel commandPane = new JPanel();
12:         BoxLayout horizontal = new BoxLayout(commandPane,
13:             BoxLayout.X_AXIS);
14:         commandPane.setLayout(horizontal);
15:         JButton subscribe = new JButton("Subscribe");
16:         JButton unsubscribe = new JButton("Unsubscribe");
17:         JButton refresh = new JButton("Refresh");
18:         JButton save = new JButton("Save");
19:         commandPane.add(subscribe);
20:         commandPane.add(unsubscribe);
21:         commandPane.add(refresh);
22:         commandPane.add(save);
23:         // create bottom panel
24:         JPanel textPane = new JPanel();
25:         JTextArea text = new JTextArea(4, 70);
26:         JScrollPane scrollPane = new JScrollPane(text);
27:         // put them together
28:         FlowLayout flow = new FlowLayout();
29:         setLayout(flow);
30:         add(commandPane);
31:         add(scrollPane);
```

LISTING 11.2   Continued

```
32:          setVisible(true);
33:      }
34:
35:      private void setLookAndFeel() {
36:          try {
37:              UIManager.setLookAndFeel(
38:                  "com.sun.java.swing.plaf.nimbus.NimbusLookAndFeel"
39:              );
40:              SwingUtilities.updateComponentTreeUI(this);
41:          } catch (Exception exc) {
42:              System.err.println("Couldn't use the system "
43:                  + "look and feel: " + exc);
44:          }
45:      }
46:
47:      public static void main(String[] arguments) {
48:          Stacker st = new Stacker();
49:      }
50: }
```

When the class is compiled and run, the output should resemble Figure 11.2.

11

FIGURE 11.2
A user interface
with buttons
arranged with
the box layout
manager.

This application creates a JPanel container named commandPane in line 11, creates a box layout manager associated with that pane in lines 12–13, and sets that manager for the panel in line 14.

The panel of buttons along the top edge of the interface is stacked horizontally. If the second argument to the box layout constructor were BoxLayout.Y_AXIS, the buttons would be arranged vertically instead.

Grid Layout

The grid layout manager arranges components into a grid of vertical columns and horizontal rows like the days on a 12-month calendar. Components are added first to the top row of the grid, beginning with the leftmost grid cell and continuing to the right. When all the cells in the top row are full, the next component is added to the leftmost cell in the second row of the grid—if there *is* a second row—and so on.

Grid layout managers are created with the GridLayout class, which belongs to the java.awt package. Two arguments are sent to the GridLayout constructor: the number of rows and the number of columns in the grid.

The following statement creates a grid layout manager with 10 rows and 3 columns:

```
GridLayout gr = new GridLayout(10, 3);
```

As with flow layout, you can specify a vertical and horizontal gap between components with two extra arguments (or by calling the setHgap() or setVgap() methods). The following statement creates a grid layout with 10 rows and 3 columns, a horizontal gap of 5 pixels, and a vertical gap of 8 pixels:

```
GridLayout gr2 = new GridLayout(10, 3, 5, 8);
```

The default gap between components arranged in grid layout is 0 pixels in both vertical and horizontal directions.

Listing 11.3 shows the Bunch application, which creates a grid with 3 rows, 3 columns, and a 10-pixel gap between components in both the vertical and horizontal directions.

LISTING 11.3   The Full Text of Bunch.java

```
 1: import java.awt.*;
 2: import java.awt.event.*;
 3: import javax.swing.*;
 4:
 5: public class Bunch extends JFrame {
 6:
 7:     public Bunch() {
 8:         super("Bunch");
 9:         setSize(260, 260);
10:         setDefaultCloseOperation(JFrame.EXIT_ON_CLOSE);
11:         setLookAndFeel();
12:         JPanel pane = new JPanel();
13:         GridLayout family = new GridLayout(3, 3, 10, 10);
14:         pane.setLayout(family);
15:         JButton marcia = new JButton("Marcia");
16:         JButton carol = new JButton("Carol");
17:         JButton greg = new JButton("Greg");
18:         JButton jan = new JButton("Jan");
19:         JButton alice = new JButton("Alice");
20:         JButton peter = new JButton("Peter");
21:         JButton cindy = new JButton("Cindy");
22:         JButton mike = new JButton("Mike");
23:         JButton bobby = new JButton("Bobby");
```

LISTING 11.3   Continued

```
24:          pane.add(marcia);
25:          pane.add(carol);
26:          pane.add(greg);
27:          pane.add(jan);
28:          pane.add(alice);
29:          pane.add(peter);
30:          pane.add(cindy);
31:          pane.add(mike);
32:          pane.add(bobby);
33:          add(pane);
34:          setVisible(true);
35:      }
36:
37:      private void setLookAndFeel() {
38:          try {
39:              UIManager.setLookAndFeel(
40:                  "com.sun.java.swing.plaf.nimbus.NimbusLookAndFeel"
41:              );
42:              SwingUtilities.updateComponentTreeUI(this);
43:          } catch (Exception exc) {
44:              System.err.println("Couldn't use the system "
45:                  + "look and feel: " + exc);
46:          }
47:      }
48:
49:      public static void main(String[] arguments) {
50:          Bunch frame = new Bunch();
51:      }
52: }
```

11

Figure 11.3 shows this application.

FIGURE 11.3
Nine buttons
arranged in a 3×3
grid layout.

The Bunch application displays nine buttons in a grid. The buttons are added to a pane in lines 24–32, and the pane is added to the frame in line 33.

One thing to note about the buttons in Figure 11.3 is that they expanded to fill the space available to them in each cell. This is an important difference between grid layout and some of the other layout managers, which display components at a much smaller size by using the preferred size of those components.

Border Layout

The layout managers introduced so far have been fairly simple. The next one employs a more complex arrangement called border layout.

This layout is created by using the BorderLayout class in the java.awt package, which divides a container into five sections: north, south, east, west, and center. The five areas in Figure 11.4 show how these sections are arranged.

FIGURE 11.4
Components arranged by a border layout manager.

In border layout, the components represented by the four compass points fill their sections, and the center component gets all the space that's left over. Ordinarily, this results in an arrangement with a large central component and four smaller components around it. The preferred sizes of the components are not followed by the layout manager.

A border layout is created with either the BorderLayout() or BorderLayout(int, int) constructors. The first constructor creates a border layout with no gap between any of the components. The second constructor uses arguments to specify the horizontal gap and vertical gap, in that order, and setVgap() and setHgap() also are available.

After you create a border layout and set it up as a container's layout manager, components are added using a call to the add() method that's different from the ones seen previously:

add(*Component*, *String*)

The first argument is the component that should be added to the container.

The second argument is a BorderLayout class variable that indicates the region of the border layout to which the component should be assigned. The class variables NORTH, SOUTH, EAST, WEST, and CENTER can be used for this argument.

The following statement adds a button called quitButton to the north portion of a border layout:

```
JButton quitButton = new JButton("quit");
add(quitButton, BorderLayout.NORTH);
```

The Border application, shown in Listing 11.4, creates the GUI shown earlier in Figure 11.4.

LISTING 11.4   The Full Text of Border.java

```
 1: import java.awt.*;
 2: import javax.swing.*;
 3:
 4: public class Border extends JFrame {
 5:
 6:     public Border() {
 7:         super("Border");
 8:         setSize(240, 280);
 9:         setDefaultCloseOperation(JFrame.EXIT_ON_CLOSE);
10:         setLookAndFeel();
11:         setLayout(new BorderLayout());
12:         JButton nButton = new JButton("North");
13:         JButton sButton = new JButton("South");
14:         JButton eButton = new JButton("East");
15:         JButton wButton = new JButton("West");
16:         JButton cButton = new JButton("Center");
17:         add(nButton, BorderLayout.NORTH);
18:         add(sButton, BorderLayout.SOUTH);
19:         add(eButton, BorderLayout.EAST);
20:         add(wButton, BorderLayout.WEST);
21:         add(cButton, BorderLayout.CENTER);
22:         setVisible(true);
23:     }
24:
25:     private void setLookAndFeel() {
26:         try {
27:             UIManager.setLookAndFeel(
28:                 "com.sun.java.swing.plaf.nimbus.NimbusLookAndFeel"
29:             );
30:             SwingUtilities.updateComponentTreeUI(this);
31:         } catch (Exception exc) {
32:             System.err.println("Couldn't use the system "
33:                 + "look and feel: " + exc);
```

11

LISTING 11.4   The Full Text of Border.java

```
34:            }
35:        }
36:
37:     public static void main(String[] arguments) {
38:            Border frame = new Border();
39:        }
40: }
```

The Border application is a frame that sets its layout manager in a new way in line 11. The call to the new `BorderLayout()` constructor returns a `BorderLayout` object, which then becomes the argument to the `setLayout()` method.

Line 11 is equivalent to the following two statements:

```
BorderLayout bl = new BorderLayout();
setLayout(bl);
```

The advantage of the technique employed in line 11 is that there's no need to create a variable and assign the `BorderLayout` object to it. That object's never needed after the layout manager is designated for the frame.

The application creates the six buttons in lines 12–16 and assigns them to positions in the border layout in lines 17–21.

TIP

> When you run the application, increase the window size several times to see how the components respond. As the window becomes larger, the center component grows accordingly. The other components stay the same. This is an advantage of the grid and border layout managers.

Mixing Layout Managers

At this point, you might be wondering how Java's layout managers can be used on the GUIs you want to design for your own programs. Choosing a layout manager is an experience akin to Goldilocks checking out the home of the three bears: This one is too square! This one is too disorganized! This one is too strange!

To find the layout that is just right, you often have to combine more than one manager within the same interface.

You can do so by putting several containers inside a larger container and giving each of the smaller containers its own layout manager.

The container to use for these smaller containers is the panel, which is created from the JPanel class in the java.awt package. Panels are simple containers used to group components. Keep in mind two things when working with panels:

- The panel is filled with components before it is put into a larger container.
- The panel has its own layout manager.

Panels are created with a simple call to the constructor of the JPanel class, as shown in the following example:

```
JPanel pane = new JPanel();
```

You set the layout method for a panel by calling the setLayout() method on that panel. Here's how to create a layout manager and apply it to a JPanel object called pane:

```
FlowLayout flo = new FlowLayout();
pane.setLayout(flo);
```

You add components to a panel by calling the panel's add() method, which works the same for panels as it does for other containers.

The following statements create a text field and add it to a JPanel object called pane:

```
JTextField nameField = new JTextField(80);
pane.add(nameField);
```

You'll see several examples of panel use in the rest of today's applications.

As you gain experience with layout managers, you get a feel for which ones to use in specific situations. For instance, border layout is good for putting a status line at the bottom and a toolbar at the top, and grid layout is effective for rows and columns of text fields and labels that take the same size.

Card Layout

A card layout manager differs from the other layout managers because it hides some components from view. A card layout is a group of containers or components displayed one at a time, in the same way that a blackjack dealer reveals one card at a time from a deck. Each container in the group is called a *card*.

If you have used a wizard in an installation program, you have seen card layout. Each step in the installation process has its own card. Often, a Next button advances from one card to the next.

The most common way to use a card layout is to use a panel container for each card. Components are added to the panels first, and then the panels are added to the container that employs card layout.

A card layout is created from the CardLayout class in the java.awt package with a simple constructor:

```
CardLayout cc = new CardLayout();
```

The setLayout() method makes this the layout manager for the container, as in the following statement:

```
setLayout(cc);
```

After you set a container to use the card layout manager, you must use the add(*Component*, *String*) method to add components.

The first argument to the add() method specifies the container or component that serves as a card. If it is a container, all components must have been added to it before the card is added.

The second argument is a string that names the card. This can be anything you want to call the card, such as "Card 1", "Card 2", "Card 3", or some other naming scheme.

The following statement adds a panel object named options to a container and names this card "Options Card":

```
add(options, "Options Card");
```

When a container using card layout is displayed for the first time, the visible card is the first card added to the container.

You can display subsequent cards by calling the show() method of the layout manager, which takes two arguments:

- The container holding all the cards
- The name of the card

The following statement calls the show() method of a card layout manager called cc:

```
cc.show(this, "Fact Card");
```

The this keyword would be used in a frame governed by card layout. It refers to the object inside which the cc.show() statement appears. In this example, "Fact Card" is the name of the card to reveal. A card is added to the container that has been given this name.

When a card is shown, the previously displayed card is hidden automatically. Only one card in a card layout can be shown at a time.

In a program that uses the card layout manager, a card change generally is triggered by a user's action. For example, in an installation program, a user could choose a folder where the program should be saved and click the Next button to see the next card.

Using Card Layout in an Application

The next project demonstrates both card layout and the use of different layout managers within the same GUI.

The SurveyWizard class is a panel that implements a wizard interface: a series of simple questions accompanied by a Next button that is used to see the subsequent question. The last question has a Finish button instead and is shown in Figure 11.5.

FIGURE 11.5

Using a card layout for a wizard-style interface.

The easiest way to implement a card-based layout is to use panels. This project uses several panels:

- The SurveyWizard class is a panel that holds all the cards.
- The SurveyPanel helper class is a panel that holds one card.
- Each SurveyPanel object contains three panels stacked on top of each other.

The SurveyWizard and SurveyPanel classes are both panels, the easiest component to use when working with card layout. Each card is created as a panel and is added to a containing panel that will be used to show them in sequence.

This takes place in the SurveyWizard() constructor, using two instance variables, a card layout manager, and an array of three SurveyPanel objects:

```
SurveyPanel[] ask = new SurveyPanel[3];
CardLayout cards = new CardLayout();
```

The constructor sets the class to use the layout manager, creates each SurveyPanel object, and then adds it to the class:

```
setLayout(cards);
String question1 = "What is your gender?";
String[] responses1 = { "female", "male", "not telling" };
ask[0] = new SurveyPanel(question1, responses1, 2);
add(ask[0], "Card 0");
```

11

Each SurveyPanel object is created with three arguments to the constructor: the text of the question, an array of possible responses, and the element number of the default answer.

In the preceding code, the question "What is your gender?" has the responses "female," "male," and "not telling." The response at position 2, "not telling," is set as the default.

The SurveyPanel constructor uses a label component to hold the question and an array of radio buttons to hold the responses:

```
SurveyPanel(String ques, String[] resp, int def) {
    question = new JLabel(ques);
    response = new JRadioButton[resp.length];
    // more to come
}
```

The class uses grid layout to arrange its components into a grid with three vertical columns and one horizontal row. Each component placed in the grid is a panel.

First, a panel is created to hold the question label:

```
JPanel sub1 = new JPanel();
JLabel quesLabel = new JLabel(ques);
sub1.add(quesLabel);
```

The default layout for panels, flow layout with centered alignment, determines the placement of the label on the panel.

Next, a panel is created to hold the possible responses. A for loop iterates through the string array that holds the text of each response. This text is used to create a radio button. The second argument of the JRadioButton() constructor determines whether it is selected. This is implemented with the following code:

```
JPanel sub2 = new JPanel();
for (int i = 0; i < resp.length; i++) {
    if (def == i) {
        response[i] = new JRadioButton(resp[i], true);
    } else {
        response[i] = new JRadioButton(resp[i], false);
    }
    group.add(response[i]);
    sub2.add(response[i]);
}
```

The last panel holds the Next and Finish buttons:

```
JPanel sub3 = new JPanel();
nextButton.setEnabled(true);
sub3.add(nextButton);
finalButton.setEnabled(false);
sub3.add(finalButton);
```

Now that the three panels have been fully set up, they are added to the `SurveyPanel` interface, which completes the work of the constructor method:

```
GridLayout grid = new GridLayout(3, 1);
setLayout(grid);
add(sub1);
add(sub2);
add(sub3);
```

There's one extra wrinkle in the `SurveyPanel` class—a method that enables the Finish button and disables the Next button when the last question has been reached:

```
void setFinalQuestion(boolean finalQuestion) {
    if (finalQuestion) {
        nextButton.setEnabled(false);
        finalButton.setEnabled(true);
    }
}
```

In a user interface that uses card layout, the display of each card usually takes place in response to an action by the user.

These actions are called events, which are covered on Day 12, "Responding to User Input."

A brief preview demonstrates how the `SurveyPanel` class is equipped to handle button clicks.

The class implements `ActionListener`, an interface in the `java.awt.event` package:

```
public class SurveyWizard extends JPanel implements ActionListener {
    // more to come
}
```

This interface indicates that the class can respond to action events, which represent button clicks, menu choices, and similar user input.

Next, each button's `addActionListener(Object)` method is called:

```
ask[0].nextButton.addActionListener(this);
ask[0].finalButton.addActionListener(this);
```

Listeners are classes that monitor specific kinds of user input. The argument to `addActionListener()` is the class that's looking for action events. Using `this` as the argument indicates that the `SurveyPanel` class handles this job.

The `ActionListener` interface includes only one method:

```
public void actionPerformed(Action evt) {
    // more to come
}
```

This method is called when a component being listened to generates an action event. In the `SurveyPanel` class, this happens whenever a button is clicked.

In `SurveyPanel`, this method uses an instance variable that keeps track of which card to display:

```
int currentCard = 0;
```

Every time a button is clicked and the `actionPerformed()` method is called, this variable is incremented, and the card layout manager's `show(Container, String)` method is called to display a new card. If the last card has been displayed, the Finish button is disabled.

Listing 11.5 shows the full `SurveyWizard` class with the complete `actionPerformed()` method.

LISTING 11.5   The Full Text of SurveyWizard.java

```
 1: import java.awt.*;
 2: import java.awt.event.*;
 3: import javax.swing.*;
 4:
 5: public class SurveyWizard extends JPanel implements ActionListener {
 6:     int currentCard = 0;
 7:     CardLayout cards = new CardLayout();
 8:     SurveyPanel[] ask = new SurveyPanel[3];
 9:
10:     public SurveyWizard() {
11:         super();
12:         setSize(240, 140);
13:         setLayout(cards);
14:         // set up survey
15:         String question1 = "What is your gender?";
16:         String[] responses1 = { "female", "male", "not telling" };
17:         ask[0] = new SurveyPanel(question1, responses1, 2);
18:         String question2 = "What is your age?";
19:         String[] responses2 = { "Under 25", "25-34", "35-54",
20:             "Over 54" };
21:         ask[1] = new SurveyPanel(question2, responses2, 1);
22:         String question3 = "How often do you exercise each week?";
23:         String[] responses3 = { "Never", "1-3 times", "More than 3" };
24:         ask[2] = new SurveyPanel(question3, responses3, 1);
```

LISTING 11.5 Continued

```
25:            ask[2].setFinalQuestion(true);
26:            addListeners();
27:        }
28:
29:        private void addListeners() {
30:            for (int i = 0; i < ask.length; i++) {
31:                ask[i].nextButton.addActionListener(this);
32:                ask[i].finalButton.addActionListener(this);
33:                add(ask[i], "Card " + i);
34:            }
35:        }
36:
37:        public void actionPerformed(ActionEvent evt) {
38:            currentCard++;
39:            if (currentCard >= ask.length) {
40:                System.exit(0);
41:            }
42:            cards.show(this, "Card " + currentCard);
43:        }
44: }
45:
46: class SurveyPanel extends JPanel {
47:        JLabel question;
48:        JRadioButton[] response;
49:        JButton nextButton = new JButton("Next");
50:        JButton finalButton = new JButton("Finish");
51:
52:        SurveyPanel(String ques, String[] resp, int def) {
53:            super();
54:            setSize(160, 110);
55:            question = new JLabel(ques);
56:            response = new JRadioButton[resp.length];
57:            JPanel sub1 = new JPanel();
58:            ButtonGroup group = new ButtonGroup();
59:            JLabel quesLabel = new JLabel(ques);
60:            sub1.add(quesLabel);
61:            JPanel sub2 = new JPanel();
62:            for (int i = 0; i < resp.length; i++) {
63:                if (def == i) {
64:                    response[i] = new JRadioButton(resp[i], true);
65:                } else {
66:                    response[i] = new JRadioButton(resp[i], false);
67:                }
68:                group.add(response[i]);
69:                sub2.add(response[i]);
70:            }
71:            JPanel sub3 = new JPanel();
72:            nextButton.setEnabled(true);
73:            sub3.add(nextButton);
```

11

LISTING 11.5   Continued

```
74:            finalButton.setEnabled(false);
75:            sub3.add(finalButton);
76:            GridLayout grid = new GridLayout(3, 1);
77:            setLayout(grid);
78:            add(sub1);
79:            add(sub2);
80:            add(sub3);
81:        }
82:
83:        void setFinalQuestion(boolean finalQuestion) {
84:            if (finalQuestion) {
85:                nextButton.setEnabled(false);
86:                finalButton.setEnabled(true);
87:            }
88:        }
89: }
```

The SurveyWizard class is a JPanel component that creates a card layout manager as an instance variable in line 7 and assigns it to the panel in line 13. This class lacks a main() method, so it must be added to another program's user interface to be tested.

The SurveyFrame application, shown in Listing 11.6, contains a frame that displays a survey panel.

LISTING 11.6   The Full Text of SurveyFrame.java

```
 1: import java.awt.*;
 2: import javax.swing.*;
 3:
 4: public class SurveyFrame extends JFrame {
 5:     public SurveyFrame() {
 6:         super("Survey");
 7:         setSize(290, 140);
 8:         setDefaultCloseOperation(JFrame.EXIT_ON_CLOSE);
 9:         setLookAndFeel();
10:         SurveyWizard wiz = new SurveyWizard();
11:         add(wiz);
12:         setVisible(true);
13:     }
14:
15:     private void setLookAndFeel() {
16:         try {
17:             UIManager.setLookAndFeel(
18:                 "com.sun.java.swing.plaf.nimbus.NimbusLookAndFeel"
19:             );
20:             SwingUtilities.updateComponentTreeUI(this);
```

LISTING 11.6   Continued

```
21:          } catch (Exception exc) {
22:              System.err.println("Couldn't use the system "
23:                  + "look and feel: " + exc);
24:          }
25:      }
26:
27:      public static void main(String[] arguments) {
28:          SurveyFrame surv = new SurveyFrame();
29:      }
30: }
```

A SurveyWizard object is created in line 10 and is added to the frame in line 11. The running application was shown earlier in Figure 11.5.

Grid Bag Layout

The last of the layout managers available through Java is grid bag layout, a sophisticated extension of the grid layout manager. Like grid layout, grid bag layout arranges components into rows and columns of individual cells. A grid bag layout differs from grid layout in these ways:

11

- A component can take up more than one cell in the grid.
- The proportions between different rows and columns do not have to be equal.
- A component does not have to fill the entire cell (or cells) it occupies.
- A component can be aligned along any edge of a cell.

A grid bag layout requires the GridBagLayout and GridBagConstraints classes, which belong to the java.awt package. GridBagLayout is the layout manager, and GridBagConstraints defines the placement of components in the grid.

The constructor for the grid bag layout manager takes no arguments and can be applied to a container like any other manager. The following statements could be used in a frame's constructor method to use grid bag layout in that container:

```
GridBagLayout bag = new GridBagLayout();
setLayout(bag);
```

In a grid bag layout, each component uses a GridBagConstraints object to dictate the cell or cells it occupies in the grid, its size, and other aspects of its presentation.

A GridBagConstraints object has 11 instance variables that determine component placement:

- gridx—The x position of the cell that holds the component (or, if it spans several cells, the x position of the upper-left portion of the component)
- gridy—The y position of the cell or its upper-left portion
- gridwidth—The number of cells the component occupies in a horizontal direction
- gridheight—The number of cells the component occupies in a vertical direction
- weightx—A value that indicates the component's size relative to other components on the same row of the grid
- weighty—A value that indicates the component's size relative to other components on the same column of the grid
- anchor—A value that determines where the component is displayed within its cell (if it doesn't fill the entire cell)
- fill—A value that determines whether the component expands horizontally or vertically to fill its cell
- insets—An Insets object that sets the white space around the component inside its cell
- ipadx—The amount by which to expand the component's width beyond its minimum size
- ipady—The amount by which to expand the component's height

With the exception of insets, all these variables can hold integer values.

The easiest way to use this class is to create a constraint with no arguments and set its variables individually. Variables not explicitly set use their default values.

The following code creates a grid bag layout and a constraint used to place components in the grid:

```
GridBagLayout gridbag = new GridBagLayout();
GridBagConstraints constraint = new GridBagConstraints();
setLayout(gridbag);
```

The constraint can be configured with a set of assignment statements:

```
constraint.gridx = 0;
constraint.gridy = 0;
constraint.gridwidth = 2;
constraint.gridheight = 1;
constraint.weightx = 100;
constraint.weighty = 100;
constraint.fill = GridBagConstraints.NONE;
constraint.anchor = GridBagConstraints.CENTER;
```

This code sets up a constraint that can be used to put a component at grid position (0,0) that is two cells wide and one cell tall.

The component's size within its cell and position are set with class variables of GridBagConstraints. The component is centered in its cell (an anchor value of CENTER) and does not expand to fill the entire cell (a fill value of NONE).

The weightx and weighty values make sense only in relation to the same values for other components, as described in detail later in this section.

A component is added to a grid bag layout in two steps:

1. The layout manager's setConstraints(*Component*, *GridBagConstraints*) method is called with the component and constraint as arguments.

2. The component is added to a container that uses that manager.

The following statements continue the preceding example, adding a button to the layout:

```
JButton okButton = new JButton("OK");
gridbag.setConstraints(okButton, constraint);
pane.add(okButton);
```

A constraint must be set before each component in the grid is placed.

11

Designing the Grid

Because grid bag layout is complex, it helps to do some preparatory work before using it. You can sketch the desired user interface on graph paper or take notes in some other form.

Figure 11.6 shows a rough sketch on graph paper for the layout of a panel in an email program's user interface.

FIGURE 11.6
Designing a user
interface on a grid.

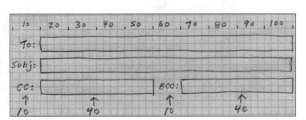

The panel shown in Figure 11.6 contains a group of labels and text fields that will be filled out when a message is sent.

A grid bag layout suits this interface because it contains components of different widths. All the labels have the same width, but the To and Subject text fields are larger than the CC and BCC fields. In grid bag layout, each component must have its own cell and cannot share it with any other components. A component can take up more than one cell.

The sketch shown in Figure 11.6 does not indicate individual cells, but it does mark off values from 0 to 100 to indicate the width of components. These are intended as percentage values rather than exact sizes, which is a convenient way to calculate weightx and weighty values.

NOTE At this point, you might be wondering why percentage values from 0 to 100 aren't running vertically alongside the sketch. The email interface doesn't need them. All the components have the same height (and, thus, the same weighty value).

After the user interface has been sketched to show the relative sizes of components, the cell position and size of each component can be determined.

The width of each component in the email interface was set to multiples of 10, making it easy to use a grid with 10 columns.

Like grid layout, cells begin with (0,0) in the upper-left corner. The x-coordinate is the column, and the y-coordinate is the row. They increase as you move to the left and downward, respectively.

Figure 11.7 shows the (x,y) position and the width of each component, in cells.

FIGURE 11.7
Choosing cells for components in the grid.

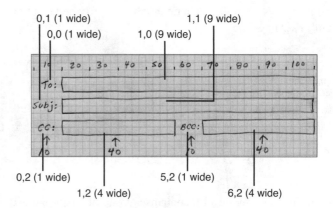

Creating the Grid

After making a sketch on graph paper, you can write the code necessary to implement that sketch as a Java user interface.

The following statements in the email panel's constructor set it to use grid bag layout and add a To label and text field to the panel:

```
public MessagePanel() {
    GridBagLayout gridbag = new GridBagLayout();
    setLayout(gridbag);
    // add the label
    JLabel toLabel = new JLabel("To: ");
    GridBagConstraints constraint = new GridBagConstraints();
    constraint.gridx = 0;
    constraint.gridy = 0;
    constraint.gridwidth = 1;
    constraint.gridheight = 1;
    constraint.weightx = 10;
    constraint.weighty = 100;
    constraint.fill = GridBagConstraints.NONE;
    constraint.anchor = GridBagConstraints.EAST;
    gridbag.setConstraints(toLabel, constraint);
    add(toLabel);
    // add the text field
    JTextField to = new JTextField();
    constraint = new GridBagConstraints();
    constraint.gridx = 1;
    constraint.gridy = 0;
    constraint.gridwidth = 9;
    constraint.gridheight = 1;
    constraint.weightx = 90;
    constraint.weighty = 100;
    constraint.fill = GridBagConstraints.HORIZONTAL;
    constraint.anchor = GridBagConstraints.WEST;
    gridbag.setConstraints(to, constraint);
    add(to);
}
```

11

The label and text fields each use their own constraint (reusing the constraint variable). Their gridx and gridy values put the label at position (0,0) and the text field at position (0,1). The gridwidth values make the label one cell wide and the text field nine cells wide.

The fields use the fill value differently. The label has NONE, so it does not expand in either direction, and the text field has HORIZONTAL, so it expands horizontally only. (The other possible values are VERTICAL and BOTH.)

The fields also use anchor differently. The label is aligned along the right edge of the cell through the EAST class variable. The text field aligns to the left edge through WEST.

Each of the compass directions and CENTER can be used: NORTH, NORTHEAST, EAST, SOUTHEAST, SOUTH, SOUTHWEST, WEST, and NORTHWEST.

The most complex aspect of grid bag constraints are the weightx and weighty values. These variables hold arbitrary integer (or double) values that indicate how big components should be in relation to each other.

The To label has a weightx of 10, and the adjacent text field has a weightx of 90, using the same scale as the sketch shown in Figure 11.6. These values make the text field nine times as large as the label. The values are arbitrary: If the label were 3 and the text field were 27, the field would still be nine times as large.

When you don't need to give components different weights, use the same value throughout a row or column. For instance, the To label and field both have weighty values of 100, so they have the same height as any other components below them in the same column.

Setting up grid bag constraints requires a lot of repetitive code. To save you some typing, the email panel's class has a method to set a component's constraint and add it to the panel:

```
private void addComponent(Component component, int gridx, int gridy,
    int gridwidth, int gridheight, int weightx, int weighty, int fill,
    int anchor) {

    GridBagConstraints constraint = new GridBagConstraints();
    constraint.gridx = gridx;
    constraint.gridy = gridy;
    constraint.gridwidth = gridwidth;
    constraint.gridheight = gridheight;
    constraint.weightx = weightx;
    constraint.weighty = weighty;
    constraint.fill = fill;
    constraint.anchor = anchor;
    gridbag.setConstraints(component, constraint);
    add(component);
}
```

This method doesn't use the insets, ipadx, and ipady variables of the GridBagConstraints class, so they retain their default values.

The following statements call this addComponent() method to add a Subject label and text field to the panel:

```
JLabel subjectLabel = new JLabel("Subject: ");
addComponent(subjectLabel, 0, 1, 1, 1, 10, 100, GridBagConstraints.NONE,
    GridBagConstraints.EAST);
JTextField subject = new JTextField();
addComponent(subject, 1, 1, 9, 1, 90, 100, GridBagConstraints.HORIZONTAL,
    GridBagConstraints.WEST);
```

The panel is completed with statements to add CC and BCC labels and fields:

```
// add a CC label at (0,2) 1 cell wide
JLabel ccLabel = new JLabel("CC: ");
addComponent(ccLabel, 0, 2, 1, 1, 10, 100, GridBagConstraints.NONE,
    GridBagConstraints.EAST);
// add a CC text field at (1,2) 4 cells wide
JTextField cc = new JTextField();
addComponent(cc, 1, 2, 4, 1, 40, 100, GridBagConstraints.HORIZONTAL,
    GridBagConstraints.WEST);
// add a BCC label at (5,2) 4 cells wide
JLabel bccLabel = new JLabel("BCC: ");
addComponent(bccLabel, 5, 2, 1, 1, 10, 100, GridBagConstraints.NONE,
    GridBagConstraints.EAST);
// add a BCC text field at (6,2) 4 cells wide
JTextField bcc = new JTextField();
addComponent(bcc, 6, 2, 4, 1, 40, 100, GridBagConstraints.HORIZONTAL,
    GridBagConstraints.WEST);
```

11

These four components share the same row, which makes their weightx values important. The labels are set to 10 each, and the text fields are set to 40 each, as noted in the initial sketch.

The MessagePanel class, shown in Listing 11.7, contains the source code of the email panel.

LISTING 11.7 The Full Text of MessagePanel.java

```
 1: import java.awt.*;
 2: import javax.swing.*;
 3:
 4: public class MessagePanel extends JPanel {
 5:     GridBagLayout gridbag = new GridBagLayout();
 6:
 7:     public MessagePanel() {
 8:         super();
 9:         GridBagConstraints constraints;
10:         setLayout(gridbag);
11:
12:         JLabel toLabel = new JLabel("To: ");
13:         JTextField to = new JTextField();
```

LISTING 11.7 Continued

```
14:            JLabel subjectLabel = new JLabel("Subject: ");
15:            JTextField subject = new JTextField();
16:            JLabel ccLabel = new JLabel("CC: ");
17:            JTextField cc = new JTextField();
18:            JLabel bccLabel = new JLabel("BCC: ");
19:            JTextField bcc = new JTextField();
20:
21:            addComponent(toLabel, 0, 0, 1, 1, 10, 100,
22:                GridBagConstraints.NONE, GridBagConstraints.EAST);
23:            addComponent(to, 1, 0, 9, 1, 90, 100,
24:                GridBagConstraints.HORIZONTAL, GridBagConstraints.WEST);
25:            addComponent(subjectLabel, 0, 1, 1, 1, 10, 100,
26:                GridBagConstraints.NONE, GridBagConstraints.EAST);
27:            addComponent(subject, 1, 1, 9, 1, 90, 100,
28:                GridBagConstraints.HORIZONTAL, GridBagConstraints.WEST);
29:            addComponent(ccLabel, 0, 2, 1, 1, 10, 100,
30:                GridBagConstraints.NONE, GridBagConstraints.EAST);
31:            addComponent(cc, 1, 2, 4, 1, 40, 100,
32:                GridBagConstraints.HORIZONTAL, GridBagConstraints.WEST);
33:            addComponent(bccLabel, 5, 2, 1, 1, 10, 100,
34:                GridBagConstraints.NONE, GridBagConstraints.EAST);
35:            addComponent(bcc, 6, 2, 4, 1, 40, 100,
36:                GridBagConstraints.HORIZONTAL, GridBagConstraints.WEST);
37:        }
38:
39:    private void addComponent(Component component, int gridx, int gridy,
40:            int gridwidth, int gridheight, int weightx, int weighty, int fill,
41:            int anchor) {
42:
43:            GridBagConstraints constraints = new GridBagConstraints();
44:            constraints.gridx = gridx;
45:            constraints.gridy = gridy;
46:            constraints.gridwidth = gridwidth;
47:            constraints.gridheight = gridheight;
48:            constraints.weightx = weightx;
49:            constraints.weighty = weighty;
50:            constraints.fill = fill;
51:            constraints.anchor = anchor;
52:            gridbag.setConstraints(component, constraints);
53:            add(component);
54:        }
55: }
```

This class isn't an application, so it can't be run. After the panel has been compiled, it can be used in any GUI. (Presumably this panel would be incorporated into an email program's interface for writing messages.)

The MessageFrame class in Listing 11.8 is a simple application that displays a frame with a MessagePanel added to it.

LISTING 11.8   The Full Text of MessageFrame.java.

```
 1: import javax.swing.*;
 2:
 3: public class MessageFrame extends JFrame {
 4:     public MessageFrame() {
 5:         super("Message");
 6:         setSize(380, 120);
 7:         setDefaultCloseOperation(JFrame.EXIT_ON_CLOSE);
 8:         setLookAndFeel();
 9:         MessagePanel mPanel = new MessagePanel();
10:         add(mPanel);
11:         setVisible(true);
12:     }
13:
14:     private void setLookAndFeel() {
15:         try {
16:             UIManager.setLookAndFeel(
17:                 "com.sun.java.swing.plaf.nimbus.NimbusLookAndFeel"
18:             );
19:             SwingUtilities.updateComponentTreeUI(this);
20:         } catch (Exception exc) {
21:             System.err.println("Couldn't use the system "
22:                 + "look and feel: " + exc);
23:         }
24:     }
25:
26:     public static void main(String[] arguments) {
27:         MessageFrame frame = new MessageFrame();
28:     }
29: }
```

11

The panel is created in line 9 and added to the frame in line 10. This application is shown in Figure 11.8.

FIGURE 11.8
Viewing the panel in an application's user interface.

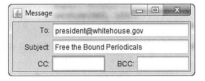

Because the panel does not stipulate its own size, the frame's dimensions determine the panel's height and width. This demonstrates how Swing's grid and grid bag layouts give components the flexibility to adapt to the space available to them in an interface.

If you didn't want the panel to assume the size of its container, its layout manager could be set to null:

```
setLayout(null);
```

As this project illustrates, grid bag layout is much more complex than the other layout managers in Java. If you can design the same interface by mixing other managers, that approach is likely to be easier to maintain in the future, especially when you aren't the only programmer working on the code.

Cell Padding and Insets

The email panel example doesn't use three GridBagConstraints variables: insets, ipadx, and ipady. The ipadx and ipady constraints control *padding*, the extra space around an individual component. By default, no components have extra space around them (which is easiest to see in components that fill their cells). The ipadx variable adds space to either side of the component, and ipady adds it above and below.

The horizontal and vertical gaps that appear when you create a new layout manager (or use ipadx and ipady in grid bag layouts) are used to determine the amount of space between components in a panel. *Insets*, however, are used to determine the amount of space around the panel itself. The Insets class includes values for the top, bottom, left, and right insets, which then are used when the panel is drawn.

Insets determine the amount of space between the edges of a panel and that panel's components.

The following statement creates an Insets object that specifies 20 pixels of insets above and below and 13 pixels to the left and right:

```
Insets whitespace = new Insets(20, 13, 20, 13);
```

You can establish insets in any container by overriding its getInsets() method and returning an Insets object, as in this example:

```
public Insets getInsets() {
    return new Insets(10, 30, 10, 30);
}
```

Summary

When it comes to designing a user interface in Java, you've seen today that abstract expressionism goes only so far. Getting the desired user interface layout in a Swing application requires the use of layout managers.

These managers require some adjustment for people who are used to more precise control over where components appear on an interface.

You now know how to use the five different layout managers and panels. As you work with Swing, you'll find that it can approximate any kind of interface through the use of nested containers and different layout managers.

After you master the development of a user interface in Java, your programs can offer an interface that works on multiple platforms without modification.

Q&A

Q I really dislike working with layout managers; they're either too simplistic or too complicated (the grid bag layout, for example). Even with a lot of tinkering, I can never get my user interface to look like I want it to. All I want to do is define the sizes of my components and put them at an (x,y) position on the screen. Can I do this?

A It's possible, but problematic. Java was designed in such a way that a program's GUI could run equally well on different platforms and with different screen resolutions, fonts, screen sizes, and the like. Relying on pixel coordinates can cause a program that looks good on one platform to be unusable on others. Layout disasters such as components overlapping each other or getting cut off by the edge of a container may result. Layout managers, by dynamically placing elements on the screen, get around these problems. Although there might be some differences in the end results on different platforms, they are less likely to be catastrophic.

If none of that is persuasive, here's how to ignore my advice: Set the content pane's layout manager with `null` as the argument. Create a `Rectangle` object (from the `java.awt` package) with the (x,y) position, width, and height of the component as arguments. Finally, call the component's `setBounds(Rectangle)` method with that rectangle as the argument.

The following application displays a 300×300-pixel frame with a Click Me button at the (x,y) position 10, 10 that is 120 pixels wide by 30 pixels tall:

```
import java.awt.*;
import javax.swing.*;
```

11

```
public class Absolute extends JFrame {
    public Absolute() {
        super("Example");
        setSize(300, 300);
        Container pane = getContentPane();
        pane.setLayout(null);
        JButton myButton = new JButton("Click Me");
        myButton.setBounds(new Rectangle(10, 10, 120, 30));
        pane.add(myButton);
        setContentPane(pane);
        setVisible(true);
    }

    public static void main(String[] arguments) {
        Absolute ex = new Absolute();
    }
}
```

You can find out more about setBounds() in the Component class. You can find the documentation for the Java class library at http://docs.oracle.com/javase/7/docs/api.

Quiz

Review today's material by taking this three-question quiz. Answers are at the end of the book.

Questions

1. What is the default layout manager for a panel in Java?

    A. None

    B. BorderLayout

    C. FlowLayout

2. Which layout manager uses a compass direction or a reference to the center when adding a component to a container?

    A. BorderLayout

    B. MapLayout

    C. FlowLayout

3. If you want a grid layout in which a component can take up more than one cell of the grid, which layout should you use?

    A. GridLayout

    B. GridBagLayout

    C. None; it isn't possible to do that.

Certification Practice

The following question is the kind of thing you could expect to be asked on a Java programming certification test. Answer it without looking at today's material or using the Java compiler to test the code.

Given:

```java
import java.awt.*;
import javax.swing.*;

public class ThreeButtons extends JFrame {
    public ThreeButtons() {
        super("Program");
        setSize(350, 225);
        setDefaultCloseOperation(JFrame.EXIT_ON_CLOSE);
        JButton alpha = new JButton("Alpha");
        JButton beta = new JButton("Beta");
        JButton gamma = new JButton("Gamma");
        JPanel content = new JPanel();
        // answer goes here
        content.add(alpha);
        content.add(beta);
        content.add(gamma);
        add(content);
        pack();
        setVisible(true);
    }

    public static void main(String[] arguments) {
        ThreeButtons b3 = new ThreeButtons();
    }
}
```

Which statement should replace // answer goes here to make the frame display all three buttons side by side?

  A. content.setLayout(null);

  B. content.setLayout(new FlowLayout());

  C. content.setLayout(new GridLayout(3,1));

  D. content.setLayout(new BorderLayout());

The answer is available on the book's website at www.java21days.com. Visit the Day 11 page and click the Certification Practice link.

Exercises

To extend your knowledge of the subjects covered today, try the following exercises:

1. Create a user interface that displays a calendar for a single month, including headings for the seven days of the week and a title for the month across the top.

2. Create an interface that incorporates more than one layout manager.

Where applicable, exercise solutions are offered on the book's website at www.java21days.com.

DAY 12

Responding to User Input

Designing a Java program with a graphical user interface (GUI) isn't very useful if the user can't do anything to it. To make the program completely functional, you must make the interface receptive to user events.

Swing handles events with a set of interfaces called event listeners. You create a listener object and associate it with the user interface component being monitored.

Today, you will learn how to add listeners of all kinds to your Swing programs, including those that handle action events, mouse events, and other interaction.

When you're finished, you will have created a full Java application using the Swing set of classes.

Event Listeners

If a class wants to respond to a user event in Java, it must implement the interface that deals with the events. This interface is not the same thing as a GUI. The interface is an abstract type that defines methods a class must implement.

Interfaces that handle user events are called event listeners.

Each listener handles a specific kind of event.

The `java.awt.event` package contains all the basic event listeners, as well as the objects that represent specific events. These listener interfaces are some of the most useful:

- `ActionListener`—*Action events*, which are generated when a user performs an action on a component, such as clicking a button
- `AdjustmentListener`—*Adjustment events*, which are generated when a component is adjusted, such as when a scrollbar is moved
- `FocusListener`—*Keyboard focus events*, which are generated when a component such as a text field gains or loses the focus
- `ItemListener`—*Item events*, which are generated when an item such as a check box is changed
- `KeyListener`—*Keyboard events*, which occur when a user enters text using the keyboard
- `MouseListener`—*Mouse events*, which are generated by mouse clicks, a mouse entering a component's area, and a mouse leaving a component's area
- `MouseMotionListener`—*Mouse movement events*, which track all movement by a mouse over a component
- `WindowListener`—*Window events*, which are generated when a window is maximized, minimized, moved, or closed

Just as a Java class can implement multiple interfaces, a class that takes user input can implement as many listeners as needed. The `implements` keyword in the class declaration is followed by the name of the interface. If more than one interface has been implemented, their names are separated by commas.

The following class is declared to handle both action and text events:

```
public class Suspense extends JFrame implements ActionListener,
    TextListener {
    // ...
}
```

To refer to these event listener interfaces in your programs, you can import them individually or use an `import` statement with a wildcard to make the entire package available:

```
import java.awt.event.*;
```

Setting Up Components

When you make a class an event listener, you have set up a specific type of event to be heard by that class. However, the event won't actually be heard unless you follow up with a second step: You must add a matching listener to the GUI component. That listener generates the events when the component is used.

After a component is created, you can call one (or more) of the following methods on the component to associate a listener with it:

- `addActionListener()`—JButton, JCheckBox, JComboBox, JTextField, JRadioButton, and JMenuItem components
- `addFocusListener()`—All Swing components
- `addItemListener()`—JButton, JCheckBox, JComboBox, and JRadioButton components
- `addKeyListener()`—All Swing components
- `addMouseListener()`—All Swing components
- `addMouseMotionListener()`—All Swing components
- `addTextListener()`—JTextField and JTextArea components
- `addWindowListener()`—JWindow and JFrame components

12

CAUTION

> Modifying a component after adding it to a container is an easy mistake to make in a Java program. You must add listeners to a component and handle any other configuration before the component is added to any containers; otherwise, these settings are disregarded when the program is run.

The following example creates a `JButton` object and associates an action event listener with it:

```
JButton zap = new JButton("Zap");
zap.addActionListener(this);
```

All the listener adding methods take one argument: the object that is listening for events of that kind. Using this indicates that the current class is the event listener. You could specify a different object, as long as its class implements the right listener interface.

Event-Handling Methods

When you associate an interface with a class, the class must contain methods that implement every method in the interface.

In the case of event listeners, the windowing system calls each method automatically when the corresponding user event takes place.

The ActionListener interface has only one method: actionPerformed(). All classes that implement ActionListener must have a method with the following structure:

```
public void actionPerformed(ActionEvent event) {
    // handle event here
}
```

If only one component in your program's GUI has a listener for action events, you will know that this actionPerformed() method is called only in response to an event generated by that component.

This makes it simpler to write the actionPerformed() method. All the method's code responds to that component's user event.

But when more than one component has an action event listener, you must use the method's ActionEvent argument to figure out which component was used and act accordingly in your program. You can use this object to discover details about the component that generated the event.

ActionEvent and all other event objects are part of the java.awt.event package.

Every event-handling method is sent an event object of some kind. You can use the object's getSource() method to determine which component sent the event, as in the following example:

```
public void actionPerformed(ActionEvent event) {
    Object source = evt.getSource();
}
```

The object returned by the getSource() method can be compared to components by using the == operator. The following statements extend the preceding example to handle user clicks on buttons named quitButton and sortRecords:

```
if (source == quitButton) {
    quit();
}
if (source == sortRecords) {
    sort();
}
```

The quit() method is called if the quitButton object generated the event, and the sort() method is called if the sortRecords button generated the event.

Many event-handling methods call a different method for each kind of event or component. This makes the event-handling method easier to read. In addition, if a class has more than one event-handling method, each one can call the same methods to get work done.

Java's instanceof operator can be used in an event-handling method to determine the class of component that generated the event. The following example can be used in a program with one button and one text field, each of which generates an action event:

```
void actionPerformed(ActionEvent event) {
    Object source = event.getSource();
    if (source instanceof JTextField) {
        calculateScore();
    } else if (source instanceof JButton) {
        quit();
    }
}
```

If the event-generating component belongs to the JTextField class, the calculateScore() method is called. If the component belongs to JButton, the quit() method is called instead.

The TitleChanger application, shown in Listing 12.1, displays a frame with two JButton components, which are used to change the text on the frame's title bar. Create a new empty Java file called TitleChanger, and enter the class's source code.

LISTING 12.1   The Full Text of TitleChanger.java

```
1: import java.awt.event.*;
2: import javax.swing.*;
3: import java.awt.*;
4:
5: public class TitleChanger extends JFrame implements ActionListener {
6:     JButton b1;
7:     JButton b2;
8:
```

12

LISTING 12.1 Continued

```
 9:    public TitleChanger() {
10:        super("Title Bar");
11:        setDefaultCloseOperation(JFrame.EXIT_ON_CLOSE);
12:        setLookAndFeel();
13:        b1 = new JButton("Rosencrantz");
14:        b2 = new JButton("Guildenstern");
15:        b1.addActionListener(this);
16:        b2.addActionListener(this);
17:        FlowLayout flow = new FlowLayout();
18:        setLayout(flow);
19:        add(b1);
20:        add(b2);
21:        pack();
22:        setVisible(true);
23:    }
24:
25:    public void actionPerformed(ActionEvent evt) {
26:        Object source = evt.getSource();
27:        if (source == b1) {
28:            setTitle("Rosencrantz");
29:        } else if (source == b2) {
30:            setTitle("Guildenstern");
31:        }
32:        repaint();
33:    }
34:
35:    private void setLookAndFeel() {
36:        try {
37:            UIManager.setLookAndFeel(
38:                "com.sun.java.swing.plaf.nimbus.NimbusLookAndFeel"
39:            );
40:            SwingUtilities.updateComponentTreeUI(this);
41:        } catch (Exception exc) {
42:            System.err.println("Couldn't use the system "
43:                + "look and feel: " + exc);
44:        }
45:    }
46:
47:    public static void main(String[] arguments) {
48:        TitleChanger frame = new TitleChanger();
49:    }
50: }
```

After you run this application with the Java interpreter, the program's interface should resemble what's shown in Figure 12.1.

FIGURE 12.1
The TitleChanger
application.

Only 13 lines are needed to respond to action events in this application:

- Line 1 imports the `java.awt.event` package.
- Line 5 implements the `ActionListener` interface.
- Lines 15–16 add action listeners to both `JButton` objects.
- Lines 25–33 respond to action events that occur from the two `JButton` objects. The evt object's `getSource()` method determines the event's source. If it is equal to the b1 button, the frame's title is set to `Rosencrantz`; if it is equal to b2, the title is set to `Guildenstern`. A call to `repaint()` is needed so that the frame is redrawn after any title change that might have occurred in the method.

Working with Methods

The following sections detail the structure of each event-handling method and the methods that can be used within them.

In addition to the methods described, the `getSource()` method can be used on any event object to determine which object generated the event.

Action Events

Action events occur when a user completes an action using components such as buttons, check boxes, menu items, text fields, and radio buttons.

A class must implement the `ActionListener` interface to handle these events. In addition, the `addActionListener()` method must be called on each component that should generate an action event—unless you want to ignore that component's action events.

The `actionPerformed(ActionEvent)` method is the only method of the `ActionListener` interface. It takes the following form:

```
public void actionPerformed(ActionEvent event) {
    // ...
}
```

In addition to the `getSource()` method, you can use the `getActionCommand()` method on the `ActionEvent` object to discover more information about the event's source.

12

By default, the action command is the text associated with the component, such as the label on a button. You also can set a different action command for a component by calling its setActionCommand(*String*) method. The string argument should be the action command's desired text.

The following statements create a button and menu item and give both of them the action command "Sort Files":

```
JButton sort = new JButton("Sort");
JMenuItem menuSort = new JMenuItem("Sort");
sort.setActionCommand("Sort Files");
menuSort.setActionCommand("Sort Files");
```

> **TIP**
>
> Action commands are useful in a program in which more than one component should cause the same thing to happen. By giving both components the same action command, you can handle them with the same code in an event-handling method.

Focus Events

Focus events occur when any component gains or loses input focus on a GUI. *Focus* describes the component that is active for keyboard input. If one of the fields has the focus (in a user interface with several editable text fields), the cursor blinks in the field. Any text entered goes into this component.

Focus applies to all components that can receive input. You can give a component the focus by calling its requestFocus() method with no arguments, as in this example:

```
JButton ok = new JButton("OK");
ok.requestFocus();
```

To handle a focus event, a class must implement the FocusListener interface, which has two methods: focusGained(*FocusEvent*) and focusLost(*FocusEvent*). They take the following forms:

```
public void focusGained(FocusEvent event) {
    // ...
}

public void focusLost(FocusEvent event) {
    // ...
}
```

To determine which object gained or lost the focus, the getSource() method can be called on the FocusEvent object sent as an argument to the two methods.

Listing 12.2 contains Calculator, a Java application that displays the sum of two numbers. Focus events are used to determine when the sum needs to be recalculated. In NetBeans create a new Java file with the source code of this listing.

LISTING 12.2   The Full Text of Calculator.java

```java
 1: import java.awt.event.*;
 2: import javax.swing.*;
 3: import java.awt.*;
 4:
 5: public class Calculator extends JFrame implements FocusListener {
 6:     JTextField value1, value2, sum;
 7:     JLabel plus, equals;
 8:
 9:     public Calculator() {
10:         super("Add Two Numbers");
11:         setSize(350, 90);
12:         setDefaultCloseOperation(JFrame.EXIT_ON_CLOSE);
13:         setLookAndFeel();
14:         FlowLayout flow = new FlowLayout(FlowLayout.CENTER);
15:         setLayout(flow);
16:         // create components
17:         value1 = new JTextField("0", 5);
18:         plus = new JLabel("+");
19:         value2 = new JTextField("0", 5);
20:         equals = new JLabel("=");
21:         sum = new JTextField("0", 5);
22:         // add listeners
23:         value1.addFocusListener(this);
24:         value2.addFocusListener(this);
25:         // set up sum field
26:         sum.setEditable(false);
27:         // add components
28:         add(value1);
29:         add(plus);
30:         add(value2);
31:         add(equals);
32:         add(sum);
33:         setVisible(true);
34:     }
35:
36:     public void focusGained(FocusEvent event) {
37:         try {
38:             float total = Float.parseFloat(value1.getText()) +
39:                 Float.parseFloat(value2.getText());
40:             sum.setText("" + total);
```

12

LISTING 12.2   Continued

```
41:            } catch (NumberFormatException nfe) {
42:                value1.setText("0");
43:                value2.setText("0");
44:                sum.setText("0");
45:            }
46:        }
47:
48:        public void focusLost(FocusEvent event) {
49:            focusGained(event);
50:        }
51:
52:        private void setLookAndFeel() {
53:            try {
54:                UIManager.setLookAndFeel(
55:                    "com.sun.java.swing.plaf.nimbus.NimbusLookAndFeel"
56:                );
57:                SwingUtilities.updateComponentTreeUI(this);
58:            } catch (Exception exc) {
59:                System.err.println("Couldn't use the system "
60:                    + "look and feel: " + exc);
61:            }
62:        }
63:
64:        public static void main(String[] arguments) {
65:            Calculator frame = new Calculator();
66:        }
67: }
```

Figure 12.2 shows the application.

FIGURE 12.2
The Calculator
application.

In this application, focus listeners are added to the first two text fields, value1 and value2, and the class implements the FocusListener interface.

The focusGained() method is called whenever either of these fields gains the input focus (lines 36–46). In this method, the sum is calculated by adding the values in the other two fields. If either field contains an invalid value, such as a string, a NumberFormatException is thrown, and all three fields are reset to "0".

The focusLost() method accomplishes the same behavior by calling focusGained() with the focus event as an argument.

One thing to note about this application is that event-handling behavior is not required to collect numeric input in a text field. This is taken care of automatically by any component in which text input is received.

Item Events

Item events occur when an item is selected or deselected on components such as buttons, check boxes, or radio buttons. A class must implement the ItemListener interface to handle these events.

The itemStateChanged(*ItemEvent*) method is the only method in the ItemListener interface. It takes the following form:

```
void itemStateChanged(ItemEvent event) {
    // ...
}
```

To determine in which item the event occurred, the getItem() method can be called on the ItemEvent object.

You also can see whether the item was selected or deselected by using the getStateChange() method. This method returns an integer that equals either the class variable ItemEvent.DESELECTED or ItemEvent.SELECTED.

The FormatChooser application, shown in in Listing 12.3, illustrates the use of item events, displaying information about a selected combo box item in a label. Create it with NetBeans as an empty Java file with the class name FormatChooser.

12

LISTING 12.3 The Full Text of FormatChooser.java

```
 1: import java.awt.*;
 2: import java.awt.event.*;
 3: import javax.swing.*;
 4:
 5: public class FormatChooser extends JFrame implements ItemListener {
 6:     String[] formats = { "(choose format)", "Atom", "RSS 0.92",
 7:         "RSS 1.0", "RSS 2.0" };
 8:     String[] descriptions = {
 9:         "Atom weblog and syndication format",
10:         "RSS syndication format 0.92 (Netscape)",
11:         "RSS/RDF syndication format 1.0 (RSS/RDF)",
12:         "RSS syndication format 2.0 (UserLand)"
13:     };
```

LISTING 12.3 Continued

```
14:     JComboBox formatBox = new JComboBox();
15:     JLabel descriptionLabel = new JLabel("");
16:
17:     public FormatChooser() {
18:         super("Syndication Format");
19:         setSize(420, 150);
20:         setDefaultCloseOperation(JFrame.EXIT_ON_CLOSE);
21:         setLayout(new BorderLayout());
22:         for (int i = 0; i < formats.length; i++) {
23:             formatBox.addItem(formats[i]);
24:         }
25:         formatBox.addItemListener(this);
26:         add(BorderLayout.NORTH, formatBox);
27:         add(BorderLayout.CENTER, descriptionLabel);
28:         setVisible(true);
29:     }
30:
31:     public void itemStateChanged(ItemEvent event) {
32:         int choice = formatBox.getSelectedIndex();
33:         if (choice > 0) {
34:             descriptionLabel.setText(descriptions[choice-1]);
35:         }
36:     }
37:
38:     public Insets getInsets() {
39:         return new Insets(50, 10, 10, 10);
40:     }
41:
42:     private static void setLookAndFeel() {
43:         try {
44:             UIManager.setLookAndFeel(
45:                 "com.sun.java.swing.plaf.nimbus.NimbusLookAndFeel"
46:             );
47:         } catch (Exception exc) {
48:             System.err.println("Couldn't use the system "
49:                 + "look and feel: " + exc);
50:         }
51:     }
52:
53:     public static void main(String[] arguments) {
54:         FormatChooser.setLookAndFeel();
55:         FormatChooser fc = new FormatChooser();
56:     }
57: }
```

This application extends the combo box example from Day 9, "Working with Swing."
Figure 12.3 shows how it looks after a choice has been made.

FIGURE 12.3
The output of the
FormatChooser
application.

The application creates a combo box from an array of strings and adds an item listener to the component (lines 22–25). Item events are received by the itemStateChanged(*ItemEvent*) method (lines 31–36), which changes a label's text based on the index number of the selected item. Index 1 corresponds with "Atom", 2 with "RSS 0.92", 3 with "RSS 1.0", and 4 with "RSS 2.0".

Key Events

Key events occur when a key is pressed on the keyboard. Any component can generate these events, and a class must implement the KeyListener interface to support them.

The KeyListener interface has three methods: keyPressed(*KeyEvent*), keyReleased(*KeyEvent*), and keyTyped(*KeyEvent*). They take the following forms:

```
public void keyPressed(KeyEvent event) {
    // ...
}

public void keyReleased(KeyEvent event) {
    // ...
}

public void keyTyped(KeyEvent event) {
    // ...
}
```

12

KeyEvent's getKeyChar() method returns the character of the key associated with the event. If no Unicode character can be represented by the key, getKeyChar() returns a character value equal to the class variable KeyEvent.CHAR_UNDEFINED.

For a component to generate key events, it must be able to receive the input focus. Text fields, text areas, and other components that accept keyboard input support this ability automatically. For other components, such as labels and panels, the setFocusable(*boolean*) method should be called with an argument of true, as in the following code:

```
JPanel pane = new JPanel();
pane.setFocusable(true);
```

Mouse Events

Mouse events are generated by a mouse click, a mouse entering a component's area, or a mouse leaving the area. Any component can generate these events, which are implemented by a class through the `MouseListener` interface, which has five methods:

- `mouseClicked(`*`MouseEvent`*`)`
- `mouseEntered(`*`MouseEvent`*`)`
- `mouseExited(`*`MouseEvent`*`)`
- `mousePressed(`*`MouseEvent`*`)`
- `mouseReleased(`*`MouseEvent`*`)`

Each method takes the same basic form as `mouseReleased(`*`MouseEvent`*`)`:

```
public void mouseReleased(MouseEvent event) {
    // ...
}
```

The following methods can be used on `MouseEvent` objects:

- `getClickCount()`—Returns as an integer the number of times the mouse was clicked
- `getPoint()`—Returns as a `Point` object the (x,y) coordinate within the component where the mouse was clicked
- `getX()`—Returns the x position
- `getY()`—Returns the y position

Mouse Motion Events

Mouse motion events occur when the mouse is moved over a component. As with other mouse events, any component can generate mouse motion events. A class must implement the `MouseMotionListener` interface to support them.

The `MouseMotionListener` interface has two methods: `mouseDragged(`*`MouseEvent`*`)` and `mouseMoved(`*`MouseEvent`*`)`. They take the following forms:

```
public void mouseDragged(MouseEvent event) {
    // ...
}
```

```
public void mouseMoved(MouseEvent event) {
    // ...
}
```

Unlike the other event-listener interfaces you have dealt with up to this point, MouseMotionListener does not have its own event type. Instead, MouseEvent objects are used.

Because of this, you can call the same methods you would for mouse events: getClick(), getPoint(), getX(), and getY().

The next project you will undertake demonstrates how to detect and respond to mouse events. The MousePrank application, shown in Listing 12.4, consists of two classes, MousePrank and PrankPanel, that implement a user interface button that tries to avoid being clicked.

Create a new empty Java file in NetBeans with the class name MousePrank, and enter the code shown in Listing 12.4. The techniques demonstrated in this class will be described after you create the application and see how it runs.

LISTING 12.4   The Full Text of MousePrank.java

```
 1: import java.awt.*;
 2: import java.awt.event.*;
 3: import javax.swing.*;
 4:
 5: public class MousePrank extends JFrame implements ActionListener {
 6:     public MousePrank() {
 7:         super("Message");
 8:         setDefaultCloseOperation(JFrame.EXIT_ON_CLOSE);
 9:         setSize(420, 220);
10:         BorderLayout border = new BorderLayout();
11:         setLayout(border);
12:         JLabel message = new JLabel("Click OK to close this program.");
13:         add(BorderLayout.NORTH, message);
14:         PrankPanel prank = new PrankPanel();
15:         prank.ok.addActionListener(this);
16:         add(BorderLayout.CENTER, prank);
17:         setVisible(true);
18:     }
19:
20:     public void actionPerformed(ActionEvent event) {
21:         System.exit(0);
22:     }
23:
24:     public Insets getInsets() {
25:         return new Insets(40, 10, 10, 10);
26:     }
27:
28:     private static void setLookAndFeel() {
29:         try {
30:             UIManager.setLookAndFeel(
```

12

LISTING 12.4   Continued

```
31:                       "com.sun.java.swing.plaf.nimbus.NimbusLookAndFeel"
32:                   );
33:            } catch (Exception exc) {
34:                System.err.println("Couldn't use the system "
35:                    + "look and feel: " + exc);
36:            }
37:        }
38:
39:        public static void main(String[] arguments) {
40:            MousePrank.setLookAndFeel();
41:            new MousePrank();
42:        }
43: }
44:
45: class PrankPanel extends JPanel implements MouseMotionListener {
46:        JButton ok = new JButton("OK");
47:        int buttonX, buttonY, mouseX, mouseY;
48:        int width, height;
49:
50:        PrankPanel() {
51:            super();
52:            setLayout(null);
53:            addMouseMotionListener(this);
54:            buttonX = 110;
55:            buttonY = 110;
56:            ok.setBounds(new Rectangle(buttonX, buttonY,
57:                70, 20));
58:            add(ok);
59:        }
60:
61:        public void mouseMoved(MouseEvent event) {
62:            mouseX = event.getX();
63:            mouseY = event.getY();
64:            width = (int)getSize().getWidth();
65:            height = (int)getSize().getHeight();
66:            if (Math.abs((mouseX + 35) - buttonX) < 50) {
67:                buttonX = moveButton(mouseX, buttonX, width);
68:                repaint();
69:            }
70:            if (Math.abs((mouseY + 10) - buttonY) < 50) {
71:                buttonY = moveButton(mouseY, buttonY, height);
72:                repaint();
73:            }
74:        }
75:
76:        public void mouseDragged(MouseEvent event) {
77:            // ignore this event
78:        }
79:
```

LISTING 12.4   Continued

```
80:    private int moveButton(int mouseAt, int buttonAt, int border) {
81:        if (buttonAt < mouseAt) {
82:            buttonAt--;
83:        } else {
84:            buttonAt++;
85:        }
86:        if (buttonAt > (border - 20)) {
87:            buttonAt = 10;
88:        }
89:        if (buttonAt < 0) {
90:            buttonAt = border - 80;
91:        }
92:        return buttonAt;
93:    }
94:
95:    public void paintComponent(Graphics comp) {
96:        super.paintComponent(comp);
97:        ok.setBounds(buttonX, buttonY, 70, 20);
98:    }
99: }
```

The MousePrank class is a frame that holds two components arranged with border lay-out—the label "Click OK to close this program." and a panel with an OK button on it. Figure 12.4 shows the user interface for this application.

FIGURE 12.4
The running MousePrank application.

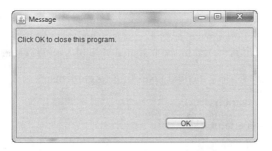

12

Because the button does not behave normally, it is implemented with the PrankPanel class, a subclass of JPanel. This panel includes a button that is drawn at a specific position on the panel instead of being placed by a layout manager. This technique was described at the end of Day 11, "Arranging Components on a User Interface."

First, the panel's layout manager is set to null, which causes it to stop using flow layout as its default manager:

```
setLayout(null);
```

Next, the button is placed on the panel using setBounds(*Rectangle*), the same method that determines where a frame or window will appear on a desktop.

A Rectangle object is created with four arguments: its x position, y position, width, and height. Here's how PrankPanel draws the button:

```
JButton ok = new JButton("OK");
int buttonX = 110;
int buttonY = 110;
ok.setBounds(new Rectangle(buttonX, buttonY, 70, 20));
```

Creating the Rectangle object as the argument to setBounds() is more efficient than creating an object with a name and using that object as the argument. You don't need to use the object anywhere else in the class, so it doesn't need a name. The following statements accomplish the same thing in two steps:

```
Rectangle box = new Rectangle(buttonX, buttonY, 70, 20);
ok.setBounds(box);
```

The class has instance variables that hold the button's (x,y) position, buttonX and buttonY. They start out at (110,110) and change whenever the mouse comes within 50 pixels of the center of the button.

You track mouse movements by implementing the MouseListener interface and its two methods, mouseMoved(*MouseEvent*) and mouseDragged(*MouseEvent*).

The panel uses mouseMoved() and ignores mouseDragged().

When the mouse moves, a mouse event object's getX() and getY() methods return its current (x,y) position, which is stored in the instance variables mouseX and mouseY.

The moveButton(*int, int, int*) method takes three arguments:

- The button's x or y position
- The mouse's x or y position
- The panel's width or height

This method moves the button away from the mouse in either a vertical or horizontal direction, depending on whether it is called with x-coordinates and the panel height or y-coordinates and the width.

After the button's position has moved, the repaint() method is called, which causes the panel's paintComponent(*Graphics*) method to be called in lines 95–98.

Every component has a `paintComponent()` method that can be overridden to draw the component. The button's `setBounds()` method displays it at the current (x,y) position in line 97.

Window Events

Window events occur when a user opens or closes a window object, such as a `JFrame` or `JWindow`. Any component can generate these events, and a class must implement the `WindowListener` interface to support them.

The `WindowListener` interface has seven methods:

- `windowActivated(`*`WindowEvent`*`)`
- `windowClosed(`*`WindowEvent`*`)`
- `windowClosing(`*`WindowEvent`*`)`
- `windowDeactivated(`*`WindowEvent`*`)`
- `windowDeiconified(`*`WindowEvent`*`)`
- `windowIconified(`*`WindowEvent`*`)`
- `windowOpened(`*`WindowEvent`*`)`

They all take the same form as the `windowOpened()` method:

```
public void windowOpened(WindowEvent event) {
    // ...
}
```

The `windowClosing()` and `windowClosed()` methods are similar, but one is called as the window is closing, and the other is called after it is closed. In fact, you can take action in a `windowClosing()` method to stop the window from being closed.

Using Adapter Classes

A Java class that implements an interface must include all its methods, even if it doesn't plan to do anything in response to some of them.

This requirement can make it necessary to add a lot of empty methods when you're working with an event-handling interface such as `WindowListener`, which has seven methods.

As a convenience, Java offers *adapters*, Java classes that contain empty do-nothing implementations of specific interfaces. By subclassing an adapter class, you can implement only the event-handling methods you need by overriding those methods. The rest inherit those do-nothing methods.

12

The java.awt.event package includes FocusAdapter, KeyAdapter, MouseAdapter, MouseMotionAdapter, and WindowAdapter. They correspond to the expected listeners for focus, keyboard, mouse, mouse motion, and window events.

Listing 12.5 is a Java application that displays the most recently pressed key, monitoring keyboard events through a subclass of KeyAdapter. Enter this source code in a new empty Java class file named KeyChecker in NetBeans.

LISTING 12.5   The Full Text of KeyChecker.java

```
 1: import java.awt.*;
 2: import java.awt.event.*;
 3: import javax.swing.*;
 4:
 5: public class KeyChecker extends JFrame {
 6:     JLabel keyLabel = new JLabel("Hit any key");
 7:
 8:     public KeyChecker() {
 9:         super("Hit a Key");
10:         setSize(300, 200);
11:         setDefaultCloseOperation(JFrame.EXIT_ON_CLOSE);
12:         setLayout(new FlowLayout(FlowLayout.CENTER));
13:         KeyMonitor monitor = new KeyMonitor(this);
14:         setFocusable(true);
15:         addKeyListener(monitor);
16:         add(keyLabel);
17:         setVisible(true);
18:     }
19:
20:     private static void setLookAndFeel() {
21:         try {
22:             UIManager.setLookAndFeel(
23:                 "com.sun.java.swing.plaf.nimbus.NimbusLookAndFeel"
24:             );
25:         } catch (Exception exc) {
26:             System.err.println("Couldn't use the system "
27:                 + "look and feel: " + exc);
28:         }
29:     }
30:
31:     public static void main(String[] arguments) {
32:         KeyChecker.setLookAndFeel();
33:         new KeyChecker();
34:     }
35: }
36:
37: class KeyMonitor extends KeyAdapter {
38:     KeyChecker display;
39:
```

LISTING 12.5   Continued

```
40:     KeyMonitor(KeyChecker display) {
41:         this.display = display;
42:     }
43:
44:     public void keyTyped(KeyEvent event) {
45:         display.keyLabel.setText("" + event.getKeyChar());
46:         display.repaint();
47:     }
48: }
```

The KeyChecker application is implemented as a main class of that name and a KeyMonitor helper class.

KeyMonitor is a subclass of KeyAdapter, an adapter class for keyboard events that implements the KeyListener interface. In lines 44–47, the keyTyped method overrides the same method in KeyAdapter, which does nothing.

When a key is pressed, the key is discovered by calling getKeyChar() of the user event object. This key becomes the text of the keyLabel label in the KeyChecker class. This application is shown in Figure 12.5.

FIGURE 12.5
The running
KeyChecker appli-
cation.

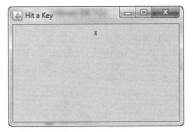

12

Using Inner Classes

One of the challenges of taking user input in Java is to keep the code as short and simple as possible. The need to implement event listeners and all their methods, even for undesired input, requires a lot of coding.

In the KeyChecker application, an adapter class was used to shorten the amount of programming required to handle key events.

A technique to shorten it further would be to use inner classes, which were covered on Day 6, "Packages, Interfaces, and Other Class Features."

Inner classes are defined within a class, as if they were a method or variable. An adapter class is created as an inner class in this statement:

```
KeyAdapter monitor = new KeyAdapter() {
    public void keyTyped(KeyEvent event) {
        keyLabel.setText("" + event.getKeyChar());
        repaint();
    }
};
```

The KeyAdapter object overrides one method, keyTyped(*KeyEvent*), to receive keyboard input. The KeyChecker2 class shown in Listing 12.6 has two advantages over its predecessor. As you create it in NetBeans, see if you can figure out what they are.

LISTING 12.6   The Full Text of KeyChecker2.java

```
 1: import java.awt.*;
 2: import java.awt.event.*;
 3: import javax.swing.*;
 4:
 5: public class KeyChecker2 extends JFrame {
 6:     JLabel keyLabel = new JLabel("Hit any key");
 7:
 8:     public KeyChecker2() {
 9:         super("Hit a Key");
10:         setSize(300, 200);
11:         setDefaultCloseOperation(JFrame.EXIT_ON_CLOSE);
12:         setLayout(new FlowLayout(FlowLayout.CENTER));
13:         KeyAdapter monitor = new KeyAdapter() {
14:             public void keyTyped(KeyEvent event) {
15:                 keyLabel.setText("" + event.getKeyChar());
16:                 repaint();
17:             }
18:         };
19:         setFocusable(true);
20:         addKeyListener(monitor);
21:         add(keyLabel);
22:         setVisible(true);
23:     }
24:
25:     private static void setLookAndFeel() {
26:         try {
27:             UIManager.setLookAndFeel(
28:                 "com.sun.java.swing.plaf.nimbus.NimbusLookAndFeel"
29:             );
30:         } catch (Exception exc) {
31:             System.err.println("Couldn't use the system "
32:                 + "look and feel: " + exc);
```

LISTING 12.6 Continued

```
33:             }
34:         }
35:
36:         public static void main(String[] arguments) {
37:             KeyChecker2.setLookAndFeel();
38:             new KeyChecker2();
39:         }
40:     }
```

The application functions identically to the KeyChecker version.

The advantages of this version are that it is shorter, does not require the creation of a separate class, and it does not need to make use of the this variable in the inner class to be able to change the label in line 15. The inner class can access the variables and methods of its own class.

Inner classes also can be anonymous, which are objects of the class not assigned to a variable.

The TitleChanger application developed today, which used action events to change a frame's title in response to button clicks, could be simplified by using anonymous inner classes. An anonymous inner class becomes the argument to the button's addActionListener() method, as you can see:

```
JButton b1
b1.addActionListener(new ActionListener() {
    public void actionPerformed(ActionEvent evt) {
        setTitle("Rosencrantz");
    }
});
b2.addActionListener(new ActionListener() {
    public void actionPerformed(ActionEvent evt) {
        setTitle("Guildenstern");
    }
});
```

The anonymous inner class is an object that implements the ActionListener interface. The object's actionPerformed() method is overridden to set the frame's title when the corresponding button is clicked. Because each button has its own listener, it's simpler than using one listener for multiple interface components.

Inner classes look more complicated than separate classes, but they can simplify and shorten your Java code.

12

Summary

Event handling is added to a GUI in Swing through these fundamental steps:

- A listener interface is added to the class that will contain the event-handling methods.
- A listener is added to each component that will generate the events to handle.
- The methods are added, each with an `EventObject` class as the only argument to the method.
- Methods of that `EventObject` class, such as `getSource()`, are used to learn which component generated the event and what kind of event it was.

When you know these steps, you can work with each of the different listener interfaces and event classes. You also can learn about new listeners as they are added to Swing with new components.

Q&A

Q Can a program's event-handling behavior be put into its own class instead of being included with the code that creates the interface?

A It can, and many programmers will tell you that this is a good way to design your programs. Separating interface design from your event-handling code allows you to develop the two separately. This makes it easier to maintain the project; related behavior is grouped and isolated from unrelated behavior.

Q Is there a way to differentiate between the buttons on a `mouseClicked()` event?

A Yes. This feature of mouse events wasn't covered today because right and middle mouse buttons are platform-specific features that are unavailable on some systems where Java programs run.

All mouse events send a `MouseEvent` object to their event-handling methods. Call the object's `getModifiers()` method to receive an integer value that indicates which mouse button generated the event.

Check the value against three class variables. It equals `MouseEvent.BUTTON1_MASK` if the left button was clicked, `MouseEvent.BUTTON2_MASK` if the middle button was clicked, and `MouseEvent.BUTTON3_MASK` if the right button was clicked. See `MouseTest.java` on the Day 12 page of the book's website at www.java21days.com for an example that implements this technique.

For more information, see the Java class library documentation for the MouseEvent class. Visit the web page http://docs.oracle.com/javase/7/docs/api and click the java.awt.event hyperlink to view the classes in that package.

Quiz

Review today's material by taking this three-question quiz. Answers are at the end of the book.

Questions

1. If you use this in a method call such as addActionListener(this), what object is being registered as a listener?

    A. An adapter class

    B. The current class

    C. No class

2. What is the benefit of subclassing an adapter class such as WindowAdapter (which implements the WindowListener interface)?

    A. You inherit all the behavior of that class.

    B. The subclass automatically becomes a listener.

    C. You don't need to implement any WindowListener methods you won't be using.

3. What kind of event is generated when you press Tab to leave a text field?

    A. FocusEvent

    B. WindowEvent

    C. ActionEvent

12

Certification Practice

The following question is the kind of thing you could expect to be asked on a Java programming certification test. Answer it without looking at today's material or using the Java compiler to test the code.

Given:

```
import java.awt.event.*;
import javax.swing.*;
import java.awt.*;
```

```
public class Interface extends JFrame implements ActionListener {
    public boolean deleteFile;

    public Interface() {
        super("Interface");
        JLabel commandLabel = new JLabel("Do you want to delete the file?");
        JButton yes = new JButton("Yes");
        JButton no = new JButton("No");
        yes.addActionListener(this);
        no.addActionListener(this);
setLayout( new BorderLayout() );
        JPanel bottom = new JPanel();
        bottom.add(yes);
        bottom.add(no);
        add("North", commandLabel);
        add("South", bottom);
pack();
        setVisible(true);
    }

    public void actionPerformed(ActionEvent evt) {
        JButton source = (JButton) evt.getSource();
        // answer goes here
            deleteFile = true;
        else
            deleteFile = false;
    }

    public static void main(String[] arguments) {
        new Interface();
    }
}
```

Which of the following statements should replace // answer goes here to make the application function correctly?

A. `if (source instanceof JButton)`

B. `if (source.getActionCommand().equals("yes"))`

C. `if (source.getActionCommand().equals("Yes"))`

D. `if source.getActionCommand() == "Yes"`

The answer is available on the book's website at www.java21days.com. Visit the Day 12 page and click the Certification Practice link.

Exercises

To extend your knowledge of the subjects covered today, try the following exercises:

1. Create an application that uses `FocusListener` to ensure that a text field's value is multiplied by –1 and is redisplayed whenever a user changes it to a negative value.
2. Create a calculator that adds or subtracts the contents of two text fields whenever the appropriate button is clicked, displaying the result as a label.

Where applicable, exercise solutions are offered on the book's website at www.java21days.com.

DAY 13
Creating Java2D Graphics

Today, you work with Java classes that put the graphics in graphical user interface. Java2D is a set of classes that support high-quality, scalable, two-dimensional images, color, and text.

Java2D, which includes classes in the `java.awt` and `javax.swing` packages, can be used for each of these visually appealing tasks:

- Drawing text
- Drawing shapes such as circles and polygons
- Using different fonts, colors, and line widths
- Filling shapes with colors and patterns

The Graphics2D Class

Everything in Java2D begins with the Graphics2D class in the java.awt package, which represents a graphics context, an environment in which something can be drawn. A Graphics2D object can represent a component on a graphical user interface, printer, or another display device.

Graphics2D is a subclass of the Graphics class that extends and improves its visual capabilities.

Before you can start using the Graphics2D class, you need a surface on which to draw.

Several user interface components can act as a canvas for graphical operations, including panels and windows.

As soon as you have a component to use as a canvas, you can draw text, lines, ovals, circles, arcs, rectangles, and other polygons on that object.

One component that's suitable for this purpose is JPanel in the javax.swing package. This class represents panels in a graphical user interface that can be empty or contain other components.

The following code creates a frame and a panel and then adds the panel to the frame:

```
JFrame main = new JFrame("Welcome Screen");
JPanel pane = new JPanel();
main.add(pane);
```

Like many user interface components in Java, panels have a paintComponent(*Graphics*) method that is called automatically when the component needs to be redisplayed.

Several things could cause paintComponent() to be called:

- The graphical user interface containing the component is displayed for the first time.
- A window that was displayed on top of the component is closed.
- The graphical user interface containing the component is resized.

By creating a subclass of JPanel, you can override the panel's paintComponent() method and put all your drawing operations in this method.

As you might have noticed, a Graphics object is sent to an interface component's paintComponent() method—not the Graphics2D you need. To create a Graphics2D object that represents the component's drawing surface, you must use casting to convert it, as in the following example:

```
public void paintComponent(Graphics comp) {
    Graphics2D comp2D = (Graphics2D) comp;
    // ...
}
```

After a comp2D object has been cast from the Graphics object sent to the method as an argument, all drawing methods use this new object. The Graphics object will not be used again.

The Graphics Coordinate System

Java2D classes use the same (x, y) coordinate system you have used when setting the size of frames and other components in your Swing applications.

Java's coordinate system uses pixels as its unit of measure. The origin coordinate (0, 0) is in the upper-left corner of a component.

The value of x-coordinates increases to the right of (0, 0), and y-coordinates increase downward.

When you set a frame's size by calling its setSize(*int*, *int*) method, the frame's upper-left corner is at (0, 0), and its lower-right corner is at the two arguments sent to setSize().

The following statement creates a frame 425 pixels wide by 130 pixels tall with its lower-right corner at (425, 130):

```
setSize(425, 130);
```

CAUTION | Java2D differs from other drawing systems in which the (0, 0) origin is at the lower left and y values increase in an upward direction.

13

All pixel values are integers; you can't use decimal numbers to display something at a position between two integer values.

Figure 13.1 shows Java's graphical coordinate system visually, with the origin at (0, 0). Two of the points of a rectangle are at (20, 20) and (60, 60).

FIGURE 13.1
The Java graphics
coordinate system.

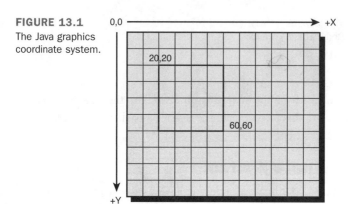

Drawing Text

Text is the easiest thing to draw in Java2D. To draw text, call a Graphics2D object's drawString(*String, int, int*) method with three arguments:

- The string to display
- The x-coordinate where it should be displayed
- The y-coordinate where it should be displayed

The (x, y) coordinates used in the drawString() method represent the pixel at the lower-left corner of the string.

The following paintComponent() method draws the string "Free the bound periodicals" at the coordinates (22, 100):

```
public void paintComponent(Graphics comp) {
    Graphics2D comp2D = (Graphics2D) comp;
    comp2D.drawString("Free the bound periodicals", 22, 100);
}
```

This example uses a default font. To use a different font, you must create an object of the Font class in the java.awt package.

Font objects represent a font's name, style, and point size. A Font object is created by sending three arguments to its constructor:

- The font's name
- The font's style
- The font's point size

A font's name can be its physical name, such as Arial, Courier New, Garamond, or Turman Grotesk. If the font is present on the computer running the application, it is used. If the font is not present, the default font is used.

The name also can be one of five logical fonts: Dialog, DialogInput, Monospaced, SanSerif, or Serif. These fonts can be used to specify the kind of font to use without requiring a specific font. This often is a better choice because some font families might not be present on all implementations of Java.

Three Font styles can be selected by using class variables: PLAIN, BOLD, and ITALIC. These constants are integers, and you can add them to combine effects.

The following statement creates a 24-point Dialog font that is bold and italicized:

```
Font f = new Font("Dialog", Font.BOLD + Font.ITALIC, 24);
```

After you have created a font, you can use it by calling the setFont(Font) method of the Graphics2D class with the font as the argument.

The setFont() method sets the current font, which will be used for all subsequent calls to the drawString() method on the same Graphics2D object until another font is set.

The following paintComponent() method creates a new Font object, sets the current font to that object, and draws the string "I'm deeply font of you" in 72-point type at the coordinates (13, 100):

```
public void paintComponent(Graphics comp) {
    Graphics2D comp2D = (Graphics2D) comp;
    Font f = new Font("Arial Narrow", Font.PLAIN, 72);
    comp2D.setFont(f);
    comp2D.drawString("I'm deeply font of you", 13, 100);
}
```

Java applications can ensure that a font is available by including it with the program and loading it from a file. This technique requires the Font class method createFont(int, InputStream), which returns a Font object representing that font.

13

Input streams, which are covered on Day 15, "Working with Input and Output," are objects that can load data from a source such as a disk file or web address. The following statements load a font from a file named Verdana.ttf in the same folder as the class file that uses it:

```
try {
    File ttf = new File("Verdana.ttf");
    FileInputStream fis = new FileInputStream(ttf);
    Font font = Font.createFont(Font.TRUETYPE_FONT, fis);
```

```
} catch (IOException¦FontFormatException exc) {
    System.out.println("Error: " + exc.getMessage());
}
```

The `try-catch` block handles input/output errors, which must be considered when data is loaded from a file. The `File`, `FileInputStream`, and `IOException` classes are part of the `java.io` package and are discussed in depth on Day 15.

When a font is loaded with `createFont()`, the `Font` object is 1 point and plain style. To change the size and style, call the font object's `deriveFont(int, int)` method with two arguments: the desired style and size.

Improving Fonts and Graphics with Antialiasing

If you displayed text using the skills introduced up to this point, the font's appearance would look crude compared to what you've come to expect from other software. Characters would be rendered with jagged edges, especially on curves and diagonal lines.

Java2D can draw fonts and graphics much more attractively using its support for *antialiasing*, a rendering technique that smooths out rough edges by altering the color of surrounding pixels.

This functionality is off by default. To turn it on, call a `Graphics2D` object's `setRenderingHint()` method with two arguments:

- A `RenderingHint.Key` object that identifies the rendering hint being set
- A `RenderingHint.Key` object that sets the value of that hint

The following code enables antialiasing on a `Graphics2D` object named `comp2D`:

```
comp2D.setRenderingHint(RenderingHints.KEY_ANTIALIASING,
    RenderingHints.VALUE_ANTIALIAS_ON);
```

By calling this method in the `paintComponent()` method of a component, you can cause all subsequent drawing operations to employ antialiasing.

Finding Information About a Font

To make text look good in a graphical user interface, you often must figure out how much space the text is taking up on an interface component.

The `FontMetrics` class in the `java.awt` package provides methods to determine the size of the characters being displayed with a specified font, which can be used for things such as formatting and centering text.

The FontMetrics class can be used to find out detailed information about the current font, such as the width or height of characters it can display.

To use this class's methods, you must create a FontMetrics object using the getFontMetrics() method. The method takes a single argument: a Font object.

Table 13.1 shows some of the information you can find using font metrics. All these methods should be called on a FontMetrics object.

Table 13.1   Font Metrics Methods

Method Name	Description
stringWidth(*String*)	Given a string, returns the full width of that string in pixels
charWidth(*char*)	Given a character, returns the width of that character
getHeight()	Returns the font's total height

Listing 13.1 shows how the Font and FontMetrics classes can be used. The TextFrame application displays a string at the center of a frame, using font metrics to measure the string's width using the selected font.

LISTING 13.1   The Full Text of TextFrame.java

```
 1: import java.awt.*;
 2: import java.awt.event.*;
 3: import javax.swing.*;
 4:
 5: public class TextFrame extends JFrame {
 6:     public TextFrame(String text, String fontName) {
 7:         super("Show Font");
 8:         setSize(425, 150);
 9:         setDefaultCloseOperation(JFrame.EXIT_ON_CLOSE);
10:         TextFramePanel sf = new TextFramePanel(text, fontName);
11:         add(sf);
12:         setVisible(true);
13:     }
14:
15:     public static void main(String[] arguments) {
16:         if (arguments.length < 1) {
17:             System.out.println("Usage: java TextFrame message font");
18:             System.exit(-1);
19:         }
20:         TextFrame frame = new TextFrame(arguments[0], arguments[1]);
21:     }
22:
23: }
24:
```

13

LISTING 13.1   Continued

```
25: class TextFramePanel extends JPanel {
26:     String text;
27:     String fontName;
28:
29:     public TextFramePanel(String text, String fontName) {
30:         super();
31:         this.text = text;
32:         this.fontName = fontName;
33:     }
34:
35:     public void paintComponent(Graphics comp) {
36:         super.paintComponent(comp);
37:         Graphics2D comp2D = (Graphics2D)comp;
38:         comp2D.setRenderingHint(RenderingHints.KEY_ANTIALIASING,
39:             RenderingHints.VALUE_ANTIALIAS_ON);
40:         Font font = new Font(fontName, Font.BOLD, 18);
41:         FontMetrics metrics = getFontMetrics(font);
42:         comp2D.setFont(font);
43:         int x = (getSize().width - metrics.stringWidth(text)) / 2;
44:         int y = getSize().height / 2;
45:         comp2D.drawString(text, x, y);
46:     }
47: }
```

The TextFrame application takes two command-line arguments, which you can set in NetBeans by choosing Project, Set Project Configuration, Customize. To run the application with this configuration, choose Run, Run Project.

Figure 13.2 shows how the application looks with a text message displayed in the font Times New Roman. When you run the application, resize the frame window to see how the text moves so that it remains centered.

FIGURE 13.2
Displaying centered text in a graphical user interface.

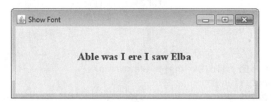

The TextFrame application consists of two classes: a frame and a panel subclass called TextFramePanel. The text is drawn on the panel by overriding the paintComponent(*Graphics*) method and calling drawing methods of the Graphics2D class inside the method.

The getSize() method calls in lines 43 and 44 use the panel's width and height to determine where the text should be displayed. When the application is resized, the panel also is resized, and paintComponent() is called automatically.

Color

The Color class (in the java.awt package) and ColorSpace class (in java.awt.color) can be used to make a graphical user interface more colorful. With these classes, you can set the color for use in drawing operations, as well as the background color of an interface component and other windows. You also can translate a color from one color system into another.

By default, Java uses colors according to the sRGB color system, which describes each shade by the amounts of red, green, and blue it contains (R, G, and B). Each of the three components can be represented as an integer between 0 and 255. Black is 0, 0, 0—the absence of any red, green, or blue. White is 255, 255, 255—the maximum amount of all three colors. You also can represent sRGB values using three floating-point numbers ranging from 0 to 1.0. Java can represent millions of colors between the two extremes using sRGB.

A color system is called a *color space*, and sRGB is only one such space. There also is XYZ, which was created by an international conference in 1931. Java supports the use of any color space desired as long as a ColorSpace object is used that defines the description system. You also can convert from any color space to sRGB, and vice versa.

Java's internal representation of colors using sRGB is just one color space used in a program. An output device such as a monitor or printer also has its own color space.

When you display or print something of a designated color, the output device might not support the designated color. In this circumstance, a different color is substituted or a dithering pattern is used to approximate the unavailable color.

The practical reality of color management is that the color you designate with sRGB will not be available on all output devices. If you need more precise control of the color, you can use ColorSpace and other classes in the java.awt.color package.

13

For most needs, the built-in use of sRGB to define colors should be sufficient.

Using Color Objects

Colors are represented by Color objects, which can be created with a constructor or by using one of the small number of standard colors available in the Color class.

You can call the `Color()` constructor to create a color with three integers that represent the sRGB value of the desired color or three floating-point numbers that serve the same purpose:

```
Color c1 = new Color(0.807F, 1F, 0F);

Color c2 = new Color(255, 204, 102);
```

The c1 object describes a neon green color, and c2 is butterscotch.

NOTE

It's easy to confuse floating-point literals such as 0F and 1F with hexadecimal numbers, which were discussed on Day 2, "The ABCs of Programming." Colors often are expressed in hexadecimal, such as when a background color is set on a web page using Cascading Style Sheets. The Java classes and methods you work with don't take hexadecimal arguments, so when you see a literal such as 1F or 0F, you're dealing with floating-point numbers.

Testing and Setting the Current Colors

The current color for drawing is designated by using the `setColor()` method of the `Graphics2D` class. This method must be called on the `Graphics2D` object that represents the area on which something is being drawn.

Several of the most common colors are available as class variables in the `Color` class. These colors use the following `Color` variables (sRGB values appear in parentheses):

black (0, 0, 0)	magenta (255, 0, 255)
blue (0, 0, 255)	orange (255, 200, 0)
cyan (0, 255, 255)	pink (255, 175, 175)
darkGray (64, 64, 64)	red (255, 0, 0)
gray (128, 128, 128)	white (255, 255, 255)
green (0, 255, 0)	yellow (255, 255, 0)
lightGray (192, 192, 192)	

The following statement sets the color for a `Graphics2D` object named comp2D by using one of the standard class variables:

```
comp2D.setColor(Color.pink);
```

If you have created a `Color` object, it can be set in a similar fashion:

```
Color brush = new Color(255, 204, 102);
comp2D.setColor(brush);
```

After you set the current color, subsequent methods to draw strings and other graphics will use that color.

You can set the background color for a component, such as a panel or frame, by calling the component's setBackground(*Color*) method.

The setBackground() method sets the component's background color, as in this example:

```
setBackground(Color.white);
```

If you want to find out what the current color is, you can use the getColor() method on a Graphics2D object, or the getBackground() method on the component.

The following statement sets the current color of comp2D—a Graphics2D object—to the same color as a component's background:

```
comp2D.setColor(getBackground());
```

Drawing Lines and Polygons

All the basic drawing commands covered today are Graphics2D methods called within a component's paintComponent() method.

This is an ideal place for all drawing operations because paintComponent() is automatically called any time the component needs to be redisplayed.

If another program's window overlaps the component and it needs to be redrawn, putting all the drawing operations in paintComponent() ensures that no part of the drawing is left out.

Java2D features include the following:

- The ability to draw empty polygons and polygons filled with a solid color
- Special fill patterns, such as gradients and patterns
- Strokes that define the width and style of a drawing stroke
- Antialiasing to smooth edges of drawn objects

13

User and Device Coordinate Spaces

One concept introduced with Java2D is the difference between an output device's coordinate space and the coordinate space you refer to when drawing an object. Coordinate space is any 2D area that can be described using (x, y) coordinates.

For all drawing operations prior to Java, the only coordinate space used was the device coordinate space. You specified the (x, y) coordinates of an output surface, such as a panel, and those coordinates were used to draw text and other elements.

Java2D requires a second coordinate space that you refer to when creating an object and actually drawing it. This is called the *user coordinate space.*

Before any 2D drawing has occurred in a program, the device space and user space have the (0, 0) coordinates in the same place—the upper-left corner of the drawing area.

The user space's (0, 0) coordinates can move as a result of the 2D drawing operations being conducted. The x- and y-axes even can shift because of a 2D rotation. You learn more about the two coordinate systems as you work with Java2D.

Specifying the Rendering Attributes

The next step in 2D drawing is to specify how a drawn object is rendered. Java2D offers a wide range of attributes for designating color, including line width, fill patterns, transparency, and many other features.

Fill Patterns

Fill patterns control how a drawn object will be filled in. With Java2D, you can use a solid color, gradient fill, texture, or pattern of your own devising.

A fill pattern is defined by using the setPaint(*Paint*) method of Graphics2D with a Paint object as its only argument. Any class that can be a fill pattern, including GradientPaint, TexturePaint, and Color, can implement the Paint interface. Using a Color object with setPaint() is the same thing as using a solid color as the pattern.

A *gradient fill* is a gradual shift from one color at one coordinate point to another color at a different coordinate point. The shift can occur once between the points—which is called an *acyclic gradient*—or it can happen repeatedly, which is a *cyclic gradient.*

Figure 13.3 shows examples of acyclic and cyclic gradients between white and a darker color. The arrows indicate the points that the colors shift between.

FIGURE 13.3
Acyclic and cyclic
gradient shifts.

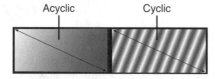

The coordinate points in a gradient do not refer directly to points on the Graphics2D object being drawn onto. Instead, they refer to user space and even can be outside the object being filled with a gradient.

Figure 13.4 illustrates this. Both rectangles are filled using the same GradientPaint object as a guide. One way to think of a gradient pattern is as a piece of fabric that has been spread over a flat surface. The shapes being filled with a gradient are the patterns cut from the fabric, and more than one pattern can be cut from the same piece of cloth.

FIGURE 13.4
Two rectangles
using the same
GradientPaint.

A call to the GradientPaint constructor method takes the following format:

```
GradientPaint gp = new GradientPaint(
    x1, y1, color1, x2, y2, color2);
```

The point (x1, y1) is where the color represented by color1 begins, and (x2, y2) is where the shift ends at color2.

If you want to use a cyclic gradient shift, an extra argument is added at the end:

```
GradientPaint gp = new GradientPaint(
    x1, y1, color1, x2, y2, color2, true);
```

The last argument is a Boolean value that is true for a cyclic shift. A false argument can be used for acyclic shifts, or you can omit this argument; acyclic shifts are the default behavior.

After you have created a GradientPaint object, set it as the current paint attribute by using the setPaint() method. The following statements create and select a gradient:

```
GradientPaint pat = new GradientPaint(0f, 0f, Color.white,
    100f, 45f, Color.blue);
comp2D.setPaint(pat);
```

All subsequent drawing operations to the comp2D object use this fill pattern until another one is chosen.

13

Setting a Drawing Stroke

Java2D allows you to vary the width of drawn lines by using the setStroke() method with a BasicStroke.

A simple BasicStroke constructor takes three arguments:

- A float value representing the line width, with 1.0 as the norm
- An int value determining the style of cap decoration drawn at the end of a line
- An int value determining the style of juncture between two line segments

The endcap- and juncture-style arguments use BasicStroke class variables. Endcap styles apply to the ends of lines that do not connect to other lines. Juncture styles apply to the ends of lines that join other lines.

Possible endcap styles are CAP_BUTT for no endpoints, CAP_ROUND for circles around each endpoint, and CAP_SQUARE for squares. Figure 13.5 shows each endcap style. As you can see, the only visible difference between the CAP_BUTT and CAP_SQUARE styles is that CAP_SQUARE is longer because of the added square endcap.

FIGURE 13.5
Endpoint cap styles.

CAP_BUTT CAP_ROUND CAP_SQUARE

Possible juncture styles include JOIN_MITER, which joins segments by extending their outer edges, JOIN_ROUND, which rounds off a corner between two segments, and JOIN_BEVEL, which joins segments with a straight line. Figure 13.6 shows examples of each juncture style.

FIGURE 13.6
Endpoint juncture styles.

JOIN_MITER JOIN_ROUND JOIN_BEVEL

The following statements create a BasicStroke object and make it the current stroke:

```
BasicStroke pen = new BasicStroke(2.0f,
    BasicStroke.CAP_BUTT,
    BasicStroke.JOIN_ROUND);
comp2D.setStroke(pen);
```

The stroke has a width of 2 pixels, plain endpoints, and rounded segment corners.

Creating Objects to Draw

After you have created a Graphics2D object and specified the rendering attributes, the final two steps are to create the object and draw it.

You create a drawn object in Java2D by defining it as a geometric shape using a class in the java.awt.geom package. You can draw lines, rectangles, ellipses, arcs, and polygons.

The Graphics2D class does not have a different method for each shape you can draw. Instead, you define the shape and use it as an argument to draw() or fill() methods.

Lines

Lines are created using the Line2D.Float class. This class takes four arguments: the (x,y) coordinates of one endpoint followed by the (x,y) coordinates of the other. Here's an example:

```
Line2D.Float ln = new Line2D.Float(60F, 5F, 13F, 28F);
```

This statement creates a line between (60, 5) and (13, 28). Note that an F is used with the literals sent as arguments. Otherwise, the Java compiler would assume that the values were integers.

Rectangles

Rectangles are created by using the Rectangle2D.Float class or Rectangle2D.Double class. The difference between the two is that one takes float arguments, and the other takes double arguments.

Rectangle2D.Float takes four arguments: x-coordinate, y-coordinate, width, and height. The following is an example:

```
Rectangle2D.Float rc = new Rectangle2D.Float(10F, 13F, 40F, 20F);
```

This creates a rectangle at 10, 13 that is 40 pixels wide by 20 pixels tall.

Ellipses

Ellipses can be created with the Ellipse2D.Float class. It takes four arguments: x-coordinate, y-coordinate, width, and height.

The following statement creates an ellipse at (113, 25) with a width of 22 pixels and a height of 40 pixels:

```
Ellipse2D.Float ee = new Ellipse2D.Float(113, 25, 22, 40);
```

Arcs

Of all the shapes you can draw in Java2D, arcs are the most complex to construct.

13

Arcs are created with the Arc2D.Float class, which takes five arguments:

- The (x,y) coordinates of an invisible ellipse that would include the arc if it were drawn
- The width and height of the ellipse
- The starting degree of the arc
- The number of degrees it travels on the ellipse
- An integer describing how the arc is closed

The number of degrees the arc travels is specified in a counterclockwise direction by using negative numbers.

Figure 13.7 shows where degree values are located when determining an arc's starting degree. The arc's starting angle ranges from 0 to 359 degrees counterclockwise. On a circular ellipse, 0 degrees is at the 3 o'clock position, 90 degrees is at 12 o'clock, 180 degrees is at 9 o'clock, and 270 degrees is at 6 o'clock.

FIGURE 13.7
Determining the starting degree of an arc.

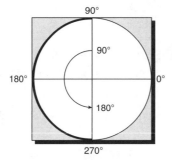

The last argument to the Arc2D.Float constructor uses one of three class variables: Arc2D.OPEN for an unclosed arc, Arc2D.CHORD to connect the arc's endpoints with a straight line, and Arc2D.PIE to connect the arc to the center of the ellipses like a pie slice. Figure 13.8 shows each of these styles.

FIGURE 13.8
Arc closure styles.

Arc2D.OPEN   Arc2D.CHORD   Arc2D.PIE

The `Arc2D.OPEN` closure style does not apply to filled arcs. A filled arc that has `Arc2D.OPEN` as its style will be closed using the same style as `Arc2D.CHORD`.

The following statement creates an `Arc2D.Float` object:

```
Arc2D.Float arc = new Arc2D.Float(
    27F, 22F, 42F, 30F, 33F, 90F, Arc2D.PIE);
```

This creates an arc for an oval at (27, 22) that is 42 pixels wide by 30 pixels tall. The arc begins at 33 degrees, extends 90 degrees clockwise, and is closed like a pie slice.

Polygons

You create polygons in Java2D by defining each movement from one point on the polygon to another. A polygon can be formed from straight lines, quadratic curves, or Bézier curves.

The movements to create a polygon are defined as a `GeneralPath` object, which also is part of the `java.awt.geom` package.

A `GeneralPath` object can be created without any arguments, as shown here:

```
GeneralPath polly = new GeneralPath();
```

The `moveTo()` method of `GeneralPath` is used to create the first point on the polygon. The following statement would be used if you wanted to start `polly` at the coordinate 5, 0:

```
polly.moveTo(5f, 0f);
```

After creating the first point, the `lineTo()` method is used to create lines that end at a new point. This method takes two arguments: the (x,y) coordinates of the new point.

The following statements add three lines to the `polly` object:

```
polly.lineTo(205f, 0f);
polly.lineTo(205f, 90f);
polly.lineTo(5f, 90f);
```

The `lineTo()` and `moveTo()` methods require `float` arguments to specify coordinate points.

13

If you want to close a polygon, the closePath() method is used without any arguments, as shown here:

```
polly.closePath();
```

This method closes a polygon by connecting the current point with the point specified by the most recent moveTo() method. You can close a polygon without this method by using a lineTo() method that connects to the original point.

After you have created an open or closed polygon, you can draw it like any other shape using the draw() and fill() methods. The polly object is a rectangle with points at (5, 0), (205, 0), (205, 90), and (5, 90).

Drawing Objects

After you have defined the rendering attributes, such as color and line width, and have created the object to be drawn, you're ready to draw something in all its 2D glory.

All drawn objects use the same Graphics2D class's methods: draw() for outlines and fill() for filled objects. These take an object as the only argument.

Drawing a Map

The next project you will create is an application that draws a simple map using 2D drawing techniques. Create the Map class in NetBeans.

LISTING 13.2   The Full Text of Map.java

```
 1: import java.awt.*;
 2: import java.awt.geom.*;
 3: import javax.swing.*;
 4:
 5: public class Map extends JFrame {
 6:     public Map() {
 7:         super("Map");
 8:         setSize(360, 350);
 9:         setDefaultCloseOperation(JFrame.EXIT_ON_CLOSE);
10:         MapPane map = new MapPane();
11:         add(map);
12:         setVisible(true);
13:     }
14:
15:     public static void main(String[] arguments) {
16:         Map frame = new Map();
17:     }
18:
19: }
20:
```

LISTING 13.2 Continued

```
21: class MapPane extends JPanel {
22:     public void paintComponent(Graphics comp) {
23:         Graphics2D comp2D = (Graphics2D)comp;
24:         comp2D.setColor(Color.blue);
25:         comp2D.setRenderingHint(RenderingHints.KEY_ANTIALIASING,
26:             RenderingHints.VALUE_ANTIALIAS_ON);
27:         Rectangle2D.Float background = new Rectangle2D.Float(
28:             0F, 0F, (float)getSize().width, (float)getSize().height);
29:         comp2D.fill(background);
30:         // Draw waves
31:         comp2D.setColor(Color.white);
32:         BasicStroke pen = new BasicStroke(2F,
33:         BasicStroke.CAP_BUTT, BasicStroke.JOIN_ROUND);
34:         comp2D.setStroke(pen);
35:         for (int ax = 0; ax < 340; ax += 10)
36:             for (int ay = 0; ay < 340 ; ay += 10) {
37:                 Arc2D.Float wave = new Arc2D.Float(ax, ay,
38:                     10, 10, 0, -180, Arc2D.OPEN);
39:                 comp2D.draw(wave);
40:             }
41:         // Draw Florida
42:         GradientPaint gp = new GradientPaint(0F, 0F, Color.green,
43:             350F,350F, Color.orange, true);
44:         comp2D.setPaint(gp);
45:         GeneralPath fl = new GeneralPath();
46:         fl.moveTo(10F, 12F);
47:         fl.lineTo(234F, 15F);
48:         fl.lineTo(253F, 25F);
49:         fl.lineTo(261F, 71F);
50:         fl.lineTo(344F, 209F);
51:         fl.lineTo(336F, 278F);
52:         fl.lineTo(295F, 310F);
53:         fl.lineTo(259F, 274F);
54:         fl.lineTo(205F, 188F);
55:         fl.lineTo(211F, 171F);
56:         fl.lineTo(195F, 174F);
57:         fl.lineTo(191F, 118F);
58:         fl.lineTo(120F, 56F);
59:         fl.lineTo(94F, 68F);
60:         fl.lineTo(81F, 49F);
61:         fl.lineTo(12F, 37F);
62:         fl.closePath();
63:         comp2D.fill(fl);
64:         // Draw ovals
65:         comp2D.setColor(Color.black);
66:         BasicStroke pen2 = new BasicStroke();
67:         comp2D.setStroke(pen2);
68:         Ellipse2D.Float e1 = new Ellipse2D.Float(235, 140, 15, 15);
69:         Ellipse2D.Float e2 = new Ellipse2D.Float(225, 130, 15, 15);
```

13

LISTING 13.2   Continued

```
70:            Ellipse2D.Float e3 = new Ellipse2D.Float(245, 130, 15, 15);
71:            comp2D.fill(e1);
72:            comp2D.fill(e2);
73:            comp2D.fill(e3);
74:        }
75: }
```

In the Map application, line 2 imports the classes in the java.awt.geom package. This statement is required because import java.awt.*; in line 1 handles only classes, not packages, available under java.awt.

Line 23 creates the comp2D object used for all 2D drawing operations. It's a cast of the Graphics object that represents the panel's visible surface.

Lines 32–34 create a BasicStroke object that represents a line width of 2 pixels and then makes this the current stroke with the setStroke() method of Graphics2D.

Lines 35–40 use two nested for loops to create waves from individual arcs.

Lines 42 and 43 create a gradient fill pattern from the color green at (0, 0) to orange at (50, 50). The last argument to the constructor, true, causes the fill pattern to repeat itself as many times as needed to fill an object.

Line 44 sets the current gradient fill pattern using the setPaint() method and the gp object just created.

Lines 45–63 create the polygon shaped like the author's home state and draw it. This polygon is filled with a green-to-orange gradient pattern.

Line 65 sets the current color to black. This replaces the gradient fill pattern for the next drawing operation because colors are also fill patterns.

Line 66 creates a new BasicStroke() object with no arguments, which defaults to a 1-pixel line width.

Line 67 sets the current line width to the new BasicStroke object pen2.

Lines 68–70 create three ellipses at (235, 140), (225, 130), and (245, 130). Each is 15 pixels wide by 15 pixels tall, making them circles.

Figure 13.9 shows the application running.

FIGURE 13.9
The Map
application.

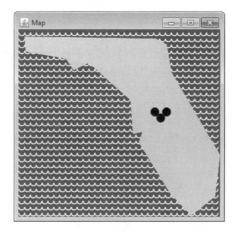

Summary

You now have some tools to improve the looks of a Java program. You can draw with lines, rectangles, ellipses, polygons, fonts, colors, and patterns onto a frame, a panel, and other user interface components using Java2D.

Java2D uses the same two methods for each drawing operation—draw() and fill(). Different objects are created using classes of the java.awt.geom package, and these are used as arguments for the drawing methods of Graphics2D.

Tomorrow, on Day 14, "Developing Swing Applications," you'll learn how to create applications that are launched from a web page using Java Web Start technology.

Q&A

13

Q **What does the uppercase F refer to in source code today? It is added to coordinates, as in the method polly.moveTo(5F, 0F). Why is F used for these coordinates and not others, and why is a lowercase f used elsewhere?**

A The F or f indicates that a number is a floating-point number rather than an integer, and uppercase and lowercase can be used interchangeably. If you don't use one of them, the Java compiler assumes that the number is an int value. Many methods and constructors in Java require floating-point arguments but can handle integers because an integer can be converted to floating-point without changing its value. For this reason, constructors such as Arc2D.Float() can use arguments such as 10 and 180 instead of 10F and 180F.

Q The section "Improving Fonts and Graphics with Antialiasing" mentioned a class called `RenderingHint.Key`. Why does this class have two names separated by a period? What does this signify?

A The use of two names to identify a class indicates that it is an inner class. The first class name is the enclosing class, followed by a period and the name of the inner class. In this case, the `Key` class is an inner class within the `RenderingHint` class.

Quiz

Review today's material by taking this three-question quiz. Answers are at the end of the book.

Questions

1. What object is required before you can draw something in Java using Swing?

   A. `Graphics2D`

   B. `WindowListener`

   C. `JFrame`

2. Which of the following is not a valid Java statement to create a `Color` object?

   A. `Color c1 = new Color(0F, 0F, 0F);`

   B. `Color c2 = new Color(0, 0, 0);`

   C. Both are valid.

3. What does `getSize().width` refer to?

   A. The width of the interface component's window

   B. The width of the frame's window

   C. The width of any graphical user interface component in Java

Certification Practice

The following question is the kind of thing you could expect to be asked on a Java programming certification test. Answer it without looking at today's material or using the Java compiler to test the code.

Given:

```
import java.awt.*;
import javax.swing.*;
```

```
public class Result extends JFrame {
    public Result() {
        super("Result");
 JLabel width = new JLabel("This frame is " +
            getSize().width + " pixels wide.");
        add("North", width);
        setSize(220, 120);
    }

    public static void main(String[] arguments) {
        Result r = new Result();
        r.setVisible(true);
    }
}
```

What will be the reported width of the frame, in pixels, when the application runs?

A. 0 pixels

B. 120 pixels

C. 220 pixels

D. The width of the user's monitor

The answer is available on the book's website at www.java21days.com. Visit the Day 13 page and click the Certification Practice link.

Exercises

To extend your knowledge of the subjects covered today, try the following exercises:

1. Create an application that draws a circle, with its radius, (x,y) position, and color all determined by arguments.

2. Create an application that draws a pie graph.

Where applicable, exercise solutions are offered on the book's website at www.java21days.com.

13

DAY 14

Developing Swing Applications

The first exposure many people have to the Java programming language is applets—small, security-restricted Java programs that run on web pages. Java Web Start, a protocol for downloading and running Java programs, makes it possible to launch applications from a web page as if they were applets.

Today, you learn how to create these web-launched Java programs as you explore the following topics:

- How to install and run Java applications in a web browser

- How to publish your application's files and deploy it

- How Swing applications can run into performance slowdowns on time-consuming tasks

- How to address these problems using SwingWorker, a class that performs Swing work in its own thread

Java Web Start

One of the issues you must deal with as a Java programmer is how to make your software available to your users.

Java applications require a Java interpreter, so one must be included with the application, previously installed on a computer, or installed by users. The easiest solution (for you) is to require that users download and install the Java Runtime Environment from Oracle's website at www.java.com.

Regardless of how you deal with the requirement for an interpreter, you distribute an application like any other program—making it available for download, distributing it on a CD, or using some other means. A user must run an installation program to set it up, if one is available, or copy the files and folders manually.

Java eases the challenges of software deployment with Java Web Start, a way to run Java applications presented on a web page and stored on a web server. Here's how it works:

1. A programmer packages an application and all the files it needs into a JAR archive, along with a file that uses the Java Network Launching Protocol (JNLP), part of Java Web Start.

2. The file is stored on a web server with a web page that links to that file.

3. A user loads the page with a browser and clicks the link.

4. If the user does not have the Java Runtime Environment, a dialog box opens, asking whether the JRE should be downloaded and installed. The full installation is 98MB in size.

5. The Java Runtime Environment installs and runs the program, opening new frames and other interface components like any other application. The program is saved in a cache, so it can be run again later without requiring installation.

To see Java Web Start in action, visit Oracle's Java Web Start site at www.oracle.com/technetwork/java/javase/javawebstart. Click the Code Samples & Apps link, and then the Demos link. The Web Start Demos page, shown in Figure 14.1, contains pictures of several Java applications, each with a Click to Launch! button you can use to run the application.

Click the Click to Launch! button of one of the applications. If you don't have the Java Runtime Environment yet, a dialog box opens, asking whether you want to download and install it.

FIGURE 14.1
Presenting Web
Start applications
on a web page.

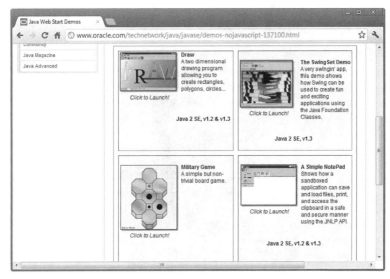

The runtime environment includes the Java Plug-in, a Java virtual machine that adds support for the current version of the language to browsers. The environment also can be used to run applications, regardless of whether they use Java Web Start.

When an application is run using Java Web Start, a title screen appears briefly, and then the application's graphical user interface appears.

NOTE
If you have installed the JDK, you probably have the Java Runtime Environment on your computer already.

Figure 14.2 shows one of the demo applications that Oracle offers, a military strategy game in which three black dots attempt to keep a red dot from moving into their territory.

As you can see in Figure 14.2, the application looks no different from any other application. Unlike applets, which are presented in conjunction with a web page, applications launched with Java Web Start run in their own windows, as if they were run from a command line.

One thing that's different about a Java Web Start application is the security that can be offered to users. When an application attempts to do something, such as read or write files, the user can be asked for permission.

14

FIGURE 14.2
Running a Java
Web Start
application.

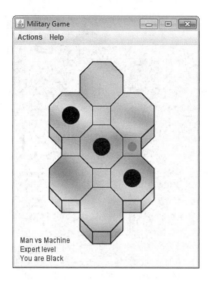

For example, another of the demo programs is a text editor. When you try to save a file
for the first time with this application, the Security Warning dialog box opens, as shown
in Figure 14.3.

FIGURE 14.3
Choosing an appli-
cation's security
privileges.

If the user does not permit something that requires such authorization, the application
cannot function fully. The kinds of things that trigger a security dialog box are reading
and writing files, loading network resources from servers other than the one hosting the
program, and the like.

After Java Web Start has run an application, it is stored on a user's computer in a cache,
enabling it to be run again later without installation. The only exception is when a new
version of the application becomes available. In this case, the new version is downloaded
and installed automatically in place of the existing one.

You can run a Java Web Start application viewer included with the JDK to see the applications that have been cached. You can run them and change some of their settings. The

application is called javaws.exe and can be found in the folder where the JDK was installed, in a `bin` subfolder.

> **NOTE**
>
> Although you run a Java Web Start application for the first time using a web browser, that's not a requirement. To see this, run the Java Web Start application viewer, select a program, and choose Application, Install Shortcuts. A shortcut to run the application is added to your desktop. You can use it to run the program without a browser.

The default security restrictions in place for a Java Web Start application can be overridden if it is stored in a digitally signed Java archive. The user is presented with the signed security certificate, which documents the program's author and the certificate granting authority vouching for its identity, and is asked whether to accept or reject it. The application won't run unless the certificate has been accepted.

Using Java Web Start

Any Java application can be run using Java Web Start as long as the web server that offers the application is configured to work with the technology and all the class files and other files it needs have been packaged together.

To prepare an application to use Java Web Start, you must save the application's files in a Java archive file, create a special Java Web Start configuration file for the application, and upload the files to the web server.

The configuration file that must be created uses JNLP, an Extensible Markup Language (XML) file format that specifies the application's main class file, its JAR archive, and other things about the program.

> **NOTE**
>
> XML is introduced during Day 20, "XML Web Services." Because the format of JNLP files is relatively self-explanatory, you don't need to know much about XML to create a JNLP file.

14

The next project you will undertake is using Java Web Start to launch and run PageData, an application that displays information about web pages.

Creating a JNLP File

The first thing you must do is package all of an application's class files into a Java archive file, along with any other files it needs. NetBeans creates a JAR file automatically for each project you build in the IDE.

Because you've been using one project for all the projects in the preceding 13 days, a new project is needed:

1. Choose File, New Project. The New Project dialog appears.
2. Choose Java in the Categories pane and Java Applications in the Projects pane and then click Next. The New Java Application dialog opens.
3. Enter PageData as the Project Name.
4. Select the Create Main Class checkbox.
5. Enter PageData in the text field next to Create Main Class.
6. Click Finish.

The file PageData.java opens in NetBeans' source code editor with some starter code entered for you. Delete all this code and enter the code shown in Listing 14.1 as the PageData class.

LISTING 14.1   The Full Text of PageData.java

```
 1: import java.awt.*;
 2: import java.awt.event.*;
 3: import java.net.*;
 4: import java.io.*;
 5: import javax.swing.*;
 6:
 7: public class PageData extends JFrame implements ActionListener,
 8:     Runnable {
 9:
10:     Thread runner;
11:     String[] headers = { "Content-Length", "Content-Type",
12:         "Date", "Public", "Expires", "Last-Modified",
13:         "Server" };
14:
15:     URL page;
16:     JTextField url;
17:     JLabel[] headerLabel = new JLabel[7];
18:     JTextField[] header = new JTextField[7];
19:     JButton readPage, clearPage, quitLoading;
20:     JLabel status;
21:
```

LISTING 14.1   Continued

```
22:    public PageData() {
23:        super("Page Data");
24:        setDefaultCloseOperation(JFrame.EXIT_ON_CLOSE);
25:        setLookAndFeel();
26:        setLayout(new GridLayout(10, 1));
27:
28:        JPanel first = new JPanel();
29:        first.setLayout(new FlowLayout(FlowLayout.RIGHT));
30:        JLabel urlLabel = new JLabel("URL:");
31:        url = new JTextField(22);
32:        urlLabel.setLabelFor(url);
33:        first.add(urlLabel);
34:        first.add(url);
35:        add(first);
36:
37:        JPanel second = new JPanel();
38:        second.setLayout(new FlowLayout());
39:        readPage = new JButton("Read Page");
40:        clearPage = new JButton("Clear Fields");
41:        quitLoading = new JButton("Quit Loading");
42:        readPage.setMnemonic('r');
43:        clearPage.setMnemonic('c');
44:        quitLoading.setMnemonic('q');
45:        readPage.setToolTipText("Begin Loading the Web Page");
46:        clearPage.setToolTipText("Clear All Header Fields Below");
47:        quitLoading.setToolTipText("Quit Trying to Load the Web Page");
48:        readPage.setEnabled(true);
49:        clearPage.setEnabled(false);
50:        quitLoading.setEnabled(false);
51:        readPage.addActionListener(this);
52:        clearPage.addActionListener(this);
53:        quitLoading.addActionListener(this);
54:        second.add(readPage);
55:        second.add(clearPage);
56:        second.add(quitLoading);
57:        add(second);
58:
59:        JPanel[] row = new JPanel[7];
60:        for (int i = 0; i < 7; i++) {
61:            row[i] = new JPanel();
62:            row[i].setLayout(new FlowLayout(FlowLayout.RIGHT));
63:            headerLabel[i] = new JLabel(headers[i]+":");
64:            header[i] = new JTextField(22);
65:            headerLabel[i].setLabelFor(header[i]);
66:            row[i].add(headerLabel[i]);
67:            row[i].add(header[i]);
68:            add(row[i]);
69:        }
70:
```

14

LISTING 14.1   Continued

```
 71:            JPanel last = new JPanel();
 72:            last.setLayout(new FlowLayout(FlowLayout.LEFT));
 73:            status = new JLabel("Enter a URL address to check.");
 74:            last.add(status);
 75:            add(last);
 76:            pack();
 77:            setVisible(true);
 78:        }
 79:
 80:        public void actionPerformed(ActionEvent evt) {
 81:            Object source = evt.getSource();
 82:            if (source == readPage) {
 83:                try {
 84:                    page = new URL(url.getText());
 85:                    if (runner == null) {
 86:                        runner = new Thread(this);
 87:                        runner.start();
 88:                    }
 89:                    quitLoading.setEnabled(true);
 90:                    readPage.setEnabled(false);
 91:                }
 92:                catch (MalformedURLException e) {
 93:                    status.setText("Bad URL: " + page);
 94:                }
 95:            } else if (source == clearPage) {
 96:                for (int i = 0; i < 7; i++)
 97:                    header[i].setText("");
 98:                quitLoading.setEnabled(false);
 99:                readPage.setEnabled(true);
100:                clearPage.setEnabled(false);
101:            } else if (source == quitLoading) {
102:                runner = null;
103:                url.setText("");
104:                quitLoading.setEnabled(false);
105:                readPage.setEnabled(true);
106:                clearPage.setEnabled(false);
107:            }
108:        }
109:
110:        public void run() {
111:            URLConnection conn;
112:            try {
113:                conn = this.page.openConnection();
114:                conn.connect();
115:                status.setText("Connection opened ...");
116:                for (int i = 0; i < 7; i++)
117:                    header[i].setText(conn.getHeaderField(headers[i]));
118:                quitLoading.setEnabled(false);
119:                clearPage.setEnabled(true);
```

LISTING 14.1   Continued

```
120:                    status.setText("Done");
121:                    runner = null;
122:                }
123:            catch (IOException e) {
124:                    status.setText("IO Error:" + e.getMessage());
125:                }
126:        }
127:
128:        private static void setLookAndFeel() {
129:            try {
130:                UIManager.setLookAndFeel(
131:                    "com.sun.java.swing.plaf.nimbus.NimbusLookAndFeel"
132:                );
133:            } catch (Exception exc) {
134:                // ignore error
135:            }
136:        }
137:
138:
139:        public static void main(String[] arguments) {
140:            PageData frame = new PageData();
141:        }
142: }
```

After you've saved the project, build it in NetBeans by choosing Run, Clean and Build Project. This extra step is required because you will deploy this application on the web instead of simply running it on your computer.

The PageData application takes a web address (URL) as input and loads data associated with the page at that address. This program uses some networking techniques that will be explored fully during Day 17, "Communicating Across the Internet."

Next, the application needs an icon that will be displayed when it is loaded and used in menus and desktops. The icon for a Java Web Start application can be in either GIF or JPEG format and should be 64 pixels wide by 64 pixels tall.

For this project, if you don't want to create a new icon, you can download pagedataicon.gif from the book's website. Go to www.java21days.com and open the Day 14 page. Right-click the pagedataicon.gif link and save the file to a folder on your computer.

Next, click the Files tab to bring that pane to the front in NetBeans, as shown in Figure 14.4.

14

Files tab

FIGURE 14.4

Adding a file to a
project in
NetBeans.

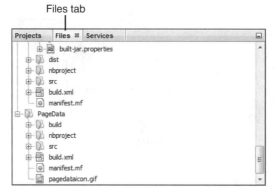

Scroll down to the PageData folder icon, and drag `pagedataicon.gif` from that folder
into NetBeans. The file appears in the Files listing, as shown in Figure 14.4.

The final thing you must do is create the JNLP file that describes the application. Listing
14.2 is a JNLP file used to distribute the PageData application.

You can create this file in NetBeans:

1. Choose File, New File. The New File dialog opens.

2. Choose Other in the Categories pane.

3. Choose JNLP File in the File Types pane.

4. Click Next. The New JNLP File dialog appears.

5. Enter `PageData` in the File Name field. In the Created File field, you see that
   NetBeans automatically adds the file extension `.jnlp` to the filename.

6. Click Finish.

NetBeans creates a new JNLP file in the source code editor, starting you with some text
in XML format. Delete all this text and enter the code shown in Listing 14.2. Then save
the file.

LISTING 14.2   The Full Text of `PageData.jnlp`

```
1: <?xml version="1.0" encoding="utf-8"?>
2: <!-- JNLP File for the PageData Application -->
3: <jnlp
4:    codebase="http://cadenhead.org/book/java-21-days/java"
5:    href="PageData.jnlp">
6:    <information>
7:      <title>PageData Application</title>
```

LISTING 14.2   Continued

```
 8:        <vendor>Rogers Cadenhead</vendor>
 9:        <homepage href="http://www.java21days.com"/>
10:        <icon href="pagedataicon.gif"/>
11:        <offline-allowed/>
12:     </information>
13:     <resources>
14:        <j2se version="1.7"/>
15:        <jar href="PageData.jar"/>
16:     </resources>
17:     <security>
18:        <all-permissions/>
19:     </security>
20:     <application-desc main-class="PageData"/>
21: </jnlp>
```

Because a JNLP file is structured as XML data, everything within the < and > symbols is a tag. Tags are placed around the information that the tag describes. There's an opening tag before the information and a closing tag after it.

For example, line 7 of Listing 14.2 contains the following text:

`<title>PageData Application</title>`

In order from left to right, this line contains the opening tag `<title>`, the text `PageData Application`, and the closing tag `</title>`. The text between the tags, "PageData Application," is the application's title. Java Web Start will display the title as the application is being loaded. The title also will be used in menus and shortcuts.

The difference between opening tags and closing tags is that closing tags begin with a slash character (`/`), and opening tags do not. In line 8, `<vendor>` is the opening tag, `</vendor>` is the closing tag, and these tags surround the name of the vendor who created the application. I've used my name here. Delete it and replace it with your own name, taking care not to alter the `<vendor>` or `</vendor>` tags around it.

Some tags have an opening tag only, such as line 11:

`<offline-allowed/>`

The `offline-allowed` tag indicates that the application can be run even if the user is not connected to the Internet. If it were omitted from the JNLP file, the opposite would be true, and the user would be forced to go online before running this application.

In XML, all tags that do not have a closing tag end with `/>` instead of `>`.

14

Tags also can have attributes, which are another way to define information in an XML file. An attribute is a name inside a tag that is followed by an equals sign and some text within quotes.

For example, consider line 9 of Listing 14.2:

```
<homepage href="http://www.java21days.com"/>
```

This is the homepage tag, and it has one attribute, href. The text between the quote marks is used to set the value of this attribute to http://www.java21days.com. This defines the application's home page—the web page that users should visit if they want to read more about the program and how it works.

The PageData JNLP file defines a simple Java Web Start application that runs with no security restrictions, as defined in lines 17–19:

```
<security>
  <all-permissions/>
</security>
```

In addition to the tags that have already been described, Listing 14.2 defines other information required by Java Web Start.

Line 1 specifies that the file uses XML and the UTF-8 character set. This same line can be used on any of the JNLP files you create for applications.

Line 2 is a comment. Like comments in Java classes, this text is provided solely for the benefit of humans looking at this file. Java Web Start ignores it.

The jnlp element, which begins on line 3 and ends on line 21, must surround all the other tags that configure Web Start.

This tag has two attributes, codebase and href, which indicate where the JNLP file for this application can be found. The codebase attribute is the uniform resource locator (URL) of the folder that contains the JNLP file. The href attribute is the name of the file or a relative URL that includes a folder and the name (such as "pub/PageData.jnlp").

In Listing 14.2, the attributes indicate that the application's JNLP file is at the following web address:

```
http://cadenhead.org/book/java-21-days/java/PageData.jnlp
```

The information element (lines 6–12) defines information about the application. Elements can contain other elements in XML, and in Listing 14.2, the information element contains title, vendor, homepage, icon, and offline-allowed tags.

The title, vendor, homepage, and offline-allowed elements were described earlier.

The icon element (line 10) contains an href attribute that indicates the name (or folder location and name) of the program's icon. Like all file references in a JNLP file, this element uses the codebase attribute to determine the full URL of the resource. In this example, the icon element's href attribute is pagedataicon.gif, and the codebase is "http://cadenhead.org/book/java21days/java", so the icon file is at the following web address:

http://cadenhead.org/book/java21days/java/pagedataicon.gif

The resources element (lines 13–16) defines resources used by the application when it runs.

The j2se element has a version attribute that indicates which version of the Java interpreter should run the application. This attribute can specify a general version (such as "1.6" or "1.7"), a specific version (such as "1.7.0-ea"), or a reference to multiple versions. A general version number can be followed by a plus sign. The tag <j2se version="1.5+"> sets up an application to be run by any Java interpreter from version 1.5 upward.

NOTE	When you use the j2se element to specify multiple versions, Java Web Start does not use a beta version to run an application. The only way to run an application with a beta release is to indicate that release specifically.

The jar element has an href attribute that specifies the application's JAR file. This attribute can be a filename or a reference to a folder and filename, and it uses codebase. In the PageData example, the JAR file is in http://cadenhead.org/book/java21days/java/PageData.jar.

The application-desc element indicates the application's main class file and any arguments that should be used when that class is executed.

The main-class attribute identifies the name of the class file, which is specified without the .class file extension.

If the class should be run with one or more arguments, place argument elements within an opening <application-desc> tag and a closing </application-desc> tag.

14

The following XML specifies that the PageData class should be run with two arguments: http://java.com and yes:

```
<application-desc main-class="PageData">
  <argument>http://java.com</argument>
  <argument>yes</argument>
</application-desc>
```

You can test the PageData application from my web server or upload it to your own and edit the JNLP file accordingly.

If you are trying it on your own server, after you have created the PageData.jnlp file, change line 5 of Listing 14.2 so that it refers to the folder on a web server where your application's JAR file, icon file, and JNLP file will be stored.

Upload all three of the project's files to this folder and then run your browser and load the JNLP file using its full web address. If your web server is configured to support Java Web Start, the application is loaded and begins running, as shown in Figure 14.5.

FIGURE 14.5
Running PageData using Java Web Start.

For this application to be run without restriction, the PageData.jar file must be digitally signed. For real-world applications, this requires the services of a certificate-granting authority such as Thawte or VeriSign and can cost $1,000 or more per year.

For testing purposes, the keystore and jarsigner tools in the JDK can be used to create a key and use it to digitally sign a JAR file.

The first step is to use keytool to create a key and assign it an alias and password:

```
keytool -genkey -alias examplekey -keypass swordfish
```

The -genkey argument generates a new key, which in this example is named examplekey and has the password swordfish. If this is the first time keytool has been used, you're prompted for a password that protects access to the key database, which is called a *keystore.*

After a key has been placed in the keystore, it can be used with the jarsigner tool to sign an archive file. This tool requires the keystore and key passwords and the key's alias. Here's how the PageData.jar archive could be signed with the examplekey key:

```
jarsigner -storepass password -keypass swordfish PageData.jar examplekey
```

The keystore password in this example is password. The security certificate used to sign the archive will last 90 days and will be described as an "untrusted source" when the Java Web Start application is run.

NOTE

> There's no easy way to avoid being described as "untrusted." The only way to establish your trustworthiness is to go through one of the professional certificate-granting companies.
>
> Java developer Roedy Green offers a guide to Java security certification that lists several companies and the prices they charge. Visit the web page http://mindprod.com/jgloss/certificate.html.

Supporting Web Start on a Server

If your server does not support Java Web Start, you might see the text of your JNLP file loaded in a page, and the application will not open.

A web server must be configured to recognize that JNLP files are a new type of data that should cause a Java application to run. This is usually accomplished by setting the MIME type associated with files that have the extension JNLP.

MIME, which is an acronym for Multipurpose Internet Mail Extensions, is a protocol for defining Internet content such as email messages, attached files, and any file that can be delivered by a web server.

On an Apache web server, the server administrator can support JNLP by adding the following line to the server's mime.types (or .mime.types) file:

```
application/x-java-jnlp-file JNLP
```

14

If you can't get Java Web Start working on your server, you can test this project on the book's official site. Load the web page http://cadenhead.org/book/java-21-days/java/PageData.jnlp.

CAUTION	Java Web Start applications should look exactly like applications do when run by other means. However, there appear to be a few bugs in how much space is allocated to components on a graphical user interface. On a Windows system, you might need to add 50 pixels to the height of an application before employing it in Java Web Start. Otherwise, the text fields are not tall enough to display numbers.

Additional JNLP Elements

The JNLP format has other elements that can affect the performance of Java Web Start.

It can be used to change the title graphic that appears when the application is launched, run signed applications that have different security privileges, run an application using different versions of the Java interpreter, and other options.

Security

By default, all Java Web Start applications are denied access to some features of a user's computer unless the user has given permission. This is similar to how the functionality of applets is limited.

If your application's JAR file has been digitally signed to verify its authenticity, you can run it without these security restrictions by using the `security` element.

This element is placed inside the `jnlp` element, and it contains one element of its own: `all-permissions`. To remove security restrictions for an application, add this to a JNLP file:

```
<security>
  <all-permissions/>
</security>
```

Descriptions

If you want to provide more information about your application for users of Java Web Start, you can place one or more `description` elements inside the `information` element.

Four kinds of descriptions can be provided using the `kind` attribute of the `description` element:

- `kind="one-line"`—A succinct one-line description, used in lists of Web Start applications
- `kind="short"`—A paragraph-long description, used when space is available

- `kind="tooltip"`—A ToolTip description
- No `kind` attribute—A default description, used for any other descriptions not specified

All these are optional. Here's an example that provides descriptions for the PageData application:

```
<description>The PageData application.</description>
<description kind="one-line">An application to learn more about web
servers and pages.</description>
<description kind="tooltip">Learn about web servers and
pages.</description>
<description kind="short">PageData, a simple Java application that
takes a URL and displays information about the URL and the web
server that delivered it.</description>
```

Icons

The PageData JNLP file includes a 64×64 icon, `pagedataicon.gif`, used in two different ways:

- When the PageData application is being loaded by Java Web Start, the icon is displayed in a window next to the program's name and author.
- If a PageData icon is added to a user's desktop, the icon is used at a different size: 32×32.

When an application is loading, you can use a second `icon` element to specify a graphic that will be displayed in place of the icon, title, and author. This graphic is called the application's *splash screen,* and it is specified with the `kind="splash"` attribute, as in this example:

```
<icon kind="splash" href="pagedatasplash.gif" width="300"
height="200" />
```

The `width` and `height` attributes, which also can be used with the other kind of icon graphic, specify the image's display size in pixels.

This second `icon` element should be placed inside the `information` element.

14

| NOTE | For more information on using the technology with your own applications, visit Oracle's Java Web Start site: http://oracle.com/technetwork/java/javase/javawebstart. |

Improving Performance with SwingWorker

The responsiveness of a Swing application depends largely on how well the software handles time-consuming tasks in response to user input.

Applications ordinarily execute tasks in one thread. So if something takes a long time to accomplish, such as loading a large file or parsing data from an XML document, the user might notice a lag in performance while this is taking place.

Swing programs also require all user-interface components to be running within the same thread.

The best way to take care of both requirements is to use SwingWorker, a class in the javax.swing package that's designed to run time-consuming tasks in their own worker thread and report the results.

SwingWorker is an abstract class that must be subclassed by applications that require a worker:

```
public class DiceWorker extends SwingWorker {
    // ...
}
```

The doInBackground() method should be overridden in the new class to perform the task, as in the following example. It rolls six-sided dice many times and tracks the results:

```
doInBackground() {
    int sum = 0;
    for (int i = 0; i < timesToRoll; i++) {
        for (int j = 0; j < 3; j++) {
            sum += Math.floor(Math.random() * 6);
        }
    }
    result[sum] = result[sum] + 1;
    return result;
}
```

Today's next project is a Swing application that rolls three six-sided dice a user-selected number of times and tabulates the results. Sixteen text fields represent the possible values, which range from 3 to 18.

The application is developed as two classes: the DiceRoller frame, which holds the graphical user interface, and the DiceWorker Swing worker, which handles the dice rolls.

Because the application allows the user to roll the dice thousands or even millions of times, putting this task in a worker keeps the Swing interface responsive to user input.

Listing 14.3 contains the worker class, DiceWorker. Create this as an empty Java file in NetBeans with that class name. In the New File dialog, be sure the Project selected is Java21, not PageData.

LISTING 14.3   The Full Text of DiceWorker.java

```
 1: import javax.swing.*;
 2:
 3: public class DiceWorker extends SwingWorker {
 4:     int timesToRoll;
 5:
 6:     // set up the Swing worker
 7:     public DiceWorker(int timesToRoll) {
 8:         super();
 9:         this.timesToRoll = timesToRoll;
10:     }
11:
12:     // define the task the worker performs
13:     protected int[] doInBackground() {
14:         int[] result = new int[16];
15:         for (int i = 0; i < this.timesToRoll; i++) {
16:             int sum = 0;
17:             for (int j = 0; j < 3; j++) {
18:                 sum += Math.floor(Math.random() * 6);
19:             }
20:             result[sum] = result[sum] + 1;
21:         }
22:         // transmit the result
23:         return result;
24:     }
25: }
```

There's no way to do anything with this class until you create the next one, DiceRoller.

A Swing worker needs only one method, doInBackground(), which performs the task in the background. The method must use the protected level of access control and return a value produced by the work. DiceWorker creates a 16-element integer array that contains dice-roll results.

Another class can use this worker in three steps:

1. Call the worker's DiceWorker(*int*) constructor with the number of rolls as the argument.

14

2. Call the worker's addPropertyChangeListener(*Object*) method to add a listener that will be notified when the task is complete.

3. Call the worker's execute() method to begin the work.

The execute() method causes the worker's doInBackground() method to be called.

A property change listener is an event listener from java.beans, the JavaBeans package that establishes ways in which components on a user interface can interact with each other.

In this case, a Swing worker wants to announce that its work is finished, which could take place long after the worker began its work. Listeners are the best way to handle notifications of this kind because they free a graphical user interface to handle other things.

The property change listener interface has one method:

```
public void propertyChange(PropertyChangeEvent event) {
    // ...
}
```

The DiceRoller class, shown in Listing 14.4, presents a graphical user interface that can display dice-roll results and begin a set of rolls.

LISTING 14.4   The Full Text of DiceRoller.java

```
 1: import java.awt.*;
 2: import java.awt.event.*;
 3: import java.beans.*;
 4: import javax.swing.*;
 5:
 6: public class DiceRoller extends JFrame implements ActionListener,
 7:     PropertyChangeListener {
 8:
 9:     // the table for dice-roll results
10:     JTextField[] total = new JTextField[16];
11:     // the "Roll" button
12:     JButton roll;
13:     // the number of times to roll
14:     JTextField quantity;
15:     // the Swing worker
16:     DiceWorker worker;
17:
18:     public DiceRoller() {
19:         super("Dice Roller");
20:         setDefaultCloseOperation(JFrame.EXIT_ON_CLOSE);
```

LISTING 14.4   Continued

```
21:             setLookAndFeel();
22:             setSize(850, 145);
23:
24:             // set up top row
25:             JPanel topPane = new JPanel();
26:             GridLayout paneGrid = new GridLayout(1, 16);
27:             topPane.setLayout(paneGrid);
28:             for (int i = 0; i < 16; i++) {
29:                 // create a textfield and label
30:                 total[i] = new JTextField("0", 4);
31:                 JLabel label = new JLabel((i + 3) + ": ");
32:                 // create this cell in the grid
33:                 JPanel cell = new JPanel();
34:                 cell.add(label);
35:                 cell.add(total[i]);
36:                 // add the cell to the top row
37:                 topPane.add(cell);
38:             }
39:
40:             // set up bottom row
41:             JPanel bottomPane = new JPanel();
42:             JLabel quantityLabel = new JLabel("Times to Roll: ");
43:             quantity = new JTextField("0", 5);
44:             roll = new JButton("Roll");
45:             roll.addActionListener(this);
46:             bottomPane.add(quantityLabel);
47:             bottomPane.add(quantity);
48:             bottomPane.add(roll);
49:
50:             // set up frame
51:             GridLayout frameGrid = new GridLayout(2, 1);
52:             setLayout(frameGrid);
53:             add(topPane);
54:             add(bottomPane);
55:
56:             setVisible(true);
57:         }
58:
59:     // respond when the "Roll" button is clicked
60:     public void actionPerformed(ActionEvent event) {
61:         int timesToRoll;
62:         try {
63:             // turn off the button
64:             timesToRoll = Integer.parseInt(quantity.getText());
65:             roll.setEnabled(false);
66:             // set up the worker that will roll the dice
67:             worker = new DiceWorker(timesToRoll);
68:             // add a listener that monitors the worker
69:             worker.addPropertyChangeListener(this);
```

14

LISTING 14.4 Continued

```
 70:                // start the worker
 71:                worker.execute();
 72:            } catch (Exception exc) {
 73:                System.out.println(exc.getMessage());
 74:                exc.printStackTrace();
 75:            }
 76:    }
 77:
 78:    // respond when the worker's task is complete
 79:    public void propertyChange(PropertyChangeEvent event) {
 80:        try {
 81:            // get the worker's dice-roll results
 82:            int[] result = (int[]) worker.get();
 83:            // store the results in text fields
 84:            for (int i = 0; i < result.length; i++) {
 85:                total[i].setText("" + result[i]);
 86:            }
 87:        } catch (Exception exc) {
 88:            System.out.println(exc.getMessage());
 89:            exc.printStackTrace();
 90:        }
 91:    }
 92:
 93:    private static void setLookAndFeel() {
 94:        try {
 95:            UIManager.setLookAndFeel(
 96:                "com.sun.java.swing.plaf.nimbus.NimbusLookAndFeel"
 97:            );
 98:        } catch (Exception exc) {
 99:            // ignore error
100:        }
101:    }
102:
103:    public static void main(String[] arguments) {
104:        new DiceRoller();
105:    }
106: }
```

This class can be run as an application. Choose Run, Run File in NetBeans.

Most of `DiceRoller` creates and lays out the user-interface components: 16 text fields, a Times to Roll text field, and a Roll button.

The `actionPerformed()` method responds to a click of the Roll button by creating a Swing worker that will roll the dice, adding a property change listener and starting work.

Calling `worker.execute()` in line 71 causes the worker's `doInBackground()` method to be called.

When the worker is finished rolling the dice, the `propertyChange()` method of `DiceRoller` receives a property change event.

This method receives the result of `doInBackground()` by calling the worker's `get()` method (line 82), which must be cast to an integer array:

```
int[] result = (int[] worker.get();
```

The application is shown in Figure 14.6.

FIGURE 14.6
Tabulating dice-roll results prepared by SwingWorker.

Summary

The topics covered today are two capabilities that enhance Java's capabilities for application development: browser-based program deployment and Swing performance improvements through the use of threads.

With Java Web Start, users no longer need to run an installation program to set up a Java application and the interpreter that executes the class. Web Start takes care of this automatically after the user's browser has been equipped to use the Java Runtime Environment.

Support for Web Start is offered through the Java Network Launching Protocol (JNLP), an XML file format used to define and set up Java Web Start.

The `SwingWorker` class improves Swing application performance by putting a time-consuming task in its own thread. The class handles all the work required to start and stop the thread behind the scenes.

When you create a subclass of `SwingWorker`, you can focus on the task that must be performed.

14

Q&A

Q I have written a Java applet that I want to make available using Java Web Start. Should I convert it to an application or go ahead and run it as is?

A If you would be converting your program to an application simply to run it with Web Start, that's probably unnecessary. The purpose of the applet-desc tag is to make it possible to run applets without modification in Java Web Start. The only reason to undertake the conversion is if you want to change other things about your program, such as the switch from init() to a constructor method.

Q How can I make sure that a SwingWorker object has finished working?

A Call the worker's isDone() method, which returns true when the task has finished executing.

Note that this method returns true no matter how the task completes. So if it is canceled or interrupted or fails in some other manner, it returns true.

The isCancelled() method can be used to check whether the task was canceled.

Quiz

Review today's material by taking this three-question quiz. Answers are at the end of the book.

Questions

1. What interface must be implemented for you to be notified when a SwingWorker has finished executing?

   A. ActionListener

   B. PropertyChangeListener

   C. SwingListener

2. Which XML element is used to identify the name, author, and other details about a Java Web Start-run application?

   A. jnlp

   B. information

   C. resources

3. What security restrictions apply to a Java Web Start application?

   A. There are no restrictions.

   B. The same restrictions that are in place for applications.

   C. The restrictions are chosen by the user.

Certification Practice

The following question is the kind of thing you could expect to be asked on a Java pro-gramming certification test. Answer it without looking at today's material or using the Java compiler to test the code.

Given:

```java
import java.awt.*;
import javax.swing.*;

public class SliderFrame extends JFrame {
    public SliderFrame() {
        super();
        setDefaultCloseOperation(JFrame.EXIT_ON_CLOSE);
        Container pane = getContentPane();
        JSlider value = new JSlider(0, 255, 100);
        setContentPane(pane);
        setSize(325, 150);
        setVisible(true);
    }

    public static void main(String[] arguments) {
        new SliderFrame();
    }
}
```

What will happen when you attempt to compile and run this source code?

- **A.** It compiles without error and runs correctly.
- **B.** It compiles without error but does not display anything in the frame.
- **C.** It does not compile because the content pane is empty.
- **D.** It does not compile because of the `new SliderFrame()` statement.

The answer is available on the book's website at www.java21days.com. Visit the Day 14 page and click the Certification Practice link.

14

Exercises

To extend your knowledge of the subjects covered today, try the following exercises:

1. Turn one of the applications created during the first two weeks into one that can be launched with Java Web Start.

2. Create a new JNLP file that runs the PageData application using version 1.3 of the Java interpreter and force users to be connected to the Internet when it is run.

Where applicable, exercise solutions are offered on the book's website at www.java21days.com.

WEEK 3:
Java Programming

DAY 15
Working with Input and Output

Many of the programs you create with Java need to interact with some kind of data source. Information can be stored on a computer in many ways, including files on a hard drive or DVD, pages on a website, and even bytes in the computer's memory.

You might expect to need a different technique to handle each different storage device. Fortunately, that isn't the case.

In Java, information can be stored and retrieved using a communications system called streams, which are implemented in the `java.io` package and are enhanced by the `java.nio.file` package.

Today, you'll learn how to create input streams to read information and output streams to store information. You'll work with the following:

- Byte streams, which are used to handle bytes, integers, and other simple data types
- Character streams, which handle text files and other text sources

You can deal with all data in the same way when you know how to work with an input stream, whether the information is coming from a disk, the Internet, or even another program. The same is true of using output streams to transmit data.

Introduction to Streams

In Java, all data is written and read using streams. Streams, like the bodies of water that share the same name, carry something from one place to another.

A stream is a path traveled by data in a program. An input stream sends data from a source into a program, and an output stream sends data from a program to a destination.

You will deal with two types of streams today: byte streams and character streams. *Byte streams* carry integers with values that range from 0 to 255. A diverse assortment of data can be expressed in byte format, including numeric data, executable programs, Internet communications, and bytecode—the class files run by a Java virtual machine.

In fact, every kind of data imaginable can be expressed using either individual bytes or a series of bytes combined.

Character streams are a specialized type of byte stream that handles only textual data. They're distinguished from byte streams because Java's character set supports Unicode, a standard that includes many more characters than could be expressed easily using bytes.

Any kind of data that involves text should use character streams, including text files, web pages, and other common types of text.

Using a Stream

The procedure for using either a byte stream or character stream in Java is largely the same. Before you start working with the specifics of the `java.io` and `java.nio.file` classes, it's useful to walk through the process of creating and using streams.

For an input stream, the first step is to create an object associated with the data source. For example, if the source is a file on your hard drive, a `FileInputStream` object could be associated with this file.

After you have a stream object, you can read information from that stream by using one of the object's methods. `FileInputStream` includes a `read()` method that returns a byte read from the file.

When you're finished reading information from the stream, you call the `close()` method to indicate that you're finished using the stream.

For an output stream, you begin by creating an object associated with the data's destination. One such object can be created from the `BufferedWriter` class, which represents an efficient way to create text files.

The write() method is the simplest way to send information to the output stream's destination. For instance, a BufferedWriter write() method can send individual characters to an output stream.

As with input streams, the close() method is called on an output stream when you have no more information to send.

15

Filtering a Stream

The simplest way to use a stream is to create it and then call its methods to send or receive data, depending on whether it's an output stream or input stream.

Many of the classes you will work with today achieve more sophisticated results when a filter is associated with a stream before reading or writing any data.

A *filter* is a type of stream that modifies how an existing stream is handled. Think of a dam on a mountain stream. The dam regulates the flow of water from the points upstream to the points downstream. The dam is a type of filter. Remove it, and the water would flow in a less-controlled fashion.

The procedure for using a filter on a stream is as follows:

1. Create a stream associated with a data source or data destination.
2. Associate a filter with that stream.
3. Read data from or write data to the filter rather than the original stream.

The methods you call on a filter are the same as the methods you would call on a stream. There are read() and write() methods, just as there would be on an unfiltered stream.

You even can associate a filter with another filter, so the following path for information is possible: An input stream associated with a text file is filtered through a Spanish-to-English translation filter, which is then filtered through a no-profanity filter. Finally, it is sent to its destination—a human being who wants to read it.

If this is confusing in the abstract, you will have opportunities to see the process in practice in the following sections.

Handling Exceptions

Several exceptions in the java.io package might occur when you are working with files and streams.

A FileNotFoundException occurs when you try to create a stream or file object using a file that couldn't be located.

An EOFException indicates that the end of a file has been reached unexpectedly as data was being read from the file through an input stream.

These exceptions are subclasses of IOException. One way to deal with all of them is to enclose all input and output statements in a try-catch block that catches IOException objects. Call the exception's toString() or getMessage() methods in the catch block to find out more about the problem.

Byte Streams

All byte streams are a subclass of either InputStream or OutputStream. These classes are abstract, so you cannot create a stream by creating objects of these classes directly. Instead, you create streams through one of their subclasses, such as the following:

- FileInputStream and FileOutputStream are byte streams stored in files on disk, CD-ROM, or other storage devices.
- DataInputStream and DataOutputStream are a filtered byte stream from which data such as integers and floating-point numbers can be read.

InputStream is the superclass of all input streams.

File Streams

The byte streams you'll work with most often are likely to be file streams. They are used to exchange data with files on your disk drives, CD-ROMs, or other storage devices you can refer to by using a folder path and filename.

You can send bytes to a file output stream and receive bytes from a file input stream.

File Input Streams

A file input stream can be created with the FileInputStream(*String*) constructor. The *String* argument should be the filename. You can include a path reference with the filename, which enables the file to be in a different folder from the class loading it. The following statement creates a file input stream from the file scores.dat:

```
FileInputStream fis = new FileInputStream("scores.dat");
```

Path references can be indicated in a manner specific to a platform, such as this example to read a file on a Windows system:

```
FileInputStream f1 = new FileInputStream("\\data\\calendar.txt");
```

NOTE   Because Java uses backslash characters in escape codes, the code \\ must be used in place of \ in path references in Windows.

Here's a Linux example:

```
FileInputStream f2 = new FileInputStream("/data/calendar.txt");
```

A better way to refer to paths is to use the class variable separator in the File class, which works on any operating system:

```
char sep = File.separator;
FileInputStream f2 = new FileInputStream(sep + "data"
    + sep + "calendar.txt");
```

After you create a file input stream, you can read bytes from the stream by calling its read() method. This method returns an integer containing the next byte in the stream. If the method returns –1, which is not a possible byte value, this signifies that the end of the file stream has been reached.

To read more than one byte of data from the stream, call its read(*byte[]*, *int*, *int*) method. The arguments to this method are as follows:

- A byte array where the data will be stored
- The element inside the array where the data's first byte should be stored
- The number of bytes to read

Unlike the other read() method, this does not return data from the stream. Instead, it returns either an integer that represents the number of bytes read or –1 if no bytes were read before the end of the stream was reached.

The following statements use a while loop to read the data in a FileInputStream object called diskfile:

```
int newByte = 0;
while (newByte != -1) {
    newByte = diskfile.read();
    System.out.print(newByte + " ");
}
```

This loop reads the entire file referenced by diskfile one byte at a time and displays each byte, followed by a space character. It also displays –1 when the end of the file is reached; you could guard against this easily with an if statement.

The ByteReader application, shown in in Listing 15.1, uses a similar technique to read a file input stream. The input stream's `close()` method is used to close the stream after the last byte in the file is read. Always close streams when you no longer need them; doing so frees system resources. Create the `ByteReader` class as an empty Java file in NetBeans.

LISTING 15.1   The Full Text of `ByteReader.java`

```
 1: import java.io.*;
 2:
 3: public class ByteReader {
 4:     public static void main(String[] arguments) {
 5:         try (
 6:             FileInputStream file = new
 7:                 FileInputStream("save.gif")
 8:             ) {
 9:
10:             boolean eof = false;
11:             int count = 0;
12:             while (!eof) {
13:                 int input = file.read();
14:                 System.out.print(input + " ");
15:                 if (input == -1)
16:                     eof = true;
17:                 else
18:                     count++;
19:             }
20:             file.close();
21:             System.out.println("\nBytes read: " + count);
22:         } catch (IOException e) {
23:             System.out.println("Error -- " + e.toString());
24:         }
25:     }
26: }
```

This application reads the byte data from the `save.gif` file in the main folder of the Java21 project. That file was used during Day 10, "Building a Swing Interface."

When you run the program, each byte in `save.gif` is displayed, followed by a count of the total number of bytes. Here's partial output:

Output ▼

```
9 0 33 254 79 67 111 112 121 114 105 103 104 116 32
50 48 48 48 32 98 121 32 83 117 110 32 77 105 99 114
111 115 121 115 116 101 109 115 44 32 73 110 99 46
32 65 108 108 32 82 105 103 104 116 115 32 82 101
```

```
115 101 114 118 101 100 46 13 10 74 76 70 32 71 82
32 86 101 114 32 49 46 48 13 10 0 59 -1
Bytes read: 266
```

File Output Streams

A file output stream can be created with the FileOutputStream(*String*) constructor. The usage is the same as with the FileInputStream(*String*) constructor, so you can specify a path along with a filename.

You have to be careful when specifying the file associated with an output stream. If it's the same as an existing file, the original is wiped out when you start writing data to the stream.

You can create a file output stream that appends data after the end of an existing file with the FileOutputStream(*String*, *boolean*) constructor. The string specifies the file, and the Boolean argument should equal true to append data instead of overwriting existing data.

The file output stream's write(*int*) method is used to write bytes to the stream. After the last byte has been written to the file, the stream's close() method closes the stream.

To write more than one byte, you can use the write(*byte[]*, *int*, *int*) method. This works in a manner similar to the read(*byte[]*, *int*, *int*) method described previously. The arguments to this method are the byte array containing the bytes to output, the starting point in the array, and the number of bytes to write.

The ByteWriter application, shown in Listing 15.2, writes an integer array to a file output stream.

LISTING 15.2   The Full Text of ByteWriter.java

```
 1: import java.io.*;
 2:
 3: public class ByteWriter {
 4:     public static void main(String[] arguments) {
 5:         int[] data = { 71, 73, 70, 56, 57, 97, 13, 0, 12, 0, 145, 0,
 6:             0, 255, 255, 255, 255, 255, 0, 0, 0, 0, 0, 0, 0, 44, 0,
 7:             0, 0, 0, 13, 0, 12, 0, 0, 2, 38, 132, 45, 121, 11, 25,
 8:             175, 150, 120, 20, 162, 132, 51, 110, 106, 239, 22, 8,
 9:             160, 56, 137, 96, 72, 77, 33, 130, 86, 37, 219, 182, 230,
10:             137, 89, 82, 181, 50, 220, 103, 20, 0, 59 };
11:         try (FileOutputStream file = new
12:             FileOutputStream("pic.gif")) {
13:
14:             for (int i = 0; i < data.length; i++) {
```

LISTING 15.2   Continued

```
15:                     file.write(data[i]);
16:                 }
17:                 file.close();
18:             } catch (IOException e) {
19:                 System.out.println("Error -- " + e.toString());
20:             }
21:     }
22: }
```

The following things take place in this program:

- Lines 5–10 create an integer array called `data` and fill it with elements.
- Lines 11 and 12 create a file output stream with the filename `pic.gif` in the main project folder in NetBeans.
- Lines 14–16 use a `for` loop to cycle through the `data` array and write each element to the file stream.
- Line 17 closes the file output stream.

The `FileOutputStream` object is created inside the parentheses of the `try` statement to make sure its resources are freed up when the block finishes executing, even in case of an error. This is a new feature of Java 7.

After you run this program, you can display the `pic.gif` file in any web browser or graphics-editing tool. It's a small image file in GIF format, as shown in Figure 15.1.

FIGURE 15.1
The `pic.gif` file (enlarged).

Filtering a Stream

Filtered streams are streams that modify the information sent through an existing stream. They are created using the subclasses `FilterInputStream` and `FilterOutputStream`.

These classes do not handle any filtering operations themselves. Instead, they have subclasses, such as `BufferInputStream` and `DataOutputStream`, which handle specific types of filtering.

Byte Filters

Information is delivered more quickly if it can be sent in large chunks, even if those chunks are received faster than they can be handled.

For example, consider which of the following book-reading techniques is faster:

- A friend lends you a book, and you read it.
- A friend lends you a book one page at a time and doesn't give you a new page until you have finished the previous one.

Obviously, the first technique is faster and more efficient. The same benefits are true of buffered streams in Java.

A *buffer* is a storage place where data can be kept before it is needed by a program that reads or writes that data. By using a buffer, you can get data without always going back to the original source of the data.

Buffers are essential when reading extremely large files. Without them, the data from the file could take up all of a Java virtual machine's memory.

Buffered Streams

A buffered input stream fills a buffer with data that hasn't been handled yet. When a program needs this data, it looks to the buffer before going to the original stream source.

Buffered byte streams use the `BufferedInputStream` and `BufferedOutputStream` classes.

A buffered input stream is created using one of the following constructors:

- `BufferedInputStream(InputStream)` creates a buffered input stream for the specified *InputStream* object.
- `BufferedInputStream(InputStream, int)` creates the specified *InputStream* buffered stream with a buffer of size *int*.

The simplest way to read data from a buffered input stream is to call its `read()` method with no arguments. This action normally returns an integer from 0 to 255 representing the next byte in the stream. If the end of the stream has been reached and no byte is available, –1 is returned.

You also can use the read(*byte*[], *int*, *int*) method available for other input streams, which loads stream data into a byte array.

A buffered output stream is created using one of these two constructors:

- BufferedOutputStream(*OutputStream*) creates a buffered output stream for the specified *OutputStream* object.

- BufferedOutputStream(*OutputStream*, *int*) creates the specified *OutputStream* buffered stream with a buffer of size *int*.

The output stream's write(*int*) method can be used to send a single byte to the stream, and the write(*byte*[], *int*, *int*) method writes multiple bytes from the specified byte array. The arguments to this method are the byte array, array starting point, and number of bytes to write.

NOTE	Although the write() method takes an integer as input, the value should be from 0 to 255. If you specify a number higher than 255, it is stored as the remainder of the number divided by 256. You can test this when running the project you will create later today.

When data is directed to a buffered stream, it is not output to its destination until the stream fills or the buffered stream's flush() method is called.

The next project, the BufferDemo application, writes a series of bytes to a buffered output stream associated with a text file. The first and last integers in the series are specified as two arguments.

After writing to the text file, BufferDemo creates a buffered input stream from the file and reads the bytes back in. Listing 15.3 contains the source code.

LISTING 15.3   The Full Text of BufferDemo.java

```
 1: import java.io.*;
 2:
 3: public class BufferDemo {
 4:     public static void main(String[] arguments) {
 5:         int start = 0;
 6:         int finish = 255;
 7:         if (arguments.length > 1) {
 8:             start = Integer.parseInt(arguments[0]);
 9:             finish = Integer.parseInt(arguments[1]);
```

LISTING 15.3 Continued

```
10:            } else if (arguments.length > 0) {
11:                start = Integer.parseInt(arguments[0]);
12:            }
13:            ArgStream as = new ArgStream(start, finish);
14:            System.out.println("\nWriting: ");
15:            boolean success = as.writeStream();
16:            System.out.println("\nReading: ");
17:            boolean readSuccess = as.readStream();
18:    }
19: }
20:
21: class ArgStream {
22:     int start = 0;
23:     int finish = 255;
24:
25:     ArgStream(int st, int fin) {
26:         start = st;
27:         finish = fin;
28:     }
29:
30:     boolean writeStream() {
31:         try (FileOutputStream file = new
32:                 FileOutputStream("numbers.dat");
33:             BufferedOutputStream buff = new
34:                 BufferedOutputStream(file)) {
35:
36:             for (int out = start; out <= finish; out++) {
37:                 buff.write(out);
38:                 System.out.print(" " + out);
39:             }
40:             buff.close();
41:             return true;
42:         } catch (IOException e) {
43:             System.out.println("Exception: " + e.getMessage());
44:             return false;
45:         }
46:     }
47:
48:     boolean readStream() {
49:         try (FileInputStream file = new
50:                 FileInputStream("numbers.dat");
51:             BufferedInputStream buff = new
52:                 BufferedInputStream(file)) {
53:
54:             int in;
55:             do {
56:                 in = buff.read();
57:                 if (in != -1)
58:                     System.out.print(" " + in);
```

```
59:                } while (in != -1);
60:                buff.close();
61:                return true;
62:            } catch (IOException e) {
63:                System.out.println("Exception: " + e.getMessage());
64:                return false;
65:            }
66:        }
67: }
```

This program's output depends on the two arguments specified when it was run. If you use 4 and 13, the following output is shown:

Output ▼

```
Writing:
 4 5 6 7 8 9 10 11 12 13
Reading:
 4 5 6 7 8 9 10 11 12 13
```

It also can be run without arguments, using 1 and 255 as default values.

This application consists of two classes: BufferDemo and a helper class called ArgStream. BufferDemo gets the two arguments' values, if they are provided, and uses them in the ArgStream() constructor.

The writeStream() method of ArgStream is called in line 15 to write the series of bytes to a buffered output stream, and the readStream() method is called in line 17 to read back those bytes.

Even though they are moving data in two directions, the writeStream() and readStream() methods are substantially the same. They take the following format:

- The filename, numbers.dat, is used to create a file input or output stream.
- The file stream is used to create a buffered input or output stream.
- The buffered stream's write() method is used to send data, or the read() method is used to receive data.
- The buffered stream is closed.

Because file streams and buffered streams throw IOException objects if an error occurs, all operations involving the streams are enclosed in a try-catch block for this exception.

TIP

The Boolean return values in `writeStream()` and `readStream()` indicate whether the stream operation was completed successfully. They aren't used in this program, but it's good practice to let callers of these methods know if something goes wrong.

Console Input Streams

One of the things many experienced programmers miss when they begin learning Java is the ability to read textual or numeric input from the console while running an application. No input method is comparable to the output methods `System.out.print()` and `System.out.println()`.

Now that you can work with buffered input streams, you can put them to use receiving console input.

The `System` class, part of the `java.lang` package, has a class variable called `in` that is an `InputStream` object. This object receives input from the keyboard through the stream.

You can work with this stream as you would any other input stream. The following statement creates a new buffered input stream associated with the `System.in` input stream:

```
BufferedInputStream command = new BufferedInputStream(System.in);
```

The next project, the `ConsoleInput` class, contains a class method you can use to receive console input in any of your Java applications. Enter the code shown in Listing 15.4 in your editor and save the file as `ConsoleInput.java`.

LISTING 15.4   The Full Text of `ConsoleInput.java`

```
 1: import java.io.*;
 2:
 3: public class ConsoleInput {
 4:     public static String readLine() {
 5:         StringBuilder response = new StringBuilder();
 6:         try (BufferedInputStream buff = new
 7:             BufferedInputStream(System.in)) {
 8:
 9:             int in;
10:             char inChar;
11:             do {
12:                 in = buff.read();
13:                 inChar = (char) in;
14:                 if ((in != -1) & (in != '\n') & (in != '\r')) {
```

LISTING 15.4   Continued

```
15:                    response.append(inChar);
16:                }
17:            } while ((in != -1) & (inChar != '\n') & (in != '\r'));
18:            buff.close();
19:            return response.toString();
20:        } catch (IOException e) {
21:            System.out.println("Exception: " + e.getMessage());
22:            return null;
23:        }
24:    }
25:
26:    public static void main(String[] arguments) {
27:        System.out.print("\nWhat is your name? ");
28:        String input = ConsoleInput.readLine();
29:        System.out.println("\nHello, " + input);
30:    }
31: }
```

The ConsoleInput class includes a main() method that demonstrates how it can be used. When you compile and run it as an application, the output should resemble the following:

Output ▼

```
What is your name? Amerigo Vespucci

Hello, Amerigo Vespucci
```

ConsoleInput reads user input through a buffered input stream using the stream's read() method, which returns –1 when the end of input has been reached. This occurs when the user presses the Enter key, a carriage return (character '\r'), or a newline (character '\n').

Data Streams

If you need to work with data that isn't represented as bytes or characters, you can use data input and data output streams. These streams filter an existing byte stream so that each of the following primitive types can be directly read from or written to the stream: boolean, byte, double, float, int, long, and short.

A data input stream is created with the DataInputStream(InputStream) constructor. The argument should be an existing input stream such as a buffered input stream or a file input stream.

A data output stream requires the DataOutputStream(*OutputStream*) constructor, which indicates the associated output stream.

The following read and write methods apply to data input and output streams, respectively:

- readBoolean(), writeBoolean(*boolean*)
- readByte(), writeByte(*integer*)
- readDouble(), writeDouble(*double*)
- readFloat(), writeFloat(*float)*
- readInt(), writeInt(*int*)
- readLong(), writeLong(*long*)
- readShort(), writeShort(*int*)

Each input method returns the primitive data type indicated by the method's name. For example, the readFloat() method returns a float value.

There also are readUnsignedByte() and readUnsignedShort() methods that read in unsigned byte and short values. Java doesn't support these data types, so they are returned as int values.

NOTE   Unsigned bytes have values ranging from 0 to 255. This differs from Java's byte variable type, which ranges from –128 to 127. Along the same lines, an unsigned short value ranges from 0 to 65,535, instead of the –32,768 to 32,767 range supported by Java's short type.

A data input stream's different read methods do not all return a value that can be used to indicate that the end of the stream has been reached.

As an alternative, you can wait for an EOFException (end-of-file exception) to be thrown when a read method reaches the end of a stream. The loop that reads the data can be enclosed in a try block, and the associated catch statement should handle only EOFException objects. You can call close() on the stream and take care of other cleanup tasks inside the catch block.

This is demonstrated in the next project. Listings 15.5 and 15.6 contain two programs that use data streams. The PrimeWriter application writes the first 400 prime numbers as

integers to a file called 400primes.dat. The PrimeReader application reads the integers
from this file and displays them.

LISTING 15.5   The Full Text of PrimeWriter.java

```
 1: import java.io.*;
 2:
 3: public class PrimeWriter {
 4:     public static void main(String[] arguments) {
 5:         int[] primes = new int[400];
 6:         int numPrimes = 0;
 7:         // candidate: the number that might be prime
 8:         int candidate = 2;
 9:         while (numPrimes < 400) {
10:             if (isPrime(candidate)) {
11:                 primes[numPrimes] = candidate;
12:                 numPrimes++;
13:             }
14:             candidate++;
15:         }
16:
17:         try (
18:             // Write output to disk
19:             FileOutputStream file = new
20:                 FileOutputStream("400primes.dat");
21:             BufferedOutputStream buff = new
22:                 BufferedOutputStream(file);
23:             DataOutputStream data = new
24:                 DataOutputStream(buff);
25:             ) {
26:
27:             for (int i = 0; i < 400; i++)
28:                 data.writeInt(primes[i]);
29:             data.close();
30:         } catch (IOException e) {
31:             System.out.println("Error -- " + e.toString());
32:         }
33:     }
34:
35:     public static boolean isPrime(int checkNumber) {
36:         double root = Math.sqrt(checkNumber);
37:         for (int i = 2; i <= root; i++) {
38:             if (checkNumber % i == 0)
39:                 return false;
40:         }
41:         return true;
42:     }
43: }
```

LISTING 15.6   The Full Text of PrimeReader.java

```
 1: import java.io.*;
 2:
 3: public class PrimeReader {
 4:     public static void main(String[] arguments) {
 5:         try (FileInputStream file = new
 6:                 FileInputStream("400primes.dat");
 7:             BufferedInputStream buff = new
 8:                 BufferedInputStream(file);
 9:             DataInputStream data = new
10:                 DataInputStream(buff)) {
11:
12:             try {
13:                 while (true) {
14:                     int in = data.readInt();
15:                     System.out.print(in + " ");
16:                 }
17:             } catch (EOFException eof) {
18:                 buff.close();
19:             }
20:         } catch (IOException e) {
21:             System.out.println("Error -- " + e.toString());
22:         }
23:     }
24: }
```

Most of the PrimeWriter application is taken up with logic to find the first 400 prime numbers. After you have an integer array containing the first 400 primes, it is written to a data output stream in Listing 15.5 in lines 17–33.

This application is an example of using more than one filter on a stream. The stream is developed in a three-step process:

1. A file output stream associated with a file called 400primes.dat is created.
2. A new buffered output stream is associated with the file stream.
3. A new data output stream is associated with the buffered stream.

The writeInt() method of the data stream is used to write the primes to the file.

The PrimeReader application is simpler because it doesn't need to do anything regarding prime numbers. It just reads integers from a file using a data input stream.

Lines 5–10 of PrimeReader are nearly identical to statements in the PrimeWriter application, except that input classes are used instead of output classes.

The `try-catch` block that handles `EOFException` objects is in lines 12–22 of Listing 15.6. The work of loading the data takes place inside the `try` block.

The `while(true)` statement creates an endless loop. This isn't a problem; an `EOFException` automatically occurs when the end of the stream is encountered at some point as the data stream is being read. The `readInt()` method in line 14 of Listing 15.6 reads integers from the stream.

The last several output lines of the PrimeReader application should resemble the following:

Output ▼

```
2137 2141 2143 2153 2161 2179 2203 2207 2213 2221 2237 2239 2243 22
51 2267 2269 2273 2281 2287 2293 2297 2309 2311 2333 2339 2341 2347
 2351 2357 2371 2377 2381 2383 2389 2393 2399 2411 2417 2423 2437 2
441 2447 2459 2467 2473 2477 2503 2521 2531 2539 2543 2549 2551 255
7 2579 2591 2593 2609 2617 2621 2633 2647 2657 2659 2663 2671 2677
2683 2687 2689 2693 2699 2707 2711 2713 2719 2729 2731 2741
```

Character Streams

After you know how to handle byte streams, you have most of the skills needed to handle character streams as well. Character streams are used to work with any text represented by the ASCII character set or Unicode, an international character set that includes ASCII.

Examples of files that you can work with through a character stream are plain text files, Hypertext Markup Language (HTML) documents, and Java source files.

The classes used to read and write these streams are all subclasses of `Reader` and `Writer`. These should be used for all text input instead of dealing directly with byte streams.

Reading Text Files

`FileReader` is the main class used when reading character streams from a file. This class inherits from `InputStreamReader`, which reads a byte stream and converts the bytes into integer values that represent Unicode characters.

A character input stream is associated with a file using the `FileReader(String)` constructor. The string indicates the file, and it can contain path folder references in addition to a filename.

The following statement creates a new `FileReader` called `look` and associates it with a text file called `index.txt`:

```
FileReader look = new FileReader("index.txt");
```

After you have a file reader, you can call the following methods on it to read characters from the file:

- `read()` returns the next character on the stream as an integer.

- `read(char[], int, int)` reads characters into the specified character array with the indicated starting point and number of characters read.

The second method works like similar methods for the byte input stream classes. Instead of returning the next character, it returns either the number of characters that were read or −1 if no characters were read before the end of the stream was reached.

The following method loads a text file using the `FileReader` object `text` and displays its characters:

```
FileReader text = new FileReader("readme.txt");
int inByte;
do {
    inByte = text.read();
    if (inByte != -1)
        System.out.print( (char)inByte );
} while (inByte != -1);
System.out.println("");
text.close();
```

Because a character stream's `read()` method returns an integer, you must cast this to a character before displaying it, storing it in an array, or using it to form a string. Every character has a numeric code that represents its position in the Unicode character set. The integer read from the stream is this numeric code.

If you want to read an entire line of text at a time instead of reading a file character by character, you can use the `BufferedReader` class in conjunction with a `FileReader`.

The `BufferedReader` class reads a character input stream and buffers it for better efficiency. You must have an existing `Reader` object of some kind to create a buffered version. The following constructors can be used to create a `BufferedReader`:

- `BufferedReader(Reader)` creates a buffered character stream associated with the specified `Reader` object, such as `FileReader`.

- `BufferedReader(Reader, int)` creates a buffered character stream associated with the specified `Reader` and with a buffer of size `int`.

A buffered character stream can be read using the read() and read(*char[]*, *int*, *int*) methods described for FileReader. You can read a line of text using the readLine() method.

The readLine() method returns a String object containing the next line of text on the stream, not including the character or characters that represent the end of a line. If the end of the stream is reached, the value of the string returned equals null.

An end-of-line is indicated by any of the following:

- A newline character ('\n')
- A carriage return character ('\r')
- A carriage return followed by a newline ("\n\r")

The project contained in Listing 15.7 is a Java application, SourceReader, which reads its own source file through a buffered character stream.

LISTING 15.7 The Full Text of SourceReader.java

```
1: import java.io.*;
2:
3: public class SourceReader {
4:     public static void main(String[] arguments) {
5:         try (
6:             FileReader file = new
7:                 FileReader("SourceReader.java");
8:             BufferedReader buff = new
9:                 BufferedReader(file)) {
10:
11:             boolean eof = false;
12:             while (!eof) {
13:                 String line = buff.readLine();
14:                 if (line == null) {
15:                     eof = true;
16:                 } else {
17:                     System.out.println(line);
18:                 }
19:             }
20:             buff.close();
21:         } catch (IOException e) {
22:             System.out.println("Error -- " + e.toString());
23:         }
24:     }
25: }
```

Much of this program is comparable to projects created earlier today:

- **Lines 6 and 7**—An input source is created: the FileReader object associated with the file SourceReader.java.
- **Lines 8 and 9**—A buffering filter is associated with that input source: the BufferedReader object buff.
- **Lines 11–19**—A readLine() method is used inside a while loop to read the text file one line at a time. The loop ends when the method returns the value null.

The SourceReader application's output is the text file SourceReader.java.

Writing Text Files

The FileWriter class is used to write a character stream to a file. It's a subclass of OutputStreamWriter, which has behavior to convert Unicode character codes to bytes.

There are two FileWriter constructors: FileWriter(*String*) and FileWriter(*String, boolean*). The string indicates the name of the file that the character stream will be directed into, which can include a folder path. The optional Boolean argument should equal true if the file is to be appended to an existing text file. As with other stream-writing classes, you must be careful not to accidentally overwrite an existing file when you're appending data.

Three methods of FileWriter can be used to write data to a stream:

- write(*int*) writes a character.
- write(*char[], int, int*) writes characters from the specified character array with the indicated starting point and number of characters written.
- write(*String, int, int*) writes characters from the specified string with the indicated starting point and number of characters written.

The following example writes a character stream to a file using the FileWriter class and the write(*int*) method:

```
FileWriter letters = new FileWriter("alphabet.txt");
for (int i = 65; i < 91; i++)
    letters.write( (char)i );
letters.close();
```

The close() method is used to close the stream after all characters have been sent to the destination file. The following is the alphabet.txt file produced by this code:

ABCDEFGHIJKLMNOPQRSTUVWXYZ

The `BufferedWriter` class can be used to write a buffered character stream. This class's objects are created with the `BufferedWriter(Writer)` or `BufferedWriter(Writer, int)` constructors. The `Writer` argument can be any of the character output stream classes, such as `FileWriter`. The optional second argument is an integer indicating the size of the buffer to use.

`BufferedWriter` has the same three output methods as `FileWriter`: `write(int)`, `write(char[], int, int)`, and `write(String, int, int)`.

Another useful output method is `newLine()`, which sends the preferred end-of-line character (or characters) for the platform being used to run the program.

> **TIP**
>
> The different end-of-line markers can create conversion hassles when files are transferred from one operating system to another, such as when a Windows 7 user uploads a file to a web server that's running the Linux operating system. Using `newLine()` instead of a literal (such as `'\n'`) makes your program more user-friendly across different platforms.

The `close()` method is called to close the buffered character stream and make sure that all buffered data is sent to the stream's destination.

Files and Paths

In all the examples thus far, a string has been used to refer to the file that's involved in a stream operation. This often is sufficient for a program that uses files and streams, but if you want to copy or rename files or handle other tasks, you can use a `Path` object from the `java.nio.file` package.

`Path` represents a file or folder reference. It is an improvement on the `File` class in the `java.io` package. The following statement gets a path matching the specified string:

```
Path source = FileSystems.getDefault().getPath("essay.txt");
```

This is a two-step process. First, a class method of the `FileSystems` class is called. The `getDefault()` method returns a `FileSystem` object that represents the computer's way of storing files. Both of these classes also are in the `java.nio.file` package.

As soon as you have that `FileSystem` object, its `getPath(String)` method returns a `Path` object matching that specified file or folder reference.

A `File` object can be created from a `Path` by calling the `toFile()` method of the latter class, as in this statement:

```
File sourceFile - source.toFile();
```

A `Path` object can be created from a `File` by calling its `toPath()` method.

You can call several class methods of the `Files` class in the `java.nio.file` package when working with files.

The `move(Path, Path)` class method renames a file from the first path argument to the second.

The `delete(Path)` class method deletes that file.

Just like any file-handling operation, these methods must be handled with care to avoid deleting the wrong files and folders or wiping out data.

These methods throw a `SecurityException` if the program does not have the security to perform the file operation in question, a `NoSuchFileException` if the paths do not exist, and an `IOException` for other IO errors. If you try to delete a folder that is not empty, a `NoSuchFileException` exception occurs. Therefore, these exceptions need to be dealt with through a `try-catch` block or a `throws` clause in a method declaration.

The `AllCapsDemo` application in Listing 15.8 converts all the text in a file to uppercase characters. The file is pulled in using a buffered input stream, and one character is read at a time. After the character is converted to uppercase, it is sent to a temporary file using a buffered output stream. `File` objects are used instead of strings to indicate the files involved, which makes it possible to rename and delete files as needed.

LISTING 15.8   The Full Text of `AllCapsDemo.java`

```
 1: import java.io.*;
 2: import java.nio.file.*;
 3:
 4: public class AllCapsDemo {
 5:     public static void main(String[] arguments) {
 6:         if (arguments.length < 1) {
 7:             System.out.println("You must specify a filename as an argument");
 8:             System.exit(-1);
 9:         }
10:         AllCaps cap = new AllCaps(arguments[0]);
11:         cap.convert();
12:     }
13: }
14:
```

LISTING 15.8   Continued

```
15: class AllCaps {
16:     String sourceName;
17:
18:     AllCaps(String sourceArg) {
19:         sourceName = sourceArg;
20:     }
21:
22:     void convert() {
23:         try {
24:             // Create file objects
25:             Path source = FileSystems.getDefault().getPath(sourceName);
26:             Path temp = FileSystems.getDefault().getPath("tmp_" + sourceName);
27:
28:             // Create input stream
29:             FileReader fr = new FileReader(source.toFile());
30:             BufferedReader in = new BufferedReader(fr);
31:
32:             // Create output stream
33:             FileWriter fw = new FileWriter(temp.toFile());
34:             BufferedWriter out = new
35:                 BufferedWriter(fw);
36:
37:             boolean eof = false;
38:             int inChar;
39:             do {
40:                 inChar = in.read();
41:                 if (inChar != -1) {
42:                     char outChar = Character.toUpperCase( (char)inChar );
43:                     out.write(outChar);
44:                 } else
45:                     eof = true;
46:             } while (!eof);
47:             in.close();
48:             out.close();
49:
50:             Files.delete(source);
51:             Files.move(temp, source);
52:         } catch (IOException|SecurityException se) {
53:             System.out.println("Error -- " + se.toString());
54:         }
55:     }
56: }
```

Before running the program, you need a text file that can be converted to all capital letters. One option is to make a copy of AllCapsDemo.java and give it a name like

`TempFile.java`. This file should be stored in the root project folder in NetBeans and specified as a command-line argument.

This program does not produce any output. Load the converted file into a text editor to see the results of the application.

Summary

Today, you learned how to work with streams in two directions: pulling data into a program over an input stream and sending data from a program using an output stream.

You used character streams to handle text and byte streams for any other kind of data. Filters were associated with streams to alter how information was delivered through a stream or to alter the information itself.

In addition to these classes, `java.io` offers other types of streams you might want to explore. Piped streams are useful when communicating data among different threads, and byte array streams can connect programs to a computer's memory.

Because the stream classes in Java are so closely coordinated, you already possess most of the knowledge you need to use these other types of streams. The constructors, read methods, and write methods are largely identical.

Streams are a powerful way to extend the functionality of your Java programs because they offer a connection to any kind of data you might want to work with.

Tomorrow, you will use streams to read and write Java objects.

Q&A

Q A C program that I use creates a file of integers and other data. Can I read this using a Java program?

A You can, but one thing you have to consider is whether your C program represents integers in the same manner that a Java program represents them. As you might recall, all data can be represented as an individual byte or a series of bytes. An integer is represented in Java using 4 bytes arranged in what is called big-endian order. You can determine the integer value by combining the bytes from left to right. A C program implemented on an Intel PC is likely to represent integers in little-endian order, which means that the bytes must be arranged from right to left to determine the result. You might have to learn about advanced techniques, such as bit shifting, to use a data file created with a programming language other than Java.

Q **Can relative paths be used when specifying the name of a file in Java?**

A Relative paths are determined according to the current user folder, which is stored in the system properties `user.dir`. You can find out the full path to this folder by using the `System` class in the main `java.lang` package, which does not need to be imported.

Call the `System` class `getProperty(String)` method with the name of the property to retrieve, as in this example:

```
String userFolder = System.getProperty("user.dir");
```

The method returns the path as a string.

Q **The `FileWriter` class has a `write(int)` method that's used to send a character to a file. Shouldn't this be `write(char)`?**

A The `char` and `int` data types are interchangeable in many ways; you can use an `int` in a method that expects a `char`, and vice versa. This is possible because each character is represented by a numeric code that is an integer value. When you call the `write()` method with an `int`, it outputs the character associated with that integer value. When calling the `write()` method, you can cast an `int` value to a `char` to ensure that it's being used as you intended.

Quiz

Review today's material by taking this three-question quiz. Answers are at the end of the book.

Questions

1. What happens when you create a `FileOutputStream` using a reference to an existing file?

    A. An exception is thrown.

    B. The data you write to the stream is appended to the existing file.

    C. The existing file is replaced with the data you write to the stream.

2. What two primitive types are interchangeable when you're working with streams?

    A. `byte` and `boolean`

    B. `char` and `int`

    C. `byte` and `char`

3. In Java, what is the maximum value of a `byte` variable and the maximum value of an unsigned byte in a stream?

    A. Both are 255.

    B. Both are 127.

    C. 127 for a `byte` variable and 255 for an unsigned byte.

15

Certification Practice

The following question is the kind of thing you could expect to be asked on a Java programming certification test. Answer it without looking at today's material or using the Java compiler to test the code.

Given:

```java
import java.io.*;

public class Unknown {
    public static void main(String[] arguments) {
        String command = "";
        BufferedReader br = new BufferedReader(new
            InputStreamReader(System.in));
        try {
            command = br.readLine();
        }
        catch (IOException e) { }
    }
}
```

Will this program successfully store a line of console input in the `String` object named `command`?

    A. Yes.

    B. No, because a buffered input stream is required to read console input.

    C. No, because it won't compile successfully.

    D. No, because it reads more than one line of console input.

The answer is available on the book's website at www.java21days.com. Visit the Day 15 page and click the Certification Practice link.

Exercises

To extend your knowledge of the subjects covered today, try the following exercises:

1. Write a modified version of the HexReader program from Day 7, "Exceptions and Threads," that reads two-digit hexadecimal sequences from a text file and displays their decimal equivalents.

2. Write a program that reads a file to determine the number of bytes it contains and then overwrites all those bytes with 0s. (For obvious reasons, don't test this program on any file you intend to keep because the file's data will be wiped out.)

Where applicable, exercise solutions are offered on the book's website at www.java21days.com.

DAY 16
Serializing and Examining Objects

An essential concept of object-oriented programming is the representation of data. In an object-oriented language such as Java, an object represents two things:

- Behavior: The things an object can do

- Attributes: The data that differentiates the object from other objects

Combining behavior and attributes is a departure from other programming languages, where a program is defined as a set of instructions that manipulate data. The data is a separate thing, such as how word processing software is considered to be a program that creates and edits text documents. The data is separate from the software that manipulates it.

Object-oriented programming blurs the line between program and data. An object in a language such as Java encapsulates both instructions (behavior) and data (attributes).

Today, you discover two ways in which a Java program can take advantage of this representation:

- Object serialization, the ability to read and write an object using streams

- Reflection, in which one object can learn details about another object

Object Serialization

As you learned during Day 15, "Working with Input and Output," Java handles access to external data via the use of a class of objects called streams. A *stream* is an object that carries data from one place to another. Some streams carry information from a source into a Java program. Others go the opposite direction and take data from a program to a destination.

A stream that reads a web page's data into an array in a Java program is an example of the former. A stream that writes a `String` array to a disk file is an example of the latter.

Two types of streams were introduced during Day 15:

- Byte streams, which read and write a series of integer values ranging from 0 to 255
- Character streams, which read and write textual data

These streams separate the data from the Java class that works with it. To use the data later, you must read it in through a stream and convert it into a form the class can use, such as a series of primitive data types or objects.

A third type of stream, an *object stream*, makes it possible for data to be represented as objects rather than as some external form.

Object streams, such as byte and character streams, are part of the `java.io` package. Working with them requires many of the same techniques you used during Day 15.

For an object to be saved to a destination such as a disk file, it must be converted to serial form.

NOTE

> Serial data is sent one element at a time, like a line of cars on an assembly line. You might be familiar with the serial port on a computer, which is used to send information as a series of bits, one after the other. Another way to send data is in parallel, transferring more than one element simultaneously.

When you implement the `Serializable` interface, an object indicates that it can be used with streams. This interface, which is part of the `java.io` package, differs from other interfaces with which you have worked. It does not contain any methods that must be included in the classes that implement it. The sole purpose of the `Serializable` interface is to indicate that objects of that class can be stored and retrieved in serial form.

Objects can be serialized to disk on a single computer or can be serialized across a network such as the Internet, even in a case in which different operating systems are involved. You can create an object on a Windows machine, serialize it to a Linux machine, and load it back into the original Windows machine without error. Java transparently works with the different formats for saving data on these systems when objects are serialized.

A programming concept involved in object serialization is *persistence*—an object's capability to exist and function outside the program that created it.

Normally, an object that is not serialized is not persistent. When the program that uses the object stops running, the object ceases to exist.

16

Serialization enables object persistence because the stored object continues to serve a purpose even when no Java program is running. The stored object contains information that can be restored in a program so that it can resume functioning.

When an object is saved to a stream in serial form, all objects to which it contains references also are saved. This makes it easier to work with serialization; you can create one object stream that takes care of numerous objects at the same time.

When several objects contain references to the same object, Java automatically ensures that only one copy of that object is serialized. Each object is assigned an internal serial number; successive attempts to save that object store only that number.

You can exclude some of an object's variables from serialization to save disk space or prevent information that presents a security risk from being saved. As you will see later today, this requires the use of the `transient` modifier.

Object Output Streams

An object is written to a stream via the `ObjectOutputStream` class.

An object output stream is created with the `ObjectOutputStream(OutputStream)` constructor. The argument to this constructor can be either of the following:

- An output stream representing the destination where the object should be stored in serial form
- A filter associated with the output stream leading to the destination

As with other streams, you can chain more than one filter between the output stream and the object output stream.

The following code creates an output stream and an associated object output stream:

```
FileOutputStream disk = new FileOutputStream(
    "SavedObject.dat");
ObjectOutputStream disko = new ObjectOutputStream(disk);
```

The object output stream created in this example is called `disko`. Methods of the `disko` class can be used to write serializable objects and other information to a file called `SavedObject.dat`.

After you have created an object output stream, you can write an object to it by calling the stream's `writeObject(Object)` method.

The following statement calls this method on `disko`, the stream created in the preceding example:

```
disko.writeObject(userData);
```

This statement writes an object called `userData` to the `disko` object output stream. The class represented by `userData` must be serializable for it to work.

An object output stream also can be used to write other types of information with the following methods:

- `write(int)` writes the specified integer to the stream, which should be a value from 0 to 255.
- `write(byte[])` writes the specified byte array.
- `write(byte[], int, int)` writes a subset of the specified byte array. The second argument specifies the first array element to write, and the last argument represents the number of subsequent elements to write.
- `writeBoolean(boolean)` writes the specified `boolean`.
- `writeByte(int)` writes the specified integer as a byte value.
- `writeBytes(String)` writes the specified string as a series of bytes.
- `writeChar(int)` writes the specified character.
- `writeChars(String)` writes the specified string as a series of characters.
- `writeDouble(double)` writes the specified `double`.
- `writeFloat(float)` writes the specified `float`.
- `writeInt(int)` writes the specified `int`, which, unlike the argument to `write(int)`, can be any `int` value.
- `writeLong(long)` writes the specified `long`.
- `writeShort(short)` writes the specified `short`.

The ObjectOutputStream constructor and all methods that write data to an object output stream throw IOException objects. These must be accounted for using a try-catch block or a throws clause.

Listing 16.1 is a Java application that consists of two classes: ObjectWriter and Message. The Message class represents an email message. This class has from and to objects that store the names of the sender and recipient, a now object that holds a Date value representing when the email was sent, and a text array of String objects that holds the message. There also is an int called lineCount that keeps track of the number of lines in the message.

When you design a program that transmits and receives email, it makes sense to use some kind of stream to save these messages to disk. The information that constitutes the message must be saved in some form as it is transmitted from one place to another. It also might need to be saved until the recipient can read it.

Messages can be preserved by saving each message element separately to a byte or character stream. In the example of the Message class, the from and to objects could be written to a stream as strings, and the text object could be written as an array of strings. The now object is a little trickier because there isn't a way to write a Date object to a character stream. However, it could be converted into a series of integer values representing each part of a date: hour, minutes, seconds, and so on. Those could be written to the stream.

Using an object output stream makes it possible to save Message objects without first translating them into another form.

The ObjectWriter class, shown in Listing 16.1, creates a Message object, sets up values for its variables, and saves the object to a file called Message.obj via an object output stream. Create a new empty Java file in NetBeans and call the class ObjectWriter.

LISTING 16.1 The Full Text of ObjectWriter.java

```
1: import java.io.*;
2: import java.util.*;
3:
4: public class ObjectWriter {
5:     public static void main(String[] arguments) {
6:         Message mess = new Message();
7:         String author = "Sam Wainwright, London";
8:         String recipient = "George Bailey, Bedford Falls";
9:         String[] letter = { "Mr. Gower cabled you need cash. Stop.",
10:             "My office instructed to advance you up to twenty-five",
11:             "thousand dollars. Stop. Hee-haw and Merry Christmas." };
12:         Date now = new Date();
```

16

LISTING 16.1   Continued

```
13:            mess.writeMessage(author, recipient, now, letter);
14:            try {
15:                FileOutputStream fo = new FileOutputStream(
16:                    "Message.obj");
17:                ObjectOutputStream oo = new ObjectOutputStream(fo);
18:                oo.writeObject(mess);
19:                oo.close();
20:                System.out.println("Object created successfully.");
21:            } catch (IOException e) {
22:                System.out.println("Error -- " + e.toString());
23:            }
24:        }
25: }
26:
27: class Message implements Serializable {
28:     int lineCount;
29:     String from, to;
30:     Date when;
31:     String[] text;
32:
33:     void writeMessage(String inFrom,
34:             String inTo,
35:             Date inWhen,
36:             String[] inText) {
37:
38:         text = new String[inText.length];
39:         for (int i = 0; i < inText.length; i++)
40:             text[i] = inText[i];
41:         lineCount = inText.length;
42:         to = inTo;
43:         from = inFrom;
44:         when = inWhen;
45:     }
46: }
```

You should see the following output after you compile and run the ObjectWriter application:

Output ▼

```
Object created successfully.
```

Object Input Streams

An object is read from a stream using the ObjectInputStream class. As with other streams, working with an object input stream is similar to working with an object output stream. The primary difference is the change in the data's direction.

An object input stream is created with the ObjectInputStream(*InputStream*) constructor. This constructor throws four exceptions: IOException, StreamCorruption
Exception, SecurityException, and NullPointerException. IOException, common
to stream classes, occurs whenever any kind of input/output error occurs during the data
transfer. StreamCorruptionException is specific to object streams, and it indicates that
the data in the stream is not a serialized object. SecurityException notes a violation of
security policy, and NullPointerException occurs when an object has a null value.

An object input stream can be constructed from an input stream or a filtered stream.

The following code creates an input stream and an object input stream to go along
with it:

16

```
try {
    FileInputStream disk = new FileInputStream(
        "SavedObject.dat");
    ObjectInputStream obj = new ObjectInputStream(disk);
} catch (IOException ie) {
    System.out.println("IO error -- " + ie.toString());
}
```

This object input stream is set up to read from an object stored in a file called
SavedObject.dat. If the file does not exist or cannot be read from disk for some
reason, an IOException is thrown. If the file isn't a serialized object, a thrown
StreamCorruptionException indicates this problem.

An object can be read from an object input stream by using the readObject() method,
which returns an Object. This object immediately can be cast into the class to which it
belongs, as in the following example:

```
WorkData dd = (WorkData) disk.readObject();
```

This statement reads an object from the disk object stream and casts it into an object of
the class WorkData. In addition to IOException, this method throws OptionalData
Exception, ClassNotFoundException, and InvalidClassException errors.

OptionalDataException indicates that the stream contains data other than serialized
object data, which makes it impossible to read an object from the stream.

ClassNotFoundException occurs when the object retrieved from the stream belongs to a
class that could not be found. When objects are serialized, the class is not saved to the
stream. Instead, the name of the class is saved to the stream, and the Java virtual machine
loads the class when the object is loaded from a stream.

Other types of information can be read from an object input stream using the following methods:

- read() reads the next byte from the stream, which is returned as an int.
- read(*byte[]*, *int*, *int*) reads bytes into the specified byte array. The second argument specifies the first array element where a byte should be stored. The last argument represents the number of subsequent elements to read and store in the array.
- readBoolean() reads a boolean value from the stream.
- readByte() reads a byte value from the stream.
- readChar() reads a char value from the stream.
- readDouble() reads a double value from the stream.
- readFloat() reads a float value from the stream.
- readInt() reads an int value from the stream.
- readLine() reads a String from the stream.
- readLong() reads a long value from the stream.
- readShort() reads a short value from the stream.
- readUnsignedByte() reads an unsigned byte value and returns it as an int.
- readUnsignedShort() reads an unsigned short value and returns it as an int.

Each of these methods throws an IOException if an input/output error occurs as the stream is being read.

When an object is created when an object stream is read, it is created entirely from the variable and object information stored in that stream. No constructor method is called to create variables and set them up with initial values. There's no difference between this object and the one originally serialized.

Listing 16.2 is a Java application that reads an object from a stream and displays its variables to standard output. The ObjectReader application loads the object serialized to the file message.obj. Create a new Java class named ObjectReader in the same project where ObjectWriter is stored.

LISTING 16.2   The Full Text of ObjectReader.java

```
1: import java.io.*;
2: import java.util.*;
3:
4: public class ObjectReader {
```

LISTING 16.2   Continued

```
 5:     public static void main(String[] arguments) {
 6:         try {
 7:             FileInputStream fi = new FileInputStream(
 8:                 "message.obj");
 9:             ObjectInputStream oi = new ObjectInputStream(fi);
10:             Message mess = (Message) oi.readObject();
11:             System.out.println("Message:\n");
12:             System.out.println("From: " + mess.from);
13:             System.out.println("To: " + mess.to);
14:             System.out.println("Date: " + mess.when + "\n");
15:             for (int i = 0; i < mess.lineCount; i++)
16:                 System.out.println(mess.text[i]);
17:             oi.close();
18:         } catch (Exception e) {
19:             System.out.println("Error -- " + e.toString());
20:         }
21:     }
22: }
```

The output is as follows:

Output ▼

```
Message:

From: Sam Wainwright, London
To: George Bailey, Bedford Falls
Date: Wed Jun 13 15:15:53 EDT 2012

Mr. Gower cabled you need cash. Stop.
My office instructed to advance you up to twenty-five
thousand dollars. Stop. Hee-haw and Merry Christmas.
```

Transient Variables

When you create an object that can be serialized, one design consideration is whether all the object's instance variables should be saved.

In some cases, an instance variable must be created from scratch each time the object is restored. A good example is an object referring to a file or input stream. Such an object must be created anew when it is part of a serialized object loaded from an object stream, so it doesn't make sense to save this information when serializing the object.

It's a good idea to exclude from serialization a variable that contains sensitive information. If an object stores the password needed to gain access to a resource, that password is more at risk if it is serialized into a file. The password also might be detected if it is part of an object restored over a stream that exists on a network.

A third reason not to serialize a variable is to save space on the storage file that holds the object. If its values can be established without serialization, you might want to omit the variable from the process.

To prevent an instance variable from being included in serialization, the transient modifier is used.

This modifier is included in the variable's declaration, preceding the variable's class or data type. The following statement creates a transient variable called limit:

```
public transient int limit = 55;
```

Checking an Object's Serialized Fields

An important thing to consider when serializing objects is how easily a malicious programmer could tamper with an object in serial form. The file format for serialized objects in Java is neither encrypted nor particularly complex.

When you re-create an object from its serial form, you can't rely on a constructor method to ensure that its fields have permissible values.

Instead, if you want to check that an object read from a stream contains acceptable values, the object can include a readObject(*ObjectInputStream*) method.

This method throws IOException and ClassNotFoundException exceptions and takes the following form:

```
private void readObject(ObjectInputStream ois) {
    ois.defaultReadObject();
}
```

Note that it is private. In the method, the defaultReadObject() method of the object stream reads serialized fields into the object, where they can be checked to ensure that the values are acceptable.

If not, an IOException can be thrown to indicate that an error related to serialization has occurred.

The following method could be added to the Message class to reject a serialized object that has an empty from value:

```
private void readObject(ObjectInputStream ois)
    throws IOException, ClassNotFoundException {
```

```
ois.defaultReadObject();
    if (from.length() < 1) {
        throw new IOException("Null sender in message.");
    }
}
```

Inspecting Classes and Methods with Reflection

On Day 3, "Working with Objects," you learned how to create `Class` objects that represent the class to which an object belongs. Every object in Java inherits the `getClass()` method, which identifies that object's class or interface. The following statement creates a `Class` object named `keyclass` from an object referred to by the variable `key`:

```
Class keyClass = key.getClass();
```

By calling the `getName()` method of a `Class` object, you can find out the class's name:

```
String keyName = keyClass.getName();
```

These features are part of Java's support for reflection, a technique that enables one Java class—such as a program you write—to learn details about another class.

Through reflection, a Java program can load a class it knows nothing about; find that class's variables, methods, and constructors; and work with them.

One use of reflection is to determine a serialized object's class when it is read.

Inspecting and Creating Classes

The `Class` class, which is part of the `java.lang` package, is used to learn about and create classes, interfaces, and even primitive types.

In addition to using `getClass()`, you can create `Class` objects by appending `.class` to the name of a class, interface, array, or primitive type, as in the following examples:

```
Class keyClass = KeyClass.class;
```

```
Class thr = Throwable.class;
```

```
Class floater = float.class;
```

```
Class floatArray = float[].class;
```

You also can create `Class` objects by using the `forName()` class method with a single argument: a string containing the name of an existing class. The following statement creates a `Class` object representing a `JLabel`, one of the classes of the `javax.swing` package:

```
Class lab = Class.forName("javax.swing.JLabel");
```

The `forName()` method throws a `ClassNotFoundException` if the specified class cannot be found, so you must call `forName()` within a `try-catch` block or handle it in some other manner.

To retrieve a string containing the name of a class represented by a `Class` object, call `getName()` on that object. For classes and interfaces, this name includes the name of the class and a reference to the package to which it belongs. For primitive types, the name corresponds to the type's name (such as `int`, `float`, or `double`).

`Class` objects that represent arrays are handled a little differently when `getName()` is called on them. The name begins with one left bracket character (`[`) for each dimension of the array: `float[]` would begin with `[`, `int[][]` with `[[`, `KeyClass[][][]` with `[[[`, and so on.

If the array is a primitive type, the next part of the name is a single character representing the type, as shown in Table 16.1.

TABLE 16.1   Type Identification for Primitive Types

Character	Primitive Type
B	byte
C	char
D	double
F	float
I	int
J	long
S	short
Z	boolean

For arrays of objects, the brackets are followed by an `L` and the name of the class. For example, if you called `getName()` on a `String[][]` array, the result would be `[[Ljava.lang.String`.

You also can use the `Class` class to create new objects. Call the `newInstance()` method on a `Class` object to create the object and cast it to the correct class.

For example, if you have a `Class` object named `thr` that represents the `Throwable` interface, you can create a new object as follows:

```
Throwable thr2 = (Throwable) thr.newInstance();
```

The `newInstance()` method throws several kinds of exceptions:

- `IllegalAccessException`—You do not have access to the class, either because it is not `public` or because it belongs to a different package.
- `InstantiationException`—You cannot create a new object because the class is abstract.
- `SecurityException`—You do not have permission to create an object of this class.

When `newInstance()` is called and no exceptions are thrown, the new object is created when the constructor of the corresponding class is called with no arguments.

NOTE

> You cannot use this technique to create a new object that requires arguments to its constructor method. Instead, you must use a newInstance() method of the Constructor class, as you will see later today.

Working with Each Part of a Class

Although `Class` is part of the `java.lang` package, the primary support for reflection is the `java.lang.reflect` package, which includes the following classes:

- `Field` manages and finds information about class and instance variables.
- `Method` manages class and instance methods.
- `Constructor` manages constructors, the special methods for creating new instances of classes.
- `Array` manages arrays.
- `Modifier` decodes modifier information about classes, variables, and methods (which were described on Day 6, "Packages, Interfaces, and Other Class Features").

Each of these reflection classes has methods for working with an element of a class.

A `Method` object holds information about a single method in a class. To find out about all methods contained in a class, create a `Class` object for that class and call

16

getDeclaredMethods() on that object. An array of Method[] objects is returned that represents all methods in the class not inherited from a superclass. If no methods meet that description, the array's length is 0.

The Method class has several useful instance methods:

- getParameterTypes() returns an array of Class objects representing each argument contained in the method signature.

- getReturnType() returns a Class object representing the method's return type, whether it's a class or primitive type.

- getModifiers() returns an int value that represents the modifiers that apply to the method, such as whether it is public, private, and the like.

Because the getParameterTypes() and getReturnType() methods return Class objects, you can use getName() on each object to find out more about it.

The easiest way to use the int returned by getModifiers() is to call the Modifier class method toString() with that integer as an argument. For example, if you have a Method object named current, you can display its modifiers with the following code:

```
int mods = current.getModifiers();
System.out.println(Modifier.toString(mods));
```

The Constructor class has some of the same methods as the Method class, including getModifiers() and getName(). One method that's missing, as you might expect, is getReturnType(); constructors do not contain return types.

To retrieve all constructors associated with a Class object, call getConstructors() on that object. An array of public Constructor objects is returned.

To retrieve a specific constructor, first create an array of Class objects that represent every argument sent to the constructor. When this is done, call getConstructors() with that Class array as an argument.

For example, if there is a KeyClass(String, int) constructor, you can create a Constructor object to represent this with the following statements:

```
Class kc = KeyClass.class;
Class[] cons = new Class[2];
cons[0] = String.class;
cons[1] = int.class;
Constructor c = kc.getConstructor(cons);
```

The getConstructor(Class[]) method throws a NoSuchMethodException if there isn't a constructor with arguments that match the Class[] array.

After you have a `Constructor` object, you can call its `newInstance(Object[])` method to create a new instance using that constructor.

Inspecting a Class

To bring together all this material, Listing 16.3 is a short Java application named MethodInspector that uses reflection to inspect the methods in a class. Create a class called `MethodInspector` in NetBeans as an empty Java file and fill it with the text of this listing.

LISTING 16.3   The Full Text of MethodInspector.java

```
 1: import java.lang.reflect.*;
 2:
 3: public class MethodInspector {
 4:     public static void main(String[] arguments)  {
 5:         Class inspect;
 6:         try {
 7:             if (arguments.length > 0)
 8:                 inspect = Class.forName(arguments[0]);
 9:             else
10:                 inspect = Class.forName("MethodInspector");
11:             Method[] methods = inspect.getDeclaredMethods();
12:             for (int i = 0; i < methods.length; i++) {
13:                 Method methVal = methods[i];
14:                 Class returnVal = methVal.getReturnType();
15:                 int mods = methVal.getModifiers();
16:                 String modVal = Modifier.toString(mods);
17:                 Class[] paramVal = methVal.getParameterTypes();
18:                 StringBuffer params = new StringBuffer();
19:                 for (int j = 0; j < paramVal.length; j++) {
20:                     if (j > 0)
21:                         params.append(", ");
22:                     params.append(paramVal[j].getName());
23:                 }
24:                 System.out.println("Method: " + methVal.getName() + "()");
25:                 System.out.println("Modifiers: " + modVal);
26:                 System.out.println("Return Type: " + returnVal.getName());
27:                 System.out.println("Parameters: " + params + "\n");
28:             }
29:         } catch (ClassNotFoundException c) {
30:             System.out.println(c.toString());
31:         }
32:     }
33: }
```

The MethodInspector application displays information about the public methods in the class you specify at the command line (or `MethodInspector` itself, if you don't specify a

16

class). To try the program, set up a command-line argument that is the full name of a Java class.

If you run the application on the `java.util.Random` class, the program's output is the following (with some methods omitted for brevity):

Output ▼

```
Method: next()
Modifiers: protected
Return Type: int
Parameters: int

Method: readObject()
Modifiers: private
Return Type: void
Parameters: java.io.ObjectInputStream

...

Method: setSeed()
Modifiers: public synchronized
Return Type: void
Parameters: long
```

By using reflection, the MethodInspector application can learn every method of a class.

A `Class` object is declared in line 5 and assigned an object in line 8 or line 10. If a class name is specified as a command-line argument when `MethodInspector` is run, the `Class.forName()` method is called with that argument. Otherwise, `MethodInspector` is used as the argument.

After the `Class` object is created, its `getDeclaredMethods()` method is used in line 11 to find all the methods contained in the class (with the exception of methods inherited from a superclass). These methods are stored as an array of `Method` objects.

The `for` loop in lines 12–28 cycles through each method in the class, storing its return type, modifiers, and arguments and then displaying them.

Displaying the return type is straightforward: Each method's `getReturnType()` method is stored as a `Class` object in line 14, and that object's name is displayed in line 26.

When a method's `getModifiers()` method is called in line 15, an integer is returned that represents all modifiers used with the method. The class method `Modifier.toString()` takes this integer as an argument and returns the names of all modifiers associated with it.

Lines 19–23 loop through the array of Class objects that represents the arguments associated with a method. The name of each argument is added to a StringBuffer object named params in line 22.

Reflection is most commonly used by tools such as class browsers and debuggers as a way to learn more about the class of objects being browsed or debugged.

NOTE	Reflection also is needed with JavaBeans to create Java classes that can be manipulated in a programming environment. These classes, called *beans*, let you create Java applications by loading beans into an interface, customizing them, and controlling their interactions.

16

Although it is a powerful technique for creating dynamic programs, reflection comes at a cost. The classes created and used through reflection cannot be checked for errors when a program is compiled. Instead, any errors must be detected while the program runs.

Summary

Although Java always has been a network-centric language, the topics covered today show how the language has been extended in new directions.

Object serialization shows how objects created with Java have a life span beyond that of a Java program. You can create objects in a program that are saved to a storage device such as a hard drive and are re-created later, after the original program has ceased to run.

Object persistence is an effective way to save elements of a program for later use.

Reflection enables a class to learn the class of an object on the fly, determining its methods and variables and making use of them.

Q&A

Q Are object streams associated with the Writer and Reader classes that are used to work with character streams?

A The ObjectInputStream and ObjectOutputStream classes are independent of the byte stream and character stream superclasses in the java.io package, although they contain many of the same methods as the byte classes.

You shouldn't need to use `Writer` or `Reader` classes in conjunction with object streams. You can accomplish the same things via the object stream classes and their superclasses (`InputStream` and `OutputStream`).

Q Are `private` variables and objects saved when they are part of an object that's being serialized?

A Yes. As you might recall from today's discussion, no constructors are called when an object is loaded into a program using serialization. Therefore, all variables and objects not declared `transient` are saved to prevent the object from losing something that might be necessary to its function.

Saving `private` variables and objects might present a security risk in some cases, especially when the variable is being used to store a password or some other sensitive data. Using `transient` prevents a variable or object from being serialized.

Quiz

Review today's material by taking this three-question quiz. Answers are at the end of the book.

Questions

1. What is returned when you call `getName()` on a `Class` object that represents a `String[]` array?

   A. `java.lang.String`

   B. `[Ljava.lang.String`

   C. `[java.lang.String`

2. What is persistence?

   A. An object's capability to exist after the program that created it has stopped running

   B. A class's capability to support multiple threads

   C. An error-handling technique

3. What `Class` method is used to create a new `Class` object using a string containing the name of a class?

   A. `newInstance()`

   B. `forName()`

   C. `getName()`

Certification Practice

The following question is the kind of thing you could expect to be asked on a Java programming certification test. Answer it without looking at today's material or using the Java compiler to test the code.

Given:

```java
public class ClassType {
    public static void main(String[] arguments) {
        Class c = String.class;
        try {
            Object o = c.newInstance();
            if (o instanceof String)
                System.out.println("True");
            else
                System.out.println("False");
        } catch (Exception e) {
            System.out.println("Error");
        }
    }
}
```

16

What will be the output of this application?

A. true

B. false

C. Error

D. The program will not compile.

The answer is available on the book's website at www.java21days.com. Visit the Day 16 page and click the Certification Practice link.

Exercises

To extend your knowledge of the subjects covered today, try the following exercises:

1. Use reflection to write a Java program that takes a class name as a command-line argument and checks whether it is an application. All applications have a main() method with public static as modifiers, void as a return type, and String[] as the only argument.

2. Write a program that creates a new object using Class objects and the newInstance() method that serializes the object to disk.

Where applicable, exercise solutions are offered on the book's website at www.java21days.com.

DAY 17

Communicating Across the Internet

Java was developed initially as a language that would control a network of interactive consumer devices. Connecting machines was one of the main purposes of the language when it was designed, and that remains true today.

The `java.net` package makes it possible to communicate over a network, providing cross-platform abstractions to make connections, transfer files using common web protocols, and create sockets.

Used in conjunction with input and output streams, reading and writing files over the network becomes as easy as reading or writing files on disk.

The `java.nio` package expands Java's input and output classes.

Today, you write networking Java programs that do each of the following:

- Load a document over the web
- Mimic a popular Internet service
- Serve information to clients

Networking in Java

Networking allows different computers to make connections with each other and exchange information. In Java, basic networking is supported by classes in the java.net package, including support for connecting and retrieving files through Hypertext Transfer Protocol (HTTP) and File Transfer Protocol (FTP), as well as working at a lower level with sockets.

You can communicate with systems on the Net in three simple ways:

- Load a web page and any other resource with a uniform resource locator (URL).
- Use the socket classes, Socket and ServerSocket, which open standard socket connections to hosts and read to and write from those connections.
- Call getInputStream(), a method that opens a connection to a URL and can extract data from that connection.

Opening a Stream Over the Net

As you learned during Day 15, "Working with Input and Output," you can pull information through a stream into your Java programs in several ways. The classes and methods you choose depend on the format of the information and what you want to do with it.

One of the resources you can reach from your Java programs is a text document on the web, whether it's a Hypertext Markup Language (HTML) file, Extensible Markup Language (XML) file, or some other kind of plain-text document.

You can use a four-step process to load a text document off the web and read it line by line:

1. Create a URL object that represents the resource's web address.
2. Create an HttpURLConnection object that can load the URL and make a connection to the site hosting it.
3. Use the getContent() method of that HttpURLConnection object to create an InputStreamReader that can read a stream of data from the URL.
4. Use that input stream reader to create a BufferedReader object that can efficiently read characters from an input stream.

Much interaction occurs between the web document and your Java program. The URL is used to set up a URL connection, which is used to set up an input stream reader, which is used to set up a buffered input stream reader. The need to deal with any exceptions that occur along the way adds more complexity to the process.

Before you can load anything, you must create a new instance of the class URL that represents the address of the resource you want to load. URL is an acronym for *uniform resource locator*, and it refers to the unique address of any document or other resource accessible on the Internet.

URL is part of the java.net package, so you must import the package or refer to the class by its full name in your programs.

To create a new URL object, use one of four constructors:

- URL(*String*) creates a URL object from a full web address such as "http://www.java21days.com" or "ftp://ftp.freebsd.org".

- URL(*URL, String*) creates a URL object with a base address provided by the specified URL and a relative path provided by the String.

- URL(*String, String, int, String*) creates a new URL object from a protocol (such as "http" or "ftp"), hostname (such as "www.cnn.com" or "web.archive.org"), port number (80 for HTTP), and filename or pathname.

- URL(*String, String, String*) is the same as the previous constructor minus the port number.

17

When you use the URL(*String*) constructor, you must deal with MalformedURLException exceptions, which are thrown if the string does not appear to be a valid URL. These objects can be handled in a try-catch block:

```
try {
    URL load = new URL("http://www.samspublishing.com");
} catch (MalformedURLException e) {
    System.out.println("Bad URL");
}
```

The WebReader application, shown in Listing 17.1, uses the four-step technique to open a connection to a website and read a text document from it. When the document is fully loaded, it is displayed in a text area. Create this class in NetBeans.

LISTING 17.1 The Full Text of WebReader.java

```
1: import javax.swing.*;
2: import java.net.*;
3: import java.io.*;
4:
5: public class WebReader extends JFrame {
6:     JTextArea box = new JTextArea("Getting data ...");
7:
8:     public WebReader() {
9:         super("Get File Application");
```

LISTING 17.1 Continued

```
10:             setDefaultCloseOperation(JFrame.EXIT_ON_CLOSE);
11:             setSize(600, 300);
12:             JScrollPane pane = new JScrollPane(box);
13:             add(pane);
14:             setVisible(true);
15:         }
16:
17:     void getData(String address) throws MalformedURLException {
18:             setTitle(address);
19:             URL page = new URL(address);
20:             StringBuilder text = new StringBuilder();
21:             try {
22:                 HttpURLConnection conn = (HttpURLConnection)
23:                     page.openConnection();
24:                 conn.connect();
25:                 InputStreamReader in = new InputStreamReader(
26:                     (InputStream) conn.getContent());
27:                 BufferedReader buff = new BufferedReader(in);
28:                 box.setText("Getting data ...");
29:                 String line;
30:                 do {
31:                     line = buff.readLine();
32:                     text.append(line);
33:                     text.append("\n");
34:                 } while (line != null);
35:                 box.setText(text.toString());
36:             } catch (IOException ioe) {
37:                 System.out.println("IO Error:" + ioe.getMessage());
38:             }
39:         }
40:
41:     public static void main(String[] arguments) {
42:             if (arguments.length < 1) {
43:                 System.out.println("Usage: java WebReader url");
44:                 System.exit(1);
45:             }
46:             try {
47:                 WebReader app = new WebReader();
48:                 app.getData(arguments[0]);
49:             } catch (MalformedURLException mue) {
50:                 System.out.println("Bad URL: " + arguments[0]);
51:             }
52:         }
53: }
```

The WebReader application requires one command-line argument—a web address—that can be set in NetBeans in the project configuration.

You can choose any URL. Try http://tycho.usno.navy.mil/cgi-bin/timer.pl for the U.S. Naval Observatory timekeeping site or http://random.yahoo.com/bin/ryl for a random link from the Yahoo! directory. Figure 17.1 shows the RSS feed loaded from www.rssboard.org/rss-feed.

FIGURE 17.1

Running the WebReader application.

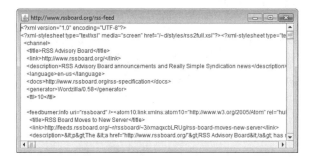

17

Two thirds of the WebReader class is devoted to running the application, creating the user interface, and creating a valid URL object. The web document is loaded over a stream and is displayed in a text area in the getData() method.

Four objects are used: URL, HttpURLConnection, InputStreamReader, and BufferedReader. These objects work together to pull the data from the Internet to the Java application. In addition, two objects are created to hold the data when it arrives: a String and a StringBuilder.

Lines 22–24 open an HTTP URL connection, which is necessary to get an input stream from that connection.

Lines 25–26 use the connection's getContent() method to create a new input stream reader. The method returns an input stream representing the connection to the URL.

Line 27 uses that input stream reader to create a new buffered input stream reader—a BufferedReader object called buff.

After you have this buffered reader, you can use its readLine() method to read a line of text from the input stream. The buffered reader puts characters in a buffer as they arrive and pulls them out of the buffer when requested.

The do-while loop in lines 30–34 reads the web document line by line, appending each line to the StringBuilder object created to hold the page's text.

After all the data has been read, line 35 converts the string builder into a string with the toString() method. Then it puts that result in the program's text area by calling the component's setText(*String*) method.

The `HttpUrlConnection` class includes several methods that affect the HTTP request or provide more information:

- `getHeaderField(int)` returns a string containing an HTTP header such as `"Server"` (the web server hosting the document) or `"Last-Modified"` (the date the document was last changed). Headers are numbered from 0 upward. When the end of the headers is reached, this method returns `null`.

- `getHeaderFieldKey(int)` returns a string containing the name of the numbered header (such as `"Server"` or `"Last-Modified"`) or `null`.

- `getResponseCode()` returns an integer containing the HTTP response code for the request, such as 200 (for valid requests) or 404 (for documents that could not be found).

- `getResponseMessage()` returns a string containing the HTTP response code and an explanatory message (such as `"HTTP/1.0 200 OK"`). The `HttpUrlConnection` class contains integer class variables for each of the valid response codes, including `"HTTP_OK"`, `"HTTP_NOT_FOUND"`, and `"HTTP_MOVED_PERM"`.

- `getContentType()` returns a string containing the MIME type of the web document; some possible types are `"text/html"` for web pages and `"text/xml"` for XML files.

- `setFollowRedirects(boolean)` determines whether URL redirection requests should be followed (`true`) or ignored (`false`). When redirection is supported, a URL request can be forwarded by a web server from an obsolete URL to its correct address.

The following code could be added to WebReader's `getData()` method after line 24 to display headers along with the text of a document:

```
String key;
String header;
int i = 0;
do {
    key = conn.getHeaderFieldKey(i);
    header = conn.getHeaderField(i);
    if (key == null) {
        key = "";
    } else {
        key = key + ": ";
    }
    if (header != null) {
        text.append(key);
        text.append(header);
        text.append("\n");
```

```
    }
    i++;
} while (header != null);
text.append("\n");
```

Sockets

For networking applications beyond what the URL and URLConnection classes offer (for example, for other protocols or for more general networking applications), Java provides the Socket and ServerSocket classes as an abstraction of standard Transmission Control Protocol (TCP) socket programming techniques.

The Socket class provides a client-side socket interface similar to standard UNIX sockets. Create a new instance of Socket to open a connection, where *hostName* is the host to connect to and *portNumber* is the port number:

```
Socket connection = new Socket(hostName, portNumber);
```

17

After you create a socket, set its time-out value, which determines how long the application waits for data to arrive. This is handled by calling the socket's setSoTimeOut(*int*) method with the number of milliseconds to wait as the only argument:

```
connection.setSoTimeOut(50000);
```

When you use this method, any effort to read data from the socket represented by connection waits for only 50,000 milliseconds (50 seconds). If the time-out is reached, an InterruptedIOException is thrown, which gives you an opportunity in a try-catch block to either close the socket or try to read from it again.

If you don't set a time-out in a program that uses sockets, it might hang indefinitely, waiting for data.

TIP

This problem is usually avoided by putting network operations in their own thread and running them separately from the rest of the program, as covered during Day 7, "Exceptions and Threads."

After the socket is open, you can use input and output streams to read from and write to that socket:

```
BufferedInputStream bis = new
    BufferedInputStream(connection.getInputStream());
DataInputStream in = new DataInputStream(bis);
```

```
BufferedOutputStream bos = new
    BufferedOutputStream(connection.getOutputStream());
DataOutputStream out = new DataOutputStream(bos);
```

You don't need names for all these objects; they are used only to create a stream or stream reader. For an efficient shortcut, combine several statements, as in this example using a `Socket` object named `sock`:

```
DataInputStream in = new DataInputStream(
    new BufferedInputStream(
        sock.getInputStream()));
```

In this statement, the call to `sock.getInputStream()` returns an input stream associated with that socket. This stream is used to create a `BufferedInputStream`, and the buffered input stream is used to create a `DataInputStream`.

The only variables you are left with are `sock` and `in`, the two objects needed as you receive data from the connection and close it afterward. The intermediate objects—a `BufferedInputStream` and an `InputStream`—are needed only once.

After you're finished with a socket, don't forget to close it by calling the `close()` method. This also closes all the input and output streams you might have set up for that socket. For example:

```
connection.close();
```

Socket programming can be used for many services delivered using TCP/IP networking, including telnet, Simple Mail Transfer Protocol (SMTP) for incoming mail, Network News Transfer Protocol (NNTP) for Usenet news, and finger.

The last of these, finger, is a protocol for asking a system about one of its users. By setting up a finger server, a system administrator enables an Internet-connected machine to answer requests for user information. Users can provide information about themselves by creating `.plan` files, which are sent to anyone who uses finger to find out more about them.

Although it has fallen into disuse because of security concerns, finger was once a popular way for Internet users to share facts about themselves and their activities before blogs and social media took off. You could use finger on a friend's account at another college or company to see whether that person was online and read the person's current `.plan` file.

As an exercise in socket programming, the Finger application is a rudimentary finger client. Enter Listing 17.2 as a new class named `Finger` in NetBeans.

LISTING 17.2   The Full Text of Finger.java

```
1: import java.io.*;
2: import java.net.*;
3: import java.util.*;
4:
5: public class Finger {
6:     public static void main(String[] arguments) {
7:         String user;
8:         String host;
9:         if ((arguments.length == 1) && (arguments[0].indexOf("@") > -1)) {
10:             StringTokenizer split = new StringTokenizer(arguments[0],
11:                 "@");
12:             user = split.nextToken();
13:             host = split.nextToken();
14:         } else {
15:             System.out.println("Usage: java Finger user@host");
16:             return;
17:         }
18:         try (Socket digit = new Socket(host, 79);
19:             BufferedReader in = new BufferedReader(
20:                 new InputStreamReader(digit.getInputStream())));
21:             ) {
22:
23:             digit.setSoTimeout(20000);
24:             PrintStream out = new PrintStream(digit.getOutputStream());
25:             out.print(user + "\015\012");
26:
27:             boolean eof = false;
28:             while (!eof) {
29:                 String line = in.readLine();
30:                 if (line != null) {
31:                     System.out.println(line);
32:                 } else {
33:                     eof = true;
34:                 }
35:             }
36:             digit.close();
37:         } catch (IOException e) {
38:             System.out.println("IO Error:" + e.getMessage());
39:         }
40:     }
41: }
```

When making a finger request, specify a username followed by an at sign (@) and a hostname, the same format as an email address. One example is icculus@icculus.org, the finger address of game developer Ryan Gordon. You can request his .plan file by running the Finger application with that address as the only command-line argument.

If icculus has an account on the icculus.org finger server, running the Finger application displays his .plan file and perhaps other information. The server also lets you know when a user can't be found.

The Finger application uses the StringTokenizer class to convert an address in user@host format into two String objects: user and host (lines 10–13).

The following socket activities are taking place:

- **Line 18**—A new Socket is created using the hostname and port 79, the port traditionally reserved for finger services.
- **Line 19–21**—The socket is used to create an InputStream, which in turn is used to create a BufferedReader.
- **Line 23**—A timeout of 20 seconds is set for the socket.
- **Line 24**—The socket is used to get an OutputStream, which feeds into a new PrintStream object.
- **Line 25**—The finger protocol requires that the username be sent through the socket, followed by a carriage return (\015) and linefeed (\012). This is handled by calling the print() method of the new print stream.
- **Lines 28–35**—The program loops as lines are read from the buffered reader. The end of output from the server causes in.readLine() to return null, ending the loop.

The same techniques used to communicate with a finger server through a socket can be used to connect to other popular Internet services. You could turn it into a telnet or web-reading client with a port change in line 18 and little other modification.

TIP

The Finger application makes use of the new try-with-resources capability of Java 7 in lines 18–21 of Listing 17.2. Declaring the socket and reader within the try statement's parentheses ensures that both of these resources will be closed even when the connection fails with an exception.

Socket Servers

Server-side sockets work similarly to client sockets, with the exception of the accept() method. A server socket listens on a TCP port for a connection from a client; when a client connects to that port, the accept() method accepts a connection from that client. By using both client and server sockets, you can create applications that communicate with each other over the network.

To create a server socket and bind it to a port, create a new instance of ServerSocket with a port number as an argument to the constructor, as in the following example:

```
ServerSocket servo = new ServerSocket(8888);
```

Use the accept() method to listen on that port (and to accept a connection from any clients if one is made):

```
servo.accept();
```

After the socket connection is made, you can use input and output streams to read from and write to the client.

To extend the behavior of the socket classes—for example, to allow network connections to work across a firewall or proxy—you can use the abstract class SocketImpl and the interface SocketImplFactory to create a new transport-layer socket implementation. This approach allows those classes to be portable to other systems with different transport mechanisms. The problem with this mechanism is that although it works for simple cases, it prevents you from adding other protocols on top of TCP and from having multiple socket implementations for each Java runtime.

Because the Socket and ServerSocket classes are not final, you can create subclasses of these classes that use either the default socket implementation or your own implementation. This allows much more flexible network capabilities.

Designing a Server Application

Here's an example of a Java program that uses the Socket classes to implement a simple network-based server application.

The TimeServer application makes a connection to any client that connects to port 4415, displays the current time, and then closes the connection.

For an application to act as a server, it must monitor at least one port on the host machine for client connections. Port 4415 was chosen arbitrarily for this project, but it could be any number from 1024 to 65,535.

NOTE

The Internet Assigned Numbers Authority controls the usage of ports 0 to 1023 but claims are staked to the higher ports on a more informal basis. When choosing port numbers for your own client/server applications, it's a good idea to do research on what ports others are using. Search the Web for references to the port you want to use, and then search for the phrases "registered port numbers" and "well-known port numbers" to find lists of in-use ports. A good guide to port usage is available at www.sockets.com/services.htm.

17

When a client is detected, the server creates a Date object that represents the current date and time and then sends it to the client as a String.

In this exchange of information between the server and client, the server does almost all the work. The client's only responsibility is to establish a connection to the server and display messages received from the server.

Although you could develop a simple client for a project like this, you also can use any telnet application to act as the client, as long as it can connect to a port you designate. (Windows includes a command-line application called telnet that you can use for this purpose.)

Listing 17.3 contains the full source code for the server application, a class called TimeServer.

LISTING 17.3   The Full Text of TimeServer.java

```
 1: import java.io.*;
 2: import java.net.*;
 3: import java.util.*;
 4:
 5: public class TimeServer extends Thread {
 6:     private ServerSocket sock;
 7:
 8:     public TimeServer() {
 9:         super();
10:         try {
11:             sock = new ServerSocket(4415);
12:             System.out.println("TimeServer running ...");
13:         } catch (IOException e) {
14:             System.out.println("Error: couldn't create socket.");
15:             System.exit(1);
16:         }
17:     }
18:
19:     public void run() {
20:         Socket client = null;
21:
22:         while (true) {
23:             if (sock == null)
24:                 return;
25:             try {
26:                 client = sock.accept();
27:                 BufferedOutputStream bos = new BufferedOutputStream(
28:                     client.getOutputStream());
29:                 PrintWriter os = new PrintWriter(bos, false);
30:                 String outLine;
31:
```

LISTING 17.3 Continued

```
32:                    Date now = new Date();
33:                    os.println(now);
34:                    os.flush();
35:
36:                    os.close();
37:                    client.close();
38:                } catch (IOException e) {
39:                    System.out.println("Error: couldn't connect to client.");
40:                    System.exit(1);
41:                }
42:            }
43:        }
44:
45:    public static void main(String[] arguments) {
46:        TimeServer server = new TimeServer();
47:        server.start();
48:    }
49:
50: }
```

17

The TimeServer application creates a server socket on port 4415. When a client connects, a PrintWriter object is constructed from a buffered output stream so that a string—the current time—can be sent to the client.

After the string has been sent, the writer's flush() and close() methods end the data exchange and close the socket to await new connections.

Testing the Server

The TimeServer application must be running for a client to be able to connect to it. The server displays only one line of output if the application is running successfully:

Output ▼

```
TimeServer running ...
```

With the server running, you can connect to the server on port 4415 of your computer using a telnet program.

Do the following to run telnet on Windows:

- With earlier versions of Windows, choose Start, Run to open the Run dialog box, and then type telnet in the Open field and press Enter. A telnet window opens.

To make a telnet connection using this program, select Connect, Remote System. A Connect dialog box opens. Enter localhost in the Host Name field, enter 4415 in the Port field, and leave the default value vt100 in the TermType field.

- With Windows XP and 2003, choose Start, Run to open the Run dialog box. Type telnet to run that program. Then type the command open localhost 4415 in the Open field and press Enter.
- With Windows Vista and Windows 7, choose Start, All Programs, Accessories, Run to open the Run dialog box. Type telnet to run that program. Then type the command open localhost 4415 in the Open field and press Enter.

CAUTION

> The telnet program may be disabled by default on Windows Vista and Windows 7. To enable it, open the Control Panel, choose Programs and Features, and click Turn Windows features on or off. The Windows Features dialog opens. Select the Telnet Client checkbox and click OK.

The hostname localhost represents your own computer—the system running the application. You can use it to test server applications before deploying them permanently on the Internet.

Depending on how Internet connections have been configured on your system, you might need to log on to the Internet before a successful socket connection can be made between a telnet client and the TimeServer application.

If the server is on another computer connected to the Internet, you would specify that computer's hostname or IP address rather than localhost.

When you use telnet to make a connection with the TimeServer application, it displays the server's current time and closes the connection. The output of the telnet program should be something like the following:

Output ▼

```
Sat May 12 01:00:15 EDT 2012

Connection to host lost.
Press any key to continue...
```

The java.nio Package

The java.nio package expands the language's networking capabilities with classes useful for reading and writing data; working with files, sockets, and memory; and handling text.

Two related packages also are used often when you are working with the new input/output features: java.nio.channels and java.nio.charset.

Buffers

The java.nio package includes support for buffers—objects that represent data streams stored in memory.

Buffers often are used to improve the performance of programs that read input or write output. They enable a program to put a lot of data in memory, where it can be read, written, and modified more quickly.

A buffer corresponds with each of the primitive data types in Java:

- ByteBuffer
- CharBuffer
- DoubleBuffer
- FloatBuffer
- IntBuffer
- LongBuffer
- ShortBuffer

Each of these classes has a static method called wrap() that can be used to create a buffer from an array of the corresponding data type. The only argument to the method should be the array.

For example, the following statements create an array of integers and an IntBuffer that holds the integers in memory as a buffer:

```
int[] temperatures = { 90, 85, 87, 78, 80, 75, 70, 79, 85, 92, 99 };
IntBuffer tempBuffer = IntBuffer.wrap(temperatures);
```

A buffer keeps track of how it is used, storing the position where the next item will be read or written. After the buffer is created, its get() method reads the data at the current

17

position in the buffer. The following statements extend the previous example and display everything in the integer buffer:

```
for (int i = 0; tempBuffer.remaining() > 0; i++)
    System.out.println(tempBuffer.get());
```

Another way to create a buffer is to set up an empty buffer and then put data in it. To create the buffer, call the static method `allocate(int)` of the desired buffer class with the size of the buffer as an argument.

You can use five `put()` methods to store data in a buffer (or replace the data already there). The arguments used with these methods depend on the kind of buffer you're working with. These methods are used with an integer buffer:

- `put(int)` stores the integer at the current position in the buffer and then increments the position.

- `put(int, int)` stores an integer (the second argument) at a specific position in the buffer (the first argument).

- `put(int[])` stores all the elements of the integer array in the buffer, beginning at the first position in the buffer.

- `put(int[], int, int)` stores all or a portion of an integer array in the buffer. The second argument specifies the position in the buffer where the first integer in the array should be stored. The third argument specifies the number of elements from the array to store in the buffer.

- `put(IntBuffer)` stores the contents of an integer buffer in another buffer, beginning at the first position in the buffer.

As you put data in a buffer, you often must keep track of the current position so that you know where the next data will be stored.

To find out the current position, call the buffer's `position()` method. An integer is returned that represents the position. If this value is 0, you're at the start of the buffer.

Call the `position(int)` method to change the position to the argument specified as an integer.

Another important position to track when using buffers is the limit—the last place in the buffer that contains data.

It isn't necessary to figure out the limit when the buffer is always full; in that case, you know the buffer's last position has something in it.

However, if there's a chance your buffer might contain less data than you have allocated, you should call the buffer's `flip()` method after reading data into the buffer. This sets the current position to the start of the data you just read and sets the limit to the end.

If the buffer is 1,024 bytes in size and the page contains 1,500 bytes, the first attempt to read data loads the buffer with 1,024 bytes, filling it.

The second attempt to read data loads the buffer with only 476 bytes, leaving the rest empty. If you call `flip()` afterward, the current position is set to the beginning of the buffer, and the limit is set to 476.

The following code creates an array of Fahrenheit temperatures, converts them to Celsius, and then stores the Celsius values in a buffer:

```
int[] temps = { 90, 85, 87, 78, 80, 75, 70, 79, 85, 92, 99 };
IntBuffer tempBuffer = IntBuffer.allocate(temps.length);
for (int i = 0; i < temps.length; i++) {
    float celsius = ( (float) temps[i] - 32 ) / 9 * 5;
    tempBuffer.put( (int) celsius );
}
tempBuffer.position(0);
for (int i = 0; tempBuffer.remaining() > 0; i++) {
    System.out.println(tempBuffer.get());
}
```

17

After the buffer's position is set back to the start, the buffer's contents are displayed.

Byte Buffers

You can use the buffer methods introduced so far with byte buffers, but byte buffers also offer additional useful methods.

For starters, byte buffers have methods to store and retrieve data that isn't a byte:

- `putChar(char)` stores 2 bytes in the buffer that represent the specified `char` value.
- `putDouble(double)` stores 8 bytes in the buffer that represent a `double` value.
- `putFloat(float)` stores 4 bytes in the buffer that represent a `float` value.
- `putInt(int)` stores 4 bytes in the buffer that represent an `int` value.
- `putLong(long)` stores 8 bytes in the buffer that represent a `long` value.
- `putShort(short)` stores 2 bytes in the buffer that represent a `short` value.

Each of these methods puts more than 1 byte in the buffer, moving the current position forward by the same number of bytes.

There also are methods to retrieve nonbytes from a byte buffer: `getChar()`, `getDouble()`, `getFloat()`, `getInt()`, `getLong()`, and `getShort()`.

Character Sets

Character sets, which are offered in the `java.nio.charset` package, are a set of classes used to convert data between byte buffers and character buffers.

The three main classes are as follows:

- `Charset` is a Unicode character set with a different byte value for each different character in the set.
- `CharsetDecoder` is a class that transforms a series of bytes into a series of characters.
- `CharsetEncoder` is a class that transforms a series of characters into a series of bytes.

Before you can perform any transformations between byte and character buffers, you must create a `Charset` object that maps characters to their corresponding byte values.

To create a character set, call the `forName(String)` static method of the `Charset` class, specifying the name of the set's character encoding.

Java supports six character encodings:

- **US-ASCII**—The 128-character ASCII set that makes up the Basic Latin block of Unicode (also called ISO646-US)
- **ISO-8859-1**—The 256-character ISO Latin Alphabet No. 1 character set (also called ISO-LATIN-1)
- **UTF-8**—A character set that includes US-ASCII and the Universal Character Set (also called Unicode), a set composed of thousands of characters used in the world's languages
- **UTF-16BE**—The Universal Character Set represented as 16-bit characters with bytes stored in big-endian byte order
- **UTF-16LE**—The Universal Character Set represented as 16-bit characters with bytes stored in little-endian byte order
- **UTF-16**—The Universal Character Set represented as 16-bit characters with the order of bytes indicated by an optional byte-order mark

The following statement creates a `Charset` object for the ISO-8859-1 character set:

```
Charset isoset = Charset.forName("ISO-8859-1");
```

After you have a character set object, you can use it to create encoders and decoders. Call the object's newDecoder() method to create a CharsetDecoder and the newEncoder() method to create a CharsetEncoder.

To transform a byte buffer into a character buffer, call the decoder's decode(*ByteBuffer*) method, which returns a CharBuffer containing the bytes transformed into characters.

To transform a character buffer into a byte buffer, call the encoder's encode(*CharBuffer*) method. A ByteBuffer is returned containing the characters' byte values.

The following statements convert a byte buffer called netBuffer into a character buffer using the ISO-8859-1 character set:

```
Charset set = Charset.forName("ISO-8859-1");
CharsetDecoder decoder = set.newDecoder();
netBuffer.position(0);
CharBuffer netText = decoder.decode(netBuffer);
```

17

> **CAUTION**
>
> Before the decoder is used to create the character buffer, the call to position(0) resets the current position of the netBuffer to the start. When you're working with buffers for the first time, it's easy to overlook this, resulting in a buffer with much less data than you expected.

Channels

A common use for a buffer is to associate it with an input or output stream. You can fill a buffer with data from an input stream or write a buffer to an output stream.

To do this, you must use a channel—an object that connects a buffer to the stream. Channels are part of the java.nio.channels package.

You can associate channels with a stream by calling the getChannel() method available in some of the stream classes in the java.io package.

The FileInputStream and FileOutputStream classes have getChannel() methods that return a FileChannel object. This file channel can be used to read, write, and modify the data in the file.

The following statements create a file input stream and a channel associated with that file:

```
try {
    String source = "prices.dat";
    FileInputStream inSource = new FileInputStream(source);
    FileChannel inChannel = inSource.getChannel();
} catch (FileNotFoundException fne) {
    System.out.println(fne.getMessage());
}
```

After you have created the file channel, you can find out how many bytes the file contains by calling its `size()` method. This is necessary if you want to create a byte buffer to hold the file's contents.

Bytes are read from a channel into a `ByteBuffer` with the `read(ByteBuffer, long)` method. The first argument is the buffer. The second argument is the current position in the buffer, which determines where the file's contents will begin to be stored.

The following statements extend the last example by reading a file into a byte buffer using the `inChannel` file channel:

```
long inSize = inChannel.size();
ByteBuffer data = ByteBuffer.allocate( (int)inSize );
inChannel.read(data, 0);
data.position(0);
for (int i = 0; data.remaining() > 0; i++) {
    System.out.print(data.get() + " ");
}
```

The attempt to read from the channel generates an `IOException` error if a problem occurs. Although the byte buffer is the same size as the file, this isn't a requirement. If you are reading the file into the buffer so that you can modify it, you can allocate a larger buffer.

The next project you undertake incorporates the new input/output features you have learned about so far: buffers, character sets, and channels.

The BufferConverter application reads a small file into a byte buffer, displays the contents of the buffer, converts it to a character buffer, and then displays the characters.

Enter the code shown in Listing 17.4 as the new Java class `BufferConverter`.

LISTING 17.4   The Full Text of `BufferConverter.java`

```
 1: import java.nio.*;
 2: import java.nio.channels.*;
 3: import java.nio.charset.*;
 4: import java.io.*;
 5:
 6: public class BufferConverter {
 7:     public static void main(String[] arguments) {
 8:         try {
 9:             // read byte data into a byte buffer
10:             String data = "friends.dat";
11:             FileInputStream inData = new FileInputStream(data);
12:             FileChannel inChannel = inData.getChannel();
13:             long inSize = inChannel.size();
14:             ByteBuffer source = ByteBuffer.allocate( (int) inSize );
15:             inChannel.read(source, 0);
16:             source.position(0);
17:             System.out.println("Original byte data:");
18:             for (int i = 0; source.remaining() > 0; i++) {
19:                 System.out.print(source.get() + " ");
20:             }
21:             // convert byte data into character data
22:             source.position(0);
23:             Charset ascii = Charset.forName("US-ASCII");
24:             CharsetDecoder toAscii = ascii.newDecoder();
25:             CharBuffer destination = toAscii.decode(source);
26:             destination.position(0);
27:             System.out.println("\n\nNew character data:");
28:             for (int i = 0; destination.remaining() > 0; i++) {
29:                 System.out.print(destination.get());
30:             }
31:             System.out.println();
32:         } catch (FileNotFoundException fne) {
33:             System.out.println(fne.getMessage());
34:         } catch (IOException ioe) {
35:             System.out.println(ioe.getMessage());
36:         }
37:     }
38: }
```

17

Before you run the file, you need a copy of `friends.dat`, the small file of byte data used in the application. To download it from the book's website at www.java21days.com, open the Day 17 page, click the `friends.dat` hyperlink, and save the file in the same place as `BufferConverter.class`.

TIP You also can create your own file. In NetBeans, choose File, New File. In the New File dialog, choose the category Other and the file type Empty File. Give it the filename `friends.dat`. In the source code editor, type a sentence or two in the document and save the file.

If you use the copy of `friends.dat` from the book's website, the output of the BufferConverter application is as follows:

Output ▼

```
Original byte data:
70 114 105 101 110 100 115 44 32 82 111 109 97 110 115 44 32
99 111 117 110 116 114 121 109 101 110 44 32 108 101 110 100
32 109 101 32 121 111 117 114 32 101 97 114 115 46 13 10 13
10

New character data:
Friends, Romans, countrymen, lend me your ears.
```

The BufferConverter application uses the techniques introduced today to read data and represent it as bytes and characters, but you could have accomplished the same thing with the original input/output package, `java.io`.

For this reason, you might wonder why it's worth learning the new package at all.

One reason is that buffers enable you to manipulate large amounts of data much more quickly. You'll find out another reason in the next section.

Network Channels

A popular feature of the `java.nio` package is its support for nonblocking input and output over a networking connection.

In Java, blocking refers to a statement that must complete execution before anything else happens in the program. All the socket programming you have done up to this point has used blocking methods exclusively. For example, in the TimeServer application, when the server socket's `accept()` method is called, nothing else happens in the program until a client makes a connection.

As you can imagine, it's problematic for a networking program to wait until a particular statement is executed because numerous things can go wrong. Connections can be broken. A server could go offline. A socket connection could appear to be stalled because a blocked statement is waiting for something to happen.

For example, a client application that reads and buffers data over HTTP might be waiting for a buffer to be filled even though no more data remains to be sent. The program will appear to have halted because the blocked statement never finishes executing.

With the `java.nio` package, you can create networking connections and read to and write from them using nonblocking methods.

Here's how it works:

- Associate a socket channel with an input or output stream.
- Configure the channel to recognize the kind of networking events you want to monitor, such as new connections, attempts to read data over the channel, and attempts to write data.
- Call a method to open the channel.
- Because the method is nonblocking, the program continues executing so that you can handle other tasks.
- If one of the networking events you are monitoring takes place, your program is notified—a method associated with the event is called.

This is comparable to how user-interface components are programmed in Swing. An interface component is associated with one or more event listeners and is placed in a container. If the interface component receives input being monitored by a listener, an event-handling method is called. Until that happens, the program can handle other tasks.

To use nonblocking input and output, you must work with channels instead of streams.

Nonblocking Socket Clients and Servers

The first step in developing a nonblocking client or server is creating an object that represents the Internet address to which you are connecting. This task is handled by the `InetSocketAddress` class in the `java.net` package.

If the server is identified by a hostname, call `InetSocketAddress(String, int)` with two arguments: the server's name and port number.

If the server is identified by its IP address, use the `InetAddress` class in `java.net` to identify the host. Call the static method `InetAddress.getByName(String)` with the host's IP address as the argument. The method returns an `InetAddress` object representing the address, which you can use in calling `InetSocketAddress(InetAddress, int)`. The second argument is the server's port number.

Nonblocking connections require a socket channel, another of the classes in the `java.nio` package. Call the `open()` static method of the `SocketChannel` class to create the channel.

17

A socket channel can be configured for blocking or nonblocking communication. To set up a nonblocking channel, call the channel's configureBlocking(*boolean*) method with an argument of false. Calling it with true makes it a blocking channel.

After the channel is configured, call its connect(*InetSocketAddress*) method to connect the socket.

On a blocking channel, the connect() method attempts to establish a connection to the server and waits until it is complete, returning a value of true to indicate success.

On a nonblocking channel, the connect() method returns immediately with a value of false. To figure out what's going on over the channel and respond to events, you must use a channel-listening object called a Selector.

A Selector is an object that keeps track of things that happen to a socket channel (or another channel in the package that is a subclass of SelectableChannel).

To create a Selector, call its open() method, as in the following statement:

```
Selector monitor = Selector.open();
```

When you use a Selector, you must indicate the events you want to monitor. You do so by calling a channel's register(*Selector*, *int*, *Object*) method.

The three arguments to register() are the following:

- The Selector object you have created to monitor the channel
- An int value that represents the events being monitored (also called selection keys)
- An Object that can be delivered along with the key, or null otherwise

Instead of using an integer value as the second argument, it's easier to use one or more class variables from the SelectionKey class: SelectionKey.OP_CONNECT to monitor connections, SelectionKey.OP_READ to monitor attempts to read data, and SelectionKey.OP_WRITE to monitor attempts to write data.

The following statements create a Selector to monitor a socket channel called wire for reading data:

```
Selector spy = Selector.open();
channel.register(spy, SelectionKey.OP_READ, null);
```

To monitor more than one kind of key, add together the SelectionKey class variables. For example:

```
Selector spy = Selector.open();
channel.register(spy, SelectionKey.OP_READ + SelectionKey.OP_WRITE, null);
```

After the channel and selector have been set up, you can wait for events by calling the selector's `select()` or `select(long)` methods.

The `select()` method is a blocking method that waits until something has happened on the channel.

The `select(long)` method is a blocking method that waits until something has happened or the specified number of milliseconds has passed, whichever comes first.

Both `select()` methods return the number of events that have taken place, or 0 if nothing has happened. You can use a `while` loop with a call to the `select()` method as a way to loop until something happens on the channel.

After an event has taken place, you can find out more about it by calling the selector's `selectedKeys()` method, which returns a `Set` object containing details on each of the events.

Use this `Set` object as you would any other set, creating an `Iterator` to move through the set by using its `hasNext()` and `next()` methods.

17

The call to the set's `next()` method returns an object that should be cast to a `SelectionKey`. This object represents an event that took place on the channel.

Three methods in the `SelectionKey` class can be used to identify the key in a client program: `isReadable()`, `isWritable()`, and `isConnectible()`. Each returns a `boolean` value. (A fourth method is used when you're writing a server: `isAcceptable()`.)

After you retrieve a key from the set, call the key's `remove()` method to indicate that you will do something with it.

The last thing to find out about the event is the channel on which it took place. Call the key's `channel()` method, which returns the associated `SocketChannel`.

If one of the events identifies a connection, you must make sure that the connection has been completed before using the channel. Call the key's `isConnectionPending()` method, which returns `true` if the connection is still in progress and `false` if it is complete.

To deal with a connection that is still in progress, you can call the socket's `finishConnect()` method, which attempts to complete the connection.

Using a nonblocking socket channel involves the interaction of numerous new classes from the `java.nio` and `java.net` packages.

To give you a more complete picture of how these classes work together, the day's final project is FingerServer, a web application that uses a nonblocking socket channel to handle finger requests.

Enter the code shown in Listing 17.5 as the class `FingerServer` and save the application.

LISTING 17.5   The Full Text of `FingerServer.java`

```
 1: import java.io.*;
 2: import java.net.*;
 3: import java.nio.channels.*;
 4: import java.util.*;
 5:
 6: public class FingerServer {
 7:
 8:     public FingerServer() {
 9:         try {
10:             // Create a nonblocking server socket channel
11:             ServerSocketChannel sockChannel = ServerSocketChannel.open();
12:             sockChannel.configureBlocking(false);
13:
14:             // Set the host and port to monitor
15:             InetSocketAddress server = new InetSocketAddress(
16:                 "localhost", 79);
17:             ServerSocket socket = sockChannel.socket();
18:             socket.bind(server);
19:
20:             // Create the selector and register it on the channel
21:             Selector selector = Selector.open();
22:             sockChannel.register (selector, SelectionKey.OP_ACCEPT);
23:
24:             // Loop forever, looking for client connections
25:             while (true) {
26:                 // Wait for a connection
27:                 selector.select();
28:
29:                 // Get list of selection keys with pending events
30:                 Set keys = selector.selectedKeys();
31:                 Iterator it = keys.iterator();
32:
33:                 // Handle each key
34:                 while (it.hasNext()) {
35:
36:                     // Get the key and remove it from the iteration
37:                     SelectionKey selKey = (SelectionKey) it.next();
38:
39:                     it.remove();
40:                     if (selKey.isAcceptable()) {
41:
42:                         // Create a socket connection with the client
43:                         ServerSocketChannel selChannel =
44:                             (ServerSocketChannel) selKey.channel();
45:                         ServerSocket selSocket = selChannel.socket();
46:                         Socket connection = selSocket.accept();
```

LISTING 17.5   Continued

```
47:
48:                            // Handle the finger request
49:                            handleRequest(connection);
50:                            connection.close();
51:                    }
52:                }
53:            }
54:        } catch (IOException ioe) {
55:            System.out.println(ioe.getMessage());
56:        }
57:    }
58:
59:    private void handleRequest(Socket connection) throws IOException {
60:
61:        // Set up input and output
62:        InputStreamReader isr = new InputStreamReader (
63:            connection.getInputStream());
64:        BufferedReader is = new BufferedReader(isr);
65:        PrintWriter pw = new PrintWriter(new
66:            BufferedOutputStream (connection.getOutputStream()),
67:            false);
68:
69:        // Output server greeting
70:        pw.println("Nio Finger Server");
71:        pw.flush();
72:
73:        // Handle user input
74:        String outLine = null;
75:        String inLine = is.readLine();
76:
77:        if (inLine.length() > 0) {
78:            outLine = inLine;
79:        }
80:        readPlan(outLine, pw);
81:
82:        // Clean up
83:        pw.flush();
84:        pw.close();
85:        is.close();
86:    }
87:
88:    private void readPlan(String userName, PrintWriter pw) {
89:        try {
90:            FileReader file = new FileReader (userName + ".plan");
91:            BufferedReader buff = new BufferedReader(file);
92:            boolean eof = false;
93:
94:            pw.println("\nUser name: " + userName + "\n");
95:
```

17

LISTING 17.5   Continued

```
 96:                while (!eof) {
 97:                    String line = buff.readLine();
 98:
 99:                    if (line == null) {
100:                        eof = true;
101:                    } else {
102:                        pw.println(line);
103:                    }
104:                }
105:
106:                buff.close();
107:            } catch (IOException e) {
108:                pw.println("User " + userName + " not found.");
109:            }
110:        }
111:
112:        public static void main(String[] arguments) {
113:            FingerServer nio = new FingerServer();
114:        }
115: }
```

The finger server requires one or more user .plan files stored in text files. These files should have names that take the form *username*.plan—for example, linus.plan, lucy.plan, and franklin.plan. Before running the server, create one or more plan files in the root folder of the Java21 project.

When you're done, run the finger server. The application waits for incoming finger requests, creating a nonblocking server socket channel and registering one kind of key for a selector to look for: connection events.

Inside a while loop that begins on line 25, the server calls the Selector object's select() method to see whether the selector has received any keys, which would occur when a finger client makes a connection. When it has, select() returns the number of keys, and the statements inside the loop are executed.

After the connection is made, a buffered reader is created to hold a request for a .plan file. The syntax for the command is simply the username of the .plan file being requested.

While the finger server is running, you can test this application with the finger client. Create a custom project configuration in NetBeans to set the command-line argument of the finger user:

- Choose Run, Set Project Configuration, Customize. The Project Properties dialog opens.
- In the Main Class text field, enter `Finger`.
- In the Arguments text field, enter `franklin@localhost` and click OK.
- Run the application by choosing Run, Run Project.

The output is as follows when you request the user franklin on the computer localhost:

Output ▼

```
Nio Finger Server

User name: franklin

Franklin Armstrong plan file (franklin@localhost)
```

Run the application again with `lucy@localhost` to see Lucy's `.plan` file, and finally with `linus@localhost` to look for Linus.

CAUTION

The plan files must be in the root folder of the Java21 project for the FingerServer application to find them. If they were saved somewhere else, you can move them by dragging and dropping in NetBeans. Click the Files tab in the Projects pane to see a list of the project's files. Find the plan files and drag them to the same folder that holds `friends.dat`.

Summary

Today, you learned how to use URLs, URL connections, and input streams in combination to pull data from the web into your program.

Networking can be extremely useful. The WebReader project is a rudimentary web browser. It can load a web page or RSS file into a Java program and display it. However, it doesn't do anything to make sense of the markup tags, presenting the raw text delivered by a web server.

You created a socket application that implements the basics of the finger protocol, a method for retrieving user information on the Internet.

17

You also learned how client and server programs are written in Java using the nonblocking techniques in the `java.nio` package.

To use nonblocking techniques, you learned about the fundamental classes of Java's new networking package: buffers, character encoders and decoders, socket channels, and selectors.

Q&A

Q How can I do **POST** form submissions?

A You can mimic what a browser does to send forms using POST. Create a URL object for the form-submission address, such as `"http://www.example.com/cgi/mail2.cgi"`, and then call this object's `openConnection()` method to create a `URLConnection` object. Call the connection's `setDoOutput()` method to indicate that you will be sending data to this URL. Then send the connection a series of name-value pairs that hold the data, separated by ampersand characters (&).

For instance, suppose the `mail2.cgi` form is a CGI program that sends mail with `name`, `subject`, `email`, and `comments` fields, and you have created a `PrintWriter` stream called `pw` connected to this CGI program. You can post information to it using the following statement:

```
pw.print("name=YourName&subject=Book&email=you@yourdomain.com&"
    + "comments= A+POST+example """);
```

Quiz

Review today's material by taking this three-question quiz. Answers are at the end of the book.

Questions

1. Which of the following is *not* an advantage of the new `java.nio` package and its related packages?

    A. Large amounts of data can be manipulated quickly with buffers.

    B. Networking connections can be nonblocking for more reliable use in your applications.

    C. Streams are no longer necessary to read and write data over a network.

2. In the finger protocol, which program makes a request for information about a user?

   A. The client

   B. The server

   C. Both can make that request.

3. Which method is preferred for loading the data from a web page into your Java application?

   A. Creating a Socket and an input stream from that socket

   B. Creating a URL and an HttpURLConnection from that object

   C. Loading the page using the method toString()

Certification Practice

17

The following question is the kind of thing you could expect to be asked on a Java programming certification test. Answer it without looking at today's material or using the Java compiler to test the code.

Given:

```java
import java.nio.*;

public class ReadTemps {
    public ReadTemps() {
        int[] temperatures = { 78, 80, 75, 70, 79, 85, 92, 99, 90, 85, 87 };
        IntBuffer tempBuffer = IntBuffer.wrap(temperatures);
        int[] moreTemperatures = { 65, 44, 71 };
        tempBuffer.put(moreTemperatures);
        System.out.println("First int: " + tempBuffer.get());
    }
}
```

What will be the output when this application is run?

   A. First int: 78

   B. First int: 71

   C. First int: 70

   D. None of the above

The answer is available on the book's website at www.java21days.com. Visit the Day 17 page and click the Certification Practice link.

Exercises

To extend your knowledge of the subjects covered today, try the following exercises:

1. Write an application that stores some of your favorite web pages on your computer so that you can read them while you are not connected to the Internet.

2. Modify the FingerServer application to use the `try-with-resources` capability of Java 7.

Where applicable, exercise solutions are offered on the book's website at www.java21days.com.

DAY 18

Accessing Databases with JDBC 4.1 and Derby

Almost all Java programs deal with data in some way. So far you have used primitive types, objects, arrays, hash tables, and other data structures.

Today, you work with data in a more sophisticated way by exploring Java Database Connectivity (JDBC), a class library that connects Java programs to relational databases.

Java 7 includes Java DB, a compact relational database that makes it easier than ever to incorporate a database into your applications. Java DB is Oracle's name for Apache Derby, an open source database maintained by the Apache Software Foundation.

Today, you explore JDBC in the following ways:

- Using JDBC drivers to work with different relational databases

- Accessing a database with Structured Query Language (SQL)

- Reading records from a database using SQL and JDBC

- Adding records to a database using SQL and JDBC

- Creating a new Java DB database and reading its records

Java Database Connectivity

Java Database Connectivity (JDBC) is a set of classes that can be used to develop client/server applications that work with databases developed by Microsoft, Sybase, Oracle, Informix, MySQL, and other sources.

With JDBC, you can use the same methods and classes in Java programs to read and write records and perform other kinds of database access. A class called a *driver* acts as a bridge to the database source. There are drivers for each of the popular databases.

Client/server software connects a user of information with a provider of that information, and it's one of the most common forms of programming. You use it every time you use the web: A web browser client requests pages, image files, and other documents using a uniform resource locator (URL). Web servers provide the requested information, if it can be found, for the client.

One of the biggest obstacles faced by database programmers is the wide variety of database formats in use, each with its own proprietary method of accessing data.

To simplify using relational database programs, a standard language called Structured Query Language (SQL) was developed. This language supplants the need to learn different database-querying languages for each database format. Java DB supports SQL.

In database programming, a request for records in a database is called a *query*. Using SQL, you can send complex queries to a database and get the records you're looking for in any order you specify.

Consider the example of a database programmer at a student loan company who has been asked to prepare a report on the most delinquent loan recipients. The programmer could use SQL to query a database for all records in which the last payment was more than 180 days ago and the amount due is more than $0.00. SQL also can be used to control the order in which records are returned, so the programmer can get the records in the order of Social Security number, recipient name, amount owed, or another field in the loan database.

All this is possible with SQL. The programmer doesn't need any of the proprietary languages associated with popular database formats.

CAUTION | SQL is strongly supported by many database formats, so, in theory, you should be able to use the same SQL commands for each database tool that supports the language. However, you will still need to learn the idiosyncrasies of a specific database format when accessing it through SQL.

SQL is the industry-standard approach to accessing relational databases. JDBC supports SQL, enabling developers to use a wide range of database formats without knowing the specifics of the underlying database. JDBC also supports the use of database queries specific to a database format.

The JDBC class library's approach to accessing databases with SQL is comparable to existing database-development techniques, so interacting with a SQL database by using JDBC isn't much different from using traditional database tools. Java programmers who already have some database experience can hit the ground running with JDBC.

The JDBC library includes classes for each of the tasks commonly associated with database usage:

- Making a connection to a database
- Creating a statement using SQL
- Executing that SQL query in the database
- Viewing the resulting records

These JDBC classes all are part of the `java.sql` package.

Database Drivers

Java programs that use JDBC classes can follow the familiar programming model of issuing SQL statements and processing the resulting data. The format of the database and the platform it was prepared on don't matter.

This platform and database independence is made possible by a driver manager. The classes of the JDBC class library are largely dependent on driver managers, which keep track of the drivers required to access database records. You'll need a different driver for each database format that's used in a program, and sometimes you might need several drivers for versions of the same format. Java DB includes its own driver.

JDBC also includes a driver that bridges JDBC and another database-connectivity standard, ODBC.

Examining a Database

NetBeans has extensive support for database programming. Before you begin writing code, you can use it to connect to a database, learn about the tables it contains, and see the data in those tables.

To connect to a Java DB database, first you must start the database server.

In the Projects pane, click the Services tab to bring it to the front, as shown in Figure 18.1. The Databases item includes a Java DB item. Right-click it and choose Start Server.

18

Java DB   Services

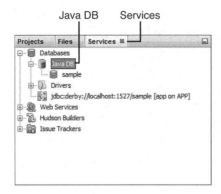

The server starts and displays text in the Output pane that shows what it is doing:

Output ▼

```
2012-05-24 00:31:50.960 GMT : Security manager installed using the Basic
 server security policy.
2012-05-24 00:31:51.205 GMT : Apache Derby Network Server - 10.6.2.1 -
 (999685) started and ready to accept connections on port 1527
```

This output indicates that the server is running on port 1527 and is ready to take connections. Keep this window open so that you can monitor the server while it runs.

In the Services pane under Java DB is a sample database named sample. Connect to this database by right-clicking sample and choosing Connect.

An item in the Services pane changes from a broken icon into an unbroken one: jdbc:derby://localhost:1527/sample.

This is an active connection to the database. Expand this item and then expand SYS, Tables, and SYSTABLES. A list of fields in the SYSTABLES table appears, as shown in Figure 18.2.

You can view the records in this table by right-clicking SYSTABLES and choosing View Data. Two things appear in other panes on NetBeans.

A SQL command appears where the source code editor normally appears:

```
select * from SYS.SYSTABLES
```

This command, which is called a SQL query, selects all fields from SYS.SYSTABLES. The asterisk character (*) could be replaced with the name of one or more fields, separated by commas.

FIGURE 18.2
Examining tables
in a Java DB
database.

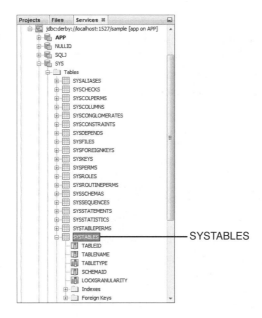

SYSTABLES

Another pane displays the result of this command: all the data in this table, organized
into rows and columns. Each column is a field, and each row is a record in the table.

18

Figure 18.3 shows the contents of the SYSTABLES table. This is the table you'll be writing
Java code to access.

FIGURE 18.3
Displaying data-
base records in
a table.

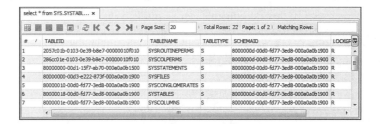

Reading Records from a Database

Your first project today is a Java application that connects to a sample Java DB database
included with NetBeans and that reads records from a table.

Working with a database in a Java program is relatively easy if you are conversant
with SQL.

The first task in a JDBC program is to load the driver (or drivers) that will be used to connect to a data source. A driver is loaded with the `Class.forName(String)` method. `Class`, part of the `java.lang` package, can be used to load classes into the Java virtual machine. The `forName(String)` method loads the class named by the specified string. This method can throw a `ClassNotFoundException`.

Programs that use Java DB can use `org.apache.derby.jdbc.ClientDriver`, a driver included with the database. Loading this class into a Java interpreter requires the following statement:

```
Class.forName("org.apache.derby.jdbc.ClientDriver");
```

After the driver has been loaded, you can establish a connection to the data source by using the `DriverManager` class in the `java.sql` package.

The `getConnection(String, String, String)` method of `DriverManager` can be used to set up the connection. It returns a reference to a `Connection` object representing an active data connection.

This method has three arguments:

- A string identifying the data source and the type of database connectivity used to reach it
- A username
- A password

The last two items are needed only if the data source is secured with a username and password. If it isn't, these arguments can be null strings (`""`).

Here's the string to use when connecting to the `sample` database:

```
jdbc:derby://localhost:1527/sample
```

You've already seen this string in the Services tab of the Projects pane, where it is an item that represents a database connection.

This string identifies the type of database (jdbc:derby:), the host and port of the database server (localhost:1527), and the name of the database (sample). Note the two slash characters (/) after the database type and the one slash after the host and port.

The second and third arguments to use are app and APP, capitalized as shown. They're the username and password.

The following statement could be used to connect to a database called payroll with a username of doc and a password of 1rover1:

```
Connection payday = DriverManager.getConnection(
    "jdbc:derby://localhost:1527/payroll",
    "doc", "1rover1");
```

After you have a connection, you can reuse it each time you want to retrieve information from or store information to that connection's data source.

The getConnection() method and all others called on a data source throw SQLException errors if something goes wrong as the data source is being used. SQL has its own error messages, and they are passed along as part of SQLException objects.

TIP	NetBeans shows the information required to connect to a database, including the driver class, database connection string, username, and password. Right-click the database connection, such as jdbc:derby://localhost:1527/sample, and choose Properties from the pop-up menu. A dialog containing the class and other information about the connection appears.

A SQL statement is represented in Java by a Statement object. Statement is an interface, so it can't be instantiated directly. However, an object that implements the interface is returned by the createStatement() method of a Connection object, as in the following example:

18

```
Statement lookSee = payday.createStatement();
```

After you have a Statement object, you can use it to conduct a SQL query by calling the object's executeQuery(String) method. The String argument should be a SQL query that follows the syntax of that language.

CAUTION	It's beyond the scope of today's lesson to teach SQL, a rich data-retrieval and storage language that has its own book in this series: *Sams Teach Yourself SQL in 21 Days*, 4th Edition, by Ron Plew and Ryan Stephens (ISBN: 978-0-672-32451-2). Although you need to learn SQL to do any extensive work with it, much of the language is easy to pick up from any examples you can find, such as those you will work with today.

The following is an example of a SQL query that could be used on the `sample` database:

```
select TABLEID, TABLENAME from SYS.SYSTABLES
    where (TABLETYPE = 'S') order by TABLENAME;
```

This SQL query retrieves several fields for each record in the database for which the TABLETYPE field equals S. The records returned are sorted according to their TABLENAME field. The lowercase parts of the command are SQL keywords. The uppercase parts are aspects of the table.

The following Java statement executes that query on a `Statement` object named `looksee`:

```
ResultSet set = looksee.executeQuery(
    "select TABLEID, TABLENAME from SYS.SYSTABLES "
    + " where (TABLETYPE = 'S') order by TABLENAME";
);
```

Although SQL queries end with a semicolon character (`;`), one is not needed in the argument to `executeQuery()`.

If the SQL query has been phrased correctly, the `executeQuery()` method returns a `ResultSet` object holding all the records that have been retrieved from the data source.

> **NOTE**
>
> To add records to a database instead of retrieving them, you should call the statement's `executeUpdate()` method. You work with this method later.

When a `ResultSet` is returned from `executeQuery()`, it is positioned at the first record that has been retrieved. The following methods of `ResultSet` can be used to pull information from the current record:

- `getDate(String)` returns the `Date` value stored in the specified field name (using the `Date` class in the `java.sql` package, not `java.util.Date`).
- `getDouble(String)` returns the `double` value stored in the specified field name.
- `getFloat(String)` returns the `float` value stored in the specified field name.
- `getInt(String)` returns the `int` value stored in the specified field name.
- `getLong(String)` returns the `long` value stored in the specified field name.
- `getString(String)` returns the `String` stored in the specified field name.

These are just the simplest methods available in the `ResultSet` interface. Which methods you should use depends on the form that the field data takes in the database. But methods such as `getString()` and `getInt()` can be more flexible in the information they retrieve from a record.

You also can use an integer as the argument to any of these methods, such as `getString(5)`, instead of a string. The integer indicates which field to retrieve (1 for the first field, 2 for the second field, and so on).

A `SQLException` is thrown if a database error occurs as you try to retrieve information from a resultset. You can call this exception's `getSQLState()` and `getErrorCode()` methods to learn more about the error.

After you have pulled the information you need from a record, you can move to the next record by calling the `next()` method of the `ResultSet` object. This method returns a `false` Boolean value when it tries to move past the end of a resultset.

Normally, you can move through a resultset once from start to finish, after which you can't retrieve its contents again.

When you're finished using a connection to a data source, you can close it by calling the connection's `close()` method with no arguments.

Listing 18.1 is the SysTableReporter application, which uses the Java DB driver and a SQL statement to retrieve records from a table in the `sample` database. Four fields are retrieved from each record indicated by the SQL statement: `TABLEID`, `TABLENAME`, `TABLETYPE`, and `SCHEMAID`. The resultset is sorted according to the `TABLENAME` field, and these fields are displayed.

Before creating this application, you must add the `JavaDB` library to the project in NetBeans:

1. Click the Projects tab in the Projects pane to bring it to the front.
2. Scroll down to the bottom of the pane and right-click the `Libraries` folder.
3. Click Add Library from the pop-up menu that appears. The Add Library dialog opens.
4. Choose `JavaDB` under Available Libraries and click Add Library.

   The library now appears in the Libraries folder.

18

Create the SysTableReporter class in NetBeans with the source code of the listing.

LISTING 18.1 The Full Text of SysTableReporter.java

```
 1: import java.sql.*;
 2:
 3: public class SysTableReporter {
 4:     public static void main(String[] arguments) {
 5:         String data = "jdbc:derby://localhost:1527/sample";
 6:         try (
 7:             Connection conn = DriverManager.getConnection(
 8:                 data, "app", "APP");
 9:             Statement st = conn.createStatement()) {
10:
11:             Class.forName("org.apache.derby.jdbc.ClientDriver");
12:
13:             ResultSet rec = st.executeQuery(
14:                 "select * " +
15:                 "from SYS.SYSTABLES " +
16:                 "order by TABLENAME");
17:             while(rec.next()) {
18:                 System.out.println("TABLEID:\t" + rec.getString(1));
19:                 System.out.println("TABLENAME:\t" + rec.getString(2));
20:                 System.out.println("TABLETYPE:\t" + rec.getString(3));
21:                 System.out.println("SCHEMAID:\t" + rec.getString(4));
22:                 System.out.println();
23:             }
24:             st.close();
25:         } catch (SQLException s) {
26:             System.out.println("SQL Error: " + s.toString() + " "
27:                 + s.getErrorCode() + " " + s.getSQLState());
28:         } catch (Exception e) {
29:             System.out.println("Error: " + e.toString()
30:                 + e.getMessage());
31:         }
32:     }
33: }
```

When this program is run with the starting data from the sample database, the output is as follows (truncated for space):

Output ▼

```
TABLEID:    c013800d-00d7-ddbd-08ce-000a0a411400
TABLENAME:  SYSALIASES
TABLETYPE:  S
SCHEMAID:   8000000d-00d0-fd77-3ed8-000a0a0b1900
```

```
TABLEID:     80000056-00d0-fd77-3ed8-000a0a0b1900
TABLENAME:   SYSCHECKS
TABLETYPE:   S
SCHEMAID:    8000000d-00d0-fd77-3ed8-000a0a0b1900

...

TABLEID:     c013800d-00d7-c025-4809-000a0a411200
TABLENAME:   SYSTRIGGERS
TABLETYPE:   S
SCHEMAID:    8000000d-00d0-fd77-3ed8-000a0a0b1900

TABLEID:     8000004d-00d0-fd77-3ed8-000a0a0b1900
TABLENAME:   SYSVIEWS
TABLETYPE:   S
SCHEMAID:    8000000d-00d0-fd77-3ed8-000a0a0b1900
```

Writing Records to a Database

In the SysTableReporter application, you retrieved data from a database using a SQL
statement prepared as a string:

```
select * from SYS.SYSTABLES order by TABLENAME;
```

This is a common way to use SQL. You could write a program that asks a user to enter a
SQL query and then displays the result. (However, this isn't a good idea. SQL queries
can be used to delete records, tables, and even entire databases.)

The java.sql package also supports another way to create a SQL statement: a prepared
statement.

A prepared statement, which is represented by the PreparedStatement class, is a SQL
statement that is compiled before it is executed. This enables the statement to return data
more quickly and is a better choice if you are executing a SQL statement repeatedly in
the same program.

To create a prepared statement, call a connection's prepareStatement(*String*) method
with a string that indicates the structure of the SQL statement.

To indicate the structure, you write a SQL statement in which parameters have been
replaced with question marks.

Here's an example for a connection object called cc:

```
PreparedStatement ps = cc.prepareStatement(
    "select * from SYS.SYSTABLES where (TABLETYPE=?) "
    + "ORDER BY TABLENAME");
```

18

Here's another example with more than one question mark:

```
PreparedStatement ps = cc.prepareStatement(
    "insert into SYS.SYSTABLES VALUES(?, ?, ?, ?, ?)");
```

The question marks in these SQL statements are placeholders for data. Before you can execute the statement, you must put data in each of these places using one of the methods of the `PreparedStatement` class.

To put data into a prepared statement, you must call a method with the position of the placeholder followed by the data to insert.

For example, to put the string `"xyzzy"` in the first prepared statement, call the `setString(int, String)` method:

```
ps.setString(1, "xyzzy");
```

The first argument indicates the placeholder's position, numbered from left to right. The first question mark is 1, the second is 2, and so on.

The second argument is the data to put in the statement at that position.

The following methods are available:

- `setAsciiStream(int, InputStream, int)`—At the position indicated by the first argument, inserts the specified `InputStream`, which represents a stream of ASCII characters. The third argument indicates how many bytes from the input stream to insert.

- `setBinaryStream(int, InputStream, int)`—At the position indicated by the first argument, inserts the specified `InputStream`, which represents a stream of bytes. The third argument indicates how many bytes to insert from the stream.

- `setCharacterStream(int, Reader, int)`—At the position indicated by the first argument, inserts the specified `Reader`, which represents a character stream. The third argument indicates how many characters to insert from the stream.

- `setBoolean(int, boolean)`—Inserts a `boolean` value at the position indicated by the integer.

- `setByte(int, byte)`—Inserts a `byte` value at the indicated position.

- `setBytes(int, byte[])`—Inserts an array of bytes at the indicated position.

- `setDate(int, Date)`—Inserts a `Date` object (from the `java.sql` package) at the indicated position.

- `setDouble(int, double)`—Inserts a `double` value at the indicated position.

- `setFloat(int, float)`—Inserts a `float` value at the indicated position.

- setInt(*int*, *int*)—Inserts an int value at the indicated position.
- setLong(*int*, *long*)—Inserts a long value at the indicated position.
- setShort(*int*, *short*)—Inserts a short value at the indicated position.
- setString(*int*, *String*)—Inserts a String value at the indicated position.

There's also a setNull(*int*, *int*) method that stores SQL's version of a null (empty) value at the position indicated by the first argument.

The second argument to setNull() should be a class variable from the Types class in java.sql to indicate what kind of SQL value belongs in that position.

There are class variables for each of the SQL data types. This list, which is not complete, includes some of the most commonly used variables: BIGINT, BIT, CHAR, DATE, DECIMAL, DOUBLE, FLOAT, INTEGER, SMALLINT, TINYINT, and VARCHAR.

The following code puts a null CHAR value at the fifth position in a prepared statement called ps:

```
ps.setNull(5, Types.CHAR);
```

The next project demonstrates the use of a prepared statement to add stock quote data to a database. Quotes are collected from Yahoo!.

18

As a service to people who follow the stock market, Yahoo! offers a Download Spreadsheet link on its main stock quote page for each ticker symbol.

To see this link, look up a stock quote on Yahoo! or go directly to a page such as this one:

```
http://quote.yahoo.com/q?s=fb&d=v1
```

Below the price chart, you can find a Download Data link. Here's what the link to Facebook looks like:

```
http://download.finance.yahoo.com/d/quotes.csv?s=FB&f=sl1d1t1c1ohgv&e=.csv
```

You can click this link to open the file or save it to a folder on your system. The file, which is only one line long, contains the stock's price and volume data saved at the last market close. Here's an example of what Facebook's data looked like on May 23, 2012:

```
"FB",32.00,"5/23/2012","4:00pm",+1.00,31.41,32.50,31.36,73721136
```

The fields in this data, in order, are the ticker symbol, closing price, date, time, price change since yesterday's close, daily low, daily high, daily open, and volume.

The QuoteData application uses each of these fields except one—the time, which isn't particularly useful because it's always the time the market closed.

The following takes place in the program:

- A stock's ticker symbol is used as a command-line argument.
- A QuoteData object is created with the ticker symbol as an instance variable called ticker.
- The object's retrieveQuote() method is called to download the stock data from Yahoo! and return it as a String.
- The object's storeQuote() method is called with that String as an argument. It saves the stock data to a database using a JDBC-ODBC connection.

Before you can run the application, you must have a database table designed to hold these stock quotes.

You can create a new table for this purpose in the sample database in NetBeans by following these steps:

1. In the Services tab of the Projects pane, open the APP item under the jdbc:derby://localhost:1527/sample item.

2. Right-click this item's Tables folder and choose Create Table from the pop-up menu. The Create Table dialog opens, as shown in Figure 18.4.

FIGURE 18.4
Creating a new database table in NetBeans.

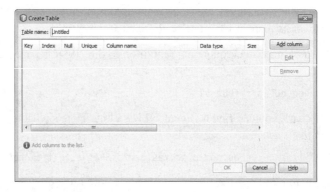

3. In the Table Name field, enter STOCKS.

4. Click Add column. The Add Column dialog opens.

5. In the Name field, enter TICKER.

6. In the Type field, choose VARCHAR.

7. In the Size field, enter 10.

8. Click OK. The new field appears in the dialog.

9. Repeat steps 4–8 for fields named PRICE, DATE, CHANGE, LOW, HIGH, PRICEOPEN, and VOLUME. The type and size are always VARCHAR and 10, respectively.

10. Click OK. The STOCKS table appears in the Tables folder.

Now that you have a database table, you can create the QuoteData application, shown in Listing 18.2, to store stock data in a new record of that table. Create the class QuoteData in NetBeans.

LISTING 18.2   The Full Text of QuoteData.java

```java
 1: import java.io.*;
 2: import java.net.*;
 3: import java.sql.*;
 4: import java.util.*;
 5:
 6: public class QuoteData {
 7:     private String ticker;
 8:
 9:     public QuoteData(String inTicker) {
10:         ticker = inTicker;
11:     }
12:
13:     private String retrieveQuote() {
14:         StringBuilder builder = new StringBuilder();
15:         try {
16:             URL page = new URL("http://quote.yahoo.com/d/quotes.csv?s=" +
17:                 ticker + "&f=sl1d1t1c1ohgv&e=.csv");
18:             String line;
19:             URLConnection conn = page.openConnection();
20:             conn.connect();
21:             InputStreamReader in= new InputStreamReader(
22:                 conn.getInputStream());
23:             BufferedReader data = new BufferedReader(in);
24:             while ((line = data.readLine()) != null) {
25:                 builder.append(line);
26:                 builder.append("\n");
27:             }
28:         } catch (MalformedURLException mue) {
29:             System.out.println("Bad URL: " + mue.getMessage());
30:         } catch (IOException ioe) {
31:             System.out.println("IO Error:" + ioe.getMessage());
32:         }
33:         return builder.toString();
34:     }
35:
36:     private void storeQuote(String data) {
```

18

LISTING 18.2 Continued

```
37:            StringTokenizer tokens = new StringTokenizer(data, ",");
38:            String[] fields = new String[9];
39:            for (int i = 0; i < fields.length; i++) {
40:                fields[i] = stripQuotes(tokens.nextToken());
41:            }
42:            String datasource = "jdbc:derby://localhost:1527/sample";
43:            try (
44:                Connection conn = DriverManager.getConnection(
45:                    datasource, "app", "APP")
46:                ) {
47:
48:                Class.forName("org.apache.derby.jdbc.ClientDriver");
49:                PreparedStatement prep2 = conn.prepareStatement(
50:                    "INSERT INTO " +
51:                    "APP.STOCKS(TICKER, PRICE, DATE, CHANGE, LOW, " +
52:                    "HIGH, PRICEOPEN, VOLUME) " +
53:                    "VALUES(?, ?, ?, ?, ?, ?, ?, ?)");
54:                prep2.setString(1, fields[0]);
55:                prep2.setString(2, fields[1]);
56:                prep2.setString(3, fields[2]);
57:                prep2.setString(4, fields[4]);
58:                prep2.setString(5, fields[5]);
59:                prep2.setString(6, fields[6]);
60:                prep2.setString(7, fields[7]);
61:                prep2.setString(8, fields[8]);
62:                prep2.executeUpdate();
63:                conn.close();
64:            } catch (SQLException sqe) {
65:                System.out.println("SQL Error: " + sqe.getMessage());
66:            } catch (ClassNotFoundException cnfe) {
67:                System.out.println(cnfe.getMessage());
68:            }
69:        }
70:
71:    private String stripQuotes(String input) {
72:        StringBuilder output = new StringBuilder();
73:        for (int i = 0; i < input.length(); i++) {
74:            if (input.charAt(i) != '\"') {
75:                output.append(input.charAt(i));
76:            }
77:        }
78:        return output.toString();
79:    }
80:
81:    public static void main(String[] arguments) {
82:        if (arguments.length < 1) {
83:            System.out.println("Usage: java QuoteData tickerSymbol");
84:            System.exit(0);
85:        }
```

LISTING 18.2   Continued

```
86:            QuoteData qd = new QuoteData(arguments[0]);
87:            String data = qd.retrieveQuote();
88:            qd.storeQuote(data);
89:        }
90: }
```

Before you run the application, you must set a command-line argument. Choose Run, Set Project Configuration, Customize, and then enter the main class QuoteData and the argument of a valid ticker symbol, such as FB or GOOG.

The application stores the stock data but does not display any output.

To see that it worked, right-click the STOCKS table in the Services tab and choose View Data. The table records are displayed; they should include at least one day's data for the requested stock ticker symbol, as shown in Figure 18.5.

FIGURE 18.5
Records in the
STOCKS table.

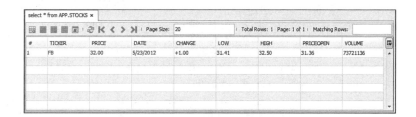

The retrieveQuote() method (lines 13–34) downloads the quote data from Yahoo! and saves it as a string. The techniques used in this method were covered on Day 17, "Communicating Across the Internet."

The storeQuote() method (lines 36–69) uses the SQL techniques covered in this section.

The method begins by using the StringTokenizer class to split the quote data into a set of tokens, using the comma character (,) as the delimiter between each token. The tokens then are stored in a String array with nine elements.

The array contains the same fields as the Yahoo! data in the same order: ticker symbol, closing price, date, time, price change, low, high, open, and volume.

Next, a data connection to the QuoteData data source is created using the Java DB database driver (lines 42–46).

18

This connection then is used to create a prepared statement (lines 49–53). This statement uses the `insert into` SQL statement, which causes data to be stored in a database. In this case, the database is `sample`, and the `insert into` statement refers to the `APP.STOCKS` table in that database.

The prepared statement has eight placeholders. Only eight are needed, instead of nine, because the application does not use the time field from the Yahoo! data.

A series of `setString()` methods puts the elements of the `String` array into the prepared statement, in the same order that the fields exist in the database: ticker symbol, closing price, date, price change, low, high, open, and volume (lines 54–61).

Because some fields in the Yahoo! data are dates, floating-point numbers, and integers, you might think that it would be better to use `setDate()`, `setFloat()`, and `setInt()` for that data. This application stores all the stock data as strings because that's more likely to work regardless of the database software being used.

CAUTION

Some databases you could use, including Microsoft Access, do not support some of these methods when you are using SQL to work with the database, even though they exist in Java. If you try to use an unsupported method, such as `setFloat()`, a `SQLException` error occurs.

It's easier to send a database strings and let the database program automatically convert them into the correct format. This is likely to be true when you are working with other databases; the level of SQL support varies based on the product and driver involved.

After the statement has been prepared and all the placeholders are filled, the statement's `executeUpdate()` method is called in line 62. This either adds the quote data to the database or throws a SQL error.

The private method `stripQuotes()` is used to remove quotation marks from Yahoo!'s stock data. This method is called in line 40 to take care of three fields that contain extraneous quotes: the ticker symbol, date, and time.

Moving Through Resultsets

The default behavior of resultsets permits one trip through the set using its `next()` method to retrieve each record.

By changing how statements and prepared statements are created, you can produce resultsets that support these additional methods:

- `afterLast()` moves to a place immediately after the last record in the set.
- `beforeFirst()` moves to a place immediately before the first record in the set.
- `first()` moves to the first record in the set.
- `last()` moves to the last record in the set.
- `previous()` moves to the previous record in the set.

These actions are possible when the resultset's policies have been specified as arguments to a database connection's `createStatement()` and `prepareStatement()` methods.

Normally, `createStatement()` takes no arguments, as in this example:

```
Connection payday = DriverManager.getConnection(
    "jdbc:odbc:Payroll", "Doc", "1rover1");
Statement lookSee = payday.CreateStatement();
```

For a more flexible resultset, call `createStatement()` with three integer arguments that set up how it can be used. Here's a rewrite of the preceding statement:

```
Statement lookSee = payday.createStatement(
    ResultSet.TYPE_SCROLL_INSENSITIVE,
    ResultSet.CONCUR_READ_ONLY,
    ResultSet.CLOSE_CURSORS_AT_COMMIT);
```

18

The same three arguments can be used in the `prepareStatement(String, int, int, int)` method after the text of the statement.

The `ResultSet` class includes other class variables that offer more options in how sets can be read and modified.

Summary

Today, you learned to read and write database records using classes that work with any of the popular relational databases. The techniques used to work with Java DB can be used with Microsoft Access, MySQL, and other programs. The only thing that needs to be changed is the database driver class and the strings used to create a connection.

Using Java Database Connectivity (JDBC), you can incorporate existing data-storage solutions into your Java programs.

You can connect to several different relational databases in your Java programs by using JDBC and Structured Query Language (SQL), a standard language for reading, writing, and managing a database.

Q&A

Q What's the difference between Java DB and more well-known databases such as Access and MySQL? Which should I use?

A Java DB is intended for database applications that have simpler needs than Access and comparable databases. The entire application takes up 2MB of space, making it easy to bundle with Java applications that require database connectivity.

Oracle employs Java DB in several parts of the Java Enterprise Edition, which demonstrates that it can deliver strong, reliable performance on important tasks.

Quiz

Review today's material by taking this three-question quiz. Answers are at the end of the book.

Questions

1. What does a `Statement` object represent in a database program?

   A. A connection to a database

   B. A database query written in Structured Query Language

   C. A data source

2. Which Java class represents SQL statements that are compiled before they are executed?

   A. `Statement`

   B. `PreparedStatement`

   C. `ResultSet`

3. What does the `Class.forName(String)` method accomplish?

   A. It provides the name of a class.

   B. It loads a database driver that can be used to access a database.

   C. It deletes an object.

Certification Practice

The following question is the kind of thing you could expect to be asked on a Java programming certification test. Answer it without looking at today's material or using the Java compiler to test the code.

Given:

```java
public class ArrayClass {

    public static ArrayClass newInstance() {
        count++;
        return new ArrayClass();
    }

    public static void main(String arguments[]) {
        new ArrayClass();
    }

    int count = -1;
}
```

Which line in this program prevents it from compiling successfully?

A. `count++;`

B. `return new ArrayClass();`

C. `public static void main(String arguments[]) {`

D. `int count = -1;`

18

The answer is available on the book's website at www.java21days.com. Visit the Day 18 page and click the Certification Practice link.

Exercises

To extend your knowledge of the subjects covered today, try the following exercises:

1. Modify the SysTableReporter application to pull fields from another table in SYS.
2. Write an application that reads and displays records from the Yahoo! stock quote database.

Where applicable, exercise solutions are offered on the book's website at www.java21days.com.

DAY 19
Reading and Writing RSS Feeds

Today, you work with Extensible Markup Language (XML), a formatting standard that enables data to be completely portable.

You'll explore XML in the following ways:

- Representing data as XML
- Discovering why XML is a useful way to store data
- Using XML to publish web content
- Reading and writing XML data

The XML format employed throughout the day is Really Simple Syndication (RSS), a popular way to publish web content and share information on site updates. RSS has been adopted by millions of sites.

Using XML

One of Java's main selling points is that the language produces programs that can run on different operating systems without modification. The portability of software is a big convenience in today's computing environment, where Windows, Linux, Mac OS, and a half dozen other operating systems are in wide use and many people work with multiple systems.

XML, which stands for Extensible Markup Language, is a format for storing and organizing data that is independent of any software program that works with the data.

Data that is compliant with XML is easier to reuse for several reasons.

First, the data is structured in a standard way, making it possible for software programs to read and write the data as long as they support XML. If you create an XML file that represents your company's employee database, several dozen XML parsers can read the file and make sense of its contents.

This is true no matter what kind of information you collect about each employee. If your database contains only the employee's name, ID number, and salary, XML parsers can read it. If it contains 25 items, including birthday, blood type, and hair color, parsers can read that, too.

Second, the data is self-documenting, making it easier for people to understand a file's purpose just by looking at it in a text editor. Anyone who opens your XML employee database should be able to figure out the structure and content of each employee record without any assistance from you.

This is evident in Listing 19.1, which contains an RSS file. Because RSS is an XML dialect, it is structured under the rules of XML. Enter this code in NetBeans (category Other, type Empty File) and save it as `workbench.rss`. (You also can download a copy of it from the book's website at www.java21days.com on the Day 19 page.)

LISTING 19.1   The Full Text of `workbench.rss`

```
1: <?xml version="1.0" encoding="utf-8"?>
2: <rss version="2.0">
3:   <channel>
4:     <title>Workbench</title>
5:     <link>http://workbench.cadenhead.org/</link>
6:     <description>Programming, publishing, politics, and popes</description>
7:     <docs>http://www.rssboard.org/rss-specification</docs>
8:     <item>
9:       <title>Tech Journalist Quits the Internet</title>
```

LISTING 19.1   Continued

```
10:          <link>http://workbench.cadenhead.org/news/3678</link>
11:          <pubDate>Wed, 02 May 2012 13:43:40 -0400</pubDate>
12:          <guid isPermaLink="false">tag:cadenhead.org,2012:weblog.3678</guid>
13:          <enclosure length="2498623" type="audio/mpeg"
14:             url="http://mp3.cadenhead.org/3678.mp3" />
15:      </item>
16:      <item>
17:          <title>My First Trip into a Debate Spin Room</title>
18:          <link>http://workbench.cadenhead.org/news/3674</link>
19:          <pubDate>Fri, 27 Jan 2012 19:36:35 -0500</pubDate>
20:          <guid isPermaLink="false">tag:cadenhead.org,2012:weblog.3674</guid>
21:      </item>
22:      <item>
23:          <title>Anthony Weiner and the Infidelity Police</title>
24:          <link>http://workbench.cadenhead.org/news/3664</link>
25:          <pubDate>Tue, 07 Jun 2011 10:37:06 -0400</pubDate>
26:          <guid isPermaLink="false">tag:cadenhead.org,2012:weblog.3664</guid>
27:      </item>
28:    </channel>
29: </rss>
```

Can you tell what the data represents? Although the ?xml tag at the top might be indeci-
pherable, the rest is clearly a website database of some kind.

The ?xml tag in the first line of the file has a version attribute with a value of "1.0" and
an encoding attribute of "utf-8". This establishes that the file follows the rules of XML
1.0 and is encoded with the UTF-8 character set.

Data in XML is surrounded by tag elements that describe the data. Opening tags begin
with a < character followed by the name of the tag and a > character. Closing tags begin
with the </ characters followed by a name and a > character. In Listing 19.1, for example, <item> on line 8 is an opening tag, and </item> on line 15 is a closing tag.
Everything within those tags is considered to be the value of that element.

Elements can be nested within other elements, creating a hierarchy of XML data that
establishes relationships within that data. In Listing 19.1, everything in lines 9–14 is
related; each element defines something about the same website item.

Elements also can include attributes, which are made up of data that supplements the rest
of the data associated with the element. Attributes are defined within an opening tag element. The name of an attribute is followed by an equals sign and text within quotation
marks.

19

In line 12 of Listing 19.1, the `guid` element includes an `isPermaLink` attribute with a value of `"false"`. This indicates that the element's value, `tag:cadenhead.org,2012:weblog.3678`, is not a permalink, the URL at which the item can be loaded in a browser.

XML also supports elements defined by a single tag rather than a pair of tags. The tag begins with a < character followed by the name of the tag and ends with the `/>` characters. The RSS file includes an `enclosure` element in lines 13 and 14 that describes an MP3 audio file associated with the item.

XML encourages the creation of data that's understandable and usable even if the user doesn't have the program that created it and cannot find any documentation that describes it.

For the most part, you can understand the purpose of the RSS file shown in Listing 19.1 simply by looking at it. Each item represents a web page that has been updated recently.

TIP	Publishing new site content over RSS and a similar format, Atom, has become one of the best ways to build readership on the web. Thousands of people subscribe to RSS files, which are called feeds, using reader software such as Google Reader and My Yahoo!.
	Rogers Cadenhead, the author of this book, is the chairman of the RSS Advisory Board, the group that publishes the RSS 2.0 specification. For more information on the format, visit the board's website at www.rssboard.org or subscribe to its RSS feed at www.rssboard.org/rss-feed.
	There's also another version of RSS, RDF Site Summary, that's used on some sites for its feeds. Find out more at http://web.resource.org/rss/1.0.

Data that follows XML's formatting rules is said to be well-formed. Any software that can work with XML reads and writes well-formed XML data.

By insisting on well-formed markup, XML simplifies the task of writing programs that work with the data. RSS makes website updates available in a form that software can easily process. The RSS feed for Workbench at http://feeds.cadenhead.org/workbench has two distinct audiences: humans reading the blog through their preferred RSS reader, and computers that do something with this data. Twitter, Facebook, and many other sites can pull data from an RSS feed and present it to users.

Designing an XML Dialect

Although XML is described as a language and is compared to Hypertext Markup Language (HTML), it's actually much larger in scope. XML is a markup language that defines how to define a markup language.

That's an odd distinction to make, and it sounds like something you'd encounter in a philosophy textbook. This concept is important to understand, though, because it explains how XML can be used to define data as varied as health-care claims, genealogical records, newspaper articles, and molecules.

The X in XML stands for Extensible, and it refers to organizing data for your own purposes. Data that's organized using the rules of XML can represent anything you want:

- A programmer at a telemarketing company can use XML to store data on each outgoing call, saving the time of the call, the number, the operator who made the call, and the result.

- A hobbyist can use XML to keep track of the annoying telemarketing calls she receives, noting the time of the call, the company, and the product being peddled.

- A programmer at a government agency can use XML to track complaints about telemarketers, saving the name of the marketing firm and the number of complaints.

Each of these examples uses XML to define a new language that suits a specific purpose. Although you could call them XML languages, they're more commonly described as XML dialects or XML document types.

An XML dialect can be designed using a Document Type Definition (DTD) that indicates the potential elements and attributes it covers.

A special !DOCTYPE declaration can be placed in XML data, right after the initial ?xml tag, to identify its DTD. Here's an example:

```
<!DOCTYPE Library SYSTEM "librml.dtd">
```

The !DOCTYPE declaration is used to identify the DTD that applies to the data. When a DTD is present, many XML tools can read XML created for that DTD and determine whether the data follows all the rules. If it doesn't, it is rejected with a reference to the line that caused the error. This process is called *validating the XML*.

One thing you'll run into as you work with XML is data that has been structured as XML but wasn't defined using a DTD. Most versions of RSS files do not require a DTD. This data can be parsed (presuming it's well-formed), so you can read it into a program

19

and do something with it, but you can't check its validity to make sure that it's organized correctly according to the rules of its dialect.

> **TIP**
>
> To give you an idea of what kinds of XML dialects have been created, Cover Pages offers a list at http://xml.coverpages.org/xmlApplications.html.

Processing XML with Java

Java supports XML through the Java API for XML Processing, a set of packages for reading, writing, and manipulating XML data.

The `javax.xml.parsers` package is the entry point to the other packages. These classes can be used to parse and validate XML data using two techniques: the Simple API for XML (SAX) and the Document Object Model (DOM). However, they can be difficult to implement, which has inspired other groups to offer their own class libraries to work with XML.

You'll spend the remainder of the day working with one of these alternatives: the XML Object Model (XOM) library, an open source Java class library that makes it extremely easy to read, write, and transform XML data.

> **TIP**
>
> To find out more about the Java API for XML Processing, visit Oracle's Java website at http://docs.oracle.com/javase/7/docs/technotes/guides/xml.

Processing XML with XOM

One of the most important skills you can develop as a Java programmer is the ability to find suitable packages and classes that can be employed in your own projects. For obvious reasons, using a well-designed class library is much easier than developing one on your own.

Although the Java Class Library contains thousands of well-designed classes that cover a comprehensive range of development needs, Oracle isn't the only supplier of packages that may prove useful to your efforts.

Other companies, groups, and individuals offer dozens of Java packages under a variety of commercial and open source licenses. Some of the most notable come from Apache Jakarta, a Java development project of the Apache Software Foundation. It has produced the web application framework Struts, the Log4J logging class library, and many other popular libraries.

Another terrific open source Java class library is the XOM library. This tree-based package for XML processing strives to be simple to learn, easy to use, and uncompromising in its adherence to well-formed XML.

The library was developed by the programmer and author Elliotte Rusty Harold based on his experience with XML processing in Java.

The project originally was envisioned as a fork of JDOM, a popular tree-based model for representing an XML document. Harold has contributed code to that open source project and participated in its development.

Instead of forking the JDOM code, Harold decided to start from scratch and adopt some of its core design principles in XOM.

The library embodies the following principles:

- XML documents are modeled as a tree, with Java classes representing nodes on the tree such as elements, comments, processing instructions, and document type definitions. A programmer can add and remove nodes to manipulate the document in memory, a simple approach that can be implemented gracefully in Java.
- All XML data produced by XOM is well-formed and has a well-formed namespace.
- Each element of an XML document is represented as a class with constructors.
- Object serialization is not supported. Instead, programmers are encouraged to use XML as the format for serialized data, enabling it to be readily exchanged with any software that reads XML, regardless of the programming language in which it was developed.
- The library relies on another XML parser to read XML documents and fill trees. XOM uses a SAX parser that must be downloaded and installed separately. Apache Xerces 2.6.1 and later versions should work.

XOM is available for download from www.xom.nu. The current version is 1.2.8, which includes Xerces 2.8 in its distribution.

19

CAUTION

> XOM is released according to the terms of the open source GNU Lesser General Public License (LGPL). The license grants permission to distribute the library without modification with Java programs that use it.
>
> You also can make changes to the XOM class library as long as you offer them under the LGPL. The full license is published online at www.xom.nu/license.xhtml.

XOM can be downloaded as a zip archive or TAR.GZ archive. Download the library and extract the files on a folder on your computer and then follow these steps to add it to NetBeans:

1. Choose Tools, Libraries. The Library Manager opens.

2. Click Create New Library. The New Library dialog appears.

3. Enter XOM 1.2.8 as the Library Name and click OK.

4. Back in the Library Manager, click Add JAR/Folder.

5. Browse to the folder where you extracted the XOM archive and open it.

6. In that folder, choose the file xom-1.2.8.jar.

7. Click Add JAR/Folder.

8. Back in the Library Manager, click OK.

After you have added the library to NetBeans, you need to add it to the current project so that you can use XOM classes in your programs:

1. In the Projects pane, scroll down past the .java files until you see a folder named Libraries.

2. Right-click this folder and choose Add Library. The Add Library dialog appears.

3. Choose XOM 1.2.8 and click OK.

An item for XOM appears under Libraries in the Projects pane.

Creating an XML Document

The first application you will create, RssWriter, creates an XML document that contains the start of an RSS feed. The document is shown in Listing 19.2. (You don't have to type in this listing.)

LISTING 19.2   The Full Text of `feed.rss`

```
1: <?xml version="1.0"?>
2: <rss version="2.0">
3:   <channel>
4:     <title>Workbench</title>
5:     <link>http://workbench.cadenhead.org/</link>
6:   </channel>
7: </rss>
```

The base `nu.xom` package contains classes for a complete XML document (`Document`), and the nodes a document can contain (`Attribute`, `Comment`, `DocType`, `Element`, `ProcessingInstruction`, and `Text`).

The RssStarter application uses several of these classes. First, an `Element` object is created by specifying the element's name as an argument:

```
Element rss = new Element("rss");
```

This statement creates an object for the root element of the document, `rss`. `Element`'s one-argument constructor can be used because the document does not employ a feature of XML called namespaces; if it did, a second argument would be necessary: the element's namespace uniform resource identifier (URI). The other classes in the XOM library support namespaces in a similar manner.

In the XML document shown in Listing 19.2, the `rss` element includes an attribute named `version` with the value `"2.0"`. An attribute can be created by specifying its name and value in consecutive arguments:

```
Attribute version = new Attribute("version", "2.0");
```

Attributes are added to an element by calling its `addAttribute()` method with the attribute as the only argument:

```
rss.addAttribute(version);
```

The text contained within an element is represented by the `Text` class, which is constructed by specifying the text as a `String` argument:

```
Text titleText = new Text("Workbench");
```

When an XML document is composed, all its elements end up inside a root element that is used to create a `Document` object—a `Document` constructor is called with the root element as an argument. In the RssStarter application, this element is called `rss`. Any `Element` object can be the root of a document:

```
Document doc = new Document(rss);
```

In XOM's tree structure, the classes representing an XML document and its constituent parts are organized into a hierarchy below the generic superclass nu.xom.Node. This class has three subclasses in the same package: Attribute, LeafNode, and ParentNode.

To add a child to a parent node, call the parent's appendChild() method with the node to add as the only argument. The following code creates two elements—a parent called channel and one child element, link:

```
Element channel = new Element("channel");
Element link = new Element("link");
Text linkText = new Text("http://workbench.cadenhead.org/");
link.appendChild(linkText);
channel.appendChild(link);
```

The appendChild() method appends a new child below all other children of that parent. The preceding statements produce this XML fragment:

```
<channel>
    <link>http://workbench.cadenhead.org/</link>
</channel>
```

The appendChild() method also can be called with a String argument instead of a node. A Text object representing the string is created and added to the element:

```
link.appendChild("http://workbench.cadenhead.org/");
```

After a tree has been created and filled with nodes, it can be displayed by calling the Document method toXML(), which returns the complete and well-formed XML document as a String.

Listing 19.3 shows the complete application. Create the RssStarter class in NetBeans with this listing as the source.

LISTING 19.3   The Full Text of RssStarter.java

```
 1: import java.io.*;
 2: import nu.xom.*;
 3:
 4: public class RssStarter {
 5:     public static void main(String[] arguments) {
 6:         // create an <rss> element to serve as the document's root
 7:         Element rss = new Element("rss");
 8:
 9:         // add a version attribute to the element
10:         Attribute version = new Attribute("version", "2.0");
11:         rss.addAttribute(version);
12:         // create a <channel> element and make it a child of <rss>
```

LISTING 19.3   Continued

```
13:            Element channel = new Element("channel");
14:            rss.appendChild(channel);
15:            // create the channel's <title>
16:            Element title = new Element("title");
17:            Text titleText = new Text("Workbench");
18:            title.appendChild(titleText);
19:            channel.appendChild(title);
20:            // create the channel's <link>
21:            Element link = new Element("link");
22:            Text linkText = new Text("http://workbench.cadenhead.org/");
23:            link.appendChild(linkText);
24:            channel.appendChild(link);
25:
26:            // create a new document with <rss> as the root element
27:            Document doc = new Document(rss);
28:
29:            // Save the XML document
30:            try (
31:                FileWriter fw = new FileWriter("feed.rss");
32:                BufferedWriter out = new BufferedWriter(fw);
33:            ) {
34:                out.write(doc.toXML());
35:            } catch (IOException ioe) {
36:                System.out.println(ioe.getMessage());
37:            }
38:            System.out.println(doc.toXML());
39:        }
40: }
```

The RssStarter application displays the XML document it creates on standard output and saves it to a file called feed.rss.

XOM automatically precedes a document with an XML declaration.

The XML produced by this application contains no indentation; elements are stacked on the same line.

CAUTION   XOM preserves significant white space only when representing XML data. The spaces between elements in the RSS feed contained in Listing 19.2 are strictly for presentation purposes and are not produced automatically when XOM creates an XML document. A subsequent example demonstrates how to control indentation.

19

Modifying an XML Document

The next project, the DomainEditor application, makes several changes to the XML document that was just produced by the RssStarter application, `feed.rss`. The text enclosed by the `link` element is changed to http://www.cadenhead.org/, and a new `item` element is added:

```
<item>
  <title>Free the Bound Periodicals</title>
</item>
```

Using the `nu.xom` package, XML documents can be loaded into a tree from several sources: a `File`, `InputStream`, `Reader`, or URL (which is specified as a `String` instead of a `java.net.URL` object).

The `Builder` class represents a SAX parser that can load an XML document into a `Document` object. Constructor methods can be used to specify a particular parser or to let XOM use the first available parser from this list: Xerces 2, Crimson, Piccolo, GNU Aelfred, Oracle, XP, Saxon Aelfred, or Dom4J Aelfred. If none of these is found, the parser specified by the system property `org.xml.sax.driver` is used. Constructors also determine whether the parser is validating or nonvalidating.

The `Builder()` and `Builder(true)` constructors both use the default parser—most likely a version of Xerces. The presence of the Boolean argument `true` in the second constructor configures the parser to be validating. It would be nonvalidating otherwise. A validating parser throws a `nu.xom.ValidityException` if the XML document doesn't validate according to the rules of its document type definition.

The `Builder` object's `build()` method loads an XML document from a source and returns a `Document` object:

```
Builder builder = new Builder();
File xmlFile = new File("feed.rss");
Document doc = builder.build(xmlFile);
```

These statements load an XML document from the file `feed.rss` barring one of two problems: A `nu.xom.ParseException` is thrown if the file does not contain well-formed XML, and a `java.io.IOException` is thrown if the input operation fails.

Elements are retrieved from the tree by calling a method of their parent node.

A `Document` object's `getRootElement()` method returns the document's root element:

```
Element root = doc.getRootElement();
```

In the XML document `feed.rss`, the root element is `domains`.

Elements with names can be retrieved by calling their parent node's
getFirstChildElement() method with the name as a String argument:

```
Element channel = root.getFirstChildElement("channel");
```

This statement retrieves the channel element contained in the rss element (or null if
that element could not be found). Like other examples, this is simplified by the lack of a
namespace in the document; there also are methods where a name and namespace are
arguments.

When several elements within a parent have the same name, the parent node's
getChildElements() method can be used instead:

```
Elements children = channel.getChildElements()
```

The getChildElements() method returns an Elements object containing each of the elements. This object is a read-only list and does not change automatically if the parent
node's contents change after getChildElements() is called.

Elements has a size() method containing an integer count of the elements it holds. This
can be used in a loop to cycle through each element in turn, beginning with the one at
position 0. There's a get() method to retrieve each element; call it with the integer position of the element to be retrieved:

```
for (int i = 0; i < children.size(); i++) {
    Element link = children.get(i);
}
```

This for loop cycles through each child element of the channel element.

Elements without names can be retrieved by calling their parent node's getChild()
method with one argument: an integer indicating the element's position within the
parent node:

```
Text linkText = (Text) link.getChild(0);
```

This statement creates the Text object for the text "http://www.cadenhead.org/
workbench/" found within the link element. Text elements always are at position 0
within their enclosing parent.

To work with this text as a string, call the Text object's getValue() method, as in this
statement:

```
if (linkText.getValue().equals("http://workbench.cadenhead.org/"))
    // ...
}
```

19

The DomainEditor application only modifies a `link` element enclosing the text `"http://workbench.cadenhead.org/"`. The application makes the following changes: The text of the `link` element is deleted, the new text `"http://www.cadenhead.org/"` is added in its place, and then a new `item` element is added.

A parent node has two `removeChild()` methods to delete a child node from the document. Calling the method with an integer deletes the child at that position:

```
Element channel = domain.getFirstChildElement("channel");
Element link = dns.getFirstChildElement("link");
link.removeChild(0);
```

These statements would delete the `Text` object contained within the channel's first `link` element.

Calling the `removeChild()` method with a node as an argument deletes that particular node. Extending the previous example, the `link` element could be deleted with this statement:

```
channel.removeChild(link);
```

Listing 19.4 shows the source code of the DomainEditor application. Create this class in NetBeans.

LISTING 19.4   The Full Text of `DomainEditor.java`

```
 1: import java.io.*;
 2: import nu.xom.*;
 3:
 4: public class DomainEditor {
 5:     public static void main(String[] arguments) throws IOException {
 6:         try {
 7:             // create a tree from the XML document feed.rss
 8:             Builder builder = new Builder();
 9:             File xmlFile = new File("feed.rss");
10:             Document doc = builder.build(xmlFile);
11:
12:             // get the root element <rss>
13:             Element root = doc.getRootElement();
14:
15:             // get its <channel> element
16:             Element channel = root.getFirstChildElement("channel");
17:
18:             // get its <link> elements
19:             Elements children = channel.getChildElements();
20:             for (int i = 0; i < children.size(); i++) {
21:
```

LISTING 19.4   Continued

```
22:                    // get a <link> element
23:                    Element link = children.get(i);
24:
25:                    // get its text
26:                    Text linkText = (Text) link.getChild(0);
27:
28:                    // update any link matching a URL
29:                    if (linkText.getValue().equals(
30:                        "http://workbench.cadenhead.org/")) {
31:
32:                        // update the link's text
33:                        link.removeChild(0);
34:                        link.appendChild("http://www.cadenhead.org/");
35:                    }
36:                }
37:
38:                // create new elements and attributes to add
39:                Element item = new Element("item");
40:                Element itemTitle = new Element("title");
41:
42:                // add them to the <channel> element
43:                itemTitle.appendChild(
44:                    "Free the Bound Periodicals"
45:                );
46:                item.appendChild(itemTitle);
47:                channel.appendChild(item);
48:
49:                // Save the XML document
50:                try (
51:                    FileWriter fw = new FileWriter("feed2.rss");
52:                    BufferedWriter out = new BufferedWriter(fw);
53:                ) {
54:                    out.write(doc.toXML());
55:                } catch (IOException ioe) {
56:                    System.out.println(ioe.getMessage());
57:                }
58:                System.out.println(doc.toXML());
59:            } catch (ParsingException pe) {
60:                System.out.println("Error parsing document: " +
pe.getMessage());
61:                pe.printStackTrace();
62:                System.exit(-1);
63:            }
64:        }
65: }
```

The DomainEditor application displays the modified XML document to standard output and saves it to a file named feeds2.rss.

Formatting an XML Document

As described earlier, XOM does not retain insignificant white space when representing XML documents. This is in keeping with one of XOM's design goals—to disregard anything that has no syntactic significance in XML. (Another example of this is how text is treated identically whether it is created using character entities, CDATA sections, or regular characters.)

Today's next project is the DomainWriter application. It adds a comment to the beginning of the XML document feeds2.rss and serializes it with indented lines, producing the version shown in Listing 19.5.

LISTING 19.5 The Full Text of feeds2.rss

```
 1: <?xml version="1.0" encoding="ISO-8859-1"?>
 2: <!--File created Mon May 14 16:11:17 EDT 2012-->
 3: <rss version="2.0">
 4:    <channel>
 5:      <title>Workbench</title>
 6:      <link>http://www.cadenhead.org/</link>
 7:      <item>
 8:        <title>Free the Bound Periodicals</title>
 9:      </item>
10:    </channel>
11: </rss>
```

The Serializer class in nu.xom offers control over how an XML document is formatted when it is displayed or stored serially. Indentation, character encoding, line breaks, and other formatting are established by objects of this class.

You can create a Serializer object by specifying an output stream and character encoding as arguments to the constructor:

```
FileOutputStream fos = new FileOutputStream("feed3.rss");
Serializer output = new Serializer(fos, "ISO-8859-1");
```

These statements serialize a file using the ISO-8859-1 character encoding.

Serializer supports 22 encodings, including ISO-10646-UCS-2, ISO-8859-1 through ISO-8859-10, ISO-8859-13 through ISO-8859-16, UTF-8, and UTF-16. There's also a Serializer() constructor that takes only an output stream as an argument; this uses the UTF-8 encoding by default.

You set indentation by calling the serializer's setIndentation() method with an integer argument specifying the number of spaces:

```
output.setIndentation(2);
```

You can write an entire XML document to the serializer destination by calling the serializer's `write()` method with the document as an argument:

```
output.write(doc);
```

The DomainWriter application inserts a comment atop the XML document instead of appending it at the end of a parent node's children. This requires another method of the parent node, `insertChild()`, which is called with two arguments—the element to add and the integer position of the insertion:

```
Builder builder = new Builder();
Document doc = builder.build(arguments[0]);
Comment timestamp = new Comment("File created " +
    new java.util.Date());
doc.insertChild(timestamp, 0);
```

The comment is placed at position 0 atop the document, moving the domains tag down one line but remaining below the XML declaration.

Listing 19.6 is the application's source code.

LISTING 19.6   The Full Text of DomainWriter.java

```
 1: import java.io.*;
 2: import nu.xom.*;
 3:
 4: public class DomainWriter {
 5:     public static void main(String[] arguments) throws IOException {
 6:         try {
 7:             // Create a tree from an XML document
 8:             // specified as a command-line argument
 9:             Builder builder = new Builder();
10:             Document doc = builder.build("feed2.rss");
11:
12:             // Create a comment with the current time and date
13:             Comment timestamp = new Comment("File created "
14:                 + new java.util.Date());
15:
16:             // Add the comment above everything else in the
17:             // document
18:             doc.insertChild(timestamp, 0);
19:
20:             // Create a file output stream to a new file
21:             FileOutputStream fos = new FileOutputStream("feed3.rss");
22:
23:             // Using a serializer with indention set to 2 spaces,
24:             // write the XML document to the file
25:             Serializer output = new Serializer(fos, "ISO-8859-1");
```

19

LISTING 19.6   Continued

```
26:                output.setIndent(2);
27:                output.write(doc);
28:            } catch (ParsingException pe) {
29:                System.out.println("Error parsing document: " + pe.getMessage());
30:                pe.printStackTrace();
31:                System.exit(-1);
32:            }
33:        }
34: }
```

The DomainWriter application reads the file `feed2.rss` as input and creates a new modified version called `feed3.rss`.

Evaluating XOM

The applications you've created cover the core features of the main XOM package and are representative of its straightforward approach to XML processing.

There also are smaller `nu.xom.canonical`, `nu.xom.converters`, `nu.xom.xinclude`, and `nu.xom.xslt` packages to support XInclude, Extensible Stylesheet Language Transformations (XSLT), canonical XML serialization, and conversions between the XOM model for XML and the one used by DOM and SAX.

Listing 19.7 is an application that works with XML from a dynamic source: RSS feeds of recently updated web content from the feed's producer. The RssFilter application searches the feed for specified text in headlines, producing a new XML document that contains only the matching items and shorter indentation. It also modifies the feed's title and adds an RSS 0.91 document type declaration if one is needed in an RSS 0.91 format feed.

LISTING 19.7   The Full Text of `RssFilter.java`

```
1: import nu.xom.*;
2:
3: public class RssFilter {
4:     public static void main(String[] arguments) {
5:
6:         if (arguments.length < 2) {
7:             System.out.println("Usage: java RssFilter rssFile searchTerm");
8:             System.exit(-1);
9:         }
10:
11:         // Save the RSS location and search term
```

LISTING 19.7   Continued

```
12:         String rssFile = arguments[0];
13:         String searchTerm = arguments[1];
14:
15:         try {
16:             // Fill a tree with an RSS file's XML data
17:             // The file can be local or something on the
18:             // Web accessible via a URL.
19:             Builder bob = new Builder();
20:             Document doc = bob.build(rssFile);
21:
22:             // Get the file's root element (<rss>)
23:             Element rss = doc.getRootElement();
24:
25:             // Get the element's version attribute
26:             Attribute rssVersion = rss.getAttribute("version");
27:             String version = rssVersion.getValue();
28:
29:             // Add the DTD for RSS 0.91 feeds, if needed
30:             if ( (version.equals("0.91")) & (doc.getDocType() == null) ) {
31:                 DocType rssDtd = new DocType("rss",
32:                     "http://my.netscape.com/publish/formats/rss-0.91.dtd");
33:                 doc.insertChild(rssDtd, 0);
34:             }
35:
36:             // Get the first (and only) <channel> element
37:             Element channel = rss.getFirstChildElement("channel");
38:
39:             // Get its <title> element
40:             Element title = channel.getFirstChildElement("title");
41:             Text titleText = (Text)title.getChild(0);
42:
43:             // Change the title to reflect the search term
44:             titleText.setValue(titleText.getValue() + ": Search for " +
45:                 searchTerm + " articles");
46:
47:             // Get all of the <item> elements and loop through them
48:             Elements items = channel.getChildElements("item");
49:             for (int i = 0; i < items.size(); i++) {
50:                 // Get an <item> element
51:                 Element item = items.get(i);
52:
53:                 // Look for a <title> element inside it
54:                 Element itemTitle = item.getFirstChildElement("title");
55:
56:                 // If found, look for its contents
57:                 if (itemTitle != null) {
58:                     Text itemTitleText = (Text) itemTitle.getChild(0);
59:
60:                     // If the search text is not found in the item,
```

19

LISTING 19.7   Continued

```
61:                      // delete it from the tree
62:                      if (itemTitleText.toString().indexOf(searchTerm) == -1)
63:                          channel.removeChild(item);
64:                  }
65:              }
66:
67:              // Display the results with a serializer
68:              Serializer output = new Serializer(System.out);
69:              output.setIndent(2);
70:              output.write(doc);
71:          } catch (Exception exc) {
72:              System.out.println("Error: " + exc.getMessage());
73:              exc.printStackTrace();
74:          }
75:      }
76: }
```

Run the application after setting the command-line arguments by selecting Run, Set Project Configuration. The first argument is the feed to check, and the second is the word to search for in its titles. One feed that can be used to test the application is http:// feeds.sportsfilter.com/sportsfilter from SportsFilter. Check it for words such as Heat, Yankees, or Cowboys.

Comments in the application's source code describe its functionality.

XOM's design is strongly informed by one overriding principle: enforced simplicity.

On the website for the class library, Elliotte Rusty Harold states that XOM "should help inexperienced developers do the right thing and keep them from doing the wrong thing. The learning curve needs to be really shallow, and that includes not relying on best practices that are known in the community but are not obvious at first glance."

The new class library is useful for Java programmers whose Java programs require a steady diet of XML.

Summary

Today, you learned the basics of another popular format for data representation, Extensible Markup Language (XML), by exploring one of the most popular uses of XML—RSS feeds.

In many ways, XML is the data equivalent of the Java language. It liberates data from the software used to create it and the operating system the software runs on, just as Java can liberate software from a particular operating system.

By using a class library such as the open source XML Object Model (XOM) library, you can easily create and retrieve data from an XML file.

A big advantage of representing data using XML is that you can always get that data back. If you decide to move the data into a relational database or some other form, you can easily retrieve the information. The data being produced as RSS feeds can be mined by software in countless ways, today and in the future.

You also can transform XML into other forms such as HTML through a variety of technology, both in Java and through tools developed in other languages.

Q&A

Q What's the difference between RSS 1.0, RSS 2.0, and Atom?

A RSS 1.0 is a syndication format that employs the Resource Description Framework (RDF) to describe items in the feed. RSS 2.0 shares a common origin with RSS 1.0 but does not make use of RDF. Atom is another syndication format that was created after RSS 1.0 and RSS 2.0. The IETF has adopted Atom as an Internet standard.

All three formats are suitable for offering web content in XML that can be read with a reader such as Bloglines or My Yahoo! or that can be read by software and stored, manipulated, or transformed.

Q Why is Extensible Markup Language called XML instead of EML?

A None of the founders of the language appears to have documented the reason for choosing XML as the acronym. The general consensus in the XML community is that it was chosen because it "sounds cooler" than EML. Before you snicker at that explanation, the language's creator chose the name Java for the new programming language using the same criteria, turning down more technical-sounding alternatives such as DNA and WRL.

It's possible that the founders of XML were trying to avoid confusion with a programming language called EML (Extended Machine Language), which predates Extensible Markup Language.

19

Quiz

Review today's material by taking this three-question quiz. Answers are at the end of the book.

Questions

1. What does RSS stand for?

   A. Really Simple Syndication

   B. RDF Site Summary

   C. Both

2. What method *cannot* be used to add text to an XML element using XOM?

   A. `addAttribute(String, String)`

   B. `appendChild(Text)`

   C. `appendChild(String)`

3. When all the opening element tags, closing element tags, and other markup are applied consistently in a document, what adjective describes the document?

   A. Validating

   B. Parsable

   C. Well-formed

Certification Practice

The following question is the kind of thing you could expect to be asked on a Java programming certification test. Answer it without looking at today's material or using the Java compiler to test the code.

Given:

```java
public class NameDirectory {
    String[] names;
    int nameCount;

    public NameDirectory() {
        names = new String[20];
        nameCount = 0;
    }

    public void addName(String newName) {
        if (nameCount < 20)
            // answer goes here
    }
}
```

The `NameDirectory` class must be able to hold 20 different names. What statement should replace `// answer goes here` for the class to function correctly?

A. `names[nameCount] = newName;`

B. `names[nameCount] == newName;`

C. `names[nameCount++] = newName;`

D. `names[++nameCount] = newName;`

The answer is available on the book's website at www.java21days.com. Visit the Day 19 page and click the Certification Practice link.

Exercises

To extend your knowledge of the subjects covered today, try the following exercises:

1. Create a simple XML format to represent a book collection with three books and a Java application that searches for books with Joseph Heller as the author, displaying any that it finds.

2. Create two applications: one that retrieves records from a database and produces an XML file that contains the same information and a second application that reads data from that XML file and displays it.

Where applicable, exercise solutions are offered on the book's website at www.java21days.com.

19

DAY 20
XML Web Services

Over the years, numerous attempts have been made to create a standard protocol for remote procedure calls (RPCs). These are a way for one computer program to call a procedure in another program over a network such as the Internet.

Often, these protocols are completely language-agnostic. This allows a client program written in a language such as C++ to call a remote database server written in Java or something else without either side knowing or caring about its partner's implementation language.

RPC efforts are being driven at breakneck speed by web services—networking programs that use the web to offer data in a form easily digested by other software. Web services are being employed to share password authentication information between sites, facilitate e-commerce transactions between stores, provide business-to-business information exchange, and other innovative offerings.

One useful technology in this area is XML-RPC, a protocol for using Hypertext Transfer Protocol (HTTP) and Extensible Markup Language (XML) for remote procedure calls. Today, you learn how to implement it in Java as the following topics are covered:

- How XML-RPC was developed

- How to communicate with another computer using XML-RPC

- How to structure an XML-RPC request and an XML-RPC response

- How to use XML-RPC in Java programs

- How to send an XML-RPC request

- How to receive an XML-RPC response

Introduction to XML-RPC

Java supports one well-established technique for remote procedure calling: remote method invocation (RMI).

RMI, like some older RPC efforts, is designed to be a complex, robust solution to a large variety of remote computing tasks. This sophistication has been one of the hindrances to the adoption of existing RPC efforts. The complexity required to implement some of these solutions can be more than a programmer wants to take on simply to exchange information over a network.

A simpler alternative, XML-RPC, has become widely adopted for web services.

Client/server implementations of XML-RPC are available for most platforms and programming languages in widespread use. UserLand Software offers a directory of implementations at www.xmlrpc.com.

XML-RPC exchanges information using a combination of HTTP, the protocol of the World Wide Web, and XML, a format for organizing data independent of the software used to read and write it.

XML-RPC supports the following data types:

- `array`—A data structure that holds multiple elements of any of the other data types, including arrays
- `base64`—Binary data in Base 64 format
- `boolean`—True-false values that are either 1 (`true`) or 0 (`false`)
- `dateTime.iso8601`—A string containing the date and time in ISO 8601 format, such as 20120915T19:20:15 for 7:20 p.m. (and 15 seconds) on September 15, 2012
- `double`—8-byte signed floating-point numbers
- `int` (also called `i4`)—Signed integers ranging in value from –2,147,483,648 to 2,147,483,647, the same size as `int` values in Java
- `string`—Text
- `struct`—Name-value pairs of associated data where the name is a string and the value can be any of the other data types (comparable to the `Hashtable` class in Java)

XML-RPC also supports the `array` data type, which is used to hold arrays of any other kind of data, including arrays.

One thing noticeably absent from XML-RPC is a way to represent data as an object. The protocol wasn't designed with object-oriented programming in mind, but you can represent reasonably complex objects with the array and struct types.

By design, XML-RPC is a simple remote procedure call protocol that is well suited to programming across a network. The protocol has become one of the key elements of web services implemented by many developers of software on Windows, Macintosh, and Linux systems.

NOTE   The full XML-RPC specification is available on XML-RPC.com at www.xmlrpc.com/spec.

More than 75 implementations of XML-RPC are available today for a variety of languages and platforms.

After the release of XML-RPC, the specification was extended to create another RPC protocol called Simple Object Access Protocol (SOAP).

SOAP shares some of the design goals of XML-RPC but has been expanded to better support objects, user-defined data types, and other advanced features, resulting in a significantly more complex protocol. SOAP also has become widely popular for web services and other decentralized network programming.

NOTE   Because SOAP is an extension of XML-RPC, it raises the question of why the latter protocol is still in use.

When SOAP came out and was considerably more complex than XML-RPC, there was enough difference between the related protocols that an argument could be made for using either one, depending on the needs of a particular project.

To find out more about SOAP and public servers that can be used with SOAP clients, visit the website www.xmethods.com.

20

Communicating with XML-RPC

XML-RPC is a protocol transmitted via HTTP, the standard for data exchange between web servers and web browsers. The information it transmits is not web content. Instead, it is XML data encoded in a specific way.

Two kinds of data exchanges are conducted using XML-RPC: client requests and server responses.

Sending a Request

An XML-RPC request is XML data sent to a web server as part of an HTTP post request.

A post request normally is used to transmit data from a web browser to a web server. Java servlets, common gateway interface programs, and other software collect the data from a post request and send back Hypertext Markup Language (HTML) in response. When you submit an email from a web page or vote in an online poll, you're using either post or a similar HTTP request called get.

XML-RPC, on the other hand, simply uses HTTP as a convenient protocol for communicating with a server and receiving a response.

The request consists of two parts: the HTTP headers required by the post transmission, and the XML-RPC request, which is expressed as XML.

Listing 20.1 is an example of an XML-RPC request.

LISTING 20.1   An XML-RPC Request

```
 1: POST /XMLRPC HTTP/1.0
 2: Host: www.advogato.org
 3: Connection: Close
 4: Content-Type: text/xml
 5: Content-Length: 151
 6: User-Agent: OSE/XML-RPC
 7:
 8: <?xml version="1.0"?>
 9: <methodCall>
10:     <methodName>test.square</methodName>
11:     <params>
12:        <param>
13:           <value>
14:               <int>13</int>
15:           </value>
16:        </param>
17:     </params>
18: </methodCall>
```

In Listing 20.1, lines 1–6 are the HTTP headers, and lines 8–18 are the XML-RPC request. This listing tells you the following:

- The XML-RPC server is at www.advogato.org/XMLRPC (lines 1 and 2).
- The remote method being called is `test.square` (line 10).
- The method is being called with one argument, an integer with a value of 13 (lines 12–16).

Unlike their counterparts in Java, method names in an XML-RPC request do not include parentheses. They consist of the name of an object followed by a period and the name of the method, or simply the name of the method, depending on the XML-RPC server.

> **CAUTION**
>
> XML-RPC, which has been implemented in numerous computer-programming languages, has a few differences in terminology from Java: Methods are called procedures, and method arguments are called parameters. The Java terms are used often during today's lesson when Java programming techniques are discussed.

Responding to a Request

An XML-RPC response is XML data that is sent back from a web server like any other HTTP response. Again, XML-RPC piggybacks on an established process—a web server sending data via HTTP to a web browser—and uses it in a new way.

The response also consists of HTTP headers and an XML-RPC response in XML format.

Listing 20.2 is an example of an XML-RPC response.

LISTING 20.2 An XML-RPC Response

```
 1: HTTP/1.0 200 OK
 2: Date: Tue, 15 Mar 2012 05:19:17 GMT
 3: Server: Apache/1.3.26 (Unix) mod_virgule/1.41 PHP/4.1.2 mod_perl/1.26
 4: ETag: "PbT9cMgXsXnw52OqREFNAA=="
 5: Content-MD5: PbT9cMgXsXnw52OqREFNAA==
 6: Content-Length: 157
 7: Connection: close
 8: Content-Type: text/xml
 9:
10: <?xml version="1.0"?>
11: <methodResponse>
12:   <params>
13:     <param>
14:       <value>
15:         <int>169</int>
```

20

LISTING 20.2   Continued

```
16:        </value>
17:      </param>
18:    </params>
19: </methodResponse>
```

In Listing 20.2, lines 1–8 are the HTTP headers, and lines 10–19 are the XML-RPC response. You can learn the following things from this listing:

- The response is 157 bytes in size and is in XML format (lines 6 and 8).
- The value returned by the remote method is an integer that equals 169 (line 15).

An XML-RPC response contains only one argument, contrary to what you might expect from the params tag in line 12. If the remote method does not return a value—for example, it might be a Java method that returns void—an XML-RPC server still returns something.

This return value can be primitive data, strings, arrays of varying dimensions, and more sophisticated data structures such as key-value pairs (the kind of thing you could implement in Java using Hashtable).

NOTE

The XML-RPC request and response examples were generated by a server run by the Advogato open source advocacy site. You can find out more about its XML-RPC server at www.advogato.org/xmlrpc.html.

Several XML-RPC debuggers on the Web can be used to call remote methods, which makes it much easier to determine if a client or server is working correctly. One is available at http://w3future.com/html/xmlrpcdebugger.html.

Choosing an XML-RPC Implementation

Although you can work with XML-RPC by creating your own classes to read and write XML and exchange data over the Internet, an easier route is to use a pre-existing Java Class Library that supports XML-RPC.

One of the most popular is Apache XML-RPC, an open source project managed by the developers of the Apache web server, Tomcat Java servlet engine, Ant build tool, and other popular open source software.

The Apache XML-RPC project, which consists of the `org.apache.xmlrpc` package and three related packages, contains classes that can be used to implement an XML-RPC client and server with a small amount of your own code.

The project has a home page at the web address http://xml.apache.org/xmlrpc. Today's projects employ release 2.0. To use this project, you must download and install it.

Apache XML-RPC can be downloaded as either a zip archive or TAR.GZ archive. Download the library and extract the files on a folder on your computer. When that's done, follow these steps to add Apache XML-RPC to NetBeans:

1. Choose Tools, Libraries. The Library Manager opens.
2. Click Create New Library. The New Library dialog appears.
3. Enter `Apache XML-RPC 3.1.3` as the Library Name and click OK.
4. Back in the Library Manager, click Add JAR/Folder.
5. Browse to the folder where you extracted the archive and open it.
6. Open the lib subfolder and choose all five JAR files it contains: `commons-logging-1.1.jar`, `ws-commons-util-1.0.2.jar`, `xmlrpc-client-3.1.3.jar`, `xmlrpc-common-3.1.3.jar`, and `xmlrpc-server-3.1.3.jar`. (To select multiple files, hold down the Shift key as you click each file.)
7. Click Add JAR/Folder.
8. Back in the Library Manager click OK.

After you have added the library to NetBeans, you need to add it to the current project so that you can use the Apache XML-RPC classes in today's programs:

1. In the Projects pane, look for the folder named Libraries below the `.java` files for the classes you have created.
2. Right-click the Libraries folder and choose Add Library. The Add Library dialog appears.
3. Choose Apache XML-RPC 3.1.3 and click OK.

20

The five JAR files comprising this class library appear under Libraries in the pane.

After the library is set up, an `import` statement makes it easy to refer to the classes in a package, as in this example:

```
import org.apache.xmlrpc.*;
```

This makes it possible to refer to the classes in the main package, `org.apache.xmlrpc`, without using the full package name. You'll work with this package in the next two sections.

Using an XML-RPC Web Service

An XML-RPC client is a program that connects to a server, calls a method on a program on that server, and stores the result.

Using Apache XML-RPC, the process is comparable to calling any other method in Java. You don't have to create an XML request, parse an XML response, or connect to the server using one of Java's networking classes.

In the `org.apache.xmlrpc.client` package, the `XmlRpcClient` class represents a client. The client is set up with the `XmlRpcClientConfigImpl` class, which holds the configuration settings for the client.

The server is set by calling the configuration object's `setServerURL(URL)` method with a URL object that contains the server's address and port number.

After configuration is complete, the client's `setConfig()` method is called with that configuration as the only argument.

The following statements create a client to an XML-RPC client on the host `cadenhead.org` at the port 4413:

```
XmlRpcClientConfigImpl config = new XmlRpcClientConfigImpl();
URL server = new URL("http://cadenhead.org:4413/");
config.setServerURL(server);
XmlRpcClient client = new XmlRpcClient();
client.setConfig(config);
```

If you are calling a remote method with any arguments, they should be stored in an `ArrayList` object, a data structure that holds objects of different classes.

NOTE

> Array lists were covered on Day 8, "Data Structures." They are part of the `java.util` package.

To work with array lists, call the `ArrayList()` constructor with no arguments and call its `add(Object)` method with each object that should be added to the list. Objects can be of any class and must be added to the list in the order in which they are called in the remote method.

The following data types can be arguments to a remote method:

- `byte[]` arrays for `base64` data
- `Boolean` objects for `boolean` values

- Date objects for dateTime.iso8601 values
- Double objects for double values
- Integer objects for int values
- String objects for string values
- HashMap objects for struct values
- ArrayList objects for arrays

The Date, HashMap, and ArrayList classes are in the java.util package.

For example, if an XML-RPC server has a method that takes String and Double arguments, the following code creates an array list that holds each argument:

```
String code = "conical";
Double xValue = new Double(175);
ArrayList parameters = new ArrayList();
parameters.add(code);
parameters.add(xValue);
```

To call the remote method on the XML-RPC server, call the XmlRpcClient object's execute() method with two arguments:

- The name of the method
- The array list that holds the method's arguments

The name of the method should be specified without any parentheses or arguments. An XML-RPC server usually documents the methods that it makes available to the public.

The execute() method returns an Object that contains the response. This object should be cast to one of the data types sent to a method as arguments: Boolean, byte[], Date, Double, Integer, String, HashMap, or ArrayList.

Like other networking methods in Java, execute() throws an XmlRpcException exception that is thrown if the server reports an XML-RPC error.

Objects returned by the execute() method have the following data types: Boolean for boolean XML-RPC values, byte[] for base64 data, Date for dateTime.iso8601 data, Double for double values, Integer for int (or i4) values, String for strings, HashMap for struct values, and ArrayList for arrays.

To see all this in a working program, enter the code shown in Listing 20.3 into your text editor and save the file as SiteClient.java.

20

LISTING 20.3   The Full Text of SiteClient.java

```
 1: import java.io.*;
 2: import java.net.*;
 3: import java.util.*;
 4: import org.apache.xmlrpc.*;
 5: import org.apache.xmlrpc.client.*;
 6:
 7: public class SiteClient {
 8:     public static void main(String arguments[]) {
 9:         SiteClient client = new SiteClient();
10:         try {
11:             HashMap<String, String> response = client.getRandomSite();
12:             // Report the results
13:             if (response.size() > 0) {
14:                 System.out.println("URL: " + response.get("url")
15:                     + "\nTitle: " + response.get("title")
16:                     + "\nDescription: " + response.get("description"));
17:             }
18:         } catch (IOException ioe) {
19:             System.out.println("IO Exception: " + ioe.getMessage());
20:         } catch (XmlRpcException xre) {
21:             System.out.println("XML-RPC Exception: " + xre.getMessage());
22:         }
23:     }
24:
25:     public HashMap getRandomSite()
26:       throws IOException, XmlRpcException {
27:
28:             // Create the client
29:             XmlRpcClientConfigImpl config = new XmlRpcClientConfigImpl();
30:             URL server = new URL("http://localhost:4413/");
31:             config.setServerURL(server);
32:             XmlRpcClient client = new XmlRpcClient();
33:             client.setConfig(config);
34:             // Create the parameters for the request
35:             ArrayList params = new ArrayList();
36:             // Send the request and get the response
37:             HashMap result = (HashMap) client.execute("dmoz.getRandomSite",
38:                 params);
39:             return result;
40:     }
41: }
```

The SiteClient application connects to the **XML-RPC** server and calls the dmoz. getRandomSite() method on the server with no arguments. When it works, this method returns a HashMap that contains the site's URL, title, and description in strings with the keys "url", "title", and "description".

This class can be run, but it won't work because the XML-RPC server hasn't been implemented yet.

NOTE

> These random sites are culled from the database of the Open Directory Project, a directory of more than five million sites at www.dmoz.org. The project's data is available for redistribution by others at no cost under the terms of the Open Directory License. For more information, visit www.dmoz.org/help/getdata.html.

Creating an XML-RPC Web Service

An XML-RPC server is a program that receives a request from a client, calls a method in response to that request, and returns the result. The server maintains a list of methods that it allows clients to call; these are different Java classes called *handlers*.

Apache XML-RPC handles all the XML and networking itself, enabling you to focus on the task you want a remote method to accomplish.

There are several ways to serve methods remotely. The simplest is to use the WebServer class in the org.apache.xmlrpc.webserver package, which represents a simple HTTP web server that responds to only XML-RPC requests.

This class has two constructors:

- WebServer(*int*) creates a web server listening on the specified port number.
- WebServer(*int*, *InetAddress*) creates a web server at the specified port and IP address. The second argument is an object of the java.net.InetAddress class.

Both constructors throw IOException exceptions if an input/output problem occurs with creating and starting the server.

The web server has an XmlRpcServer object associated with it that handles tasks related to the protocol. This class is in another package, org.apache.xmlrpc.server. Call the web server's getXmlRpcServer() method with no arguments to retrieve it.

The following statements create a web server on port 4413 and an object for its XML-RPC server:

```
WebServer server = new WebServer(4413);
XmlRpcServer xmlRpcServer = server.getXmlRpcServer();
```

20

The web server does not contain the remote methods that clients call via XML-RPC. These reside in handlers.

Handlers are set up by another class in the `org.apache.xmlrpc.server` package, `PropertyHandlerMapping`. This class contains configuration settings for an XML-RPC server, which can be set with a properties file or by calling its methods. It can be created with no arguments to the constructor:

```
PropertyHandlerMapping phm = new PropertyHandlerMapping();
```

To add a handler, call the mapping object's `addHandler(String, Object)` method with two arguments.

The first argument to `addHandler()` is a name to give the handler, which can be anything you choose. Naming an XML-RPC method is comparable to naming a variable. Clients will use this name when calling remote methods.

The SiteClient application created earlier today called the remote method `dmoz.getRandomSite()`. The first part of this call—the text preceding the period—refers to a handler given the name `dmoz`.

The second argument to `addHandler()` is a `Class` object for the handler's class.

These statements add a handler named dmoz to the XML-RPC server's property mapping and then set the server to use that configuration:

```
phm.addHandler("dmoz", DmozHandlerImpl.class);
xmlRpcServer.setHandlerMapping(phm);
```

The `DmozHandlerImpl` class is the one that implements the `getRandomSite()` method and any others that can be called remotely over XML-RPC. You'll create this class in a moment.

A class that handles remote method calls can be any Java class that contains `public` methods that return a value, as long as the methods take arguments that correspond with data types supported by Apache XML-RPC: `boolean`, `byte[]`, `Date`, `double`, `HashMap`, `int`, `String`, and `ArrayList`.

You can put existing Java classes to use as XML-RPC handlers without modification as long as they do not contain `public` methods that should not be called and each `public` method returns a suitable value.

CAUTION — The suitability of return values relates to the Apache XML-RPC implementation rather than XML-RPC itself. Other implementations of the protocol are likely to have some differences in the data types of the arguments they take in remote method calls and the values they return.

Using Apache XML-RPC, the web server allows any public method in the handler to be called, so you should use access control to keep prying clients out of methods that should remain off limits.

As the first step toward creating an XML-RPC service, the following code creates a simple web server that takes XML-RPC requests. In NetBeans, use Listing 20.4 to create the DmozServer application.

LISTING 20.4   The Full Text of DmozServer.java

```
 1: import java.io.*;
 2: import org.apache.xmlrpc.*;
 3: import org.apache.xmlrpc.server.*;
 4: import org.apache.xmlrpc.webserver.*;
 5:
 6: public class DmozServer {
 7:     public static void main(String[] arguments) {
 8:         try {
 9:             startServer();
10:         } catch (IOException ioe) {
11:             System.out.println("Server error: " +
12:                 ioe.getMessage());
13:         } catch (XmlRpcException xre) {
14:             System.out.println("XML-RPC error: " +
15:                 xre.getMessage());
16:         }
17:     }
18:
19:     public static void startServer() throws IOException, XmlRpcException {
20:         // Create the server
21:         System.out.println("Starting Dmoz server ...");
22:         WebServer server = new WebServer(4413);
23:         XmlRpcServer xmlRpcServer = server.getXmlRpcServer();
24:         PropertyHandlerMapping phm = new PropertyHandlerMapping();
25:
26:         // Register the handler
27:         phm.addHandler("dmoz", DmozHandlerImpl.class);
```

20

LISTING 20.4 Continued

```
28:            xmlRpcServer.setHandlerMapping(phm);
29:
30:            // Start the server
31:            server.start();
32:            System.out.println("Accepting requests ...");
33:        }
34: }
```

This class can't be compiled successfully until you have created the handler class `DmozHandlerImpl` and a `DmozHandler` interface that it implements.

The DmozServer application creates a web server at port 4413 and an associated XML-RPC server in lines 22 and 23.

Using the server's property mapping, a handler is added to the server: a `DmozHandlerImpl` object given the name `"dmoz"`. The server's `start()` method is called to begin listening for requests.

That's all the code required to implement a functional XML-RPC server. Most of the work is in the remote methods you want a client to call. They don't require any special techniques as long as they are public and return a suitable value.

To give you a complete example you can test and modify to suit your own needs, the `DmozHandler` interface and `DmozHandlerImpl` class are provided in the next two listings.

The `DmozHandler` interface defines the public methods that can be called remotely over XML-RPC. Create a new empty Java file of this class name and fill it with Listing 20.5.

LISTING 20.5 The Full Text of `DmozHandler.java`

```
1: import java.util.*;
2:
3: public interface DmozHandler {
4:     public HashMap getRandomSite();
5: }
```

This interface contains one method, `getRandomSite()`, which returns a `HashMap`. No other methods can be called.

The `DmozHandlerImpl` class is an implementation of the `DmozHandler` interface.

The techniques employed in this class were covered during Day 18, "Accessing Databases with JDBC 4.1 and Derby." They are a good review of how to use JDBC to retrieve records from a database—in this example, a MySQL database called `cool`.

Enter the code shown in Listing 20.6 in NetBeans as the class DmozHandlerImpl.

LISTING 20.6   The Full Text of DmozHandlerImpl.java

```
 1: import java.sql.*;
 2: import java.util.*;
 3:
 4: public class DmozHandlerImpl implements  DmozHandler {
 5:
 6:     public HashMap getRandomSite() {
 7:         Connection conn = getMySqlConnection();
 8:         HashMap<String, String> response = new HashMap<>();
 9:         try {
10:             Statement st = conn.createStatement();
11:             ResultSet rec = st.executeQuery(
12:                 "SELECT * FROM cooldata ORDER BY RAND() LIMIT 1");
13:             if (rec.next()) {
14:                 response.put("url", rec.getString("url"));
15:                 response.put("title", rec.getString("title"));
16:                 response.put("description", rec.getString("description"));
17:             } else {
18:                 response.put("error", "no database record found");
19:             }
20:         } catch (SQLException sqe) {
21:             response.put("error", sqe.getMessage());
22:         }
23:         return response;
24:     }
25:
26:     private Connection getMySqlConnection() {
27:         Connection conn = null;
28:         String data = "jdbc:mysql://localhost/cool";
29:         try {
30:             Class.forName("com.mysql.jdbc.Driver");
31:             conn = DriverManager.getConnection(
32:                 data, "cool", "mrfreeze");
33:         } catch (SQLException s) {
34:             System.out.println("SQL Error: " + s.toString() + " "
35:                 + s.getErrorCode() + " " + s.getSQLState());
36:         } catch (Exception e) {
37:             System.out.println("Error: " + e.toString()
38:                 + e.getMessage());
39:         }
40:         return conn;
41:     }
42: }
```

20

Lines 28–32 of the DmozHandlerImpl application should be changed to reflect your own database, username, and password. In this class, a MySQL database named cool is accessed on the local computer with the username cool and the password mrfreeze. You also might need to change the rest of the string used to connect to the database, depending on your driver.

When the server is up and running, you can run `SiteClient` to see the data from a randomly selected website:

Output ▼

```
URL: http://www.oscommerce.com/
Title: osCommerce
Description: A free online shop program featuring order history,
shopping carts, full search capability, product reviews, secure
transactions, bestseller lists, and related items
```

NOTE
Running this particular XML-RPC server also requires a database. To download a MySQL database containing information on 1,000 websites from the Open Directory Project, visit this book's website at www.java21days.com and open the Day 20 page. The database is in a file named `dmozdata.dat` and is a text file of SQL commands that can be used to create the database on a MySQL server.

Summary

XML-RPC has been described as the "lowest common denominator" of remote procedure call protocols, but this isn't considered an insult by its originators. Most attempts to facilitate software communication over a network have been sophisticated, scaring off developers who have simpler needs.

The XML-RPC protocol can be used to exchange information with any software that supports HTTP, the *lingua franca* of the Web, and XML, a highly popular, structured format for data.

By looking at XML-RPC requests and responses, you should be able to figure out how to use the protocol even without reading the protocol specification.

However, as implementations such as Apache XML-RPC become more extensive, you can begin using it quickly without ever looking at the protocol.

Q&A

Q **When I try to return a `String` array from a remote method, Apache XML-RPC responds with an `XmlRpcException` that states that the object is not supported. Which objects does it support?**

A Apache XML-RPC returns the following data types: `Boolean` for `boolean` XML-RPC values, `byte[]` for `base64` data, `Date` for `dateTime.iso8601` data, `Double` for `double` values, `Integer` for `int` (or `i4`) values, `String` for strings, `HashMap` for `struct` values, or `ArrayList` for arrays.

These are specific to Apache XML-RPC. Other class libraries that support this format may work with different data types and classes in Java. Consult the documentation for those libraries.

Q **I'm writing an XML-RPC client to call a method that returns binary data (`base64`, in other words). The `execute()` method of `XmlRpcClient` returns an object instead of an array of bytes. How do I convert this?**

A Arrays are objects in Java, so you can use casting to convert the object returned by `execute()` to an array of bytes (assuming that the object really is an array). The following statement accomplishes this on an object named `fromServer` that contains a byte array:

```
byte[] data = (byte[]) fromServer;
```

Quiz

Review today's material by taking this three-question quiz. Answers are at the end of the book.

Questions

1. Which popular Internet protocol does XML-RPC not require?

    A. HTML

    B. HTTP

    C. XML

2. Which XML-RPC data type would be best suited to hold the number 8.67?

    A. `boolean`

    B. `double`

    C. `int`

20

3. Which XML tag indicates that the data is an XML-RPC request?

  A. methodCall

  B. methodResponse

  C. params

Certification Practice

The following question is the kind of thing you could expect to be asked on a Java programming certification test. Answer it without looking at today's material or using the Java compiler to test the code.

Given:

```
public class Operation {
    public static void main(String[] arguments) {
        int x = 1;
        int y = 3;
        if ((x != 1) && (y++ == 3))
            y = y + 2;
    }
}
```

What is the final value of y?

  A. 3

  B. 4

  C. 5

  D. 6

The answer is available on the book's website at www.java21days.com. Visit the Day 20 page and click the Certification Practice link.

Exercises

To extend your knowledge of the subjects covered today, try the following exercises:

1. The programming site Advogato offers an XML-RPC interface to read member diaries at www.advogato.org/xmlrpc.html. Write an application that reads a member's last 10 diary entries.

2. The XML-RPC interface for the weblog update service Weblogs.com is at www.weblogs.com/api.html. Write a client and server that can send and receive the `weblogUpdates.ping` method.

Where applicable, exercise solutions are offered on the book's website at www.java21days.com.

20

DAY 21
Writing Android Apps with Java

Once viewed primarily as a language for programs on a web page, Java has established itself as a powerful general-purpose programming language that can be run on desktop computers, Internet servers, tablets, appliances, and many other platforms. One platform in particular has in the past five years become an exciting and commercially lucrative area for new Java development: Android.

The Android operating system began on cell phones and quickly became the brains for a large number of other devices. All programs on Android are written in Java.

These programs, which are called apps, are developed on a free open source mobile OS that's enormously popular. Android does not require costly development tools, licensing fees, or approval by the OS developer. Anyone can create, distribute, and sell apps.

On this final day of the book, you learn about the history of Android, the things that have made it a success, and what it takes to develop programs for this OS. You learn how to create apps and run them on Android devices and emulators.

Today, these topics are covered:

- Why Android was created
- How to code your first app
- How to organize an app
- How to design the app's user interface
- How to deploy an app on emulators
- How to deploy an app on an Android phone

The History of Android

In 2007, Google launched Android in collaboration with several other tech companies and mobile phone manufacturers. They hoped to establish a new mobile platform to challenge the dominance of the Apple iPhone and RIM BlackBerry in that space. Unlike those devices, Android was designed to be open, nonproprietary, and easy for third parties to participate in. Google, Intel, Nvidia, Samsung, Sprint Nextel, and 29 other companies formed the Open Handset Alliance to promote the new platform.

Google released at no cost the Android Software Development Kit (SDK), a set of tools for developing apps that run on the OS. The T-Mobile G1, which was released in June 2008, was the first phone running Android to hit the market.

Once considered an also-ran in mobile computing, Android exploded in popularity in 2010 to rival the iPhone. Today, all major phone carriers offer Android phones, and the market for tablets and e-book readers is growing rapidly. In the first quarter of 2012, 59 percent of all new mobile phones were running Android, according to IDC.

Before Android came along, mobile software development required expensive programming tools and private developer programs. The phone makers had the power to decide who could create apps for them and what apps could be sold to their users.

Because of Android's opensource, nonproprietary nature, anyone can create and distribute apps on the platform. There's a nominal cost to submit apps to Google's app marketplace, but everything else is free.

The central hub of Android programming is the Android Developer site at http://developer.android.com. Visit it to find out more about writing software for the OS and to download the Android SDK. This site provides documentation for every class in Android's Java Class Library, tutorials for beginners, and an online reference.

Writing Android apps requires an integrated development environment (IDE) that supports the Android SDK. Although NetBeans from Oracle can be used to create apps, most programmers use another free and open source IDE called Eclipse. The standard version of Eclipse does not support Android, but an Android Plug-in for Eclipse is available that incorporates the SDK's functionality into the IDE.

Eclipse can be used to write Android apps, test them in an emulator that acts like an Android device, and deploy them on the real thing.

The Java language has been used primarily to write software that runs on a desktop computer, web server, or web browser. Android puts the language everywhere. The apps you create can be deployed on millions of phones, tablets, and other mobile devices, going with your users everywhere they go.

When James Gosling created Java while he worked at Sun Microsystems in the '90s, the company wanted it to be a language for devices such as phones, smart cards, and appliances. Its slogan was "Write once, run everywhere."

That lofty goal was set aside when the language rose to prominence first as a way to put interactive programs on web pages and then as a general-purpose language for desktop computers and servers.

Thanks to Android, that goal has been met. One industry estimate is that the operating system is running a billion Java programs on its devices around the world.

Let's make that count one billion and one.

Writing an Android App

Android apps are Java programs that use an application framework, a set of classes and files that make the job easier as long as you follow all the rules. You've already used a framework, Swing, to create graphical user interfaces. The Android SDK provides a framework that lays down a set of rules for how apps must be structured to run properly on Android devices.

Before you can write apps, you must install and configure three things: the Android SDK, Eclipse IDE, and Android Plug-in for Eclipse.

If you've never done any Android programming, you can download and configure these tools by reading Appendix C, "Setting Up an Android Development Environment."

As soon as you have those tools installed, you can get started.

Today's first project is Palindrome, an app that displays a line of text on an Android device.

After running Eclipse, look for the menu command File, New, Android Project. If you don't see this command, follow these steps:

1. Choose File, New, Other. A dialog opens listing wizards for creating things in the IDE.
2. Expand the Android folder, and choose Android Project.
3. In the Project Name field, enter `Temporary` and click Next.
4. In the next dialog, click Next.
5. In the Package Name field, enter `com.example` and click Finish.

21

Creating this dummy project serves the purpose of adding Android projects as an option on the File menu. You can now delete it: In the Package Explorer, right-click the Temporary folder and choose Delete from the pop-up menu. You'll be asked to confirm the deletion.

To begin the Palindrome project, follow these steps:

1. Choose File, New, Android Project. The New Android Project Wizard opens, as shown in Figure 21.1.

FIGURE 21.1
Starting a new Android project in Eclipse.

2. In the Project Name field, enter Palindrome.

3. Select Create New Project in Workspace.

4. The Use Default Location checkbox affects where this project will be stored on your computer. If the default is acceptable, keep this box selected. If not, deselect it, click Browse, and choose a folder for the project.

5. Click Next.

6. Every project requires a build target, which is the oldest version of the Android OS that can run the app. Because new Android releases have new capabilities, the target indicates the features that Eclipse will enable.

You might have only one target, which must be selected. If you have a choice, any target from Android 2.2 up is suitable.

7. Click Next.

8. In the Application name field, keep the name `Palindrome`.

9. Android projects must belong to a Java package. In the Package name field, enter `org.cadenhead.android`.

10. The Create Activity check box determines whether the new app is created with an `Activity` class. An activity is a task the app performs. Keep this check box selected and keep `PalindromeActivity` as its name.

11. Click Finish.

Eclipse creates the new app, and a Palindrome folder appears in the Package Explorer pane.

Organizing an Android Project

The Java programs you created in past days were made up primarily of class files. Sometimes a class needed the data in a file, such as a graphics file that contained a button icon or a text file read from an input stream.

Android projects always require external files. A new project is composed of about 20 files and folders, which are organized into a fixed folder structure. You can add files to those folders, but the starting files and folders must be present, or the app won't compile.

You can use the Eclipse Package Explorer, shown in Figure 21.2, to examine how a new Android project is organized.

In the Package Explorer, expand folders to familiarize yourself with the files and folders that a starting project contains. A new app such as Palindrome has these starting components:

- `/src` folder—The app's Java source code that you create.
- `/src/org.cadenhead.android/PalindromeActivity.java`—The activity class that automatically launches when the app runs.
- `/gen` folder—Java source code that the framework creates automatically. You must not edit these files.
- `/gen/org.cadenhead.android/BuildConfig.java`—The app's debugging configuration source code (do not edit).
- `/gen/org.cadenhead.android/R.java`—The app's resource management source code (do not edit).

21

FIGURE 21.2
Viewing the components of an Android project.

- `/assets`—File resources stored externally rather than being compiled into the app.

- `/res`—Application resources, which include animation, graphics, layout files, numbers, and strings. Subfolders `layout`, `values`, `drawable-hdpi`, `drawable-ldpi`, `drawable-mdpi`, and `drawable-xhdpi` hold specific resource types. These folders contain six resource files: four versions of `ic_launcher.png`, `main.xml`, and `strings.xml`.

- `AndroidManifest.xml`—The app's configuration file.

- `project.properties`—A build file generated by the Android Plug-in (do not edit).

These files and folders, along with a few others not described here, comprise the app framework. The first thing an Android programmer must learn is what each of these components does and how they can be edited to create an app.

You can add files to the folders of the framework to create new functionality. For example, if an app has additional screens, they are added to the `/res/layout` folder.

Creating the Program

This framework can be run successfully as an app, but it wouldn't be much to look at, because nothing has been done to it yet.

The Palindrome app needs to be edited to display a palindrome, a sentence that reads the same forwards and backwards.

Java programs can display strings with the method `System.out.println(String)`, where literals and variables can be used as the argument and concatenated. In Android apps, strings to be displayed are first saved in the resource file `strings.xml`, which is in the folder `/res/values`.

With the Package Explorer, find and expand this folder. Then double-click `strings.xml` to open it in the Resources editor, shown in Figure 21.3.

FIGURE 21.3
Creating an app's string resources.

strings.xml

Strings and other resources have a name and a value, comparable to Java variables. Two string resources appear in the Resources elements pane: `hello` and `app_name`. Resource names must be lowercase, can contain no spaces, and can use only the underscore character (_) as punctuation.

To edit one of these strings, click its name. Name and Value text fields appear, along with some guidance on how to edit strings.

In Figure 21.3, the `app_name` string resource is open for editing. The value of this resource, which defines the app's display name, was defined by the New Android Project wizard. You can change it at any time by opening this resource and editing the Value field.

21

The `hello` string resource contains text that is displayed on the app's main screen, which at this point is its only screen.

Click `hello` to edit this resource.

In the Value field, enter `Sit on a Potato Pan, Otis!`.

Android app resources such as `app_name` and `hello` are stored in XML files. The Resources editor is a simple XML editor. You also can directly edit the XML itself. Click the strings.xml tab at the bottom of the editor, shown in Figure 21.3, to load this file for direct editing.

Here's `strings.xml` in XML format:

Output ▼

```
<?xml version="1.0" encoding="utf-8"?>
<resources>
    <string name="hello">Sit on a Potato Pan, Otis!</string>
    <string name="app_name">Palindrome</string>
</resources>
```

Everything in this XML file can be edited. You can give `app_name` a new value by replacing `Palindrome` with new text. You also can change the XML tags within the < and > characters. Each `string` element's name attribute defines the name of a string resource. The value is the character data contained within the opening and closing `string` tags.

CAUTION

Editing XML directly like this is much more error-prone than using the Resources editor. Making one typo in a tag causes the app to fail to compile. The only time you might want to edit XML is when Eclipse doesn't support something you need to define in a resource. This is never the case with strings, so use the Resources editor to create and modify them.

To return to the Resources editor, click the Resources tab along the bottom edge of the editor. Click the Save button in the Eclipse toolbar or choose File, Save to save the change you made to `strings.xml`.

Before you can build and run an Android app, you must set up a debugging environment.

Using an Android Emulator

An Android Virtual Device (AVD) is an emulator that pretends it is a mobile device running the OS. The emulation isn't perfect—you can't make real phone calls on this fake Android, for instance—but it can simulate a lot of other capabilities. After you have chosen (or created) an emulator and a debug configuration, you can build the Palindrome app and have the emulator run it.

To create an Android Virtual Device, click the Android Virtual Device Manager icon in the Eclipse toolbar, shown in Figure 21.4.

FIGURE 21.4
Configuring an
Android Virtual
Device (AVD).

Android Virtual Device Manager

The manager launches with a dialog listing all virtual devices you have created (if any). To add a new emulator, follow these steps:

1. Click New. The Create new Android Virtual Device dialog opens, as shown in Figure 21.5.

FIGURE 21.5
Creating an emula-
tor to run apps.

2. In the Name field, enter StarterAVD.

3. In the Target drop-down, choose the version of Android the virtual device will run. Any version from Android 2.2 or higher is suitable.

4. In the Size field, enter 1024 as the size of the device's fake SD card and keep MiB as the choice in the associated drop-down. This creates an SD card that is 1024MB in size. Your hard drive must have this much available space. The minimum permitted size is 9MB.

5. Click Create AVD. The new emulator is created, which might take a little while (no longer than a minute, generally).

You can create more than one emulator, each with a different version of Android. Close the manager to return to the main Eclipse interface.

Creating a Debug Configuration

One more task is required before you can launch the Palindrome app. You must create a debug configuration for your app in Eclipse by following these steps:

1. Choose Run, Debug Configurations. The Debug Configurations window appears, as shown in Figure 21.6.

Android Application

FIGURE 21.6
Creating a
new debug
configuration.

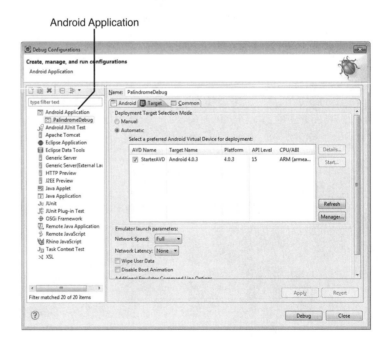

2. In the pane on the left, double-click Android Application. A new entry called New_configuration is created under that item. The pane on the right presents configuration settings for the new item.

3. In the pane on the right, change the Name field from New_configuration to PalindromeDebug.

4. Click Browse. The Project Selection dialog opens.

5. Choose the project Palindrome and then click OK.

6. Click the Target tab to bring it to the front.

7. Under Deployment Target Selection Mode, choose Automatic.

8. In the table listing virtual devices, select the StarterAVD emulator you just created.

9. Click Apply to save your changes and then click Close.

Running the App

With your newly created Android emulator and debug configuration, you finally can run your first app. Click the Palindrome folder in the Package Explorer and then click the Debug icon in the Eclipse toolbar. (It looks like a green bug.)

The Android emulator loads in its own window, which may take a minute or more, depending on how fast your computer is. The first thing that loads is a screen that displays an animated Android logo while the emulator continues to load the OS.

The emulator displays "Palindrome" in the app's title bar and one line of text on the app's screen, "Sit on a Potato Pan, Otis!," as shown in Figure 21.7. Controls to the right of the screen let you use the emulator like a phone with the mouse. You also can click the screen, although in this app there's nothing to click.

Click the Back button to close the Palindrome app and try out your new fake Android phone.

An emulator can simulate many things, such as connecting to the Internet over the computer's current connection and receiving phone calls and SMS messages.

Because it's not a real device, the apps you create must be tested on real Android phones and other devices to be sure they work.

If you have an Android device that you connect to your computer over a USB cord, you can run apps you've created when the device is set to debugging mode. The apps are deployed on the phone over USB and appear as if they were added in the Android marketplace.

21

FIGURE 21.7

Running an app in an emulator.

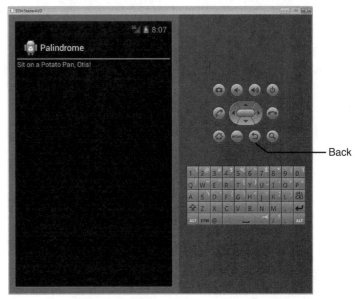

Back

On the device, enter debugging mode by choosing Home, Settings, Applications, Development. The Development settings are shown. Choose the USB debugging option.

In Eclipse, do the following:

1. Choose Run, Debug Configurations. The Debug Configurations dialog opens.
2. Click the Target tab to bring it to the front.
3. Change Deployment Target Selection Mode from Automatic to Manual.
4. Click Apply.
5. Click Close.

Connect your Android device to the computer with the USB cord. An Android bug icon should appear on the device's screen along the top edge. If you drag down this bar, you should see the message "USB Debugging Connected" (or something similar).

Back in Eclipse, click the Debug icon in the toolbar. The Android Device Chooser dialog opens, as shown in Figure 21.8.

If the Android phone has been connected successfully, it appears in the top table in Figure 21.8 under the Choose a running Android device option. Select the option, click the device, and then click OK. The app appears on the phone and runs automatically.

Even after you disconnect the USB cord, the app will be on your phone and can be run.

FIGURE 21.8
Deploying an app
on an Android
phone.

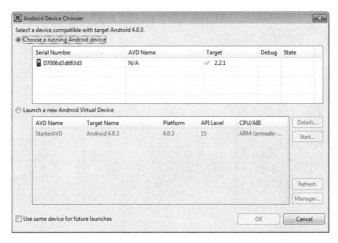

Designing an Android App

Android apps can make use of SMS messaging, location-based services, touch screen input, and the rest of the device's functionality. For a final programming project, you create an app that can make a phone call, visit a website with the browser, and load a location using Google Maps.

Create a new project in Eclipse by following these steps:

1. Select File, New, Android Project. The New Android Project wizard appears.
2. In the Project Name field, enter `Santa`.
3. Select Create New Project in Workspace and click Next.
4. Choose a Build Target in the table and click Next.
5. In the Application Name field, enter `Contact Santa Claus`, as shown in Figure 21.9.
6. In the Package Name field, enter `org.cadenhead.android`.
7. Make sure that Create Activity is checked and that `SantaActivity` is entered in the adjacent text field.
8. Click Finish.

The project appears in the Eclipse Package Explorer below the Palindrome project. To close Palindrome so that it's easier to work with the new project, right-click Palindrome in Package Explorer and choose Close Project.

The folder icon for Palindrome now appears closed. You can reopen the project by double-clicking the icon.

21

FIGURE 21.9
Creating a new
project.

Preparing Resources

Although Android apps are Java programs, a lot of the work required to create them is done in the Eclipse interface. You can accomplish many things in the Android SDK without writing Java code.

One thing you accomplish without programming is creating resources the app needs.

As shown earlier today, every new Android project begins with several folders and sub-folders that contain resources. To examine these folders, expand the Santa folder in the Package Explorer and then expand /res and all its subfolders, as shown in Figure 21.10.

The project's starting resources are several graphics files, strings in strings.xml, and graphical user interface layout files that also are in XML format. Graphics must be in PNG, JPG, or GIF format. Two additional XML files that often are added to apps are colors.xml, which defines colors used in the app, and dimens.xml, which holds dimensional measurements for text and other things that can be displayed in the app.

The /res folder contains the folders drawable-hdpi, drawable-mdpi, drawable-lpdi, and drawable-xhdpi, each containing a version of the file ic_launcher.png. This is the app's icon, the small graphic that represents it in application menus on an Android device. Each folder is for graphics of different screen resolutions.

FIGURE 21.10
Examining an
app's resources.

Because you won't be using these icons, you can delete them. Right-click the icon's file in Package Explorer and choose Delete. You must confirm each deletion to remove the file.

When these files are gone, red Xs appear in two places in Package Explorer—on the Santa folder and on `AndroidManifest.xml`, as shown in Figure 21.11. These Xs flag errors that prevent the app from compiling.

These errors were flagged because every app requires an icon. A new graphics file, `santa.png`, must be brought into the project and designated as its icon in `AndroidManifest.xml`, the file that holds the app's configuration settings.

This book's website contains `santa.png` and four other graphics files needed by this app: `browser.png`, `maps.png`, `northpole.png`, and `phone.png`. Load www.java21days.com in your browser, open the site for this edition of the book and click the Day 21 link. The graphics files are linked on this page. Download all five and save them to a folder on your computer (or the desktop).

Android's support for multiple resolutions is important for optimizing an app for different devices, but for this project it would be overkill. Instead of using the four current `drawable` folders, a new one is created.

FIGURE 21.11
Fixing errors in
an app.

Errors —

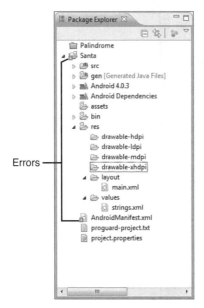

Follow these steps:

1. Click the /res folder in Package Explorer.
2. Choose File, New, Folder. The New Folder dialog appears.
3. In the Folder Name field, enter drawable.
4. Click Finish.

A new drawable folder appears inside /res. All graphics used in the Santa app are stored here rather than creating different versions for different screen resolutions.

You can add files to an Android project in Eclipse using drag and drop. Open the folder where the five files for this app were downloaded from the book's website, select them, drag them to the drawable folder in Package Explorer and drop them there.

A File Operation dialog asks whether you want to copy the files in the folder or link to them. Choose the Copy Files option and click OK.

CAUTION

Resource filenames can contain only lowercase letters, numbers, the underscore character (_), and the period character (.).

Android apps identify resources using their filenames with the extension removed. This becomes the resource's ID, which is how it will be referred to in code. The files dragged into this project have the IDs browser, maps, northpole, phone, and santa. No two resources can have the same ID, except for versions of the same graphics file in the four drawable-*dpi folders, which are treated as a single resource. An app can't be compiled in Eclipse if two resources have the same ID.

Configuring a Manifest File

If one of the new icons imported into the project is made the Santa app's icon, this eliminates the errors flagged by Eclipse in Package Explorer. You can do so by editing the resource file AndroidManifest.xml.

This file contains the app's configuration settings. Like strings.xml, this is an XML file that can be edited manually or with a special editor. The latter is the better choice because it's far less error-prone.

To choose the proper icon for the app, follow these steps:

1. In Package Explorer, double-click AndroidManifest.xml. A form titled Android Manifest opens in the main Eclipse window.

2. Click the Application tab at the bottom of the form. The app's configuration settings are displayed, as shown in Figure 21.12.

FIGURE 21.12
Viewing an app's manifest file.

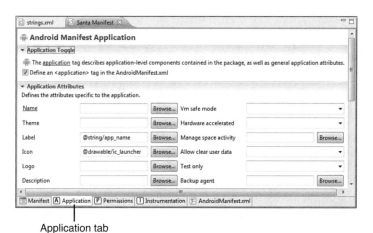

Application tab

21

3. The Icon field sets the app's icon to `@drawable/ic_launcher`, which is erroneous. Click the Browse button next to this field. A Resource Chooser dialog opens with a list of the app's graphics resources.

4. Choose santa and click OK. The Icon field value now is `@drawable/santa`.

5. Click the Save button in the main Eclipse toolbar.

Now that the app has an icon again, the red Xs disappear from the Package Explorer.

Designing the Graphical User Interface

The graphical user interface for an Android app does not use Swing because Android has its own library of user interface widgets. An app's graphical user interface is created as a collection of layouts, which are containers that hold text fields, buttons, graphics, and other widgets.

Each screen displayed to a user can have a single layout or multiple layouts. There are layouts that organize widgets into a table, stack them vertically or horizontally, and arrange them in other ways.

The Santa app has a single screen with buttons to contact Santa.

An app could be presented as multiple screens:

- A splash screen displays while the app loads
- A menu screen contains buttons to access the other screens
- A help screen explains how to use the app
- A credits screen names the app's developer
- A main screen accomplishes the app's purpose

All of an app's screens are stored in the `/res/layout` folder. A new project starts with a `main.xml` file in this folder that's set up to display when the app loads.

To work on this screen layout, double-click `main.xml` in Package Explorer. The screen opens for editing, as shown in Figure 21.13.

Along the left side of the screen editor is a Palette pane with subpanes that can be expanded when you click their names. The user interface widgets in these panes can be dragged onto the screen. The Form Widgets subpane contains several simple widgets.

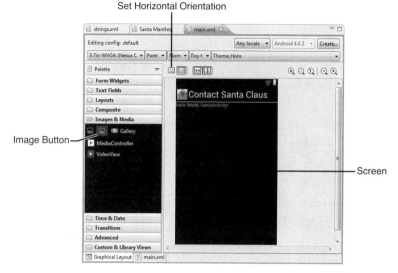

Set Horizontal Orientation

FIGURE 21.13
Editing the
`main.xml` file.

Image Button

Screen

Three graphical buttons, which are called `ImageButton` widgets in Android, must be added to the screen. Follow these steps:

1. Click the widget that contains the text "Hello World, SantaActivity!" A blue rectangle appears around the widget.

2. Press your keyboard's Delete key. The widget is removed.

3. Double-click the Images & Media subpane to expand it.

4. Drag an `ImageButton` widget (shown in Figure 21.13) from the Palette to the screen. A Resource Chooser dialog appears.

5. Choose the resource `phone` and click OK. An image button with a Dialer icon appears.

6. Drag another `ImageButton` widget to the screen. Assign it the resource `browser`. Click OK. A Browser icon appears.

7. Drag a third `ImageButton` to the screen. Assign it `maps`. Click OK. A Maps icon appears. All three icons are stacked as a column.

8. Click the Set Horizontal Orientation button above the screen (see Figure 21.13). The buttons line up in a row.

9. In the Outline pane to the right of the screen editor, double-click the LinearLayout item. The screen's properties appear in the Properties pane.

21

10. Click the value for Background and then click the ... button. The Reference Chooser opens.

11. Expand Drawable, choose northpole, and click OK. The screen's background becomes this graphic, a photo of Santa and his sled.

12. Click the Phone button. The Properties pane appears next to the editor with this widget's properties displayed.

13. Scroll down to the On Click property. In its Value field, enter processClicks (capitalized as shown).

14. Do the same for the Browser button, setting its On Click property to processClicks.

15. Do the same for the Maps button.

16. Click the Save button.

The finished screen is shown in Figure 21.14.

FIGURE 21.14
Viewing an app's user interface.

If you haven't done so lately, click the Save button to avoid losing all this work.

Writing Code

Without writing any Java code, you have completed most of this project. Android app development is much easier when you have learned how to exploit the features of the Android SDK that require no programming.

Apps are organized into activities, which are the tasks an app can perform. Every Activity is a Java class. When you created the Santa app, one of the options you specified was that an activity named SantaActivity should be created. This class runs when the app loads.

The source code for SantaActivity.java is in the /src/org.cadenhead.android folder in the Package Explorer. Double-click this file to open it in the source code editor.

The class starts out with the code shown in Listing 21.1.

LISTING 21.1 The Starting Text of SantaActivity.java

```
 1: package org.cadenhead.android;
 2:
 3: import android.app.Activity;
 4: import android.os.Bundle;
 5:
 6: public class SantaActivity extends Activity {
 7:     /** Called when the activity is first created. */
 8:     @Override
 9:     public void onCreate(Bundle savedInstanceState) {
10:         super.onCreate(savedInstanceState);
11:         setContentView(R.layout.main);
12:     }
13: }
```

If you can't see all the import statements in the editor, click the + character next to import android.app.Activity;.

All activities are subclasses of Activity in the android.app package, which contains the behavior to display a screen, receive user input, and save user preferences.

The onCreate() method defined in lines 9–12 is called when the class loads. The first thing this method does is call the same method in its superclass.

Next, it calls setContentView() to select the layout to display on the screen. The method's argument is the instance variable R.layout.main, which refers to the file main.xml in /res/layout. The ID has the name main because each resource ID is its filename with the extension removed.

The R in R.layout.main refers to R.java, a class in a /res/gen subfolder that the Android SDK creates.

21

While you were creating this app's screen, you set the buttons' On Click property to the value processClicks. This causes a method called processClicks() to be called when a user clicks those widgets.

That method must be implemented in SantaActivity. Below the last line of the onCreate() method, add these statements:

```
public void processClicks(View display) {
    Intent action;
    int id = display.getId();
}
```

This method takes one argument, a View object from the android.view package. Views are visual displays in an app. This particular View is the screen containing the Dialer, Browser, and Maps buttons.

The View object's getId() method returns the ID of the button that was clicked: imageButton1, imageButton2, or imageButton3.

This ID, which is saved in an integer variable named id, can be used in a switch conditional that takes action based on what the user clicks:

```
switch (id) {
    case (R.id.imageButton1):
        // ...
        break;
    case (R.id.imageButton2):
        // ...
        break;
    case (R.id.imageButton3):
        // ...
        break;
    default:
        break;
}
```

The first statement in the processClicks() method declares a variable for an Intent object:

```
Intent action;
```

The `Intent` class in the `android.content` package is how one `Activity` tells another `Activity` to do something. An `Intent` also can be used to communicate with the device running the app.

Three intents are created in the `processClicks()` method, each in a `case` section of the `switch` conditional:

```
action = new Intent(Intent.ACTION_DIAL, Uri.parse(
    "tel:877-446-6723"));
action = new Intent(Intent.ACTION_VIEW, Uri.parse(
    "http://www.noradsanta.org"));
action = new Intent(Intent.ACTION_VIEW, Uri.parse(
    "geo:0,0?q=101 Saint Nicholas Dr., North Pole, AK"));
```

An `Intent()` constructor takes two arguments:

- The action to take, selected by a class variable
- The data associated with the action

The three `Intents` tell the Android device to set up an outgoing phone call to Santa's NORAD hotline at 877-446-6723, visit the website www.noradsanta.org, and load Google Maps with an address at the North Pole.

The `startActivity(Intent)` statement turns an intent into action:

```
startActivity(action);
```

For security reasons, the call is not made by the first intent. Instead, the device's dialer is opened with that number ready to be called.

Listing 21.2 contains the full text of the `SantaActivity` class. Add the `import` statements in lines 3–7 and the `processClicks()` method to what you already have entered. Then double-check the listing to be sure your code matches this listing.

LISTING 21.2   The Full Text of SantaActivity.java

```
 1: package org.cadenhead.android;
 2:
 3: import android.app.Activity;
 4: import android.content.Intent;
 5: import android.net.Uri;
 6: import android.os.Bundle;
 7: import android.view.View;
 8:
 9: public class SantaActivity extends Activity {
10:     public static final String TAG = "Santa";
```

21

LISTING 21.2   Continued

```
11:
12:      /** Called when the activity is first created. */
13:      @Override
14:      public void onCreate(Bundle savedInstanceState) {
15:          super.onCreate(savedInstanceState);
16:          setContentView(R.layout.main);
17:      }
18:
19:      public void processClicks(View display) {
20:          Intent action = null;
21:          int id = display.getId();
22:
23:          switch (id) {
24:              case (R.id.imageButton1):
25:                  action = new Intent(Intent.ACTION_DIAL,
26:                      Uri.parse("tel:877-446-6723"));
27:                  break;
28:              case (R.id.imageButton2):
29:                  action = new Intent(Intent.ACTION_VIEW,
30:                      Uri.parse("http://www.noradsanta.org"));
31:                  break;
32:              case (R.id.imageButton3):
33:                  action = new Intent(Intent.ACTION_VIEW,
34:                      Uri.parse("geo:0,0?q=101 Saint Nicholas Dr., North Pole,
                        AK"));
35:                  break;
36:              default:
37:                  break;
38:          }
39:          startActivity(action);
40:      }
41: }
```

As you save the file, Eclipse automatically compiles the class if there are no errors. Otherwise, red Xs appear in the Package Explorer in any file where an error has been detected.

When there are no errors, you're almost ready to run the app. The last task left is to create a new debug configuration for this project:

1. Click the arrow next to the Debug button in the Eclipse toolbar and choose Debug Configurations. The Debug Configurations dialog appears.

2. Double-click Android Application in the pane on the left to create a new configuration with the name New_configuration.

3. In the Name field, enter SantaDebug.

4. Click Browse, choose the project Santa, and click OK.

5. Click the Target tab.

6. Select Automatic as the Deployment Target Selection Mode.

7. Select StarterAVD as the Android virtual device.

8. Click Apply.

9. Click Close.

The new debug configuration is created.

To run the app, click the arrow next to the Debug button and choose SantaDebug (if it is in the menu).

If not, choose Debug, Debug Configurations, and then choose SantaDebug and click Debug. The Android Device Chooser opens. Select Launch a New Android Virtual Device, select StarterAVD, and click OK.

The emulator loads Android OS and then runs the Santa app.

In the emulator, the app's Dialer and Browser buttons should work, but Maps might have problems.

The app also can be run on an Android device, if you've got one working with the Android SDK and the phone has been set to debugging mode.

Click the arrow next to Debug, and choose SantaDebug. Select Choose a Running Android Device, select your device, and click OK.

Figure 21.15 shows the app running in an emulator. When the phone is shifted from portrait mode to landscape mode, the app shifts accordingly.

NOTE

For more on Android, refer to *Sams Teach Yourself Android Application Development in 24 Hours*, 2nd Edition, by Lauren Darcey and Shane Conder (ISBN 978-0-13-278686-7). The Android Developer site also has an online reference at http://developer. android.com/reference.

FIGURE 21.15
Calling Santa
Claus.

Summary

For the last three weeks, you've had a chance to work with the syntax and the core classes that make up the Java language and the Java Class Library. You've ventured into sophisticated topics such as JDBC, Internet networking, and data structures, and you've explored class libraries such as the XML Object Model library and Android.

Now you are ready to tackle the biggest challenge yet: Turning an empty source code file into a robust and reliable program implemented as a set of Java classes using object-oriented programming.

This book has an official website at www.java21days.com with answers to frequently asked questions, source code for the entire book, error corrections, and supplementary material.

Now get to work on the next billion-dollar tech startup. In your IPO, don't forget the author who was there when you taught yourself Java.

Q&A

Q Do I need to create Android virtual devices for older versions of the Android SDK?

A Probably, because you want an app to run on as many different versions of the Android operating system as possible. A large variety of Android devices are in use today, and not all are being updated to the current OS. Some can't be updated.

To ensure that your app has the widest possible audience, use the Android SDK Manager—available as one of the buttons in the Eclipse toolbar—to install older versions of Android.

Most devices are running Android version 2.1 or higher. Writing an app that works in early versions of Android will restrict the features it can use because new Android capabilities that came out in subsequent releases won't be available.

Quiz

Review today's material by taking this three-question quiz. Answers are at the end of the book.

Questions

1. What Android object enables an app to communicate with the device running the app?

   A. Intent

   B. View

   C. Activity

2. Which resource file contains an app's string resources?

   A. main.xml

   B. strings.xml

   C. R.java

3. Can an app have resource files named icon.gif and icon.png?

   A. Yes

   B. No

   C. Ask again later.

21

Certification Practice

The following question is the kind of thing you could expect to be asked on a Java programming certification test. Answer it without looking at today's material or using the Java compiler to test the code.

Given:

```
public class CharCase {
    public static void main(String[] arguments) {
        float x = 9;
        float y = 5;
        char c = '1';
        switch (c) {
            case 1:
                x = x + 2;
            case 2:
                x = x + 3;
            default:
                x = x + 1;
        }
        System.out.println("Value of x: " + x);
    }
}
```

What will be the value of x when it is displayed?

A. 9.0

B. 10.0

C. 11.0

D. The program will not compile.

The answer is available on the book's website at www.java21days.com. Visit the Day 21 page and click the Certification Practice link.

Exercises

To extend your knowledge of the subjects covered today, try the following exercises:

1. Modify the Palindrome app to display a different palindrome and show a graphic as the screen's background.

2. Modify the Santa app with the phone number, website address, and map location of another famous person.

Where applicable, exercise solutions are offered on the book's website at www.java21days.com.

Appendixes

APPENDIX A

Using the NetBeans Integrated Development Environment

Although it's possible to create Java programs with nothing more than the Java Development Kit and a text editor, the experience is considerably more pleasant when you use an integrated development environment (IDE).

The first 20 days of this book employ NetBeans, a free IDE that Oracle offers to Java programmers. NetBeans is a program that makes it easier to organize, write, compile, and test Java software. It includes a project and file manager, graphical user interface designer, and many other tools. One killer feature is a code editor that automatically detects Java syntax errors as you type.

Now in version 7.1, NetBeans has become a favorite of professional Java developers, offering functionality and performance that used to be available only in commercial development tools at no cost. It's also one of the easiest IDEs for Java novices to use.

In this appendix, you install NetBeans and learn how to use it in projects created in this book.

Installing NetBeans

From inauspicious beginnings, the NetBeans IDE has grown to become one of the leading programming tools for Java developers. James Gosling, creator of the Java language, wrote in the Foreword to *NetBeans Field Guide*: "I use NetBeans for all my Java development." I've become a convert as well.

NetBeans supports all facets of Java programming for the three editions of the language—Java Standard Edition (JSE), Java Enterprise Edition (JEE), and Java Mobile Edition (JME). It also supports web application development, web services, JavaBeans, and Android development.

You can download the software, available for Windows, Mac OS, and Linux, from www.netbeans.org. NetBeans is available for download bundled with the Java Development Kit. Choose this option if you don't already have the kit on your computer.

If you'd like to ensure that you're downloading the same version of NetBeans used to write this book, visit the book's website at www.java21days.com. Click the book's cover to open the site for this edition and then look for the Download JDK and Download NetBeans 7.1 links. You'll be steered to the proper file.

Creating a New Project

The JDK and NetBeans are downloaded as installation wizards that set up the software on your system. You can install the software in any folder and menu group you like, but it's best to stick with the default setup options unless you have a good reason to do otherwise.

When you run NetBeans for the first time after installation, you see a start page that displays links to news, programming tutorials, and blogs, as shown in Figure A.1. You can read these within the IDE using NetBeans' built-in web browser.

A NetBeans project consists of a set of related Java classes, files used by those classes, and Java class libraries. Each project has its own folder. You can explore and modify the files in the folder outside of NetBeans using text editors and other programming tools, like any other Java source code you create outside of NetBeans.

To begin a new project, click the New Project button shown in Figure A.1 or select File, New Project. The New Project Wizard opens, as shown in Figure A.2.

New project

FIGURE A.1
The NetBeans
user interface.

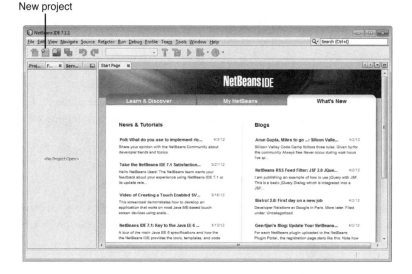

FIGURE A.2
The New Project
Wizard.

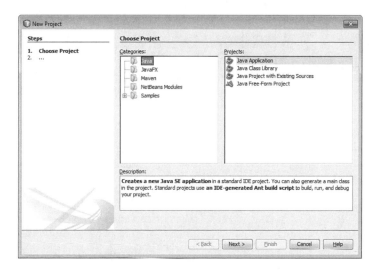

NetBeans can create several different types of Java projects, but during this book you can focus on just one: Java Application.

For your first project (and most of the projects in this book), choose the Java category and the project type Java Application; then click Next. The wizard asks you to choose a name and location for the project.

The Project Location text field identifies the root folder of the programming projects you create with NetBeans. In Windows, this is a subfolder of My Documents called NetBeansProjects. All projects you create are stored inside this folder, each in its own subfolder.

In the Project Name text field, enter Java21. The Create Main Class text box changes in response to the input, recommending java21.Java21 as the name of the main Java class in the project. Change this to Spartacus and click Finish, accepting all other defaults. NetBeans creates the project and its first class.

Creating a New Java Class

When NetBeans creates a new project, it sets up all the necessary files and folders and creates the main class. Figure A.3 shows the first class in your project, Spartacus.java, open in the source editor.

Save All Files

Project pane

FIGURE A.3
The NetBeans
source editor.

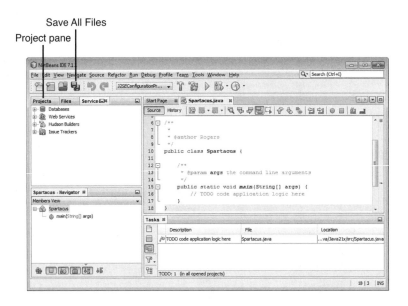

Spartacus.java is a bare-bones Java class that consists of only a main() method. All the light gray lines of code in the class are comments that exist to explain the class's purpose and function. Comments are ignored when the class is run.

To make the new class do something, add the following line of code on a new line right below the comment `// TODO code application logic here`:

```
System.out.println("I am Spartacus!");
```

The method `System.out.println()` displays a string of text—in this case, the sentence "I am Spartacus!"

Be sure to enter this code exactly as it is shown here. As you type, the source editor figures out what you're doing and displays helpful information related to the `System` class, the `out` instance variable, and the `println()` method. You'll love this stuff later, but for now, try your best to ignore it.

After you ensure that you typed the line correctly and ended it with a semicolon, click the Save All Files button on the toolbar to save the class.

Java classes must be compiled into executable bytecode before you can run them. NetBeans tries to compile classes automatically. You also can manually compile this class in two ways:

- Select Run, Compile File.
- Right-click `Spartacus.java` in the Projects pane to open a pop-up menu, and choose Compile File.

If NetBeans doesn't allow you to choose either of these options, NetBeans already has compiled the class.

If the class does not compile successfully, a white exclamation point in a red circle appears next to the filename `Spartacus.java` in the Projects pane. To fix the error, compare what you've typed in the text editor to the full source code of `Spartacus.java`, shown in Listing A.1, and resave the file.

LISTING A.1   The Full Text of `Spartacus.java`

```
 1: /*
 2:  * To change this template, choose Tools | Templates
 3:  * and open the template in the editor.
 4:  */
 5:
 6: /**
 7:  *
```

LISTING A.1 Continued

```
 8:  * @author User
 9:  */
10: public class Spartacus {
11:
12:      /**
13:       * @param args the command line arguments
14:       */
15:      public static void main(String[] args) {
16:          // TODO code application logic here
17:          System.out.println("I am Spartacus!");
18:
19:      }
20:
21: }
```

The class is defined in lines 10–21. Lines 1–9 are comments that NetBeans includes in every new class.

Running the Application

After you've created the Java application Spartacus and compiled it successfully, you can run it within NetBeans in two ways:

- Choose Run, Run File.
- Right-click Spartacus.java in the Projects pane, and choose Run File.

When you run a Java class, the compiler calls its main() method. The string "I am Spartacus!" appears in the Output pane, as shown in Figure A.4.

A Java class must have a main() method to be run. If you attempt to run a class that lacks a main() method, NetBeans responds with an error.

FIGURE A.4
Viewing program
output in the
NetBeans Output
pane.

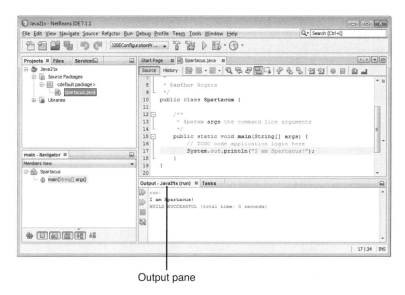

A

Output pane

Fixing Errors

Now that the Spartacus application has been written, compiled, and run, it's time to
break something to get some experience with how NetBeans responds when things go
terribly wrong. Like any Java programmer, you'll soon get plenty of practice screwing up
things on your own, but pay attention here anyway.

Return to Spartacus.java in the source editor, and remove the semicolon from the end
of the line that calls System.out.println() (line 17 in Listing A.1). Even before you
save the file, NetBeans spots the error and displays a red alert icon to the left of the line,
as shown in Figure A.5.

Hover the mouse cursor over the alert icon to see a dialog that describes the error
NetBeans thinks it has spotted.

The NetBeans source editor can identify many common programming errors and typos it
encounters as you write a Java program. It stops the file from being compiled until the
errors have been removed.

FIGURE A.5

Flagging errors in the source editor.

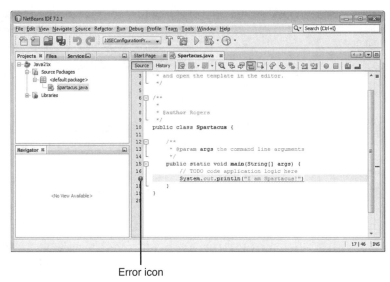

Error icon

Put the semicolon back at the end of the line. The error icon disappears, and you can save and run the class again.

These basic features of NetBeans are all you need to create and compile the Java programs in this book.

NetBeans is capable of a lot more than the features described here, but you should focus on learning Java before diving too deeply into the IDE. Use NetBeans as if it were just a simple project manager and text editor. Write classes, flag errors, and make sure you can compile and run each project successfully.

When you're ready to learn more about NetBeans, Oracle offers training and documentation resources at www.netbeans.org/kb.

APPENDIX B
This Book's Website

As much as I'd like to think otherwise, there are undoubtedly things you're unclear about after completing the 21 days of this book. Programming is a specialized, technical field that throws strange concepts and jargon at new learners, such as "instantiation," "ternary operators," and "big- and little-endian byte order."

If you have a question about any topic covered in the book, visit the book's website at www.java21days.com for assistance. Click the link for this edition of the book to visit its site.

The book's website offers the following:

- **Error corrections and clarifications**—When errors are brought to my attention, they are described on the site with the corrected text and any other material that will help.
- **Answers to reader questions**—If readers have questions that aren't covered in this book's Q&A sections, they may be presented on the site.
- **Sample files**—The source code and class files for all the programs you create during the book are available.
- **Sample Java programs**—Working versions of the programs featured in this book are available.
- **End-of-chapter features**—Solutions, including source code, for activities suggested at the end of each day and the answers to each day's quiz questions and certification practice are available.
- **Updated links to the sites mentioned in this book**—If sites mentioned in the book have moved to a new URL, they are listed.

You can email me by visiting the book's website. Click the Feedback link to be taken to a page where you can send email directly from the website.

—Rogers Cadenhead

APPENDIX C
Setting Up an Android Development Environment

Although Android apps are written in Java, creating them requires more than just the standard Java programming tools. Apps require the Java Development Kit, drivers for Android devices, and the Android Software Development Kit (SDK)—an integrated development environment (IDE) tailored to Android programming.

Eclipse is the most popular and best-supported IDE for Android and one of the most popular for general Java programming.

These tools are free and can be downloaded from the Internet. In this appendix, you set them up and make sure they can work together to run an Android app.

Getting Started

You can perform Android programming on the following operating systems:

- Windows XP or later
- Mac OS X 10.5.8 or later (x86)
- Linux

You need approximately 600MB of free disk space to install the Android SDK and another 1.2GB for the Eclipse IDE.

At this point you already should have the Java Development Kit installed because it is used in conjunction with NetBeans throughout the book to run Java programs. Android requires JDK 5.0 or later. If you still need the JDK, you can download it from http://oracle.com/technetwork/java/javase. Click the Downloads tab and look for the JDK.

Installing Eclipse

Although NetBeans supports Android development, Eclipse has emerged as the most popular choice for writing apps for the mobile platform. Android's developers designated Eclipse as the preferred environment, and they employ it throughout their official documentation and tutorials. You will find Android programming easier to master if you use Eclipse.

Eclipse, like NetBeans, provides a graphical user interface for writing Java programs. You can use it to create any kind of Java program (and it supports other programming languages as well).

Android requires Eclipse 3.5 or later.

To download Eclipse, visit www.eclipse.org/downloads.

Several versions of the IDE are available. Pick the Eclipse IDE for Java EE Developers. Java EE is the Java Enterprise Edition. This version of Eclipse includes two things you require for Android projects: Eclipse's Java Development Tools (JDT) plug-in and the Web Tools Platform (WTP).

NOTE

Eclipse also is used in popular tutorials for Android programming such as *Sams Teach Yourself Android Application Development in 24 Hours*, Second Edition, by Lauren Darcey and Shane Conder (Sams, 2011, ISBN 9780672335693). The tools set up in this appendix are used in that book as well. I've read the book, and I highly recommend it.

Eclipse is packaged as a zip archive file. There's no installation program to guide you through the process of setting it up on your computer. The zip archive contains a top-level folder called eclipse that holds all the files you need to run Eclipse.

Unzip this to the folder where you store programs. On my Windows system, I put it in the Program Files (x86) folder.

After unzipping the files, go to the eclipse folder you just created and look for the executable Eclipse application (named eclipse, naturally). Create a shortcut to this application and put it on the Start menu or somewhere else where you run programs, such as the desktop or taskbar.

C

Before launching Eclipse, you should install the Android SDK.

Installing Android SDK

The Android SDK is a free set of tools used to create, debug, and run Android applications. Eclipse uses the SDK as you're working on Android apps.

You can download the SDK from the official Android website at http://developer.android.com/sdk. It's available for Windows, Mac OS, and Linux. The SDK must be run as an administrator in Windows.

The Windows version is available as an installation wizard that walks you through the process of setting it up. The others, at the time of this writing, are a zip archive (Mac OS) or a TGZ archive (Linux).

Using either the installation wizard or a program that handles archives, put Android in a folder where you store programs—presumably the same parent folder where you placed Eclipse's folder. On my computer, I put it in Program Files (x86).

After the SDK has been installed, a tool called the SDK and AVD Manager will be run to update and enhance the SDK.

The manager, which is run using a menu command in Eclipse, makes it possible to keep the SDK current with each new release of Android. Choose the newest version of Android, Android SDK Tools, and all the items in the Extras folder. Click Install Packages to download and install them.

After you've installed the SDK, you're ready to run Eclipse for the first time.

Installing the Android Plug-in for Eclipse

The Eclipse IDE supports numerous programming languages and technologies, but not all of them are available the first time you run it. The IDE must be enhanced with plug-ins that provide the specific functionality you need.

Eclipse requires a plug-in to integrate the IDE with the Android SDK. The plug-in adds menu commands to the IDE interface related to Android and makes it possible to create and manage Android apps.

Follow these steps:

1. Launch Eclipse (as an administrator in Windows) from the folder where it was installed. The program loads with several windows and a menu bar and toolbar running across the top.

2. Select Help, Install New Software. The Install Wizard opens, which enables you to find and install plug-ins for Eclipse. Because plug-ins are downloaded from software repositories, Eclipse must be told the location of a repository.

3. Click the Add button. The Add Repository dialog opens.

4. Leave the Name field blank. In the Location field, enter the web address `http://dl-ssl.google.com/android/eclipse/` and click OK. A Developer Tools item should appear in the Install window, as shown in Figure C.1.

5. Expand this item by clicking the arrow that appears when you hover the mouse cursor over the item. You see several subitems for Android-related tools you can add to Eclipse, as shown in Figure C.1.

6. Select the check boxes for Android DDMS and Android Development Tools. (You also can add the Android Hierarchy Viewer and other tools, but they are not needed at the start of your Android programming.)

7. Click Next to review the licensing agreement, and check whether anything else needs to be installed. When you reach the end of the wizard, click Finish.

After the plug-in has been installed, close Eclipse and run it again.

FIGURE C.1
Adding new plug-ins to Eclipse.

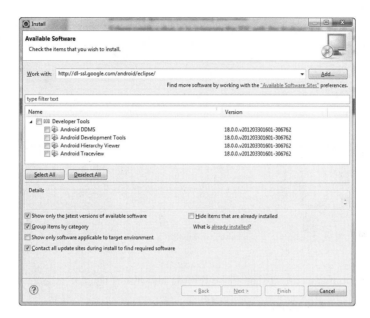

Your preferences in Eclipse must be checked to make sure that the IDE can find the Android SDK.

To check this, follow these steps:

1. Select Window, Preferences. The Preferences dialog opens with a list of categories running along the left side, as shown in Figure C.2.

2. Click Android to see the general Android preferences.

3. Make sure the SDK Location field contains the name of the folder where the Android SDK was installed. If it doesn't, click Browse to navigate to that folder and choose it using a file folder dialog.

4. After the SDK has been located, you see a table with a list of SDK targets. These targets are the versions of Android for which you can create apps using the SDK. Android apps must specify the earliest version of Android on which they are created to work. Click OK to close the dialog and save your preferences.

With the Android plug-in installed and the SDK located, you should see new menu commands in Eclipse. Two of them are Window, Android SDK Manager and Window, AVD Manager.

FIGURE C.2
Setting Android
preferences in
Eclipse.

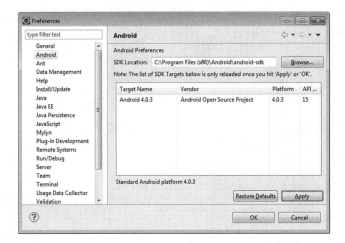

If these commands are absent, close Eclipse and restart it.

You can use the SDK manager to keep the SDK up to date:

1. Choose Window, Android SDK Manager. The manager opens, as shown in Figure C.3.

FIGURE C.3
Installing new
packages for the
Android SDK.

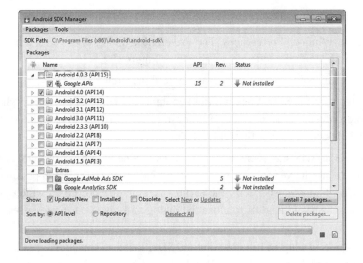

2. Select the Installed check box to see which SDK components are installed on your computer (or deselect it to hide them).

3. Select the Updates/New check box to see what is available that hasn't been installed yet.

4. In the Packages list, select the check boxes for the packages you want to install and then click the Install packages button. A dialog asks you to confirm that you want to install these packages.

You should periodically check for new updates. Android is being developed at a furious pace as new phones and other devices hit the market and the SDK adds support for them.

Setting Up Your Phone

The Android SDK includes an emulator that acts like an Android phone and that can run the apps you create. This comes in handy as you're writing an app. You can get an app working in a test environment, but at some point you need to see how it works on an actual Android phone (or another device).

C

The version of Android running on the phone must be one that Eclipse can use in the Android emulator. You can download and install multiple versions of Android in Eclipse.

You can deploy apps you write with the SDK on an Android device over your computer's USB connection. You can use the same cord you use to transfer photos and other files off the device.

Before connecting the cord, you must enable USB debugging on the phone by following these steps:

1. On the phone's Home screen, choose Menu, Settings. The Settings app opens.

2. Choose Applications, Development and check the USB debugging box.

Other devices might have this option elsewhere in the settings. It is called something like USB connection mode, USB debugging, or the like. The Android site at http://developer.android.com has documentation for how to set this option on different Android devices.

Connect the USB cord to your computer and the other end to your phone. A buglike Android icon may appear along the top edge of the device, alongside the time and icons for connection bars and the battery meter.

Drag down the top bar. You should see the USB debugging connected and USB connected messages, as shown in Figure C.4.

FIGURE C.4
Using an Android
phone in USB
debugging mode.

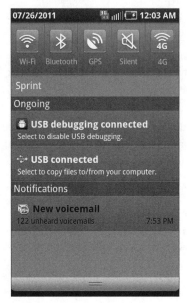

This sets up your phone, but your computer also might require some configuration to be able to connect to the device. If you have never connected to the phone over a USB cord, check your phone's documentation for how to do this. You might need to install a driver from a CD that came with the phone or the manufacturer's website.

In Windows, the Android SDK manager is run within Eclipse. You can use it to download the USB Driver Package, a collection of drivers for phones and other devices, along with other packages related to your device. Choose Window, Android SDK Manager to see what's available.

During Day 21, "Writing Android Apps for Java," you use the Android development tools to create and run an Android app. If everything's set up correctly, it should run properly on both the emulator and an Android phone.

APPENDIX D
Using the Java Development Kit

In addition to the integrated development environment NetBeans, Oracle offers the Java Development Kit (JDK), a free set of command-line programs that are used to create, compile, and run Java programs. Every new release of Java is accompanied by a new release of the development kit. The current version is JDK version 7.

Although NetBeans and other programs such as IntelliJ IDEA and Eclipse are more sophisticated, some programmers continue to use the Java Development Kit. This appendix covers how to download and install the Java Development Kit, set it up on your computer, and use it to create, compile, and run a simple Java program.

It also describes how to correct a common configuration problem faced by JDK users.

Choosing a Java Development Tool

If you're using a Microsoft Windows or Apple Mac OS system, you probably have a Java virtual machine installed that can run Java programs.

To develop Java programs, you need more than a virtual machine. You also need a compiler and other tools that are used to create, run, and test programs.

The Java Development Kit includes a compiler, virtual machine, debugger, file archiving program, and several other programs.

The kit is simpler than other development tools. It does not offer a graphical user interface, text editor, or other features that many programmers rely on.

To use the kit, you type commands at a text prompt. MS-DOS, Linux, and UNIX users will be familiar with this prompt, which is also called a command line.

Here's an example of a command you might type while using the Java Development Kit:

```
javac RetrieveMail.java
```

This command tells the javac program—the Java compiler included with the kit—to read a source code file called RetrieveMail.java and create one or more class files. These files contain compiled bytecode that a Java virtual machine can execute.

When RetrieveMail.java is compiled, one of the files will be named RetrieveMail.class. If the class file was set up to function as an application, a virtual machine can run it.

People who are comfortable with command-line environments will be at home using the Java Development Kit. Everyone else must become accustomed to the lack of a graphical point-and-click environment as they develop programs.

If you have NetBeans or another Java development tool compatible with Java 7, you don't need to use the Java Development Kit. Many different development tools can be used to create the tutorial programs in this book.

Installing the Java Development Kit

You can download the Java Development Kit from Oracle's Java website at www.oracle.com/technetwork/java.

The website's Downloads section offers links to several different versions of the Java Development Kit. It also offers the NetBeans development environment and other products related to the language. The product you should download is in the Java Standard Edition (Java SE) and is called the Java Software Development Kit version 7.

The kit is available for Windows, Mac OS, Linux, and Solaris SPARC systems.

The kit requires a computer with a Pentium 2 processor that is 266MHz or faster, has 128MB of memory, and has 300MB of free disk space.

When you're looking for this product, you might find that the Java Development Kit's version number has a number after 7, such as "JDK 7.1." To fix bugs and address security problems, Oracle periodically issues new releases of the kit and numbers them with a period and digit after the main version number. Choose the most current version of JDK 7 that's offered, whether it's numbered 7.0, 7.1, 7.2, or higher.

CAUTION | Take care not to download two similarly named products from Oracle by mistake: the Java Runtime Environment (JRE) 7.0 or the Java Standard Edition 7.0 Source Release.

To set up the kit, you must download and run an installation program (or install it from a CD). On the Java website, after you choose the version of the kit that's designed for your operating system, you can download it as a single file.

After you have downloaded the file, you'll be ready to set up the kit.

D

Windows Installation

Before installing the kit, make sure that no other Java development tools are installed on your system (assuming, of course, that you don't need any other tool at the moment). Having more than one Java programming tool installed on your computer can often cause configuration problems with the kit.

To set up the program on a Windows system, double-click the installation file or choose Start, Run from the Windows taskbar to find and run the file.

The installation wizard guides you through the process of installing the software. If you accept the terms and conditions for using the kit, you'll be asked where to install the program, as shown in Figure D.1.

The wizard suggests a folder where the kit should be installed. In Figure D.1, the wizard suggests the folder `C:\Program Files\Java\jdk1.7.0_04`. When you install the kit, the suggested name might be different.

To choose a different folder, click the Change button. Either select or create a new folder and click OK. The wizard returns to the Custom Setup options.

FIGURE D.1
Installing the JDK.

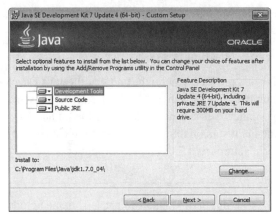

Before continuing, make note of the folder you have chosen. You'll need it later to configure the kit and fix any configuration problems that may occur.

You also are asked what parts of the kit to install. By default, the wizard installs all components of the JDK:

- **Development tools**—The executable programs needed to create Java software
- **Source code**—The source code for the thousands of classes that make up the Java Class Library
- **Public JRE**—A Java virtual machine you can distribute with the programs you create (also called a Java Runtime Environment)

If you accept the default installation, you need about 300MB of free hard disk space. You can save space by omitting everything but the program files. However, the source code and Java Runtime Environment can be useful, so it's a good idea to install them.

To prevent a component from being installed, click the hard drive icon next to its name and then choose the This Feature Will Not Be Available option.

After you choose the components to install, click the Next button to continue. You may be asked whether to set up the Java Plug-in to work with the web browsers on your system.

The Java Plug-in is a virtual machine that runs Java programs incorporated into web pages. These programs, which are called applets, can work with different virtual machines, but most browsers do not include one that supports the current version of the

Java language. Oracle offers the plug-in to provide full language support to Microsoft Internet Explorer, Mozilla Firefox, Google Chrome, and other browsers.

After you complete the configuration, the wizard installs the kit on your system.

Configuring the Java Development Kit

After the wizard installs the kit, you must edit your computer's environment variables to include references to the kit.

Experienced MS-DOS users can finish setting up the kit by adjusting two variables and then rebooting the computer:

- Edit the computer's PATH variable and add a reference to the kit's bin folder (which is C:\Program Files\Java\jdk1.7.0_04\bin if you installed the kit into the C:\Program Files\Java\jdk1.7.0_04 folder).

- Edit or create a CLASSPATH variable so that it contains a reference to the current folder—a period and semicolon (.;)—followed by a reference to the tools.jar file in the kit's lib folder (which is C:\Program Files\Java\jdk1.7.0_04\lib\tools.jar if the kit was installed into C:\Program Files\Java\jdk1.7.0_04).

For inexperienced MS-DOS users, later sections cover in detail how to set the PATH and CLASSPATH variables on a Windows system.

Users of other operating systems should follow the instructions provided by Oracle on its Java Development Kit download page.

D

Using a Command-line Interface

The kit requires the use of a command line to compile Java programs, run them, and handle other tasks.

A command line is a way to operate a computer entirely by typing commands using the keyboard, rather than by using the mouse. Very few programs designed for Windows users require the command line today.

TIP

To get to a command line in Windows, do the following:

- On Windows 7, Vista, XP, or Server 2003, choose Start, All Programs, Accessories, Command Prompt.

- On Windows 98 or Me, choose Start, Programs, MS-DOS Prompt.

- On Windows NT or 2000, choose Start, Programs, Accessories, Command Prompt.

When you open a command line in Windows, a new window opens in which you can type commands, as shown in Figure D.2.

Command line

The command line in Windows uses commands adopted from MS-DOS, the Microsoft operating system that preceded Windows. MS-DOS supports the same functions as Windows—copying, moving, and deleting files and folders; running programs; scanning and repairing a hard drive; formatting a floppy disk; and so on.

In the window, a cursor blinks on the command line whenever you can type in a new command. In Figure D.2, `C:\Users\Rogers>` is the command line.

Because MS-DOS can be used to delete files and even format your hard drive, you should learn something about the operating system before experimenting with its commands.

NOTE

If you'd like to learn a lot about MS-DOS, a good book is *Special Edition Using MS-DOS 6.22*, 3rd Edition (ISBN 978-0-78972-573-8), published by Que. The emphasis is on the words "a lot" because this book is 1,056 pages long.

However, you need to know only a few things about MS-DOS to use the kit: how to create a folder, how to open a folder, and how to run a program.

Opening Folders in MS-DOS

When you are using MS-DOS on a Windows system, you have access to all the folders you normally use in Windows. For example, if you have a Windows folder on your C: hard drive, the same folder is accessible as `C:\Windows` from a command line.

To open a folder in MS-DOS, type the command CD, followed by the name of the folder, and press Enter. Here's an example:

CD C:\TEMP

When you enter this command, the TEMP folder on your system's C: drive is opened if it exists. After you open a folder, the command line is updated with the name of that folder, as shown in Figure D.3.

MS-DOS command

FIGURE D.3
Opening a folder in a command-line window.

You also can use the CD command in other ways:

- Type CD \ to open the root folder on the current hard drive.
- Type CD *foldername* to open a subfolder matching the name you've used in place of *foldername* if that subfolder exists.
- Type CD .. to open the folder that contains the current folder. For example, if you are in C:\Windows\Fonts and you use the CD .. command, C:\Windows is opened.

It's helpful to create a folder for the projects you create in this book, such as one named J21work. If you already have done this, you can switch to that folder by using the following commands:

CD \

CD J21work

If you haven't created that folder yet, you can do so using an MS-DOS command.

D

Creating Folders in MS-DOS

To create a folder from a command line, type the command MD followed by the folder's name and press Enter, as in the following example:

```
MD C:\STUFF
```

The STUFF folder is created in the root folder of the system's C: drive. To open a newly created folder, use the CD command followed by that folder's name, as shown in Figure D.4.

Creating a folder

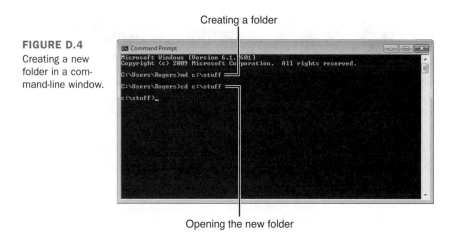

Opening the new folder

If you haven't already created a J21work folder, you can do so from a command line:

1. Change to the root folder (using the CD \ command).
2. Type the command MD J21work and press Enter.

After J21work has been created, you can go to it at any time from a command line by using this command:

```
CD \J21work
```

The last thing you need to learn about MS-DOS to use the Java Development Kit is how to run programs.

Running Programs in MS-DOS

The simplest way to run a program at the command line is to type its name and press Enter. For example, type DIR and press Enter to see a list of files and subfolders in the current folder.

You also can run a program by typing its name followed by a space and some options that control how the program runs. These options are called *arguments*.

To see an example of this, change to the root folder (using CD \) and type DIR J21work. You'll see a list of files and subfolders contained in the J21work folder if it contains any.

After you have installed the kit, run the Java virtual machine to see that it works. Type the following command at a command line:

```
java -version
```

java is the name of the Java virtual machine, and -version is an argument that tells it to display its version number.

You can see an example of this in Figure D.5, but your version number might be a little different, depending on what version of the kit you have installed.

Running a program

FIGURE D.5

Running the Java virtual machine in a command-line window.

D

If java -version works and you see a version number, it should begin with 1.7. Oracle tacks on a third number, but as long as the version number begins with 1.7, you are using the correct version of the Java Development Kit.

If you see an incorrect version number or a Bad command or filename error after running java -version, you need to make some changes to how the Java Development Kit is configured on your system.

CAUTION

Because Java 7 is the current version, you might be confused about the references to version 1.7.

Although the language is called Java 7 and the JDK is designated JDK 7.0, the kit's internal version number is 1.7.0. This internal

CAUTION (Continued)

number shows up in the -version command as well as in your choice of installation folder for the kit.

When all else fails, run the java -version command to make sure the right development tool has been installed on your system. If it begins with 1.7, you've got the right tool to develop programs for Java 7.

Correcting Configuration Errors

When you are writing Java programs for the first time, the most likely source of problems is not typos, syntax errors, or other programming mistakes. Most errors result from a misconfigured kit.

If you type java -version at a command line and your system can't find the folder that contains java.exe, you see one of the following error messages or something similar (depending on your operating system):

- Bad command or file name
- 'java' is not recognized as an internal or external command, operable program, or batch file

To correct this, you must configure your system's PATH variable.

Setting the PATH on Windows 98 or Me

On a Windows 98 or Me system, you configure the PATH variable by editing the AUTOEXEC.BAT file in the root folder of your main hard drive. MS-DOS uses this file to set environment variables and configure how some command-line programs function.

AUTOEXEC.BAT is a text file you can edit with Windows Notepad. Start Notepad by choosing Start, Programs, Accessories, Notepad from the Windows taskbar.

The Notepad text editor opens. Choose File, Open from Notepad's menu bar, go to the root folder on your main hard drive, and then open the file AUTOEXEC.BAT.

When you open the file, you see a series of MS-DOS commands, each on its own line.

The only commands you need to look for are any that begin with PATH.

The PATH command is followed by a space and a series of folder names separated by semicolons. It sets up the PATH variable, a list of folders that contain command-line programs you use.

PATH helps MS-DOS find programs when you run them at a command line.

You can see what PATH has been set to by typing the following command at a command line:

PATH

To set up the kit correctly, the folder that contains the Java virtual machine must be included in the PATH command in AUTOEXEC.BAT.

The virtual machine has the filename java.exe. If you installed JDK 7 in the C:\Program Files\Java\jdk1.7.0_04 folder on your system, java.exe is in C:\Program Files\Java\jdk1.7.0_04\bin.

If you can't remember where you installed the kit, you can look for java.exe by choosing Start, Find, Files or Folders. You might find several copies in different folders. To see which one is correct, open a command-line window and do the following for each copy you have found:

1. Use the CD command to open a folder that contains java.exe.

2. Run the command java -version in that folder.

When you know the correct folder, create a blank line at the bottom of the AUTOEXEC.BAT file and add the following:

PATH rightfoldername;%PATH%

For example, if C:\Program Files\Java\jdk1.7.0_04\bin is the correct folder, add the following line at the bottom of AUTOEXEC.BAT:

PATH c:\"Program Files"\Java\jdk1.7.0_04\bin;%PATH%

%PATH% keeps you from wiping out any other PATH commands in AUTOEXEC.BAT. Quotation marks appear around the folder name Program Files because some versions of Windows require this to handle folder names that contain spaces.

After making changes to AUTOEXEC.BAT, save the file and reboot your computer. When this is done, try the java -version command.

If it displays the correct version of the kit, your system is probably configured correctly. You'll find out for sure when you try to create a sample program later in this appendix.

Setting the Path on Windows 7, NT, 2000, or XP

On a Windows 7, NT, XP, 2000, or 2003 system, you configure the Path variable using the Environment Variables dialog box, one of the features of the system's Control Panel.

D

To open this dialog box, follow these steps:

1. Right-click the Computer icon on your desktop or the Start menu and choose Properties. The System Properties dialog box opens.

2. Click the Advanced tab or the Advanced System Settings link.

3. Click the Environment Variables button. The Environment Variables dialog box opens, as shown in Figure D.6.

FIGURE D.6
Setting environment variables in Windows NT, XP, 2000, and 2003.

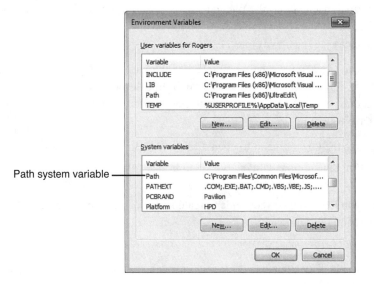

Path system variable

You can edit two kinds of environment variables: system variables, which apply to all users on your computer, and user variables, which apply only to you.

Path is a system variable that helps MS-DOS find programs when you run them at a command line. It contains a list of folders separated by semicolons.

To set up the kit correctly, the folder that contains the Java virtual machine must be included in the Path. The virtual machine has the filename java.exe. If you installed the kit in the C:\Program Files\Java\jdk1.7.0_04 folder on your system, java.exe is in C:\Program Files\Java\jdk1.7.0_04\bin.

If you can't remember where you installed the kit, you can look for java.exe by choosing Start, Search. You might find several copies in different folders. To see which one is correct, open a command-line window and do the following for each copy you have found:

1. Use the CD command to open a folder that contains java.exe.

2. Run the command java -version in that folder.

When you know the correct folder, return to the Environment Variables dialog box, select Path in the System Variables list, and click Edit. The Edit System Variable dialog box opens with Path in the Variable name field and a list of folders in the Variable value field, as shown in Figure D.7.

FIGURE D.7
Changing your system's Path variable.

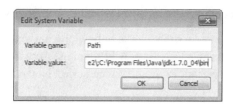

To add a folder to the Path, click the Variable Value field and move the cursor to the end without changing anything. At the end, add a semicolon followed by the name of the folder that contains the Java virtual machine.

For example, if C:\Program Files\Java\jdk1.7.0_04\bin is the correct folder, add the following text to the end of the Path variable:

;c:\Program Files\Java\jdk1.7.0_04\bin

After making the change, click OK twice: once to close the Edit System Variable dialog box and another time to close the Environment Variables dialog box.

Try it: Open a command-line window and type the command java -version.

If it displays the correct version of the Java Development Kit, your system is probably configured correctly, although you won't know for sure until you try to use the kit later in this appendix.

D

Using a Text Editor

Unlike more sophisticated Java development tools, the Java Development Kit does not include a text editor to use when you create source files.

For an editor or word processor to work with the kit, it must be able to save text files with no formatting.

This feature has different names in different editors. Look for a format option such as one of the following when you save a document or set the properties for a document:

- Plain text
- ASCII text
- DOS text
- Text-only

If you're using Windows, several editors are included with the operating system.

Windows Notepad is a no-frills text editor that works only with plain-text files. It can handle only one document at a time. Choose Start, All Programs, Accessories, Notepad to run it on Windows XP or choose Start, Programs, Accessories, Notepad on other Windows systems.

Windows WordPad is a step above Notepad. It can handle more than one document at a time and can handle both plain-text and Microsoft Word formats. It also remembers the last several documents it has worked on and makes them available from the File menu. It's also on the Accessories menu along with Notepad.

Windows users also can use Microsoft Word, but you must save files as text rather than in Word's proprietary format. (UNIX and Linux users can author programs with emacs, pico, and vi; Macintosh users have SimpleText or any of the previously mentioned UNIX tools available for Java source file creation.)

One disadvantage of using simple text editors such as Notepad or WordPad is that they do not display line numbers as you edit.

Seeing the line number helps in Java programming because many compilers indicate the line number where an error occurred. Take a look at the following error generated by the JDK compiler:

```
Palindrome.java:2: Class Font not found in type declaration.
```

The number 2 after the name of the Java source file indicates the line that triggered the compiler error. With a text editor that supports numbering, you can go directly to that line and start looking for the error.

Usually there are better ways to debug a program with a commercial Java programming package. But kit users must search for compiler-generated errors using the line number indicated by the `javac` tool. This is one of the best reasons to move on to an advanced Java development program after learning the language with the kit.

TIP

> Another alternative is to use the kit with a programmer's text editor that offers line numbering and other features. One of the most popular for Java is jEdit, a free editor available for Windows, Linux, and other systems at www.jedit.org.
>
> I use UltraEdit, an excellent programmer and web designer's editor that currently sells for $59.95. To find out more and download a trial version, visit www.ultraedit.com.

Creating a Sample Program

Now that you have installed and set up the Java Development Kit, you're ready to create a sample Java program to make sure it works.

Java programs begin as source code—a series of statements created using a text editor and saved as a text file. You can use any program you like to create these files, as long as it can save the file as plain, unformatted text.

The kit does not include a text editor, but most other Java development tools include a built-in editor for creating source code files.

D

Run your editor of choice and enter the Java program shown in Listing D.1. Be sure to correctly enter all the parentheses, braces, brackets, and quotation marks in the listing and capitalize everything in the program exactly as shown. If your editor requires a filename before you start entering anything, call it HelloUser.java.

LISTING D.1   Source Code of HelloUser.java

```
1: public class HelloUser {
2:     public static void main(String[] arguments) {
3:         String username = System.getProperty("user.name");
4:         System.out.println("Hello " + username);
5:     }
6: }
```

The line numbers and colons at the beginning of each line are not part of the program. They're included so that I can refer to specific lines by number in each program. If you're ever unsure about the source code of a program in this book, you can compare it to a copy on the book's official website at www.java21days.com.

After you finish typing in the program, save the file somewhere on your hard drive with the name HelloUser.java. Java source files must be saved with the extension .java.

> **TIP**
>
> If you have created a folder called J21work, save HelloUser.java and all other Java source files from this book in that folder. This makes it easier to find them while using a command-line window.

If you're using Windows, a text editor such as Notepad might add an extra .txt file extension to the filename of any Java source files you save. For example, HelloUser. java is saved as HelloUser.java.txt. As a workaround to avoid this problem, place quotation marks around the filename when saving a source file.

> **TIP**
>
> A better solution is to permanently associate .java files with the text editor you'll be using. In Windows, open the folder that contains HelloUser.java, and double-click the file. If you have never opened a file with the .java extension, you're asked what program to use when opening files of this type. Choose your preferred editor and select the option to make your choice permanent. From this point on, you can open a source file for editing by double-clicking the file.

The purpose of this project is to test the Java Development Kit. None of the Java programming concepts used in the six-line HelloUser program are described in this appendix.

You learn the basics of the language during the first several days of Week 1, "The Java Language." If you have figured out anything about Java simply by typing in Listing D.1, it's your own fault.

Compiling and Running the Program in Windows

Now you're ready to compile the source file with the kit's Java compiler, a program called javac. The compiler reads a .java source file and creates one or more .class files that can be run by a Java virtual machine.

Open a command-line window, and then open the folder where you saved HelloUser.java.

If you saved the file in the J21work folder inside the root folder on your main hard drive, the following MS-DOS command opens the folder:

```
cd \J21work
```

When you are in the correct folder, you can compile `HelloUser.java` by entering the following at a command prompt:

```
javac HelloUser.java
```

Figure D.8 shows the MS-DOS commands used to switch to the \J21work folder and compile `HelloUser.java`.

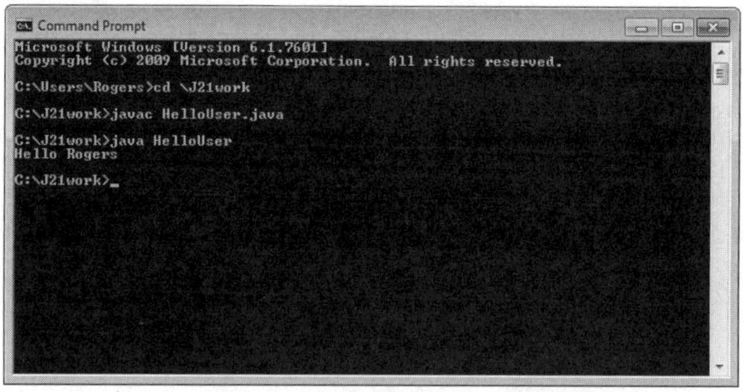

FIGURE D.8

Compiling a Java program in a command-line window.

The kit's compiler does not display a message if the program compiles successfully. If there are problems, the compiler tells you by displaying each error along with the number of the line that triggered the error.

D

If the program compiles without any errors, a file called `HelloUser.class` is created in the same folder that contains `HelloUser.java`.

The class file contains the Java bytecode that a Java virtual machine will execute. If you get any errors, go back to your original source file and make sure that you typed it in exactly as it appears in Listing D.1.

After you have a class file, you can run that file using a virtual machine. The kit's virtual machine is called `java`, and it also is run from the command line.

Run the HelloUser program by switching to the folder containing `HelloUser.class` and entering the following:

```
java HelloUser
```

You see the text "Hello" followed by a space and your username.

> **CAUTION**   When running a Java class with the kit's Java virtual machine, don't specify the .class file extension after the class's name. If you do, you'll see an error such as the following:
>
> ```
> Exception in thread "main" java.lang.NoClassDefFoundError:
> HelloUser/class
> ```

Figure D.8 shows the successful output of the HelloUser application along with the commands used to get to that point.

If you can compile the program and run it successfully, your kit is working, and you are ready to start Day 1 of this book.

If you cannot get the program to compile successfully even though you have typed it in exactly as it appears in the book, there may be one last problem with how the kit is configured on your system: The CLASSPATH environment variable might need to be configured.

Setting Up the CLASSPATH Variable

All the Java programs you write rely on two kinds of class files: the classes you create and the Java Class Library, a set of hundreds of classes that represent the functionality of the Java language.

The kit needs to know where to find Java class files on your system. In many cases, the kit can figure this out on its own by looking in the folder where it was installed.

You also can set it up yourself by creating or modifying another environment variable: CLASSPATH.

Setting the CLASSPATH on Windows 98 or Me

If you have compiled and run the HelloUser program successfully, the kit has been configured successfully. You don't need to make any more changes to your system.

On the other hand, if you see a Class not found error or NoClassDefFound error whenever you try to run a program, you need to make sure your CLASSPATH variable is set up correctly.

To do this, run Windows Notepad and choose File, Open. Go to the root folder on your system, and then open the file AUTOEXEC.BAT. A file containing several different MS-DOS commands is opened in the editor.

Look for a line in the file that contains the text SET CLASSPATH= command followed by a series of folder and filenames separated by semicolons.

CLASSPATH is used to help the Java compiler find the class files it needs. A CLASSPATH can contain folders or files. It also can contain a period character (.), which is another way to refer to the current folder in MS-DOS.

You can see your system's CLASSPATH variable by typing the following command at a command line:

```
ECHO %CLASSPATH%
```

If your CLASSPATH includes folders or files that you know are no longer on your computer, you should remove the references to them on the SET CLASSPATH= line in AUTOEXEC.BAT. Be sure to remove any extra semicolons also.

To set up the kit correctly, you must include the file containing the Java Class Library in the SET CLASSPATH= command. This file has the filename tools.jar. If you installed the kit in the C:\Program Files\Java\jdk1.7.0_04 folder on your system, tools.jar is probably in the folder C:\Program Files\Java\jdk1.7.0_04\lib.

If you can't remember where you installed the kit, you can look for tools.jar by choosing Start, Find, Files or choosing Folders from the Windows taskbar. If you find several copies, you should be able to find the correct one using this method:

D

1. Use CD to open the folder that contains the Java virtual machine (java.exe).
2. Enter the command CD ...
3. Enter the command CD lib.

The lib folder normally contains the right copy of tools.jar.

When you know the correct location, create a blank line at the bottom of the AUTOEXEC.BAT file and add the following:

```
SET CLASSPATH=%CLASSPATH%;.;rightlocation
```

For example, if the tools.jar file is in the C:\Program Files\Java\jdk1.7.0_04\lib folder, add the following line at the bottom of AUTOEXEC.BAT:

```
SET CLASSPATH=%CLASSPATH%;.;c:\"Program Files"\Java\jdk1.7.0_04\lib\tools.jar
```

After making changes to AUTOEXEC.BAT, save the file and reboot your computer. After this is done, try to compile and run the HelloUser sample program again. You should be able to accomplish this after the CLASSPATH variable has been set up correctly.

Setting the Classpath on Windows 7, NT, XP, 2000, or 2003

On a Windows 7, NT, XP, 2000, or 2003 system, you also configure the Classpath variable using the Environment Variables dialog box.

To open it, do the following:

1. Right-click the My Computer icon on your desktop or Start menu and choose Properties. The System Properties dialog box opens.

2. Click the Advanced tab to bring it to the front.

3. Click the Environment Variables button. The Environment Variables dialog box opens, as shown in Figure D.9.

FIGURE D.9
Setting environment variables in Windows 7, NT, XP, 2000, or 2003.

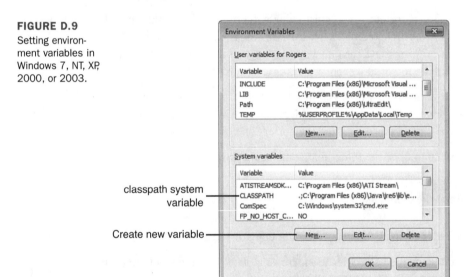

classpath system variable

Create new variable

If your system has a Classpath variable, it probably is one of the system variables. Your system may not have a Classpath variable set. Normally the kit can find class files without the variable.

However, if your system has a Classpath, it must be set up with at least two things: a reference to the current folder (a period) and a reference to a file that contains the Java Class Library, tools.jar.

If you installed the kit in the C:\Program Files\Java\jdk1.7.0_04 folder, tools.jar is in the folder C:\Program Files\Java\jdk1.7.0_04\lib.

If you can't remember where you installed the kit, you can look for `tools.jar` by choosing Start, Search from the Windows taskbar. If you find several copies, you should be able to find the correct one using this method:

1. Use `CD` to open the folder that contains the Java virtual machine (`java.exe`).
2. Enter the command `CD ...`
3. Enter the command `CD lib`.

The lib folder normally contains the right copy of `tools.jar`.

When you know the correct folder, return to the Environment Variables dialog box, shown in Figure D.9.

If your system does not have a `Classpath`, click the New button under the System Variables list. The New System Variable dialog box opens.

If your system has a `Classpath`, choose it and click the Edit button. The Edit System Variable dialog box opens.

Both boxes contain the same thing: a Variable Name field and a Variable Value field.

Enter `Classpath` in the Variable Name field and the correct value for your `Classpath` in the Variable Value field.

For example, if you installed the kit in `C:\Program Files\Java\jdk1.7.0_04`, your `Classpath` should contain the following:

`.;C:\"Program Files"\Java\jdk1.7.0_04\lib\tools.jar`

After setting up your `Classpath`, click OK twice: once to close the Edit or New System Variable dialog box and again to close the Environment Variables dialog box.

Unlike Windows 98 and Me users, you don't have to reboot the system before you can try it. Open a new command-line window and type the command `java -version`.

If it displays the correct version of the kit, your system might be configured correctly and require no more adjustments. Try creating the sample `HelloUser` program again. It should work after the `CLASSPATH` variable has been set up correctly.

D

APPENDIX E

Programming with the Java Development Kit

The Java Development Kit (JDK) can be used throughout this book to create, compile, and run Java programs.

The tools that make up the kit contain numerous features that many programmers don't explore. Some of the tools themselves might be new to you.

This appendix covers features of the kit that you can use to create more reliable, better-tested, and faster-running Java programs.

Overview of the JDK

Although you can use numerous integrated development environments to create Java programs, the most widely used may still be the Java Development Kit (JDK) from Oracle, the set of command-line tools that are used to develop software with the Java language.

There are two main reasons for the kit's popularity:

- It's free. You can download a copy at no cost from the official Java website at www.oracle.com/technetwork/java/index.html.
- It's first. Whenever a new version of the language is released, the first tools that support the new version are in the kit.

The kit uses the command line. This is also called the MS-DOS prompt, command prompt, or console under Windows and the shell prompt under UNIX. You enter commands using the keyboard, as in this example:

```
javac VideoBook.java
```

This command compiles a Java program called `VideoBook.java` using the kit's compiler. The command has two elements: the name of the compiler, `javac`, and the name of the program to compile, `VideoBook.java`. A space character separates the two elements.

Each kit command follows the same format: the name of the tool to use, followed by one or more elements indicating what the tool should do. These elements are called *arguments*.

The following illustrates the use of command-line arguments:

```
java VideoBook add DVD "Invasion of the Bee Girls"
```

This command tells the Java virtual machine to run a class file called `VideoBook` with three command-line arguments: the strings `add`, `DVD`, and `"Invasion of the Bee Girls."`

NOTE

You might think there are more than three command-line arguments because of the spaces in the string "Invasion of the Bee Girls". The quotation marks around that string cause it to be considered one command-line argument, which makes it possible to include spaces in an argument.

Some arguments used with the kit modify how a tool functions. These arguments are preceded by a hyphen character and are called *options*.

The following command shows the use of an option:

```
java -version
```

This command tells the Java virtual machine to display its version number rather than trying to run a class file. It's a good way to find out whether the kit is correctly configured to run Java programs on your system. Here's an example of the output run on a system equipped with JDK 7:

Output ▼

```
java version "1.7.0_04"
Java(TM) SE Runtime Environment, Standard Edition (build1.7.0_04-b22)
Java HotSpot(TM) 64-Bit Server VM (build 23.0-b21, mixed mode)
```

The version reflects Oracle's internal number for JDK 7, which is 1.7.

In some instances, you can combine options with other arguments. For example, if you compile a Java class that uses deprecated methods, you can see more information on these methods by compiling the class with a -deprecation option, as in the following:

```
javac -deprecation OldVideoBook.java
```

The java Virtual Machine

java, the Java virtual machine, is used to run Java applications from the command line. It takes as an argument the name of a class file to run, as in the following example:

```
java BidMonitor
```

Although Java class files end with the .class extension, this extension is not specified when the virtual machine is used. The machine also is called the Java interpreter.

The class loaded by the virtual machine must contain a class method called main() that takes the following form:

```
public static void main(String[] arguments) {
    // Method here
}
```

Some simple Java programs might consist of only one class—the one containing the main() method. In more complex programs that use other classes, the virtual machine automatically loads any other classes that are needed.

The virtual machine runs bytecode, compiled instructions that the machine executes. After a Java program is saved in bytecode as a .class file, it can be run by different

E

virtual machines without modification. If you have compiled a Java program, it will be compatible with any virtual machine that fully supports Java.

NOTE

Interestingly, Java is not the only language that you can use to create Java bytecode. NetRexx, JPython, JRuby, JudoScript, and several dozen other languages compile into .class files of executable bytecode through the use of compilers specific to those languages. Robert Tolksdorf maintains a comprehensive list of these languages at www.is-research.de/info/vmlanguages.

You can specify the class file that the Java virtual machine will run in two different ways. If the class is not part of any package, you can run it by specifying the class's name, as in the preceding java BidMonitor example. If the class is part of a package, you must specify the class by using its full package and class name.

For example, consider a SellItem class that is part of the org.cadenhead.auction package. To run this application, you would use the following command:

```
java org.cadenhead.auction.SellItem
```

Each element of the package name corresponds to its own subfolder. The Java virtual machine looks for the SellItem.class file in several different places:

- The org\cadenhead\auction subfolder of the folder where the java command was entered (If the command was entered from the C:\J21work folder, for example, the SellItem.class file can be run successfully if it is in the C:\J21work\org\cadenhead\auction folder.)
- The org\cadenhead\auction subfolder of any folder in your Classpath setting

If you're creating your own packages, an easy way to manage them is to add a folder to your Classpath that's the root folder for any packages you create, such as C:\javapackages or something similar. After creating subfolders that correspond to the name of a package, place the package's class files in the correct subfolder.

Java supports assertions, a debugging feature that works only when requested as a command-line option. To run a program using the Java virtual machine and make use of any assertions it contains, use the command line -ea, as in the following example:

```
java -ea Outline
```

The Java virtual machine executes all assert statements in the application's class and all other class files it uses, with the exception of classes from the Java Class Library.

To remove that exception and make use of all assertions, run a class with the `-esa` option.

If you don't specify one of the options that turns on the assertions feature, the virtual machine ignores all `assert` statements.

The javac Compiler

The Java compiler, `javac`, converts Java source code into one or more class files of byte-code that a Java virtual machine can run.

Java source code is stored in a file with the `.java` file extension. This file can be created with any text editor that can save a document without any special formatting codes. The terminology varies depending on the text-editing software being used, but these files are often called plain text, ASCII text, DOS text, or something similar.

A Java source code file can contain more than one class, but only one of the classes can be declared to be public. A class can contain no public classes at all if desired, although this isn't possible with applets because of the rules of inheritance.

If a source code file contains a class that has been declared to be public, the filename must match the name of that class. For example, the source code for a public class called `BuyItem` must be stored in a file called `BuyItem.java`.

To compile a file, you run the `javac` tool with the name of the source code file as an argument, as in the following:

```
javac BuyItem.java
```

You can compile more than one source file by including each separate filename as a command-line argument, such as this command:

```
javac BuyItem.java SellItem.java
```

You also can use wildcard characters such as * and ?. Use the following command to compile all `.java` files in a folder:

```
javac *.java
```

When you compile one or more Java source code files, a separate `.class` file is created for each Java class that compiles successfully.

If you are compiling a program that uses assertions, you must use the `-ea` option, as in this command:

```
javac -ea Outline.java
```

E

If the -ea option is not used and you try to compile a program that contains assertions, javac displays an error message and won't compile the file.

Another useful option when running the compiler is -deprecation, which causes the compiler to describe any deprecated methods that are being employed in a Java program.

A deprecated method is one that Oracle has replaced with a better alternative, either in the same class or in a different class. Although the deprecated method works, at some point Oracle may decide to remove it from the class. The deprecation warning is a strong suggestion to stop using that method as soon as you can.

Normally, the compiler issues a single warning if it finds any deprecated methods in a program. The -deprecation option causes the compiler to list each method that has been deprecated, as in the following command:

```
javac -deprecation SellItem.java
```

If you're more concerned with the speed of a Java program than the size of its class files, you can compile its source code with the -O option. This creates class files that have been optimized for faster performance. Methods that are static, final, or private might be compiled inline, a technique that makes the class file larger but causes the methods to be executed more quickly.

If you plan to use a debugger to look for bugs in a Java class, compile the source with the -g option to put all debugging information in the class file, including references to line numbers, local variables, and source code. (To keep all this out of a class, compile with the -g:none option.)

Normally, the Java compiler doesn't provide a lot of information as it creates class files. In fact, if the source code compiles successfully and no deprecated methods are employed, you won't see any output from the compiler. No news is good news in this case.

If you want to see more information on what the javac tool is doing as it compiles source code, use the -verbose option. The more verbose compiler describes how long it takes to complete different functions, the classes that are being loaded, and the overall time required.

The appletviewer Browser

The appletviewer tool runs Java programs that require a web browser and are presented as part of a Hypertext Markup Language (HTML) document. It takes an HTML document as a command-line argument, as in the following example:

```
appletviewer NewAuctions.html
```

If the argument is a web address instead of a reference to a file, `appletviewer` loads the HTML document at that address. For example:

`appletviewer http://www.javaonthebrain.com`

Figure E.1 shows an applet loaded from this page, a site developed by cartoonist and Java game programmer Karl Hörnell.

FIGURE E.1

Viewing Java web applets outside of a browser.

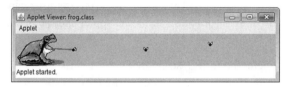

When `appletviewer` loads an HTML document, every applet on that document begins running in its own window. The size of these windows depends on the `height` and `width` attributes that were set in the applet's `html` tag.

Unlike a web browser, `appletviewer` cannot be used to view the HTML document itself. If you want to see how the applet is laid out in relation to the other contents of the document, you must use a Java-capable web browser.

CAUTION

The Java Plug-in from Oracle enables web browsers to run Java applets. The Plug-in is included in the Java Runtime Environment, a virtual machine for running Java programs that is installed along with the Java Development Kit. If it isn't already present on your system, you can download it from Oracle's website at www.java.com.

E

Using `appletviewer` is reasonably straightforward, but you might be unfamiliar with some of the menu options that are available as the viewer runs an applet.

The following menu options are available:

- The Restart and Reload options are used to restart the applet's execution. The difference between these two options is that Restart does not unload the applet before restarting it, whereas Reload does. The Reload option is equivalent to closing the applet viewer and opening it again on the same web page.
- The Start and Stop options are used to call the applet's `start()` and `stop()` methods directly.

- The Clone option creates a second copy of the same applet running in its own window.

- The Tag option displays the program's `applet` or `object` tag, along with the HTML for any `param` tags that configure the applet.

Another option on the Applet pull-down menu is Info, which calls the applet's `getAppletInfo()` and `getParameterInfo()` methods. A programmer can implement these methods to provide more information about the applet and the parameters it can handle.

The `getAppletInfo()` method returns a string that describes the applet. The `getParameterInfo()` method returns an array of string arrays that specify the name, type, and description of each parameter.

Listing E.1 contains a Java applet that demonstrates the use of these methods.

LISTING E.1 The Full Text of AppInfo.java

```
 1: import java.awt.*;
 2:
 3: public class AppInfo extends javax.swing.JApplet {
 4:     String name, date;
 5:     int version;
 6:
 7:     public String getAppletInfo() {
 8:         String response = "This applet demonstrates the "
 9:             + "use of the Applet's Info feature.";
10:         return response;
11:     }
12:
13:     public String[][] getParameterInfo() {
14:         String[] p1 = { "Name", "String", "Programmer's name" };
15:         String[] p2 = { "Date", "String", "Today's date" };
16:         String[] p3 = { "Version", "int", "Version number" };
17:         String[][] response = { p1, p2, p3 };
18:         return response;
19:     }
20:
21:     public void init() {
22:         name = getParameter("Name");
23:         date = getParameter("Date");
24:         String versText = getParameter("Version");
25:         if (versText != null) {
26:             version = Integer.parseInt(versText);
27:         }
28:     }
```

LISTING E.1   Continued

```
29:
30:     public void paint(Graphics screen) {
31:         Graphics2D screen2D = (Graphics2D) screen;
32:         screen2D.drawString("Name: " + name, 5, 50);
33:         screen2D.drawString("Date: " + date, 5, 100);
34:         screen2D.drawString("Version: " + version, 5, 150);
35:     }
36: }
```

The main function of this applet is to display the value of three parameters: Name, Date, and Version. The getAppletInfo() method returns the following string:

This applet demonstrates the use of the Applet's Info feature.

The getParameterInfo() method is a bit more complicated if you haven't worked with multidimensional arrays. The following things are taking place:

- Line 13 defines the return type of the method as a two-dimensional array of String objects.

- Line 14 creates an array of String objects with three elements: "Name", "String", and "Programmer's name". These elements describe one of the parameters that can be defined for the AppInfo applet. They describe the name of the parameter (Name in this case), the type of data that the parameter will hold (a string), and a description of the parameter ("Programmer's name"). The three-element array is stored in the p1 object.

- Lines 15 and 16 define two more String arrays for the Date and Version parameters.

- Line 17 uses the response object to store an array that contains three string arrays: p1, p2, and p3.

- Line 18 uses the response object as the method's return value.

Listing E.2 contains a web page that can be used to load the AppInfo applet.

LISTING E.2   The Full Text of AppInfo.html

```
1: <applet code="AppInfo.class" height="200" width="170">
2: <param name="Name" value="Rogers Cadenhead">
3: <param name="Date" value="05/30/12">
4: <param name="Version" value="6">
5: </applet>
```

E

Figure E.2 shows the applet running with `appletviewer`, and Figure E.3 is a screen capture of the dialog box that opens when the viewer's Info menu option is selected.

FIGURE E.2

The AppInfo applet running in `appletviewer`.

FIGURE E.3

The Info dialog box of the AppInfo applet.

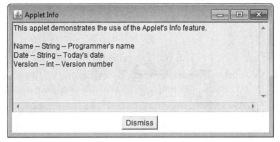

These features require a browser that makes this information available to users. The kit's `appletviewer` handles this through the Info menu option, but browsers do not offer anything like it at this time.

The javadoc Documentation Tool

The Java documentation creator, `javadoc`, takes a `.java` source code file or package name as input and generates detailed documentation in HTML format.

For `javadoc` to create full documentation for a program, a special type of comment statement must be used in the program's source code. Tutorial programs in this book use `//`, `/*`, and `*/` in source code to create *comments*—information for people who are trying to make sense of the program.

Java also has a more structured type of comment that the javadoc tool can read. This comment is used to describe program elements such as classes, variables, objects, and methods. It takes the following format:

```
/** A descriptive sentence or paragraph.
 * @tag1 Description of this tag.
 * @tag2 Description of this tag.
 */
```

A Java documentation comment should be placed immediately above the program element it is documenting and should succinctly explain what the program element is. For example, if the comment precedes a class statement, it describes the class's purpose.

In addition to the descriptive text, different items can be used to document the program element further. These items, called *tags*, are preceded by an at sign (@) and are followed by a space and a descriptive sentence or paragraph.

Listing E.3 contains a thoroughly documented version of the AppInfo applet called AppInfo2. The following tags are used in this program:

- @author—The program's author. This tag can be used only when a class is documented. It is ignored unless the -author option is used when javadoc is run.

- @version *text*—The program's version number. This also is restricted to class documentation. It requires the -version option when you're running javadoc, or the tag will be ignored.

- @return *text*—The variable or object returned by the method being documented.

- @serial *text*—A description of the data type and possible values for a variable or object that can be *serialized*—saved to disk along with the values of its variables and retrieved later.

E

LISTING E.3   The Full Text of AppInfo2.java

```
 1: import java.awt.*;
 2:
 3: /** This class displays the values of three parameters:
 4:  * Name, Date and Version.
 5:  * @author <a href="http://java21days.com/">Rogers Cadenhead</a>
 6:  * @version 6.0
 7:  */
 8: public class AppInfo2 extends javax.swing.JApplet {
 9:     /**
10:      * @serial The programmer's name.
11:      */
```

LISTING E.3   Continued

```
12:     String name;
13:     /**
14:      * @serial The current date.
15:      */
16:     String date;
17:     /**
18:      * @serial The program's version number.
19:      */
20:     int version;
21:
22:     /**
23:      * This method describes the applet for any browsing tool that
24:      * requests information from the program.
25:      * @return A String describing the applet.
26:      */
27:     public String getAppletInfo() {
28:         String response = "This applet demonstrates the "
29:             + "use of the Applet's Info feature.";
30:         return response;
31:     }
32:
33:     /**
34:      * This method describes the parameters that the applet can take
35:      * for any browsing tool that requests this information.
36:      * @return An array of String[] objects for each parameter.
37:      */
38:     public String[][] getParameterInfo() {
39:         String[] p1 = { "Name", "String", "Programmer's name" };
40:         String[] p2 = { "Date", "String", "Today's date" };
41:         String[] p3 = { "Version", "int", "Version number" };
42:         String[][] response = { p1, p2, p3 };
43:         return response;
44:     }
45:
46:     /**
47:      * This method is called when the applet is first initialized.
48:      */
49:     public void init() {
50:         name = getParameter("Name");
51:         date = getParameter("Date");
52:         String versText = getParameter("Version");
53:         if (versText != null) {
54:             version = Integer.parseInt(versText);
55:         }
56:     }
57:
58:     /**
59:      * This method is called when the applet's display window is
60:      * being repainted.
```

LISTING E.3   Continued

```
61:        */
62:       public void paint(Graphics screen) {
63:           Graphics2D screen2D = (Graphics2D)screen;
64:           screen.drawString("Name: " + name, 5, 50);
65:           screen.drawString("Date: " + date, 5, 100);
66:           screen.drawString("Version: " + version, 5, 150);
67:       }
68: }
```

The following command creates HTML documentation from the source code file
AppInfo2.java:

```
javadoc -author -version AppInfo2.java
```

The Java documentation tool creates several different web pages in the same folder as
AppInfo2.java. These pages document the program in the same manner as Oracle's official documentation for the Java Class Library.

> **TIP**
>
> To see the official documentation for Java 7 and the Java Class
> Library, visit http://docs.oracle.com/javase/7/docs/api.

To see the documentation that javadoc has created for AppInfo2, load the newly created
web page index.html on your web browser. Figure E.4 shows this page loaded with
Google Chrome.

E

FIGURE E.4
Java documenta-
tion for the
AppInfo2 program.

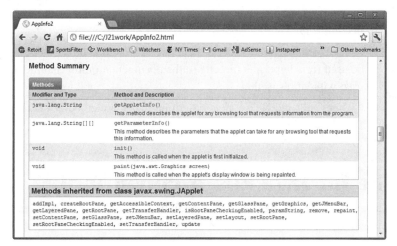

The javadoc tool produces extensively hyperlinked web pages. Navigate through the pages to see where the information in your documentation comments and tags shows up.

If you're familiar with HTML markup, you can use HTML tags such as A, TT, and B within your documentation comments. Line 5 of the AppInfo2 program uses an A tag to turn the text "Rogers Cadenhead" into a hyperlink to this book's website.

The javadoc tool also can be used to document an entire package by specifying the package name as a command-line argument. HTML files are created for each .java file in the package, along with an HTML file indexing the package.

If you want the Java documentation to be produced in a different folder than the default, use the -d option followed by a space and the folder name.

The following command creates Java documentation for AppInfo2 in a folder called C:\JavaDocs\:

```
javadoc -author -version -d C:\JavaDocs\ AppInfo2.java
```

The following list details the other tags you can use in Java documentation comments:

- @deprecated *text* provides a note that indicates that the class, method, object, or variable has been deprecated. This causes the javac compiler to issue a deprecation warning when the feature is used in a program that's being compiled.

- @exception *class description* is used with methods that throw exceptions. This tag documents the exception's class name and its description.

- @param *name description* is used with methods. This tag documents the name of an argument and a description of the values the argument can hold.

- @see *class* indicates the name of another class, which will be turned into a hyperlink to the Java documentation for that class. This can be used without restriction in comments.

- @see *class#method* indicates the name of a method of another class, which will be used for a hyperlink directly to the documentation for that method. This can be used without restriction.

- @since *text* indicates a note describing when a method or feature was added to Java's class library.

The jar Java File Archival Tool

When you deploy a Java program, keeping track of all the class files and other files required by the program can be cumbersome.

To make this easier, the kit includes a tool called jar that can pack all a program's files into a Java archive—also called a JAR file. The jar tool also can be used to unpack the files in one of these archives.

JAR files can be compressed using the zip format or packed without using compression.

To use the tool, type the command jar followed by command-line options and a series of filenames, folder names, or wildcards.

The following command packs all of a folder's class and GIF image files into a single Java archive called Animate.jar:

```
jar cf Animate.jar *.class *.gif
```

The argument cf specifies two command-line options that can be used when running the jar program. The c option indicates that a Java archive file should be created, and f indicates that the name of the archive file will follow as one of the next arguments.

You also can add specific files to a Java archive with a command such as the following:

```
jar cf MusicLoop.jar MusicLoop.class muskratLove.mp3 shopAround.mp3
```

This creates a MusicLoop.jar archive containing three files: MusicLoop.class, muskratLove.mp3, and shopAround.mp3.

Run jar without any arguments to see a list of options that can be used with the tool.

One use of jar is to put all files necessary to run a Java applet in a single JAR file. This makes it much easier to deploy the applet on the web.

The standard way of placing a Java applet on a web page is to use an applet or object tag to indicate the applet's primary class file. A Java-enabled browser then downloads and runs the applet. Any other classes and any other files that the applet needs are downloaded from the web server.

The problem with running applets in this way is that every file an applet requires—helper classes, images, audio files, text files, or anything else—requires a separate connection from a web browser to the server containing the file. This can significantly increase the amount of time it takes to download an applet and everything it needs to run.

If you can reduce the number of files the browser has to load from the server by putting many files into one Java archive, a web browser can download and run your applet more quickly. If the files in a Java archive are compressed, it loads even more quickly.

After you create a Java archive, the archive attribute is used with the applet tag to show where the archive can be found. You can use Java archives with an applet with tags such as the following:

E

```
<applet code="MusicLoop.class" archive="MusicLoop.jar" width="45" height="42">
</applet>
```

This tag specifies that an archive called `MusicLoop.jar` contains files used by the applet. Browsers and browsing tools that support JAR files will look inside the archive for files that are needed as the applet runs.

CAUTION	Although a Java archive can contain class files, the `archive` attribute does not remove the need for the code attribute. A browser still needs to know the name of the applet's main class file to load it.

When you use an `object` tag to display an applet that uses a JAR file, the applet's archive file is specified as a parameter using the `param` tag. The tag should have the `name` attribute `"archive"` and a `value` attribute with the name of the archive file.

The following example is a rewrite of the preceding example to use `object` instead of `applet`:

```
<object code="MusicLoop.class" width="45" height="42">
    <param name="archive" value="MusicLoop.jar">
</object>
```

The jdb Debugger

`jdb`, the Java debugger, is a sophisticated tool that helps you find and fix bugs in Java programs. You also can use it to better understand what is taking place behind the scenes in the Java virtual machine as a program is running. It has a large number of features, including some that might be beyond the expertise of a Java programmer who is new to the language.

You don't need to use the debugger to debug Java programs. This is fairly obvious, especially if you've been creating your own Java programs as you read this book. After the Java compiler generates an error, the most common response is to load the source code into an editor, find the line cited in the error message, and try to spot the problem. You repeat this dreaded compile-curse-find-fix cycle until the program compiles without complaint.

After using this debugging method for a while, you might think that the debugger is unnecessary to the programming process because it's such a complicated tool to master.

This reasoning makes sense when you're fixing problems that cause compiler errors. Many of these problems are simple things such as a misplaced semicolon, unmatched { and } braces, or the use of the wrong type of data as a method argument. However, when you start looking for logic errors—more subtle bugs that don't stop the program from compiling and running—a debugger is an invaluable tool.

The Java debugger has two features that are useful when you're searching for a bug that can't be found by other means: single-step execution and breakpoints. Single-step execution pauses a Java program after every line of code is executed. Breakpoints are points where execution of the program pauses. Using the Java debugger, these breakpoints can be triggered by specific lines of code, method calls, or caught exceptions.

The Java debugger works by running a program using a version of the Java virtual machine over which it has complete control.

Before you use the Java debugger with a program, you compile the program with the -g option, which causes extra information to be included in the class file. This information greatly aids in debugging. Also, you shouldn't use the -O option, because its optimization techniques might produce a class file that does not directly correspond with the program's source code.

Debugging Applications

If you're debugging an application, you can run the jdb tool with a Java class as an argument. This is shown in the following:

```
jdb WriteBytes
```

This example runs the debugger with WriteBytes.class, an application that's available from the book's website at www.java21days.com. Visit the site, select the Appendix E page, and then save the files WriteBytes.class and WriteBytes.java in the same folder from which you run the debugger.

E

The WriteBytes application writes a series of bytes to disk to produce the file pic.gif.

The debugger loads this program but does not begin running it, displaying the following output:

Output ▼

```
Initializing jdb...
>
```

You control the debugger by typing commands at the > prompt.

To set a breakpoint in a program, you use the stop in or stop at commands. The stop in command sets a breakpoint at the first line of a specific method in a class. You specify the class and method name as an argument to the command, as in the following example:

```
stop in SellItem.SetPrice
```

This command sets a breakpoint at the first line of the SetPrice() method. Note that no arguments or parentheses are needed after the method name.

The stop at command sets a breakpoint at a specific line number within a class. You specify the class and number as an argument to the command, as in the following example:

```
stop at WriteBytes:14
```

If you're trying this with the WriteBytes class, you see the following output after entering this command:

Output ▼

```
Deferring breakpoint WriteBytes:14
It will be set after the class is loaded.
```

You can set as many breakpoints as you want within a class. To see the breakpoints that are currently set, use the clear command without any arguments. The clear command lists all current breakpoints by line number rather than method name, even if they were set using the stop in command.

By using clear with a class name and line number as an argument, you can remove a breakpoint. If the hypothetical SellItem.SetPrice method were located at line 215 of SellItem, you could clear this breakpoint with the following command:

```
clear SellItem:215
```

Within the debugger, you can begin executing a program with the run command. The following output shows what the debugger displays after you begin running the WriteBytes class:

Output ▼

```
run WriteBytes
VM Started: Set deferred breakpoint WriteBytes:14

Breakpoint hit: "thread=main", WriteBytes.main(), line=14 bci=413
14                for (int i = 0; i < data.length; i++)
```

After you have reached a breakpoint in the WriteBytes class, experiment with the following commands:

- list—At the point where execution stopped, this command displays the source code of the line and several lines around it. This requires access to the .java file of the class where the breakpoint has been hit, so you must have WriteBytes.java in either the current folder or one of the folders in your Classpath.

- locals—This command lists the values for local variables that are currently in use or will soon be defined.

- print *text*—This command displays the value of the variable, object, or array element specified by *text*.

- step—This command executes the next line and stops again.

- cont—This command continues running the program at the point it was halted.

- !!—This command repeats the previous debugger command.

After trying out these commands within the application, you can resume running the program by clearing the breakpoint and using the cont command. Use the exit command to end the debugging session.

The WriteBytes application creates a file called pic.gif. You can verify that this file ran successfully by loading it with a web browser or image-editing software. You'll see a small letter J in black and white.

After you have finished debugging a program and you're satisfied that it works correctly, recompile it without the -g option.

E

Debugging Applets

You can't debug an applet by loading it using the jdb tool. Instead, use the -debug option of appletviewer, as in the following example:

```
appletviewer -debug AppInfo.html
```

This loads the Java debugger, and when you use a command such as run, appletviewer begins running also. Try this example to see how these tools interact.

Before you use the run command to execute the applet, set a breakpoint in the program at the first line of the getAppletInfo method. Use the following command:

```
stop in AppInfo.getAppletInfo
```

After you begin running the applet, the breakpoint won't be hit until you cause the getAppletInfo() method to be called. You do so by selecting Applet, Info from appletviewer's menu.

Advanced Debugging Commands

With the features you have learned about so far, you can use the debugger to stop execution of a program and learn more about what's taking place. This might be sufficient for many of your debugging tasks, but the debugger also offers many other commands. These include the following:

- up moves up the stack frame so that you can use `locals` and `print` to examine the program at the point before the current method was called.

- down moves down the stack frame so that you can examine the program after the method call.

A Java program often has places where a chain of methods is called. One method calls another method, which calls another method, and so on. At each point where a method is being called, Java keeps track of all the objects and variables within that scope by grouping them. This grouping is called a *stack*, as if you were stacking these objects like a deck of cards. The various stacks in existence as a program runs are called the stack frame.

By using up and down along with commands such as `locals`, you can better understand how the code that calls a method interacts with that method.

You also can use the following commands within a debugging session:

- `classes` lists the classes currently loaded into memory.
- `methods` lists the methods of a class.
- `memory` shows the total amount of memory and the amount that isn't currently in use.
- `threads` lists the threads that are executing.

The `threads` command numbers all the threads. This enables you to use the `suspend` command followed by a number to pause that thread, as in `suspend 1`. You can resume a thread by using the `resume` command followed by the thread's number.

Another convenient way to set a breakpoint in a Java program is to use the `catch` *text* command, which pauses execution when the `Exception` class named by *text* is caught.

You also can cause an exception to be ignored by using the `ignore` *text* command with the `Exception` class named by *text*.

Using System Properties

One obscure feature of the kit is that the command-line option -D can modify the performance of the Java Class Library.

If you have used other programming languages before learning Java, you might be familiar with environment variables, which provide information about the operating system in which a program is running. An example is the Classpath setting, which indicates the folders where the Java virtual machine should look for a class file.

Because different operating systems have different names for their environment variables, a Java program cannot read them directly. Instead, Java includes a number of different system properties that are available on any platform with a Java implementation.

Some properties are used only to get information. The following system properties are among those that should be available on any Java implementation:

- java.version is the version number of the Java virtual machine.
- java.vendor is a string identifying the vendor associated with the Java virtual machine.
- os.name is the operating system in use.
- os.version is the version number of that operating system.

Other properties can affect how the Java Class Library performs when being used inside a Java program. An example is the java.io.tmpdir property, which defines the folder that Java's input and output classes use as a temporary workspace.

You can set a property at the command line by using the -D option followed by the property name, an equals sign, and the property's new value, as in this command:

```
java -Duser.timezone=Asia/Jakarta Auctioneer
```

The use of the system property in this example sets the default time zone to Asia/Jakarta before running the Auctioneer class. This affects any Date objects in a Java program that do not set their own zone.

These property changes are not permanent; they apply only to that particular execution of the class and any classes it uses.

E

TIP

In the `java.util` package, the `TimeZone` class includes a class method called `getProperties()` that returns a string array containing all the time zone identifiers that Java supports.

The following code displays these identifiers:

```
String[] ids = java.util.TimeZone.getAvailableIDs();
for (int i = 0; i < ids.length; i++) {
    System.out.println(ids[i]);
}
```

You also can create your own properties and read them using the `getProperty()` method of the `System` class, which is part of the `java.lang` package.

Listing E.4 contains the source code of a simple program that displays the value of a user-created property.

LISTING E.4   The Full Text of `ItemProp.java`

```
1: class ItemProp {
2:     public static void main(String[] arguments) {
3:         String n = System.getProperty("item.name");
4:         System.out.println("The item is named " + n);
5:     }
6: }
```

If you run this program without setting the `item.name` property on the command line, the output is the following:

Output ▼

```
The item is named null
```

You can set the `item.name` property using the `-D` option, as in this command:

```
java -Ditem.name="Microsoft Bob" ItemProp
```

The output is the following:

Output ▼

```
The item is named Microsoft Bob
```

The -D option is used with the Java virtual machine. To use it with appletviewer as well, all you have to do differently is precede the -D with -J. The following command shows how this can be done:

```
appletviewer -J-Dtimezone=Asia/Jakarta AuctionSite.html
```

This example causes appletviewer to use the default time zone Asia/Jakarta with all applets on the web page AuctionSite.html.

E

Quiz Answers

Chapter 1

1. B. A class is an abstract template used to create objects that are similar to each other.

2. B. You define how the subclass is different from its superclass. The things that are similar are already defined for you because of inheritance. Answer A is technically correct, but if everything in the subclass is identical to the superclass, there's no reason to create the subclass.

3. C. Instance methods refer to a specific object's behavior. Class methods refer to the behavior of all objects belonging to that class.

Chapter 2

1. B. In Java, a `boolean` can be only `true` or `false`. If you put quotation marks around the value, it is treated like a `String` rather than one of the two `boolean` values.

2. C. Constant names are capitalized to make them stand out from other variables.

3. C. The `short` primitive data type has that range of values.

Chapter 3

1. B. The `new` operator is followed by a call to the object's constructor.

2. C. Class methods can be called without creating an object of that class.

3. B. The = operator does not copy values from one object to another. Instead, it makes both variables refer to the same object.

Chapter 4

1. A. In a do-while loop, the while conditional statement appears at the end of the loop. Even if it is initially false, the statements in the loop are executed once.

2. C. Before Java 7, neither objects nor strings could be used in case.

3. B. The length variable is an integer that returns the array's size.

Chapter 5

1. B. Answer A is a good idea, but variable name conflicts can be a source of subtle errors in your Java programs.

2. B. Customarily, instance variables are declared right after the class declaration and before any methods. It's necessary only that they be outside all methods.

3. A. The quotation marks are not included in the argument when it is passed to the program.

Chapter 6

1. C. All other packages must be imported if you want to use short class names such as LinkedList instead of full package and class names such as java.util.LinkedList.

2. B. This convention assumes that all Java package developers will own an Internet domain or have access to one so that the package can be made available for download.

3. A. All public methods must remain public in subclasses. Access control in a subclass can be more public or the same as its subclass, but it can't be more private.

Chapter 7

1. B. The return statement exits the block.

2. C. The kinds of errors you'll want to note in your programs generally belong in the Exception hierarchy.

3. C. The Runnable interface requires only the run() method.

Chapter 8

1. C. In past versions of Java, to store primitive types such as int in a map, objects had to be used to represent their values (such as Integer for integers). This is no longer true. Primitive types are converted automatically to the corresponding object class through a process called autoboxing.

2. A. The index numbers of each item in an array list can change as items are added or removed. Because "Chance" becomes the second item in the list after "Evers" is removed, it is retrieved by calling get(1).

3. B. HashMap implements the interface, as does a similar class called Hashtable.

Chapter 9

1. B. A JTextArea requires a container to support scrolling, but it is not a container itself.

2. C. Any component can be added to a scroll pane, but most are unlikely to need scrolling.

3. C. This is a trick question. Calling setSize() has nothing to do with a window's position on the desktop. You must call setBounds() rather than setSize() to choose where a frame will appear.

Chapter 10

1. B. Progress bars are useful when used to display the progress of a file-copying or file-extracting activity.

2. C. Swing duplicates all the simple user interface components included in the Abstract Windowing Toolkit.

3. B. The toolbar can be dragged to the top, right, left, or bottom of the interface and also out of the interface.

Chapter 11

1. C. To keep a panel from using flow layout, you can set its layout manager to null.

2. A. Border layout has class variables NORTH, SOUTH, EAST, WEST, and CENTER.

3. B. Grid bag layout enables a component to take up multiple grid cells.

Chapter 12

1. B. The current class must implement the correct listener interface and the required methods.

2. C. Because most listener interfaces contain more methods than you will need, using an adapter class as a superclass saves the hassle of implementing empty methods just to implement the interface.

3. A. A user interface component loses focus when the user stops editing that component and moves to a different part of the interface.

Chapter 13

1. A. The `Graphics2D` object is cast from a `Graphics` object and represents a graphics context for a graphical user interface component.

2. C. Both are valid ways to create the object. You also can use hexadecimal values to create a `Color`, as in this example:
   ```
   Color c3 = new Color(0xFF, 0xCC, 0x66);
   ```

3. C. You can call `getSize().width` and `getSize().height` on any user interface component.

Chapter 14

1. B. The `PropertyChangeListener` in the `java.beans` package receives a `propertyChange()` event when the worker finishes.

2. B. The application is described using elements contained within an opening `<information>` tag and a closing `</information>` tag.

3. C. A Java Web Start application has few restrictions. They are limited to important functionality such as saving files or opening Internet connections. These restrictions are dropped if a user explicitly grants those privileges as the application runs.

Chapter 15

1. C. That's one of the things to look out for when using output streams; you can easily wipe out existing files.

2. B. Because Java represents a `char` internally as an integer value, you often can use the two interchangeably in method calls and other statements.

3. C. The `byte` primitive data type has values ranging from –128 to 127, whereas an unsigned byte can range from 0 to 255.

Chapter 16

1. B. The bracket indicates the array's depth, the L indicates that it is an array of objects, and the class name that follows is self-explanatory.

2. A. Persistence saves objects to disk or another storage medium via serialization so that they can be re-created later.

3. B. If the class is not found, a `ClassNotFoundException` is thrown.

Chapter 17

1. C. The `java.nio` classes work in conjunction with streams. They don't replace them.

2. A. The client requests information, and the server sends back something in response. This is traditionally how client/server applications function, although some programs can act as both client and server.

3. B. Sockets are good for low-level connections, such as when you are implementing a new protocol. For existing protocols such as HTTP, some classes are better suited to that protocol—`URL` and `HttpURLConnection`, in this case.

Chapter 18

1. B. The class, part of the `java.sql` package, represents a SQL statement.

2. B. Because it is compiled, `PreparedStatement` is a better choice when you need to execute the same SQL query numerous times.

3. B. This static method loads a database driver.

Chapter 19

1. C. One version, RSS 2.0, claims Really Simple Syndication as its name. The other, RSS 1.0, claims RDF Site Summary.

2. A. Answers B and C both work. One adds the contents of a `Text` element as the element's character data, and the other adds the string.

3. C. For data to be considered XML, it must be well-formed.

Chapter 20

1. A. XML-RPC uses HTTP (Hypertext Transfer Protocol) to transport data that is formatted as XML (Extensible Markup Language). HTML (Hypertext Markup Language) is not used.

2. B. All floating-point numbers such as 8.67 are represented by the `double` type in XML-RPC. There are not two different floating-point types, as there are in Java (`float` and `double`).

3. A. The `methodCall` tag is used only in requests, `methodResponse` is used only in responses, and `params` is used in both.

Chapter 21

1. A. The `Intent` also can be used for one `Activity` to tell another to take an action.

2. B. The `main.xml` file is a screen, and `R.java` defines resource IDs.

3. B. No, because both files would be given the same identifier, `icon`.

Index

Symbols

A

AppInfo2 application,
645-647

ItemProp application, 656

CodeKeeper class, 232

CodeKeeper2 class, 243-244

collection, garbage, 69

color

background colors, 377

dithering, 375

drawing colors, setting,
376-377

finding current color, 377

sRGB color system, 375

XYZ color system, 375

Color class, 375

Color objects, 375

color spaces, 375

colors, Color objects, 375

ColorSpace class, 375

combining

layout managers, 316-317

methods, nested, 76

combo boxes, 269-270

event handling

action events, 345-346

item events, 349-350

ComicBooks class, 239-240

command line, 636

arguments, 636

options, 636-637

**command-line interfaces,
617-618**

command-line tools, javac, 628

commands

Applet menu, 641-642

arguments, 636

jar, 648-650

jdb (debugger)

!!, 653

catch, 654

classes, 654

clear, 652

cont, 653

down, 654

exit, 653

ignore, 654

list, 653

locals, 653

memory, 654

methods, 654

print, 653

resume, 654

run, 652

step, 653

stop at, 652

stop in, 652

suspend, 654

threads, 654

up, 654

JDK, format, 636

MS-DOS

CD, 619, 628

CLASSPATH variable,
630-633

MD, 620

PATH variable, 622-625

SET CLASSPATH=, 631

Start menu

Find, 623

Run, 615

comment notation, 46

comments, 45

notation, 46

source code, 644

comparing

instances, 85

objects, 85-86

comparison operators, 56-57

compilation errors, 95

compiler (javac), 639-640

compiler errors, 242

compilers, 614

compiling

files, 639-640

multiple, 639

Java programs in Windows,
628-630

programs, 617

troubleshooting, 630

complexity, code (Java), 206

**complications, multiple
interfaces, 169**

components, 258

aligning, 306-307

border layouts, 314-315

card layouts, 317-318

flow layouts, 307-309

grid bag layouts, 325-327

grid layouts, 312

panels, 317

associating with event
listeners, 341-342

check boxes, 266-267

combo boxes, 269-270

to containers, adding,
250, 256

creating, 255-256

dialog boxes, 278

confirm dialog boxes, 279

Info sample application,
283-284

input dialog boxes,
280-281

message dialog boxes, 281

option dialog boxes,
282-283

disabled, 258

drop-down lists, 269-270

icons, 259-261

labels, 261-262

methods, stop( ), 214

to panels, adding, 317

progress bars, 293

radio buttons, 266-267

resizing, 258

scroll panes, 288-289

scrollbars, configuring, 265

scrolling panes, 265

How can we make this index more useful? Email us at indexes@samspublishing.com

Sams Teach Yourself

Java™

in 21 Days

"If you get only one Java book, it should be Sams Teach Yourself Java in 21 Days"
—PC Magazine

Covering Java 7 and Android

Rogers Cadenhead

SAMS

Safari
Books Online

FREE
Online Edition

WITHDRAWN

Your purchase of *Sams Teach Yourself Java in 21 Days* includes access to a free online edition for 45 days through the **Safari Books Online** subscription service. Nearly every Sams book is available online through **Safari Books Online**, along with thousands of books and videos from publishers such as Addison-Wesley Professional, Cisco Press, Exam Cram, IBM Press, O'Reilly Media, Prentice Hall, Que, and VMware Press.

Safari Books Online is a digital library providing searchable, on-demand access to thousands of technology, digital media, and professional development books and videos from leading publishers. With one monthly or yearly subscription price, you get unlimited access to learning tools and information on topics including mobile app and software development, tips and tricks on using your favorite gadgets, networking, project management, graphic design, and much more.

Activate your FREE Online Edition at
informit.com/safarifree

STEP 1: Enter the coupon code: HCPMOGA.

STEP 2: New Safari users, complete the brief registration form.
Safari subscribers, just log in.

If you have difficulty registering on Safari or accessing the online edition,
please e-mail customer-service@safaribooksonline.com

 Addison Wesley Adobe Press ALPHA Cisco Press FT Press FINANCIAL TIMES IBM Press Microsoft Press New Riders O'REIL

 Peachpit Press PRENTICE HALL que Redbooks SAMS SAS Publishing  vmware PRESS WILEY